THE INSIDERS' GUIDE TO
WILMINGTON
& North Carolina's Southern Coast

THE INSIDERS' GUIDE® TO
WILMINGTON
& North Carolina's Southern Coast

by
Bill DiNome
and
Carol Deakin

Co-published and marketed by:
By The Sea Publications Inc.
Hanover Center P.O. Box 5386
Wilmington, NC 28403
(910) 763-8464

Insiders' Guide
105 Budleigh St.
P.O. Box 2057
Manteo, NC 27954
(919) 473-6100
www.insiders.com

•

FIFTH EDITION
1st printing

•

Copyright ©1998
by By The Sea Publications

•

Printed in the United States
of America

•

All rights reserved. No part of this book may be reproduced in any form without permission, in writing, from the publisher, except by a reviewer who wishes to quote brief passages in connection with a review in a magazine or newspaper.

Publications from The Insiders' Guide® series are available at special discounts for bulk purchases for sales promotions, premiums or fundraisings. Special editions, including personalized covers, can be created in large quantities for special needs. For more information, please write to Karen Bachman, Falcon Publishing, Inc., P.O. Box 2057, Manteo, NC 27954, or call (800) 765-2665 Ext. 241.

ISBN 1-57380-066-X

By The Sea Publications, Inc.

President and Publisher
Jay Tervo

Sales and Marketing
Rosemarie Gabriele
Matt Hege
Herb Hilliard

Administrative Manager
Gerry Tyhacz

Administrative Assistant
Sandy Putnam

Creative Services
Marylee Hanna

Creative Consultant
Ashley Ware

Insiders' Guide

Publisher/Editor-in-Chief
Beth P. Storie

Advertising Director/
General Manager
Michael McOwen

Creative Services Director
Giles MacMillan

Art Director
David Haynes

Managing Editor
Dave McCarter

Project Editor
Pat von Brook

Project Artist
Carolyn McClees

Insiders' Guide
An imprint of Falcon Publishing Inc.
A Landmark Communications company.

Preface

Welcome to the fifth edition of *The Insiders' Guide® to Wilmington and North Carolina's Southern Coast* — the most reliable and comprehensive collection of facts and tips available for the coastal region extending from Topsail Island to the South Carolina border.

As in years past, you'll find recommendations on where to hear a symphony or mosh to rock 'n' roll, charter a dive trip or shop for antiques. You'll find out where to rent a Jet Ski, study yoga, buy original art, avoid traffic snarls, volunteer your time for a good cause, store your boat, locate emergency medical clinics and repair your bike. Those relocating here will find the chapters on real estate, retirement, healthcare, commerce and schools invaluable.

This guide is not merely a checklist of things to do or places to go. Rather, it is designed to give you a sense of the character of the region and its offerings. We've tried to include information that will prove useful not only to short-term visitors but also to newcomers who plan to stay. Even longtime residents and natives may gain new perspectives. Interspersed throughout the book are vignettes, multiple perspectives, and histories about the places, people and events that have shaped this coastal area.

Two important changes have been incorporated into this edition: We've revised and simplified the price code in the Restaurants chapter for ease of comparison among restaurants in our region and with restaurants listed in other Insiders' Guide® books. And in addition to our Weekly and Long-Term Vacation Rentals chapter, we've created a chapter for hotels and motels and one for bed and breakfast inns. We hope that together they will facilitate your search for just the kind of vacation accommodation you desire.

Keep in mind that you'll also find us on the World Wide Web at www.insiders.com. There you can view each and every chapter in this book, investigate other locales in the ever-growing Insiders' Guide® series and e-mail us your questions and comments. We'd love to hear from you.

See you on the beach!

About the Authors

Carol Deakin

Carol Deakin is a freelance writer, illustrator and designer who lives in historic downtown Wilmington. She is currently enrolled in graduate studies at East Carolina University in Greenville, North Carolina, working on her Master's degree in Rehabilitation Studies.

Deakin co-authored the first five editions of *The Insiders' Guide® to Wilmington & North Carolina's Southern Coast* with Bill DiNome. Additionally, she authored *Wilmington: Treasure on the Atlantic*, a pictorial perspective on the city she loves.

She regards Wilmington as the finest place she has ever lived.

Bill DiNome

Bill is the seventh-born in a family of 12 children. He is a native of New York City who left because it got too crowded. His relationship with that city has since much improved, emotionally and financially, and he loves it still.

Bill has been earning his living as a writer (mostly) since the mid-1980s, since the time that working as a musician began feeling like real work. He prefers writing because he can work in his underwear.

His many interests include backpacking, travel, cinema, history and mythology, mucking about in caves and chocolate, not necessarily in that order.

Acknowledgments

Carol . . .

I would like to gratefully acknowledge the unflagging support of publisher Jay Tervo, a fine human being and good friend who has made the experience of co-authoring this book a pleasure. Jay has been consistently upbeat — even in moments of deadline crisis — and I have deeply appreciated his humanity throughout the production of five editions.

I also thank my friend and co-author Bill DiNome, a heck of a nice guy and a great writer. Bill, one of my favorite "damn Yankees," has embraced his Southern home and brought the important element of fascination — perhaps a better word would be "enthrallment" — to his research and writing about the Cape Fear area.

I thank my friend Elizabeth Darrow for helping me to balance a hectic schedule that includes being a full-time student in graduate school at East Carolina University this year. There were many weekends when I sat glued to the computer screen tapping out chapters of this book while she attended to many of my other life responsibilities.

Finally, I thank all the folks in Manteo who toil constantly to maintain the high quality of Insiders' Guide® books. Bill and I may get to have our names on the book, but dozens of other people made the book possible. I would especially like to salute the production staff because they're the ones who manage to bring it all together so beautifully by press time.

Bill . . .

Bouquets of Jovian moon blossoms to Deborah Flora, my wife, best friend, comic relief and reality check. Forever in my memory will ring her words of encouragement: "Get to work!" Her son, Taj, deserves monster props for putting up with me. Sincerest thanks also to the Kirk of our *Enterprise*, our publisher Jay Tervo.

Brava! to my coauthor Carol "Caller ID-No Surprises" Deakin. Special thanks to Mimi Cunningham and her staff at UNCW's University Relations office; Betty Parks; the late Betty Polzer; the inimitable Harry Warren at the Cape Fear Museum; and one Bulkington. Fanfares, knighthood and their favorite chocolates to the many others who fielded my questions, set me straight, produced this book and helped me wrestle this beast to the mat once again — great teachers all.

Special thanks . . .

Insiders' Publishing and By The Sea Publications would like to thank and acknowledge the suppliers of the cover photographs. Cover: Bellamy Mansion Museum (top left) and the Cape Fear Coast Convention and Visitors Bureau. Spine: Cape Fear Coast Convention and Visitors Bureau.

Silver Screen Tours
～ presents ～

TOURS
of
Screen Gems Studios

1223 North 23rd Street
Wilmington, NC 28405

TOUR DIRECTOR: James Crews
(910)675-8479
Saturday & Sunday
10:00am / 12:00pm / 2:00pm

Reservations welcome for this walking tour.

Table of Contents

Getting Around 1
Area Overview 13
Hotels and Motels 37
Bed and Breakfast Inns 55
Weekly and Long-Term Vacation Rentals 69
Camping 81
Restaurants 87
Nightlife 121
Shopping 131
Attractions 161
Annual Events 189
The Arts 203
Kidstuff 217
Daytrips 241
Watersports 251
Sun, Sand and Sea 269
Fishing 275
Marinas and the Intracoastal Waterway 287
Sports, Fitness and Parks 297
Golf 327
Real Estate 343
Retirement 371
Healthcare 379
Schools and Child Care 387
Higher Education and Research 401
Volunteer Opportunities 411
Media 419
Commerce and Industry 425
Worship 431

Directory of Maps

Wilmington and the Southern Coast x
Topsail Island to Calabash xi
Downtown Wilmington xiv

Wilmington and the Southern Coast

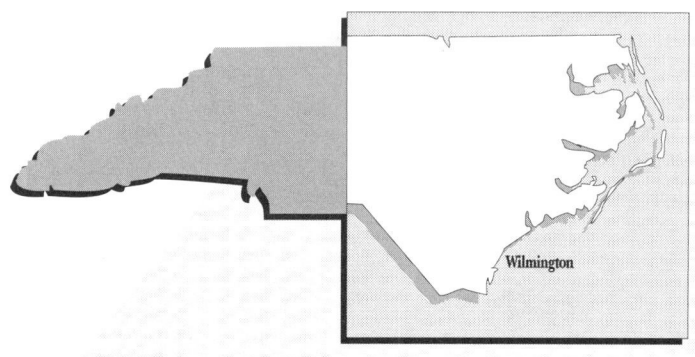

Topsail Island to Calabash

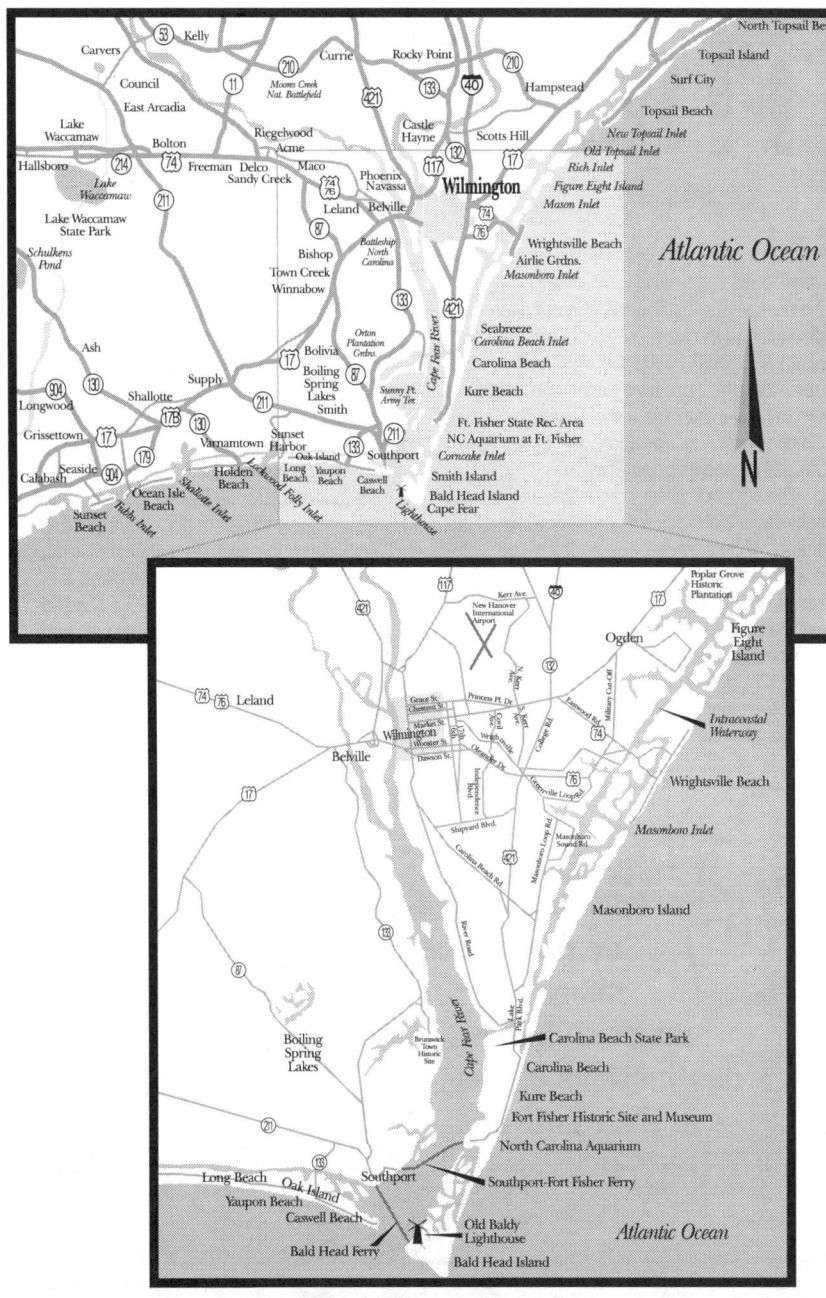

How to Use This Book

The Insiders' Guide® to Wilmington and North Carolina's Southern Coast encompasses the Barrier Islands and the coastal plain from New Inlet, at the northern tip of Topsail Island, south and west to the South Carolina state line. Near the figurative and literal center of this narrow swath lies the city of Wilmington, the economic anchor and port city for Lower Cape Fear and its populace.

The fold-out, color map inside the book's front cover provides a schematic view of the region, while a three-page series of more detailed maps follows the table of contents. Of these, each map after the first offers an "exploded" view of the preceding map's inset, culminating in a detailed street map of downtown Wilmington.

The Getting Around chapter should prove additionally useful, especially if you're new to the area. There you'll get your bearings on Wilmington in relation to the mid-Atlantic states as well as find information on local highways and byways, public and private surface transportation, air travel, the state-run Southport-Fort Fisher ferry and established bicycle paths. Historic and demographic profiles of each community within our coverage area are found in the Area Overview chapter.

This guide is structured functionally, with chapters arranged according to activities and subjects, for example, restaurants, kidstuff, nightlife, arts, golf, retirement, etc. Where appropriate, the chapter is divided into locales, starting with Wilmington and then spinning off toward the outlying beach communities.

Every chapter stands on its own — read them in any order you desire; handy cross-

references will lead you to other chapters where there's additional information on a particular subject or it's covered from a different perspective. Also, a comprehensive index appears at the back of the book.

You'll also find some useful and entertaining surprises between these covers. Along the bottom of many pages are Insiders' Tips, offering practical suggestions, useful leads and mere curiosities about our region. The tips offer quick, interesting insights into local styles and activities.

You're also bound to notice the various Close-ups (not listed in the table of contents or the index) that focus on interesting people, threads of folklore or shards of history that many of us hold close to our hearts. It is our hope that reading these Close-ups will fill you with the spirit of the region and suggest the unique mindset of its longtime residents.

Every attempt has been made to present accurate, up-to-date information. Naturally things change, businesses come and go, hotels renovate. Even the shoreline moves (sometimes more quickly than we'd like). So please let us know about any information you read here that's at odds with what you find in your travels. If you know of or discover an outstanding establishment or activity that you think deserves to be listed here but isn't, please drop us a note. Write to us at By The Sea Publications, Hanover Center Box 5386, Wilmington, NC 28403; or make comments on our web site: www.insiders.com/explore.

And when the reading of this guide results in a pleasurable experience, "tell 'em we sent ya'."

Downtown Wilmington

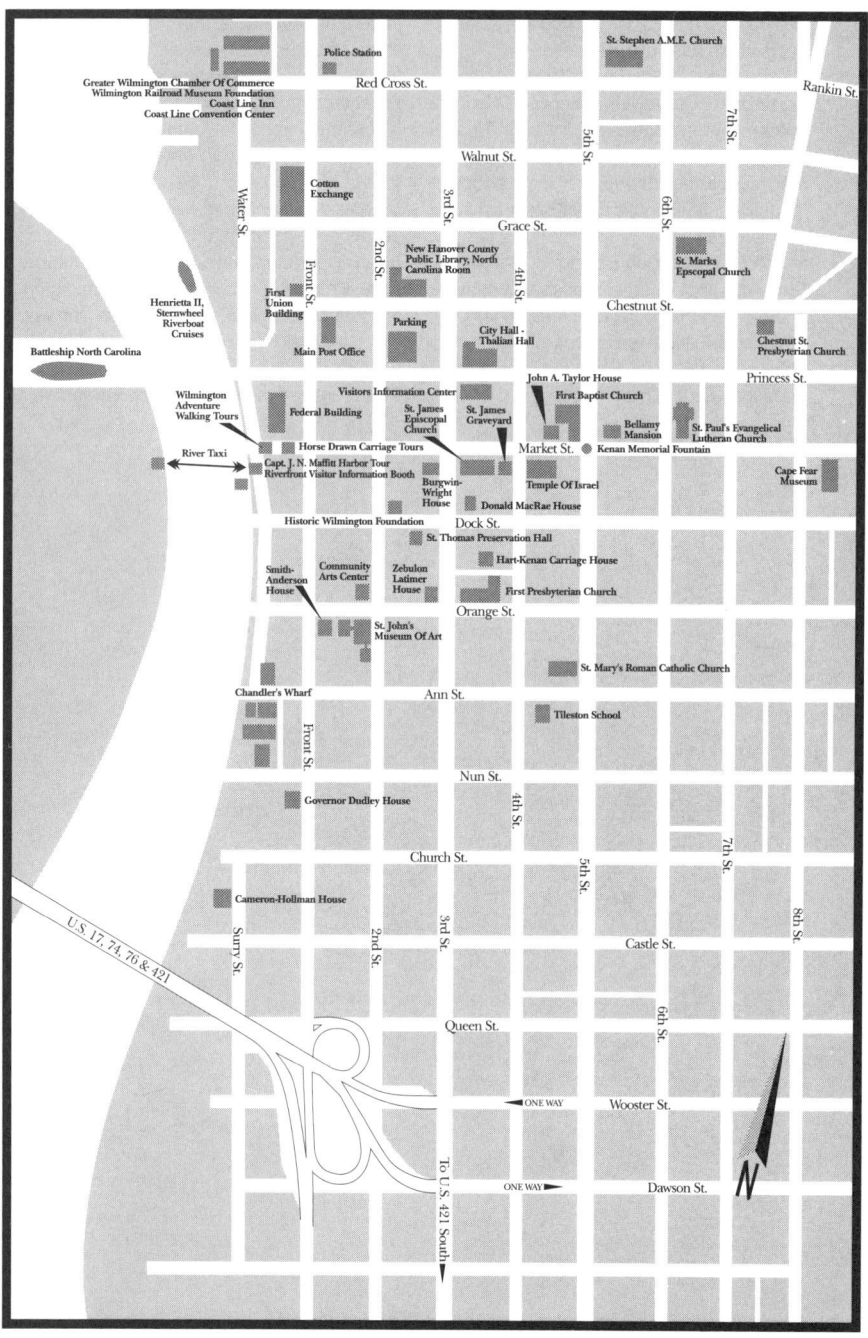

Getting Around

Cape Fear is the southernmost cape of three along the North Carolina Coast. The "greater" Cape Fear area consists of four oceanfront counties. New Hanover, which embraces the city of Wilmington, is the state's smallest county geographically and among the state's wealthiest. It is a triangular area bordered by the Atlantic Ocean on the east, the Cape Fear River on the west, and Pender County to the north (the county line there being the Northeast Cape Fear River). Pender County includes Figure Eight Island and the southern half of Topsail Island. The northern half of Topsail is in Onslow County. On the west side of the Cape Fear River and south to the state line lies Brunswick County, one of the fastest-growing counties in the state.

To orient yourself to Wilmington and the immediate area, grab a copy of the guide map published by the Cape Fear Coast Convention and Visitors Bureau, (910) 341-4030 or (800) 222-4757. It's a great downtown street map and is available free at the Visitors Information Center at the Old Courthouse in Wilmington, 24 N. 3rd Street, as well as at many hotels and from the Chamber of Commerce, 1 Estell Lee Place, (910) 762-2611.

Roadways

Roadways into the greater Wilmington area continue to be widened and repaved as the region's increasing popularity places greater demands on the infrastructure. Recent improvements include the widening of Market Street west of Colonial Drive and the new Smith Creek Parkway (currently in its second phase of construction), which extends all the way from Eastwood Road east of Market Street to 23rd Street, not far from the airport. When finished, it will loop around Wilmington's north side from the river nearly to the sea — a boon to beachgoers. Traffic still piles up in places, but compared to other cities, Wilmington's road problems are minor. Folks from larger cities chuckle when they hear locals complaining about the traffic.

First, some bearings: Situated at the eastern terminus of Interstate 40, Wilmington is about 12 hours from New York City (600 miles); seven hours from Washington, D.C. (374 miles); four hours from Charlotte (197 miles); three-and-a-half hours from Charleston, South Carolina (169 miles); and one-and-a-half-hours from Myrtle Beach (72 miles). The interchange between I-40 and Interstate 95 is near Benson, one-and-a-half hours from Wilmington (about 75 miles). Driving from Raleigh will take about two hours (127 miles).

Interstates and Highways

I-40 will be your most likely choice if you're coming a long distance from points west (I-40 extends all the way to Barstow, California) or from I-95. The local stretch of I-40 is named after one of Wilmington's most famous former residents, basketball star Michael Jordan. It's a fairly dull ride unless counting surfboards on car racks excites you.

Services along the stretch between the I-40/I-95 interchange and Wilmington are limited, often located well off the highway, and they close early; fuel up beforehand if you'll be traveling at night. There is only one public rest area along the way, about an hour outside Wilmington. I-40 ends as it enters Wilmington from the north and converges with N.C. Highway 132. It then assumes the name College Road.

From western North Carolina (Whiteville, Rockingham, Charlotte), U.S. Highway 74 is a direct link to downtown Wilmington. It joins U.S. Highway 76 out of Florence, South Carolina, N.C. Highway 211 from Southport, and U.S. Highway 17 from the south.

U.S. 17, the "Ocean Highway," is the road to remember from Calabash to Topsail, as it intersects every main route to the sea. Entering the region from the south, U.S. 17 intersects N.C. Highway 179, which veers seaward through Calabash. N.C. 179 hugs the Intracoastal Waterway, giving access to the pontoon bridge to Sunset Beach (Sunset Boulevard) and to the Ocean Isle Beach high-span (N.C. Highway 904) before leaning northward into Shallotte, where it rejoins U.S. 17 Business. In Shallotte (pronounced "shu-LOTTE"), U.S. 17 Business intersects N.C. Highway 130 (Holden Beach Road), a direct route to that beach community.

Continuing northward, U.S. 17 joins N.C. Highway 211 near the town of Supply. N.C. 211 leads directly into the picturesque village of Southport and is named, appropriately enough, the Southport-Supply Road.

Traveling northward again from Supply, U.S. 17 joins N.C. Highway 87 and U.S. highways 74 and 76, then crosses the Cape Fear Memorial Bridge into downtown Wilmington. U.S. 17 joins Market Street as it exits the northeast side of town. It then passes through Ogden, Scotts Hill, Hampstead and Holly Ridge. U.S. 17 intersects N.C. 210 and N.C. 50, both leading to Topsail Island (that's "TOP-sul"), converging at the drawbridge into Surf City (Roland Avenue). Until 1993, this intersection boasted Topsail Island's only traffic light. Now there's a flashing light in Topsail Beach, too. Time marches on.

On Topsail Island, N.C. 50 turns south toward Topsail Beach, while N.C. 210 turns north, passing through North Topsail Beach then back onto the mainland across the New River Inlet Bridge, which affords a superb view of the Intracoastal Waterway. N.C. 210 rejoins U.S. 17 just minutes outside Jacksonville.

Drivers take note: Speed limits at the beaches can be a test of patience and are strictly enforced. Seat belt checkpoints are common throughout the area. Relax, take it slowly and enjoy.

Streets and Byways

College Road extends north and south through Wilmington about midway between, and nearly parallel to, the seashore and the Cape Fear River. As the name suggests, it borders the University of North Carolina at Wilmington (UNCW) campus. Flanked by strip malls and massive shopping centers, College Road is among the least attractive and most frustrating roadways in the region, so avoid it during rush hours and holiday shopping frenzies. To the south, it joins Carolina Beach Road (N.C. Highway 421) at Monkey Junction.

Carolina Beach Road is the direct southerly extension of S. 3rd Street as it leaves downtown Wilmington. This road gives access to Pleasure Island (Carolina Beach, Kure Beach, Fort Fisher) all the way to Federal Point.

After crossing the Cape Fear Memorial Bridge as one, N.C. 74 and 76 go their separate ways. They both run roughly east and west, N.C. 74 serving the north side of Wilmington and N.C. 76 the south side. N.C. 74 consists of Market Street from downtown past the S. College Road overpass, and the Smith Creek Parkway. N.C. 76 assumes even more names: from the Cape Fear Memorial Bridge to 17th Street it's Dawson Street (Wooster Street in the opposite direction), then it's Oleander Drive to just beyond Bradley Creek, then Wrightsville Avenue as it heads toward the beach. Confused? Don't sweat; driving it is easy. These two routes lovingly reunite at the drawbridge onto Harbor Island (Causeway Drive) and Wrightsville Beach.

Wrightsville Avenue, known as the "shell

INSIDERS' TIP

Need a ride to the Raleigh-Durham International Airport? Call the Wilmington Shuttle, (910) 791-6678 or (800) 273-9206, for departure information or to reserve a seat.

GOLD'S GYM®

Aerobics & Fitness
A Licensee of Gold's Gym Enterprises, Inc.

Free One-On-One Instruction to help you:
✓ Lose Weight ✓ Tone Up ✓ Lower Blood Pressure & Cholesterol
✓ Reduce Stress ✓ Increase Energy ✓ Improve Health

We Offer:
✓ The Largest selection of workout & cardio equipment in New Hanover County ✓ Variety of aerobics classes 7 days/week ✓ Free Kids' Care
✓ Special Rates for students & senior citizens

2 Convenient Locations

Long Leaf Mall
350-8289

Market Place Mall
392-3999

---

road" once upon a time because it was paved with oyster shells, was the original beach-bound road from Wilmington. Today its western terminus is at 17th and Dock streets, immediately south of Market Street. It runs diagonally, at a southeasterly glance, until it nearly parallels Oleander Drive all the way to the intersection of Military Cutoff Road (near the stuccoed St. Andrews On-the-Sound Episcopal Church). At this point, Wrightsville Avenue becomes N.C. 76 on its way to the drawbridge to Harbor Island and Wrightsville Beach. It is a heavily used road, especially between 17th Street and College Road and over the mile or two nearest the bridge, and warrants entering at intersections with stop lights to save time.

The Intracoastal Waterway

Our region is particularly accessible to boaters from Canada to the Keys. You can sail "outside" through open ocean waters or "inside" via the Intracoastal Waterway. From New River Inlet at the northern tip of Topsail Island to the South Carolina border, scores of marinas await you along nearly 90 miles of protected waterway. See our chapter on Marinas and the Intracoastal Waterway for detailed information.

Bike Paths

Wilmington is behind the times in regarding bicycles as a viable form of transportation. Busy city roadways have little or no room for cyclists, and roadways that do are frustratingly circuitous. (On that point, be sure to avoid Market Street in Wilmington at all costs.)

Outside of Wilmington, however, level landscape and predominantly well-maintained roads make touring the coastal plain by bicycle mostly excellent. Three state-funded Bicycling Highways pass through Wilmington and along the neighboring coast. They're marked by rectangular road signs bearing a green ellipse, a bicycle icon and the route number. The River-to-Sea Bike Route (Route 1) stretches from Riverfront Park at the foot of Market Street in Wilmington to Wrightsville Beach, a ride of just under 9 miles. You'll have to cross one improved railroad-crossing and a busy thoroughfare nearby. Exercise caution on the Bradley Creek bridge, which has badly uneven road seams and debris.

The Ports of Call route (Route 3) is a 319-mile seaside excursion from the South Carolina border to the Virginia line. Approximately 110 miles of it lie along the southern coast, giving access to miles of beaches and downtown Wilmington.

The Cape Fear Run (Route 5) links Raleigh to Southport. This 166-mile route crosses

WILMINGTON INTERNATIONAL AIRPORT

1740 Airport Boulevard
Wilmington, North Carolina 28405
(910) 341-4333
Fax: (910) 341-4365
www.airport-wilmington.com

*Southeastern North Carolina's
Gateway to the World --
With non-stop airline service to 4 major airport hubs
and connecting service to
141 Domestic and 28 International Markets.*

Airlines:
U S Airways   800-428-4322
Atlantic Southeast Airline,
"The Delta Connection"   800-282-3424
Midway/Corporate Express   800-446-4392
United Express
   (Atlantic Coast Airlines)   800-241-6522
Federal Inspection Services for Arriving International Flights:
   United States Customs
   United States Department of Agriculture
   United States Immigration & Naturalization Service

Fixed Base Operators:
(Serving Business & General
Aviation around-the-clock)
Aeronautics   (910) 763-4691
Air Wilmington   (910) 763-0146
ISO Aero Service (910) 763-8898

A 24 hour Landing Rights Airport for International Traffic.

---

the Cape Fear River twice and intersects the Ports of Call.

Obtain free maps and information from the North Carolina Department of Transportation Bicycle Program, P.O. Box 25201, Raleigh, NC 27611, (919) 733-2804. Although the maps are updated regularly, be ready to improvise when it comes to information on campgrounds and detours. The Wilmington Bike Map is a must for local cycling. Get your free copy from the City Transportation Planning Department, P.O. Box 1810, Wilmington, NC 28402, (910) 341-7888.

Area Transportation

Buses

The Wilmington Transit Authority (WTA) operates six bus lines that link outlying neighborhoods, the university, shopping centers and downtown. One-way fare is 75¢, 35¢ for senior citizens and the handicapped, and a transfer is 10¢ (5¢ for seniors, the handicapped and students). Discount ticket books are available from any bus driver — 11 rides for $7.50, $6 for senior citizens, the handicapped and students (student tickets are good only for students in grades 1 through 12, on weekdays during the school year). UNCW students and faculty with valid IDs ride free. Buses run from 6:30 AM until about 7:30 PM. There is no bus service on Sunday and major holidays, including Martin Luther King, Jr. Day.

Routes include East Wilmington-Long Leaf Park (Route 1); Market Street-UNCW (Route 2); Oleander Shopping Centers (Route 3); New Hanover Regional Medical Center-Brooklyn (Route 5); Independence and Long Leaf malls-UNCW (Route 6); and two UNCW Shuttles (north and south). No, we didn't overlook Route 4 — there isn't one. Door-to-door transportation is available for disabled travelers who qualify.

The "Wilmington Public Transit Guide," which contains a map and a table of sched-

ules, is available at the Visitors Information Center and on buses. For more information call the WTA at (910) 343-0106 Monday through Friday from 8 AM to 5 PM or TDD at (910) 763-9011.

Taxicabs and Limousines

The going rate for cabs within Wilmington city limits is $1.35 plus $1.60 per mile. Cab drivers will stop when hailed if they're between calls. In addition to the usual services, many taxicab companies will unlock your car if you've locked yourself out. Most charge $15.

Limousine service typically runs in the $50-per-hour range and may require some hourly minimum (often three hours). If pickup and dropoff locations are outside the company's primary service area (city limits most likely), travel time is usually charged. For service on holidays and weekends during the wedding season, most companies require reservations well in advance plus a credit card deposit.

Wilmington
Taxicab Companies
Lett's Taxi Service, (910) 458-3999
Port City Taxi Inc., (910) 762-1165
Yellow Cab, (910) 762-3322
Limousine Services
Affordable Affluence Inc., (910) 251-8999
After Dark Limousine Service, (910) 392-3355
Best Holiday Limousine Service, (910) 799-5565
Formal Limousine Service, (910) 395-1191
Prestige Limousine Service, (910) 399-4484

Carolina Beach, Kure Beach
Beach Buggy Taxi, (910) 458-0450

Southport-Oak Island and South Brunswick
A-Plus Taxi Service, (910) 278-6373
Easy Way Transport Service, (910) 579-9926

Van Service

Van transportation between Wilmington and Raleigh-Durham Airport (RDU) is provided by the Wilmington Shuttle, (910) 791-6678, or (800) 273-9206 outside Wilmington, which offers regularly scheduled shuttle service seven days a week. Additional shuttles are added on Sundays in December to accommodate holiday travelers. Pickups and dropoffs in Wilmington are at Shoney's on S. College Road. The Wilmington Shuttle also offers service to Camp Lejeune, making pickups and dropoffs at Shoney's in Jacksonville. Reservations are required. One way service (either direction) costs $50, and discounts apply for groups of two or more.

Beds Express
OVER 40 MODELS ON SALE NOW

We've Got It All Under One Roof!
- Over 40 Models of Bedding
- Bunkbeds
- Futons - Wood, Metal- Twin, Full, Queen
- Daybeds
- Brass Beds
- Bedroom Sets
- and more!

We've Got The Low Price!

We've Got The Service — **A Tremendous Selection**

- 30 Comfort Trial Period
- Weeknight / Weekend Delivery

Open 7 Days a Week

6010 F, Oleander Dr. *(Next to Barstools Unlimited)*

350-8876 *"Quality Bedding at Affordable Prices"*

Car Rentals

Along with the national chains and independents listed here, several new car dealerships also lease cars long-term.

Budget Rent A Car, (910) 762-8910, (800) 527-0700

Enterprise Rentals, 5601 Market Street, Wilmington, (910) 799-4042, (800) 325-8007

Hertz, Wilmington International Airport, (910) 762-1010, (800) 654-3131

National Car Rental, Wilmington International Airport, (910) 762-8000, (800) CAR-RENT

Triangle Rental, 4124 Market Street, Wilmington, (910) 251-9812

Ferries

Southport-Fort Fisher Ferry
(800) 368-8969

This two-ship, vehicle-carrying ferry can be (and is) viewed both as a mode of transportation that saves miles of driving and as one of the least expensive scenic tours. On the approximately 30-minute cruise, the ferry provides a panoramic view of the mouth of the Cape Fear River above Southport. The passenger lounges of the *Southport* and the *Gov. Daniel Russell* are climate-controlled. The ships pass dredge-spoil islands where brown pelicans nest and waters frequented by dolphins.

On the Brunswick County side, huge yellow cranes mark the Military Ocean Terminal at Sunny Point, the largest distribution center in the country for military supplies.

Other sights include Old Baldy, North Carolina's oldest lighthouse, on Bald Head Island; Price's Creek Lighthouse, which guided Confederate blockade runners through New Inlet during the Civil War; and the Oak Island Lighthouse, the nation's brightest. (For information on tours and attractions, see our Attractions chapter.)

The Fort Fisher terminal is near the southern terminus of N.C. 421 at Federal Point, on the right. The Southport terminal is on Ferry Road, just off N.C. 211, about 3 miles north of town.

The summer schedule (March 25 through November 17) is:

Departs Southport	Departs Fort Fisher
5:30 AM	6:15 AM
7:00 AM	7:45 AM
8:30 AM	-
9:15 AM	9:15 AM
10:00 AM	10:00 AM
10:45 AM	10:45 AM
11:30 AM	11:30 AM
2:15 PM	2:15 PM
1:00 PM	1:00 PM
1:45 PM	1:45 PM
2:30 PM	2:30 PM
3:15 PM	3:15 PM

GETTING AROUND • 7

Affordable Affluence
COMPLETE TRANSPORTATION SOURCE

For both Business and Pleasure
- **Limousines • Cars • Vans**
- **Classic • Vintage**

Weddings • Proms • Concerts • Parties

Airport Transportation to and from Raleigh, Wilmington & Myrtle Beach

251-8999 FAX 251-9009

4:00 PM	4:00 PM
4:45 PM	4:45 PM
-	5:30 PM
6:15 PM	7:00 PM
7:45 PM	8:30 PM

The winter schedule (November 18 through March 30) is:

Departs Southport	Departs Fort Fisher
5:30 AM	6:15 AM
7:00 AM	7:45 AM
8:30 AM	9:15 AM
10:00 AM	10:45 AM
11:30 AM	12:15 PM
1:00 PM	1:45 PM
2:30 PM	3:15 PM
4:00 PM	4:45 PM

One-way fares are as follows: pedestrians, 50¢; bicycles, $1; vehicles 20 feet or longer, $3; vehicles or combinations measuring up to 32 feet, $6. Call in advance if ferrying larger vehicles.

Rates and schedules are subject to change. For statewide ferry information call (800) BY-FERRY.

Bald Head Island Ferry
Foot of W. 9th St., Southport
• **(910) 457-7390, (800) 234-1666**

The ferry between Southport and Bald Head Island is strictly for passengers. Travel on the island is by foot, bicycle or electric cart; no passenger cars allowed. An individual round-trip ferry ticket is $15 for adults, $8 for children ages 3 through 12. Children 2 and younger ride free.

In Southport, the ferry terminal is at Indigo Plantation at the foot of 9th Street. It departs on the hour from 8 AM to 10 PM, with some exceptions depending on the day, seven days a week. Ferries leave Bald Head every hour on the half-hour, again with minor exceptions. Parking costs $4 or $5 per day depending on which lot you use (shorter walk, higher price!). Special summer ferry packages that include passage, parking, lunch and a historic tour are available.

Long-Distance Bus Lines

Long-distance bus service to Wilmington is provided by Greyhound, (800) 231-2222, and Carolina Trailways, (910) 762-6625, at the Wilmington bus terminal, 201 Harnett Street between N. 3rd and N. Front streets.

Airports

Wilmington (formerly New Hanover) International Airport is the prime entry point for most people flying into the greater Wilmington area. Myrtle Beach International Airport in South Carolina is nearly the same distance from Shallotte as the Wilmington airport (about 38 miles), so visitors to Calabash and the South

The Days of Ballrooms and Beach Cars

Before the days of gas stations and weekend traffic, the best way to get to Wrightsville Beach was the "Beach Car," the electric trolley that ran from Princess and Front streets in downtown Wilmington to what was once the biggest beach attraction south of Atlantic City: Wrightsville Beach's Lumina Pavilion.

The trolley began operating in 1902, replacing an older railway train. The route roughly paralleled the "shell road" (now Wrightsville Avenue) and ran along today's Park Avenue, where a couple of the old station shelters still remain. Operated by the Tidewater Power Company, the trolley cars were orange with cream trim, carried 68 passengers each, and made the trip from downtown to the beach in as little as 35 minutes. Five-car trains ran during the height of the season.

In 1903, the Tidewater Power Company purchased an oceanfront lot for $10 at Station 7, the end of the line, where it built the Lumina Pavilion, named for the thousands of incandescent lights that made the building visible from far out at sea. Constructed entirely of heart pine, it was opened on June 3, 1905, and underwent two major expansions in subsequent years.

The pavilion featured a vast promenade, bowling lanes, a ladies' parlor, an upstairs restaurant and downstairs lunch service, dressing rooms, slot machines and other amusements, but the gem of the pavilion was its second-floor dance hall. The enormous dance floor accommodated hundreds of dancers, and the high-ceilinged room was festooned with bunting and flags. Some of the era's most famous orchestras and big bands played there, including Kay Kaiser, Guy Lombardo and Cab Calloway. (Wilmington was the biggest city in North Carolina at the time.) Curiously, a writer in

— continued on next page

The "Beach Car" trolley picks up passengers outside Wilmington, c. 1915.

1910 recalled that opera was favored by Lumina audiences over so-called popular music of the day.

Other attractions included dance contests, beauty pageants, beach games such as sack races and water sports, and convention dances. Swimmers could rent bathing suits emblazoned with "Lumina" on the front. An especially unusual attraction was motion pictures. The owners erected a screen about 50 yards into the surf and projected silent movies that could be viewed from seating on the beach or from the promenade. The screen was moved closer when "talkies" appeared. This tradition lives on in the annual Lumina Daze celebration, which benefits the Wrightsville Beach Museum of History. (See our Annual Events chapter.)

Manners were carefully observed at the Lumina. Jacket and tie were essential. Cheek-to-cheek dancing? Unacceptable! Mrs. Bessie Martin, the Lumina's permanent chaperon, saw to that. No alcoholic beverages or rude behavior were permitted, either — Tuck Savage saw to that. Some called Tuck a "supervisor"; today we'd call him a bouncer.

Admission was free before World War I. After that, the trolley to the beach cost 35¢, which included admission to the Lumina.

The trolley line even influenced the birth of Wilmington's early suburbs — Carolina Place, Carolina Heights, Oleander, Audubon, and Winter Park grew up along the route. Then, in the 1930s, the first automobile route was built to Harbor Island. Billboards sprung up: "In a hurry? Take the Causeway." It wasn't long before the road spanned Banks Channel, and another road was paved down the length of the island in 1935. Soon the trolley became a throwback to a more sluggish era, and it declined in popularity. Its last run took place April 27, 1940. The only beach car alleged to remain today is in Annabelle's Restaurant on Oleander Drive.

The Lumina remained viable a while longer. Hot dogs and surf accessories were sold downstairs. Rock concerts were occasionally held there in the 1960s, but by the early '70s the ballroom stood perpetually dark, and in 1973 the pavilion was torn down. The Lumina lives on in many place names around the beach and, like the old Oceanic Hotel and the Harbor Island Casino, it won't be totally forgotten any time soon. The Lumina and the beach trolley are reminders that perhaps being in a hurry really isn't what the beach is all about.

The photo of the trolley here is one of 250 photos in *Wrightsville Beach, A Pictorial History* by the nonprofit Wrightsville Beach Preservation Society. For a copy of the book write to the society at P.O. Box 584, Wrightsville Beach, NC 28480, or call (910) 256-2569.

Brunswick Islands might do well to check flight availability at Myrtle Beach. If your destination is Oak Island, Southport, or points north and you're traveling by commercial airline, you'd do better flying into New Hanover. Small aircraft destined for Brunswick County can use Brunswick County Airport, just outside Southport.

Wilmington International Airport
1740 Airport Blvd., Wilmington
• **(910) 341-4125**

Wilmington International (which, incidentally, has no direct international flights) is an entirely 21st-century facility, complete with baby-changing areas accessible to dads — even the palm trees in the atrium will remain forever green, thanks to the wonders of polyurethane. Yet it has plenty of that charm peculiar to small airports. The airport fronts 23rd Street, 2 miles north of Market Street, and is within 10 minutes of downtown Wilmington by car and about 20 minutes from Wrightsville Beach.

Three airlines serve greater Wilmington — the number of daily flights varies with the

A ride on the Southport-Fort Fisher Ferry is like a half-hour cruise.

tourist season. Atlantic Southeast Airlines (ASA), (800) 282-3424, is the Delta connection to Atlanta; Midway Corporate Express Airlines, (800) 555-6565, provides daily flights to destinations throughout the eastern United States via Raleigh-Durham; and USAir, (800) 428-4322, offers daily flights via Charlotte.

Short-term parking rates are $1 per half hour, with a maximum 24-hour charge of $5.25. Long-term parking costs $1 per hour, with a maximum charge of $4.50 per day. A limited amount of metered parking (25¢ for 20 minutes) is available just beyond the terminal (on the left when facing the building).

Brunswick County Airport
4019 Long Beach Rd., Southport
• **(910) 457-6483**

This fast-growing, full-service airport, which has a small terminal, hangars, fuel service and a 4,000-foot paved and lighted runway, can accommodate general aviation aircraft from the smallest ultralights to fairly sizable private jets. Especially convenient to Bald Head Island and the Southport-Oak Island area, the airport supports instrument approaches (GPS, NDB) and offers a variety of services, including flight instruction. Tie-down fees for piston aircraft are $5 per day, $30 per month and $270 per year.

Brunswick County Airport is also the East Coast summer home of Blue Yonder Flying Machines, purveyors of the Quicksilver ultralight aircraft (see the Flying section in our Sports, Fitness and Parks chapter). The airport is on the mainland side of the Oak Island Bridge, on N.C. Highway 133.

Car rental at the Brunswick County Airport is provided by A-Plus, (910) 278-6373, which offers older-model "ugly ducklings" at reasonable rates.

Ocean Isle Airstrip
N.C. Hwys. 179 and 904, Ocean Isle Beach • **(910) 579-6222**

This landing strip (4,000 feet, paved) accommodates only small, private, piston aircraft. Usage is free to the public on a first-come basis. There is no fuel available, and pilots must provide their own tie-downs. The airstrip is managed by Ocean Isle Realty.

Olsten Staffing Services℠

The Working Solution®

FLEXIBLE. RESPONSIVE.

STAFFING SERVICES
- Office Automation
- General Office
- Production/Distribution/Assembly
- Legal/Accounting/Technical

TOP BENEFITS
- Long and short-term assignments
- Competitive pay
- Training

343-8763 • Fax: 763-7416
513 Market Street, Wilmington, NC 28401

Air Charters, Rentals, Leasing

You can charter small aircraft at Wilmington International Airport for a bird's-eye view of the southern coast. Most companies offer 24-hour charter service, sales, service and rentals, and all offer flight training. Unless otherwise noted, all the companies listed below are based at Wilmington International.

Aeronautics, (910) 763-4691
Air Wilmington, (910) 763-0146
ISO Aero Service Inc. of Wilmington, (910) 763-8898
Ocean Aire Aviation Inc., Brunswick County Airport, Southport, (910) 457-0710

BEACHES • ENTERTAINMENT • SHOPPING • FISHING • DINNING

RESTAURANTS

Stella Mae's Cafe...Homestyle cooking, fun atmosphere, daily specials. Dine in or take out.
6C N. Lake Park Blvd. 458-3778

Breakfast Cafe'...
Hearty Breakfast & Bountiful Lunch, daily 6am-2pm
700 N. Lake Park Blvd. 458-8897

The Cottage... *"Casual Dining at it's Best"* Lunch or Dinner. Closed on Sun.
1 N. Lake Park Blvd. 458-4383

The Old Philadelphia Grill...
Authentic Philly specialties: Cheese Steaks, Subs, Deli Sandwiches, Dogs & Burgers.
1018 N. Lake Park Blvd.
(Federal Point Shopping Center)
458-7886

Tang Chinese Cuisine...
Lunch and dinner buffet. Free delivery, full ABC Permits. Mon.-Sat.
11:30-3:00 & 5-10pm / Sun.12pm-9:30pm
977 N. Lake Park Blvd. 458-7254 or 7683

SHOPPING

The Checkered Church...
Fine Gifts, Pine Furniture, Yankee Candles.
800 St. Joseph Street 458-3140

PK's... Fine Jewelry, "Atocha Charms", Unusual Gift Items, Cruise Wear Clothing.
8 S. Lake Park Blvd.
458-3090

The Yankee Trader...
Unique nautical gifts, sterling silver jewelry, Snow Babies, Boyds Bears and More. Your Island Christmas Shop.
9 S. Lake Park Blvd. 458-0097

ICE CREAM PARLORS

Squigley's Ice Cream & Treats...
4050 Flavors. 208 S. Lake Park Blvd.
458-8779

BOATING/FISHING/CRUISING

Dockside... Watersports, Wave Runners (PWC) 7 Boat Rentals. 458-0220

SPECIALTY SHOPS

The Civil War Shop... Buy • Sell • Trade Consignment • Appraisals
209 S. Lake Park Blvd. 458-4244

Hemingway's ... New & Used books. 14K & Silver Nautical Jewelry, Cards, Stationery, Giftwrap, Candles, Lamps, Pottery & More!
1140-H N. Lake Park Blvd..
458-8883

Sassy Glass... Come see our exciting selection of jewelry, stained glass, prints, candles, sculptures, lamps, pottery.
104 N. Lake Park Blvd. 458-8489

AMUSEMENT PARK

Jubilee Park... Waterslides, 21 rides, 3 race tracks, arcade, snack bar, ice cream shop, giftshop. Catering & group rates.
421 South to Carolina Beach. 458-9017

Fun Land... Family oriented arcade. Check out the new Alpine Skiers, Cruising World, Suzuka Motor Cycles, Big Screen TV's, Pool Tables & Air Hockey. Special announcement in June!
On the Boardwalk. 458-8531

LAUNDRY

SunSpree Dry Cleaning & Laundry...
Dry Cleaning and coin laundry plus wash, dry and fold service.
702 S. Lake Park Blvd. 458-3505

Area Overview

Greater Wilmington and the Cape Fear region from Topsail Island in the north to Sunset Beach and Calabash in the south are geographically, socially, culturally, economically and historically tied to the water. While the ocean gets top billing in terms of geographical attraction, it was the existence of a relatively narrow river that gave rise to successful European settlement. The Cape Fear River, a deep, often fast-moving body of water begins as a trickle near Greensboro, North Carolina, meanders through Fayetteville and empties into the Atlantic Ocean 30 miles south of downtown Wilmington.

The Cape Fear River

In 1524 when Spanish explorer Giovanni da Verrazano took his French-financed expedition into an unknown river in a wild place, he ushered in a new historical period that would slowly lead to European development of the area.

Verrazano wrote glowingly of the area in his journal: "The open country rising in height above the sandy shore with many faire fields and plaines, full of mightie great woods, some very thicke and some thinne, replenished with divers sorts of trees, as pleasant and delectable to behold, as if possible to imagine."

Despite the explorer's enthusiastic description, very little happened in terms of development at that time. More than a hundred years would pass before attempted European settlement when members of the Massachusetts Bay Colony attempted to colonize the region in 1660. Their effort failed and it was some time before a new settlement ventured into the region. A group of English settlers from Barbados established Charles Town on the west bank of the river shortly thereafter, but their effort failed in 1667 because of hostile coastal Indians, pirates, weak supply lines, mosquitos and other problems that drove the residents south where they founded the City of Charleston in South Carolina. Perhaps one of the greatest reasons for failure was, ironically, the very river that sparked interest in settlement.

In 1879, settler George Davis in James Sprunt's *Chronicles of the Cape Fear River,* vividly describes part of the problem with settlement caused by the river: "Looking to the cape for the idea and reason of its name, we find that it is the southernmost point of Smith's Island — a naked, bleak elbow of sand, jutting far out into the ocean. Immediately in front of it are the Frying Pan Shoals, pushing out still farther, twenty miles, to sea. Together, they stand for warning and for woe; and together they catch the long majestic roll of the Atlantic as it sweeps through a thousand miles of grandeur and power from the Arctic toward the Gulf. It is the playground of billows and tempests, the kingdom of silence and awe, disturbed by no sound save the sea gull's shriek and the breakers' roar. Its whole aspect is suggestive, not of repose and beauty, but of desolation and terror. Imagination can not adorn it. Romance cannot hallow it. Local pride cannot soften it."

Queen Elizabeth had opened the area to English colonization as early as 1662. The Town of Brunswick was founded by English settlers on the west bank of the river in 1725 but withered away as more strategically located Wilmington, on the high east bank, began to prosper. Wilmington was founded in 1732 and incorporated in February 1740 by an act of the North Carolina General Assembly.

Incorporation says something for the tenacity of successful settlers who managed to tame what was apparently a very wild place. But they understood, as do their descendants, that the river posed more opportunities than obstacles. The positioning of the City of Wilmington on a bluff created a port relatively safe from storms. And what created a challenge for early settlers would prove to be a protective barrier against outside invaders from England during the Revolutionary War and Union troops during the Civil War.

Wilmington: The Port City

Previously known as New Carthage, New Liverpool, Liverpool, New Town and Newton, this east-bank settlement was named Wilmington by Governor Gabriel Johnston to honor his friend Spencer Compton, Earl of Wilmington. By 1740 the incorporated City of Wilmington was the largest in North Carolina, with a population of 13,500 city residents in a county that numbered 28,000 residents.

Wilmington prospered as a major port, shipbuilding center and producer of pine forest products. Tar, turpentine and pitch were central to the economy, and lumber from the pine forests was a lucrative economic resource. At one time, Wilmington was the site of the largest cotton exchange in the world. The waterfront bustled with sailing ships, and steam ships crowded together to pick up or unload precious cargo.

James Sprunt's chronicles, published in 1916, paint a vivid picture in the book's foreword. Sprunt writes: "From early youth, I have loved the Cape Fear River, the ships and the sailors which it bears upon its bosom. As a boy I delighted to wander along the wharves where the sailing ships were moored with their graceful spars and rigging in relief against the skyline, with men aloft whose uncouth cries and unknown tongues inspired me with a longing for the sea, which I afterwards followed, and for the faraway countries whence they had come."

Downtown Wilmington remains the historical core of the community and is still in many ways the neighborhood that defines the region. Suburbs may flourish, but there is something fascinating — even compelling — about the historic homes and buildings downtown, with their intimate proximity to the river. Both visitors and residents are affected by a sense of lingering ghosts. Important events happened here, in places that are still standing . . . places that have not been obscured by modern architecture or lost in the trends of a constantly changing American culture.

Home to the county's seat of government for more than and two-and-a-half centuries, this urban area has been on the forefront of historic changes. Throughout its history, downtown Wilmington has been a focal point for virtually everything that has shaped the region's sense of identity and unity. British and Union troops advanced upon it with some difficulty, managing to temporarily occupy the resilient city, but their claims were weak at best. Wilmington was the fall-back position for a weary Lord Cornwallis and his ragged troops at the end of the Revolutionary War, and it was the last Southern port to fall during the Civil War. Despite the temporary setbacks of conquest, Wilmington was never claimed by the outsiders who assailed her.

The best perspective on Wilmington's rich and colorful history can be found at the Cape Fear Museum, 814 Market Street, (910) 343-4350, where the unique format allows visitors to walk through time in chronological order.

The 20th Century

Wilmingtonians born in this century will likely express an lifelong awareness of isolation regarding their hometown. Despite several booming eras in its history — the present one included — Wilmington has lagged behind much of North Carolina in many respects throughout the 20th century.

Wilmington's primary connection to the outside world, before the extension of Interstate 40 from Raleigh in 1991, was the Wilmington and Weldon Railroad. The rail system — the world's longest line at the time with 167 miles — was built in the middle of the 19th century. The railroad promised and delivered prosperity, as goods shipped from all over the world up the Cape Fear to the city could in turn be sent inland at a profit.

Thus, at the end of the 19th century, Wilmington had become the largest city in North

---

www.insiders.com

See this and many other **Insiders' Guide®** destinations online — in their entirety.

Visit us today!

Abundant and exotic plant life is a constant feature on North Carolina's Southern beaches.

16 • AREA OVERVIEW

Carolina and sported a robust economy. But in 1960 the Wilmington and Weldon Railroad's main office closed and the tracks went largely unused. More than 4,000 families were transferred to Jacksonville, Florida.

Poor roads increasingly separated Wilmington from commerce with the rest of the state. While the Triad and Triangle areas of North Carolina thrived amid a network of interstate highway systems, Wilmington has felt like the distant cousin 100 miles removed. Although U.S. Highway 421 was fine for tourists on their way to area beaches, commerce and industry needed the speed and convenience of an interstate. Having a two-lane blacktop highway as the main artery of access to the city proved to be a profound liability that severely isolated Wilmington for decades.

Compounding the woes of a slipping local economy, problems with race relations erupted in Wilmington in the 1970s, putting the city on the international map as the home of the Wilmington Ten, a group of black citizens arrested for inciting race riots.

This was a grave time for Wilmington — race riots, white flight from the downtown area, a devastated economy and social despair. Tourists ignored downtown. Beautiful homes fell into disrepair in neighborhoods that were regarded as unsafe. Forlorn, vacant buildings stared blankly over the river, crime was rampant and much of downtown's commerce came to revolve around seedy bars and unsavory dealings.

Happily, in the early 1970s, a few voices began to question why the urban center of Wilmington should be abandoned. The Wilmington Historic Foundation demanded to know why such valuable architecture should be allowed to rot. City government eyed the situation and decided to create the Historic District Commission. Die-hard merchants banded together in the establishment of the Downtown Wilmington Association. DARE, the Downtown Area Revitalization Effort, was organized as a public-private successor to the Mayor's Task Force on Revitalization.

Thousands of people are responsible for

putting downtown back together. It would take volumes to mention the organizations that contributed to its renewal and the many who toiled alone in pursuit of private dreams that would merge with others to form a collective vision. Their efforts have resulted in the restoration and maintenance of a national treasure. Wilmington boasts one of the largest districts on the National Historic Register, with homes dating from as early as the mid-1700s.

Meticulously restored Victorian, Georgian, Italianate and antebellum homes, from grand mansions to cottages, attest to the previous and current determination of the citizens to maintain the special charm of the neighborhood. In fact, the grassroots movement to save the downtown area was made up of many people who actually live there. The 200-block downtown historic district is not a mere museum — it is home to real people who do real things to make a living. The neighborhood wasn't merely restored for the sake of remembering the past, it's a place where life goes forward.

Greater Wilmington Today

The $23 million expansion of the then New Hanover International Airport — now the Wilmington International Airport — in September 1990 and the linking of Wilmington with I-40 in June 1991 were significant events that opened what some locals may now describe as a "Pandora's Box." These still relatively new access routes have promoted discovery of the region and nurtured a greater than 19.2 percent population increase between 1990 and 1998.

Explosive growth has both good and bad points. On the positive side, there is change in terms of better services, more interesting cultural offerings and a much higher level of overall sophistication. Outsiders have brought some pleasant cultural additions with them: fresh bagels, international cuisine, new entertainment venues, demands for more diversity in the market and interesting accents. On the negative side, there are traffic problems, strained public school facilities and, much to the chagrin of natives, waiting lines at the better restaurants.

There have been heated discussions in recent years over land use, zoning and the prospect of annexation as Wilmington struggles to strike a balance between general quality of life and her citizen's individual rights to do profitable business. In short, growth has presented some knotty problems that will require vision and, frankly, guts on the part of the government representatives charged with protecting the region's environmental and economic future.

Downtown Wilmington continues to be a success story in progress. In the last decade of the 20th century, the Cape Fear River has become a second focal point of the city's booming tourist industry, vying for tourist attention with the beaches. Downtown hotels, shops and restaurants situated on its banks enjoy brisk business all year long.

Beyond the river, the area has experienced a building boom that is unprecedented in the whole of the 20th century. Shopping centers that boast national chains such as Target, Barnes & Noble Booksellers, The Gap and Home Depot have elevated the region's shopping choices. Upscale specialty stores have also appeared throughout the area.

Real estate has been a lively business in the last decade of the century, with new neighborhoods being developed so quickly that natives have been heard to say they occasionally get lost because of the changing scenery. The new home market is dominated by single-family homes that average $200,000.

Wilmington remains the educational hub of the southeastern North Carolina coast, with the University of North Carolina at Wilmington and Cape Fear Community College within its boundaries. Mount Olive College, Shaw University and Miller-Motte Business College are also located in Wilmington.

The city also holds the distinction of being the cultural center for not only this corner of the state but the whole North Carolina coastline. Performances by touring and home-based theater, dance and music companies enliven the local stages of Thalian Hall Center for the Performing Arts downtown and Kenan Auditorium and Trask Coliseum on the campus of UNCW. Writers, artists and musicians are evident in abundance. St. John's Museum of Art, located downtown but slated to move into grand new facilities in the suburbs within two years, is a showcase of regional and international artists.

General Statistics

Wilmington occupies most of New Hanover County. Geographically the second-smallest county in the state with only 185 square miles, New Hanover had a population of approximately 143,354 as of 1996, gaining 23,000 people since 1990. Some of these folks were homegrown as babies, but 19,000 moved here. Wilmington proper has about 60,000 residents. Projections suggest the population may double by the year 2030. County population density is more than 700 people per square mile, which is in stark contrast to neighboring Pender and Brunswick counties, where there are 33 and 60 people per square mile, respectively. Despite these numbers, these areas are experiencing what some describe as overflow from Wilmington. Look for density figures to

James E. Moore

INSURANCE

SINCE 1954
♦
Homeowners
♦
Automobile
♦
Business
♦
Life & Health

Located at the Galleria
6800 Wrightsville Avenue Suite 2
Wilmington, NC 28403
(910) 256-5333 ♦ (800) 256-3244

Come By to "Sea" Us

Cape Fear Coast's
2 Visitor Information Centers:

**Downtown-24 N. Third St.
Riverfront (Apr-Oct)
(foot of Market St.)**

FREE INFORMATION

Visitor Guides

Accommodations

Golf Guides

Restaurant Guides

Maps

Historic Wilmington • Carolina Beach
Kure Beach • Wrightsville Beach

OR CALL FOR FREE GUIDES

Cape Fear Coast Convention & Visitors Bureau
24 N. Third St., Wilmington, N.C. 28401
910/341-4030 1-800-222-4757
www.cape-fear.nc.us

WILMINGTON, NC
FINE FOODS OVERLOOKING THE CAPE FEAR RIVER

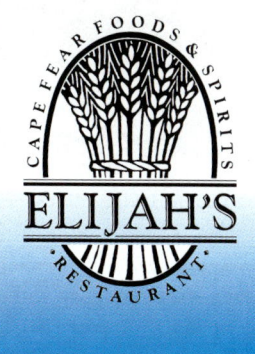

An American Seafood Grill and Oyster Bar with Outside Dining in Historic Chandler's Wharf.

910-343-1448

Innovations on Southern Regional Cooking in the Historic Craig House with Riverfront Deck.

910-343-0200

OPEN SEVEN DAYS A WEEK ALL YEAR

FOLLOW MARKET STREET TO THE CAPE FEAR, TURN LEFT ON WATER STREET, THREE BLOCKS TO CHANDLER'S WHARF

Two To Six Acre Private Estates

WhiteBridge offers the best of everything in its recreation facilities, surroundings and its distinguished quality homes. And just as important, it has an atmosphere that appeals to those rare people who expect a level of personal privacy within a protected community and have the ability to obtain it.

Discover uncommon choices in residential living at WhiteBridge. Expertly developed estate sites, from two to six acres, provide a lush backdrop for distinguished homes. At WhitBridge, lifestyle choices are diverse. Homesites overlook elegant ponds, pristine meadows or are tucked into hardwood forests.

- Only 75 lots on 300 acres of land, with finished homes also available.
- A neighborhood protected by architectural controls and restrictions without confining your lifestyle. Privacy with social amenities including swimming pool with outdoor pavilion, tennis courts, miles of natural trails and a 20-acre bird sanctuary
- Custom homes by WhiteBridge Construction available.
- Homes on estate-sized lots from the 300's.

WHITEBRIDGE

The Alternative To Heavily Restricted Half-Acre Living

Located on Hwy. 17, just 11 minutes North of Wilmington
For more information, stop by or write: P.O. Box 963, Hampstead, NC 28443

(919) 270-2000 • (800) 480-2007

WILCOX & WILCOX BUILDERS/DEVELOPERS
BROKERS PROTECTED

Exercise Today
Wilmington's #1 Woman's Health Club
We have designed & created
an environment with ladies in mind!

- Aerobics
- Jazzercise
- Yoga
- Air Walkers
- Steppers
- Treadmills
- Life Cycles
- Weight Training
- Nutritional Guidance
- Child Care Available
- Unwind in our Sauna, Steam Or Whirlpool

Call Today for Two Free Weeks of Fitness

397-0003
6832 Market St. • Ogden Shopping Center

---

be much higher as this book comes to press. In terms of age, the 25 to 54 age group has the biggest presence in the area.

The population explosion in the entire Cape Fear area has been fueled by many factors, including easier accessibility by land and air, an extremely pleasant four-season climate, scenic beauty, entrepreneurial opportunities and the discovery of the area by the film industry.

Educational opportunities also draw people. UNCW, long a relatively dormant institution, has taken off in the past decade. Chancellor James Leutze, host of the popular Public Television series *Globe Watch*, lends a visionary style of leadership to the university that emphasizes international awareness. The 661-acre campus is among the fastest-growing universities in the 16-campus UNC system. It offers degrees in 60 areas of concentration, including a marine sciences program that was recently ranked fifth-best in the world.

The public school system prides itself on innovation. With a $100.4 million budget, the system devotes 70 percent of its monies to direct instructional costs. There are 30 schools in the New Hanover County Public School System, organized as kindergarten through 5th grades, 6th through 8th, and 9th through 12th, with an estimated 21,000 students.

Employment in the area is concentrated in the services sector and wholesale/retail trade. These two areas account for half the jobs in the county. Unemployment is at approximately 6 percent, although this figure fluctuates regularly and seasonally. Manufacturing accounts for only slightly more than 15 percent of the local jobs. The retail sales business is something of a phenomenon in Greater Wilmington, placing the area sixth in retail sales within the state.

Tourism and its related industries, of course, are vital to the Cape Fear-area economy. At this writing, more than 80,000 people visit the Cape Fear Coast Convention and Visitors Bureau in downtown Wilmington annually. An estimated 1.6 million visitors vacation on the Cape Fear coast and its surrounding islands each year. Despite two damaging hurricanes in 1996, the area's appeal has not diminished. Area beaches have been largely restored as of this edition. Be assured that Topsail Island and Figure Eight Island are getting themselves back together.

People who may be considering a move to the area should understand something very important about the local economy: Wages are generally low. The median family income here in 1995 was $34,000. That's slightly higher than the average for the state of North Carolina, but much lower than in some of North Carolina's inland cities and certainly lower than wages in other areas of the nation. Some Insiders suspect salaries are going to improve

20 • AREA OVERVIEW

Wilmington's old courthouse houses the Cape Fear Coast Convention and Visitors Bureau.

in the near future. The film industry, for example, has already brought a different perspective to the area in terms of salaries.

Retirement is beginning to figure significantly in the area's social and economic spheres. People who might have gone to Florida to retire find the southern coast of North Carolina immensely appealing because of the climate and the relatively inexpensive cost of living.

Recreational opportunities are abundant. Some of the finest golf courses and tennis facilities in the country are in New Hanover County (see our Golf and Sports, Fitness and Parks chapters). Boating, sailing and in-the-water recreation are readily accessible. Fishing is both an industry and a serious sport, with purses as large as $50,000 for the biggest fish landed in the U.S. Open King Mackerel Tournament.

The Wilmington area climate is moderate compared with the continental standard. The growing season for plants is long, averaging 244 days. Some types of plants grow

Victoria's Interiors

**Decorating with a difference...
because the difference is *Victoria's***

- Upholstery
- Slipcovers
- Window Treatments
- Cornices
- Bed Coverings
- Headboards
- Accent Pull-Overs
- Trimmings
- Specialty Items
- Standard Fabrics
- Stand Alone Fabrics

**763-1440
3505 Market Street**

THE BASKET CASE

located in the
Cotton Exchange
308 Nutt St.
(910) 763-3956
Monday - Saturday
10-6pm
Sundays 1-5pm

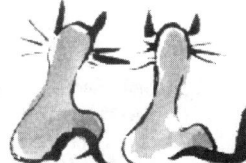

"UNCUSTOMARY-GIFTS"

all year, as temperatures average 47 degrees in January and 79.8 degrees in August. Midsummer temperatures average 88 degrees; the average low in the winter is 36.4 degrees. The maritime location makes the climate of Wilmington unusually mild for its latitude.

New Hanover County

Downtown Wilmington Today

Downtown Wilmington pulsates. Aside from being the center of government for the city and New Hanover County, it has become a magnet for retail stores, financial institutions, the cultural arts, entertainment, filmmaking, dining and scenic beauty. Although tourism is crucial, it's also important to note that the businesses in the downtown Central Business District create a combined economic impact of a half-billion dollars a year on the local economy.

Nightlife is abundant. Dance clubs, jazz bars, live soaps, local and touring musicals, rock 'n' roll, rhythm and blues venues and more can be found in the 55-block area of the downtown commercial district.

Perhaps the nicest thing about downtown Wilmington — and something that separates it from the rest of the city and nearby communities — is its pleasant and fascinating walkability. The Riverwalk, with its view of the Battleship *North Carolina* moored on the western shore, is a great place to stroll, grab a hot dog from a street vendor, listen to free music and gaze at the river.

Because Wilmington is a prominent international port of call, it's likely that a stroller will see an occasional ship being escorted by tugs up the river. Military ships from other nations frequent the city, and there is a service — Dial-A-Sailor — that allows residents to invite sailors into their homes for dinner and cross-cultural exchange. The *Star-News* publishes an announcement when the ships are in town along with the Dial-A-Sailor phone number. The HMS *Bristol*, hailing from England, drops into town now and then, drawing excited locals who throng the docks to greet the crew. As a courtesy, this ship and others offer free tours of their oceangoing quarters.

A walk through the residential area, lush with live oaks draped in Spanish moss, beautiful azaleas and native oleander, is a plant enthusiast's delight. Most of the homes downtown have private gardens that are occasionally opened to the public during special events such as the Azalea Festival in the spring and Riverfest in the fall.

Downtown residents often leave their cars at home when they go out to shop, dine or bank because these destinations are mere blocks away. Given the strenuously enforced drinking-and-driving laws, it's a wise diner who can enjoy a little wine and not have to worry about driving home. There's also a strong sense of downtown identity that inclines residents toward spending their dollars with downtown merchants and restaurateurs because, after all, they're neighbors.

The film industry lends an exciting opportunity for spotting the occasional celebrity or just watching the process of making movies. Filmmaking now accounts for 12 percent of the local economy and promises to grow in the years ahead because of the interest the movie industry has in the region. Stars spotted in recent years include Katherine Hepburn, Alec Baldwin, Kim Basinger, Patrick Swayze, Julie Harris and Anthony Hopkins. Linda Lavin, Broadway star and a woman known affectionately as "Alice," from the '70s TV series, lives on Front Street when she isn't in New York.

INSIDERS' TIP

Springbrook Farms, the horse-and-carriage tour company operating in downtown Wilmington, has special Halloween, Easter and Christmas rides at family prices. Inquire at the first block of Market Street beside the river where the carriage departs.

Wilmington Suburbs

As Wilmington sprawls toward the beaches, so must this guide. With the advent of technologies that allowed people to easily move longer distances over the land, the boundaries of Wilmington increasingly pushed toward the sea in two directions: south and east. At the end of the century, there has been dramatic expansion to the north and west. It has become difficult to tell where Wilmington ends and New Hanover County begins.

With the dawn of the 20th century, the automobile and an electric trolley system allowed large numbers of Wilmingtonians to make greater use of the surrounding land. Downtown Wilmington radiates from its urban center through diverse neighborhoods in a crazy quilt of suburban areas to the north, east and south. The would-be resident can choose from modest to grand neighborhoods nestled among live oaks or pines. There is a neighborhood for every taste and budget (see our Real Estate chapter).

Most older neighborhoods located along or near the old trolley lines are conveniently close to Independence Mall on Oleander Drive, the largest shopping center in the region with 128 stores. Its shopping appeal is enhanced by the proximity of other centers and services.

Newer neighborhoods are springing up in profusion throughout Wilmington and New Hanover County. As residential populations expand into previously undeveloped areas closer to the Intracoastal Waterway and the various sounds, commercial businesses are following and creating community subcenters. Even gated residential communities find their borders flanked by shopping and service facilities, so it is a rare location that could be considered remote in New Hanover County today.

Many communities up and down the coastline from Wilmington feature excellent golf courses, tennis courts and community clubhouses for resident use. Courses and some club memberships are open to nonresidents for fees.

Carolina Beach

Carolina Beach is just twenty minutes down the road from downtown Wilmington on the narrow slip of land pressed between the Cape Fear River and the Atlantic Ocean dubbed Pleasure Island. Established in 1857, when Joseph Winner planned the streets and lots for the 50 acres of beach property he had purchased, the island's only access then was by water. In 1866, a steamship began carrying vacationers down the Cape Fear River to Snow's Cut, and a small railroad took them the rest of the way into Carolina Beach.

Carolina Beach has undergone a dramatic transformation during the 1990s. Once considered a wild party spot, it is now a heavily residential community dedicated to creating a wholesome family environment. Recent years have seen the cultivation of improved services, pleasant landscaping, attention to zoning and tangible citizen action to make Carolina Beach an attractive visitor destination. There's a busy central business district centered around an active yacht basin. The boardwalk is undergoing revitalization with an increase in the number of family-oriented establishments, including a planned arcade and restaurants.

A drive through Carolina Beach reveals a pleasant 1950s-style beach of modest cottages, increasingly more upscale single-family dwellings and an abundance of three- and four-story condominiums. Unfortunately, these taller structures were built on the oceanfront and tend to obstruct the view of the sea for several congested blocks on the north end. Newer development to the south is much more spread out and lower in height along the shoreline.

INSIDERS' TIP

Downtown Wilmington put up new, clear signs for parking times in 1998. Free spaces on the street range up to 2 hours. If you need more time, there are two public parking decks readily apparent on North Front Street facing the river and on North Second Street behind the post office.

In the heart of Carolina Beach is Jubilee Park, one of two amusement parks on the southern coast. Nearby, you'll find waterslides, miniature golf courses and other things that appeal to the kids. The town also has a movie theater, grocery stores and bait shops. The beachfront motels — including several vintage motor courts — offer a "blast from the past." If you were a kid during the '50s and your parents took you on vacation to the beach, this was the kind of place where you probably stayed. Some of the best beachfront lodging values are offered in these spots.

Anglers will love Carolina Beach. The surf promises wonderful bounty all year long, and there are plenty of tackle shops and piers as well as the opportunity to experience deep-sea fishing from the sterns of a number of charter boats berthed in the municipal yacht basin. Several annual fishing tournaments are based on the abundance of mackerel, and you can pay a nominal entry fee for a chance to reap as much as $50,000 for the winning fish.

At the extreme northern end of the island the beach is open to four-wheel drive vehicles. While there is a certain allure to driving right off the street onto the sand of this expansive space, don't do it if you are in a car. Getting stuck in the sand is as easy and frustrating as getting stuck in the snow.

Carolina Beach also offers one of the few state parks in the region. For a modest fee, you can camp and enjoy the wonders of nature. Venus's-flytrap, a carnivorous plant, is abundant in the park. This plant, a relic from prehuman existence on the planet, only grows naturally within a 60-mile radius of Wilmington.

Away from the seasonal bustle at the center of town, Carolina Beach is a quiet community of about 5,000 regular residents. That number jumps five times at the peak of the vacation season. The community is growing in appeal to locals from Wilmington for one big reason: It isn't crowded, yet. You have plenty of elbow room on the beach; there is no problem finding parking at the bargain rate of $2 a day in the central business district; and some of the better vacation rental deals are here. Many a Wilmingtonian has given Wrightsville Beach over to visitors for the summer in the past few years and turned to Carolina Beach for a quiet spot on the sand.

Kure Beach

Carolina Beach dissolves into the town of Kure Beach just to the south. Kure Beach (pronounced "cure-ee") is a younger community. Development began in the 1870s when Hans Andersen Kure moved from Denmark and bought large tracts of land in the middle of the island. Apparently, things moved slowly because Kure Beach wasn't incorporated until 1947. Today, it is overwhelmingly residential, dotted with modest cottages, new houses and several old-style beach motels. Several apartment buildings cluster together in one spot, but there is little else in the way of tall buildings here because condominiums are not allowed. In fact, new structures may not be built taller than 35 feet.

You'll find neither arcade nor amusement park here. There is very little in the way of shopping. A permanent population of only about 700 residents makes for a very close community, but Kure Beach's small size should not lead visitors to think they're out in the boondocks. The town maintains its own municipal services and fire protection, and a local planner describes the community as being "like any big city, only smaller."

Kure Beach will remain small because it is surrounded by buffer zones. The Fort Fisher State Recreation Area and Historic Site is on the south side, and the U.S. government owns the west side as part of the military terminal at Sunny Point across the Cape Fear River. Of course, there's the ocean, too.

If you're looking for peace and quiet in a friendly setting, Kure Beach is the place to go. A word to visitors who bring their dogs: Kure Beach never allows dogs on the beach, not even on a leash. This is the only beach community within the range of this guide that has this policy on a year-round basis.

Fort Fisher

Farther south, toward the point where the Cape Fear River and the Atlantic Ocean finally converge, the summer homes increase in size and opulence near Fort Fisher. Twisted live oaks cover the landscape and increase in density until, at last, natural flora overtakes architecture.

There are several spots of interest near

> **"Talk Of The Town"**
> Your Morning News Magazine of the Airwaves!
>
> Local News • Weather • Breaking News • Newsmaker Interviews • Traffic • Sports
>
> WEEKDAYS 6 AM - 9 AM
> NEWSTALK 980
> WAAV

the end of the island. Fort Fisher, an earthworks fort of significance during the Civil War, appears on the right. The North Carolina Aquarium at Fort Fisher, a fine facility that boasts a touch tank and a close-up encounter with live sharks, comes up on the left. Near the aquarium is a beach where anglers in four-wheel drive vehicles flock to take in the bounty of the waters. At the end of it all is the Fort Fisher-Southport Ferry, possibly the best $3 cruise in the world (see our Getting Around chapter). The beach on the south end of Fort Fisher is open to four-wheel drive vehicles.

All in all, these southernmost beaches of New Hanover County offer 7.5 miles of very pleasant vacationing and living.

Wrightsville Beach

Wrightsville Beach is a special place for both the resident and the visitor and quite unlike the commercial beaches that often come to mind when one thinks of the coast. There is no carnival atmosphere — no Ferris wheels or gaudy displays of beach merchandise (well, maybe just one that locals try hard to overlook), no bumper boats, no arcade. Instead, Wrightsville Beach is primarily an affluent residential community that has its roots in Wilmington.

For nearly a century, Wrightsville Beach has been the main retreat from summer heat for residents of Wilmington. Many of the homes are owned by city residents whose families have maintained ownership through the decades, and that is not likely to change during the rest of the century.

Wrightsville Beach was incorporated in 1899 as a resort community. The Tidewater Power Company built a trolley system from downtown to the beach, providing the only land access to the island until 1935. The company, which owned the island, was interested in development and built the Hotel Tarrymore in 1905 to attract visitors and revenue. Later named The Oceanic, this grand hotel burned down in 1934, along with most structures on the northern half of the island. Lumina, a beach pavilion, was

Welcome to "Wilmywood"

Believe it or not, more movies are filmed each year in Wilmington than in any other American city except Los Angeles and New York. TV's long-running *Matlock* series, starring Andy Griffith, was filmed here, as were TV's *American Gothic,* many commercials, music videos and industrial films.

At the heart of this phenomenon is EUE/Screen Gems Studios, a 32-acre complex on N. 23rd Street. Some of the studio's eight sound stages — totaling more than 100,000 square feet — are among the largest in the East. And you've probably seen the backlot several times on screen, although you probably thought you were looking at the streets of New York City, New Orleans, Beirut, Detroit or Bucharest.

The spark that ignited Wilmington's steadily burning film industry came in 1983 when Stephen King's *Firestarter* was filmed at the studios, then owned by Dino DeLaurentis. Carolco Pictures (makers of the *Terminator* films) bought the studio in 1989, then EUE/Screen Gems in 1996. Wilmington's ideal weather, its variety of locations, accessibility to transportation and low labor costs offer the film industry an effective formula for success.

So it's not surprising so many Wilmingtonians have film experience. Local musicians performed in *The Radioland Murders*. Local dancers went *Stomping at the Savoy*. Scores of locals earn their livings as "techies." Hundreds more work as on-screen extras. At least one Wilmington city councilman may be seen in TV commercials. The Cape Fear Filmmakers Accord, (910) 763-3456, is a consortium of crews, staff and screenwriters that publishes its own directory.

State-of-the-art recording studios serving the film industry also thrive around town. It's not unusual to see major Hollywood celebrities frequenting local restaurants and clubs while they're in town for a shoot. And fees collected for film permits go toward downtown beautification projects.

— continued on next page

The streets of a bygone New York City came to life on the studio backlot for the filming of *Billy Bathgate*.

AREA OVERVIEW • 27

Just a glance at the following sample of movies and TV shows made in and around Wilmington (the list is always growing) makes it clear why Wilmington has earned the nickname "Wilmywood":

Virus, 29th Street, Dawson's Creek, Against Her Will: The Carrie Buck Story, Alan and Naomi, Betsy's Wedding, Billy Bathgate, Blue Velvet, Crimes of the Heart, The Crow, Dream a Little Dream, Empire, Everybody Wins, Fall Time, Golden Years, Justice and a Small Town: The Sandra Prine Story, Lolita, Margaret: A Burning Passion, The Member of the Wedding, Noble House, Out of Carolina, Raw Deal, Simple Justice, Sleeping With the Enemy, The Squeeze, A Stoning in Fulham County, To Gillian on Her 37th Birthday, Too Young the Hero, Truman Capote's One Christmas, Tune In Tomorrow, Virus, When We Were Colored, Windmills of the Gods, and *Year of the Dragon.*

And who could forget *Amos & Andrew, Bad With Numbers, Cannibal Vampire Schoolgirls from Outer Space, Cyborg, Date with an Angel, The Exorcist III, Firestarter, King Kong Lives, Little Monsters, Loose Cannons, The Lost Capone, Super Mario Bros., Teenage Mutant Ninja Turtles, Teenage Mutant Ninja Turtles II: The Secret of the Ooze, Weeds,* and *Weekend at Bernie's.*

The sound stages and back lot of EUE/Screen Gems are open for public tours at noon and 2 PM every Saturday. The tour lasts about an hour and costs $5. Reservations are recommended. Call (910) 675-8479.

also built by the Tidewater Power Company to attract visitors. On the site of the current Oceanic Restaurant at the south end of the beach, Lumina offered a festive place where locals gathered for swimming, dancing and outdoor movies. The building was demolished in 1973.

Development of the beach continued steadily until 1954 when Hurricane Hazel, a monster of a storm, came ashore and wreaked devastation on the island's homes and buildings. Hazel also shoaled the channel between Wrightsville Beach and adjacent Shell Island. Developers, seeing an opportunity for expansion, filled in the remaining water and joined the islands together. Today, the area is the site of the Shell Island Resort Hotel and numerous condominiums and large homes.

In the aftermath of two hurricanes in 1996, the resort hotel finds itself precariously close to an advancing inlet. North Carolina has very strict laws regarding seawalls because of their negative impact on the rest of a beach, and the state has denied permission to Shell Island's condominium owners to erect a hard wall. It's a serious example of how important it is to keep a respectable distance from the sea. Litigation surrounds this unhappy situation at this writing and, given the fickle nature of the sea, it's hard to predict how things are going to go. Temporary sandbags are in place and there's talk of dredging the inlet, but only time will tell the fate of this building.

Today's Wrightsville Beach is a very busy and prosperous place. The area is still a stronghold of long-term residents who summer in family homes built to catch the ocean breeze. The permanent residential population is approximately 3,050, but that figure swells considerably in the summer. With a land mass of nearly a square mile, this island manages to maintain its charm despite increasing numbers of visitors. At the peak of the summer season, there are 12,000 overnight visitors and 30,000 daytrippers on the island each day. Surprisingly, brisk commercial development in the form of marinas, restaurants and other services has not seriously changed the residential orientation of the island.

INSIDERS' TIP

Get a glimpse of what life at old Wrightsville Beach was like at the Wrightsville Beach Museum of History, (910) 256-2569, 303 W. Salisbury St., Wrightsville Beach. (Where else?)

A visitor to Wrightsville Beach is bound to be impressed by the clean and uncluttered nature of the place. The residential atmosphere encourages a dedication to keeping the beach clean. Lifeguards oversee the safety of swimmers in the summer season, and the beach patrol keeps an eye on the area to make sure laws are obeyed. Alcohol and glass containers are not allowed on the beach. If you have questions, just ask one of the friendly lifeguards.

Boaters, sun worshippers, swimmers, surfers and anglers will find much to appreciate and enjoy about the setting. Public access points, liberally sprinkled across the island, make a day in the sun a free experience for daytrippers — with the notable exception of parking. Always an issue at Wrightsville Beach, the parking situation was exacerbated by the completion of I-40 in 1991. In 1997, traffic counts indicated that 48,000 cars passed over the bridge headed to Wrightsville Beach on the Fourth of July alone. Insiders know the island is extremely crowded during peak summer weekends and are therefore more inclined to leave those times to visitors. On those weekends, visitors are advised to arrive before 9:30 AM and bring plenty of quarters for the parking meters. (A quarter buys 30 minutes.) Parking lots at area restaurants and hotels are vigilantly guarded, and residents are not inclined to allow unknown cars to occupy their driveways for more than three seconds. Towing is very strictly enforced in no-parking zones.

Opportunities for water-related sports and entertainment are plentiful on Wrightsville Beach. Some of the most luxurious marinas along the North Carolina coast are clustered around the bridge at the Intracoastal Waterway and offer a full range of services. Charter boats, both power and sail, are available in abundance. Jet Ski rental, windsurfing, kayaking and sailing lessons are there for the asking. Bait, tackle, piers and more than enough advice on the best way to fish are all easy to find. Visitors who bring their own boats will appreciate the free boat ramp just north of the first bridge onto Harbour Island, the island between the mainland and Wrightsville Beach.

A visit to Wrightsville Beach, whether for a day or for a vacation, is bound to be a memorable experience that will be repeated time after time. The island is wonderfully walkable, and you can find everything you need for a comfortable and memorable vacation almost any time of the year.

Figure Eight Island

Figure Eight Island is a private, residential, oceanfront resort community just north of Wrightsville Beach. It has moved closer to Wrightsville in recent years as the inlet has shifted to the south. This island is, in the most extreme sense, a highly restricted residential island of very expensive homes. It's a favorite hideaway for stars and political bigwigs who want privacy when they're visiting the area. Vice President Gore and family, for example, enjoyed a vacation here in 1997.

The development includes a yacht club, marina, tennis courts and a boat ramp. The island is connected to the mainland by a causeway bridge, and a guard will only let you onto the island if you've called ahead to someone on the island, such as a friend or a real estate agent, and are on the list at the gate.

The celebrity orientation of the island doesn't mean regular folk can't rent homes and enjoy a private vacation. In fact, the island is very hospitable to vacationers and welcomes guests to its uncrowded shores. You can rent opulent vacation homes here (there are no modest ones) by calling Figure Eight Realty at (910) 686-4400. Some of the larger Wilmington real estate companies may also handle properties on this exclusive island (see our chapter on Weekly and Long-Term Rentals).

Masonboro Island

South of Wrightsville Beach and north of Carolina Beach is Masonboro Island. One of the last and largest pristine barrier islands remaining on the southern North Carolina coast, this island is accessible only by boat. If you are fortunate enough to have a shoal-draft boat, just look for a spot to put in among the reeds — probably alongside other boats — and tie a meaningful line to the shore with your anchor because, as in all areas of the Cape Fear region, the tides have wide fluctuation.

Although parts of the island belong to private landowners, no development is allowed. Masonboro is a component of the North Carolina National Estuarine Research Reserve. The island is home to gray foxes, cotton rats, a variety of birds, river otters and several species of aquatic life.

You can spot the island by the large number of pleasure craft clustered on the Masonboro Sound side. If you want to be more alone, pass by this gathering and look for small passages farther to the south on the island. Access is only limited by the draft of your boat and how easily you can push it off when you run aground. Gather your gear and hike a short way to the ocean beach, where it's a special pleasure to take a picnic and relax on the uncrowded beach. There are no facilities so be prepared to rough it. If you make the trip in the fall, be sure to take along insect repellant because the yellow flies can be extremely annoying.

Pender and Onslow Counties

Topsail Island

Topsail (pronounced "TOP-sull") Island has the distinction of spanning two counties. In a way, county affiliation seems insignificant because the island is an entity unto itself. This long island — 27 miles— is north of Wilmington, about a 45-minute drive.

Topsail Island allegedly got its name from pirates who would hide in the coves awaiting the view of a top of a sail. Once a ship was seen it could be easily ambushed in the channel and relieved of its cargo. Eventually, merchant seamen learned to look for sails over in the coves, and pirating went on the skids.

In 1946 Topsail Island was taken over by the U.S. Navy to begin Project Bumblebee, a missile program that was a predecessor to Florida's rocket program at Cape Canaveral. The first supersonic missiles in the country were tested on this remote island. It was, technically, a secret project, although residents in the mainland area must have noticed the launching of 200 prototype missiles between 1946 and 1948.

Remains of the project can be observed on the island. Seven concrete missile observation towers, including two that have been converted into homes, remain on the island. The launch pad is now the patio for the Jolly Roger Hotel.

Topsail is another fishing community. Topsail Inlet is subject to shoaling, a constant concern. Commercial fishermen with considerable experience traverse the tricky inlet; pleasure boaters are strongly advised to go south to Masonboro Inlet south of Wrightsville Beach for sure passage into the Atlantic. Hurricane Fran carved a new inlet through the island, but it isn't navigable.

The island is a haven for sea turtles, and the residents are vigilant in their protection of these creatures. The Topsail Turtle Project, an all-volunteer operation, dedicates itself each season to the preservation and protection of sea turtles.

Topsail Island is largely a residential community. It took a serious whacking from Hurricane Fran, but the community is recovering. Frankly, it lost its marina, several restaurants, quite a few homes and its piers, but the resolve of islanders is returning the beautiful island to its former appeal. After all, the view of the ocean is still the same.

Surf City is the "big city" of the island, in the center and connected to the mainland by a 40-year-old swing bridge on N.C. Highways 50/210. Although this is a modest, small town by anyone's standards, it serves the island well with restaurants, a grocery store, gift shops and other commercial enterprises. Surf City was part of what has been described locally as the "miracle mile" in Hurricane Fran's aftermath, avoiding the destruction that was particularly evident farther north.

Brunswick County

Southport

Southport is reachable by both ferry and scenic highway. Leaving Wilmington, take the Cape Fear Memorial Bridge and hang a fast left onto N.C. Highway 133 just off U.S. Highways 17, 74 and 76. If you miss it, you can also take N.C. Highway 87, although the N.C.

133 route is very beautiful and offers several attractions, including Orton Plantation, the Carolina Power & Light nuclear plant with its visitor center, and Brunswick Town, site of the first European colony in the region. For information on the ferry route and schedule, see our Getting Around chapter.

The city of Southport is steeped in history. This coastal community saw the establishment of North Carolina's first fort in 1754: Fort Johnston. A small community of river pilots, fishermen and tradespeople grew up around the fort. In 1792, the town of Smithville was created. In 1808, Smithville became the county seat of Brunswick County. For the remainder of the century, the town made plans to link rail service with the existing river traffic to make the community a major southern port, and the city was renamed Southport.

The town is widely regarded as the Fourth of July Capital of North Carolina. Southport celebrated the Fourth of July just after the signing of the Declaration of Independence in 1776. History records that in 1795, citizens gathered at Fort Johnston and observed a 13-gun military salute to the original 13 states. In 1813, a Russian warship anchored in the harbor fired a 13-gun salute, and it was on this Fourth of July that fireworks were used for the first time to close the celebration. In 1972, the Fourth of July Festival was chartered and incorporated as the official North Carolina Fourth of July Festival, and it has become a tremendously popular four-day event for residents and visitors.

Southport, listed on the National Register of Historic Places, is ranked by both Rand McNally and Kiplinger as one of the most desirable places in the United States to retire to. The live oak-lined streets, charming architecture, quaint shops — most notably an abundance of antiques shops — as well as year-round golf, boating and fishing seasons, create an enormously pleasant environment. This is the place for people who genuinely want to really kick back and enjoy beautiful coastal scenery. With a year-round population of 2,400, there's still plenty of elbow room.

Park your car — it's free — and just walk around until you discover shops, restaurants and views that please you. It's an extremely casual community that invites visitors to pause and savor a slow pace of life that is fast disappearing in nearby Wilmington.

Bald Head Island

Just off the coast of Southport and the mainland, at the mouth of the Cape Fear River, is the pristine island of Bald Head. The island is easily identifiable in the distance by the wide-based Bald Head Island lighthouse, a structure built in 1817, retired in 1935 and cataloged as the oldest lighthouse in North Carolina.

Once a favorite hiding spot for pirates such as Blackbeard and Stede Bonnet, Bald Head Island is now an affluent residential and resort community of about 80 year-round residents that can only be reached by the island's private ferry or personal boat. The island is graciously open to the public, and the summer population can reach 3,000 with visitors renting vacation homes and playing golf. (See our Golf chapter for course and rates.)

It is probably safe to say this is one of the most unspoiled beach and maritime forest areas on the North Carolina coast. Despite residential development, as well as a few commercial amenities such as a restaurant, bed and breakfast, general store with deli, marina, golf course, specialty store and electric cart and bike rental business, the island's natural beauty is still protected.

The island has 14 miles of beaches, unspoiled dunes, creeks and forests. The 2,000 acres of land are surrounded by 10,000 acres of salt marshes. The owners have deeded nearby Middle Island and Bluff Island to the state and The Nature Conservancy. The Bald Head Island Conservancy, a nonprofit organization, was formed to ensure that the unique natural resources of the island are maintained and preserved.

The Sea Turtle Program, featured on public television, protects and monitors these wonderful creatures. Turtle nesting on Bald Head Island accounts for 50 percent of all turtle eggs laid in North Carolina. There is an Adopt-a-Nest Program that pairs concerned humans with turtles in an effort to protect the nest and encourage the hatchlings toward the sea. Studies in which female turtles were tagged have revealed that pregnant turtles return to the same site every other year. Due to the

Discover the Undiscovered

Southport – Oak Island Chamber of Commerce

Southport • Long Beach
Yaupon Beach • Boiling Spring Lakes
Caswell Beach • Bald Head Island

Call
1-800-457-6964
for our 1998
Vacation & Resident's
Guide

Look for us on the INTERNET'S World Wide Web
http://www.oak-island.com/chamber
http://www.southport.net/chamber.html

many species of birds found on the island, the Audubon Society conducts an annual count here as part of its national program.

Something quite special about the island is the absence of cars. Gasoline-powered engines, with the exception of security and maintenance vehicles, are not allowed. The residents and visitors who rent lovely homes all drive electric carts or ride bicycles. The resulting lack of noise pollution and exhaust fumes is one of the finest features of the place. A visitor can come for the day by private ferry service from Indigo Plantation in Southport. The cost is $15 roundtrip. Day parking in Southport is $4, although this is subject to change. For a longer stay, there are many rental units on the island. The cost, compared to rental on much of the mainland, is slightly on the upper end, but so is the experience for the visitor who wants to really get away from it all in quiet style.

Despite Bald Head Island's private status, the welcome mat is always out for visitors. There are several daytripper packages available that include lunch or dinner, historic tours and ferry service. The lighthouse is open all year, and there is no fee. The well-appointed marina welcomes transients. For information on Bald Head Island's numerous amenities, call (800) 234-1666.

Oak Island

Just across the water from Bald Head Island and Southport is Oak Island, a narrow strip of land that is separated into three beach communities: Caswell Beach, Yaupon Beach and Long Beach.

Caswell Beach is the site of Fort Caswell, a military stronghold that dates from 1826. Fort Caswell is now owned by the North Carolina Baptist Assembly and welcomes visitors of all denominations each year. The community has some summer homes, but the area has mostly permanent residences. The year-round population is 191, but up to 1,200 people can be staying on this part of Oak Island in the summer.

Yaupon Beach is a haven for live oaks and is named for a species of holly that grows in the area. Known as a family beach, Yaupon is populated mainly by its 780 permanent residents, most of whom are retirees. Recreational areas include a championship golf course, nine beach access points, a picnic area on the Elizabeth River estuary system and fishing piers.

As the name implies, Long Beach occupies the longest stretch of beach on Oak Island, but its greater claim to fame is the fact that it is Brunswick County's largest town, with a population of more than 4,150. There are 52 access points to the absolutely uncrowded beaches, and you'll find a few restaurants and motels. For the most part, a visitor will enjoy renting a house for an extended vacation here. In fact, vacation rental is the liveliest business on the beach, with approximately 14 rental companies operating on Oak Island.

South Brunswick Islands

Of the three islands in the group known as the South Brunswick Islands, Holden Beach is the longest. Stretching 11 miles along the Atlantic, the island is a jogger's paradise. The village has about 768 permanent residents, and visitors will find a host of opportunities for assimilating themselves into this exceedingly quiet family community. The beach and the sea are the central attractions in this town, which prides itself on a serene quality of life.

Ocean Isle Beach is the center island, offering 8 miles of beach with a total resort experience: restaurants, specialty shops, public tennis courts, access to all watersports and a waterslide. This beach has the only high-rise on the South Brunswick Islands. There is an airport that makes getting to Ocean Isle accessible by air, but don't expect to see commercial jets at this relatively small facility. Home to almost 650 full-time residents, Ocean Isle welcomes visitors to a peaceful place.

Sunset Beach, described as a diminutive island gem, is only 3 miles long. Despite its size, this island has experienced a 150-percent population increase between 1990 and 1997, with a current year-round population of 720. Reachable by a one-lane pontoon bridge, making it the only island without a high-rise bridge in Brunswick County, there is sometimes a bit of a wait to get to Sunset in the high tourist season. However, the island is well worth the wait. This bridge will probably be replaced by a high-rise bridge eventually if the

South Brunswick Islands
CHAMBER OF COMMERCE

Shallotte
NC
17
SC
Calabash
Sunset Beach
Ocean Isle Beach
Holden Beach
Atlantic Ocean

For Information:
P.O. Box 1380
Shallotte, NC
28459

Uncrowded.

Unhurried.

Unforgettable.

1-800-426-6644

Pelicans from along the Cape Fear River pay a visit to a local fishing dock.

Department of Transportation has its way, but that discussion has been going on for years. Islanders like their bridge the way it is for the most part because it tends to keep traffic levels down.

Again, this island is residential in character. Some of the best bargains in vacation rental are here, and the visitor who wants a quiet coastal place will do very well to book a house on this beach. As with all of the beaches on the southern coast, quality golfing is available on the mainland. For fishing enthusiasts, there is a full-service pier.

Sunset Beach offers a special delight: a walk to Bird Island at low tide. Bird Island is completely untouched by development at this writing. A walk through the shallow inlet at low tide is easy for children as well as adults. Frequently, there are informal guided tours, announced by posters attached to street markers on the beach, so it's easy to hook up with locals who are pleased to share their knowledge of the island with you. The environment is purely natural and deeply comforting, where people of the 20th century can experience life as it was before the development of the land.

Calabash

Just a few miles from Sunset Beach is the town of Calabash. This charming seaport is known widely as the "Fried Seafood Capital of the World," with 17 restaurants serving battered-and-fried shrimp, fish and oysters in a style that is indigenous to North Carolina. There have been some health-conscious changes in the oil used by many Calabash restaurants, but the taste is still authentic Calabash style.

Calabash merged with Carolina Shores in 1993, increasing the number of permanent residents from 221 to 1,200 overnight. Carolina Shores is an affluent, golf course community comprised of mostly retirees. While it wasn't an easy merger, things seem to have settled down considerably. Yet, as this book goes to press, there are new rumors of secession. Currently, the town has about 1,500 residents.

Shallotte

The town of Shallotte serves as the hub for services for Brunswick County's beach communities. In fact, it is perhaps best-known as the commercial mecca of the county. Because of its mainland location and island proximity, Shallotte offers residents and visitors the convenience of larger-town living and services. The town has a year-round population of approximately 2,000.

Area Chambers of Commerce

Chambers of Commerce are great resources for gaining an understanding of the big picture in terms of a community's business, educational, entertainment and institutional flavor. Although this organization is not generally in the tourism business, it has brochure racks filled with information of interest to the visitor, newcomer and even the long-time resident who just wants to know what's going on. Staff members are always courteous and interested in providing information to visitors.

Greater Wilmington Chamber of Commerce, 1 Estell Lee Place, Wilmington, (910) 762-2611

Carolina Beach Chamber of Commerce, 201 Lumberton Avenue, Carolina Beach, (910) 458-8434

Topsail Area Chamber of Commerce and Tourism, 205 S. Topsail Drive, Topsail Island, (910) 328-4722, (800) 626-2780

Hampstead Chamber of Commerce, U.S. Highway 17, Hampstead, (910) 270-9642, (800) 833-2483

Southport/Oak Island Chamber of Commerce, 4841 Long Beach Road S.E., Southport, (910) 457-6964

South Brunswick Islands Chamber of Commerce, 4948 Main Street, Shallotte, (910) 754-6644, (800) 426-6644

Myrtle Beach Area Chamber of Commerce, 1200 N. Oak Street, Myrtle Beach, S.C., (803) 626-7444

Carolina Beach teems with small, family-run motels concentrated within a small area.

Hotels and Motels

The number of hotel and motel accommodations in Wilmington has taken a dramatic leap, with new units being built at a record rate, particularly in the area surrounding the intersections of S. College Road, Market Street and New Centre Drive. But even though resort hotels, efficiency apartments and simple motel lodgings truly abound, don't count on coming to town without a reservation if you're traveling on holiday weekends — even Valentine's Day!

Full-service resort and business hotels are strategically located in desirable areas such as Wilmington's riverfront and Wrightsville Beach. In smaller towns such as Surf City, Carolina Beach, Yaupon Beach and others, lower-priced oceanfront motels are more common. In Wilmington, the motel strip is Market Street west of College Road, with some overflow onto College Road itself.

You can find motels of every price range there, from the budget Motel 6 to the pricier Ramada Inn. Carolina Beach teems with small, family-run motels concentrated within a small area — no fewer than 15 line Carolina Beach Avenue N. within a half-mile of Harper Avenue. In general, beach motels, especially the older ones, are known for their great locations rather than their stylish decor.

There are no hotels or motels on Bald Head Island. Daily accommodations are limited to one large bed and breakfast inn (see our Bed and Breakfast Inns chapter). Some rental homes are available for stays as short as a weekend (see our Weekly and Long-Term Cottage Rentals chapter).

We've listed here a cross-section of accommodations — inexpensive and expensive, elegant and downscale, busy and peaceful. Of course there are many others, but the ones here all share the kind of quality we feel comfortable recommending to our own friends and family.

Price Code

Since prices are subject to change without notice, we provide only price guidelines based on double-occupancy per night during the summer ("high" season). Guidelines do not reflect the 6 percent state and 3 percent local taxes. Most establishments offer lower rates during the off-season, but always confirm rates and necessary amenities before reserving. It may also pay to inquire about corporate, senior citizen or long-term discounts even when such discounts are not mentioned in our descriptions. Most establishments accept major credit cards, but personal checks tend to be accepted only when making payment well in advance.

$	Less than $75
$$	$75 to $120
$$$	$120 to $150
$$$$	$150 and more

Wilmington

Coast Line Inn
$$-$$$ • 503 Nutt St. • (910) 763-2800

On the Riverwalk at the historic Coast Line Center, Coast Line has 50 rooms, each with a fine river view. The decor is warmly appointed with artwork, and the rooms are meticulously maintained. Computer/modem hookups and coffee makers are available in every room. Complimentary continental breakfasts are placed in baskets outside your room if desired, and laundry service is available. The River's Edge Lounge on the fourth floor is a great place to enjoy sunsets and, on Wednesday and Friday nights, live entertainment. The lounge opens at 5 PM Monday through Saturday. The Coast Line Inn is within easy, safe walking distance of many fine restaurants.

The adjacent Coast Line Convention Center, 501 Nutt Street, (910) 763-6739, occupies a historic building that was once part of Wilmington's railroad depot, serving what was then one of the world's most important cotton exchanges. The convention center consists of more than 10,000 square feet of space, which can be reconfigured into four rooms of various sizes. It provides a unique setting and ambiance for conferences, seminars, trade and fashion shows, banquets, weddings or practically any other function. There's plenty of parking, and additional hotel accommodations are within easy walking distance.

Comfort Inn Wilmington
$-$$ • 151 S. College Rd.
• (910) 791-4841

The Comfort Inn provides excellent amenities for the price, which explains its popularity among families and business travelers alike. It is a newly remodeled, 146-room establishment midway between downtown Wilmington and the beach. Laundry and valet services, complimentary beverages in the lobby/lounge, free local telephone calls, an outdoor pool and free guest membership to Gold's Gym (located close by) contribute to the Comfort Inn's value. Continental breakfasts and daily newspapers are available each morning in the lobby.

Children younger than 18 stay free when sharing their parents' room. Handicapped-accessible rooms and corporate discounts are available, and all guests are entitled to a 10-percent discount at certain local restaurants. If you forget any personal toiletries, the staff will provide them free. Meeting rooms can accommodate up to 50 people for board meetings and conferences. Reservations may also be made through a central booking service, (800) 221-2222, or by fax (910) 790-9100.

Courtyard Marriott
$-$$ • 151 Van Campen Blvd.
• (910) 395-8224

Debuting in 1997, this 128-room hotel offers comfortable accommodations especially suitable to the business traveler. Rooms include large work desks, fold-out sofas, ironing equipment, cable TV with video games, coffee machines, two-line telephones with voice mail, and data ports. Roll-aways and cribs are available, as well as dry-cleaning service (except Sundays), self-service laundry facilities and a fitness room.

The eponymous courtyard features a pool, whirlpool spa, and gazebo amid colorful landscaping. Beneath the high-peaked ceiling of the lobby cafe, a moderately priced breakfast buffet (free for kids three and under) is available daily from 7 to 11 AM. In the evenings you can relax beside the fireplace in the lounge, where drinks are served nightly from 5 to 11 PM (except Sundays). The hotel also has meeting and banquet space available. The Courtyard Marriott is accessible via Imperial Drive—turn right from the southbound lanes of S. College Road just south of the Market Street overpass.

Front Street Inn
$$$-$$$$ • 215 S. Front St.
• (910) 762-6442

Full of Southwestern ambiance, rooms at the Front Street Inn feature original American art and decor inspired by such namesakes as Monet, Hemingway, Cousteau and O'Keeffe. Full kitchens, wet bars, French doors and exposed brick are typical, and some rooms feature canopied beds, futon sofas and Jacuzzis. The inn occupies the renovated Salvation Army building (1923) across the street from Chandler's Wharf and has great views of river sunsets from the second-floor balcony.

The Sol y Sombra bar and breakfast room

INSIDERS' TIP

Appreciate the value of shoes at the beach: The asphalt and sand get very hot, and there are sand spurs in the grass and dunes. Also, day-sailing in Banks Channel is often over oyster beds.

COASTLINE INN
AND
CONVENTION CENTER
Riverfront Rooms, Suites
and Intimate Lounge

Facilities for Meetings, Conventions, Trade Shows and Events for up to 1,000 people

*Come Enjoy Historic Wilmington
on the Cape Fear River*

Accommodations (910)763-2800 • Reservations (800)617-7732
Meeting/Convention Info • (910) 763-6739
503 Nutt Street • Wilmington, NC 28401
http://coast-inn.wilmington.net
email:clinn@wilmington.net

North Carolina's Southern coast is also a great place to slow down.

offers continental fare (organic coffee, fruit, yogurt, biscotti) plus beer, wine and champagne, unless room service is preferred. Innkeepers Stefany and Jay Rhodes will cater to any reasonable request (how about supplying chocolates and flowers for an anniversary surprise?). There is plenty of off-street parking. Corporate and long-term rates are available.

Holiday Inn
$$-$$$ • 4903 Market St.
• (910) 799-1440

With 232 guest rooms, this is Wilmington's largest hotel, providing full-service amenities such as coffee and newspapers each morning. Other conveniences include guest laundry and valet service, room service, a courtesy van, banquet space for up to 100 people, cable TV and On Command Video, and a "Forget Me Not" program providing personal toiletries to guests who forgot their own. The Holiday Inn boasts an outdoor Olympic-size swimming pool and the Glass Garden Restaurant and Lounge next door.

Holiday Inn Express Hotel & Suites
$$-$$$ • 160 Van Campen Blvd.
• (910) 392-3227, (888) 489-8889

Among the newest hotels in Wilmington, this one provides a range of amenities, from king- and double-bedded rooms to suites featuring whirlpool baths or Jacuzzis. All rooms include cable TV with Nintendo, coffee makers, voice-mail telephones and data hookups. Complimentary continental breakfasts may be taken in front of the fireplace in the comfortable living room-style lounge or overlooking the outdoor pool. Other amenities include a fitness room, boardroom, coin-operated laundry, complimentary daily newspaper, and meeting facilities to accommodate up to 150 people.

To find the Holiday Inn Express, turn right onto Imperial Drive from the southbound lanes of S. College Road just south of the Market Street overpass.

Howard Johnson Plaza Hotel and Conference Center
$$$-$$$$ • 5032 Market St.
• (910) 392-1101, (800) 833-4721

A full-service hotel offering expanded amenities such as in-room coffee makers, the Plaza is 3 miles from downtown and 7 miles from Wrightsville Beach. It is especially well-suited to corporate travelers, having courtesy airport transportation, telephone/computer jacks in all 124 guest rooms, office equipment and meeting facilities to accommodate up to 500 people. Guests may also avail themselves of the indoor heated pool and whirlpool, sauna, fitness center, laundry and valet service and premium cable TV. The hotel has electronic card lock room keys, three suites and Rigby's Restaurant and Lounge adjoining the main building.

Courtyard by Marriott Wilmington

- 128 guest rooms
- Six suites w/refrigerators and microwaves
- Full hot breakfast buffet
- Lounge open evenings
- Outdoor pool w/jacuzzi
- Exercise room
- Guest laundry facility
- Complimentary coffee 24 hours
- Banquet facilities
- Rooms offer in room coffee, irons and ironing boards, voice mail, pay movies and nintendo

151 Van Campen Blvd. Wilmington, NC 28403
Reservations: 910•395•8224(direct) ♦ **800•321•2211**(Marriott Worldwide)

The Inn at St. Thomas Court
$$$-$$$$ • 101 S. Second St.
• (910) 343-1800, (800) 525-0909

The St. Thomas is a beautifully designed and sophisticated 34-unit accommodation just two blocks from the Cape Fear River. Room decor ranges from country French and Southwestern to antebellum and embraces tasteful artwork, replica antique furnishings, handsome rugs over wide-plank floors and modern conveniences. Continental breakfast baskets are delivered to your door at the time you request. Some rooms are fully equipped with kitchenettes, wet bars and washer/dryers and are suitable for long stays; some have microwave ovens. Second-floor terraces have comfortable chairs for each room.

Ample off-street parking is available. The attentive staff will help arrange tee times at golf courses throughout the region and assist with planning recreational activities. Office services such as fax and photocopying are available, and rooms are equipped with computer data ports.

The inn also owns the new City Club at de Rosset, an exclusive private club offering its members high-end dining and facilities for social and business meetings at the fully restored de Rosset House, one of Wilmington's grandest antebellum mansions, across Dock Street from the inn. For the public, the City Club offers magnificent overnight accommodations consisting of six luxurious upstairs suites. Each suite is uniquely decorated; all use 19th-century style to good effect, with such details as decorative stenciling, working gas fireplaces and original heart-pine floors. The Cupola Suite offers a panoramic view from the cupola at the top of the building.

Ramada Inn Conference Center
$$-$$$ • 5001 Market St.
• (910) 799-1730

Services and affordability make the Ramada an excellent choice for business people and tourists alike. Situated about midway between downtown Wilmington and Wrightsville Beach, the 100-room establishment provides top-notch amenities in keeping with corporate-chain standards. These include airport transportation, room service, valet and laundry service, cable TV and an outdoor pool. An executive suite features a boardroom with a refrigerator and wet bar, conference table and adjoining rooms.

The Ramada can accommodate banquets for up to 400 people. There is no charge for children younger than 18 staying with parents. The adjoining nightclub is among Wilmington's more popular, featuring Top 40 dance music and shagging. The adjoining restaurant serves breakfast, lunch and dinner. The club and restaurant are open every day. Reservations may

Few walks are as rewarding as those beside the surf.

be made through a central booking service at (800) 228-2828.

Sleep Inn
$-$$ • 5225 Market St.
• (910) 313-6665, (800) 62-SLEEP

Affordable and well maintained, Sleep Inn is among the several new accommodations built in 1997. It offers 108 modest, motel-style rooms with queen or double beds, roomy showers, key-card security locks, cable TV, modem ports and automatic air-conditioning units. Some rooms are connecting. The outdoor pool and fitness room add to the value. Roll-away beds, copier and fax machines and meeting rooms for up to 36 people are available. Hot beverages are available free all day in the lobby lounge as are daily newspapers while supplies last. The motel is 0.2 miles west of the Market Street overpass.

Wilmington Hilton
$$$ • 301 N. Water St. • (910) 763-5900, (800) 445-8667

Situated on the Riverwalk, the Hilton is one of downtown Wilmington's premier full-service hotels and corporate meeting centers, with 178 guest rooms, half of which overlook the river. The Hilton is scheduled for a major expansion in 1988-99. There is no charge for children, regardless of age, if they share rooms with their parents. The Hilton's new Poolside & Cabana Bar, complete with ceiling fans and palm trees, is a great place for a sunset cocktail, and on Friday evenings in the summer the pool deck is the scene of the Sunset Celebration, a popular live-music party (see our Nightlife chapter).

On the concierge level, complimentary beverages are served to guests in the evening and continental breakfasts in the morning. Compton's is the hotel's fine restaurant and lounge, serving grilled steaks, seafood and Sunday brunch. The hotel's fitness room and poolside Jacuzzi are popular. Eleven meeting rooms, including the Grand Ballroom, can accommodate up to 600 persons with food service. Courtesy vans provide complimentary airport transportation. If you're arriving by boat, call well in advance to arrange docking out front.

INSIDERS' TIP

New residents of the Topsail-Holly Ridge area can get to know their new hometown by contacting the Topsail Area Newcomers Network (TANN), a year-round group organized by the Topsail Chamber of Commerce, (910) 328-4722.

CAROLINA TEMPLE APARTMENTS
An Island Inn
"Directly on the Ocean"

Phone: 910/256-2773
Fax: 910/256-3878
E-mail: swright168@aol.com
P.O. Box 525
Wrightsville Beach, NC 28480
Late March - November

Completely furnished, air conditioned apartments. All with kitchenettes and private baths. Large, spacious porches. Ocean and sound front beaches. Pier with boat slips. Office: 550 Waynick Blvd.

Wrightsville Beach

Blockade Runner Resort Hotel
$$$$ • 275 Waynick Blvd.
• (910) 256-2251, (800) 541-1161

The Blockade Runner is a top-quality oceanfront resort. All 150 rooms have water views, either oceanfront or soundside, some with balconies. Each room has a refrigerator with mini-bar, coffee maker, hair dryer, plush bathrobes and ironing equipment; some rooms also have a microwave oven. A sumptuous breakfast buffet for two is included with every room, every day. Amenities also include beach furniture for guests, a health spa, free van shuttle to certain attractions on the island, the Aquarium Lounge, and the Ocean Terrace Restaurant, which has a wide ocean view and new outdoor dining deck.

The hotel's oceanside deck also features a cabana bar adjoining the heated indoor/outdoor pool. Live entertainment is available free to guests four nights a week in season (including magic shows for the family on Tuesdays). Room service and bicycles are available, tennis courts are nearby (the hotel provides shuttles) and a sailing center on Banks Channel offers watercraft rentals and lessons for which packages can be arranged. Children's Sand Camper programs and golf packages are also offered, and children 11 and younger stay free when with parents. Conference facilities and banquet services can accommodate up to 250 and 225 people, respectively. A complementary airport limousine is available, and corporate rates are available all year.

For a change of pace, inquire about The Cottage, a 13-room, full-service lodging next door that offers room service, spacious porches and all the amenities of the Blockade Runner.

Carolina Temple Apartments
$-$$, no credit cards • 550 Waynick Blvd. • (910) 256-2773

This is the kind of beach-cottage accommodation our parents remember from their childhood. Carolina Temple Apartments consists of two historic plantation-style cottages built by the Temple family after the turn of the century. The property runs from the sound side of the island to the ocean, yet the buildings are set back like a well-kept secret.

The inn was once Station 6 along the Wrightsville Beach trolley line (ask to see the old photos), and the pride with which the place is run is evident everywhere. Both buildings are classics: central hallways; spacious, breezy, wraparound porches furnished with large rockers and the occasional well-placed hammock; a high sun deck overlooking the ocean; louvered outer doors to each of the 16 apartments. The rooms are not large but they are beautifully

Once one of Wilmington's most desirable places to stay, The Orton hotel stood at 109-117 N. Front Street.

maintained, comprising one-, two- and three-room air-conditioned suites with private baths, ceiling fans and fully equipped kitchenettes.

The apartments are perfect for couples and families (up to six people). The decor is tropical, with luminous beach colors and Caribbean-style folk art. The dune-front patio, surrounded by palms and oleander, is a cool, shaded place to relax. There's a communal TV room with a video library for the youngsters. Rentals from June through August mostly require a one-week minimum (Sunday to Sunday), but split weeks sometimes become available. In spring and autumn, split weeks are always available, and the inn closes in winter.

This is an excellent bargain relative to the area. Extras include a small soundside beach perfect for toddlers, laundry facility, complimentary morning coffee, soundside docking facilities, cribs, and weekend continental breakfasts during spring and fall. Note that towels are extra during the summer.

Landfall Park Hampton Inn & Suites
$$$-$$$$ • 1989 Eastwood Rd.
• (910) 256-9600

The moment you walk into the lodge-style lobby, you sense the quality. The free-standing stone chimney above a two-sided gas fireplace is surrounded by oversize rattan chairs and plush sofa on one side and by the handsome Eagle Bar lounge on the other. With 90 standard rooms and 30 suites, the inn provides high-end amenities, complete with bell staff, just minutes from the beach and next door to one of the area's better restaurants. All suites feature a full kitchen with microwave, stove, dishwasher and refrigerator.

The Signature Suite provides "celebrity" accommodations, with a double-sided fire-

Golden Sands Motel

An Oceanfront Inn for the Whole Family

P.O. Box 759
U.S. Highway 421 South

(910) 458-8334

---

place, entertainment center and two-person whirlpool bath. Executive one- and two-bedroom suites are enticing to movie-production staff and other business travelers seeking high quality. Desk and data modem are standard.

The Landfall Park Hampton Inn serves upscale, 18-item continental breakfasts (6 to 10 AM daily) and provides valet service on weekdays. A dedicated boardroom and large meeting room (for 30 to 80 people) are suitable for corporate retreats or small receptions. Of special interest are the large kidney-shaped pool set in a lush garden landscape, a fitness room, a 24-hour sweet shop, rattan rocking chairs on a collonaded porch (a great place for breakfast) and the Gazebo Bar in summer. Landfall Park is on the mainland, less than a half-mile from the drawbridge.

Summer Sands Motel
$$-$$$ • 104 S. Lumina Ave.
- **(910) 256-4175, (800) 336-4849**

This comfortable 32-suite efficiency motel sits in the heart of "downtown" Wrightsville Beach within a short walk of restaurants, shopping, laundry facilities and the strand, and rooms are ideal for two adults and two kids. Guest rooms have balconies, queen-size beds and queen-size sofabeds, and the rooms facing Banks Channel provide the better view, especially at sunset. An outdoor pool is open in the summer. Monthly stays are available off-season only (November through March).

Surf Suites
$$$$ • 711 S. Lumina Ave.
- **(910) 256-2275**

Calling itself the first and largest "motelminium" on the island and open year round, the Surf offers 46 resort-quality suites with separate bedrooms, full bath, dining areas, queen-size sleeper sofas, cable TV, telephones and private oceanfront balconies. Amenities include an outdoor pool, a sun deck and full maid and linen service. Commercial rates are available, and there is a $10 fee for each additional guest.

Carolina Beach and Kure Beach

Atlantic Towers
$$-$$$ • 1615 S. Lake Park Blvd., Carolina Beach • (910) 458-8313, (800) BEACH-40

This 11-story establishment offers modest, well-kept condominium suites with separate bedrooms and full kitchens. Each suite accommodates up to six guests. All 137 condos are oceanfront, and each has a telephone, cable TV, private balcony, an exterior terrace

Atlantic Towers
On The Ocean

Oceanfront Condos with Balconies
1 Bedroom or 2 Bedrooms, Fully
Furnished, Oceanfront Pool, Video
Game Room

1615 S. Lake Park Blvd.
Carolina Beach, NC 28428

FREE Brochure or Reservations
1-800-BEACH-40

---

entrance, maid service and elevator service. The outdoor pool deck is in view of the ocean and stands beside a gazebo — a perfect place for a picnic.

Beach Harbour Resort
$$$-$$$$ • 302 Canal Dr., Carolina Beach • (910) 458-4185, (910) 458-8667

Consisting of privately owned time-shares, Beach Harbor invites short-term guests to its clean one- and two-bedroom suites. Rooms vary in size, but each has a balcony, living and dining areas, a full kitchen, cable TV, a sleeper sofa and a washer and dryer. Local calls are free. The resort has an outdoor pool, and most parking is shaded. Beach Harbour is directly across from Harbor Master's Restaurant & Lounge and the Carolina Beach Marina. Call ahead for information on availability.

Cabana De Mar Motel
$$-$$$ • 31 Carolina Ave. N., Carolina Beach • (910) 458-4456, (800) 333-8499

One of the most attractive and well-appointed motel accommodations in Carolina Beach, Cabana De Mar resembles a condominium complex more than a motel. Its 71 condominium suites (one to three bedrooms) are small yet pleasant, with cable TV, elevator access and daily housekeeping service. Some rooms face the ocean and have modest private balconies. Streetside suites are the best value. Laundry rooms are available, but some rooms are equipped with washer/dryers. The motel is within a short walk of central Carolina Beach's attractions and restaurants.

Golden Sands Motel
$$-$$$ • 1206 S. Lake Park Blvd., Carolina Beach • (910) 458-8334

This family-oriented oceanfront motel offers 88 air-conditioned rooms, most with ocean views, in three buildings. Amenities include terraces, compact refrigerators, convertible sofas, phones, TVs and microwaves. Most rooms are nonsmoking. Complimentary coffee is available at all hours in the motel gift shop. One of the motel's two outdoor pools and an outdoor tiki bar are within sight of the surf. An on-site restaurant, Steamers Pierhouse, was due to be completed in mid-1998. The motel's pier offers a good view of the beach strand.

King's Motel
$$-$$$ • 318 Carolina Beach Ave. N., Carolina Beach • (910) 458-5594

Highly practical, if not aesthetically sophisticated, King's rooms include basic motel lodgings as well as fully equipped efficiencies (there is no separation between the twin double beds and the kitchen area in the efficiencies). All

> We could tell you Surfside & Paradise Inn are GREAT, but we would rather tell you what the experts have to say...
>
> *"Paradise Inn is a good bargain with a great location just yards from the surf"*
> *"Surfside offers a good balance among convenience, amenities and price"* – Insiders' Guide®

PARADISE INN
310 Carolina Beach Ave. North
P.O. Box 1585 • Carolina Beach, NC 28428
(910) 458-8264

Surfside MOTOR LODGE OCEANFRONT
234 Carolina Beach Ave. North
P.O. Box 1690 • Carolina Beach, NC 28428
(910) 458-8338

---

are well-maintained and sanitary and include cable TV, air conditioning and heat, dinettes and a full bath. Many of the 42 rooms (distributed in three buildings) have ocean views and balconies. One building is a duplex cottage suitable for up to seven and eight guests in respective apartments. The oceanside pool has a slide.

Paradise Inn
$$-$$$ • 310 Carolina Beach Ave. N., Carolina Beach • (910) 458-8264

The Paradise is a good bargain with a great location just yards from the surf. Forty-three units include singles, doubles, efficiencies and three-bedroom cottages complete with a pool, oceanfront breezeway with lounge chairs, outdoor grills and cable TV. The Paradise is within walking distance of downtown Carolina Beach and all the attractions and restaurants to be found there.

Surfside Motor Lodge
$$-$$$ • 234 Carolina Beach Ave. N., Carolina Beach • (910) 458-8338

Situated just steps from the beach and one block from the amusements of the Carolina Beach boardwalk, this 80-unit complex offers a variety of accommodations ranging from singles to separate three-bedroom cottages, all with full baths (two baths in the larger units). Two pools are a big plus, as are the outdoor grills, cable TV and oceanfront views. The Surfside offers a good balance of convenience, amenities and price.

Docksider Inn-Oceanfront
$$-$$$ • 202 N. Ft. Fisher Blvd., Kure Beach • (910) 458-4200

This establishment may seem unassuming on the outside, but it's shipshape inside and one of the finest choices for lodging on Pleasure Island. Specially tailored to romantic getaways, the Docksider has 34 clean, modest units (oceanfront and ocean view), almost half of which are efficiencies that include full-size refrigerators. The Captain's Cabins are oceanfront rooms featuring "breakfast in bed" extras (gourmet delights and snacks), VCR, wet bar, coffee maker, toaster and more. The Docksider has a pool with an elevated deck and its own "Sunketch," a high, secluded deck

---

INSIDERS' TIP

Consider vacationing during the shoulder seasons — spring and fall. The weather's fine and crowds are thin. And in early autumn, ocean temperatures in our region are still comfortable.

that's perfect for viewing sunsets, all just steps away from the blue Atlantic.

The inn offers AARP discounts to seniors 55 and older for midweek stays year-round. Inquire also about other midweek discounts. On weekends during the high season, two-night minimums apply. The Docksider Inn is just north of K Street in downtown Kure Beach.

Seven Seas Inn
$$-$$$ • 130 Ft. Fisher Blvd., Kure Beach • (910) 458-8122

The Seven Seas is a family-oriented establishment still in prime form. Comprising three buildings — oceanfront, ocean view and pool view — Seven Seas has 32 clean, comfortable rooms in a variety of configurations. Large efficiencies and motel accommodations are roomy and equipped with double beds, telephones, cable TV, individually controlled air conditioning and heat and microwave ovens. The well-kept grounds include fine pool facilities with a shaded cabana, benches and beautiful cactus beds, and a bait and tackle shop. Children will appreciate the game room. When entering Kure Beach by the main road, which is Second Avenue (U.S. 421), look for the enormous agave plant on the ocean side of the road.

Southport-Oak Island

Blue Water Point Marina Resort Motel
$-$$ • 57th Pl., Long Beach • (910) 278-1230

Quiet and located on the soundside of Oak Island, this small yet comfortable, 30-room motel is especially convenient to boaters. The motel offers rooms with waterway views, double or twin beds, showers, TVs and telephones; an outdoor pool in season; and various patios and sun decks with a fine sunset view. The marina rents floating docks and boat slips with a water depth of 6 feet at mean low tide. City-owned boat ramps adjoining the marina are available free.

Other amenities include an adjoining restaurant and lounge (open from March 1 to November 1), ship's store and tackle shop, charter boat rentals and head boats, plus rentals of pontoon boats, john boats, beach chairs and umbrellas. Motel guests are eligible for a 50-percent discount on head boat tickets and all rentals.

Riverside Motel
$ • 103 W. Bay St., Southport • (910) 457-6986

This small eight-room establishment commands an excellent waterfront view of Southport's harbor with Bald Head Island to the left and Fort Caswell to the right. Situated between the Ships Chandler Restaurant and the Cape Fear Pilot Tower, the Riverside is one of Southport's three multiple-unit accommodations downtown. The cozy double-occupancy rooms are equipped with two double beds, microwave ovens, cable TV, refrigerators, coffee makers, toasters and telephones (local calls are free). The rooms are small and well-kept, and nearly everything in Southport is a short walk away.

Sea Captain Motor Lodge
$ • 608 W. West St., Southport • (910) 457-5263

The Sea Captain, near the Southport Marina, is the largest motel in Southport. Each of the 96 units is modern, well-kept and equipped with a refrigerator, telephone and TV. Accommodations include single motel rooms, efficiencies and two-room efficiency apartments with separate sleeping areas. An Olympic-size outdoor pool and shaded gazebo are centrally located among the lodge's four buildings, and there are two adjoining dining facilities: the Sea Captain Restaurant for breakfast and lunch and the Harbourside Lounge for dinner (see our Restaurants chapter.)

Ocean Crest Motel
$-$$ • 1411 E. Beach Dr., Long Beach • (910) 278-3333

The Ocean Crest is one of the premier oceanfront motels in Long Beach. Streetside rooms for up to four guests each offer the best value. All oceanfront rooms feature private balconies, and you can choose between one- and two-bedroom units with kitchenettes or efficiencies. The carpeted rooms are clean and bright and tastefully furnished. All are equipped with individually controlled air conditioning and heat, cable TV and private telephones. The Ocean Crest adjoins the fishing

North Carolina's Southern coast offers magnificent scenery.

pier of the same name and the Windjammer Restaurant. The complex includes a handsome oceanfront townhouse on the premises with a gas fireplace, two private balconies, a full kitchen, two bedrooms, laundry facilities and two-and-a-half baths.

Driftwood Motel
$ • 604 Ocean Dr., Yaupon Beach
• (910) 278-6114

This attractive two-story motel has an oceanfront location, an outdoor pool, laundry facilities, outdoor grills and picnic tables, plus a refrigerator, telephone and cable TV in every room, all at a reasonable cost. The second-floor verandas provide wonderful views, especially at sunset, and are equipped with deck chairs and tables for relaxing in the ocean breeze. Recently remodeled, the Driftwood offers neat, carpeted rooms, each with its own air conditioning and heat, and a full kitchen is available for all guests to share. Adjoining the kitchen is an outdoor play area for children. The Driftwood is open year round.

Island Resort
$-$$ • 500 Ocean Dr., Yaupon Beach
• (910) 278-5644

Island Resort provides at least partial ocean views from most of its neatly kept rooms, plus the option of a freshwater pool and outdoor hot tub. There are 10 motel rooms and 11 efficiency apartments consisting of one or two bedrooms and mini-kitchens. Amenities include laundry facilities, an oceanside gazebo with grills and a private beach access. The Island Resort is open all year.

Southwinds Motel
$-$$ • 700 Ocean Dr., Yaupon Beach
• (910) 278-5442

Including singles, doubles and efficiency suites, the accommodations are comfortable at Southwinds, an older, well-run operation. It is ideally situated across the street from the beach strand, the Yaupon Beach Fishing Pier and two restaurants. Rooms are quaint and equipped with cable TV, air conditioning and a telephone. The larger accommodations have fully equipped kitchens, sleeper sofas and double beds. Roll-aways are available at a small cost, and a children's play area is always available. A cabana adjoins the pool, and an outdoor grill and picnic area are nearby.

South Brunswick Islands

Gray Gull Motel
$ • 3263 Holden Beach Rd. S.W., Holden Beach • (910) 842-6775

Don't be fooled by the low rates. This family-owned motel, the only one at Holden Beach, is very well maintained and courteously run.

Each of the 17 carpeted rooms has cable TV and a telephone as well as easy access to the outdoor pool and picnic tables. The Gray Gull is on the mainland side of the Intracoastal Waterway, just minutes from the beach. The office is in the hardware store next door, where anglers can also buy tackle. Cancellations require 24 hours notice.

Cooke's Inn Motel
$ • 12 Causeway Dr., Ocean Isle Beach
• (910) 579-9001

Cooke's has 35 very clean rooms (three are handicapped accessible) with individual air conditioning and heat, twin and double beds, telephones, refrigerators and cable TV. The outdoor pool and sun deck are close to the parking lot, but with the beach only 200 yards away, they aren't the No. 1 attractions anyway. Cooke's, family owned and operated, is also convenient to dining and entertainment, much of it within walking distance.

Plaza Motel
$-$$ • 19 Causeway Dr., Ocean Isle Beach • (910) 579-6019

Occupying the second floor of a building one-and-a-half blocks from the beach, the Plaza consists of 10 simple and neat double-occupancy rooms and two two-room suites. Each has air conditioning, a view of the waterway and sound, TV and telephone. Boat slips with access to the Intracoastal Waterway and charter boat service are available on site. The adjoining grocery-and-supply store (which carries fishing tackle and video rentals), the gas station, and the Plaza Marina earn the Plaza Motel high marks for convenience.

Ocean Isle Inn
$$-$$$ • 37 W. First St., Ocean Isle Beach • (910) 579-0750, (800) 352-5988

The 70-room Ocean Isle Inn features private oceanfront balconies and tranquil soundside views of the marshes and the Intracoastal Waterway. The outdoor pool and deck overlook the ocean and have access to the beach; bathers can use the indoor heated pool and hot tub all year long. The carpeted rooms are carefully maintained and handsome. Each is equipped with a refrigerator, cable TV and telephone, and daily maid service is provided. Some rooms connect. Handicapped facilities and elevators are also available.

Guests are entitled to complimentary continental breakfasts and can purchase golf packages offering a choice of play on more than 65 area courses. The Ocean Isle Inn's conference space offers quiet, off-the-beaten-path facilities for business meetings. Be sure to inquire about midweek Supersavers during the off-season, weekly rates, and AAA and AARP discounts.

The Winds Oceanfront Clarion Inn
$$-$$$$ • 310 E. First St., Ocean Isle Beach • (910) 579-6275, (800) 334-3581

This oceanfront resort is an excellent choice for its range of accommodations and prices. Studios, mini-suites, deluxe rooms, one- and two-bedroom suites and separate houses are all richly appointed and comfortable. Many have indoor whirlpools, and all have kitchen facilities. The grounds are fastidiously landscaped to resemble the tropics, with palms, banana trees and flowering plants nestling a series of boardwalks and decks. The heated outdoor pool is enclosed in winter.

Choose among a sauna, outdoor Jacuzzi, exercise room, beach bocci, shuffleboard, volleyball and, nearby, tennis to pass the time. In summer, sailboat and bike rentals are available on the premises. Honeymoon and golf packages (available at 90 championship courses) are easily arranged. Some rooms are handicapped accessible, and complimentary continental breakfasts are available.

Topsail Island Area

GOOD AREA — WALK TO LOTS OF STUFF

The Jolly Roger Motel
$-$$ • 803 Ocean Blvd., Topsail Beach • (910) 328-4616, (800) 633-3196

From rooms with one double bed each to apartment suites, the Jolly Roger has a wide variety of room sizes and amenities, which include daily maid service, cable TV, fully equipped kitchens and baths and room-controlled air conditioning. Fully carpeted efficiency apartments and two-room suites also feature sleeper sofas. Rooms on the second and third floors of the large new annex provide the best ocean views and balconies (not

The Winds
Clarion Inn & Suites

An Island Beach & Golf Resort

Luxurious oceanfront rooms and one, two and three bedroom suites with kitchens, overlooking palm trees, lush subtropical gardens and our breathtaking island beach.

Complimentary continental breakfast buffet, heated pool (encl. in winter), jet spas, sauna, exercise room, shuffleboard, bikes, sailboats, ocean kayaks, beach volleyball, beach service, free tennis, free summer golf and dining & shopping discounts.

Golf in the heart of Coastal Carolina's most requested courses. Golf Packages with a choice of 98 courses start at $43. Oyster Bay, Marsh Harbour, Sea Trail and dozens more of the Myrtle Beach area's most requested courses are within 5 to 15 minutes.

1-800-334-3581

310 E. First St., Ocean Isle Beach, NC 28469-3309 *Fax:* 1-910-579-2884
E-mail: Info@TheWinds.com *Web:* http://www.TheWinds.com

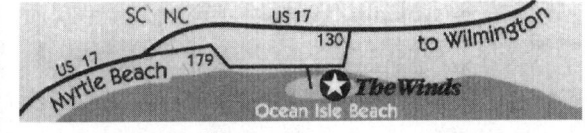

but rates for rooms facing inland are ally cheaper. The hotel office is at Jolly Roger Fishing Pier next door, where you can also arrange deep-sea fishing trips.

St. Regis Resort
$$$$ • 2000 New River Inlet Rd., N. Topsail Beach • (910) 328-0778, (800) 682-4882

Each of this resort's 224 privately owned units offers ocean-view balconies, two full baths, fully equipped kitchens and washer/dryer facilities. The one-, two- and three-bedroom suites are clean and modern, and even the one-bedroom suites can accommodate four people. Some rooms include a Jacuzzi. The resort comprises three tall buildings fronted by a private beach. Two pools are available, one heated and enclosed by a solarium. Whirlpools, a sun deck, a fitness center, tennis courts, a chipping and putting green and volleyball facilities will satisfy almost every style of vacation. There is also a gift shop, The Pavilion, in Building 1. A 30-day notice is required for cancellations.

You'll find New River Inlet Road branching off New River Drive (N.C. 210) before the high-span bridge. Tetterton Management Company is the exclusive on-site management for this hotel.

Sea Vista Motel S. END
$$-$$$ • 1521 Ocean Blvd., Topsail Beach • (910) 328-2171, (800) 732-8478

Much of Sea Vista's business consists of regular guests. Some of the reasons for that may be its quiet location and its large, bright rooms with full-size appliances, cable TV, balconies and individually controlled air conditioning. Within an easy walk are the Topsail Sound fishing pier and a restaurant. Since individual rooms are privately owned and the decor and furnishings vary, repeat guests often request certain rooms, But all 35 rooms are comfortable and clean and were recently refurbished.

ONE ONLY

The accommodations consist of eight efficiencies, five mini-efficiencies and two apartments, which do not enjoy a direct ocean view. The honeymoon suite is an efficiency with a private balcony perched atop the center of the oceanfront building. Discounts apply for senior adults and seven-day stays, and children stay free. Pets are allowed with a $20 surcharge. Call for information on availability.

Surfside Motel
$ • 122 N. Shore Dr., Surf City
• (910) 328-4099

Surfside garners plenty of repeat business from families and fishermen who appreciate its unpretentious style, its quietness, and its location right behind the beach dune and within walking distance of restaurants and shopping. Single rooms and doubles (the latter featuring refrigerators and microwave ovens) are small but well-kept and offer double beds, cable TV, and air conditioning, but no telephones. Roll-aways are available for $5 extra.

For those who spend their waking hours fishing, a downstairs room without a window may be a worthwhile bargain. The motel's dune crossover features a dune-top deck with a shower. Weekend stays during the high season require a two-night minimum. Surfside is one block north of Roland Avenue (the bridge causeway).

The Topsail Motel   MUST DRIVE TO ANY REST. etc
$$-$$$ • 1195 N. Anderson Blvd., Topsail Beach • (910) 328-3381, (800) 726-1795

Consisting of one- and two-bed oceanfront rooms with kitchenettes, two- and three-bed efficiency suites and oceanfront apartments with full kitchens — 30 units in all — the Topsail Motel offers basic motel amenities and a superb dune-front location. Ground-floor rooms have enclosed patios, and second-floor rooms have a deck balcony. Rooms are equipped with cable TV, telephone and individual air conditioning-heating unit. The lawn area is a fine vantage point for an ocean view. Weekly rates offering a one-night discount are available. The motel is 5 miles south of the Surf City stoplight. Call for information on availability.

Villa Capriani Resort
$$$$ • 790 New River Inlet Rd., N. Topsail Beach • (910) 328-1900, (800) 934-2400

Reminiscent of the grand resorts of the Riviera, Villa Capriani is a beautifully landscaped complex that offers on-site dining, tennis and entertainment. The building is constructed of sand-colored stucco with terra cotta roofs and archways. Covered balconies overlook a multilevel courtyard featuring three oceanfront pools (including a baby pool), waterfalls, hot tubs and a cabana bar with a fine ocean view. Choose from oceanfront, ocean view and courtyard view (which overlooks the pools and the ocean).

Suites with one, two or three bedrooms are available, fully appointed with full kitchens and washers/dryers. The rooms are well-kept, fully carpeted and furnished in contemporary style. Palliotti's Restaurant is off the courtyard opposite a handsome lounge. An on-site activities director sees to it that no guest can justifiably complain of boredom at Villa Capriani. Entertainment options include live outdoor music, karaoke, line dancing and children's programs in summer. Tetterton Management Company is the on-site management company.

OCEAN PIER INN - NEXT TO JOLLY ROGER (handwritten note)

ROSEHILL INN
BED & BREAKFAST

HISTORIC WILMINGTON

••• *Experience The Romance* •••

Laurel Jones & Dennis Fietsch, Innkeepers

114 South Third Street • Wilmington, North Carolina 28401
(800) 815-0250 • **(910) 815-0250**
Fax: (910) 815-0350
Visit our website: www.rosehill.com

North Carolina
BED & BREAKFASTS AND INNS

Triple Diamond Award

AAA Approved

Bed and Breakfast Inns

Travelers are often delighted by the high caliber of bed and breakfast inns in Wilmington, which are comparable to the finest inns anywhere. Most inns here occupy meticulously kept historic homes. Some are as casual as a pajama party while others are steeped in Victorian elegance. And innkeepers are typically knowledgeable about the area and will usually assist you with directions and in making reservations for shows, meals, charters and golf packages.

Bed and breakfast inns typically do not allow pets, smoking indoors or very young children unless by prior arrangement. Most establishments accept major credit cards and personal checks, especially for making payment in advance. Be aware that cancellations, even when made with the required notice, may incur an administrative fee, although you'll find most innkeepers in the region to be reasonable and fair. Also note that many bed and breakfasts require a full weekend lodging during the Azalea Festival and Riverfest (see our Annual Events chapter).

Price Code

Since prices are subject to change without notice, we provide only price guidelines based on per-night rates during the summer ("high season"). Guidelines do not reflect the 6 percent state and 3 percent local taxes. Some inns offer lower rates during the off-season, but always confirm rates and necessary amenities before reserving. It may also pay to inquire about corporate discounts even if they are not mentioned in our descriptions.

$	Less than $75
$$	$75 to $120
$$$	$120 to $150
$$$$	$150 and more

Wilmington

219 South 5th Bed and Breakfast
$$ • 219 S. 5th St. • (910) 763-5539, (800) 219-7634

In keeping with its slogan, 219 South 5th is indeed "uniquely unpretentious." The Greek Revival Deans-Maffit House (1871) offers three guest rooms of an essentially country French and English style accented with Victorian antiques. Two of the rooms have fireplaces, and the inn includes an efficiency suite. Some rooms have a private bath, some share a bath. The backyard, with its small circular koi pond and attractive loggia, has a nostalgic and relaxing character. Hearty hot breakfasts are a balance of formality and familiarity, blending the use of china, antique glasses and hefty coffee mugs. Off-street parking is accessible from a side street.

Camellia Cottage
$$$ • 118 S. 4th St. • (910) 763-9171, (800) 763-9171

Standing on a brick-paved street four blocks from the river, Camellia Cottage is a richly appointed, high-peaked Queen Anne Shingle home (built in 1889) that was once the home of prominent Wilmington artist

CATHERINE'S INN

Comfortable Yet Elegant
- With Antiques & Reproductions
- Full Breakfast
- Private Baths
- Corporate Rates

410 S. Front St.
In Historic Downtown Wilmington
North Carolina 28401

(910) 251-0863
Toll Free: **(800) 476-0723**
Fax: **(910) 772-9550**

Wilmington's Premier Bed & Breakfast on the Cape Fear River

Henry J. MacMillan. Some of his work remains in the home. In fact, artwork abounds throughout Camellia Cottage, from murals on the wraparound piazza outside to handpainted fireplace tiles.

Camellia Cottage offers three spacious guest rooms and one suite, each with its own character. Queen-size, antique-style beds dressed in English linen, private baths and gas-fired hearths are standard. Morning coffee service is provided at your door, and beverages are available in the afternoon. Traditional Southern breakfasts are served with crystal, china and silver. The music room, parlor and sun room are always available to guests. Guests with allergies, take note of the resident cat, dog and finches.

Catherine's Inn
$$ • 410 S. Front St. • (910) 251-0863, (800) 476-0723

Catherine's occupies the Forshee-Sprunt home (1888), an Italianate structure distinguished by a wraparound front porch and two-story screened-in rear porch, an especially inviting setting for breakfast. It is one of the few bed and breakfast inns directly overlooking the Cape Fear River, with a superior sunset vantage point, especially from the two-tiered formal gardens or gazebo. In one of the Victorian double parlors, a piano awaits the musically gifted.

The five bedrooms are elegant — one features a sleigh bed, another, antique dolls — and each is adorned with fresh flowers and local artwork. Each room has a king- or queen-size bed and private bath. Coffee is delivered to the rooms before breakfast, which is always a hearty affair. Complimentary beer, wine and soda are always available, plus cake and coffee in the evenings and complimentary liqueur at bedtime. You may play horseshoes and croquet on the 300-foot rear lawn, and there's plenty of off-street parking. Bicycles are at your disposal.

Chandler's Wharf Inn
$$-$$$ • 2 Ann St. • (910) 815-3510

This distinctive inn offers a good river view (especially from the second-floor suite) and

---

INSIDERS' TIP

Pocomoke's Juice Bar in the Jacobi Hardware Co. Warehouse, 15 S. Water Street in Wilmington, (910) 762-1942, makes delicious vegetable juices to order, plus many other refreshing delights. It's a great place to pause while sightseeing!

·OVERLOOKING THE CAPE FEAR RIVER·

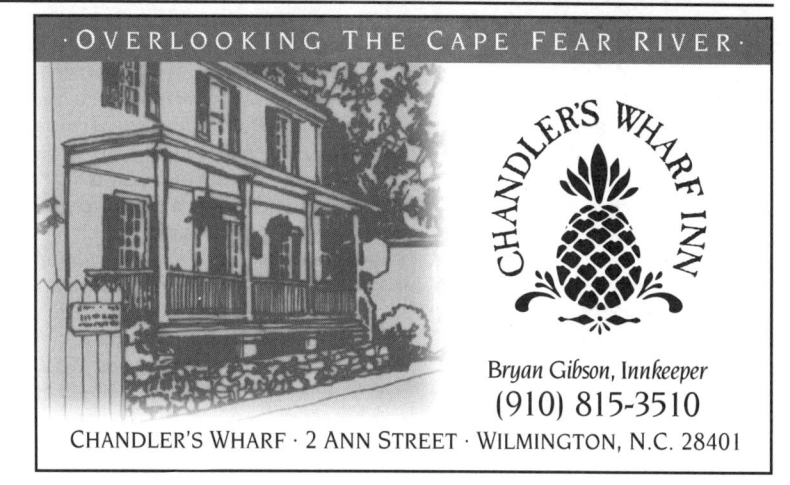

Bryan Gibson, Innkeeper
(910) 815-3510
CHANDLER'S WHARF · 2 ANN STREET · WILMINGTON, N.C. 28401

the kind of character only a building nearly 150 years old can have. Situated on the cobblestone street of Chandler's Wharf in the Reston-Richardson House (c. 1850), across from two fine restaurants and shopping, the inn offers two suites featuring antique reproduction furnishings, including a queen-size pencil-post bed upstairs.

The decor has been described as English country, but is the epitome of antebellum America, with its heart-pine flooring and intimate scale. Each suite features a sitting room with gas fireplace, private shower, coffee maker, refrigerator, cable TV, bathrobes, ironing equipment and a personal phone line with an answering machine. For breakfast, choose between excellent hot meals (prepared between 7:30 and 10:30 AM at the Pilot House across the street and delivered to your room for an extra charge) or a continental breakfast (included). Room service (also provided by the Pilot House) is available throughout the day as long as the restaurant kitchen is open.

Chandler's Wharf Inn stands in the midst of everything downtown Wilmington has to offer.

Curran House
$$ • 312 S. 3rd St. • (910) 763-6603, (800) 763-6603

Curran House, just three blocks from Wilmington's riverfront, strikes a balance between historic ambiance and put-up-your-feet comfort. Innkeepers Vickie and Greg Stringer have furnished their downstairs parlor with plush ottomans for just that purpose, and it's an inviting place to browse through one of their many interesting books or play a board game. Full breakfasts, served from 8:30 to 9:30 AM, include homemade breads and muffins with such mainstays as frittatas. Fresh-ground coffee awaits you in the upstairs hallway each morning, and snacks and beverages are available all day.

One guest room boasts a king-size four-poster bed. Rattan and some unusual painted furnishings add an island flavor to another room. A third, a European-style room with a massive king-size sleigh bed, offers bath facilities (including a claw-foot tub) behind a tall Venetian screen. All rooms include wing-back easy chairs, private bath, a pair of warm terry robes, hair dryer, telephone, cable TV and VCR and both hypoallergenic and down pillows. Guests are welcome to use the video library of recent films.

Curran House occupies the McKay-Green House (1837), which features Queen Anne and Italianate details, decorative fireplaces (nonfunctional) and four porches (one with a bench swing). The second-floor porch in the rear is screened — a great place for morning coffee. There's plenty of off-street parking as well as table tennis and badminton, a fax machine and photocopier. Ask about the Valentine's Day special and other holiday packages.

Graystone Inn
$$$-$$$$ • 100 S. 3rd St.
• (910) 763-2000

If Bellamy Mansion stands as the epitome of Civil War-era elegance, Graystone Inn must be its 20th-century successor. This palatial mansion, built in 1906 and completely remodeled in early 1998, is the most imposing structure downtown and a historic landmark. The vast ground floor includes a masterpiece of a library, paneled in mahogany. From the great hall, a grand Renaissance-style staircase made of handcarved oak rises three stories, culminating in the ballroom. Outdoors, the garden and terraces are exquisite. The Graystone is frequently used as a movie set.

Several of the guest rooms are as large as entire suites in some hotels. Each room features a private bath with period fixtures (most with claw-foot tubs), telephone and data port. Five bedrooms have fireplaces. The Graystone makes a prestigious venue for weddings, receptions, meetings, and other events for up to 150 people, and its location is ideal for walking to all downtown Wilmington attractions. Room rates include full breakfast and beverage service throughout the day.

Hoge-Wood House Bed and Breakfast
$$ • 407 S. Third St. • (910) 762-5299

Offering two upstairs guest rooms with private bathrooms (with showers), refrigerators stocked with beverages, TV, and a telephone, the Hoge-Wood House is exceedingly casual, plain and homey. You'll find fresh flowers practically everywhere in the house. The downstairs parlor is cozy and warm, with comfy wing-back chairs, and the library, with its ceiling-high bookshelves, is ideal for relaxing with some good reading.

The inn's affable proprietors, Page and Larry Tootoo (pronounced "Toto"), emphasize flexibility in their service, which extends to soliciting guest requests for morning meals. (Tip: Larry makes a great pecan waffle.) Full country breakfasts are served family-style on seasonal ceramic and china dinnerware with silverware over a classic library table. Coffee lovers will appreciate the Kona served daily.

One guest room features a high brass queen-size bed; the other a double bed with queen-size sleeper sofa. (A third, comparably large guest room, also with private bath, is expected to be ready before the new year.) Snacks are available downstairs. Bicycles are available to guests. The Hoge-Wood House has plenty of off-street parking and stands within walking distance of all downtown attractions. A one-night stay is costlier than the per-night rate for longer stays.

Live Oaks Bed & Breakfast
$$ • 318 S. 3rd St. • (910) 762-6733, (888) 762-6732

Live Oaks effectively combines Victorian decor and various relaxing settings with its convenient downtown location. The clapboard Queen Anne structure, the Burris-Poisson House (1883), features beautiful Stick Style (a.k.a. Carpenter Gothic) detailing and numerous places to kick back, including front and back furnished wraparound porches and a walled garden with shade trees, pergola, a hammock and benches. Best of all is the water garden with gurgling falls and a pond. The inn's three guest rooms range from intimate to spacious. The Garden Room has a private entrance off the rear second-story porch. All rooms are furnished with antiques and queen-size beds and feature private baths, central air conditioning and fireplaces.

The living room, in addition to its Victorian seating and lace curtains, is graced by bright 11-foot windows, a classic Weaver organ, a gramophone and a crystal chandelier. The library's handsome French doors open on to an enclosed sun porch — ideal for sunset-watching. Furnishings in the dining room include velvet-upholstered chairs you may recognize from the locally shot movie, *The Road to Wellville*. Innkeepers Margi and Doug

Graystone Inn

A European-Style Bed & Breakfast Inn, located in the Heart of Historic Wilmington

- Full Breakfast
- In Room Telephone & PC Data Ports
- Private Baths
- 7 Rooms, Including 2 Elegant Suites
- Wedding, Reception & Meeting Facilities Available
- Corporate Accounts Welcome

100 S. Third Street Wilmington, NC 28401
(910) 763-2000 • Fax: (910) 763-5555 • (888) 763-4773

Erickson serve homemade breakfasts over china and unique pressed-glass goblets.

Amenities include laundry service, complimentary refreshments and snacks, TV in the library and a guest refrigerator upstairs. Airport pickup and dropoff is available by arrangement. A one-night's deposit is required for reservations.

The River Inn
$$-$$$ • 314 S. Front St.
• (910) 763-4891

Among Wilmington's premier bed and breakfast inns, The River Inn directly overlooks the Cape Fear River. Proprietor Jenny McKinnon Wright has endowed her magnificent turreted Queen Anne home (built 1899) with unvarying elegance without forgoing comfort. Full silver-service breakfasts bring a cosmopolitan flair to Southern-style cooking, with such homemade treats as sweet potato breads, superb frittatas and specially blended coffees.

Of particular interest are the inn's convenient downtown location, its back porch with an excellent river view and the exquisite period furnishings, including some art deco pieces, an 1860s crystal chandelier, a magnificent open staircase, original parquet floors and leaded glass.

Each of the inn's three rooms features a private bath, a fireplace and antiques. The room occupying the turret has an antique pencil-post tester bed. Two adjoining rooms with river views may serve as a suite. The River Inn's ambiance is sociable, bright and never too refined for guests to congregate in the kitchen to share conversation and refreshments. Cancellations require a three-day notice.

Rosehill Inn Bed and Breakfast
$$$-$$$$ • 114 S. 3rd St.
• (910) 815-0250, (800) 815-0250

The elegant Rosehill Inn takes its place among the most exclusive bed and breakfast inns anywhere. It's a luxurious getaway as appropriate to corporate travelers as to honeymooners. The faithfully restored classic Greek Revival home, the Savage-Bacon House (1848),

Historic Wilmington's Most Elegant Bed and Breakfast

The Verandas

910-251-2212

www.verandas.com

is tastefully adorned with fine antiques and period wall coverings. It features a wraparound front porch, a magnificent pulpit staircase and large gardens with a columned pergola.

The inn has six guest rooms, each with its own fireplace (nonfunctioning), a writing desk, bathrobes and a private bath. The Heritage Room boasts a New Orleans gate bed made from antique cast-iron fence parts. The Wedgewood Room echoes the design of the fine china of the same name. Morning coffee service, use of bicycles, beverage service in the two parlors and nightly turndown service with a cordial and sweets are provided. Breakfasts offer such delights as crab rarebit and morning sherbet. The Rosehill Inn stands three blocks from the Cape Fear River.

Taylor House Inn Bed and Breakfast
$$ • 14 N. 7th St. • (910) 763-7581, (800) 382-9982

Taylor House's unassuming exterior conceals an interior of surprising grandeur, replete with vast ceilings, enormous rooms, rich oak woodwork, parquet floors, 10 fireplaces and a magnificent open staircase. Downstairs, a library and separate parlor offer ample room to relax. Formal breakfasts are by candlelight, served on handpainted china and crystal stemware. The five guest rooms in this 1905 home are carefully appointed, each with a private bath, period furnishings and phones. One room features a canopied bed. Television is available upon request. Cancellations require 72-hour notice. Convenient to all of downtown Wilmington, the Taylor House is on a brick-paved street just off Market Street.

The Verandas
$$$-$$$$ • 202 Nun St. • (910) 251-2212

For its sheer grandeur and balance of luxury and comfort, The Verandas is a premier bed and breakfast inn. Its elegance is never intimidating, thanks to proprietors who are affable and laid-back, and the price is a good value for such opulence. The Verandas occupies the Beery mansion (1853), just three blocks from the river in the quiet historic district. It is a massive, white clapboard edifice with four inviting verandas (porches, if you will), an oval garden terrace and screened breakfast patio. Enormous parlors downstairs, with 12-foot ceilings and chandeliers, are meticulously decorated, not overdone, and full of light. Original artwork abounds.

Most of the eight, enormous guest rooms, some as large as 400 square feet, are designed after world-famous hotel suites. All are corner rooms with fireplaces, individual climate control, desk, telephone with modem jack, TV and VCR, sitting area and private bath. The bathrooms are all spacious and have wainscoting and supplemental heat. Some rooms upstairs have views of nothing but rooftops and tall chimneys or centuries-old treetops.

Most beds are new kings and queens of classic design. Take a look, if possible, at the nautically designed Boat House Room, which features a king-size bed. A unique attraction is the cupola, high above the city for an unbroken daytime view or evening toast.

Fresh coffee is available daily. Breakfasts, typically including fruits, baked goods, juices and a hearty main course, may be enjoyed on the patio or terrace. Meals are served on tapestry place mats, silverware and crystal. With advance notice, special dietary needs can be accommodated. Stays at the Verandas require two-night minimums on festival weekends and holidays. Corporate discounts apply.

The Wine House
$$ • 311 Cottage Ln. • (910) 763-0511

Perhaps Wilmington's most unusual bed and breakfast inn, The Wine House (the Levi-Hart Wine House, to be exact) looks just as you might expect a wine house dating from about 1863 to look. It's a rustic, two-room clapboard building with shuttered windows, standing apart from the owner's residence behind a brick-walled courtyard. Its location on an easy-to-miss lane lends the Wine House an out-of-the-way feeling, right in the heart of downtown Wilmington. Each room is furnished with antiques, a wet bar, a queen-size bed and refrigerator and has heart-pine floors, a private bath and a fireplace. Breakfasts are continental. Bicycles are available for exploring the city.

The Worth House
$$ • 412 S. 3rd St. • (910) 762-8562, (800) 340-8559

Francie and John Miller's bed and breakfast inn is a scrupulously restored Queen Anne-style turreted house with a wraparound front porch and a tastefully simple interior that includes a library and parlor. Television is available in the sitting rooms. Special touches include private baths, working fireplaces in most rooms, the accessibility of fax and modem hookups, a laundry room, a large backyard and an ongoing jigsaw puzzle. Breakfasts are hearty and homemade and may be enjoyed in some rooms or on the second-floor porch.

Most of the seven guest rooms are large, and beds are classic, including four-poster, antique queen-size and king-size plantation. Ask about the Azalea Room with its glassed-in veranda or the Hibiscus Room with its sitting room nestled in the corner turret. There is also a two-room upstairs suite with a TV room, perfect for families or groups. Beverages are available to guests all day. The Worth House welcomes children older than 8. Ask about special seasonal and three- to five-night packages.

Carolina Beach and Kure Beach

The Beacon House Inn Bed and Breakfast
$$ • 715 Carolina Beach Ave. N., Carolina Beach • (910) 458-6244, (910) 458-7322

Way back when, the builders got this one right — central breezeways on each floor, running from oceanside balcony to soundside balcony, permit the coastal breezes to cool the building all day. The interior has a country-home atmosphere, with a downstairs common room with a fireplace.

The nine nonsmoking guest rooms have Queen Anne decor, including cheval mirrors, and are decorated with a lighthouse theme. Rooms are equipped with ceiling fans and paired doors, one of each being louvered to take advantage of that hallway breeze. There is one bath for every two rooms. Full country breakfasts include homemade breads and jams and may be taken on the upstairs balcony overlooking the ocean.

A separate cottage with a full kitchen is available by the week and accommodates up to eight people (breakfast is not included in cottage rental). Children are welcome at the cottages. Beacon House is a block from the ocean between Carolina Beach's two fishing piers. The innkeepers also offer dinner, assistance arranging recreational packages and plenty of hospitality.

Ocean Princess Inn
$$-$$$ • 824 Fort Fisher Blvd., Kure Beach • (910) 458-6712

Ocean Princess Inn is ideally suited to the romantic adult getaway: peaceful, secluded, close by the Fort Fisher State Historic Site and

State Recreation Area and graced with every modern amenity, now including a small bar with all ABC permits. Set far back from the road amid windswept live oaks, the inn is a beachy establishment with high decks that offer ocean views. Each guest room features a choice between breakfast basket (a complimentary continental selection) and full breakfast, plus private entrances, TV, coffee maker, refrigerator, microwave and telephone. Six rooms offer Jacuzzis, one of which is on the deck outdoors with an ocean view. A minisuite is handicapped accessible.

Guests can gather in the large, comfortable downstairs den with fireplace. Original local artwork adorns the building. A major attraction is the in-ground heated pool, complete with cabana, Jacuzzi and hot-and-cold showers. The Ocean Princess can accommodate small functions plus conferences of up to 24 people.

Bald Head Island

Theodosia's Bed and Breakfast
$$$-$$$$ • Harbour Village
• (910) 457-6563, (800) 656-1812

This, the island's first bed and breakfast inn, is of a quality one expects at Bald Head and occupies an imposing gabled, modern Victorian structure near the marina. The decor and size of the 10 carefully appointed rooms are diverse, variously incorporating floral and Virgin Island motifs, queen-size and double beds, and wrought-iron and wood detailing. Everywhere there are porches or balconies offering spectacular views of the harbor, river or island marshes. All rooms have private baths (one with Jacuzzi) or showers, cable TV and telephones. The ground-floor guest room is handicapped-accessible. Two rooms occupy the adjoining Carriage House.

Innkeepers Lydia and Frank Love formally serve full breakfasts to guests' individual tables. Meals vary in accent among English, Smoky Mountain and Mexican, with local coastal touches as well. Nightly or weekly stays include plenty of little extras such as refreshments, evening desserts and complimentary golf carts and bicycles (Bald Head Island's only permitted mechanized transportation). The inn was named in honor of the daughter of America's most famous duelist, Aaron Burr. She disappeared off the North Carolina coast in 1812 and her ghost is said to fancy Bald Head Island these days. Children may find Theodosia's formality uncomfortable. A seven-day cancellation notice is requested.

Southport-Oak Island

Lois Jane's Riverview Inn
$$ • 106 W. Bay St., Southport
• (910) 457-6701, (800) 457-1152

Directly overlooking the mouth of the Cape Fear River near the old harbor pilot's tower, this beautifully restored 1892 home has been owned by only one family since its construction. It is a quiet getaway within easy walking distance of Southport's restaurants, river walk, shops and museum. It is currently the only bed and breakfast accommodation in Southport. Porches on the river side of the building are ideal for rocking away the time.

Two rooms with private baths and two with a shared bath have queen-size, four-poster beds and period furnishings that have been part of the home for years. The rooms to the front of the building have beautiful river views, and one room has its own entrance to the communal upstairs porch. Full breakfasts, including homemade breads and muffins, are served daily in the dining room, and afternoon hors d'oeuvres and evening sweets are additional touches. Special breakfast arrangements can be made with advance notice. Coffee is placed in the hallway outside the guest rooms each morning, and a small refrigerator is available there with beverages and snacks. Cancellations require at least 24-hour notice for refunds.

South Brunswick Islands

Breakfast Creek Bed & Breakfast
$ • 4361 Ocean Breeze Ave. S.W., Shallotte • (910) 754-3614

With a veranda overlooking the Atlantic at Shallotte Inlet, Breakfast Creek Bed & Breakfast is a contemporary home within minutes of Holden and Ocean Isle beaches. The home sits on more than an acre of landscaped property filled with live oaks and gardens and bor-

BED AND BREAKFAST INNS • 63

North Carolina beaches are perfect places to get your feet wet.

Photo: Cape Fear Coast Convention and Visitors Bureau

The Historic Wilmington Foundation

During the 1960s and '70s, the 200-block area of residential downtown Wilmington was falling into disrepair. Social and economic circumstances were driving Wilmingtonians away from the neighborhood to the safety of the suburbs. Beautiful old homes that were no longer livable — and had become tax burdens to owners who would not live in them and could not rent them — began to be demolished. The sight of losing these houses one after another sounded an alarm in Wilmingtonians that reverberated throughout the community. Concerned citizens feared not only the complete destruction of the houses but of a piece of local history as well.

Although privately owned, these homes, with their distinctive architecture that ranges from Italianate to Antebellum to Neo-Classical to Mediterranean to Victorian, share their history with every visitor who stands on the sidewalk and looks at them. Years before the Civil War, General U.S. Grant attended a wedding at the Governor Dudley mansion, a downtown home overlooking the river. In another home, young Woodrow Wilson studied his homework by candlelight. In yet another, youthful journalist David Brinkley straightened his tie, collected his notepad and headed off to cover a story at the nearby Cape Fear Hotel.

Aside from the value of memories and the interesting lessons of history, perhaps this community's greatest current importance is simply its livability. A stroll through Historic Downtown Wilmington today reveals little of the hard times that gripped the neighborhood during the 1970s. Beautifully restored 18th- and 19th- century homes gleam with new paint and catch the eye with fascinating architectural detail. Passersby can't help but notice the meticulously kept gardens and neighbors engaged in ongoing renovation projects. There is almost always a ladder in view and a proud homeowner tending to maintenance of a home that, while private, is a national treasure.

— continued on next page

The deRosset House, former home of the Historic Wilmington Foundation, is now the City Club.

The convivial and prosperous atmosphere of today's downtown neighborhood is the result of a tremendous amount of work on the part of many individuals and groups. The City of Wilmington, the Downtown Area Redevelopment Effort, the Lower Cape Fear Historical Society and others share credit for what must have seemed a daunting task.

One organization that has toiled quietly behind the scenes for three decades to save the neighborhood is the Historic Wilmington Foundation. Formed in 1966, its members came together to question the alarming loss of historic homes and a community that could never be duplicated again in American history. Under the leadership of R.V. Asbury and Thomas H. Wright, Sr., an army of volunteers came forth to address a critical component in the reclaiming of downtown: saving the architecture by stopping demolitions and providing for alternative funding to help home buyers finance renovations. It was the beginning of preservation efforts in Wilmington.

The foundation purchased endangered homes, identified their historical significance, established protective covenants with buyers and gave momentum to what became a massive domino effect. Early in the effort, the foundation funded the purchase of more than 50 homes through North Carolina's first revolving fund. As the renovation process progressed, neighbors who had endured the community's worst times took heart and began to repair their own homes.

A house that became something of a beacon to the neighborhood was purchased in 1985 by the Historic Wilmington Foundation to serve as its office. The deRosset House at the corner of South Second and Dock streets is a 10,000 square-foot Greek Revival home dating from 1841. Renovations in 1874 added the cupola and gave the building an Italianate style. The house was purchased for $35,000 and, according to the foundation's Executive Director Elizabeth Buxton, it had been vacant since the 1950s and was in terrible disrepair. Although the foundation renovated office space in the basement and spent 12 years painstakingly restoring the home, a time came when the house was a serious financial drain on the organization.

As with all foundation purchases, the deRosset House was returned to the market and, in 1997, was sold to Tom Scott and Mike Compton, visionary developers who are currently renovating the home to its former grandeur. "It surprised some people that we sold it," says Ms. Buxton, "But that's our purpose. It has always been our mission to save architecturally significant homes and return them to the community for use. These gentlemen understand historic rehabilitation and we're pleased to see one of the grandest antebellum houses being put back into use."

Mr. Scott and Mr. Compton, owners of the Inn at St. Thomas across the street from the deRosset House, are currently engaged in a $1.5 million restoration project of the house that will result not only in preservation of an important part of Wilmington's history, but will also create a valuable and appropriate resource for the community — it will open in the near future as the City Club, creating a setting where, no doubt, more of Wilmington's significant history will be made.

The Historic Wilmington Foundation has temporarily moved to offices on Fifth Street and, with the transition, is able to refocus its efforts on wider preservation efforts throughout the city and county. "With the sale of the deRosset House, we will once again be able to operate the revolving fund to purchase threatened historic properties," says Ms. Buxton.

The mission statement of the foundation says it all: To preserve and restore historic buildings, sites and resources; to advocate compatible new development; to educate the public in preservation principles and techniques; and to enhance the livability of our rich Lower Cape Fear Heritage.

For more information on the Historic Wilmington Foundation, call (910) 762-2511.

dering a wildlife-filled salt marsh. Marinas on the Intracoastal Waterway are a short walk away, and charter fishing and golf courses are available close by. Two rooms and a suite, all with private baths, are equipped with central air conditioning, ceiling fans and TV. Breakfast Creek is a good, affordable option for those who don't mind not being directly on the beach.

Crescent Moon Inn
$-$$ • 965 Sabbath Home Rd. S.W., Holden Beach • (910) 842-1190

This modern bed and breakfast inn is only 1.5 miles from Holden Beach, and the owners have arranged for guest parking at the beach at no additional cost. Add to this the proximity to the area's dozens of golf courses and easy access to both Wilmington and Myrtle Beach. Crescent Moon Inn is a large white-brick building with a rear deck shaded by tall sycamore, curly-bark birch, apple and pear trees. Guests are welcome to use the screened-in outdoor Jacuzzi. Flower and herb beds are carefully tended. The decor is attractive and casual, full of earth tones and pastels, fiber rugs, wicker and rattan. Breakfasts range from continental to homemade baked goods, juices and cereals. Beverages and snacks are available all day.

The guest rooms have peaked ceilings with beams and skylights and are furnished with king-size, queen-size and twin beds. Two nights minimum are required for stays from June through August and during festival weekends and holidays. Sabbath Home Road runs nearly parallel to the Intracoastal Waterway, about 8 miles south of U.S. Highway 17. Holden Beach Road (N.C. 130) from Shallotte, Mt. Pisgah Road or Stone Chimney Road will get you there from Highway 17. Crescent Moon Inn's driveway is directly opposite the entrance to the Sea Trace development.

Goose Creek Bed & Breakfast
$-$$ • 1901 Egret St. S.W., Ocean Isle Beach • (910) 754-5849, (800) 275-6540

If being eight minutes from the beach isn't a deterrent, this bed and breakfast inn on the mainland side of the Intracoastal Waterway is an excellent choice. Reasonably priced, this establishment offers comfortable, large bedrooms, more than 2,000 square feet of lighted outdoor decking with comfy rockers and porch swing,

Historic Downtown Wilmington has many charming bed and breakfast inns.

plus central air and a working fireplace in a non-smoking home on quiet, navigable Goose Creek. You can fish from the pier or take a boat tour with your host, a USCG-certified captain. Breakfasts typically include homemade breads, pastries and omelets, served buffet-style. For a real treat, ask about the custard-baked French toast. Guests often prefer to eat on the screened porch overlooking the creek.

The four guest rooms are on the third floor, seemingly nestled among the trees, and can be configured as suites with private or shared bathrooms. Guests are welcome to use the projection TV, pool table, and kayak. Goose Creek Bed & Breakfast is close to numerous golf courses and restaurants. Note that the proprietors own two well-behaved golden retrievers. Cancellations within 10 days of your stay are subject to a $10 service fee, and no refunds are made for cancellations within 48 hours of your scheduled arrival. Guests without reservations are welcome.

Topsail Island Area

Bed & Breakfast at Mallard Bay
$-$$ • 960 Mallard Bay Rd., Hampstead
• (910) 270-3363

This contemporary beach-style home is a single-suite inn directly over looking the Intracoastal Waterway across from Topsail Island. It is the only bed and breakfast inn in the Hampstead are and is a short ride from the beach, many golf courses and downtown Wilmington. The large grounds are extremely quiet, the view excellent, and the Harbour Village Marina is within easy walking distance.

The two-room suite is upstairs and features a four-poster bed, antiques, full private bath, TV, VCR and a sitting room with a queen-size sofa bed — perfect for couples or small families with children older than 12. A spacious, high deck is ideal for sunbathing, and a canoe is available for exploring the waterway.

Innkeeper Phoebe Hood serves full country breakfasts on weekends, continental breakfasts on weekdays and complimentary wine and cheese each afternoon. Laundry facilities are available at no extra cost. Weekly rates are available, an open year-round. A seven-day policy is in effect.

The Pink Palace of Topsail
$-$$ • 1222 S. Shore Dr., Surf City
• (910) 328-5114

Casual and comfortable, the Pink Palace is an oceanfront bed and breakfast inn offering private beach access, a choice of three open-air decks (one shaded), a screened-in porch ideal for viewing sunsets and an outdoor hot tub with an ocean view accommodating up to eight people. Innkeeper Micki Tucker hosts guests from September through May, and rooms are available by the week during the summer. Four of its five guest rooms, each with playful murals painted by the innkeeper's daughter, open onto a bright living area with a wet bar. Full American breakfasts are served upstairs, where there is also a loft-like reading nook with books. Two-night minimums are requested for weekend stays.

The Pink Palace, the only pink building of its size in the area, is 1.5 miles south of the Surf City light, at the intersection of S. Shore Drive and S. Topsail Drive (N.C. 50).

Davies Realty

Beach Rentals and Sales

- Resort Real Estate Sales
- Investment Property
- Relocation Specialists
- Homes • Condominiums
- Vacation Rentals
- Free Market Analysis
- Residential & Commercial

Serving Pleasure Island Carolina Beach & Kure Beach

"Community Specialists"

Full Service Realtors

910-458-0444 • Toll Free 1-800-685-4614

View our Real Estate Listings and Beach Rentals on the
INTERNET: www.factnet.com/davies.html
EMAIL: daviesrlty@aol.com

Weekly and Long-Term Vacation Rentals

The southern North Carolina coast has many outstanding hotels, motels, inns and bed and breakfasts for vacationers, but there's another way to stay: rental homes. Every island from Topsail in the north to Sunset Beach in the south has at least half a dozen home rental companies with properties for short-term rental that range from opulent to modest. Choose from million-dollar homes, well-appointed condos, cheery cottages and even fishing trailers to meet your own preferences and budget. Most rentals are booked through a rental agency (a list of agencies is included below).

Most people have three reasons for choosing to rent a home instead of staying in a hotel for a week: it's usually less expensive to rent a cottage than a hotel room for a longer period of time; you can fit a bunch of family and friends into one comfortable place; and the setting is casual — you can dress the way you like and never have to worry about getting up to greet housekeeping when they tap on your door to clean.

This latter brings up a big difference between hotels and rental homes: there's no staff on hand to wait on guests. No room service, either. A bed left unmade in the morning will stay that way unless you take care of it. Same thing for taking out the garbage, cleaning the bathrooms and doing the laundry. A vacation rental home is, simply put, your home away from home and you're responsible for how well it runs.

Guests who don't mind the added responsibility of cooking and cleaning while on vacation will discover the special pleasures a rental home offers. There's enormous freedom in terms of scheduling the day to suit oneself. A kitchen at the beach is a bonus to cooks who appreciate the availability of fresh seafood at nearby markets. And there's an inclination for renters to make their chosen vacation home a tradition, returning year after year to a place that increasingly feels like their own home.

Accommodations and Locations

Choosing a home usually begins with a decision about proximity to the water. The benefits of an oceanfront house or apartment include an unobstructed view of the ocean, a short walk for a swim in the waves and the ability to keep an eye on the kids from the house as they play on the sand. However, these are the most expensive rentals. A home a block or two from the ocean can save hundreds of dollars in the vacation budget and still be a delight.

Soundside housing is less expensive than oceanfront but more expensive than homes in the middle of the island. If you have a boat and the house has a pier, or if you simply appreciate quiet coastal views, this can be a very exciting location that may be worth the extra cost.

Most homes are well-appointed in terms of furnishings, dishes, coffee-makers, and pots and pans. Usual features are heat and air and cable TV. Some nicer homes have stereo systems and VCRs. A condominium unit may include tennis courts, a pool and even a golf course for renter use.

Although you're expected to bring along or rent your provisions — including linens and beach chairs — rental homes usually have staples on hand, including foils and wraps, cleaning products and even residual groceries. It isn't uncommon to find fresh items in the pantry and refrigerator, such as butter, jams and jellies, soft drinks — sometimes beer — left by previous renters. There is an unspoken rule that unused items that will last are left for the next occupants to enjoy. In this way, houses manage to have salt and pepper, sugar and other staples on hand at all times. It's a nice welcome on the first night after check-in when even the best packer realizes condiments have been neglected.

A Few Rules

It is important to note that vacation home rental entails rules and regulations that reflect the family orientation of this kind of arrangement. A rental agency's primary allegiance is to the homeowner. The agency maintains the properties for the owners and assumes responsibility for renting the homes to reliable tenants.

There is an age requirement for renting most vacation homes through real estate management companies. Generally, the primary renter must be at least 21 years old, although some companies require the primary renter to be 25. An exception to this may involve marital status. If you're younger than 25 and married, you probably qualify, but companies will differ. Individual inquiry is recommended. Some companies that don't have an actual age requirement take a long, hard look at younger customers, especially in large groups.

Most rental agreements forbid house parties on the premises and that's the main reason for the age concern, especially in the quieter beach communities. Rowdiness is very much unappreciated on all area beaches, and a noisy party may cause you to forfeit your rental agreement without a refund. Most homes have a written maximum-occupancy regulation, and you are required to honor it. This bodes well for families seeking a peaceful location for vacationing.

There is a general expectation that you'll leave the house as clean as you found it. Some rental agencies will provide cleaning service

WEEKLY AND LONG-TERM VACATION RENTALS • 71

Seasoned boaters know to never leave the dock without binoculars.

Resort Property Sales & Rentals

Call for free summer rental brochure

ERA-Brittain & Associate Realtors
1322 Airlie Road • P.O. Box 916
Wrightsville Beach, NC 28480
910-256-2224 • 800-362-9031

and linens for a fee if you are not particularly inclined toward domestic concerns on your getaway. If you don't clean up and haven't made arrangements for maid service, your deposit will be applied toward this work. The minimum charge is $50.

Cleaning supplies are usually already in the house because a prior vacationer bought them and left them there. It's a nice gesture on your part to do the same, even if current supplies seem ample, and it's essential for you to provide cleaning supplies if none have been left for you. Owners supply vacuum cleaners, mops and brooms. You are responsible for putting out the garbage — just like at home. Some beaches have recycling programs, and you'll be instructed in how to participate in the event that yours does.

Most rental homes have telephones, and you're on your honor not to use them in any way for which the owners would be charged. If your vacation home doesn't have a phone, most rental companies will arrange to get emergency messages to you. Of course, the proliferation of mobile phones makes this issue less important.

Pets

Pets are absolutely not allowed. If Fido must come with you, ask your rental agent about the services of local kennels. Since your pet is not allowed on most beaches in the summer season, you might want to leave him at home in friendly surroundings. Also, please note this region has a seasonal flea problem, which more than anything else dictates this policy. As a local Realtor has written in a brochure, "it only takes two fleas" to cause a flea problem in a house. If you smuggle in a pet and the housekeeping staff that follows you discovers fleas, be assured that your deposit will be used to pay for fumigation.

Rates

Prices fall in a wide range from $300 to $3,800 a week, depending on your choice of

Plan Your Vacation With Us!

SOLD

Howard Perry and Walston REALTORS®

Better Homes and Gardens®

From economy to luxury accommodations short or long term lengths of stay, WE HAVE IT ALL!
Wrightsville Beach - Bald Head Island
Call for free brochure
P.O. Box 293 • 222 Causeway Dr.
Wrightsville Beach, NC 28480
(910) 256-2181 • 800-529-7653

P.O. Box 526 • 2400 N. Lumina Ave.
Duneridge Resort
Wrightsville Beach, NC 28480
(910) 256-3101 • 800-822-4588

---

beach, luxury factor and season. Bald Head Island, Wrightsville Beach and Figure Eight Island are at the high end. Topsail, Carolina Beach and the Brunswick Beaches (Oak Island, Holden Beach, Ocean Isle Beach and Sunset Beach) offer a broader array of less-pricey accommodations but also have their share of high-end properties. Most agencies will require a deposit, and there are various stipulations in the agreement that you need to be familiar with; for example, a state tax of 6 percent and county room tax of 3 percent are added to the cost.

Rental rates are subject to change without notice. Winter rates may be as much as 30 percent less. A deposit of 50 percent is generally required to confirm reservations. Major credit cards are usually accepted, but other methods of payment are available depending upon the agency's policies. Some accept personal checks provided they arrive 30 days in advance of your arrival.

Rental Agencies

The following rental agencies are only some of the fine companies from which you may choose. By no means do we include them all, as it would take an entire book to do so. Select the beach of your choice and contact the area's convention and visitors bureau or local Board of Realtors for the names of other rental companies. Chambers of commerce also carry brochures about rental companies — see our Area Overview chapter for a list of local chambers.

Wrightsville Beach

ERA Brittain & Associates Realtors
1322 Airlie Rd., Crocker's Landing
• (910) 256-2224, (800) 362-9031

This company rents homes and condominiums exclusively on Wrightsville Beach. It has many oceanfront rentals.

Bryant Real Estate
1001 N. Lumina Ave. • (910) 256-3764, (800) 322-3764

This is the oldest vacation rental agency on Wrightsville Beach, and it handles diverse properties ranging from homes to condominiums or duplexes. It also offers rentals in Wilmington.

Howard, Perry and Walston Coastal Rental Properties
222 Causeway Dr. • (910) 256-2181, (800) 529-7653

This company represents numerous properties on the oceanfront, Intracoastal Water

Coastal Condo-Let

FREE BROCHURE

Vacation Rentals and Sales
Federal Point Shopping Center
1020 N. Lake Park Blvd. #12
Carolina Beach, NC 28428

http://www.condolet.com
email: condolet@wilmington.net

1-800-994-5222 • 910-458-5658

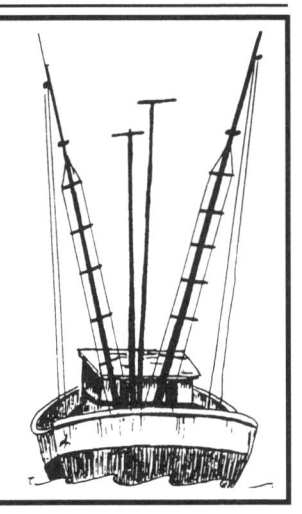

---

way and surrounding properties on Wrightsville Beach and in Wilmington. The company markets properties on Bald Head Island, including single-family homes and condominiums.

Intracoastal Realty Corporation
605 Causeway Dr. • (910) 256-3780, (800) 346-2463

This company offers about 200 properties, largely upscale but with a few old-style beach cottages, in a mix of condominiums and single-family homes primarily on Wrightsville Beach.

Figure Eight Island

Figure Eight Realty
15 Bridge Rd., Wilmington
• (910) 686-4400, (800) 279-6085

Although many Wrightsville Beach Realtors handle rental properties on Figure Eight Island, this is the only company actually on the private island. It handles luxury properties — all single-family homes overlooking the ocean, sound or marshes.

Carolina Beach and Kure Beach

Atlantic Towers
1615 S. Lake Park Blvd., Carolina Beach
• (910) 458-8313, (800) 232-2440

Extensively remodeled and offering attractive condominium units — including deluxe units — Atlantic Towers is situated right on the beach. It offers nightly rentals and short-term and weekly rentals at discounted prices.

Bullard Realty
1404 S. Lake Park Blvd., Carolina Beach
• (910) 458-4028, (800) 327-5863

Bullard Realty, working since 1985 on the island, offers vacation rental condominiums and cottages on Carolina and Kure beaches.

Carolina Beach Realty
307 Lake Park Blvd., Carolina Beach
• (910) 458-4444

Carolina Beach Realty rents single-family

INSIDERS' TIP

Brunswick beaches run from east to west, so the sun both rises and sets over the ocean.

Visit our Kingdom by the Sea... without paying a King's Ransom.

On the North Carolina Oceanfront. Wide Beaches spacious 1 to 4 bedroom condominiums with full amenities, plus a variety of dining, entertainment, fishing, golf and more.

1001 N. Lake Park Blvd. Carolina Beach, NC 28428

UNITED Beach Vacations

Call For Our Color Brochure And Attractive Rates

1-800-334-5806

---

homes and condominiums in Carolina Beach, Kure Beach and Fort Fisher.

Coastal Condo-Let
1020 N. Lake Park Blvd. #12, Carolina Beach • (910) 458-5658, (800) 994-5222

Properties range across the island from Carolina Beach in the north to Fort Fisher in the south for this large company. Established in 1984, it handles condominiums, cottages, apartments and larger homes.

Davies Realty
1009 N. Lake Park Blvd., Carolina Beach • (910) 458-0444, (800) 685-4614

This company offers largely high-quality oceanfront or oceanview condominium rentals from Carolina Beach to Fort Fisher.

Gardner Realty
(910) 458-8503, (800) 697-7924

Gardner Realty offers a large selection of rental properties, including apartments, con-

Surf's up!

Hobbs Realty & Holden Beach

RENT, BUY, and BUILD with the Leaders in Customer Satisfaction.

*A Family Tradition of Excellence.
We Offer a large selection of oceanfront homes, over 150 cottages to choose from.
Free Color Brochure • Toll Free: 800-655-3367*

114 Ocean Blvd. West • Holden Beach, NC 28462
(910) 842-2002 • www.hobbsrealty.com

---

dominiums and single-family homes on Carolina Beach, Kure Beach and Fort Fisher.

Lighthouse Realty
201 Fort Fisher Blvd., Kure Beach
• (910) 458-3300

This small real estate company rents both residential and commercial properties on all of Pleasure Island and throughout New Hanover County.

United Beach Vacations
1001 N. Lake Park Blvd., Carolina Beach
• (910) 458-9073, (800) 334-5806

This large company manages rental units, including condominiums and single-family homes on Carolina Beach, Kure Beach and Fort Fisher.

Southport, Bald Head Island, Oak Island

Bald Head Island Information Center
5079 Southport Supply Rd., Southport
• (800) 234-1666

At this writing, this pristine island has 100 rental properties. Each rental includes the use of at least one four-passenger electric golf cart for transportation around the island, where cars are not allowed.

Coldwell Banker Southport-Oak Island Realty
300 Country Club Dr., Yaupon Beach
• (910) 278-6011, (800) 243-8132

Weekly resort rentals are available through this large company, which manages 400 cottages, duplexes and condominiums on Oak Island.

Century 21 Dorothy Essey & Associates Inc., Realtors
6102 E. Oak Island Dr., Long Beach
• (910) 278-RENT, (800) 849-2322

This company offers properties for rental on Oak Island, in Southport and in Boiling Spring Lakes.

Margaret Rudd & Associates Inc., Realtors
210 Country Club Dr., Yaupon Beach
• (910) 278-6523, (800) 733-5213

There are 250 rental properties managed by this company on Oak Island, most of which are single-family homes and condominiums. This office is open seven days a week.

There's nothing like a lazy fall afternoon for some intense fishing.

Ocean 1 Realty
4310 E. Beach Dr., Long Beach
• (910) 278-6677, (800) 231-4882

The oldest rental agency on Oak Island, this company has been serving vacation rental needs for more than 30 years.

Walter Hill & Associates
4324 E. Beach Dr., Long Beach
• (910) 278-5405

Formerly named Scruggs & Morrison Realty, this company handles single-family homes and duplexes on Oak Island.

Shannon's Services Inc.
4902 E. Beach Dr., Long Beach
• (910) 278-5251

The oldest rental agency on the beach, this company handles rentals of single-family homes and duplexes on Oak Island.

South Brunswick Islands

Atlantic Vacations Resorts and Real Estate
131 Ocean Blvd. W., Holden Beach
• (910) 842-8000, (800) 252-7000

This company offers vacation rentals of private homes, condominiums and duplexes ranging from two to 10 bedrooms in all locations on Holden Beach.

Brick Landing Plantation
1900 Goose Creek Rd., Ocean Isle Beach
• (910) 754-4373, (800) 438-3006

This resort/golf community offers golf packages that include accommodations, breakfast and green fees for 18 holes. Tennis can be substituted for one round of golf. Rental of condominiums or townhomes includes maid service at departure.

Brunswickland Realty
123 Ocean Blvd., Holden Beach
- (910) 842-6949, (800) 842-6949

In business since the 1970s, this company manages single-family cottages and larger homes.

Hobbs Realty
114 Ocean Blvd. W., Holden Beach
- (910) 842-2002, (800) 655-3367

Hobbs Realty manages 150 rental properties on Holden Beach, including oceanfront, canal and second- and third-row homes. The company accepts MasterCard and Visa and requires no reservation fee. Housekeeping services are available. Discounts are offered during the winter season until May 31. Year-round rentals are also available.

Island Realty Vacations
19 Causeway Dr., Ocean Isle Beach
- (910) 579-3599, (800) 589-3599

This company offers cottages and condominiums exclusively on Ocean Isle Beach.

Alan Holden Vacations
128 Ocean Blvd. W., Holden Beach
- (910) 842-6061, (800) 720-2200

This busy agency manages more than 325 rental properties, mostly cottages and duplexes as well as a few condos, on Holden Beach. It now offers golf packages.

R.H. McClure Realty Inc.
24 Causeway Dr., Ocean Isle Beach
- (910) 579-3586, (800) 332-5476

Single-family homes and duplexes are handled by this company on Ocean Isle Beach.

McMillan Real Estate
113 Causeway Dr., Ocean Isle Beach
- (910) 579-9100, (800) 353-3533

This company rents a full range of houses and condominiums on Ocean Isle Beach.

Sloane Realty
16 Causeway Dr., Ocean Isle Beach
- (910) 579-6216, (800) 843-6044

The largest and oldest vacation rental business on Ocean Isle Beach has condos and cottages available.

Sunset Properties
419 Sunset Blvd., Sunset Beach
- (910) 579-9900, (800) 446-0218 in N.C., (800) 525-0182 outside N.C.

This large company handles the rental of vacation homes and duplexes exclusively on Sunset Beach.

Sunset Vacations
401 S. Sunset Blvd., Sunset Beach
- (910) 579-9000, (800) 331-6428

This company offers a wide assortment of attractive single-family homes for rental on Sunset Beach.

Topsail Island

Beach Properties of Topsail Island, Inc.
(910) 328-0719, (800) 753-2975

Beach Properties rents homes and condominium units all over Topsail Island. Owner Patsy Jordan was the recipient of the 1997 Realtor of the Year Award.

Jean Brown Real Estate
522-A&B, New River Dr., Surf City
- (910) 328-1640, (800) 745-4480

This large residential sales company has been in the vacation rental business for four seasons and offers properties ranging from large, single-family houses to mobile homes.

Coldwell Banker Coastline Realty
965 Old Folkstone Rd., Topsail Way Shopping Center, Sneads Ferry
- (910) 327-7711, (800) 497-5463

This company offers mostly oceanfront vacation rentals that include condominiums (with swimming pools and tennis courts), townhomes, single-family homes and "basic little beach cottage" for nostalgia buffs.

The Kennedy Company Realty and Management
200 North Shore Village, Sneads Ferry
• (910)327-2526, (910) 800-682-3460

Established in 1984, Kennedy Company handles real estate rentals exclusively on North Topsail Beach. Rentals include 120 condominiums and townhomes, all with swimming pools (including some indoor pools) and tennis courts. It accepts all major credit cards, including American Express. A deposit is required for rentals.

Lewis Realty
412 Roland Ave., Surf City
• (910) 328-5211, (800) 233-5211

This small rental agency has rental properties in Surf City and on Topsail Island. The properties are mainly single-family cottages.

Cathy Medlin Real Estate
406 Roland Ave., Surf City
• (910) 328-2323, (800) 622-6886

This 19-year veteran of real estate sales also offers the widest range of rental homes and condominiums on Topsail Island.

Topsail Realty
712 S. Anderson Blvd., Topsail Beach
• (910) 328-5241, (800) 526-6432

This well-established company handles 180 properties that are mostly single-family homes in the quiet oceanfront town of Topsail Beach on the island's southern end. It also manages rentals for Serenity Point, a development of attractive townhomes on the southern tip of the island.

Ward Realty
116 S. Topsail Dr., Surf City
• (910) 328-3221, (800) 782-6216

"The original developers of Topsail Island," this company handles properties for weekly or weekend vacation rentals.

Mountain Aire
BY NEWMAR

Wilmington FACT
Did you know that:
HOWARD RVCENTER is the #1 Luxury/Highline Coach Dealer in the Mid-Atlantic?

imagine
the comforts of *home.*

You'll find the comforts of home in the a Mountain Aire by Newmar. Choose from five interiors with lighter oak as our standard woodgrain and frosted maple or cherry options. In addition there are two new exterior colors. Luxury and classic style are standard in all our RVs.

HOWARD RV CENTER

- Mid-Atlantic #1 Luxury/Highline Coach Dealer
- Out of state deliveries
- Full service, parts and accessories
- One of the largest inventories in mid-atlantic region
- A wide selection of brand names including:
  NEWMAR *DUTCH STAR*
  NEWMAR *MOUNTAIN AIRE*
  NEWMAR *LONDON AIRE*

800-852-7148
www.hrvc.com
**6811 MARKET STREET
WILMINGTON, NC 28405**

HOWARD RV CENTER

Camping

These ever-changing shores have witnessed an epic succession of campers, from ancient Siouan and Algonquian gatherers whose shell middens littered the coast, to ill-fated European settlers who initially could gain no foothold on the low-lying land, to today's tourists who play the nomad on soil once thick with plantation rice and cotton. Despite the fact that most of the finest tracts of coastline have been built over, campers can still live — if only for a few days — a simpler life at the edge of the quiet spectacle of the Atlantic.

For the most part there isn't much roughing it when camping around here. Campgrounds nearest the beaches are generally RV towns with ample amenities. So, if you'd like to take along the kitchen sink, you may as well take your electric bug-zapper too. But, if you wear your home on your back and have the use of a small boat, leave the parking-lot-style camping behind for the isolation of Masonboro Island. In the off-season, your only neighbors may be pelicans and rabbits.

Bicycle campers will find campgrounds about a day's ride apart except in the Wilmington vicinity, where campgrounds are more numerous. In any event, camping the southern coast is ideal for visitors on a budget, anglers who want to walk to the water each morning and anyone for whom recreation is re-creation.

Naturally, the highest rates at private campgrounds apply during the summer and holiday weekends, averaging from about $13 to $24. Some campgrounds charge less, others more. Tent sites are cheaper than RV sites. At most private grounds, weekly rates often discount the seventh day if payment is made in advance. Rentals by the month or longer are extremely limited from April to August. Some campgrounds offer camper storage for a monthly fee.

As the Boy Scouts say, be prepared, especially for blistering sun, sudden electrical storms with heavy downpours, voracious marsh mosquitoes and insidious "no-see-ums" in summer. Temperatures in the region generally are mild, except for the occasional frost in winter. Average summer peak temperature is 88; average winter low, 36. April and October average the least rainfall, about three inches each, while July averages the most, nearly eight inches. Be prepared for rain in any season.

Sunscreen is essential. Hats and eye protection are wise and insect repellent useful. For tent camping, a waterproof tent fly is a must, and a tarp or dining fly is handy when cooking. Pack longer tent stakes or sand stakes for protection against high winds. Stay abreast of weather reports, especially during hurricane season, and always bring a radio. A lightweight camp stove and cook set will come in handy when restaurants aren't convenient and at the many sites where fires are prohibited.

The primary creature hazards are poisonous snakes, which are prevalent in forested areas, and ticks, which have been known to carry disease. Raccoons and other small nocturnal animals are seldom more than a nuisance, although rabid animals are occasionally reported in the rural interior. Normally, the animals posing the greatest threat are human, which is why open fires and alcoholic beverages are restricted in most campgrounds. Beware of poison ivy, poison oak and poison sumac in brushwood and forests.

For hikers or cyclists carrying packs, there are two noteworthy local retail outlets for equipment. In business for more than 50 years, Canady's Sport Center, 3220 Wrightsville Avenue, (910) 791-6280, is an excellent outdoor outfitter with a varied inventory (closed on Sunday). Also remarkable is Cape Fear Outfitters in the Plaza East Shopping Center, 1934-A Eastwood Road near Wrightsville Beach, (910) 256-1258 (open seven days a week). They carry a less varied but complete line of equipment for sale and rent. Your other choices for field gear are discount stores such as Kmart, 815 S. College Road, (910) 799-5360, which keeps a decent inventory of fishing and hunting gear in season, and the two area Wal-Mart stores, 352 S. College Road, (910) 392-4034, and 5511 Carolina Beach Road at Monkey Junction, (910) 452-0944 — good choices for novices and tailgate campers.

We've provided here a list of the area's nicest, most popular camping destinations. (For information on children's summer camps, refer to our Kidstuff chapter.)

Wilmington

Camelot RV Park & Campground
7415 Market St. • (910) 686-7705

Twenty minutes from downtown Wilmington, Camelot is better situated for getting to all the local attractions than for getting away from it all. Moreover, the Tomaselli family has endowed its establishment with plenty of its own resort quality. Camelot is Woodall-rated (the most recognized approval among private campgrounds). The tree-shaded grounds include a large swimming pool, a playground, volleyball, horseshoes, a fishing pond, a dump station, 100 campsites (pull-through and tent sites) and full and partial hookups. Independence Day is especially festive at Camelot, with musical entertainment.

The lodge has clean, tiled restrooms, hot showers, laundry facilities, a grocery and supply store, a game room and mail service. There is even a TV lounge. Near the campground entrance is a convenience store and gas station. Weekly and monthly rates are available, and reservations are accepted.

Carolina Beach Family Campground
9641 River Rd. • (910) 392-3322

This wooded, shady, 120-site campground is conveniently situated for cyclists touring the Ports of Call Route and the Cape Fear Run (see our Sports, Fitness and Parks chapter). The large RV and tent sites are complemented by a swimming pool, hot showers, laundry facilities, a craft room, small grocery store, and easy access to many area attractions. Partial and full hookups are available as well as air conditioning, electricity and heat. The campground is about a quarter-mile from Carolina Beach Road (U.S. 421) on the Wilmington side of the Snow's Cut bridge.

Masonboro Island

Accessible only by boat, Masonboro Island is the last and largest undisturbed barrier island remaining on the southern North Carolina coast. It is the fourth component of the North Carolina National Estuarine Research Reserve (see our Higher Education and Research chapter), and deservedly so. This migrating ribbon of sand and uphill terrain about 8 miles in length is immediately south of Wrightsville Beach and offers the camper a secluded, primitive experience in the most pristine environment left on the Cape Fear coast. It is also used by anglers, bird watchers, the occasional hunter, students and surfers (who prefer the north end). Everything you'll need must be packed in, and everything you produce should be packed out — everything!

Of the reserve's more than 5,000 acres, about 4,400 acres are tidal marsh and mud flats, so most folks land at the extreme north or south ends, on or near the sandy beaches by the inlets. Pitch camp behind the dunes only and use a cook stove; there is little or no firewood. While the North Carolina Division of Coastal Management hopes to limit its involvement with the island and preserve its traditional uses, it does prohibit polluting the island and camping on and in front of the dune ridge.

Wildlife here is remarkable and fragile. During the warm months, Masonboro Island is one of the most successful nesting areas for loggerhead turtles, a threatened species. Piping plovers, also threatened, feed at the island in winter. Keep your eyes on the marshes for

North Carolina's Southern coast offers a multitude of camping opportunities.

river otters and, at low tide, raccoons. Gray foxes, cotton rats and tiny marsh rabbits all frequent the small maritime forest.

The marshes, flats and creeks at low tide are excellent places to observe and photograph great blue and little blue herons, tricolor herons, snowy and great egrets, oystercatchers, clapper rails and many other flamboyant birds. Brown pelicans, various terns and gulls, American ospreys and shearwaters all live on Masonboro, if not permanently then at least for some part of their lives. Endangered peregrine falcons are very occasional seasonal visitors.

We recommend plenty of sun protection and insect repellent, perhaps even mosquito netting, in the warm months, and trash bags always. Keep in mind that some of the island is still privately owned, especially the north end, and all of it is fragile. The University of North Carolina at Wilmington is in the midst of a visitor-impact study that will attempt to assess the viability of continued camping here. Visitors' behavior and scientific scrutiny together will have some influence on whether Masonboro Island becomes severely restricted, so responsible usage is paramount. For more information about Masonboro Island, see the Islands section in our Attractions chapter.

Carolina Beach

Carolina Beach State Park
Dow Rd. • (910) 458-8206

Once a campsite for Paleo-Indians, colonial explorers and Confederate troops, Carolina Beach State Park remains a gem among camping destinations. Watersports enthusiasts are minutes from the Cape Fear River, Masonboro Sound and the Atlantic. There is a full-service marina with two launching ramps. Need we mention the great fishing? The park is a birdwatcher's paradise and home to lizards, snakes (mostly harmless), rare frogs, carnivorous plants (protected) and occasionally alligators, opossums, gray foxes and river otters.

Five miles of hiking trails wind through several distinct habitats, including maritime forest, pocosin (low, flat, swampy regions) and savanna. Hikers on the Sugar Loaf Trail pass over tidal marsh and dunes and along three lime-sink ponds. Cypress Pond, the most unusual, is dominated by a dwarf cypress swamp forest.

Dense vegetation lends the campsites a fair amount of privacy. Each site has a table and grill, and sites are available on a first-come basis ($9 per site). Drinking water and well-kept restrooms with hot showers are close by. There is a dump station for RVs, but no hookups. Ranger-led interpretive programs deepen visitors' understanding of the region's natural bounty. Unleashed pets and possession of alcoholic beverages are prohibited.

The park is 15 miles south of Wilmington, a mile north of Carolina Beach just off U.S. 421 on Dow Road. From Wilmington, make your first right after crossing Snow's Cut bridge. (See our Sports, Fitness and Parks chapter for more information about the park.)

Southport-Oak Island

Long Beach Family Campground
5011 E. Oak Island Dr., Long Beach
• **(910) 278-5737**

Boasting access to both the beach and the nightlife of east Oak Island and located just minutes from historic Southport, this campground is understandably popular all year long. Few of the 157 sites enjoy any shade, but the tent areas are grassy and commonly host foraging sea birds. One tenting area is for groups. Full and partial hookups are available, as are flush toilets, hot showers, sewage disposal, tables, a public phone, ice, and seasonal or permanent lease sites.

South Brunswick Islands

Holden Beach Pier Family Campground
441 Ocean Blvd. W., Holden Beach
• **(910) 842-6483**

The reason these 54 sun-baked sites remain jammed all summer with campers living cheek-to-jowl may be explained by their proximity to Holden Beach Pier and the beach. This campground, not the most attractive, is recommended only to die-hard budget vacationers. All sites have water, electric hookups and shaded tables, and the grounds essentially comprise an RV village. Pets on leashes are allowed. The adjacent Holden Beach General Store is a full-service grocery and beach-supply store.

Sea Mist Camping Resort
4616 Devane Rd. S.W., Shallotte
• **(910) 754-8916**

Sea Mist's panoramic view of Shallotte Inlet and Ocean Isle Beach is enough to entice any camper, but owners Nellie and Baker Harrel don't depend on view alone. Visitors love Sea Mist's pool, reputedly the largest in Brunswick County, with its shaded deck and picnic area. Volleyball, basketball, horseshoes and tetherball are among the activities available. Use of the boat ramp carries no extra charge. This Woodall-rated resort is open year-round and has 245 spacious RV and tent sites with tables. Most have full hookups.

The restrooms, bathhouses and coin-operated laundry facilities are clean, and the camp store is open from March 1 through December 1. Perhaps best of all, Sea Mist is only 10 minutes from the attractions of Ocean Isle Beach. Leashed pets are permitted. Daily, monthly and annual rates and storage are available. Reserve early.

Sea Mist is at the Intracoastal Waterway opposite the east end of Ocean Isle Beach. Follow the blue and white camping signs along N.C. Highway 179 to Brick Landing Road and con-

---

INSIDERS' TIP

Some good campgrounds in our area are giving way to development. Try them now, before they're gone!

Follow his lead for the "best catch" of the day.

tinue to the end of the pavement. Turn left onto Devane Road. (Devane passes through Waterway Campground, (910) 754-8652, a tolerable alternative in case Sea Mist is booked. Waterway is open April 1 through December 1.)

Topsail Island

Rogers Bay Family Campway
4021 Island Dr., North Topsail Beach • (910) 328-5781

This colossal camp city (500 sites) is remarkable for its shaded and manicured grounds, recreational offerings, and superb location across the road from the sparsely populated beach of northern Topsail Island. Rabbits make frequent visits to the lawns beneath gnarled live oaks. Open all year, this Woodall-rated facility features an in-ground swimming pool, a teen recreation room, a playground, complete hookups, a dump station, three air-conditioned bathhouses, a convenience store, propane refills, camper storage and a laundry room. Nearby attractions are miniature golf and a fine full-length golf course. Weekly, monthly and yearly stays and storage space can be arranged. Permanent sites are available for sale. Weekend reservations require a minimum two-day stay (with a $10 deposit); three days are required for holiday weekends. Campfires are prohibited, and pets must be leashed at all times.

INSIDERS' TIP

Look for carnivorous plants growing wild in Carolina Beach State Park — but don't pick them!

Inland

Lake Waccamaw State Park
State Park Rd., Lake Waccamaw
• (910) 669-2928

Lake Waccamaw, named after the region's tribal natives, is the largest of the Carolina bays and is located 38 miles from Wilmington in Columbus County. It wasn't until the age of aviation that thousands of similar elliptical depressions were noticed dotting the Carolinas' coastal plain. All the depressions are oriented along northwest-southeast axes. Locals came to call them "bays," referring to the abundance of bay trees — red, sweet and loblolly — that flourish there.

About 400,000 Carolina bays exist, ranging in size from a fraction of an acre to more than 5,000 acres. Some are lakes, but most are seasonal wetlands filled with fertile peat. Their origin is still a mystery. A hypothesis that an ancient meteor shower or explosion formed them collapsed under scrutiny. A widely accepted theory is that they were formed by strong winds blowing across a sandy landscape or shallow sea during the last Ice Age.

Lake Waccamaw's shallow waters support 52 species of fish. Five species of aquatic animals living here exist nowhere else in the world. A half-mile-long nature trail and the boardwalk are worthwhile.

Visitors to Lake Waccamaw must be willing to rough it slightly. The park is undeveloped, with no more facilities than pit toilets, tables and grills. Three primitive group campsites (no water) are available by reservation or on a first-come basis. Trailer camping is not allowed. Permits may be obtained at the ranger station that, in keeping with the bays' mysterious origins, seems to keep no regular routine except an 8 AM opening and 6 PM closing time. If you're lucky, you may reach a ranger by phone at (910) 646-4748; otherwise, call Singletary State Park (another bay lake) at the number listed above. Fees are $5 per site or $1 per person, whichever is higher.

The park is about 7 miles south of U.S. Highway 74/76. Highly visible signs along that route and along N.C. Highway 214 lead the way. Entrance to the park is from Martin Road, which veers off State Road 1947.

Restaurants

As you might expect from a coastal community, seafood figures prominently almost everywhere you dine on North Carolina's southern coast. These coastal waters are among the most pristine in the east, yielding consistently high-quality seafood, and just about every restaurant worth its salt offers fresh daily catches that may include grouper, mahimahi, shark, swordfish, mackerel, triggerfish and shellfish, to name only a few.

International cuisines now available in the area include Thai, Indian, Chinese (including Szechuan), Greek, Italian, German, Japanese, Jamaican, French and Australian. The several restaurants serving Mexican food are good places to advance the perpetual quest for the perfect margarita, but by no means does the search end there. Also represented throughout our coverage area are a number of major restaurant chains (national and regional), such as Subway, Perkins, Fuddruckers, Kenny Rogers Roasters and Outback Steakhouse.

Favorite Local Foods

Naturally, the traditional regional specialties still comprise the heart and soul of Southern coastal dining. The famous Calabash-style seafood is ever-present. It gets its name from the town heralded as the seafood capital of the world for having at least 30 seafood restaurants within a square mile. Calabash-style calls for seasoned cornmeal batter and deep frying and has become synonymous with all-you-can-eat. Calabash restaurants typically serve a huge variety of piping-hot seafood in massive quantities. But that's not all there is to regional cuisine.

Lowcountry steam-offs are buckets filled with a variety of shellfish, potatoes, corn and Old Bay seasoning. When fresh oysters are in season in the fall, oyster roasts abound. While crab is popular, it's crab dip that attracts attention in these parts. Competition is stiff among restaurants boasting the best crab dip. New Year's Eve dinners may include collards and black-eyed peas, symbolic (some say) of paper money and small change, to ensure prosperity in the year to come. Okra, sweet potatoes, grits, turnip greens, mustard greens and kale are also regional favorites. Hush puppies, those delicious deep-fried dollops of sweet cornmeal dough, take the place of bread on many coastal tables.

Hoppin' John, based on black-eyed peas and rice, is a hearty dish seen in many variations. Shrimp and grits is another popular dish appearing in various incarnations from restaurant to restaurant. Boiled (often pronounced "bawled") peanuts are popular snacks, frequently available at roadside stands, and nowhere does pecan pie taste better. Iced tea flows freely, in most places by the pitcher-full, and locals prefer it very sweet.

Wilmington has made its mark in the world of the master brewers of beer. The Wilmington Brewing Company's Dergy Porter and amber ale both won silver medals in the World Beer Championships in 1996. You'll find Dergy's served at many local restaurants. And if fresh microbrewed beer is your idea of heaven, also look into Wilmington's Front Street Brewery, listed below. (Note that practically all restaurants in our area serve beer and wine, but some do not serve mixed drinks.)

Planning and Pricing

Reservations are generally not required unless your party consists of six persons or more, and many restaurants throughout the region don't accept reservations at all. It wasn't very long ago that waiting time at most Wilmington restaurants was negligible. With the town's booming growth since 1990, that has changed substantially for many restaurants (for example, Outback Steakhouse on S. College Road is jammed practically every night of the

TOMATOZ
Wilmington N.C. American Grille

Upbeat, Casual and Delicious

Pasta / Risotto
Fresh Seafood
Beef / Mixed Grill
Vegetarian Options
Sourdough Pizzas
Salads
Sandwiches
Smoked Fish
Homemade Desserts
Homemade Breads

Lunch & Dinner from 11am
Sunday Brunch 10am -3:30pm

1201 South College at the corner of Wrightsville Ave..

910-313-0541

year). At most popular eateries in Wilmington expect to find waiting lists throughout the summer, during festivals, and on most holidays.

Restaurant hours are frequently curtailed in winter, when some restaurants close entirely for a month or more. Most places serve later on Friday and Saturday nights than on weeknights. So always call ahead to verify hours and reservations. You may also want to inquire about early-bird specials and senior citizen discounts even if such information isn't included in our listings.

In keeping with the area's resort character and hot summers, dining here is generally very casual. While you might feel out of place wearing shorts at fancier restaurants such as The Pilot House, casual dress is commonplace practically everywhere else. Wearing shorts or polo shirts during the summer, even at the better restaurants, is simply practical and not frowned upon.

Most restaurants listed here accept major credit cards. We'll let you know which ones do not.

Price Code

The following price code is based on the average price for two dinner entrees only. For restaurants not serving dinner, the code reflects midpriced lunch entrees for two. The price codes do not reflect the state's 6 percent sales tax or gratuities.

$	Less than $15
$$	$15 to $25
$$$	$25 to $40
$$$$	$40 and more

Where To Eat

If your favorite restaurant isn't listed here, it may be because it's among the many fine restaurants that are impossible to miss because of reputation or location. We've made a special effort to include the more out-of-the-way places that shouldn't be missed, along with some obvious favorites. We've also tried

Celebrating 15 Years
Katy's
Grill and Bar
PUB STYLE RESTAURANT & PATIO LOUNGE

Succulent Seafood: Grilled Tuna & Salmon, Fried or Cajun Shrimp, Scallops & Soft Shelled Crabs. Big, juicy, award-winning Burgers, Veggie Burger, Wings, Soup, Sandwiches & much more!

Kids Welcome • Family Area

Open Monday thru Saturday • Dining 11am - 10pm • Lounge 4pm - 1am
ABC Permits • Reasonable prices • Late nite menu 'til 1am.
1054 S. College Rd. • Wilmington, NC • 910/395-5289

to indicate which restaurants include extras such as salads or side dishes with each entree, which yield a better bargain for the apparent buck.

Wilmington

Annabelle's Restaurant & Pub
$$ • 4106 Oleander Dr. • (910) 791-4955

Annabelle's is a family-oriented restaurant with turn-of-the-century charm, accented by gas street lamps, balcony seating, stained glass and soft lighting. Most of the seating is in high-back booths, and you can even dine inside the only trolley car known to remain from the old trolley line that once connected Wrightsville Beach and downtown. The restaurant's wide range of offerings includes center-cut sirloin and prime rib, char-grilled fish, pasta and chicken. Ribs, fajitas, crab melt, stir-fried vegetables, burgers and a sizable list of sandwiches round out a menu to suit most tastes. The Sunday "beef or bird" special is a good bargain.

All entrees include a salad, and everything Annabelle's prepares is available to go. The children's menu (for ages 12 and under) includes a free soft drink or milk with any item. The bar lounge offers lots of window seating and televised sports, and free popcorn is always available. The lounge remains open until 1 AM on weekends (midnight on weeknights). Annabelle's serves lunch and dinner daily.

Ari Rang House
$, no checks • 419 S. College Rd. • (910) 392-1292

Among the better places to enjoy sushi in Wilmington, Ari Rang House features a full Ichiban sushi bar and dining room seating. Specializing in Korean and Japanese cuisine for lunch and dinner, Ari Rang also serves dim sum (Chinese stuffed pastries), noodles (try the udon!), imported Asian beers and sake. Main courses come with soup and may include such extras as rice and kimchee (Korean spicy cabbage). The staff is friendly, and there is plenty of parking. Ari Rang serves dinner Monday through Saturday. Gift certificates are available. Be sure to explore the adjoining gift and grocery section.

Bocci
$$$ • 811 Mercer Ave. • (910) 763-0067

Touting wood-fired specialties, Bocci is a fine restaurant, featuring an ever-changing menu that combines the flavors of Italy, Asia and Cajun country. Start off with wood-grilled Portobello mushroom with toasted goat cheese, roasted eggplant and olive relish, and you'll have an idea of the richness of Bocci's offerings. Each meal begins with baked garlic

10 Convenient Locations To Serve You!

THE SUBWAY
A SANDWICH SHOULD BE.

- 1707 Dawson St.
- 1011 S. College Rd.
- Monkey Junction
- Murrayville Post
- Ogden Village Shopping Center
- 800 Shipyard Blvd.
- Wrightsboro Plaza
- Wrightsville Beach
- North 17 Shopping Center
- 5424 Oleander Dr.

and bread. The brochette of lamb is tender, the Bayou crawfish cakes piquant and the personal pizzas satisfying. Desserts tend to be excellent (try the tiramisu).

From the enormous, carved double door outside to the classic columned dining area, Bocci is visually appealing, with faux marble, "deconstructed" trompe l'oeil brick, earth-tone tile, indirect lighting and lustrous wood. Artful black-and-white photos depicting men playing bocci line the walls. An excellent selection of domestic, Italian and French wines and champagnes is available. Bocci serves dinner Monday through Saturday and provides free valet parking.

Caffe Phoenix
$$ • 9 S. Front St. • (910) 343-1395

High ceilings, original art, an interior balcony . . . what the Phoenix offers the eyes is more than complemented by a menu of consistent quality that makes it one of the most appealing dining experiences on Cape Fear. Situated in a historic glass-front building, the Phoenix is also a popular night spot. The room can become noisy with conversation, but that detracts little from its chic allure.

The regular menu has an Italian accent but includes grilled chicken, shrimp and steaks (and portions tend to be generous). Dressings and sauces are all-natural and made fresh. The special seasonal offerings are always inventive. Recorded music (often classical, jazz or Brazilian) adds to the ambiance. Caffe Phoenix serves lunch and dinner (with light fare in-between) every day except Monday. Mixed drinks, a selection of coffees and excellent homemade desserts are served until closing— an excellent choice for a romantic nightcap.

Chris's Restaurant
$ • 853 S. 17th St. • (910) 763-1791

Unassuming and family-run, this is a good choice for authentic, homemade Greek cooking as well as for sandwiches, Italian pastas, burgers and fried seafood. Local politicians and businesspeople have known about Chris's value and quality for years. The pastistsio and moussaka are very good, and you should make it a point to try the dolmathes (stuffed grape leaves) and stuffed cabbage, both local rarities. (Chris's regularly offers vegetarian items.) All main courses come with extras, which may include Grecian bread, vegetables and iced tea. The restaurant, at the corner of Dawson Street, is open for lunch and breakfast. It accommodates take-outs and custom catering.

Cowboy's Texas Bar-B-Q
$ • 264 N. Front St. • (910) 762-8007

Set into an atmospheric old basement downtown, Cowboy's specializes in a Texas-

CAROLINA'S

"WILMINGTON'S BEST KEPT SECRET"
COMFORTABLY CASUAL   DELICIOUSLY UNIQUE

EXPERIENCE A CONTEMPORARY MENU USING THE FRESHEST INGREDIENTS PRODUCING A TRULY INNOVATIVE CUISINE WITH ITALIAN, PACIFIC RIM, AND CALIFORNIA WINE COUNTRY INFLUENCES

RESERVATIONS ACCEPTED • CATERING • PRIVATE PARTIES
256-5008 • 1610 PAVILLION PLACE
LOCATED BEHIND PLAZA EAST JUST WEST OF THE DRAWBRIDGE AT WRIGHTSVILLE BEACH. OPEN FOR LUNCH AND DINNER

---

style red barbecue (pork, beef and chicken) and a toothsome brisket of beef that sets the place apart from most other barbecue restaurants. (Their Juicy-Q is "Yee-ha!") The room is filled with artifacts of cowboy culture, old, new and odd, and the floor is often strewn with peanut shells (baskets of peanuts are complementary). Cowboy's is open for lunch and dinner Tuesday through Saturday and features live music on Friday and Saturday nights.

Deluxe Cafe
$$ • 114 Market St. • (910) 251-0333

With its eclectic decor of art deco, abstract expressionism, and architectural formalism; painting, wood sculpture, and glasswork; and fresh flowers, high ceiling and clean lines, Deluxe is an aesthetically stimulating environment in which to enjoy excellent lunches and dinners. It also serves one of Wilmington's superior brunches and has a respectable list of fine wines. Artwork is placed on display by NoFo Gallery and by the proprietors' artist friends and is always for sale.

Dinner tends to be memorable, with such offerings as chevre-encrusted black grouper and pan-roasted duck breast with gorganzola butter. For brunch, ask your palate how it feels about orange-and-Gran Marnier French toast or smoked salmon brioche. For us, the response is always Pavlovian. After dinner, sit back with a 20-year-old tawny Port, and you'll know why this cafe at the very heart of downtown is garnering a dedicated following. Deluxe is open for lunch and dinner every day (it closes for a week in January).

Dragon Garden Chinese Cuisine
$$ • 341-52 S. College Rd.
• (910) 452-0708

Dragon Garden serves some of Wilmington's best regional Chinese cuisine, and you'll find some quite unusual dishes here. Outstanding items include a savory cilantro shrimp and the generously portioned house special, pan-fried noodles. Unusual appetizers include the crabmeat with cream cheese and the shrimp sizzling rice soup.

The restaurant's decor is interesting, with comfortable banquettes in a large, sectioned room with Chinese artwork, marble detailing and carved woodwork. A circular table with a lazy Susan is available for family-style dining for 10. A separate room accommodates private affairs for up to 60 people. Don't miss the extremely affordable lunch combinations and superior lunch buffet. Dinner is served every day and a dinner buffet is offered Friday through Sunday. Dragon Garden is in the University Commons shopping center, two doors down from Phar-Mor. Take-out orders are welcome.

Eddie Romanelli's
$$ • 5400 Oleander Dr. • (910) 799-7000

Romanelli's high-tone atmosphere is suffused with the richness of dark wood, red brick and full carpeting. The menu emphasizes American regional dishes, many with an Italian accent. Among the house specialties are an excellent crab dip and homemade 10-inch pizzas, some of which are unusual, such as the barbecued chicken pizza and Philly steak pizza. The menu offers a variety of appetizers (the pesto cheese toast is worth a try), sandwiches, salads with freshly made dressings and Italian baked specialties. Lunch and dinner menus are essentially the same, with dinner portions being larger and including soup and salad or a choice of potatoes or pasta.

The popular bar adjoining the restaurant has a high, raftered ceiling, skylights and handsome sectional seating, and a late-night finger-food menu is served there. Menu and drink specials are offered every day. Romanelli's is open seven days a week.

Elijah's
$$-$$$ • Chandler's Wharf, Water St. • (910) 343-1448

No one can say they've been to Wilmington until they've tried Elijah's crab dip. Directly on the Cape Fear River, Elijah's offers traditional Lowcountry fare as well as such delights as oysters Rockefeller and Cajun-spiced New York strip. Elijah's is two restaurants in one (thus the hyphenated price code) — the oyster bar, which includes outdoor deck seating, and the enclosed dining room, with its more formal presentation of seafood, poultry, pasta and choice beef.

Nautical artwork recalls the building's former incarnation as a maritime museum. The ambiance is casual, and the western exposure makes it a great place for a sundown toast. Elijah's is open seven days a week during the summer but is closed Monday from Labor Day to mid-spring. It serves lunch, dinner and Sunday brunch. Reservations are accepted only for parties of eight or more.

Elizabeth's Pizza
$ • 4304 Market St. • (910) 251-1005

Elizabeth's Pizza has long been a Wilmington favorite, and its thin, crisp-crust pizzas should not be overlooked. The restaurant is a casual place with funky artwork nostalgic for the Amalfi coast. Pasta, calzone, burgers and submarine sandwiches are served, and the eggplant manicotti (thinly sliced eggplant stuffed with ricotta) is unusual and quite good. The kids will get a kick out of the large aquariums, filled with tropical fish, that divide the room in half.

The Faded Rose
$$ • 8 N. Front St. • (910) 762-2969

Following in the footsteps of the original Faded Rose in Little Rock, Arkansas, Wilmington's Rose features affordable fare with a New Orleans flair, including gumbo, red rice and beans, blackened chicken and po-boy sandwiches (beef or shrimp) and live jazz on weekends. The selection of burgers and sandwiches is formidable, and the appetizers and luncheon plates, such as the Cajun popcorn, fried artichoke hearts and trout meuniere (deep fried with lemon-butter sauce), are welcome diversions from much of the area's more common offerings.

The Rose is a lively setting, where blues and jazz are piped in at all times, the beer cooler is actually a former bank vault (appropriately, we think), and you can order up mudbugs (crawfish, for you northerners) by the pound. A children's menu is available. Cigar-smoking is permitted in the upstairs pool lounge and after 10 PM at the bar and in the smoking section. The Rose serves lunch and dinner daily.

Front Street Brewery
$$ • 9 N. Front St. • (910) 251-1935

The Brewery is locally famous for its ales, lagers, stouts and porters, all freshly made on the premises, and for its pub-style food. The restaurant occupies the Foy-Roe Building (1883) with its original, high tin ceiling and heart-pine floors. Wrought-iron railings, historic photos, lush woodwork and a beautiful exte-

ANNABELLE'S RESTAURANT & PUB™

Great Times, Great Food, Great Fun!

Appetizers - Steaks - Pasta - Seafood - Sandwiches - Salads - Chicken - Kids Menu - Desserts - Lounge - and all ABC Permits

Lunch and Dinner - Seven Days a Week
4106 Oleander Drive 791-4955

---

rior facade are additional merits. The Brewery specializes in pot pies, fish 'n' chips and sandwiches plus generously portioned salads, steaks, seafood and poultry, all matched to suit the excellent beers. The desserts, which include homemade ice cream, should not be missed.

Usually on tap are an unfiltered, classic Hefe Weissbier, a hop-bitter Dusseldorf Alt, a popular golden ale, a hearty Irish dry stout, and their very popular raspberry wheat beer (highly recommended). Other beverages are seasonal, such as spiced ales in fall and winter, and some unusual drink specials. The Brewery is open for lunch and dinner seven days a week.

Goody Goody Omelet House
$ • 3817 Market St. • (910) 762-0444

You haven't had a real omelet until you've had a Goody Goody omelet. The hard-working folks at the griddle whip their eggs before slinging omelets that are light, thickly upholstered and humongous. Throw in the grits, biscuits and country ham and you've got yourself a Southern breakfast you can take with you all day. Goody Goody also serves lunch — burgers, fried chicken and such. It's a tiny place with small banquettes and counter seating, so arrive early. Waits are usually brief. The griddle starts to sizzle at 6 AM.

Grouper Nancy's Fine Dining & Spirits
$$$ • 501 Nutt St. • (910) 251-8009

Atmospheric and conveniently located in the Coast Line Center downtown, Grouper Nancy's has a personality that suits romantic dining as readily as family and business meals. The brick-walled room, with its high raftered ceiling, is in a historic former railroad terminal. Among the restaurant's more popular entrees, items such as the steak Diane and the New York strip steak au poivre are prepared right at your tableside. Other favorites include the Grouper Nancy (sauteed shrimp over angel hair pasta) and crab meat-stuffed filet. Six to eight specials and an 80-item wine list are standard. Many desserts are prepared on the premises, and the kids will love the Toll House cookie pie.

The colorful, somewhat casual decor includes black-and-white checked table cloths and modest train motifs. Grouper Nancy's features a full bar and invites an after-dinner cordial, espresso or cappuccino. Dinner is served Tuesday through Sunday.

Harvest Moon
$$$ • 5704 Oleander Dr.
• (910) 772-0172

This attractively designed restaurant blends Old World atmosphere (fluted col-

Here's why our gourmet pizzas are truly Incredible:

FREE Delivery — Limited Area

- Hand tossed White or Whole Wheat Crust
- California Style or Traditional Toppings
- Tomato, Olive Oil & Garlic
- Home Made Pesto & Spicy Black Bean
- Baked in Our Own Brick Ovens
- Fresh Ingredients • Prepared Daily

INCREDIBLE GOURMET PIZZA

Voted Wilmington's Best Pizza

791-7080	256-0339	686-7774
S. College Rd.	1952 Eastwood Rd.	Porters Neck Rd.
(at 17th St. Extension)	(at Plaza East)	(N. Market Street)

---

umns, faux stucco, copper and tile) with contemporary high-tech design. It serves seasonal New Southern innovations that borrow wisely from various ethnic styles. The menu is imaginative, ranging from a straightforward fried oyster-and-spinach salad to pecan-crusted venison loin. When you've got an urge for wild boar barbecue, Harvest Moon is the place to go. The chefs are especially proud of their grilled whisky flank steak and their jambalaya.

The restaurant serves lunch Monday through Friday and dinner and a late-night menu Monday through Saturday. Special requests and dietary requirements are gladly accommodated. You can put your name on the waiting list by telephone; seating, however, cannot be guaranteed for a particular time. Harvest Moon is in the Courtyard Shops On Oleander, nearly equidistant from S. College Road and the Bradley Creek bridge.

Hiro Japanese Steak and Seafood House
$$, no checks • 419 S. College Rd.
• (910) 452-3097

Hiro is unique in Wilmington as the only Japanese restaurant in town specializing in teppanyaki — that is, your food is prepared before your eyes at a teppan table. Traditional staples are served, from various tempura dishes and yakitori (skewered chicken) to steaks and seafood hibachi-style. Stand-outs include succulent lobster tail, yakinuki steak (spicy, but not very), teppanyaki shrimp flambe and several combination entrees.

Every dinner entree is accompanied by extras, including green tea on request. Portions are generous, a good value. Hiro offers a children's menu, imported beer and wine (including sake and plum wine), cocktails and a lunch menu, but no sushi. Be prepared to sit with strangers at the teppan table, which is the nature of this very social style of dining. The restaurant is in the University Landing Shopping Center.

Incredible Gourmet Pizza
$ • 3600 S. College Rd. • (910) 791-7080
$ • 1952 Eastwood Rd., Wrightsville Beach • (910) 256-0339
$ • 8211 Market St., north of Wilmington • (910) 686-7774

Incredible makes the pizza most true to its name in the known universe and, in our estimation, nearly ties with Pizza Bistro (below) for the best, most adventurous pizza in the greater Wilmington area. The crust is not too thick, not too doughy. Delivery, available within limited areas, is free. The Wilmington location is immediately east of the intersection of 17th Street Extension, about three miles south of

HOME COOKING MOM WOULD BE PROUD OF

Taste Of Country
Buffet & Catering

When we opened the first Taste of Country restaurant in 1987, our goal was to make the same kind of food that grandmother used to make...

Hwy 24 West
Warsaw, NC 28398
I-40 Exit 364
(910) 293-3213

226 S. Front Street
Wilmington, NC 28401
Downtown
(910) 343-9888

Oleander Drive. The Eastwood Road store is in the Plaza East shopping center. The newest location is in the Porter's Neck Center.

India Mahal
$ • 4610 Maple St. • (910) 799-2089

The only Indian restaurant in Wilmington, India Mahal serves the cuisine of northern India plus a few selections of Bombay and south India. Authentic in every degree, India Mahal will please both neophytes and worldlings. From the wide variety of breads and surprising appetizers to the entrees and chutneys, the selection invites over-ordering. The staff is attentive and happy to adjust the spice of any dish to taste.

India Mahal does not serve beef. Specialties include sabzian (vegetarian), lamb, sagar (seafood), tandoori dishes (fired clay, oven cooking), biryani (rice) and chicken. This is almost certainly the only place in Wilmington to find mango lassi. Luncheons are inexpensive, and take-out orders and catering are available.

The restaurant is open seven days a week for lunch and dinner. India Mahal is hidden in a row of storefronts that lies parallel to S. College Road on the northbound side. Enter the parking lot from Wrightsville Avenue (opposite Tomatoz restaurant) or from Maple Street. Look for India Mahal's red sign.

Jackson's Big Oak Barbecue
$ • 920 S. Kerr Ave. • (910) 799-1581

Repeated winner of local magazine polls for the area's best barbecue since it opened in 1984, Jackson's is a family-run business fully deserving of the praise. The barbecue is moist and tangy, the hush puppies superior, and the friendly staff is as hard-working as all get-out. The fried corn sticks are a specialty that should be a given with every meal, and if you're a fan of Brunswick stew, greens and chicken, you won't be disappointed. The dining room is rustic and familiar, a good place to greet and meet. Jackson's is open for lunch and dinner Monday through Saturday.

K-38 Baja Grill
$$ • 5410 Oleander Dr. • (910) 395-6040

The name comes from a seaside spot 38 kilometers south of the Baja border where natives prepare foods in roadside shanties for tourists and surfers. Owner Josh Vach brought home to Wilmington some of their recipes, inspirations and authentic ingredients to produce a palette of flavors and textures that stands out among those of other local Mexican restaurants.

You'll find all the standard offerings, all done well, but K-38's adapted specialties are the most impressive, particularly the chipotle barbecued shrimp (chipotle is smoked jalapeño) and pollo de Chimayo. Grilling is the preferred preparation, and all ingredients are fresh. Seekers of the perfect margarita must visit K-38.

The place itself is attractive, decorated with wrought iron, blue glass and items collected along Josh's travels. A small room on the right is perfect for parties of up to 16 people (reserve in advance), and K-38 caters off site as well. K-38 serves lunch and dinner and a fine Sunday brunch. The bar remains open until your surfing stories are exhausted.

Katy's Great Eats
$ • 1054 S. College Rd. • (910) 395-5289

As popular for its food as for its adjoining patio bar, Katy's is a friendly, laid-back establishment with a homey atmosphere and interesting decorative touches. The restaurant has long been known for its killer burgers, onion rings and chicken wings (Kluckers, B-52 Bombers). Katy's also offers fresh seafood and Cajun shrimp. Affordable, satisfying cold plates, salads, sauteed and fried seafood and subs and sandwiches are specialties. Seniors are entitled to discounts, and there is a children's menu.

The bar features a pool table and foosball plus live music on the patio Monday and Thursday evenings. Katy's is on the southbound side of S. College Road (north of Wrightsville Avenue). Doors open for lunch and dinner. Katy's closes on Sunday.

Ken's Bagels & Deli
$ • 5906 Oleander Dr. • (910) 313-0907
$ • 215 Princess St. • (910) 762-8151

With two locations, Ken's fine fresh bagels, muffins, soups, sandwiches and desserts are accessible to everyone on both sides of town. All baked goods are made at the Oleander premises and are among the best available anywhere. You can fax your orders to either location: Oleander Drive, (910) 313-0960; downtown, (910) 762-5676. Inquire about catering or free delivery in your area.

La Costa Mexican Restaurant
$$ • 3617 Market St. • (910) 772-9000

The fact that La Costa serves possibly the most authentic Mexican food available in town is evident right from the start, when complementary warm tortilla chips and salsa, both freshly made on the premises, are served. The small, A-frame building is festooned with sombreros and filled with Mexican music, and the servers are always polite and attentive. Servings tend to be more than you can comfortably finish. Among the menu's highlights are the entrees with mole sauce and the chile rellenos. Be sure to leave room for flan afterward.

Leon's Ogden Restaurant
$ • 7324 Market St., Ogden
• (910) 686-0228

Pitchers of iced tea are on the formica table when you arrive. The servers are usually on the run, and at lunch time the room fills in minutes. Something of an institution, Leon's is popular, inexpensive and not too concerned with its decor (if it could even be said to have any). But if you're looking for fresh local oysters, succulent fried clams, delicious fried chicken, southern barbecue, collards with ham or even a very respectable ostrich burger, this is the place. You get genuine southern cooking at its tastiest, plain and simple. Leon's is the kind of place to look for lemon pudding listed among the vegetables. You'll find it in the Ogden Village mall, a few minutes north of Wilmington.

Mollye's Downtown Market
$ • 188 Princess St. • (910) 772-9989

Lunch at Mollye's is quickly becoming a must-do in downtown Wilmington because the food is so fresh, healthful, inexpensive and well prepared. The setting is an inviting gourmet market. For seating, choose between the beautiful mosaic-topped counter and the mix-and-match-styled tables. The roll-ups — such as the Middle Eastern roll-up (hummus, tabouli, pepperoncini, tahini and vegetables) or the black bean hummus — are a good bet. Specials include pasta salad, tabouli and fresh fruit salad.

The Wine Bar at Mollye's is an evening wine-tasting beginning at 5 PM every day and lasting until closing. On alternate Tuesday evenings, the Wine Bar is a popular gathering place for patrons of the Cinematique film series at Thalian Hall prior to showings; people come to meet, talk (especially about film), and sample gourmet coffees and wine.

Sweet & Savory Bake Shop & Cafe
Gourmet & Regional Foods

Always Serving Our Delicious Homemade Breads, Pastries, Muffins, etc.

• *Catering Available* •

1611 Pavillion Place • Wilmington
256-0115 • fax: 256-0176

Downtown Soup Co.
211 Princess St.
772-9525

At RiverDogs
108 Walnut St.
251-1722

Nuss Strasse Cafe
$$ • 316 Nutt St. • (910) 763-5523

The old brick and exposed rafters of the historic Cotton Exchange befit this cozy establishment, which has been serving authentic German cuisine in a setting reminiscent of a Bavarian country inn since 1985. Seating is divided among three small rooms on different levels. Servers in traditional garb offer national dishes, including bratwurst, wienerwurst and Polish kielbasa as well as hearty sandwiches, hot German potato salad, homemade breads, a host of pastries, imported wines and, of course, excellent German beer (among others). Lunch and dinner are served daily. There is ample parking.

Paleo Sun Cafe
$$$ • 35 N. Front St. • (910) 762-7700

Visually impressive, Paleo Sun is a restaurant/jazz club with big-city ambiance that is never a put-off. The high-back wooden chairs are comfortable, the lighting subtle and the service personable. The regular menu tends to be culturally diverse, often unusual and includes a variety of artfully prepared seafood, poultry, meats and pasta, as well as salads and soups. Paleo Sun offers a variety of coffees and imported beers. The cafe is open for dinner and music Thursday through Sunday. A late bar menu is served to the accompaniment of live jazz. A small cover charge (usually $2) applies Friday and Saturday nights.

The Pilot House
$$$ • 2 Ann St. • (910) 343-0200

The Pilot House is among the preeminent dining establishments downtown. Overlooking the Cape Fear River at Chandler's Wharf, the restaurant occupies the historic Craig House (c. 1870) and strives for innovations on high-quality Southern regional cooking. The large menu, featuring sauteed and chargrilled seafood, pasta, heart-healthy selections and a delectable roster of appetizers, changes frequently, so plan repeat visits accordingly. The kitchen staff even grows its own herbs in front of the building.

The style of service is semiformal, with linen, Wilton pewter and teamed servers, but the management successfully steers for middle ground. You will see guests dressed in everything from Bermuda shorts to tuxedos. (Lunch is more casual than dinner.) The wine list is carefully chosen and well-rounded. The Pilot House features additional outdoor seating, weather permitting, and serves lunch and dinner Monday through Saturday. Sunday brunch is served seasonally. Reservations are recommended.

This is what snapper looks like before it gets to your plate.

Pizza Bistro
$ • 319 N. Front St. • (910) 762-1222

Although we're usually suspicious of anything calling itself "designer," Pizza Bistro, at the Cotton Exchange in Wilmington, bakes up superior, original pizza combinations and demands a visit, even if the proprietors insist on calling their best-known product "designer pizza." The steak, bacon and cheddar pizza really deserves a try. The menu of other Italian specialties, from antipasto to desert, is also worthwhile.

Counter seating is available at one side of the ovens, while table seating (including balcony seating) is available on the other. The outdoor tables are best on cool evenings when traffic is light. With strains of opera or Frank Sinatra playing on the stereo, dining here may favorably remind you of New York's Little Italy during feast days.

P.T.'s Grille
$ • 4544 Fountain Dr. • (910) 392-2293

When you want a freshly grilled burger or chicken sandwich, forget the fast-food mills. P.T.'s can't be beat. Every menu item is a package deal that includes a sandwich (whopping half-pound burgers, tender chicken breast, eight-ounce hot dogs, fresh roast beef and more), fresh-cut, spiced, skin-on french fries and a soft drink, refill included. Prices are low and quality is high. You place your order by filling in an idiot-proof order form and dropping it through the window if you're eating on the outdoor deck. Your meal is prepared to order and ready in about 10 minutes — fast food that doesn't taste like fast food.

P.T.'s Grille is west of S. College Road across from the south end of the UNCW campus. Take-out orders are welcome and may be habit-forming. P.T.'s is open every day.

Rucker John's Restaurant and More
$$ • 5511 Carolina Beach Rd. • (910) 452-1212

Casual, comfortable and providing friendly service, Rucker John's serves salads, beef, poultry, pasta and fish seven days a week for lunch and dinner. Locals frequently recommend the tender barbecued ribs. Salads are made to order, and dressings are made fresh on the premises. The ever-popular menu includes burgers, grilled seafood and croissant sandwiches. Lunch and dinner specials and drink specials change daily. A dinner salad and side dish are included with each entree.

Adjoining the oak-trimmed dining area is the lounge, with its horseshoe-shape bar, where you can catch the latest sports on TV. RJ's is located in the Myrtle Grove Shopping

"NEW YORK'S FINEST *now* **Proud to be Wilmington's"**

Designer Pizzas, Pasta, Subs, Beer, Wine & Vegetarian Dishes

The Cotton Exchange
**319 N. Front Street
(910) 762-1222**

Coming soon to Landfall Center

Center at Monkey Junction (where Carolina Beach and S. College roads meet), about 7.3 miles south of downtown Wilmington.

Szechuan 132
$$ • 419 S. College Rd. • (910) 799-1426

Szechuan 132 stands out, due in part to the personalities of the proprietor, the engaging Joseph Hou, and his staff. Much of the menu is Cantonese, but Szechuan items such as the hot and sour soup and Szechuan panfried noodles live up to their names. The decor is contemporary American. Comfortable banquettes and high-back chairs invite diners to linger. Mixed drinks are available. Excellent lunch specials average around $7 and takeout orders are accepted.

Szechuan 132 is in the University Landing Shopping Center. Lunch and dinner are served daily, and reservations are recommended for dinner. Its sister establishment downtown, Szechuan 130, 130 N. Front Street, (910) 762-5782, offers much the same quality and service as well as a daily buffet.

Taste of Country II
$ • 226 S. Front St. • (910) 343-9888

Many restaurants claim to serve "authentic" southern cooking. Taste of Country claims to and does. At its very popular all-you-can-eat buffet, you'll find an array of delights, including daily meat specials such as chicken (fried, baked and barbecued), barbecue pork, ribs, stew beef, chicken and pastry, chitterlings and turkey and dressing. Fifteen different vegetables are prepared daily, including greens, rice and gravy, and macaroni and cheese. Desserts vary, ranging from fresh cobbler (apple or peach) and banana pudding to pecan and pumpkin pies — all for a price a college student can afford: under $5 at all times except Sunday and dinner on Friday and Saturday.

This establishment is a spinoff of the original Taste of Country in nearby Warsaw, North Carolina, run by the same family. The Wilmington restaurant occupies the mid-19th-century W.G. Fowler home, with shuttered windows, original fireplaces and a view of the river from the back. The upstairs banquet room can accommodate up to 60 people. Everything prepared at Taste of Country can be packaged to go.

The restaurant is open for lunch daily and for dinner Friday and Saturday. Reservations are accepted for groups of six or more except on the busiest days, such as Mother's Day.

Texas Steakhouse & Saloon
$$$ • 1331 Military Cutoff Rd. • (910) 509-1404

If succulent steaks, ribs and prime rib make

your mouth water, you'll enjoy Texas Steakhouse, where servings are generous and prices surprisingly affordable considering the high quality of the meats. The atmosphere is what you might expect of a Texas roadhouse-style establishment: plywood walls, plenty of cowboy art, even a little NASCAR color thrown in.

The menu offers a wide variety of cuts of beef, including ribeye, New York strip and Porterhouse, all mesquite grilled. Prime rib is the signature item, and for a small extra charge per ounce, you can have any size cut you'd like above the standard à la carte cuts. All steak dinners are served with a salad and choice of side dish. Also worthwhile are the baby back ribs and pork chops. To satisfy a hearty appetite for surf-and-turf, inquire about the Duke's Meal or the Texas Two-Step appetizer (enough for two).

The menu has a number of nice surprises, such as the catfish cakes and a vegetarian plate. There's also a Young Texans menu for kids under 12. It's a safe bet that Texas Steakhouse serves every domestic brand of beer you can name off the top of your head. The enclosed bar adjoining the dining room is roomy, and small, galvanized buckets of peanuts are always in good supply.

With country music in the air, comfortable, high-back-booth seating and short sight lines with subdued lighting, Texas Steakhouse is a busy, popular place. You can't miss it from the intersection of Eastwood Road and Military Cutoff Road, about three minutes from the Wrightsville Beach drawbridge.

Tomatoz American Grille
$$ • **S. College Rd. and Wrightsville Ave.** • **(910) 313-0541**

Tomatoz is a great place to satisfy both the heartiest of appetites and the requirements of a health-conscious diet. The menu borrows freely from various cultures, Italian and Southwestern North American being the most prevalent influences. Ingredients are all natural and considered for their health value as much as for taste.

Sourdough pizzas are made fresh to order with low-fat mozzarella and are available with vegetarian toppings as well as with shrimp or chicken. The pastas, lunch entrees and specialty dishes make delicious use of turkey and seafood, with a smaller representation of beef. Fish and meats are smoked in-house. Portions are generally enormous and come with fresh-baked breads. The nachos appetizer is a meal in itself.

Tomatoz carries a good selection of beer, including some made locally. A children's menu, Sunday brunch and (lest we forget) heavenly homemade desserts round out the offerings. The chocolate mousse pie is one of our faves. All this in a unique brick building with spacious seating and attractive decor enlivened by local artwork. Most menu items are available for take-out.

Trails End Steak House
$$$ • **Trails End Rd.** • **(910) 791-2034**

For many locals over many decades, all roads have led to Trails End. Overlooking the Intracoastal Waterway near Whiskey Creek, Trails End is known for three things: steak, beef and red meat. All the steaks here — sirloin, filet of tenderloin, prime rib, Delmonico and more — are broiled over hardwood charcoal. Every entree comes with hors d'oeuvres and salad bar. Trails End is famous for the loyalty of its clientele and staff (a waiter retired in 1993 after 26 years of continuous service).

Its colorful history, dating to 1965, is related on the back of the menu and by memorabilia near the entrance (the door handles are horseshoes from the Budweiser Clydesdales). The original building was something of a windowless shack. Rebuilt in 1987 after a fire, the new building is not large (it seats less than 90), but now there are large windows yielding a marvelous waterway vista. The grill is open Monday through Saturday. Reservations are strongly recommended.

Trails End Road is about 7.5 miles south of Wilmington. To find it, take Pine Grove Drive south from Oleander Drive (at Hugh MacRae Park). Turn right onto Masonboro Loop Road. Less than a half-mile after the tiny Whiskey Creek bridge, make the first left onto Trails End Road. Proceed beyond the "End State Road" sign until the scent of charbroiled beef stops you in your tracks.

Water Street Restaurant & Sidewalk Cafe
$ • **5 Water St.** • **(910) 343-0042**

Housed in the Quince Building (1835), a former peanut warehouse on the riverfront, the

NEW YORK STYLE BAGELS!™
Breakfast & Gourmet Lunches
7 DAYS A WEEK
Bialys, Whitefish, Salad, Chopped Liver, & Nova Lox

Atlantic View Retail Center
7220 Wrightsville Ave.

(910) 256-1222 *Fax:* 256-1229

Water Street Restaurant offers moderately priced, offbeat and healthy meals all day, every day, in a softly lit, antique atmosphere that can be quite romantic. Salads (tabouli, shrimp, falafel, fruit, etc.), burgers (including chicken and veggie), burritos and pita pockets (turkey, shrimp, hummus, baba ganouj, etc.) are typical of Water Street's style. Many salad items are available to go.

Reservations are recommended for the Sunday Jazz Brunch. Sidewalk seating is in full view of the river, and live piano music is frequent. In fact, Water Street Restaurant is an attractive night spot featuring live jazz every Friday evening beginning at 8 PM. Lot parking is available at the corner of Dock and Water streets.

Wrightsville Beach

The Bridge Tender Restaurant
$$$$ • 1414 Airlie Rd. • (910) 256-3419

The Bridge Tender's tremendous local following is testimony to its consistent high quality and flexibility in pleasing its customers. Situated on the Intracoastal Waterway within view of the Wrightsville Beach drawbridge, this small establishment, founded in 1976, excels in its preparation of fresh seafood and in its nationally recognized, multiple-award-winning domestic wine list. From lamp-lit tables beneath a high, raftered ceiling, the view of the waterway marina is romantic.

All of the Bridge Tender's offerings are fresh and made from scratch, and it serves only certified Angus beef. Specials change daily, making repeat visits worthwhile. Past specials have included the mixed grill, a Maryland crab cake appetizer and Cajun-spiced shrimp served over rice. The adjoining lounge offers the same excellent scenery along with hot and cold appetizers Monday through Thursday. The Bridge Tender has all ABC permits and serves lunch and dinner Monday through Friday.

The Cafe at Sweet & Savory Bake Shop
$ • 1611 Pavillion Pl. • (910) 256-0115

Sweet & Savory first made a name for itself as one of the area's preeminent bakeries, partly by supplying many restaurants with sumptuous breads and desserts. The bake shop now presents a unique setting for a cafe (you're actually sitting in a working bakery, within sight of the ovens, work tables and flour-dusted bakers) where you can enjoy inexpensive, delicious lunches and dinners.

The cafe's forte is its variety of original sandwiches, for example, the Veggie-Deelite (which includes hummus), the Hot Tomale (turkey, pico de gallo, jalapenos, havarti and

102 • RESTAURANTS

Photo: Cape Fear Coast Convention and Visitors Bureau

Local seafood doesn't come any fresher than on these shores.

ranch dressing), the Rawhide (a cheese-added version of the French dip), and the Avo-Burger (avocado, Swiss cheese, sauteed mushrooms and garnish). The salads and freshly made dressings, soups, and croissant melts are all wonderful. Best of all, when you're done, you can readily pick up any number of breads, pastries, and sweets baked fresh and practically within arm's reach.

When in downtown Wilmington, visit the Sweet & Savory Cafe at River Dogs Grill, 108 Walnut Street, (910) 251-1722. This is a cleverly redesigned gas station, artfully painted and displaying 50-year-old ads and pictures of Wilmington, with a spacious, canopied patio in the rear. Both locations are open for lunch Monday through Saturday. The Wrightsville Beach shop is immediately east of the Plaza East shopping center.

Carolina's Food & Drink
$$ • 1610 Pavilion Pl. • (910) 256-5008

Casual and colorful and just minutes from the beach, Carolina's excels with unusual combinations of flavors borrowed from the Orient, Italy and the American South. Don't be surprised — well, OK, be surprised — when you taste grilled tuna steak with ginger and wasabi, Tuscan-style lamb chops or salads garnished with edible flowers.

The changing menu includes homemade soups, colorful salads with and without grilled meat or seafood, grilled free-range chicken, steaks and pastas plus such specialties as Carolina's own version of shrimp and grits (topped with prosciutto) and oysters tempura. Open-face pita salads, with or without grilled meat or sharp cheeses, are a treat. For lunch the restaurant serves some Italian-style hot sandwiches as well as specialty sandwiches on 8-inch and 16-inch Italian loaves. The soups and pies are homemade. Soft lighting and jazz add to an ambiance conducive to conversation.

Carolina's has all ABC permits and serves lunch and dinner every day (and does it efficiently). Reservations are accepted, and takeouts and catering are available. Carolina's adjoins Sidelines, a popular sports bar, under the same roof. Pavilion Place lies a quarter-mile west of the Wrightsville Beach drawbridge, behind Plaza East shopping center, and can be entered from either Eastwood Road or Wrightsville Avenue.

Doxey's Market and Cafe
$ • Landfall Shopping Center, Eastwood Rd. at the Military Cutoff Rd. intersection. • (910) 256-9952

Aside from being one of the area's preeminent outlets for natural groceries and products, Doxey's serves all-natural, high-quality foods at its casual in-store cafe. The salad bar and hot bar feature fresh vegetables (mostly organic), homemade salads, bean cuisine and soups. Sandwiches and daily specials are available. Patrons may dine on the premises or take their meals to go.

King Neptune
$$ • 11 N. Lumina Ave. • (910) 256-2525

King Neptune has been in business since the '50s, outlasting hurricanes and the competition but not its appeal. From soups and chowders to steamers, platters and hearty specialties that include steaks and pizza, King Neptune focuses on seafood and does it well. Many menu items have a distinctive island flair, such as the triggerfish with rum-mango sauce, Voodoo Snapper and Jamaican jerk chicken.

The restaurant's owners bring their entire staff on an annual winter sailing trip to the Caribbean, where they often collect new recipes, so it's no wonder the King Neptune staff work so well together and do such a fine job all around.

The dining room is large and bright, decorated in Caribbean colors, with local art, beach umbrellas and photographs. After dinner, the adjoining lounge is lively and offers perhaps the widest selection of rums on the cape as well as an international selection of beers. King Neptune serves dinner seven days a week and offers senior citizens discounts. Free parking is available in the lot across the street.

Logan's Cafe
$$$ • 1900 Eastwood Rd.
• (910) 256-1254

Logan's is among the most pleasant dining experiences near the beach, a bright, casual, colorful place with indoor and outdoor seating, including roomy, canopied "glider" booths outside that are a lot of fun. The lunch menu's fresh clam chowder, salads and crab cakes are delicious, as are the meats and seafood at dinner. The southwestern ravioli (served with Mexican vegetables, cheeses, and black beans finished with tequila) brings people back repeatedly. All the dishes are unique and worth trying.

Logan's is located behind the picket fence at Lumina Station and serves lunch and dinner daily.

Manhattan Bagel
$ • 7220 Wrightsville Ave.
• (910) 256-1222

This popular franchise makes no bones about celebrating Yankees, displaying poster-sized historic photos of Big Apple skyscrapers (the Empire State Building under construction!). But it's the bagels, specialty coffees, sandwiches and fixings that are the real reason to visit. Baked goods are fresh daily and come in a sumptuous variety. You'll find various spreads, from plain to fancy, packaged to go, and a selection of breakfast items, lunch salads, and bialys (try 'em, you'll like 'em! — especially toasted), all of which you can enjoy on the premises. Party platters are also available. The shop is in the Atlantic View Retail Center, immediately west of the drawbridge, and opens every day.

The Oceanic Restaurant
$$$ • 703 S. Lumina Ave.
• (910) 256-5551

Few culinary experiences are as delightful as dining on the pier at the Oceanic. As pelicans kite overhead and the surf crashes below, you could be enjoying a chilled drink, fresh blackened swordfish or some of the region's most acclaimed crab dip. Should the weather turn angry, the Oceanic's two floors of indoor seating offer panoramic views.

The Oceanic may not be innovative, but its tried-and-true menu items are satisfying, delicious and a good value. Heart-healthy menu items abound. From entree salads, seafood platters and specialties to chicken and steaks, the menu is quite varied and includes items for kids. Entrees include a variety of extras ranging from salads and she-crab soup to hush puppies, slaw, rice pilaf, vegetables, potatoes and confetti orzo. Juices used in mixed drinks are all squeezed fresh daily.

Those seeking the perfect margarita should dowse here. The maritime decor features historic photographs that are attractions in themselves. Top off your meal with a walk on the pier or beach. Breakfast is served all day on weekends, and there's a Sunday brunch. Lunch and dinner are served daily. The third-floor banquet room is available for private parties. Free parking is ample.

Ocean Terrace Restaurant
$$$$ • Blockade Runner Resort Hotel, 275 Waynick Blvd. • (910) 256-2251

With an unbroken view of the ocean, dining at the Ocean Terrace is everything you'd expect of a premier hotel. To the strains of soft jazz in a comfortable, carpeted room, the kitchen serves top-quality Angus beef, poultry, pasta, seafood and salads with distinction and creativity. Recent entrees have included corn bread-stuffed Carolina quail, 20-ounce grilled Porterhouse steak, succulent pork medallions in port wine with dried apples and cranberries, and other sumptuous feasts. Specials are always something to plan for, especially when live lobster is the main course or part of a surf-and-turf combination.

The Ocean Terrace serves lunch every day in the restaurant or the adjoining bar. Lunch specialties include hearty sandwiches and salads, including a classic Caesar and cold poached salmon. Also available are personal pizzas, appetizers (coconut beer shrimp, house-cured gravlax and more), soups and homemade desserts. Of special interest are the nightly buffets (except Monday), including the popular Seafood & Prime Rib Buffet on Saturday nights, and the Louisiana-style Jazz Brunch on Sunday featuring live music — one of the area's finest brunches. Inquire about the seasonal Friday Lobster Nights. Reservations, especially for the buffets, are strongly recommended.

Pusser's Landing
$$-$$$ • 4 Marina St. • (910) 256-8500

Famous for its West Indian and nautical ambience, its namesake rum and a menu of fresh seafood and vibrantly flavored Caribbean fare, Pusser's made its area debut in early 1997 by partnering itself with the already popular waterfront restaurant Wally's. The best of the old features remain — boat docks on the Intracoastal Waterway available to patrons, live music Friday nights, an outdoor upper deck (great for sunsets) and one of the liveliest bar scenes around.

Pusser's Landing comprises two restaurants (thus the hyphenated price code): fine dining and Sunday brunch plus the Havana

INSIDERS' TIP

The region's freshest popcorn, available in many varieties (including reduced salt) comes from Vic's Corn Popper, 1616 Shipyard Boulevard (corner of 17th Street), (910) 452-2869.

SOUTH BEACH GRILL

Open for Lunch 11am

100 S. Lumina Ave.

256-4646

Casual Dining / Serious Food
"Overlooking Banks Channel"

Nightly Dinner Specials

All ABC Permits

Room & Wine Bar (offering cigars, a place to smoke them and wine by the glass) upstairs; more casual fare at Pusser's Downstairs Pub, (910) 256-2002, offering specialty sandwiches and salads, fish 'n' chips, shepherd's pie, and more. Your attire in both rooms need not differ — neat, beach-casualwear fits right in.

Appetizers served upstairs include fried green tomatoes, onion grass (like thinly sliced onion rings), conch fritters and escargot. The hearty entrees served upstairs (including rack of lamb, seafood casserole, prime rib) come with salad, vegetable and bread. All desserts are made on the premises (the signature dessert is rum cake, naturally). The cozy decor features a fireplace, gas lights on the canopied deck and roomy wooden tables. Pusser's is open for lunch and dinner every day. Reservations are accepted upstairs only, and both restaurants are handicapped accessible.

South Beach Grill
$$ • 100 S. Lumina Ave. • (910) 256-4646

This is a most inviting place. The decor is soft on the eyes: the rich colors, the fresh flowers on each table and the dark wood of the tables and armchairs. The location, immediately south of the fixed bridge near the center of the beach, is convenient and overlooks Banks Channel (especially nice at sunset from the patio tables outside).

Most important, meals are tasty, healthy and creative, emphasizing grilled poultry and seafood, plus burgers, sandwiches and an array of interesting appetizers, such as crabmeat nachos served on flour tortillas. Highlights include the Tuna Cabo (served with mango-black bean salsa) and the Chicken Carolina (boneless breast rolled with country ham and Havarti, served with linguine Alfredo). All lunches include french fries or homemade potato chips; dinner entrees include house or Caesar salad.

Among the beer offerings is the wonderful Front Street Raspberry Wheat ale, brewed in downtown Wilmington. South Beach Grill has a children's menu and all ABC permits and welcomes take-out orders. Lunch and dinner are served every day; breakfast is served on Saturday and Sunday only. Reservations are not accepted except for very large groups (eight or more).

Vinnie's Steak House & Tavern
$$$$ • Lumina Station • (910) 256-0995

Due largely to the reputation of its progenitor in Raleigh, considered ideal for power meals, dinner deals, schmoozing and being seen, Vinnie's at Wrightsville Beach commands much the same cachet. The walls are adorned with celebrity caricatures, a la Sardi's, and the power smokers among us will appreciate the fact that cigar-smoking is PC.

Everything here speaks of high quality and high rollers — dark, elaborate woodwork in the original half of the establishment, comfortable seating and some of the area's most enviable steaks, chops and seafood. All bar drinks are top-shelf. Vinnie's is only open for dinner and drinks and gets swamped in no time — better to go at off-peak hours. Reservations are only accepted for parties of five or more.

Carolina Beach and Kure Beach

Big Daddy's Seafood Restaurant
$$ • 202 K Ave., Kure Beach
• (910) 458-8622

A Kure Beach institution for three decades, Big Daddy's serves a variety of better-quality seafood and combination platters. Seafood can be broiled, fried, chargrilled, steamed or fixed Calabash-style. These and choice steaks, prime rib and chicken are offered every day in a family-oriented, casual setting.

Highlights of Big Daddy's menu include all-you-can-eat, Lowcountry, family-style dining, an inexpensive all-you-can-eat salad bar, special plates for seniors and children and the sizable Surf and Turf Supreme (beef tenderloin with split Alaskan king crab legs). An after-dinner walk along the beach or on the Kure Beach fishing pier (both a block away) further adds to Big Daddy's appeal.

Because the restaurant consists of several rooms, its total seating capacity of about 500 people comes as a surprise; it doesn't seem that big. Rare and unusual maritime memorabilia make for entertaining distractions. Entrance to the restaurant is through a colorful gift shop offering novelties and taffy. Patrons frequently make secret wishes and cast coins into the fountain there. Located at the only stop light in Kure Beach, Big Daddy's has all ABC permits and ample parking in front and across the street.

Breakfast Café
$, no checks or credit cards • 700 N. Lake Park Blvd., Carolina Beach
• (910) 458-8897

This recently renovated, family-run restaurant serves hearty breakfasts and lunches in clean, friendly surroundings. The carpeted dining room, decorated with nautical accents, seats about 100 people and is fully handicapped-accessible. Specialties of the house include Spanish omelettes and home fries, as well as burgers and sandwiches. Take-out orders are welcome.

The Cottage
$$ • 1 N. Lake Park Blvd., Carolina Beach • (910) 458-4383

The Cottage occupies a tastefully renovated home, reputedly the oldest in Carolina Beach. The interior is modern, preserving the several ground-level rooms as separate dining areas. In keeping with the owners' motto, "Simple foods well-prepared," the cuisine is a simple, effective combination of Lowcountry and new-American approaches to seafood, chicken and beef, with a hint of Italian. The kitchen shows real strength in the appetizers, soups (ask about the tomato-dill and carrot-ginger soups) and desserts. Entrees are served with a small salad and two sides, and the preparations are fresh, natural and heart-healthy.

The lunch menu includes affordable sandwiches, salads and quiche, placing The Cottage high on the list of options when coming off the beach hungry. While waiting for your table, enjoy a drink on the front porch. Portions aren't huge, but The Cottage is most worthwhile. A children's menu is available, and kids can pass the wait with a stack of children's books. The Cottage serves imported and domestic beer and mixed drinks and is open for lunch and dinner Monday through Saturday from March 1 through New Year's Day.

Freddie's Restaurant
$$ • 111 K Ave., Kure Beach
• (910) 458-5979

Dining at Freddie's is a curiously pleasant experience. The room is cozy, almost tiny, and the seashore murals, greenery, checkered table coverings and coastal knickknacks will almost certainly make you forget you're in a cinder-block building, but not that you're in Kure Beach, North Carolina. Servers may dress in tuxedo vests, bow ties and sneakers. The owners will come by and chat. The food is hearty, well-prepared and thoroughly home

Big Daddy's

"SEAFOOD AT ITS BEST"

SEAFOOD
SPECIALIZING IN FRIED OR
BROILED OCEAN FRESH SEAFOOD
LOBSTER TAILS
ALASKAN SNOW CRABS
CHAR-BROILED FISH STEAKS
- Major Credit Cards Accepted -

STEAKS & PRIME RIB
CHOICE
WESTERN BEEF

ALL ABC PERMITS

458-8622

206 K AV. IN THE HEART OF KURE BEACH

---

made. Barbara's Famous Lasagna is just like Mom's (if Mom was Italian). The bread is crusty and fresh, as it should be.

Nightly specials are unusual — be sure to try the portobello mushroom Bolognese — and there's always a wide choice if you're a lover of meat (including chops), seafood, poultry or pasta. All entrees come with a large romaine salad with Italian dressing (naturally), bread and a side of pasta. With an appetizer you may not be able to finish dinner, so save room for espresso and dessert. Freddie's is open every day of the year — for dinner only during the week off-season and for lunch and dinner on weekends. It's a few steps from the Kure Beach Pier, under an awning painted red, white and green. Naturally.

Marina's Edge
$$ • 300 N. Lake Park Blvd., Carolina Beach • (910) 458-6001

Marina's Edge specializes in steaks and seafood, stressing healthful preparation and reasonable prices. Popular items fill out the menu, from stuffed grouper and blackened tuna or swordfish to crab leg and prime ribs, which are the all-time favorite.

Eight to 10 nightly specials might consist of ginger-glazed pork chops, barbecued shrimp, scallop marinara, chicken or veal parmigiana, which offers a special Italian twist to the norm. There is also an affordable children's menu that includes such kiddie favorites as shrimp, chicken or spaghetti.

The lounge affords comfortable seating for light meals or cocktails. The restaurant's new owner, Charlie Byrum, has added a late-night fare that sports soup, salad, sandwich, pizza and an array of appetizers. (It is rumored that if you are a weary traveler or look a bit emaciated, Charlie will bread out something more substantial.) Marina's Edge serves dinner seven days a week and offers lunch on Saturday and Sunday.

Michael's Seafood Restaurant & Market
$$$ • 1018 N. Lake Park Blvd., Carolina Beach • (910) 458-7761

Long considered one of the area's impor-

INSIDERS' TIP

Enjoy an overhead view of sand volleyball and a panorama of the Atlantic Ocean from the pier at The Oceanic in Wrightsville Beach.

You "otter" see how much wildlife there is on the coast of North Carolina.

tant fresh seafood markets, Michael's is also known for its restaurant, where seafood — naturally — plays a major role in the menu. Michael's is a casual place, with reggae often in the air and four large fish tanks that will mesmerize young and old alike. (The oyster toads are alluringly ugly.)

Michael's excels in preparing steamed and broiled seafood. The house specialty, Admiral's Delight, is a seafood feast fit for two. The seafood chowder is an award-winning recipe, having twice won the area's annual Chowder Cook-off. Also featured are such land foods as prime rib, St. Louis ribs and grilled poultry.

Appetizers include peanut-encrusted shrimp and the popular double-stuffed potatoes with jalapeño cheese and shrimp. All entrees are served with two sides, usually a steamed vegetable plus a "starch" such as red beans and rice, garlic mashed potatoes, fresh cornbread or corn sticks. The restaurant also has a lively night life focused on its 30-seat bar.

Michael's does not accept reservations, but you may call ahead to place your name on the waiting list. Lunch and dinner are served daily. The full-scale seafood market brings in live catches five times a week and carries an inventory of some 100 hot sauces from around the world. You'll find Michael's near Food Lion, where parking is plentiful.

Paradise Cafe
$ • 9 S. Lake Park Blvd., Carolina Beach • (910) 458-4020

This laid-back eatery, a short walk from the Boardwalk, is the place for zesty salads, sandwiches (even PB & J!) and soups. Sandwiches, such as the Paradise Melt and a classic Reuben, are hefty affairs, and the Carolina Beach Cheese Steak scores highly. The Paradise serves wine and beer, offers daily specials and can package your order to go. From Memorial Day to Labor Day, it's open every day for lunch and dinner; it closes on Sunday in the off season. It's in Nautica Centre, just south of Cape Fear Boulevard.

Sweetwater Cafe
$$ • 106 Carl Winner's Ave., Carolina Beach • (910) 458-0500

Sweetwater Cafe offers coastal ambiance, well-prepared fare at a good price and up-close views of the municipal docks, especially from the rooftop deck. Naturally, the menu includes plenty of local seafood, including soft-shell crab in season. Seafood entrees are available fried, Cajun-style or broiled. The restaurant's pride, however, is prime rib, recommended by Insiders.

Sweetwater also offers a raw bar menu, steamers, a variety of dinner salads, a good selection of sandwiches and burgers, do-

The Marina's Edge Restaurant

STEAKS • SEAFOOD • SPECIALS

Come enjoy our scrumptious slow roasted Prime Rib, fresh local seafood or a juicy 18oz. T-bone in our casual resort atmosphere. "Catch" a live lobster from our lobster tank or choose from our special entree board which offers 8-10 fresh features that change daily. All of our menu items are fresh and cooked to order. Our children's menu includes fried shrimp, chicken and spaghetti. Dine out on our charming veranda and enjoy the fresh air or take a break in the lounge with the 61" TV and late night bar menu.

• Take Out Available • ALL ABC Permits • MC & VISA Accepted
• Daily Drink Specials • AMEX Not Accepted

Monday - Friday open 4pm
Saturday & Sunday open 11am
300 N. Lake Park Blvd • 458-6001

mestic and imported beer and domestic wine. Indoor seating is intimate, with oil lamps on tables dressed in white linen. Seating on the outdoor decks is more ample, and the lower deck is curtained in the cool weather.

Bald Head Island

The Bald Head Island Club
$$$ • Bald Head Island • (910) 457-7300

Refined yet somewhat relaxed, the Club dining room is a warm atmosphere in which to enjoy a fine selection of seafood, chargrilled steaks, pasta, poultry and fresh desserts. The wine list offers some of the better domestic vintages. The weekly gala buffet, a sumptuous fixed-price feast, is a deservedly popular summer event for which reservations are required. Set in a building reminiscent of coastal New England, the room is modulated by wood, carpeting and floral wallpaper and commands a fine ocean view. The club does not allow T-shirts or cutoffs but does permit dress shorts during the summer.

Entry to the Club requires at least a temporary membership, which is included in accommodation rates for all properties leased through Bald Head Island Management Inc. Temporary memberships may also be arranged for day visits and group tours through the management office. The Club dining room serves dinner Tuesday through Sunday, Memorial Day to Labor Day. It is closed for the month of January and open on weekends during February. Call for information on spring and fall schedules. Reservations are always preferred.

Island Chandler Delicatessen
$ • Bald Head Island Marina
• (910) 457-7450

This is really no more than the deli counter at the Island Chandler grocery store, but the well-prepared, ready-to-eat foods (cold salads, sandwiches, cheeses, seafood, etc.) can be enjoyed at the tables on the patio overlooking the marina. Be sure to ask for some plastic utensils.

River Pilot Cafe
$$ • Bald Head Island • (910) 457-7390

Boasting the finest ocean view on the is-

INSIDERS' TIP

You can find breakfast-all-day places, which serve meals complete with grits and biscuits, all over the southern coastal area.

CAPE FEAR COFFEE & TEA COMPANY™

24 South Front St.
Wilmington, NC

Sun-Thurs 6:30 a.m. to 10:00 p.m.
Fri-Sat 6:30 a.m. to midnight
(910) 343-1500

Fresh Roasted Gourmet Coffee and Bulk Teas

Coffeehouses On the Cape

The rebirth of the coffeehouse continues to manifest itself in Wilmington with a host of new establishments joining older, familiar haunts, each with its own personality. Most shops sell gourmet coffees by the pound, teas, related paraphernalia, Italian sodas, baked goods and desserts. All shops provide board games to play, magazines and newspapers to browse, sometimes books to borrow. But perhaps the coffeehouses' greatest value is their contribution to the art of congenial socializing and slowing down, despite the caffeine — to providing forums for sharing news and announcements of cultural events, the hallmarks of a highly evolved community.

Cape Fear Coffee & Tea, 24 S. Front Street, (910) 343-1500, was one of the first coffeehouses to open in downtown Wilmington. Its several rocking chairs outdoors are extremely popular. Here you'll find the *New York Times* every day. It's also a great place to inspect, and perhaps buy, local artwork, which is always on display.

Expresso Cafe, 4555 Fountain Drive, (910) 313-0227, is a European-style coffee bar, specializing only in espressos and specialty concoctions made with Illycaffe brand arabica espresso and featuring drive-through service.

General Assembly, 300 N. Front Street, (910) 343-8890, across the street from the Cotton Exchange, is attractively designed in a Federalist/neo-Georgian style, with handsome woodwork and large windows on two sides. This shop boasts one of Wilmington's two scaled-down statues of Liberty and sells hand-packed ice cream, too.

Halfmoon's Coffee Bar, 505 Nutt Street, (910) 251-9283, in the Coastline Convention Center, is unique insofar as it's the only coffee shop we know that shares space with a hair salon, Nu Waves Hair Colour & Art Gallery. While listening to recorded jazz and

— continued on next page

blues, you can try the coffees, mochaccinos, lattes, cappuccinos and frappeccinos (yogurt, espresso, crushed ice and milk—yum!).

Java Lane, 4302 Wrightsville Avenue, (910) 313-0704, takes the name "coffeehouse" literally by having turned an entire former residence into an attractive place to enjoy your cup o' joe. Choose among easy chairs beside the living room fireplace, office-like desks in the adjoining room or a conference table in the meeting room. Java Lane frequently features informal live music, including bluegrass and jazz. Schedules tend to be weekly, but be sure to check the chalk board for updates.

Kelly's Coffee Pub, 5751 Oleander Drive in the Philips Azalea Plaza, Wilmington, (910) 392-7693, is as homey as your living room but a little smokier. (After all, this is a pub!) Jazz musicians from the university frequently stop in on Saturdays to play for tips.

Port City Java, 7 N. Front Street, (910) 762-5282, is intimate (OK, that also means small), cozy and artsy and features comfy chairs and excellent desserts. But what really distinguishes this shop is that it roasts its own coffee beans fresh daily, right around the corner. You can smell it for blocks. It also specializes in fruit smoothies and juices, non-java beverages such as Ghirardelli cocoas and the tea blend known as Chai. Also visit the Wrightsville Beach location, at Lumina Station on Eastwood Road, (910) 256-0993, where you'll find excellent grilled panini (sandwiches) among other delights.

The Wilmington Espresso Co., 5317 Wrightsville Avenue, (910) 790-5689, is a spacious coffee bar, with 1950s-style Formica-top tables and a great selection of magazines. Featuring all the pastries, biscotti, flavored coffees, smoothies and all the other specialties we've come to expect of a premier coffee shop, this one goes the extra step of having drive-through service and parking in the back. It's located very near Columbia Cape Fear Memorial Hospital (east of College Road).

---

land, the River Pilot Cafe and its adjoining lounge serve breakfast, lunch and dinner in a more casual setting than the Club dining room. Nonetheless, the expanded wine list and fine linen provide an upscale tenor to a menu that includes soups, excellent salads and burgers as well as daily meat and seafood specials. In summer, the Cafe serves the island's best breakfasts. It's also a superb vantage from which to view stunning sunsets while enjoying a meal or drink. The River Pilot is open daily during the summer, and reservations are requested for dinner.

Southport-Oak Island

The Chart House
$ • 832 N. Howe St., Southport
• (910) 457-4777

Genuine home cooking in an informal, no-frills setting makes The Chart House a popular breakfast and lunch spot for locals. Standard American breakfast items and Belgian waffles are complemented by Southern-style biscuits, country ham and grits. Breakfast is served all day. Daily lunch specials are hearty and inexpensive. Seafood offerings can be fried, grilled or blackened, and grilled meats, homemade barbecue and fish sandwiches are available.

Del's Restaurant
$$ • 6302 E. Oak Island Dr., Long Beach
• (910) 278-3338

Pleasant, small and casual, Del's specializes in Italian-style seafood and regional dishes, pizza, subs and sandwiches. Spaghetti Buckets yielding two to eight servings are something you won't see every day, except at Del's. The friendly staff serves beer, wine and wine coolers as well as a smattering of Cajun-style meat dishes. Call-in orders may be picked up at the drive-through window, and local delivery is available after 5 PM, call (910) 278-1912. Del's is open for lunch and dinner daily.

Laredo's Neon Cactus Restaurant & Cantina
$$ • 607 W. West St., Southport
• (910) 457-4543

Specializing in Tex-Mex cuisine, Laredo's also offers a partial waterfront view in a warm, softly lit setting. Many Mexican favorites are served in generous portions and very reasonable prices. The adjoining bar is a handsome room with high tables and chairs and brass detailing, and its margaritas are a local legend — get them by the pitcher! Recorded music and karaoke are featured on weekends after dinner in the lounge. Located very near the Southport Marina, Laredo's is open every day for lunch and dinner and has plenty of parking available.

Jones' Seafood House
$$ • 6404 E. Oak Island Dr., Long Beach
• (910) 278-5231

Jones' Seafood House affords patrons a casual dining experience of high quality. The menu offers all the most popular regional specialties, including fresh crabmeat patties, trout filet and grilled shrimp-and-scallop skewers. Meat lovers won't be disappointed by the variety of steaks, chicken and pork and a selection of surf-and-turf combinations. Dinner specials and a children's menu are available, and the restaurant has all ABC permits. All menu items are available for take-out. Jones' Seafood House and the lounge are open Monday through Saturday for dinner. Lunch is also served on Sundays.

Lucky Fisherman
$ • 4419 Long Beach Rd. S.E. (N.C. 133), Southport • (910) 457-9499

This lively establishment offers a huge all-you-can-eat seafood buffet every night for a mere nine clams per adult. There are usually more than 30 hot items to choose from, made from old Lowcountry recipes modified to accommodate low-cholesterol and reduced-sodium diets. The salad and dessert bars are equally expansive, and nightly specials keep the offerings varied. Entrees are available a la carte and include fresh fried or broiled fish, lobster tails, crab legs and steaks.

Early-bird specials and senior citizen discounts are available. A separate children's menu offers popular kid-size meals. Lucky Fisherman is open every day and accepts take-out orders. Reservations and special parties are welcome.

Marge's Restaurant & Waffle House
$ • 5700 E. Oak Island Dr., Long Beach
• (910) 278-3070

Among Long Beach residents Marge's is one of the most popular diner-style eateries for breakfast and lunch. No matter how crowded it gets, the food is served hot, fast and with a smile, and no one will rush you. Table-to-table conversation comes easily as folks dine on large omelets, flaky biscuits, pasta, grilled foods, fried seafood and local specialties such as hush puppies, okra and beans. Marge's is open daily for breakfast (served all day) and lunch. Take-out orders are welcome.

Port Charlie's
$$ • 317 W. Bay St., Southport
• (910) 457-4395

With a harbor view from practically every seat, Port Charlie's is many Insiders' first choice for quality seafood, steaks, pasta and consistently fine service in Southport. If too much fried fish has jaded your palate, Port Charlie's can revive it with a variety of salads, Cajun-spiced seafood and meat, chargrilled steaks and sauteed veal.

Situated next to Southport's old yacht basin, Port Charlie's features limited screened-in porch seating, an attractively rustic dining room and docking facilities for customers (come by boat!). Free snacks are occasionally served in the Marker One Lounge, which also has darts and a juke box. Port Charlie's possesses all ABC permits, serves dinner seven nights a week during the summer and provides ample free parking and senior citizen discounts.

INSIDERS' TIP

For a blast from the past, visit Merritt's Burger House on Carolina Beach Road south of Wilmington for car-side wait service.

Sandfiddler Seafood Restaurant
$$ • N.C. Hwy. 211, Southport
• (910) 457-6588

With its high-pitched roof, plainly set tables and nautical decor, this large establishment offers rustic ambiance and affordable Lowcountry cuisine. Lunch specials, served with hush puppies, slaw and fries, are low-priced, and landlubbers will find plenty of landfood to choose from, including steaks and pit-cooked pork barbecue. Most of the regional seafood staples are available, including deviled crabs, fried fantail shrimp stuffed with crabmeat and a good selection of combination platters. You can get take-out orders too.

The Sandfiddler serves lunch Monday through Friday and Sunday. Dinner is served Monday through Saturday. The restaurant is on the outskirts of Southport near N.C. 87.

Sea Captain Restaurant
$ • 608 W. West St., Southport
• (910) 457-5075

The Sea Captain serves affordable, Southern-style breakfasts and lunches in a somewhat cafeteria-style atmosphere. Guests may design their own omelets, and egg substitutes are available. Lunch specialties include Cajun-style blackened treats such as beef or shrimp burgers and chicken breast, or you can have the home-style lunch special of meat, two vegetables, rolls or hush puppies. The Sea Captain is next to the Sea Captain Motor Lodge near the Southport Marina.

Thai Peppers
$$ • 115 E. Moore St., Southport
• (910) 457-0095

An uncommon dining experience in the Lower Cape Fear, Thai Peppers demands a visit. Thai foods are influenced equally by China and India, so you'll find familiar appetizers, soups and stir-fried entrees from China but also delicious Thai hybrids. Such Thai specialties as satay (skewered meat), ajard (cucumber salad), tom kha gai (chicken coconut milk soup), a wide variety of stir-fries, rice and curries are available. Those who shy away from curry may become true believers once they sample the several varieties offered here. The fried basil leaves with meat (chicken, beef or pork), the stir-fried ginger with meat and the green curry should not be missed.

Thai food tends to be spicy, but Thai Peppers will adjust the heat of any dish to taste, avoiding pepper spice entirely if you wish. (You can always spice it yourself with the condiments on the table.) Any menu item can be prepared without meat. Excellent bargains are the lunch specials (appetizer, soup, entree and rice), which change every day. Iced Thai coffee or Thailand's Singha beer are excellent accompaniments.

Founded by Voravit "Tic" Hemawong, a native of Bangkok, Thai Peppers is casual and offers sheltered outdoor seating and ample space for large parties. Meals are often served with contemporary Thai music playing in the background. It's open for lunch and dinner Monday through Saturday. Take-out orders are welcome, and reservations are recommended for parties of more than five. The restaurant closes in January.

Windjammer Restaurant & Lounge
$$ • 1411 E. Beach Dr., Long Beach
• (910) 278-7740

The Windjammer has a solid reputation for fine dining. Through enormous oceanfront windows, the view overlooking the Ocean Crest Pier is superb. The menu emphasizes a variety of seafood served Calabash-style, sauteed or broiled. Freshly cut steaks and chicken make limited appearances. The Windjammer is the only place on the island where you can try the enormous bloomin' onion. The jalapenos stuffed with crabmeat are, as owner Wade Goin puts it, "right famous."

In a fairly large, bright room, the Windjammer features occasional live entertainment during the high season and offers breakfast and lunch buffets. It is open every day in the summer and has all ABC permits.

Yacht Basin Provision Company
$$ • 130 Yacht Basin Dr., Southport
• (910) 457-0654

This, as one perceptive youngster once put it, is "the secret place," which must be true since it even eluded the Insiders' Guide® early on. And what a discovery! A casual and entirely outdoor eatery, the Provision Company has the best decor possible, the Southport Yacht Basin and waterfront. It's a place where the honor system is still honored — beverages are self-serve and no guest checks are written. Specialties of the house include great shrimp and crab cakes, conch fritters and grouper salad.

Open for lunch and dinner seven days a week from St. Patrick's Day through mid-December, the Provision Company has all ABC permits and is something of a night spot as well. You may arrive by sea — boat slips are available. You'll find the Provision Company next to the shell shop as you come down Bay Street. Look for the funky green building that once was a provisions house.

South Brunswick Islands

Archibald's Delicatessen & Rotisserie
$ • 2991 Holden Beach Rd. S.W., Holden Beach • (910) 842-6888

We love the sandwiches and subs at Archibald's almost as much as its homemade desserts, and most people we meet around Holden Beach do, too. Take the Richie's Roaster for instance — fresh rotisserie chicken breast with provolone and garnish on a kaiser roll. Or Archie's B.L.E.S.T. — bacon, lettuce, egg salad, tomato on fresh honey-wheat bread. Don't ask about the hot apple cobbler, just add ice cream and eat it! (You'll be glad you did.) Pork ribs are another rotisserie specialty you'll want to try — if you can resist the chocolate cheesecake and fresh fruit pies.

You can design your own sandwich or sub or choose from a selection of excellent fresh salad plates and homemade soups. Sliced deli meats and cheeses, of a variety usually not seen outside the largest supermarket deli counters, are available to go. The screened-in patio is nice during mild weather. Archibald's serves lunch and, in high season, dinner in a comfortable, clean, casual shop, housed in a curious round building. It offers a modest menu of fine quality and value, and the staff can put together party platters and complete dinners as well.

Crabby Oddwaters Restaurant and Bar
$$ • 310 Sunset Blvd., Sunset Beach • (910) 579-6372

If the food weren't so darn good, this upstairs restaurant would still be worth a visit just to read the story of how it got its "damp and crawly name" (a story told in one easy-to-remember sentence of barely more than 400 words). This is a small, handsome restaurant with an enclosed deck overlooking a creek. The tables have holes in the center where you can pitch your shucked shells and, despite the plastic utensils, the ambiance and cuisine are high quality.

Local seafood of all types is the focus, featuring the unusual shrimp, scallop or combo "KaBillbobs" and wonderful nightly specials (ask about the spicy Seminole snapper). A limited choice of landfood (and, sometimes, hot jambalaya) is offered. Crabby Oddwaters is above Bill's Seafood — which is owned by a guy named Joe — on the mainland side of the pontoon bridge. It is open for dinner all year.

Duffer's Pub & Deli
$ • Shallotte Plaza, Main St., Shallotte • (910) 754-7229

Modestly priced and generously portioned subs (cold and hot), uncommon half-pound burgers made with Angus beef (try the bleu cheese) and salads are Duffer's long suit. Subs and sandwiches include a side order, and the burgers come with steak fries. Specialty cold cuts include capocolla (Italian hot ham), prosciutto and turkey pastrami, and salads are made fresh daily. Sandwiches are made to order, and meals are delivered right to your table. You can even get PB&J for the kids.

J/G's Country Bar-B-Que
$ • Barbecue Rd., Grissettown • (910) 287-3505

If you eat at a Southern-style barbecue joint only once in your life, this is the place to go. For $9 (children 11 and younger, $4) you can eat all the smoky chicken, beef and pork barbecue you can handle, along with plenty of other country-style fare, served on cardboard plates. Seating is at long picnic tables that fill half the barn. The other half accommodates the stage and dance floor for the occasional live country music (and sometimes bluegrass) and dancers who come from miles around. Music usually begins about 7 PM. Beverages are extra (pitchers of sweet tea

Daybreak off Oak Island reveals a shrimper trawling for dinner.

cost a whopping $1.50), and no alcohol is permitted.

J/G's is open for dinner Wednesday through Saturday and also for lunch on Sunday from April through October. Grissettown is north of Sunset and Ocean Isle beaches off U.S. 17. From U.S. 17, take N.C. 904 north for 1.4 miles; turn right onto Russtown Road, go 1.4 miles farther, turn right down unpaved Barbecue Road and park on the lawn.

Joe's Barbecue Kitchen
$ • U.S. 17 N. Bus., Shallotte
• (910) 754-8876

We know you've been dying to find a place where all the catfish you can eat costs less than $7 a person. Joe's is that place every Wednesday night. And its all-you-can-eat pig pickin' buffet is served on Friday and Saturday nights. But you can enjoy the full lunch and dinner menus Monday through Saturday — spare ribs, pork barbecue (plates and sandwiches), homemade Brunswick stew, fried shrimp, fish or crab, barbecued or fried chicken, peach cobbler, and more. Joe's is a single large room with massive amounts of seating, and everything can be ordered in bulk — naturally. You'll find the place immediately east of the intersection of U.S. 17 Business and N.C. 179.

Roberto's Pizzeria & Restaurant
$ • Jordan Ave., Holden Beach
• (910) 842-4999

Hailing from Philadelphia, the Roberto family brought authentic Italian-American, hand-tossed pizza to Holden Beach. And the Philly cheese steaks are right on the money too. They operate at two locations. The Holden Beach restaurant (the only restaurant on the island) closes from November through March, and the Ocean Isle Beach location, at 6773 Beach Drive (N.C. 179), (910) 579-4999, is open all year. Specialty dinners, hoagies (Philadelphians' name for subs or heroes), burgers, nightly specials and beer and wine are available to eat in, take out or have delivered locally. Both locations are open seven days a week during the summer.

Sharky's Pizza & Deli
$ • Causeway Dr., Ocean Isle Beach
• (910) 579-9177

When owners Al and Ray traded their power suits for bathing suits and opened Sharky's in 1991, their goal was to provide a good place to eat with a great view. They've succeeded. The food at Sharky's isn't fancy but is well-priced and can be enjoyed on the handicapped-accessible enclosed deck overlooking the waterway. You can tie up your boat at Sharky's dock. Thoroughly casual and fun for the whole family, Sharky's offers Lite Bites (wings, chicken tenders, etc.), thin-crust pizza, a nice selection of hot and cold subs, beer, soups and salads.

Occasionally, Sharky's hosts family-oriented holiday parties with live music, volleyball and plenty of food. Most days, the stereo pumps lively rock, country and beach music. Ray describes his clientele and staff as "a laid-back, fun-loving, music-loving bunch." Sharky's also provides free local delivery. It is next to the ABC store at the foot of the bridge.

Sugar Shack
$$ • 1609 Hale Beach Rd., Ocean Isle
• (910) 579-3844

Don't miss this place. Sugar Shack features authentic Jamaican home cooking (yes, the chef is Jamaican) in a colorful, intimate setting about a mile from the beach. Amid greenery, tropical artwork and floral table coverings, recorded reggae music adds a lively island feel most days, while live music is offered on weekends (don't be surprised if the regulars dance). Outdoor seating is also available.

Sugar Shack specializes in its own recipe for jerk seasoning — a complex blend of scallions, onions, thyme, cinnamon, nutmeg, pepper and some elusive magic. The tangy jerk chicken, pork and beef — marinated, barbecued and served with a hot 'n' sweet sauce — anchor a small but delightful menu that also includes Stamp & Go (a traditional spicy cod fritter), Brown Stewed Fish (slowly cooked red snapper) and a curried goat so tender it literally falls off the bone.

Most items are marinated, slowly simmered and richly flavored. Nothing is too spicy for the average palate, but imported hot sauce is available if you want to hurt yourself. Fine steaks and burgers are also offered. Some appetizers are enough for a meal, and the Jamaican Sampler is a good introduction. Red Stripe beer and Guinness Stout are served, of course. Other offerings include jerk chicken salads and Cobb salads, fruit dishes and homemade soups as well as burgers and grilled steaks. Take-out orders are welcome. Sugar Shack is one block south of Ocean Isle Beach Road, a few yards off N.C. 179. (Ocean Isle Beach Road intersects U.S. 17 about 3 miles east of Grissettown.) Sugar Shack is open every day in summer, serving lunch and dinner.

Twin Lakes Restaurant
$$ • 102 Sunset Blvd., Sunset Beach
• (910) 579-6373

Many tables at Twin Lakes offer a panoramic view of the region's most picturesque watercourse and draw bridge. The restaurant stands rooted in the region's long culinary tradition, having family connections to the earliest seafood days of nearby Calabash. With its tropical decor enhanced by palm trees outdoors, colorful table coverings and local art within, Twin Lakes is an attractive family restaurant that stays busy.

The menu includes meat and seafood specials that change nightly. Otherwise, seafood, vegetables and pasta make up the bulk of a tasty and affordable menu. Entrees may be ordered fried, sauteed, grilled, broiled or blackened, and the seafood is never long out of the water. Seafood salads, stir-fry and pasta combinations are all nicely done. As always, irresistible desserts are all homemade by local women (the butterscotch pie is "to die for").

Capt. Willie's Restaurant
$$ • Holden Beach Causeway, Holden Beach • (910) 842-9383

Capt. Willie's, owned and operated by one of the area's grand old families and helmed by a former Norwegian Cruise Lines chef, specializes in fresh country cooking featuring seafood (fried, broiled and blackened), plus a few steak, chicken, pork and barbecue dishes. The breakfast and lunch buffets and the evening seafood buffet are worthwhile bargains, and the ambiance is casual and friendly. Capt. Willie's is open every day for breakfast, lunch and dinner, and it stands beside the Water Slide Ice Cream shop, a short hop from the beach.

Calabash

Calabash Seafood Hut
$ • 1125 River Rd., Calabash
• (910) 579-6723

Don't be surprised to find this tiny place with a line of customers stretching around the corner. It's that popular, as much for its low,

low prices as for the food, which is as good as anywhere in Calabash. The seafood platters, offering combinations of Calabash-style fish, shrimp, oysters, crab and scallops, are huge. For only the biggest appetites would the daily lunch specials not suffice. Sandwich offerings include soft-shell crab in season. Children will enjoy many items that are not even on the children's menu.

All meals are served with a drink (refills included), coleslaw, french fries and hush puppies. The atmosphere is clean and bright, and everyone is friendly. The Hut also serves dinner, and it does a brisk take-out business through the street-side window. The Hut is closed Mondays. Call ahead for take-out.

Larry's Calabash Seafood Barn
$$ • N.C. 179, Calabash • (910) 579-6976

Unless you insist on having a view of the docks, Larry's is one of the better choices for Calabash-style seafood on the other side of town. The all-you-can-eat seafood buffet and raw bar are frequently cited by Insiders as reasons for repeat visits. Nightly specials include Italian buffets, roast beef, ham, prime rib and other country favorites.

Despite its name, Larry's bears little resemblance to a barn. Rather, it is clean, bright and spacious. Rocking chairs on the front porch are handy in case there's a wait. Larry's also serves steaks and mixed drinks and offers golfers' specials (present your scorecard for a discount), seniors' and children's menus, early-bird buffets, and discounts to large groups. Larry's is open for dinner every day from mid-March through November.

The Original Calabash Restaurant
$$ • On the waterfront, Calabash
• (910) 579-6875

Whether this is actually the first "original" Calabash restaurant is secondary to the fact that it's a decent place to try Calabash-style seafood (Insiders say Beck's Old Original Calabash Restaurant, established in 1940, was the first). The hamburgers, steaks and chicken seem like distant afterthoughts on a menu outweighed by seafood — everything from oyster stew and teriyaki shrimp to stuffed flounder in hollandaise and soft-shell crabs.

Open every day during the high season, The Original Calabash stands at the foot of River Road in a large parking area rimmed by several competitors, but you can't miss it — it's the one straight ahead with the garish flashing lights. Welcome to Calabash.

Ella's of Calabash
$$ • 1148 River Rd., Calabash
• (910) 579-6728

Ella's is among the stalwarts of Calabash that remain open most of the off-season, and it's been doing so since 1950. This is also one of the least flashy establishments; it prefers to draw patrons with good food, affordable prices and a casual, friendly atmosphere rather than with excessive prefab nautical ambiance. Ella's offers a worthwhile lunch special (choice of two seafood, plus slaw, hush puppies and fries) that's a real bargain. Steaks, chicken, oyster roasts (in season), mixed drinks and a children's menu are also available. Ella's is open daily and is almost midway between the waterfront and Beach Drive (N.C. 179).

Topsail Island

Betty's Smokehouse Restaurant
$ • N.C. Hwy. 17 N., Holly Ridge
• (910) 329-1708

Real down-home cooking is how Betty's describes its fare, and the slow-cooked barbecue is locally famous. This is one of the few places around where you'll find the bloomin' onion. Betty's serves breakfast, lunch and dinner at family prices, seven days a week. Dinner offerings include steaks (seasoned with garlic), chops, crab cakes and local seafood (mostly fried). There are also low-priced seniors' and kids' menus. Betty's is exceedingly casual and friendly and even features occasional live entertainment. You can't miss it — it's the big place with the wraparound shed roof, one block north of the Holly Ridge traffic light.

Breezeway Restaurant
$$ • Channel and Davis Sts., Topsail Beach • (910) 328-7751

An institution since 1973, the Breezeway is a family restaurant with a great panoramic view of the waterway and a knack for encouraging

Don't want to eat that catch? Turn it into art at the North Carolina Aquarium.

relaxed dining. Its Lowcountry dinners include the popular crab dip and other crab dishes (crab quesadilla, for instance), surf 'n' turf, grilled and fried chicken and prime rib. Dinner is served every night of the year. Breakfast and lunch are served on weekends in summer. Beer and wine, a children's menu and a daily homemade dessert are also available. The restaurant is adjacent to the Breezeway Motel.

Holland's Shelter Creek Restaurant
$ • N.C. 53, near Burgaw
• (910) 259-5743

Local color is seldom as brilliant as at Holland's. From the moment you step in the door, you know you're in for a country-style treat. Situated over the banks of Holly Shelter Creek, the restaurant adjoins the sport and tackle shop where you may rent canoes, buy hunting supplies or inspect photographs of prize catches. Popular among sportsmen and campers, Holland's serves shrimp, oysters, clam strips, flounder and catfish plus a variety of standard grill fare in a friendly backwoods atmosphere.

Holland's is a good 30 miles north of Wilmington (a tad longer from Surf City) on N.C. 53 north of the Holly Shelter Game Land. From I-40, travel about 7.5 miles east, toward Jacksonville. You will find it on the right-hand side next to Holland's Family Campground. The restaurant is open every day for lunch and dinner.

Oceanside Restaurant
$ • Foot of Roland Ave., Surf City
• (910) 328-0619

As in many restaurants along the Carolina coast, the Oceanside is a place where greetings are readily exchanged between strangers. Overlooking the beach, the Oceanside is a popular family eatery (especially on Sundays) that serves breakfast, lunch and dinner seven days a week. The preferred seating is naturally along the oceanfront windows, while larger groups are better accommodated on the inland side.

The aptly named Hungry Man Breakfast is a bargain. Burgers, burritos and sandwiches, including soft-shell crab in season, are typical of lunch offerings, while seafood, including combination platters, chicken and a limited choice of steaks round out the evening menu. Beer, wine and desserts are available on request, and there is ample parking. The Oceanside is open every day.

Saratoga Restaurant
$$ • **N.C. Hwy. 172 at New River Inlet, Sneads Ferry** • **(910) 327-4031**

Since 1979, word of mouth and repeat customers have kept this charming little restaurant a popular destination for quality dinners featuring broiled seafood, steaks and Italian specialties. Only minutes north of Topsail Island, the Saratoga offers casual dining in a refined atmosphere featuring a large working fireplace in winter, soft music, table linen and friendly service.

Proprietors Audrey and Orrin Hill (a former ballerina and opera singer, respectively) take pride in such showcase dishes as their shrimp and mushroom bisque and broiled oysters en brochette (skewered), along with such staples as veal scallopini Marsala and shrimp Creole.

The Saratoga opens for dinner every day except Wednesday in summer and Thursday through Sunday off-season. Beer and wine are served, and children's plates are available. Dress casually. Reservations are suggested on weekends and all summer. You'll find Saratoga Restaurant by taking N.C. 172 from U.S. 17 or N.C. 210 toward Sneads Ferry. It's on Old Ferry Road, the last sharp right turn before the New River bridge.

Soundside
$$$ • **209 N. New River Dr., Surf City** • **(910) 328-0803**

Pleasant ambiance, attentive service and quality cuisine make Soundside an above-average dining experience on Topsail. Established in 1981, Soundside overlooks a tranquil sound perfect for viewing sunsets. Tables are dressed with fresh flowers, handsome tablecloths, lamps and china. Service is semiformal.

Soundside's menu, predominantly seafood, includes unusual dishes such as the smoked salmon with pesto, jumbo shrimp Bach (sauteed shrimp baked with tomato salsa and feta) and Parmesan-crusted lemon chicken. It also serves grilled items, prime rib, soups and salads and domestic and imported wines. We suggest reservations for dinner. The excellent Sunday brunch requires no reservations. The restaurant closes during the month of January and is handicapped accessible.

For something more casual, step next door into Sundowner the Lounge, where you may enjoy all Soundside's non-entree menu items and wine by the glass on a screened porch overlooking the water. Sundowner is open seven days a week during the warm season. It's a great place for evening dessert.

TWO FLOORS OF BARNEY'S
DRINKING AND DANCING
910 • 772 • 9662

Come to scenic and historic Downtown Wilmington, and visit Barney's at 23 Market St. (where Market St. meets the Cape Fear River) for an exciting and new two floor bar. Come enjoy the comfortable feel of the downstairs bar, play pool, darts, fooseball and hang out with friends. Upstairs is a 2000 sq. ft. dance floor with the latest laser light shows. *(Come see the UFO!)* Barney's is a private club, but you can join or be a guest of any member. Join us for some incredible FUN!

Weekly Calendar

Sunday...
SIN **Night**
(Service Industry Night)
.50¢ DRAFT

Monday...
DJ **Jack Nasty**
DRINK SPECIALS

Tuesday...
College **Night**
FREE DRAFT

Wednesday...
Swing Night
w/ Davis
*Learn to Swing-
no partner needed!*
DRINK SPECIALS

Thursday...
Open Mike
Share Your Talent!

Friday...
Dance All Night with
T-Dogg

Saturday...
Ladies
In Free
with
DJ Jack Nasty

Nightlife

The term "nightlife" may have very different meanings to locals and to visitors. Plenty of residents spend summer nights searching the beaches for loggerhead turtle nests and helping protect the ones they find. Others prefer the nights for offshore fishing. Many youngsters enjoy surprising ghost crabs with their flashlights as the little critters (the crabs) make their nocturnal runs on the beach.

Taken in its usual sense of "going out to be inside someplace else," area nightlife is most concentrated in Wilmington, with its numerous clubs, bars and theaters. Outlying areas, especially the South Brunswick Islands, are famous for their unbroken quiet. But hot spots (a relative term, to be sure) also exist at Wrightsville Beach (Lumina Avenue is often choked with summertime revelers just yards from the quiet beach), Carolina Beach, Surf City and Long Beach, particularly in summer.

Stroll the Riverwalk and Front Street in downtown Wilmington. There are plenty of interesting places along the way in which to pause for a toast or a fresh cup of coffee or to hear live music. A horse-drawn carriage tour of downtown Wilmington is a pleasant introduction to the city, too.

Billiards (see listings in this chapter) and bowling (see our Sports, Fitness and Parks chapter) are fun alternatives to the usual bar scene. Browsing our Attractions chapter will reveal more ideas — for instance, a variety of evening cruise opportunities on the Cape Fear River, at Carolina Beach and at North Myrtle Beach.

Those who like to dance may choose among country two-step and line dancing, freeform disco or the area's undisputed monarch of dances, the shag (no offense to the British). You can take in an evening of square dancing, clogging and contra dancing to live music (with lessons) at various locations in Wilmington.

If you've never been contra dancing, you owe yourself a try. Contra dancing grew out of the Irish-Celtic tradition and in America was most popular during the colonial era. The Cape Fear Contra Dancers, 1409 Faulkenberry Road, (910) 395-0973 or (910) 791-6646, organizes monthly dances at area community centers or halls plus weekly dances at various night spots around Wilmington. The $12 annual membership (prorated) helps defray costs, but nonmembers are welcome.

The last couple of years have brought a local resurgence of interest in jazz, evident in the increasing number of restaurants and bars offering live jazz in the evenings, typically between Thursday and Sunday. Venues worth a visit include the Ice House, Paleo Sun Cafe, and Water Street Restaurant (all listed below). Also check out Harvest Moon (see our Restaurants chapter).

Fans of classical music should take note of several area presenters that sponsor evening concert programs from October through May. See our chapter on The Arts for more information on both concerts and theatrical productions.

Other live entertainment is fairly ubiquitous; however, you will find many nightclubs throughout the region (and the state) that are private. In order for an establishment to serve liquor, it must either earn the bulk of its revenue from the sale of food, or it must be a private club open only to members and their guests. Alcohol served in clubs that are not private is restricted to beer and wine. Membership to most clubs is inexpensive, usually between $1 and $5 per year. Weekend visitors applying for membership should know that a three-day waiting period must elapse before you can become a full member, but it's easy to be signed in as someone's guest at the door.

What follows is by no means the last word on the area's nightlife. At the end of the chapter is a section on movie theaters for those

Nightspots

Wilmington

Barbary Coast
116 S. Front St. • (910) 762-8996

Looking for a nightspot with atmosphere? Check out the Coast. It's atmosphere is like a fog at low tide, and its crew of die-hard regulars are as crusty and fun-loving as the name of the place implies — and those are just the college students. The Coast is old (and looks it), small, and serves beer and wine and plenty of it. The decor is classic flotsam and jetsam. Pool tables and an excellent jukebox draw well, but the bathrooms may repel. If Wilmington were still a pirate-plagued port, this would be the place to find them. It's a good drinkin' bar.

Bessie's
133 N. Front St. • (910) 762-0003

An eclectic clutch of lounge lizards flourish in this popular basement club, which is actually two bars in one. Bessie's features live rock and blues bands on Fridays and Saturdays, Shelf Life (live comic soap-opera) on Tuesdays, The Comically Impaired (live comedy) on Wednesdays, and live plays by local theater groups on Sundays. Bessie's attracts a varied clientele predominantly in their 20s and 30s. Once the site of historic Orton's Billiard Parlor, the club still sports five pool tables, including the one where Willie Mosconi sank a record-breaking 365 balls consecutively in 1953.

The adjoining room, full of Civil War atmosphere, is a small club called General Longstreet's Headquarters, so named because it was once co-owned by actor Tom Berenger, who portrayed the bearded Confederate in the film *Gettysburg*. The jukebox packs a solid cross section of rock. Longstreet's is open every day from lunchtime 'til 2 AM. Membership costs $5.

Breaktime Sports Bar, Billiards & Grill
127 S. College Rd. • (910) 395-6658

Wilmington's largest billiards parlor is also a popular sports bar and casual restaurant, serving sandwiches, burgers, soups, salads and more. Breaktime possesses all ABC permits as well as 21 top-quality pool tables, 15 televisions and arcade-style diversions. Neat attire is required; no tank tops. Food is served until 10 PM weekdays and midnight on weekends. The bar serves until 2 AM.

Caffe Phoenix
9 S. Front St. • (910) 343-1395

The Phoenix has an appeal that exceeds even the high quality of its food. With its soft lighting and regular art exhibits, it exudes both warmth and sophistication. No wonder it has become a favorite rookery for nocturnal birds of many an artistic feather (plus its share of poseurs) who gather for a meal or cappuccino, dessert and conversation. Sidewalk seating is best on quiet evenings. As great a place to begin an evening as it is to end one, the Phoenix is open until 1 AM and keeps a very well-stocked bar (more on the menu in our Restaurants chapter).

Cape Fear Coffee & Tea
24 S. Front St. • (910) 343-1500

Like any good coffee house, this is a fine night spot at which to meet, converse, perhaps play a game or two of chess or just relax in the

---

INSIDERS' TIP

Join the Cape Fear Contra Dancers, (910) 395-0973 or (910) 791-6646, either as a member ($12 per year) or a guest, and kick up your heels all around the Wilmington area.

"Talk Of The Town"

Your Morning News Magazine of the Airwaves!

Local News • Weather • Breaking News • Newsmaker Interviews • Traffic • Sports

WEEKDAYS 6 AM – 9 AM

NEWS·TALK 980 WAAV

rockers out front. It's popular among downtown locals — often a curious lot comprising artists, actors and writers as well as more "normal" types. The artwork and availability of information here regarding local events make it something of a cultural clearing house. The shop stays open until 10 PM Sunday through Thursday and until midnight Friday and Saturday, and the staff often plays excellent music, typically ranging from be-bop to art rock.

Club Rio
5001 Market St. • (910) 799-1730

More than just a hotel lounge (it adjoins the Ramada Inn), Club Rio is a popular dance club with the mature singles set. R&B (Friday and Saturday) and beach music (Monday and Tuesday) make up the play list, and shag lessons are offered twice weekly. Wednesday is request night. Drink specials, occasional contests, ample parking and a full bar with all ABC permits add to the club's amenities. Hotel guests are admitted free. Cover charge is $3 Monday and Tuesday and $5 Friday and Saturday.

The Comedy Club
The Hilton, 301 N. Water St.
• (910) 763-5900

The Comedy Club presents nationally headlining comedians in the hotel lounge every Friday and Saturday night from March through early autumn. It's a comfortable, attractive nightclub atmosphere where you can enjoy cocktails and some hearty laughs. Admission costs $5, and shows begin at 9 PM.

The Ice House
115 S. Water St. • (910) 763-2084

Few Wilmington nightspots enjoy the far-flung renown of The Ice House, thanks largely to its outdoor stage and patio directly overlooking the Cape Fear River, the tugboat deckhouse-turned-bar, a large selection of beer, daily live music at lunch hour (in summer) and at night year round (wide-ranging styles, but stressing the blues, beach and jazz). During the cold months, the music moves indoors, and the fireplace is especially attractive.

This year the Ice House has also added a

restaurant and serves liquor. Open jazz jam sessions take place on Sundays from 6 to 10 PM. The building itself is an old ice house with antiquated but still operable ice-making machinery. Open every day, The Ice House has long been a popular singles hangout and is always a blast. In many ways, it is to Wilmington what Sloppy Joe's is to Key West.

Katy's Great Eats
1054 S. College Rd. • (910) 395-5289

The bar at Katy's restaurant is a favorite hangout for sports fans. It's almost always buzzing with young locals who come to enjoy the games on big-screen TV and occasional live music.

Lula's
138 S. Front St. • (910) 763-0070

Tucked away in the low-ceilinged, stone-walled basement, Lula's is a cozy, tiny, pub-style private club sporting vintage celebrity photos and a huge American flag overhead. The jukebox contains an eclectic selection of rock, funk, blues, Motown and some classic Irish drinking songs. Many of the regular clientele, mostly in their 30s and younger, are familiar friends. It's an interesting place, entrance to which is gained through the rear of the building. Membership at Lula's will set you back an entire dollar a year.

Mickey Ratz
115 S. Front St. • (910) 251-1289

This cosmopolitan, progressive, private dance club features high-tech lighting, a superior sound system, two large-screen videos, live shows every Friday and Sunday night, and top-notch DJs, who provide all the energy and up-to-date music of a big-city disco. Dance music of the '80s is featured every Thursday (which is also dollar night). The clientele is largely gay but not exclusively. An outdoor patio with its own bar provides a pleasant change of ambiance in fair weather. Cover charges vary (highest for shows), and an annual membership costs $25.

Paleo Sun Cafe
35 N. Front St. • (910) 762-7700

Four nights a week, live jazz comes here, one of Wilmington's most attractive rooms and among its better places for dinner (from 4:30 PM). The soft lighting, wall-mounted Aztec-style sun god, and roomy seating are almost enough in themselves to keep you there, and the 20-foot ceiling keeps the air seeming smoke-free. The clientele tends to be mature, not stodgy. On Thursdays and Sundays the music begins around 7 PM (no cover). On Fridays and Saturdays, the music hits around 10:30 PM (shortly after the kitchen starts serving its light menu), lasts until around 2 AM, and the cover charge is $2, a pittance.

Port City Java
7 N. Front St. • (910) 762-5282

Comfortable seating, artistic decor, plenty of reading material, premium coffees and excellent desserts make this little shop a popular gathering place into the night (until midnight on weekends, 10 or 11 PM on weeknights). It's within an easy walk of practically everything downtown. If your nightlife ends around sunrise, Port City Java reopens at 6:30 AM.

Rack 'M Pub and Billiards
415 S. College Rd. • (910) 791-5668

This handsome club-style parlor cuts its pool prices in half during the daytime, and ladies play free Monday and Tuesday. Rack 'M is open every day from noon until 2 AM. You'll find it in the rear of the University Landing shopping strip, nearly opposite the Wal-Mart shopping center.

Rockits Rhythm & Sports Grille
5025 Market St. • (910) 791-2001

Rockits is a spacious sports bar featuring live, classic and current rock music on Saturday nights (no cover) and shag lessons and beach music on Fridays. Unpredictable acts — such as the occasional

---

INSIDERS' TIP

Participate in free line-dance lessons in the Holly Ridge area at Betty's Smokehouse Restaurant, 511-A U.S. Hwy. 17 N., (910) 329-1708, Tuesday nights at 7 PM.

A classic beach pose before the Lumina Pavilion buildings, c. 1925.

comic hypnotist-magician — are surprises to watch for. Always popular are the pool table, dart boards (electronic and traditional), electronic golf, Foosball table and free interactive videos. Twenty — count 'em, 20 — TVs, plus two wide-screens, keep everyone up on the most contested games. You'll find Rockits behind the Greentree Inn, where there's plenty of parking, and it's open every night until 2 AM.

The Starlight
23 N. Front St. • (910) 815-2915

A cool combination: live rock bands on weekends, movies on Sunday evenings, and a top-floor vantage point of some of downtown Wilmington's taller buildings. The Starlight is a private club (annual membership $1) and is said to be the only club in town with an elevator — not unlikely considering the number of elevators in Wilmington. Cover charges may apply.

Sunset Celebration at the Hilton
301 N. Water St. • (910) 763-5900

Every Friday evening from Memorial Day to just beyond Labor Day, the pool deck at the Hilton springs to life at 5 PM with the weekly Sunset Celebration, Wilmington's answer to "The Love Boat." Featuring local radio DJs, occasional rock bands, free buffets and a variety of contests, Sunset Celebrations are enhanced by spectacular sunsets over the Cape Fear River. They often become extremely crowded with folks in their 20s and 30s, most of them single, who come to meet new friends, dig the music, make silly toasts and imbibe until 10 PM. Cash bars offer mixed drinks and beer. Admission is free.

INSIDERS' TIP

Jazz lovers, check out the Cape Fear Jazz Appreciation Society for quality concerts, lecture-demonstrations, informative newsletters and more. Contact them via Audio Lab, 5732 Oleander Drive, (910) 28403, (910) 392-1200, fax (910) 392-1077. Individual annual memberships cost $25.

Water Street Restaurant & Sidewalk Cafe
5 S. Water St. • (910) 343-0042

The relaxed, cozy atmosphere here invites you to linger with a friend or loved one late into the night, any night of the week. Every Friday from 9 PM to 1 AM, live jazz provides extra incentive to stay (no cover charge). Regular performers include the local Dixieland Society's sextet, 30-year veterans who appear on the last Friday of each month at 5 PM. Water Street also hosts open jazz jam sessions every Sunday at 5:30 PM. The decor is colorful, somewhat rustic and warm. Sidewalk seating offers a view of the riverfront, and good food is always available.

Wave Hog Saloon
12 Dock St. • (910) 762-2827

This two-level watering hole is extremely popular among the surf-inspired — lots of "Dude-ish" spoken here. Live rock bands keep the place packed and sweaty most of the summer, though it's open year round.

Wrightsville Beach

Buddy's Crab & Oyster Bar
35 N. Lumina Ave. • (910) 256-8966

Home of the world's smallest dance floor, this little shack stays crammed with summer transients, old-time residents and former yuppies who traded burnout for beachcombing. Festooned with ships' lanterns, pulley blocks, bells, life rings, hundreds of business cards, photos and (so it's said) a 16th-century Seminole dugout, Buddy's also has a jukebox choked with 2,000 attitude-improving songs. Buddy's is open daily and closes at no more specific time than "until."

King Neptune's Pirate Lounge
11 N. Lumina Ave. • (910) 256-2525

The Pirate Lounge in the King Neptune Restaurant is as lively as its proprietor, Barnard Carroll, who did the research to accurately identify all the pirate flags hung in the room. It's the kind of decor you might expect of someone who'd rather be sailing, and, as a salt should, he places some importance on rum. His "Rum Bar" features some 19 premium rums from around the world, including Gosling's and North Carolina's own Outer Banks Rum. Microbrewed and imported beers are always in stock, and an inexpensive Pub Grub menu offers plenty of quality munchies (available for take-out). The lounge is open every day and has all ABC permits.

Carolina Beach

The Back Alley Lounge
110 Harper Ave. • (910) 458-9081

A cozy indoor/outdoor space at the back of the Hotel Astor, the Back Alley is open seven days a week, with live entertainment Tuesday through Sunday during the high season (weekends off-season). Wednesday night jam sessions are informal. Enter from the parking lot or through the restaurant.

Cobb's Corner Lounge
217 Carolina Ave. N. • (910) 458-8865

Laid-back and friendly, Cobb's Corner is a private sports bar that attracts a mature clientele, many from the nearby motels. It's also the unofficial home of the Parrot Heads in Paradise, an international nonprofit service organization founded by fans of singer and Head Parrot Jimmy Buffett. You'll find a sunny outdoor deck and darts, and the lounge is open every day during the high season. Schedules of special offerings such as cookouts and occasional live bands on the deck, usually tied to current sporting events, are consistently posted. Cobb's Corner stands directly behind Cabana De Mar. Yearly membership costs $10.

INSIDERS' TIP

Jazz lovers — feast your ears on five solid hours of the best jazz ever recorded every Saturday beginning at 8 PM on public radio WHQR-FM, 91.3. And don't miss the jazz show on Wednesday evenings at 10:10 PM either.

Southport-Oak Island

Bogey's At the Beach
5908 E. Oak Island Dr., Long Beach
• (910) 278-4400

Bogey's is a bright, clean restaurant filled on Friday and Saturday evenings with beach music and Top 40. High director's chairs lining the bar, banquettes and tables allow for viewing the latest golf and NASCAR events on TV, and there's room left over for dancing. A big plus is the open-air patio out back with its own bar and food service.

The Creek
5712 E. Oak Island Dr., Long Beach
• (910) 278-9090

Boasting the largest dance floor on Oak Island, this friendly private club features country and southern rock music, DJs on Saturday nights, karaoke on Fridays and Sundays, and occasional live bands. Weekly pool tournaments are held. Laid-back and without frills, it's just a darn good place to hang out. The Creek is at the corner of S.E. 58th Street.

Laredo's Neon Cactus Restaurant and Cantina
607 W. West St., Southport
• (910) 457-4543

It's true: Laredo's margaritas figure prominently in our mythology; but if spiked lime juice isn't focal to your night life, you're still in luck. Live entertainment happens almost every weekend in season, and DJs prevail otherwise, playing blues, beach and light jazz. It's a casual, mellow, softly lit restaurant and cantina that also serves spicy southwestern dishes and a darned good homemade salsa every day until 2 AM. (They also serve lunch daily.) Laredo's is near the Southport Marina.

Shuckers
6220 E. Oak Island Dr., Long Beach
• (910) 278-4944

Home of the Oak Island Shag Club, Shuckers is a great place for dancing into the wee hours to beach music every Friday and Saturday. DJs spin the old hits, and free shag and line-dance lessons are available on Thursday evenings. But according to some, the food here is the best thing going. Shuckers serves a full menu until 11 PM and possesses all ABC permits.

South Brunswick Islands

Steamers II Restaurant and Lounge
8 Second St., Ocean Isle Beach
• (910) 575-9009

This lively establishment, a mere block from the beach, offers live bands on weekends and recorded music the rest of the time. The music leans mostly toward beach, R&B and classic rock with a little country thrown in. (The juke box is among the few we know still spinning vinyl.) The small dance floor and electronic darts are also popular. Steamers opens early and serves breakfast, lunch and dinner every day. Golfers are especially welcome. The bar at Steamers is an attractive, three-sided affair, elevated slightly above the rest of the room, and has all ABC permits. There a light bar menu of appetizers is always available. All foods are available for take-out.

Topsail Island

The Brass Pelican
2112 N. New River Dr., Surf City
• (910) 328-4373

The ads say this is the friendliest bar on the island. The regulars say it's the coolest. Either way you can't go wrong. The Brass is a casual private club that hosts live rock and beach bands on weekends (some quite loud for a place this size), Thursday through Sunday during the summer. As in many clubs in these parts, a new face turns heads, so get involved in the weekly informal pool or dart tournaments or the occasional ping-pong match. Check out the outdoor deck.

The Mermaid
N. New River Dr., Surf City
• (910) 328-0781

This restaurant and lounge near the north side of Surf City is known for its live rock bands on weekends and holidays, volleyball and pool tournaments and occasional roughhousing. Insiders say the food is better than ever. Night owls can have breakfast here from

11 PM to 3 AM Friday and Saturday, but lunch and dinner are also served (and at more traditional hours). On other nights, karaoke, beach bingo, cards and games help maintain the Mermaid's disputed claim as Topsail Island's "original" beach bar.

Movie Theaters

There are plenty of first- and second-run theaters in the area, but films that are foreign, controversial or "artsy" have frustratingly short runs, if they run at all. It's a paradox, considering the number of films shot in Wilmington and the high level of local interest, but the situation is improving. With some shuffling of theaters by the Carmike chain and the opening in 1997 of its 12-screen complex off Market Street in Wilmington, the net number of screens from Wilmington to Southport jumped from 26 to 32, and programming everywhere seemed more varied literally overnight.

A valuable film resource is Cinematique of Wilmington, the series that brings acclaimed foreign and domestic films to town for three-day runs every other week (sometimes more often) to historic Thalian Hall, at Chestnut and Third streets, in Wilmington. Cinematique is a bargain at $5 a ticket and benefits St. John's Museum of Art and WHQR 91.3 FM, the local public radio station. Thalian Hall's antiquated seating and poor sight-lines are nuisances worth tolerating; arrive early for popular shows. Show times are usually 7:30 PM Monday through Wednesday, but schedules may change to accommodate Thalian's stage schedule. You can receive Cinematique mailings by calling (910) 343-1640 or writing: c/o WHQR, 251 N. Front Street, Wilmington, NC 28401.

All movie theaters in the region offer matinee showings every day during the summer, on holidays and most weekends throughout the year at $4.25 per ticket on average. Full-price tickets typically cost $6.25 everywhere. Since there are so few theaters outside Wilmington, we've listed all theaters together.

Carmike 12, 111 Cinema Drive, Wilmington, (910) 815-0212, is the area's newest addition and, with 12 screens, a major one, enough of a development to require a street of its own (Cinema Drive), linking Market Street and Kerr Avenue. The seats and leg room are the most generous in town.

Cinema 6, 5335 Oleander Drive, Wilmington, (910) 799-6666, is less than 4 miles from Wrightsville Beach.

College Road Cinemas, 632 S. College Road, Wilmington, (910) 395-1790, is a six-screen complex with comfortable, high-back seats. It's behind Swensen's, across the street from the UNCW campus.

Independence Mall Cinemas, 1843 Independence Boulevard, Wilmington, (910) 392-3333, with three screens, has assumed the role of budget, or second-run, theater, with ticket prices locked at $1.50 Monday through Thursday. It's right behind Independence Mall, south of Oleander Drive.

Cinema 4, 1020 Carolina Beach Road, Carolina Beach, (910) 458-3444, is a four-screen complex in the Federal Point Plaza shopping center next to Jubilee Amusement Park. Tickets cost $6 ($4 for matinees).

Surf Cinemas, 4836 Long Beach Road SE, Southport, (910) 457-0320, is convenient to the entire Southport-Oak Island area, situated south of the intersection of Long Beach Road and N.C. 211 (Southport-Supply Road).

Carmike 7 Theaters, 1038 Henderson Drive, Jacksonville, (910) 455-3374, provides film-lovers in the Topsail Island-Holly Ridge area a convenient (and better) alternative to waiting for the video release.

Cinema 6 Theater, College Plaza, Jacksonville, (910) 346-6626, is a six-screen complex also within easy reach of the Topsail Island area.

Carmike Dunes Cinema 8, 4501 N. Kings Highway in North Myrtle Beach, SC, (803) 449-

---

INSIDERS' TIP

Two jazz jams take place every Sunday in Wilmington: one at the Ice House from 6 to 10 PM, the other at Water Street Restaurant from 5:30 to 9:30 PM.

7733, is a convenient choice if you're residing in theater-less South Brunswick. It's about a 30-minute drive from Ocean Isle Beach. Prices can be as low as $2, and the box office opens for advance sales at 1:30 PM daily.

Poetry Readings

Considering the incomes of poets today, some people say the art is in its dying throes. However, considering the number of public readings and enrollment in college poetry workshops, others say we're experiencing an unprecedented poetry renaissance. The best of times, the worst of times, indeed. You, too, may take part in the revival, and at no cost — other than laying bare your soul before an audience. Recite your own work, read a classic — bring your bongos!

Throughout the year, you can explore the art of spoken music on a weekly and monthly basis in Wilmington, where among younger poets, the Beat generation is being rediscovered and reprocessed in a big way. Poetic styles at local readings range widely, from innocent lyricism to experimental riffing to adult confessional. Performers may be nervous first-timers or theatrical extroverts. The fun is often in the surprise.

The following venues are in Wilmington.

Barnes & Noble Booksellers
322 S. College Rd. • (910) 395-4825

The cafe at Barnes & Noble ensures there's enough caffeine at hand to get you through the mediocre stuff. Readings here are family-friendly and take place on the second Monday of each month beginning at 7:00 PM.

New Hanover County Public Library
201 Chestnut St. • (910) 341-4389

OK, so this one doesn't take place at night but at 2:30 PM on the fourth Sunday of the month. (We had to list it somewhere!) This is the longest-running series of poetry readings in the area and comes complete with refreshments, cookies and a well-lit, smoke-free environment. Readings typically conform to a pre-determined theme and are suitable for a general audience.

LUMINA STATION

*Offering a fresh approach to the
shopping and dining experience
in a relaxed, warm and friendly setting.*

Alligator Pie
Children's Boutique

Bristol Books
A Reader's Paradise

Elephant Ears
Fine Home Decor & Gifts

Fat Fish Trading Company
Low Country Collectibles

Intracoastal Realty
Full-Service Real Estate Co.

Logan's
Breakfast • Lunch • Dinner

Monkee's
The Ultimate in Shoes & Accessories

Port City Java
Coffee Houses & Roastery

The Quarter
Coastal Lifestyle Ladies' Clothing

R. Bryan Collections
Fine Womenswear

Vinnie's
Steak House & Tavern

Intracoastal Angler
Fly-fishing & Light Tackle Outfitters

Lumina Jewels
Fine Designer Jewelry

1900 Eastwood Road • Wilmington, NC • Open Sunday

Shopping

If you like to shop, the southern North Carolina coast offers plenty of opportunity to spend your traveler's checks or exercise your credit cards. During the 1990s, shopping centers have sprung up all around the area in such profusion that even locals find it hard to keep up with it all. Stores seem to magically appear overnight and, at this writing, there is no evidence this trend is going to change until well into the new century.

It was not too many years ago that shopping along the coast was an extremely limited experience, even in Greater Wilmington. Throughout the first three-quarters of the century, locals with the means often took shopping vacations in New York, Atlanta and Paris to search for finer clothing.

The notion of upscale shopping in the Cape Fear region was foreshadowed in 1915 when a country store named Belk Williams Company opened in three buildings on Front Street in downtown Wilmington. W.B. Berry, Jr., joined the company in 1919. In 1951, then-renamed Belk-Beery opened on South Second Street as Wilmington's first modern department store.

A previously unseen technical marvel — escalators — set Belk apart from every other store in Wilmington. Now located at Independence Mall (referred to as "THE mall") in Wilmington, as well as a second location at Landfall Center near Wrightsville Beach, Belk-Beery continues to hold its place as the region's dominant fashion and home department store, closely challenged by JC Penney and Sears.

In the 1980s, Wilmington began to attract other large chain retailers with somewhat different focuses than these successful department stores. Huge discount chains such as Wal-Mart, Sam's Club, Circuit City, Home Depot, Office Depot and Target entered the market in a dizzying rush to capitalize on what is widely acknowledged as Wilmington's obsession with bargain hunting. It was a good corporate hunch because these stores are generally packed with people in search of savings on everything from electronics to computers to lumber to 24-pack deals on bathroom tissue.

A segment of the retail market that bears special mention is specialty shops. These "mom and pop" stores comprise the majority of shopping experiences in the region. Independently owned businesses with two to six employees are the norm, a reflection of the entrepreneurial nature of the economy.

Although this book doesn't delve into food shopping, there have been exciting developments in the fare and services offered in area markets in recent years. Wilmington has previously impossible-to-find specialty ingredients, ethnic markets, health foods markets, gourmet shops, specialty bakeries, wine shops, cheese shops and all kinds of interesting additions for the pantry. In response to requests from newcomers from different regions, even the major supermarkets are delighted to test out new items if customers simply make a request.

This chapter is, regrettably, simply too small to do justice to the full range of shopping options available in the Cape Fear region, so we offer an overview and mention only a few of the thousands of shops in the area.

General Shopping

Wilmington

Downtown

Downtown shopping is wonderfully original and surprising. Aside from the one chain store, all the 100-plus stores jammed into the downtown area are independent shops that reflect the interests and tastes of their owners.

TEMPTATIONS
Gourmet Specialty Foods & Cafe

Wilmington's Premier Food Gift Store
Distinctive Gift Baskets • Stacks of Yummy Snacks • Indulgence Foods
Chocolate•Wine•Coffee•Tea•NC Specialty Foods
Shipping • Local Delivery
Cafe Lunch Served Mon.-Sat. 11:00AM-2:30PM

Store Hours: Mon.-Sat. 10-6
Hanover Center • 3501 Oleander Dr. • 763-6662

You're not likely to encounter rack after rack of the same items.

The downtown shopping experience is a step back in time — personal service by shop owners, an inquiry into the well-being of your family and, for regulars, charge accounts that don't bother with credit cards or even a signature. If you're a regular and you pass by a clothing shop where you trade, don't be surprised to have a merchant call out that she has put back a suit or dress for you try. In this scenario, you might even expect it to be bagged and tucked under your arm.

Downtown offers art galleries, antique stores, fine clothing, funky clothing, traditional shoes, crazy shoes, toys, gourmet items, CDs, wine, linens, glassware, fine and costume jewelry, collectibles, books, home furnishings, scents and more. It's a great place to find interesting imports as well.

Part of the charm of this shopping district is its compact size and pleasant walkability. Park your car in a free space on the street or, if you're shopping at one of the retail/dining centers, park at no cost in their large lots. Downtown is an open-air mall with an astonishing selection of spots in which to pause and take in the beautiful scenes between purchases. Coffee shops, delicatessens, bars, ice cream parlors, full-service restaurants and street vendors offer constant temptation while shopping. Many downtown restaurants have outdoor seating right on the sidewalk, a setup guaranteed to lure your shopping-weary feet to pause and gawk.

Viewed as an extended, outdoor mall, downtown is anchored by two large centers at the northern and southern perimeters of the central shopping district. The Cotton Exchange is a shopping/dining/office complex at the northerly end of the riverfront. Chandler's Wharf occupies the southern end. The area between is Front Street, a busy corridor lined with restaurants, galleries, banks, services and stores. Streets that cross Front Street offer many shopping possibilities as well. Downtown is also becoming known for its number of antique stores (see our close-up on antique shopping in this chapter.)

American Pie
113 Dock St. • (910) 251-2131

This is a delightful shop of contemporary American crafts and folk art. You'll discover some of the most unusual arts and crafts in Southeast at this store. If you're seriously into American folk art, ask Elaine Johansen if you can go upstairs to browse around.

The Cape Fear Christmas House
505 Nutt St. • (910) 763-1193

Welcome to 8,000 square feet of Christmas that lasts 365 days a year. Both religious and secular items, including a vast array of

BRADLEY SQUARE

Friendly People that make shopping *Fun!*

Windrose
Furniture, Gifts & Accessories with Personality & Style
799-5793

Travel Specialists
Specializing in Cruises, International Travel, Honeymoon Vacations & Emergency Medical Fares
799-7200

Nevada Bob's Golf
If you like the game, you'll love us!
799-4212

Mail Boxes Etc.
Postal, Business & Communication Services
799-7222

Cellular Plus Communications
Cellular, paging, plus... a whole lot more
360 Communications
Authorized Dealer
792-1400

PEDAL PUMP & RUN
"Bicycle and Fitness Equipment Professionals"
392-8020

Visual Concepts
"A Unique Look At Eye Care"
452-0554

Blimpie
Subs & Salads
452-3777

The Blind Spot
Accessories & Interiors More than just Blinds...
395-5221

collectibles, jam this store to the rafters. An hour in this store is enough to get a shopper in the holiday spirit, and don't be surprised, even in the heat of August, to find yourself humming a holiday tune as you leave.

CD Alley
8 Market St. • (910) 762-4003

At long last, downtown Wilmington has a store that carries new and used CDs, vinyls (which used to be called LPs or records) and tapes, especially blues, jazz, reggae and rock and roll.

Chadsworth Columns
277 N. Front St. • (910) 763-7600

A fascinating addition to Wilmington's shopping scene, this store, owned by North Carolinian Jeff Davis, has locations in London and Atlanta. His company, founded in 1987, combines modern materials and technology with classical design and workmanship to create arch columns in the manner of ancient artisans. Greek, Roman and classical columns, both interior and exterior, are created in the company's Georgia location. Some of the materials available include wood, stone and marble.

Davis is a member of the Institute for the Study of Classical Architecture at the New York Academy of Art. Consultation is by appointment, but browsers are graciously welcome in the storefront columns gallery in downtown Wilmington. For mail order information, call (800) COLUMNS. As an aside, customers of this company include the Virginia Historical Society, David Brinkley, MGM Studios and the Smithsonian.

Chandler's Wharf
2 Ann St.

This center on the river has many appealing shopping opportunities. Created by Thomas Henry Wright, Jr., in the late 1970s, it has evolved over time as a retail/dining complex, but part of it began as a ship's chandler in the 19th century. There was also a maritime museum here in the 1970s, and there are still some marine artifacts scattered about the grounds, including an old tugboat, an enormous anchor and other reminders of the complex's origins. Cobblestone streets, plank walkways, attractive landscaping and a gorgeous view of the Cape Fear River are some of the features that make shopping at Chandler's Wharf such a pleasant experience.

This center is flourishing today with some of Wilmington's most delightful stores, and it boasts two of the city's most pleasant restaurants — The Pilot House and Elijah's (see our Restaurants chapter) — and the pleasure of dining in either one is heightened by the option of enjoying your meal on outdoor decks overlooking the river. Some of the many shops here include the following.

A Proper Garden, 2 Ann Street, (910) 763-7177, has everything for your garden you never knew you needed until you walk in the door and find yourself wanting it all. Birdhouses, chimes, gazing globes, fountains, lawn ornaments, swings, hammocks and umbrellas are just some of the items here.

Salon Deja Vu, 225 S. Water Street, (910) 762-4106, has been serving area residents since 1981. Sad to say, its services are not readily available to visitors who are in town for only a brief vacation. Locals know it takes a bit of a wait to get on Norma Norwood's list of clients, and once they're on it they make sure to remain on it. Great service, exceptional coloring skills, reasonable prices and stimulating conversation make this tiny salon a big success. Norma carries an extensive line of hair care products, as well as lotions and oils for the body. The salon offers waxing.

> **www.insiders.com**
> See this and many other **Insiders' Guide®** destinations online — in their entirety.
> **Visit us today!**

INSIDERS' TIP

Free on-street parking in historic downtown Wilmington is available in 30-minute and 1- and 2-hour allotments. Look for the signs.

Island Passage

CLOTHING • SHOES • ELIXIR

BALD HEAD ISLAND • HISTORIC DOWNTOWN WILMINGTON • WRIGHTSVILLE BEACH
457-4944 762-6128 256-0407

Every candle and accessory you'll ever need for lighting up your home in an aesthetically pleasing way can be found in Candles Etc., 225 S. Water Street, (910) 762-8853. It carries scented candles, hand-dipped tapers, pillars and holders as well as novelty candles. The store moved to a larger space on the same floor in late 1996, so it's now possible to bend over to see something without knocking a display over.

One of the newest shops in Chandler's Wharf is The Gifted Gourmet, 225 South Water Street, (910) 815-0977. It carries chocolates, coffees, jams and jellies, an incredible variety of vinegars, oils, gift baskets, pestos, smoked salmon, Crook's Creamy Grits, Vidalia onion vinaigrette, brandied apricot jam, North Carolina roasted peanuts and too much more to mention.

Romax Shoppe, 225 S. Water Street, (910) 762-1865, has career and casual apparel for women. Newly expanded in 1998, it took the space of the departing clothing store The Quarter. Next door is it's sister store Romax Shoes.

Occasions, 225 S. Water Street, (910) 343-9033, is a relatively new card and gift shop and a pleasing addition to Chandler's Wharf. Tucked away in the corner next to Salon Deja Vu, it's hard to spot but well worth the look.

Owner Ellen Goodell stocks the store with a truly fresh assortment of greeting cards and postcards — shouldn't you let the people back home know what a good time you're having in Wilmington? — as well as G.R.I.T.S (Girls Raised In The South) items, giftwrap, golf gifts, D. Morgan shirts and bags, Robert J. May dog portraits, Red Farm shell and seascape cards, Terry Moore's nautical notes and Donna Robertson's fun fish prints. A card selection worth noting for college sports fans: Bernie Kosar Sports Cards.

The Cotton Exchange
321 N. Front St. • (910) 343-9896

The site of the largest cotton-exporting company in the world in the 19th century, this collection of eight buildings overlooking the Cape Fear River was converted into a shopping and dining center in the early 1970s. Its renovation marked the beginning of the restoration of downtown Wilmington. Shoppers can enjoy a bit of history as they stroll the mall's tri-level space, where displays of cotton bales, weighing equipment and photographs tell the story of the center's evolution. Parking is free in the large lot for visitors of the shopping complex.

The few stores are listed here to suggest the scope of shopping possibilities at The Cotton Exchange (all stores are located within the complex bounded by Water and Front streets).

R. Bryan & Company, (910) 763-6860, is probably one of the nicest clothing stores anywhere, featuring fine clothing for men and women in traditional and classic styles. Exclusive brand-name clothing and accessories include Burberry, H. Freeman, Robert Talbott, Pringle and Bobby Jones. The quality and service are impeccable. (A second location in Lumina Station in Wrightsville Beach offers women's clothing and accessories.)

The Beverage Boutique, (910) 762-6760, is a small store with a glorious assortment of domestic and imported wines and beers. The staff takes a keen interest in consumer needs and aims to please by finding and ordering whatever a customer wants. Wines are displayed by country and vintage for ease of selection. It also carries fine cigars.

T.S. Brown Jewelers, (910) 762-3467, specializes in gemstones (with more than a thousand loose stones on display) and settings and also has a nice assortment of fine jewelry and costume items. Handcrafted jewelry in original designs by 20 artists makes this a special place to look for unusual items. Owners Tim and Sandy Brown are also designers and will create a custom piece for you.

The Candy Barrel, (910) 762-3727, is a delicious place to browse until you make your confectionery decision. Chocolates are homemade and include several varieties of fudge. This store sells all kinds of chocolate-covered and pretzels, hard candies, taffies, toffees and fresh popcorn. You'll also find an interesting array of coffees, teas and gourmet foods.

The Kitchen Shoppe, (910) 762-1919, is a dream store for the accomplished as well as the new cook. Cookbooks, gadgets, grill items, glassware, cookware and spices make up the dazzling array of items. Owner Liz Kirby usually has a pot of coffee on for customers, and if you're a regular you just might get a piece of her chocolate cheesecake.

The Write Place, (910) 343-0617, is a card and stationery store that may well qualify for a Guiness record. It is the tiniest store imaginable, crammed with thousands of cards, gift items, buttons, T-shirts and giftwrap. When you look for merchandise you should expect to be shoulder-to-shoulder with other customers who will jockey with you for space. The selection is worth the squeeze.

One of the first stores in the complex, The Basket Case, (910) 763-3956, opened in 1979 when the very notion of a shopping complex on the site (then overlooking a dirt parking lot) was a shocking idea. Owner Jean Hanson has steadily expanded this unusual gift store, stocking it with an amazing assortment of items that will sometimes make you scratch your head in puzzlement and often make you smile. Sandicast, jewelry, greeting cards, elaborate plush hand- and arm-puppets are just some of the regular items.

Two Sisters Bookery, (910) 762-4444, is a small bookstore that carries novels, books of local interest, lots of journals for the aspiring writer, greeting cards and angels in all configurations. Service is high-quality, and the staff will locate and order any available books. It's a great stop for putting literature in your beachbag before heading out to the shore.

A lively store on the upper level the Zoo, (910) 815-3410, specializes in just about every kind of soft sculpture on a tropical or desert theme imaginable. It has a colorful selection of cloth cactus plants, fish, exotic wildlife and tropical birds. The store also has outrageous tropical luggage guaranteed not to be confused with anybody else's on the baggage carousel at the airport.

Relative newcomer Calhoun's Celtic Import, (910) 763-1990, moved into the Cotton Exchange in 1997 from just down Water Street. It specializes in fine Scottish and Irish imports that range from clothing to gifts.

Down Island Traders
111 S. Front St. • (910) 762-2112

Walk into this store and find yourself transported to Bali. The clothing, decorative accessories, jewelry and other handicrafts are reasonably priced — actually very inexpensive — and there is always something new to peruse. In addition to Indonesian items, this attractive store has merchandise from all over the world, including Southeast Asia, Africa and New Guinea.

Finkelstein's Jewelry and Music Company
6 S. Front St. • (910) 762-5662

Finkelstein's has been in business since 1906. This combination music store/jewelry store/pawnbroker is a must-stop for the visitor or resident who is drawn to any of these enterprises.

DOWN ISLAND TRADERS

Gallery and Gifts

Direct importers of Fine Art, Clothing, Decorative Accessories, Crafts & Jewelry Southeast Asia & Dutch Indonesia Antique & Reproduction Furniture

Members of Museum Store Association

111 South Front Street (Between Dock St. & Orange St.) • Wilmington, NC 28401

(910) 762-2112

Hilda Godwin's
105 Market St. • (910) 762-4472

Hilda runs a unique women's clothing shop that features fine sportswear, dresses for all occasions and accessories. While this lovely little store is wonderful for year-round shopping, things really get exciting around the holiday party season.

Jacobi Warehouse
15 S. Water St. • (910) 343-1131

This is a very unusual shopping center in the heart of downtown on the riverfront. Two old warehouses have been converted into retail space. Shops include Island Passage, (910) 762-1911, which carries an exciting mix of casual '90s clothing for women and some of the most interesting shoes you'll find in the Cape Fear region. Bijoux, (910) 251-0109, sells one-of-a-kind handcrafted jewelry, primarily silver.

Crystal Connection New Age Shop, (910) 251-0439, sells crystals, sage bundles, and things to enhance your metaphysical quest. Earth's Treasures, (910) 763-5403, offers jewelry, wood carvings, fossils, minerals and handcrafted patio sculptures and accessories.

All in all, this little center has some of the most unique and offbeat shops in the area. At the entrance, there's generally an artist waiting on the street who will be glad to render your portrait in copper. Grab a latte from the little stand just inside the Jacobi Warehouse and strike a pose.

Kingoff's Jewelers
10 N. Front St. • (910) 762-5219

A downtown jeweler since 1919, Kingoff's offers fine jewelry, watches and repairs and is the exclusive seller of the famed Wilmington Cup. Metalsmith Thomas Brown created this pewter cup to celebrate the city's success in commerce and industry, and it's a favorite gift for everyone from new babies to civic leaders. There's a second location of Kingoff's in the 'burbs at 1409 Audubon Boulevard, (910) 799-2100.

MasonArt
314 North Green Meadows Dr., Dutch Square Industrial Park • (910) 790-3990

Although this art gallery is a wholesaler, it offers custom framing and decorative artwork from its retail store at 25 percent less than retail price. It has a wide selection of prints — some signed, limited edition — that range in subject matter from beach scenes to magnolias. It has full custom-framing services.

The Old Wilmington City Market
119 S. Water St. • (910) 763-9748

This center is in a constant state of evolution and is turning into a spot with free-stand-

AUDUBON VILLAGE
Corner of Oleander Drive and Audubon Boulevard

Rebecca's Lingerie, Ltd.
(910) 313-6620
Quality lingerie and mastectomy needs

Wonder Shop
(910) 799-4511
A world of ladies' fashions in one unique place

Rag A Muffin
(910) 793-9290
Fine Children's Wear

Kingoff's Jewelers
(910) 799-2100
A full service jewelry store also
(910) 762-5219
10 North Front Street
Downtown

R. Dawson
(910) 350-3510
Hair and Nails

Hours: Monday thru Saturday, 10:00 a.m. - 6:00 p.m.

WILMINGTON'S AUDUBON-VILLAGE

ing vendors and enclosed shop spaces along the perimeter. The really good news is it has become climate-controlled! Inside are tables with freshly growing herbs and plants, cut flowers, baked goods, local artists' paintings and prints, pottery and basket, handcrafted hats, jewelry and more.

Ropa, Etc., (910) 815-0344, is in an enclosed space on the south wall. It carries an excellent assortment of Flax clothing for women, as well as shoes and accessories.

You'll also find the art of Ronald Williams, (910) 763-7944, in the market. Williams has probably painted more watercolor views of Wilmington than anyone else in the region and he sells affordably priced prints as well as originals.

Rare Cargo
112 N. Front St. • (910) 762-7636

Rare Cargo is a great place for women who love loosely structured linen and flax clothing. Mimi Kessler has a "flax list," and those who crave these clothes need to be on it to take advantage of arrivals because the shipments are snapped up quickly. Prices are incredibly good on the high-quality clothing. The store also has an interesting assortment of art T-shirts, incense, jewelry and unusual gifts. The cheery, laid-back atmosphere is an added delight.

Reeds Jewelers
27 N. Front St. • (910) 762-8748

Reeds Jewelers is part of a large chain of 100 stores, but the personal service is of a calibre one would expect of a small store. The downtown store was founded in the 1940s by Bill and Roberta Zimmer and the couple still oversees daily operations. Reeds specializes in diamonds, watches and gold and is a Rolex dealer. There is a second Reeds store at Independence Mall in Wilmington, (910)799-6810.

Scentsational
29 S. Front St. • (910) 762-2626

Scentsational has featured scents, oils, imported soaps, beeswax candles, bath items, lin-

Photo: Curtis Krueger

Loggerhead turtles make their nests along the coast.

ens and personal luxuries for nearly two decades. It sells Crabtree & Evelyn, Thymes and other favorite products. Scentsational now offers hand therapies, facials and massage therapy in the store. Look for the purple awning.

The Stork's Nest
20 Market St. • (910) 251-8008

Since 1985, this has been a great place to find everything for the infant and mother-to-be. European strollers, Madela products, Childcraft furniture, Catamini, Combi, Emmaljunga, Silver Cross, Earthlings, Avent, toys, mobiles, Japanese Weekend maternity items and other products makes this store a magnet for discerning parents and parents-to-be. Owner Polly Daniel is an experienced mother herself and brings wisdom and enthusiasm to the shopping experience. New mothers will find her advice invaluable.

Toms Drug Company
1 N. Front St. • (910) 762-3391

This is an authentic old-style drugstore that has been a landmark in downtown Wilmington since 1932. Despite a serious face-lift in 1995, the store continues to have an old Wilmington flavor. The complete pharmacy offers free citywide delivery. You can also get lots of opinions on current affairs at Toms. If you want to know, ask Faye or Susan about most anything and they'll have the answer.

Oleander Drive Area

Independence Mall is the dominant shopping area along Oleander Drive. The area

INSIDERS' TIP

Since some stores and restaurants don't take out-of-town checks, be sure to bring your credit cards or traveler's checks along.

Easy Living

All Clad Cookware • Nancy Calhoun Dishes
BBQ • Rugs • Doormats • Table Linens
Frames & Wall Art • Bath Accessories

Plaza East Shopping Center
1934B Eastwood Road
Wilmington, NC 28403

Bridal Registry • Gift Wrapping
• Shipping
Monday-Saturday 10-6, Sunday 1-5pm

256-5370

around the mall bustles with shopping possibilities too. Several smaller centers and stores offer exciting shopping opportunities.

Audubon Village
1400 Audubon Blvd.

A special strip mall that needs to be mentioned is Audubon Village, located just a bit east of Independence Mall on the other side of Oleander Drive. This small center has some very nice stores, including Kingoff's Jewelers (see the Downtown Wilmington section above).

Rebecca's Lingerie Ltd., (910) 313-6620 offers everyday undergarment items as well as lounging attire and special-occasion lingerie. Rebecca's also specializes in mastectomy needs. Discreet and sensitive service is a hallmark of Rebecca's, where state-of-the-art fitting is matched with a genuine desire to help women during and after the postsurgical transition. For other lingerie needs, Rebecca's is simply a great place to shop for oneself or for someone special.

Country Vogue, (910) 791-3082, is an upscale, ready-to-wear ladies' store that has been a Wilmington fixture for more than a half-century. It sells top-of-the-line brands including David Brooks and Robert Scott. Clothing runs the gamut from sportswear to dressy dresses, including evening and mother-of-the-bride wear.

Another Wilmington veteran retailer in Audubon Village, The Wonder Shop, (910) 799-4511, has been selling ladies clothing since 1932. Its inventory ranges from sportswear to cocktail dresses to Panache and Mycra Pac rainwear. It is the exclusive area retailer of Bleyle and also carries Canvasbacks, Austin Reed, Ann May, Teri Jon, Chetta B, UMI, Henry Lee, Kenar and Jackie Benard.

Azalea Plaza
3700 Oleander Dr.

The next strip to the east of Hanover Center is Azalea Plaza. The two centers seem to merge into one and their proximity makes this part of Oleander Drive a great place to shop for a variety of needs.

Azalea Plaza is home to superstores. At Office Depot, (910) 392-9013, you'll find an enormous selection, low prices and good customer service. This store has a large selection of computers, software, computer accessories, paper supplies, calendars, planners, office furniture, files, copier services and more.

Books-A-Million, (910) 452-1519, has at least a million books in its huge store beside Office Depot. Nicely sectioned into categories that range the spectrum of hardbacks and paperbacks, it's a place where a book-lover could easily spend hours roaming from section to section. There are large areas devoted to deeply discounted books and also racks and racks of the newest in fiction and nonfiction. It also has a large card and gift section.

SPECIALTY STORE

Birkenstock Specialists.

Birkenstock Comfortable Soles

University Landing
415 S. College Rd.
(910) 790-3878
Across from
Rock-Ola Cafe

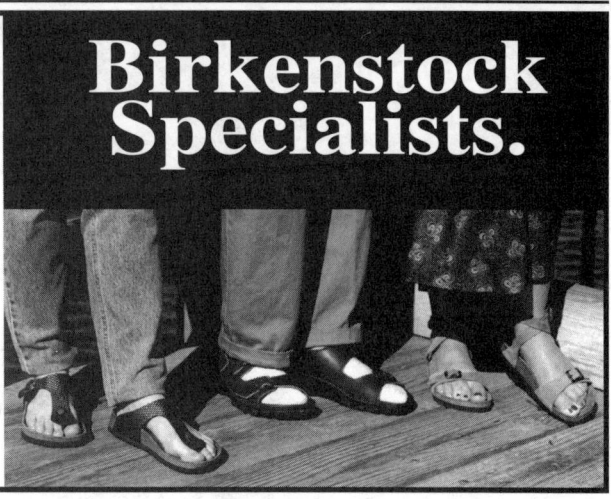

Pier 1 Imports, (910) 392-3151, is one of the largest chains offering home furnishings, accessories, candles, glassware, serving pieces, placemats, eucalyptus, rugs, clothing and more. This is the place to go for rattan or furniture at good prices, and it also has a vast selection of cushions, pillows, window treatments, knickknacks and more.

Hanover Center
3501 Oleander Dr.

This lively strip center has grown increasingly stronger in recent years and is a nice complement to Independence Mall across the street. It houses Rose's (a discount department store), Eckerd Drugs and Harris Teeter, the area's upscale supermarket chain, as well as a post office for added convenience. This is also the location of AAA Motor Club, (910) 763-8446 or (800) 477-4222.

Looking for a food gift? Temptations, (910) 763-6662, established in 1987 in Hanover Center, offers an expansive selection of gourmet treats including candies, cookies, cheese straws, nuts, sauces, pastas, coffees, teas, wines, micro-brewed beers and North Carolina specialty foods. Two refrigerated chocolate cases hold luxury chocolate. This gourmet foods and wine store also boasts a cafe where you can pick up a croissant and coffee in the morning and shop at the same time.

A & G Sportswear, (910) 762-0194, is a fine clothing store for men and women that carries sought-after linen, the area's favorite apparel fabric in summer, available in Elliott Lauren linen and Richard Malcolm Irish linen. It also has a Jams World section with several styles of affordable dresses in 100 percent washable rayon from Honolulu. Hawaiian shirts for men in this line are available in button-up rayon. Other men's lines are Greg Norman golf apparel, Ruff Hewn and Brighton Shoes and leather belts.

Independence Mall
3500 Oleander Dr. • (910) 392-1776

Independence Mall has nearly a hundred stores in a climate-controlled environment. Sears, JC Penney and Belk-Beery anchor this complex of fashion, music, computer, art supplies, food, jewelry, sporting goods and shoe stores. There are one-hour photo developing stores, sporting goods shops, jewelry stores, software stores, video stores, a half-dozen shoe stores, a cinema, music stores, apparel dealers in large quantity, restaurants, a store where everything is a dollar, beauty salons, a tobacco shop, import shops, banking services, and a B. Dalton Bookseller, (910) 791-5504.

Perry's Emporium, (910) 392-6721, with its handsome wood and leaded-glass facade, is a visually exciting store that specializes in estate jewelry, loose diamonds and antique

AUDIO VISIONS
fine home audio, video and car stereo

Experience The Ultimate In Home Theater

ADCOM • ALPINE
CLARION
DEFINITIVE TECH
DENON • KLIPSCH
MTX • NAKAMICHI
PANAMAX • PHOENIX GOLD
POLK • RUSSOUND
TOSHIBA • VELODYNE

CUSTOM HOME & CAR INSTALLATION SALES SERVICE

FEATURING: Vidikron & Toshiba Projection Televisions

Commercial & Residential Audio, Video & Telephone Systems

452-6444

5060 New Centre Dr. (Across From Bob King Truck Center)
VISIT US AT www.hometheater.com/audiovisions/

watches and has two gemologists and two appraisers on staff. The mall has a Gap, (910) 395-0028, and Garden Botanika, (910) 791-5575, two great stores with wonderful items at good prices.

Martha's Vineyard
1205 Floral Pkwy. • (910) 799-1782

This place is just down the street from Pier 1 in an eggplant-colored house between Oleander Drive and Wrightsville Avenue. It's packed with a broad range of gifts for everyone from infants to grandparents. Home accessories, garden gifts, kitchen items, pillows, kitchen and bath linens, jewelry and a large selection of golf-theme gifts line the walls and shelves. If you need jam spoons topped with little bagels or croissants, this should be your first stop!

Space Savers
1411 Floral Pkwy. • (910) 791-4949

Across the street from Pier 1 in Azalea Center is a really fun store for people who want to figure ways to store their household items. Do-it-yourself closet shelving, plastic storage containers, kitchen storage systems and endless opportunities to just put stuff away inspire the most serious packrat to spend hours here.

S. College Road

This part of Wilmington is home to the megastores. Wal-Mart, Lowe's, and Phar-Mor are some of the destinations if you need home-improvement materials, auto parts, industrial-size bags of party chips and — well, you know what you need. Sam's Club, 422 South Col-

DOWN ISLAND TRADERS

Gallery and Gifts

Direct importers of Fine Art, Clothing, Decorative Accessories, Crafts & Jewelry Southeast Asia & Dutch Indonesia Antique & Reproduction Furniture

Members of Museum Store Association

111 South Front Street (Between Dock St. & Orange St.) • Wilmington, NC 28401

(910) 762-2112

---

lege Road, (910) 392-2995, is Wilmington's only price club, and membership restrictions apply.

Barnes & Noble
322 S. College Rd. • (910) 395-4825

It's a given that this huge bookstore is going to carry every book you could ever want or need, but what is special is its extremely comfortable, inviting atmosphere. Big puffy chairs liberally sprinkled around the store invite browsers to grab a Starbuck's cup of coffee and a pastry at the store's cafe, then settle down for a read. Extremely involved in the community, Barnes & Noble has something going on every night, ranging from meeting of community groups to mini-productions by local theater companies to book clubs. The children's department is larger than most bookstores' and has a stage for story time three days a week. There's also a massive gift section with a display of unusual greeting cards, writing journals from the cheapest to the most luxurious, book accessories and calligraphy pens.

Birkenstock Comfortable Soles
415 S. College Rd., University Landing • (910) 790-3878

Opened in February of 1998, this is North Carolina's first specialty shoe store. Owner Patricia Keane, who admits that her own uncomfortable feet turned her into a lifelong fan of Birkenstocks, offers 52 styles of the shoe, which, after color and leather options, translates into 300 choices. In addition to sandals, there are clogs and a full line of shoes for people who spend a lot of time on their feet, including professionals. They all feature the trademark cork footbed – often imitated but never duplicated. If 300 styles aren't enough, you can also direct order some unusual shoes from Germany. The store is located across from the Rock-Ola Café.

McAllister & Solomon Books
4402 Wrightsville Ave. • (910) 350-0189

People who love vintage, rare or just plain hard-to-find books will really enjoy a browse through McAllister & Solomon Books, just a block off S. College Road. This store stocks used and rare books, maps, photographs, manuscripts and postcards. Books are bought, sold and traded. With 15,000 titles in store at any given time, McAllister & Solomon has access to a database of 1.4 million books daily through a computerized out-of-print search network. The staff can also do quick searches online.

Other Wilmington Areas

Audio Visions
5060 New Centre Dr. • (910) 452-6444

Come here for mid- to high-end home audio and video systems as well as great sound for your car. Audio Visions specializes in sales and installation of quality systems, including preconstruction home system designs. It features home automation that includes stereo, intercoms, satellite dishes and more. According to the owners, "we look expensive, but we're not." Everything is sold at a discount. Brands carried include Denon, Polk, Definitive Technology, Adcom, Nakamichi, Klipsch, Toshiba, Alpine, Clarion, Phoenix Gold and Vidikron.

Canady's Sport Center
3220 Wrightsville Ave. • (910) 791-6280

They say they sell "Everything for the Sportsman," and it appears to be true. Marine items, Schwinn bikes, guns, decoys, sport knives, ski outfits, boots, canoes, tents, camping supplies and hiking items are just some of the goods in this extremely reasonable and well-stocked store. The cool- and cold-weather jackets are so densely packed throughout half of the store in the winter that it's a little bit of a struggle to get through the racks, but the January sale is well worth it.

When hurricanes strike, head to Canady's because it sells Sterno — canned heat — an item surprisingly hard to find in Wilmington. Its great for heating soup when the power is out.

Daphna's House of Charms
6213 A Market St. • (910) 793-4944

This new shop carries Old Country Roses china, crystal, Pilgrim glass, Fenton glass, Oriental pieces, Heavenly Retired Angels and David Frykman collectibles. It also features silk floral arrangements and separate flowers, brassware, scented candles, figurines, nautical items, lighthouses, water fountains, shells, porcelain dolls, Williraye Studio Collection, Blue Mountain Pottery, Highland Ridge, Beanie Babies, gold and silver jewelry and collectibles by Sarah's Attic.

The Great Harvest Bread Company
4302 Market St., North 17 Shopping Center • (910) 763-0003

This bakery specializes in breads, mainly whole wheat. They grind their own wheat,

Discover THE COTTON EXCHANGE
Downtown Wilmington

The "Must Visit" gallery in Wilmington...

The Golden Gallery
for the best in local...

Watercolors
Limited Editions
Fine Art Photography
Songs and Legends

Summer Pleasures Remembered
Image 12" x 16" $30

The Cotton Exchange
(910) 762-4651

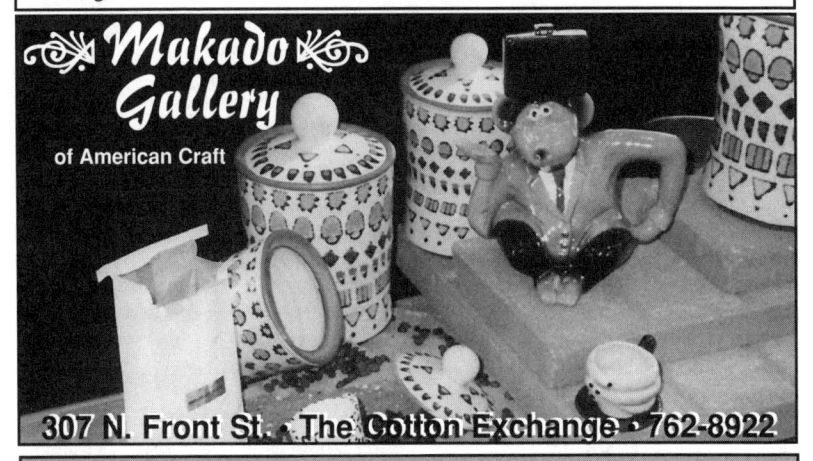

Makado Gallery
of American Craft

307 N. Front St. • The Cotton Exchange • 762-8922

FIDLER'S GALLERY AND FRAMING

Wall Art
Limited Editions
Fine Art Posters
Custom Framing

Parking Lot Level • Under Blue Awning
(910) 762-2001

Cotton Exchange
Wilmington, NC 28401

Wrigley's Clocks
Sales & Services
•
Floor • Wall • Mantle
Repair All Makes
We Make Housecalls
•
The Cotton Exchange
Wilmington, NC 28401
•
910-763-0338

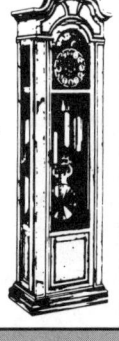

Casual Comfortable Clothing For Fun Active Women

Ad·lib
BODY & SOUL

16 Market St
Wilmington
762-2121

...AN ESCAPE FROM THE ORDINARY

Ad·lib
— HOME —
14 Market St, Wilmington
762-0303

use the highest protein wheat available and never use oils, fats or preservatives. Everything is truly from scratch. The bakery offers Breads of the Month, some of which are destined to become regular items, including spinach-feta bread, sundried tomato-pesto bread, cheddar-garlic bread and lots of fruit breads. Muffins, scones and cookies are regular items. Citing a philosophy of awareness of its role as a "village baker," Great Harvest donates its space, ingredients, staff and advertising to a local nonprofit organization one day each year and lets that agency have all the day's profits.

The Learning Express
**The Courtyard, 5704 Oleander Dr.
• (910) 397-0301**

This store's slogan is "Toys that Capture Imaginations." It's a great place for kids and their parents because everything in it offers educational opportunities. There's an extensive dress-up section, with everything from glittery flappers to a create-a-cape kit to cowgirl and cowboy duds. Puzzles range the complexity spectrum and there are science kits for all age levels.

The store also carries books, games for all ages, YoYos — including Yomega — Brio, Playmobile, Corolle dolls, Thomas the Tank Engine, replicas of Lionel engines in miniature versions that work on wooden tracks, Lost in Space keychains, Silly Putty, Manhattan Baby and Beanie Babies.

The Learning Express carries Robotix, which are kits to put together your own robots, including RoboDog and RoboRex, Legos, puppets, glow-in-the-dark alien kites, giant dolphin kites, and more. The size of the store doubled in 1997 to create 3,300 square feet of fun. It offers a Birthday Registry for kids and has a Grandparents Club, complete with discounts and free dessert at Harvest Moon restaurant nearby. Discounts for teachers, including homeschoolers, are offered as well. Call for periodic YoYo clinics.

Paula's Health Hut
3405 Wrightsville Ave. • (910) 791-0200

If you're into vitamins, health foods, diet, homeopathic products and all-natural items for your body, Paula's Health Hut is a must. It has Wilmington's largest selection of vitamins, health foods, diet and all-natural products. The courteous staff are glad to share their knowledge and latest information.

Townhouse Art & Frame Center Inc.
737 St. James Dr. • (910) 791-2113

Townhouse's store is somewhat hidden in St. James Village between the main part of the village and the back road to College Road Cinemas. Once there, you'll find an excellent

SHOPPING • 147

A keen sense of fashion goes a long way on the beach.

Toms Drug Co.

Since 1932

Forget Something?

prescriptions, toothpaste, sunglasses, film, gift items? Come See Us, We're nice, We're fun...

762-3391 • 1 North Front Street

Our Clothes Cover Your Belly

- Maternity Needs
- Nursery Selections
- European Strollers
- Infant Clothing

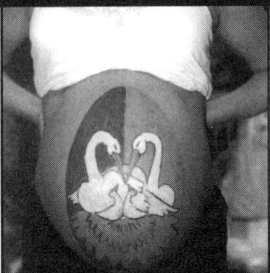

The Stork's Nest
20 Market St. • 251-8008

THE RUNWAY

ATTENTION

STYLE STARVED SHOPPERS

IT'S TIME TO GET DRESSED

- AGGRESSIVE AVANTE-GARDE STYLES
- FLIRTY PARTY/PROM WEAR
- THREADS OF THE FUNKY VARIETY
- PLATFORM SHOES FOR MEN & WOMEN
- ALL THE HOTTEST DRAG

772-2100 • 2325 MARKET

PINEHURST POTTERY

Your Treasure Chest of Savings!
- Silk Flowers and arrangements
- Candles
- Baskets
- Ribbon
- Greenery
- Statuary
- Bird Baths
- Crystal
- Pots
- Brass
- Xmas items
- Kitchen Accessories
- ...and MUCH MORE

Bargain hunting is a favorite Southern pastime! And there isn't a better place to discover the area's best values than at Pinehurst Pottery! Take in the charm and experience of Pinehurst Pottery's friendly staff in a store that's so big --you can get lost in it!

686-0338
7222 Market Street, Wilmington, just past the Ogden Light

---

selection of art supplies for everyone from students to professionals. Brushes, stretched canvas, canvas strips, colored pencils, markers, a wide range of papers, presentation portfolios and more are on display. Half of the large building is occupied by a comprehensive frame shop that offers everything from do-it-yourself to museum-standard mounting and framing.

Adjacent to Wrightsville Beach and Vicinity

Truth be told, there is not a lot of shopping on this primarily residential beach, but there's an explosion of retail growth over the bridge on the mainland side. (All the stores in this section have a Wilmington address.)

Clockwise Clocks
7040 Wrightsville Ave. • (910) 256-2576

Located near the Galleria between Airlie Road and Eastwood Road, this store is in a hard-to-spot space in a new, small commercial/retail center called Twelve Oaks. Clockwise Clocks carries mostly mechanical-wind clocks, including new pieces by Howard Miller and exquisite handmade pieces by Foster Campos — such as his mahogany Banjo Clock — as well as Comittee of London. The store carries mantle clocks, grandfather clocks and a full line of Chelsea marine clocks. It offers complete repair services and rumor has it the owner has become "clocksmith to the stars."

The Fisherman's Wife
1425 Airlie Rd. • (910) 256-5505

This store specializes in decorative accessories and gifts with a fishy theme, including home accent pieces. "Playful prints, perky pottery and funky folk art" made by hand are regular features of this store's offerings. It has a wide array of tableware, ceramic lamps, candlesticks, books, toys, T-shirts, pewter tub and sink stoppers, drawer pulls and starfish hooks, cookbooks and a year-round Christmas room.

Landfall Shopping Center
Eastwood Dr. and Military Cutoff Rd.
• (910) 256-9473

Located just minutes from Wrightsville Beach, this robust center has entered the retail arena in a brisk way in the past few years. This retail, dining and service center lies just outside the gates of the Landfall residential subdivision. It offers a smaller version of Belk-Beery Department Store and may other stores.

If you're looking for health foods, natural beauty aids, organic vegetables (something hard to find in quantity in the area) and an extensive line of Japanese cooking products, Doxey's Market and Cafe, (910) 256-9952, is a one-of-a-kind store in the Cape Fear region. The healthy fare inside makes it a favorite dining or take-out spot for the discerning vegetarian.

An exciting store for cooks and people who enjoy entertaining, The Seasoned Gourmet, (910) 256-9488, is a great addition to the culinary arts stores beginning to pepper Wilmington. There's high emphasis on cookware, including handpainted ceramics in one-of-a-kind designs by Pennsylvania artist Anita Ambrose.

The store sells KitchenAid mixers, cookbooks, linens, Wustoff knives, Cuisinart, gift baskets, gourmet foods, handpainted trays and cheeseboxes, lazy Susans and some unusual furniture. Each Tuesday on a seasonal basis, the store offers cooking classes that range from French to Asian to Southwestern and beyond. It has an impressive offering of imported cheeses.

Something Special Florist and Gifts, (910) 256-0020, bills itself as having the "most beautiful flowers in Wilmington," and, indeed, no one could disagree with that self-assessment. Designer Jerry Rivenbark creates exquisite floral arrangements, and the store offers a nice selection of gifts. It carries custom gourmet baskets, live plants, planters, pottery, cards, home accessories and gardening gifts.

Also in Landfall Center is Taverniers Jewelers, (910) 256-1122, the second location of this Wilmington business. A beautiful store, it's a fitting setting for the works of Henry Dumay, exclusively offered by Taverniers in both Carolinas. Dumay's works have been bought by Diana Ross, Princess Di, Hillary Clinton and Elizabeth Taylor.

The Julia, (910) 256-1175, moved from downtown Wilmington to the Landfall Center in 1995. Offering better women's apparel since 1916, this veteran retailer sells evening wear, daytime wear and "a bit of casual." Some of its clothing makers include Tom and Linda Platt, Mondi, Votre Nom and Tamotsu.

HobbyTown USA, (910) 256-0902, describes its merchandise as "toys for the big kids." Remote-controlled helicopters, planes and boats, train sets, racing sets and thousands of model kits are enough to bring out the kid in anyone. Sure, the real children in the family will find a lot to entertain them, but the grown-ups in the house are going to have a good time here.

If you're into outdoor sports, Aussie Island Surf Shop, (910) 256-5454, has a mind-boggling array of clothing and equipment for surfers on sea, street and snow as well as casual sport clothing and beachwear. There are lots of surfboards on display. Wave surfers can get a surf report for the area beaches by calling Aussie Island at (910) 256-5757.

J.S. Anderson, (910) 256-8893, a younger sister store to A & G Sportwear, offers a full line of Jams, complete with a Caribbean cabana display modeled after a house on Grand Caymans that store owner Steve Anderson stays in every Christmas. The store carries trendy items, including resort wear for ladies and men, Brighton shoes and leather belts and gifts.

Lumina Station
1900 Eastwood Rd. • (910) 256-0900

Lumina Station, with its Lowcountry architecture, is a stunning example of what can happen when the beauty of the natural setting is incorporated with architecture. This upscale center is a shopping and environmental plus for the community. The following is a partial description of the stores here; you'll discover many other shopping opportunities.

The Quarter, (910) 256-6011, has classic to contemporary and casual to cocktail clothing for women in such upscale lines as Lady Boudin and Robert Scott. Like its downtown counterpart, this store carries quality clothing and prides itself on personal service. At R. Bryan Collections, (910) 256-9943, a contemporary boutique for women, Sheri Bryan has assembled a collection of the latest upscale, traditional trends and wardrobe essentials for women. Alligator Pie, (910) 509-1600, is a complete children's boutique specializing in international designs in sizes newborn to 16. It also has gifts, toys, accessories and clothing.

Bristol Books, (910) 256-4490, is a small independent bookstore offering a wide range of books, magazines, newspapers, cards and fine stationery in a cozy bookstore setting. Personal service and community involvement are hallmarks of Bristol that keep it highly competitive in a market with several much larger bookstores.

Outer Banks Hammocks
7228 Wrightsville Ave. • (910) 256-4001

Outer Banks Hammocks sells its own

wilmington's

Shopping at it's best...
that's Independence Mall!
Discover an unparalleled collection
of your favorite stores,
restaurants and services...
over 85 great stores in all,
plus Belk Beery, Sears and JCPenney!

BEST SHOPPING

From fashion to footwear,
books to stereo equipment,
special gifts and more,
it's Independence Mall,
Wilmington's best shopping destination!
Welcome to the Cape Fear Coast!

destination.

INDEPENDENCE MALL

3500 Oleander Drive · Belk Beery, Sears, JCPenney and over 85 other fine stores.
Open Monday-Saturday 10 am - 9 pm. Sunday 12:30 pm - 6 pm.
Department store hours may vary.

PERRY'S EMPORIUM

Allen Perry welcomes you into his store.

A jewelry store from the past to the present. Fine antiques and estate jewelry, loose diamonds & gems. One of a kind new pieces. Full time service & two jewelers on premise.

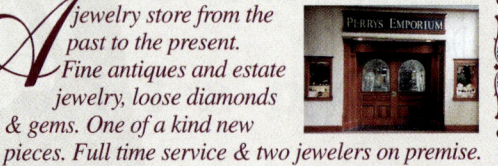

PERRY'S EMPORIUM
Independence Mall • 392-6721

Murrow furniture galleries
...for styles that are naturally you

Competitive Discount Prices

45,000 sq. ft. of beautifully decorated showrooms filled with Lexington, Baker, Century, Bernhardt, Hickory White, Pennsylvania House, Statton, Thomasville and more. Professional Interior Designers on staff.

We Ship Worldwide

3514 So. College Rd. • P.O. Box 4337, Wilmington, NC 28406 • (910) 799-4010
Hours: Monday-Friday 8:30-5:30, Saturday, 9:00-5:30

We'd Go Out More... But It's So Much Fun At Home.

THE RED DINETTE
FURNITURE AND DOMESTIC ARTS

5 North 3rd Street in Historic Downtown Wilmington
910-343-8920

Provence Ltd.

Immerse yourself in the spell of the French countryside... the taste, the scent, the color and texture of Provence.

Colorful Provencal clothing & accessories...Jardinieres & planters...Biot glassware...Faience of Provence...Handcrafted pottery from the artisans of Roussillion & Vaison la Romaine...Urns & jarres anciennes from the French countryside...Bausman furniture & French Antique imports...Lavender & rosemary honey, salad dressings, & herbs de Provence...Candles, soaps, & lavender sachets.

10am until 6pm
Monday through Saturday

The Galleria at Wrightsville Beach
6766-L Wrightsville Ave
910-256-4550

Take home a little piece of French Country

ROLEX

REEDS *Jewelers*

Independence Mall 799-6810
North Front Street 762-8748

high-quality hammocks, rope and wood-related items such as porch swings, deck chairs and hanging chairs. Owner Clark Helton has established a reputation for selling products that are durable and comfortable. Oak and ash hardwoods and soft-spun polyester rope make these hammocks hold up to the weather. Generous sizing is a plus. Hammock pillows and cushions are all made of Sunbrella. Drive by most any day and watch Helton's employees handweaving hammocks right in front of the store. It's an attraction in itself.

Plaza East Shopping Center
1946 Eastwood Rd. • (910) 256-4782

Plaza East Shopping Center has several unique specialty stores.

Airlie Moon, (910) 256-0655, has an eclectic assortment of pottery, candles, handmade blank books, sculpture, glass, body lotions and jewelry. There's a metaphysical theme to the place, too, so check out the counter for information on area meetings and groups.

At Easy Living, (910) 256-5370, you'll find cookware, a wide assortment of serving pieces, glassware, table linens and grill accessories, all perfectly suited to coastal living and entertaining. The store carries All-Clad, Nancy Calhoun dishes, rugs, wall art and doormats. A bridal registry service is available.

If you want to head into the outdoors, Cape Fear Outfitters, (910) 256-1258, is the store to visit first. It is stocked with everything you'll need to enjoy an adventure in nature: tents, sleeping bags, backpacks, outdoor clothing, kayaks and touring canoes. The store also arranges guided trips into the wilds of the Cape Fear region and rents kayaks and canoes to adventurers.

A member of a huge chain that carries boating supplies, hardware and accessories, West Marine, (910) 256-7878, is a welcome addition to the Wilmington shopping scene for boaters. As a personal service, West Marine is happy to pick up cruising boaters at the docks on the Intracoastal Waterway who want or need to shop in their store. It's open seven days a week.

Embellishments, (910) 256-5263, carries a wide selection of gifts suitable for weddings, birthdays or special holidays. It has a Bridal Registry, stationery and gifts particularly suited for bridal attendants and features handblown glass by Simon Pearce.

The Cotton Exchange is a charming complex of shops and restaurants in restored historic warehouses on Wilmington's riverfront.

Whiting & Company
The Galleria, 6800 Wrightsville Ave.
• (910) 256-3993

Casualwear for women and men in brands such as Nautica and Kenar are hallmarks of this store near Wrightsville Beach. Look to this store for hard-to-find linen clothing and sportswear.

Wrightsville Beach and Harbor Island

Redix
120 Causeway Dr., Wrightsville Beach
• (910) 256-2201

Redix is simply a gratifying store for shoppers looking for a variety of items. It is a huge beach goods store that carries everything from rafts to sandchairs to groceries to boogie boards, but it also has one of the best selections of excellent quality clothing for men and women in the whole Cape Fear region. Swimsuits, sweaters, shorts, slacks, dresses and more jam half of the large building. When Redix has sales, such as after Christmas, you can get great bargains on Liz Claiborne, Jones of New York, Robert Scott and other quality name brands.

Sweetwater Surf Shop
10 N. Lumina Ave., Wrightsville Beach
• (910) 256-3821

Sweetwater has everything the surfer will ever need — and then some. Spyder, Xanadu and Bessell are some of the quality brands of boards it carries. It also has a repair service for the occasional unhappy landing. You'll also find swimsuits, women's fashions, shoes, sunglasses and accessories.

Carolina Beach

There are several places to shop in Carolina Beach. Something important to know is that most of the smaller retail stores — as well as restaurants — have limited hours in the winter season. Many of them close up altogether until the tourist seasons kicks off anew in March or April. However, several specialty-shop merchants are parting ways with this tradition and staying open all year. This is good news for the off-season visitor.

Checkered Church
800 St. Joseph St. • (910) 458-3140

Located in a former Catholic church, this blue-and-white-checked building houses a fascinating store filled with home accent pieces. Pine furniture, prints, crocks, M.A. Hadley pottery, candlesticks, chainsaw carvings (need a full-size pelican?), windchimes, weathervanes, pillow, lamps and wreaths with a "shore decor" theme are featured. It also sells Yankee Candles, greeting cards, birdhouses, baskets and Christmas decorations.

The Gold Rose Apparel
6-B N. Lake Park Blvd. • (910) 458-9770

The Gold Rose is a quality women's clothing store that offers outfits suitable for daywear or parties. The clothing is all American-made, all washable and very reasonably priced. The Gold Rose also carries a full range of accessories with the exception of shoes. Although the store is open all year, hours are reduced in January and February.

Great Mistakes
21 Carolina Beach Ave. • (910) 458-7477

Great Mistakes carries a huge selection of overruns, closeouts and buyouts of the kinds of brand names they'd like to mention but can't. Expect to enjoy savings of 40 percent to 70 percent off retail price. This is the 10th store in a regional chain. One is in Raleigh and the rest are located on North Carolina beaches. The Carolina Beach store opened in December of 1997.

Island Appliance
716 N. Lake Park Blvd. • (910) 458-3070

This store sells and services all major brands of appliances, including window air conditioners, refrigerators and freezers, washers and dryers, dishwashers, microwaves and ranges. Some of its brand-name items include KitchenAid, Jenn-Air, Whirlpool, Roper and RCA. Low prices and free local delivery are appealing features of this appliance/service store.

Island Tackle & Hardware
15 Federal Point Shopping Center
• (910) 458-3049

This is your first stop for fishing supplies. A combination hardware and tackle store, it sells

Pull up a chair under a beautiful old oak and enjoy the sunset.

bait, offshore lures, rods and reels, line, coolers — everything an angler needs and then some. For damage done to reels by the big fish off the Carolina Beach shores, Island Tackle & Hardware also repairs reels. It is open all year because, after all, the fish never stop biting.

Linda's
201 N. Lake Park Blvd. • (910) 458-7116

Linda's is a fairly large, year-round store has a wide assortment of ladies sportswear, dresses for special evenings on the town, swimwear, costume jewelry, scarves and other accessories. You'll find resortwear made of comfortable, machine-washable, low-maintenance material in stylish cuts and colors.

PK's
10 S. Lake Park Blvd. • (910) 458-3090

PK's is a gift boutique owned by the now-retired Kure Beach postmaster, Patty Compton. She describes her clothing for women as "fun and glitzy" casual and resortwear. PK's also sells Lefton Lighthouses, crystal, salt-and-pepper sets, brass, 14K gold charms, lots of jewelry, pewter miniatures, frames by Fiji, clay art, ceramics and music boxes. Check out the assortment of unique cookie jars. The store prides itself on good prices and a high level of service, including shipping and gift wrapping.

Sassy Glass
104 N. Lake Park Blvd. • (910) 458-8489

Open at this location since 1997, Sassy Glass offers gifts, collectibles, stainglass and supplies. It carries an extensive selection of sterling silver jewelry, clocks, Brian Crabb collectibles, Windsor Bear collectibles, stainglass lamps and suncatchers, postcards, magnets, Mexican pottery, windchimes, David Fryckman collectibles, candles, framed prints, Bob Timberlake prints, Austin sculptures, water globes and musical angels.

Wings
807 N. Lake Park Blvd. • (910) 458-4488

Welcome to the ultimate beach goods store that is large enough to stay open all year in a town that is largely seasonal. Whether you want Boogie Boards, beach clothing for the family, windsocks, beach toys or T-shirts made your way, Wings is the place to find whatever you need.

Southport-Oak Island

Boat House Gifts
5606 E. Oak Island Dr., Long Beach
• (910) 278-9856

Boat House Gifts carries Tom Clark's sculptural creations, collectible sand dollars,

Swarovski Silver Crystal Miniatures, lighthouses, prints, jewelry and cards.

The Driftwood Shell Shop
122 Yacht Basin St., Southport
• (910) 457-5466

With souvenirs, jewelry, T-shirts and Sure Catch Tackle, The Driftwood, on the Southport harbor, is touted as one of the area's most complete fishing tackle centers. It's also an official weigh station to verify your tall tales. And it is packed with all kinds of seashells, including specimen shells for serious collectors.

Little Professor Book Center
4930 Long Beach Rd., S.E., Southport
• (910) 457-9653, (800) 722-2323

Located in the River Run Shopping Center, this family book store is open seven days a week. The staff is big on personal customer service, and the store's motto is "We'll help you find the books you love." Before heading out to relax on the beach, drop by for books and magazines and pick up some cards to send the folks back home.

Lynne's Hallmark Shop & Treasure Room
103 Yaupon Dr., Yaupon Beach
• (910) 278-9352

Lynn's has Hallmark greeting cards, fashion jewelry, saltwater taffy, shells, beach bags and souvenirs of your visit to the beach.

Miss Patti's Porch
122 E. Moore St., Southport
• (910) 457-5052

Miss Patti's sells handcrafted and handpainted tin pins. It specializes in the themes of cats and angels done in tinwork and also carries a wide array of country collectibles.

Northrop Mall
111 E. Moore St., Southport
• (910) 457-9569

Antique shoppers will be delighted to discover 25 antiques and collectibles dealers under one roof just a few feet down the street from the Antique Mall.

Oak Island Senior Center Craft Shop
5918 E. Oak Island Dr., Long Beach
• (910) 278-5224

This unusual shop, operated as a nonprofit organization, has gifts made by its members for sale as well as classes in crafts ranging from decoupage to pottery to paintings. It also sells arts and craft supplies.

Philomena Moultries Boutique
5813 E. Oak Island Dr., Long Beach
• (910) 278-4992, (800)491-4992

This small boutique offers an array of fine and fun gifts, Bibles, collectibles, health foods, vitamins, children's clothing, books, tapes, costume and fine jewelry and angels.

Swayne's Crafts & Things, Inc.
817 N. Howe St., Southport
• (910) 457-6589

Swayne's carries a selection of garden supplies, craft supplies for the hobbyist, fabrics, floral products, shells, gifts and souvenirs.

South Brunswick Islands

Calabash Nautical Gifts
9973 Beach Dr., Calabash
• (910) 579-2611

Drop by here when you're feeling particularly nautical and want to accessorize your home with sailorly stuff. This store also carries collectibles such as Department 56 and Tom Clark Gnomes and boasts over 3 million ornaments. You'll also find golf equipment and clothing.

Carson Cards and Gifts
Twin Creek Plaza, Shallotte
• (910) 754-9968

Carson has shelves of collectibles, including Tom Clark Gnomes, Hummel figurines, Porcelain Birds by Andrea and more, as well as a full inventory of greeting cards.

The Cockle Shell
Holden Beach Cswy., Holden Beach
• (910) 842-6030

Need some sand dollar hardener? Maybe you never thought you would need this particular item, but maybe you've never had an

SHOPPING • 155

Insiders love the Southern coast because water is always nearby.

Photo: Curtis Krueger

opportunity to find whole sand dollars like you will on the Brunswick beaches. This store not only has this mystical ingredient but also sells live hermit crabs, coral, a wide variety of seashells, books, jewelry and lamps.

Pelican Square Books & Ball Cards
1647 Seaside Rd., Sunset Beach
• (910) 579-8770

This store carries top-10 hardback and paperback books as well as a general line of books, newspapers and magazines. It has ball cards too.

Topsail Island

Topsail Island has seen tremendous growth in retail business during the past few years. Despite the primarily residential orientation of this island, there are some fun places to shop. Some businesses ceased operation after the hurricanes, but it is apparent that the island is going to see a lot of new stores and services soon.

Docksider Gifts & Shells
14061 Ocean Hwy. 50, Surf City
• (910) 328-1421

Docksider is filled with souvenirs, fresh saltwater taffy, clothing and accessories, costume and fine jewelry, postcards, puzzles, back scratchers, stuffed animals, lighthouses, crystals, shell-filled lamps, flags, nautical items, soaps, Christmas ornaments and more. As an added service, you can have the shark teeth you found on the beach wired while you wait so you can wear your treasure home and amaze your inland friends.

The Gift Basket
702 S. Anderson Blvd., Topsail Beach
• (910) 328-7111

This packed gift shop has been on the island since 1973. It is a fine gift store that offers an extensive selection of 14K gold jewelry, colorful flags and a nice variety of upper scale gifts. It carries Tom Clarke gnomes, Yankee Candles, a wide and interesting assortment of time and weather instruments, tide clocks, Michigan Rag clothing, T-shirts, rug mats, dishtowels, children's toys and books.

Island Super Store
N.C. Hwy. 210, N. Topsail
• (910) 328-5351

Three miles north of the Surf City bridge, this beach and party supplier also has a butcher shop, groceries, fresh produce, hurricane supplies, garden supplies, hardware, stuff for your boat, camping equipment, books, newspapers and virtually everything you forgot to bring on your beach vacation. Best of all, it's open seven days a week all year long.

Island Treasures
627 S. Anderson Blvd., Topsail Beach
• (910)328-4487

Island Treasures offers a wide assortment of items that, frankly, make the store pleasantly reminiscent of the venerable Redix store down at Wrightsville Beach. There's a little something for everyone, including fine resortwear (clothing by Cotton Connections, tops and bottoms by Taylor and harve' benard, as well as T-shirts, shorts and pants for men, women and children), jewelry, flags, windsocks, Boogie boards, beach supplies, beach toys, plush toys, beach umbrellas, sunglasses and gifts.

Spinnaker Surf & Sport
111 N. Shore Dr., Surf City
• (910) 328-2311

Spinnaker has kites and windsocks, surfing apparel, new and used surfboards, resort wear, Rollerblades and Jimmy Buffett/Caribbean Soul T-shirts and souvenirs.

The Topsail Island Trading Company
201 New River Dr., Surf City
• (910) 328-1905

Despite the hurricanes, this store has endured since 1986. Patterned after a Maryland lighthouse, it carries fun resort wear, T-shirts,

---

INSIDERS' TIP

Independence Mall in Wilmington offers complimentary strollers for the little ones.

quality toys and unusual gifts. Delicious fudge, freshly made in the store, is shipped across the country. The store is also the home of Topsail Scenic Boat Tours and Turtle Island Ventures, a guided kayak nature tour.

Antiques

Downtown Wilmington

Downtown Wilmington is a focal point for antique stores. They range the spectrum in size, price and quality, and antiquers can spend days exploring possibilities. You can find most of these stores along Front Street, and a knot of them are on nearby Castle Street. There is an Historic Downtown Wilmington Antique Dealers Association, and most of the stores will provide you with a map that pinpoints the other shops. Park the car anywhere along Front Street or adjacent streets and set off on foot to discover these stores. There are so many of them that they can't all be included here, so pick up the map and go on an adventure.

About Time Antiques
30 N. Front St. • (910) 762-9902

If you're into pottery, glassware, French and Victorian furniture and linens, this is a good stop on your tour of antique shops.

Angel's Antiques and Auctions
545 Castle St. • (910) 763-1210

Another of the new group of antique shops on Castle Street, you can find furniture, glassware and collectibles in this shop, which is connected in location and work to Antique Emporium.

Antique Emporium
539 Castle St. • (910) 762-0609

What isn't in this store? Not much. Lamps, weathervanes, furniture, glass, duck decoys, jewelry, china, dolls, vintage appliances and more jam the space.

Antiques of Old Wilmington
25 S. Front St. • (910) 763-6011

Walnut and mahogany furniture, glassware and accessories can all be found at this long-time store.

Butterflies Castle Antiques
606 Castle St. • (910) 251-0405

This antique store specializes in Chinese exports, a wide variety of antique furniture and an assortment of glassware.

Butte's Antiques
302 N. Front St. • (910) 343-0059

Rather than collectibles, Butte's Antiques concentrates on 18th- and 19th-century American and English furniture and related accessories. This period-furniture store buys estates and specializes in Chippendale, Queen Anne and Federal. It also has Chinese export porcelain, chandeliers and estate silver.

Michael Moore Antiques
20 S. Front St. • (910) 763-0300

This store occupies a building with Hollingsworth American Country. These businesses complement each other with Moore's collection of collectibles, toys and furniture and Hollingsworth's reproductions.

Provenance Antiques & Interiors
306 N. Front St. • (910) 343-1590

Provenance is an upscale antiques and interiors store that carries imported English and Continental antique furniture as well as porcelain, silver, prints and clocks.

Other Areas

While the bulk of the area's antique stores are clustered downtown, there are also endless opportunities to shop around the region. Listed below are a few stores in Wilmington and Southport.

The Antique Mall
108 E. Moore St., Southport
• (910) 457-4982

Antique lovers will appreciate that this store has 15 dealers in three buildings. Here you'll find an abundance of furniture and collectibles. The mall is open Monday through Saturday 10 AM to 5 PM.

Auld Stokley Antiques
7250 Market St., Wilmington
• (910) 686-9620

This store specializes in fine antique furni-

SHOPPING

ture of mahogany, walnut, oak and pine as well as primitives.

Cape Fear Antiques Center
1606 Market St., Wilmington
- **(910) 763-1837**

With more than 8,000 square feet of quality antiques, collectibles and glassware, this place could take the better part of a day to examine.

Furniture

Beds Express
6213 B Market Street, Wilmington
- **(910) 799-5022**

Bed Express offers a full line of bedding, including futons, bunk beds, brass beds and famous name brands. The staff can special order bedroom sets from oak to contemporary styles. Bed Express will soon be expanding with three additional stores in the Wilmington area.

Ecko Furniture
424 S. College Rd., Wilmington
- **(910) 452-5442**

This is a really fun place for people seeking contemporary, quality furniture on a budget. Materials and workmanship on Ecko pieces are excellent. Those undaunted by minor assembly of some of the furniture will find their efforts well rewarded in terms of aesthetics and value.

The Furniture Patch of Calabash
10283 Beach Dr. S.W., N.C. Hwy. 179, Calabash • (910) 579-2001

This company is owned by the same family that owns Murrow Furniture Galleries in Wilmington. It carries more than 350 major lines, including Lexington, Stanley, Hickory White, Hickory Chair, Kincaid, Broyhill and National Mt. Airy. As is the case with sister store Murrow, the Furniture Patch of Calabash sells top-quality furnishings at discounted prices and ships furniture all over the world. There is a designer on staff who will help customers with interior statements that range from casual to formal. The Furniture Patch of Calabash is the last company in North Carolina before crossing the South Carolina line.

Murrow Furniture Galleries
3514 S. College Rd., Wilmington
- **(910) 799-4010**

At the other end of the street from Sutton Furniture, beyond the intersection of Shipyard Boulevard, is Murrow Furniture Galleries. It has 45,000 square feet in its showroom and sells such brands as Council Craftsmen, Century, Bernhardt, Hickory Chair, Statton, Southwood, Tropitone, Woodard, Kincaid, Maitland Smith, Baker, Bradington Young and LaBarge as well as all major medium- to high-end accessory lines such as Howard Miller clocks. Murrow's furniture is discounted, and there's a full staff of designers in-house.

The Red Dinette
5 N. Third Street, Wilmington
- **(910) 343-8920**

Newly opened at a downtown location across from the Convention & Visitors Bureau, The Red Dinette (which is actually quite green in its new incarnation) has contemporary furnishings and home accessories with a decidedly unusual twist. Handpainted furniture, eclectic items and what co-owner Greg Taylor describes as "refimitive" (Greg's own word for refined primitive) are the types of merchandise that place this new store in a category all by itself. Services here include custom handpainting and finishing. It is hard to place this store in terms of category because it is a fine arts gallery in addition to being a most unusual furniture store.

Sutton-Council Furniture
421 S. College Rd., Wilmington
- **(910) 799-9000**

Also known as Sutton's Furniture, this store is an established and reliable place to buy quality furniture in Wilmington. It has more than 40,000 square feet of showroom space where you'll see such brands of furniture as Pennsylvania House, Statton, Hickory-White, Council Craftsman, the Bob Timberlake Collection, Hickory Chair, Thayer Coggin and more. Sutton-Council is a Karastan Gallery dealer.

Windrose Furniture Company
5629 Oleander Dr., Wilmington
- **(910) 799-5793**

Located in Bradley Square across the street from the Learning Express and Harvest Moon Restaurant, Windrose carries some of the most unusual handcrafted furniture and home accessories in the region. American-made, handcrafted needlepoint rugs, rice paper batik shades, items crafted in Israel, handmade fountains, pottery and interesting clocks are just some of the offerings. It sells pencil-post beds, entertainment centers, armoires and limited edition prints. An exciting line of upholstered and slip-covered furniture by J.M. Paquet, a company owned by women, is not only beautiful and comfortable (down stuffing!), but the slipcovers are also machine washable.

WILMINGTON
Morning Star
Sunday Star-News

Courtesy New Hanover County Public Library, Louis T. Moore collection.

What is now one of the most respected newspapers in North Carolina began life above a grocery store at 3 S. Water Street, Wilmington.

The *Morning Star* was owned by William H. Bernard, a Confederate veteran. In the aftermath of war, he saw the need for courageous leadership in the South.

The first issue of the *Star*, a four page evening newspaper, appeared on September, 23 1867. The following month The Wilmington *Morning Star* made its first appearance, replacing the evening paper.

In the 1920's the *Star* began publication of the afternoon *Evening News*. The corporation then published the *Star*, the *News* and the *Sunday Star-News*.

The company was bought in 1975 by the New York Times Company. Publication of the *News* ceased that same year, leaving the *Morning Star* and the *Sunday Star-News* as the surviving papers and explains the split personality in the names.

The *Morning Star* is today the oldest daily newspaper in continuous publication in North Carolina.

Attractions

History and geography have shaped the types of attractions that flourish on the southern coast. The area's rich historical legacy manifests itself in museums, monuments, churches and living structures that speak eloquently of our past. And the proximity to the sea of a culturally vibrant city and its satellite settlements lends a distinct resort quality to the entire region.

Downtown Wilmington's historic attractions might even be called organic because they are so integral to the identity of Cape Fear. Sites such as Brunswick Town, Fort Fisher and Topsail Island's Assembly Building convey specific eras and events as no textbook or commemoration can.

The historic district of downtown Wilmington practically groans under the weight of its history, and it is the most varied single attraction in the area, easily explored on foot, by boat or by horse-drawn carriage.

By 1850 Wilmington was the largest city in North Carolina. As a port city, it was on a par with other great southern ports such as Galveston and New Orleans. But when the Atlantic Coast Line Railroad company pulled out of Wilmington in the 1960s, the city went into such a rapid decline that even its skyline was flattened by the demolition of several buildings and railroad facilities on the north side of town. Downtown was all but deserted until a core of local entrepreneurs revitalized and restored their hometown. In 1974, downtown Wilmington became the state's largest urban district listed in the National Register of Historic Places.

Many of the images of Wilmington's bustling past are preserved in the North Carolina Room at the public library's main branch at 201 Chestnut Street in downtown Wilmington. Likewise, the Cape Fear Museum and the Wilmington Railroad Museum interpret the region's history in far-reaching exhibits. Together, these places (all listed below) are excellent resources for interpreting what you see today or exploring the history further.

The region is so rich in history, it would be impossible to list every historical attraction in a book this size. So as you travel to such places as Southport's Old Smithville Burial Ground, stay alert for other sites with similar stories to tell, such as Southport's old Morse Cemetery on W. West Street and the John N. Smith Cemetery on Leonard Street off Herring Drive.

Memorials are so abundant you may miss the one at Bonnet's Creek (Moore Street north of downtown Southport), at the mouth of which "Gentleman Pirate" Stede Bonnet used to hide his corsair. (This and many other sites are on the Southport Trail, listed below.) Other memorials also bear silent testimony to the past, such as the shipwrecks that are awash at low tide and may be spied from the beaches (for example, the blockade runner *Vesta*, run aground February 4, 1864, south of Tubbs Inlet in about 10 feet of water; and the blockade runner *Bendigo*, run aground January 11, 1864, a mile southwest of Lockwood Folly Inlet in about 15 feet of water).

Many attractions are typical of the seashore: excellent fishing, fine seafood dining, the many cruise opportunities. No beach resort would be complete without water slides, go-cart tracks or batting cages, so take note of these places listed in our Kidstuff chapter — they are definitely not for kids only. These amusements, as well as miniature golf, movies and bowling, are concentrated along our most heavily traveled routes.

In Wilmington, Oleander Drive east of 41st Street is the predominant amusement strip, having several more attractions than listed here. North of Ocean Isle Beach, Beach Drive (N.C. Highway 179/904) is another strip, with its share of go-carts, miniature golf and curiosities. Near the foot of Yaupon Pier on Oak Island stands an arcade and seaside miniature-golf course. Topsail Beach and Surf City share the limelight as Topsail Island's two centers of attractions. It would be redundant to list every enterprise; you're bound to stumble across them as you gravitate toward each community's entertainment center.

Not all local attractions are summertime flings. The world's largest living Christmas tree is decorated and lit nightly during the Christmas season in Wilmington. Not your average Christmas tree, it is a 400-year-old live oak in Hilton Park, a few minutes north of downtown on N.C. Highway 133/U.S. Highway 117. Another great holiday display is Calder Court, a cul-de-sac in the King's Grant subdivision. To get there, drive north on N.C. Highway 132 (College Road) about 1.25 miles beyond the Market Street overpass. Turn right onto Kings Drive and take the next two lefts, then douse the headlights to witness one of the most flamboyant demonstrations of Christmas illumination anywhere. Cars often line up all the way down the street, not one with its lights on. The show has been catching on elsewhere in the King's Grant neighborhood, with more homes being decorated each year.

It would be difficult to overstate the importance of the region's gardens, for which North Carolina is rightly famous. The fact that the North Carolina Azalea Festival, in which garden tours are focal, is based in Wilmington makes a strong case for the southern coast's horticultural significance. Annual and perennial plantings are well-supported public works. The gardens at Orton Plantation are simply spectacular in springtime.

What follows, then, are descriptions of the area's prime general attractions followed by a brief section on the southern coast's islands. Wilmington's attractions are grouped into three subsections: Downtown Wilmington, Around Wilmington and Outside Wilmington. Within each section, all attractions are listed alphabetically. At the end of the chapter is a section on air tours of the area.

Information to supplement this guide can be obtained at several locations: the Cape Fear Coast Convention & Visitors Bureau, 24 N. Third Street, (910) 341-4030, in the 1892 courthouse building; the visitors information booth at the foot of Market Street in Wilmington; public libraries, especially New Hanover County's main branch at Third and Chestnut streets in Wilmington; in Southport, the Southport 2000 Visitors' Center, 107 E. Nash Street, (910) 457-7927; the Greater Topsail Area Chamber of Commerce, 203 Roland Drive in Surf City, (910) 328-4722 or (800) 626-2780. Of course, all the area's chambers of commerce are helpful; see our Area Overview chapter for a list.

Downtown Wilmington

Battleship North Carolina
Cape Fear River • (910) 251-5797

The battleship *North Carolina*, enshrined in a berth on Eagle Island across the river from downtown Wilmington, is dedicated to the 10,000 North Carolinians who gave their lives during World War II. Commissioned in 1941, the 44,800-ton warship wields nine 16-inch turreted guns and carries nickel-steel hull armor 16 to 18 inches thick. It was this plating that undoubtedly helped her survive at least one direct torpedo hit in 1942. In fact, the "Immortal Showboat" is renowned for its relatively small number of casualties.

The battleship came to its present home in 1961. It took a swarm of tugboats to maneuver the 728-foot vessel into its berth, where the river is only 500 feet wide. Predictably, the bow became stuck in the mud. When the tugs succeeded in freeing the ship, they failed to prevent it from slamming into Fergus's Ark, a floating restaurant moored at the foot of Princess Street. Wilmington gained a battleship and lost a restaurant.

The *North Carolina* is open for tours every day of the year from 8 AM to 8 PM May 16 to September 15 and 8 AM to 5 PM September 16 to May 15. You can drive to it easily enough, but using the Battleship River Taxi is more fun (see the *Capt. Maffitt* Sightseeing Cruise below). Choose between two self-guided tours, both of which begin with a 10-minute orientation film. A full two-hour tour takes you above

Don't Miss The Boat!

*Battleship NORTH CAROLINA —
recipient of 15 battle stars..*

- Nine decks to examine including the bridge, crew's quarters, galley, sick bay, engine room, pilot house, guns and turrets
- Newly opened Radio Central Room with original receivers and switchboard equipment
- Newly opened Coding Room where the end of the war message was decoded for the Captain
- FREE and ample parking
- Picnic sites
- Gift shop

Located on the Cape Fear River across from historic downtown Wilmington

BATTLESHIP NORTH CAROLINA

OPEN EVERY DAY:
8:00 AM – 8:00 PM
(May 16 – Sept. 15)
8:00 AM – 5:00 PM
(Sept. 16 – May 15)

P.O. Box 480 • Wilmington, NC 28402 • Info Line (910)350-1817
Business Line (910)251-5797 • EMail: ncbb55@aol.com • www.city-info.com/ncbb55.html

and below decks and includes the pilot house, turrets, a rare Kingfisher float plane, crew's quarters and the galley. The hour-long tour takes in fewer decks and eliminates much of the climbing. Only the main deck is handicapped accessible.

Tours cost $8 for those 12 and older and $4 for children 6 through 11. Discounts ($1 off) apply for senior citizens age 65 and older and for active-duty military personnel. Picnic grounds and ample RV parking adjoin the berth. There is no extra charge for unscheduled appearances by old Charlie, the alligator who makes his home near the ship at the river's edge.

Bellamy Mansion Museum of Design Arts
503 Market St. • (910) 251-3700

The assertion that Bellamy Mansion is Wilmington's premiere statement of prewar opulence and wealth is impossible to contest. ("Prewar" here refers to the War Between the States, a.k.a. the Civil War, the War of Northern Aggression, the Great Unpleasantness.) This four-story, 22-room wooden palace, completed in 1861, is a classic example of Greek Revival and Italianate architecture. Its majesty is immediately evident in 14 fluted exterior Corinthian columns. Most of the craftwork is the product of African-American slave artisans, some of whom, it is said, were granted their freedom on the steps of this very building.

Before plans were set to renovate and restore the mansion in 1972, it hadn't been lived in since 1946. Volunteer guides are sure to point out the glassed-in portion of a wall left unrestored to illustrate the extent of a 1972 fire set by an arsonist. That event was linked to the disfavor in which the Bellamy Mansion has been held by some locals, who see it as a symbol of slavery, which further legitimizes the mansion's value as a historic and cultural landmark.

The mansion's museum exhibits embrace regional architecture, landscape architecture, preservation and decorative arts. The museum hosts multimedia traveling exhibits, workshops, films, lectures, slide shows and other activities. Ongoing and painstaking restoration qualifies Bellamy Mansion as an important work in progress. Outside, the gardens have recently been restored. Restoration is planned for the slave quarters (a rare example of urban slave housing) and the carriage house.

Bellamy Mansion is open to the public Wednesday to Saturday 10 AM to 5 PM and Sunday 1 to 5 PM. Fees are $6 for adults, $3 for children 6 through 12. Members of Preservation North Carolina are admitted free.

Burgwin-Wright House
224 Market St. • (910) 762-0570

When Lord Charles Cornwallis, still in danger of a rebel pursuit, fled his slim victory near Guilford Courthouse in central North Carolina in 1781, he repaired to Wilmington, then a town of 200 houses. He lodged at the gracious Georgian home of John Burgwin (pronounced "bur-GWIN"), a wealthy planter and politician, and made it his headquarters.

The home, completed in 1770, is distinguished by two-story porches on two sides and six levels of tiered gardens. The massive ballast-stone foundation remains from the previously abandoned town jail, beneath which was a dungeon where Cornwallis held his prisoners. Volunteers for the National Society of the Colonial Dames, the building's present owners, can point out the trap door leading to it. Underground, an old brick tunnel communicates to the river. Rumored to have concealed pirate treasure or slaves on the Underground Railroad, it is only a sluice for a stream called Jacob's Run.

The Burgwin-Wright House is one of the great restoration/reconstruction achievements in the state, and visitors may peruse the carefully appointed rooms and period furnishings for $3 (students, $1). The museum is open Tuesday through Saturday 10 AM to 4 PM.

INSIDERS' TIP

A great way to get to Masonboro Island is to rent a daysailer at the Blockade Runner Resort Hotel on Wrightsville Beach, provided you know how to sail.

VISIT TRYON PALACE HISTORIC SITES & GARDENS AND
EXPERIENCE TWO CENTURIES OF NORTH CAROLINA HERITAGE.

Tryon Palace
HISTORIC SITES & GARDENS

601 Pollock Street • New Bern, North Carolina • 1-800-767-1560 or 252-514-4900

Cape Fear Museum
814 Market St. • (910) 341-4350

For an overview of the cultural and natural histories of the Cape Fear region from prehistory to the present, the Cape Fear Museum, established in 1898, stands unsurpassed. A miniature re-creation of the second battle of Fort Fisher and a remarkable scale model of the Wilmington waterfront, c. 1863, are of special interest. The Michael Jordan Discovery Gallery (which includes a popular display case housing many of the basketball star's personal items) is a long-term interactive natural history exhibit for the entire family.

The Discovery Gallery includes a crawl-through beaver lodge, Pleistocene-era fossils and an entertaining Venus's-flytrap model you can feed with stuffed "bugs." Children's activities, videos, special events and acclaimed touring exhibits contribute to making the Cape Fear Museum not only one of the primary repositories of local history but also a place where learning is fun.

The museum is open Tuesday through Saturday 9 AM to 5 PM, Sunday 2 to 5 PM and is handicapped accessible. Admission is $2 for adults 18 through 65; $1 for children 5 through 17, college students with valid ID and seniors older than 65. Children younger than 5 and Museum Associates are admitted free. Admission is free to all on the first and third Sundays of each month and the first day of each month.

Capt. Maffitt Sightseeing Cruise
Riverfront Park • (910) 343-1611, (800) 676-0162

Named for Capt. John Newland Maffitt, one of the Confederacy's most successful blockade runners, the *Capt. Maffitt* is a converted World War II Navy launch affording 45-minute sightseeing cruises along the Cape Fear River with live historical narration. Cruises set out at 11 AM and 3 PM daily from Memorial Day to Labor Day. The *Capt. Maffitt* is available for charter throughout the year, and it doubles as the Battleship River Taxi during the summer. No reservations are necessary, and it runs on the quarter-hour from 10 AM to 5 PM outside of cruise times.

Chandler's Wharf
Water and Ann Sts. • (910) 815-3510

More than 100 years ago, Chandler's Wharf was choked with mercantile warehouses, its sheds filled with naval stores, tools, cotton and guano, its wharves lined with merchantmen. A disastrous (and suspicious) fire in August 1874 changed the site forever. In the late 1970s, Chandler's Wharf became an Old Wilmington riverfront reconstruction site, complete with a museum and seven historic ships moored at the adjoining docks.

Today, much of the flavor — and none of the odor — of the 1870s remains, and Chandler's Wharf is again a business district, or, more accurately, a shopping and dining district. Two historic homes transformed into shops stand on the cobblestone street, beside wooden sidewalks and the rails of the former waterfront railway. You'll find a jewelry/gemstone shop, two restaurants (Elijah's and The Pilot House) and boutiques set amid flowers, a small herb garden, benches and nautical artifacts.

On the corner immediately north, a renovated warehouse contains more shops. The tugboat *John Taxis*, reputedly the oldest in America, sits above the water's edge. (For more on wharf businesses, see our Restaurants and Shopping chapters.)

Chestnut Street United Presbyterian Church
710 N. Sixth St. • (910) 762-1074

This tiny church, built in 1858 and originally a mission chapel of First Presbyterian Church (see below), is a remarkable example of Stick Style, or Carpenter Gothic, architecture. Its exterior details include decorative bargeboards with repeating acorn pendants, board-and-batten construction, a louvered bell tower (with carillon) and paired Gothic windows.

When the congregation, then slaves, formed in 1858 under the auspices of the mother church, the chapel was surrendered by the mother church to the new, black congregation, which finally purchased the building in 1867. The congregation's many distinguished members have included the first black president of Biddle University (now Johnson C. Smith University), the publisher of Wilmington's first black newspaper, a member of the original Fisk University Jubilee Singers, the first black graduate of MIT, and North Carolina's first black physician.

First Baptist Church
529 N. Fifth St. • (910) 763-2647

Even having lost its stunning 197-foot, copper-sheathed steeple to Hurricane Fran in 1996, First Baptist is still Wilmington's tallest church, if only in the hearts of the townspeople, many of whom are rallying to rebuild it. For years this tower, the taller of two, had been known to visibly sway even in an "average" wind.

Being literally the first Baptist church in the region, this is the mother church of many other Baptist churches in Wilmington. Its congregation dates to 1808, and construction of the red brick building began in 1859. The church was not completed until 1870 because of the Civil War, when Confederate and Union forces in turn used the higher steeple as a lookout. Its architecture is Early English Gothic Revival with hints of Richardson Romanesque, as in its varicolored materials and its horizontal mass relieved by the verticality of the spires, with their narrow, gabled vents. Inside, the pews, galleries and ceiling vents are of native heart pine.

The church offices occupy an equally interesting building next door, the Conoley House (1859), which exhibits such classic Italianate elements as frieze vents and brackets, and fluted wooden columns.

First Presbyterian Church
125 S. Third St. • (910) 762-6688

Organized as early as 1760, this congregation continues to have among its members some of the most influential Wilmingtonians. The Rev. Joseph R. Wilson was pastor from 1874 until 1885; his son, Thomas Woodrow Wilson, grew up to become slightly more famous. The church itself, with its finials and soaring stone spire topped with a metal rooster (a symbol of the Protestant Reformation), blends Late Gothic and Renaissance styles,

Cape Fear Museum
One-stop shopping for regional history!

Michael Jordan
Discovery Gallery
Civil War artifacts
Fort Fisher battle diorama
Educational programs
Changing exhibitions

814 Market Street
Downtown Wilmington
910.341.4350

Hours:
Tue–Sat 9-5/ Sun 2-5
Open 7 days a week
Memorial Day through
Labor Day

Admission charged

---

and is the congregation's fourth home, the previous three having succumbed to fire.

During the Union occupation, the lectern Bible was stolen from the third church, which burned on New Year's Eve, 1925. The stolen Bible was returned years later to become all that remains of the sanctuary. Today, intricate tracery distinguishes fine stained-glass windows along the nave as well as the vast West window and the chancel rose. The 1928 E.M. Skinner organ, with its original pneumatic console, is used regularly. Handsomely stenciled beams, arches and trusses support a steep gabled roof.

Downstairs is the Kenan Chapel, with its transverse Romanesque arches. The education building behind the sanctuary is quintessential Tudor, complete with exterior beams set in stucco, wide squared arches, casement windows with diamond panes, interior ceiling beams and eccentric compound chimneys. Having undergone major renovation in the early 1990s, First Presbyterian is an impressive sight. Its carillon can be heard daily throughout the historic district.

Horse-Drawn Carriage Tour
Market St. between Water and Front Sts.
• (910) 251-8889

See historic downtown Wilmington the old-fashioned way — by horse-drawn carriage. This half-hour ride in a French-top surrey is narrated by a knowledgeable driver in 19th-century garb, who offers interesting anecdotes about the historic mansions and waterfront along the way. At busy times such as Azalea Festival and Riverfest, horse-drawn trolleys are used.

Tours operate Tuesday through Sunday 10 AM to 10 PM, April through October. In November, December and March, the carriages roll Friday 7 to 10 PM, Saturday 11 AM to 10 PM and Sunday 11 AM to 4 PM. Ride by appointment during January and February. The individual fee is $8; $4 for children 11 and younger.

Henrietta II
Docked at the Wilmington Hilton, Water St., Wilmington • (910) 343-1611, (800) 676-0162

Celebrating its 10th anniversary on the Cape Fear River, this 149-passenger sternwheel riverboat offers an ideal vantage point for viewing the riverside sights or dancing and dining in a large salon complete with bar. From April through December, the *Henrietta II* keeps a varied cruise schedule that includes Entertainment Dinner Cruises, Narrated Sightseeing Cruises, Sunset Cruises, Moonlight Cruises and special events cruises such as the Sweetheart Cruise in February,

168 • ATTRACTIONS

the Azalea Festival Cruises in April, a Fireworks Cruise on July 4, Riverfest Cruises in October, Fall Nature Cruises in November and the New Year's Eve Party Cruise.

Weddings and private-party charters are welcome year-round. Call for schedules and reservations.

Oakdale Cemetery
520 N. 15th St.

When Nance Martin died at sea in 1857, her body was preserved, seated in a chair, in a large cask of rum. Six months later she was interred at Oakdale Cemetery, cask and all. Her monument and many other curious, beautiful and historic markers are to be found within the labyrinth of Oakdale Cemetery, Wilmington's first municipal burial ground, opened in 1855.

At the cemetery office, you can pick up a free map detailing some of the more interesting interments, such as the volunteer firefighter buried with the faithful dog that gave its life trying to save his master, and Mrs. Rose O'Neal Greenhow, a Confederate courier who drowned while running the blockade at Fort Fisher in 1864. Amid the profusion of monuments lies a field oddly lacking in markers — the mass grave of hundreds of victims of the 1862 yellow fever epidemic.

The architecture of Oakdale's monuments, its Victorian landscaping and the abundance of dogwood trees make Oakdale beautiful in every season. The cemetery is open until 5 PM every day.

The Riverwalk
Riverfront Park, along Water St.

The heart and soul of downtown Wilmington is its riverfront. Once a bustling, gritty confusion of warehouses, docks and sheds — all suffused with the odor of turpentine — the wharf was the state's most important commercial port. Experience Wilmington's charm and historical continuity by strolling the Riverwalk. Dining, shopping and lodging establishments now line the red-brick road, and live entertainment takes place at the small Riverfront Stage on Saturday and Sunday evenings from June to early August. Check with the visitors information booth at the foot of Market Street for schedules.

Immediately to the north, schooners, pleasure boats and replicas of historic ships frequently visit the municipal dock. Coast Guard cutters and the occasional British naval vessel dock beyond the Federal Court House; some allow touring, especially during festivals. Benches, picnic tables, a fountain and snack vendors complete the scene, one of Wilmington's most popular.

St. James Episcopal Church and Burial Ground
25 S. Third St. • (910) 763-1628

St. James is the oldest church in continuous use in Wilmington, and it wears its age well. The parish was established in 1729 at Brunswick Town across the river (also see St. Philip's Parish, below). The congregation's original Wilmington church wasn't completed until 1770. It was seized in 1781 by Tarleton's Dragoons under Cornwallis. Tarleton had the pews removed, and the church became a stable.

The original church was taken down in 1839 and some of its materials used to construct the present church, an Early Gothic Revival building with pinnacled square towers, battlements and lancet windows. The architect, Thomas U. Walter, is best known for his 1865 cast-iron dome on the U.S. Capitol.

A repeat performance of pew-tossing took place during the Civil War, when occupying Federal forces used the church as a hospital. A letter written by the pastor asking President Lincoln for reparation still exists. The letter was never delivered, having been completed the day news arrived of Lincoln's assassination.

Within the church hangs a celebrated painting of Christ (*Ecce Homo*) captured from one of the Spanish pirate ships that attacked Brunswick Town in 1748. The sanctuary also boasts a handsome wood-slat ceiling and beam-and-truss construction. The graveyard at the corner of Fourth and Market streets was in use from 1745 to 1855 and bears considerable historic importance. Here lies the patriot Cornelius Harnett, remembered for antagonizing the British by reading the Declaration of Independence aloud at the Halifax Courthouse in 1776. He died in a British prison during the war. America's first playwright, Thomas Godfrey, is also memorialized here.

The cemetery once occupied grounds over which Market Street now stretches, which explains why utility workers periodically (and inadvertently) unearth human remains outside the present burial ground.

Visitors are welcome to take self-guided tours of the church between 9 AM and early afternoon when services are not underway. Informative brochures are available in the vestibule.

St. John's Museum of Art
114 Orange St. • (910) 763-0281

Even if St. John's didn't possess one of the world's major collections of Mary Cassatt color prints, it would still be a potent force in the Southeast's art culture. Housed in three distinctive restored buildings (one a former church), the museum boasts a fine sculpture garden, an outstanding collection of Jugtown pottery, touring exhibits, a working studio for art classes, lectures and workshops and an extensive survey of regional and national artists, all of them world-class. Educational programs for children, films, concerts and a gift shop are among the museum's offerings.

Admission is $2 per adult, $5 per family and $1 for children younger than 18. Children younger than 5 and museum members may enter free. Admission on the first Sunday of every month is free to all.

St. Marks Episcopal Church
600 Grace St. • (910) 763-3210

Established in 1875, this was the first Episcopal church for blacks in North Carolina, and it has conducted services uninterrupted since that time. The building (completed in 1875) is a simple Gothic Revival structure with a buttressed nave and octagonal bell tower.

St. Mary's Roman Catholic Church
412 Ann St. • (910) 762-5491

Numerous historical writers have referred to this Spanish Baroque edifice (built 1908-11) as a major architectural creation, often pointing out the elaborate tiling, especially inside the dome, which embraces most of this church's cross-vaulted interior space.

The plan of the brick building is based on the Greek cross, with enormous semicircular stained-glass windows in the transept vaults, arcade windows in the apse and symmetrical square towers in front. Over the main entrance, in stained glass, is an imitation of da Vinci's *Last Supper*. A coin given by Maria Anna Jones, the first black Catholic in North Carolina, is placed inside the cornerstone.

St. Paul's Evangelical Lutheran Church
603 Market St. • (910) 762-4882

Responding to the growing number of German Lutherans in Wilmington, North Carolina's Lutheran Synod organized St. Paul's in 1858. Services began in 1861, as the Civil War broke. Construction came to a halt when the German artisans working on the building volunteered for the 18th North Carolina Regiment and became the first local unit in active duty. The building was occupied, and badly damaged, by Union troops after the fall of Fort Fisher in early 1865. Horses were stabled in the building and its wooden furnishings used as firewood.

The completed church was dedicated in 1869, only to burn in 1894. It was promptly rebuilt. There have been several additions and renovations since. Today the building is remarkable for its blend of austere Greek Revival elements outside (such as the entablature, pediments and pilasters) and Gothic Revival (such as the slender spire, clustered interior piers, and large lancet windows). Also notable are its color-patterned slate roof and copper finials and the gently arcing pew arrangement. Paneling removed during renovations in 1995-96 uncovered beautiful stenciling on the ceiling panels and ribs in the vestibule, nave and chancel.

Temple of Israel
1 S. Fourth St. • (910) 762-0000

The first Jewish temple in North Carolina, this unique Moorish Revival building was erected in 1875-76 for a Reform congregation formed in 1867. Its two square towers are topped by small onion domes, and the paired, diamond-paned windows exhibit a mix of architrave shapes, including Romanesque, trefoil and Anglo-Saxon arches. The temple was shared for two years with neighboring Methodists when the Methodist church was destroyed in 1886.

Thalian Hall/City Hall
310 Chestnut St., Wilmington
• (910) 343-3664

Since its renovation and expansion in the late 1980s, the name has been, more accurately, Thalian Hall Center for the Performing Arts. And yes, it does share the same roof with City Hall. Conceived as a combined political and cultural center, Thalian Hall was built between 1855 and 1858. During its first 75 years, the hall brought every great national performer — and some surprising celebrities — to its stage: Lillian Russell, Buffalo Bill Cody, John Philip Sousa, Oscar Wilde and Tom Thumb, to name a few.

That tradition continues. Full-scale musicals, light opera and internationally renowned dance companies are only a portion of Thalian's consistent, high-quality programming. Today the center consists of two theaters — the Main Stage and the Studio Theater — plus a ballroom (which doubles as the city council chambers).

With its Corinthian columns and ornate proscenium, it's no wonder Thalian Hall is on the National Register of Historic Places. Tours are offered at 11 AM and 3 PM Monday through Friday and at 2 PM Saturday. The cost is $5 for adults, $3 for children 12 and younger. Group rates are available.

Wilmington Adventure Walking Tour
Foot of Market St. • (910) 763-1785

Lifelong Wilmington resident Bob Jenkins, the man with the straw hat and walking cane, walks fast but talks slowly, passionately and knowledgeably about his hometown. Expounding upon architectural details, family lineage and historic events, Bob whisks you through 250 years of history in about an hour. You'll see residences, churches and public buildings. Tours begin at the flagpole at the foot of Market Street at 10 AM and 2 PM daily, weather permitting. A $10 fee is charged. Although no reservations are required, it's best to call ahead, especially in summer.

Wilmington Railroad Museum
501 Nutt St. • (910) 763-2634

The dramatic transformation that Wilmington underwent when the Atlantic Coast Line Railroad closed its local operations in the late 1950s are clearly borne out by this museum's fine photographs and artifacts. Beyond history, the Railroad Museum is a kind of funhouse for people fascinated by trains and train culture. And who isn't?

For $2 ($1 for children ages 6 through 11), you can climb into a real steam locomotive and clang its bell for as long as your kids will let you. Inside, volunteers (some of whom are walking histories themselves) will guide you to exhibits explaining why the 19th-century Wilmington & Weldon Railroad was called the "Well Done," and that the ghost of beheaded flagman Joe Baldwin is behind the Maco Light — at least one volunteer claims to have seen it. Ask about the museum's Memories book in which visitors are encouraged to share their favorite train memories; it includes entries by famous people who have visited Wilmington.

The museum building was the railroad's freight traffic office and is listed on the National Register of Historic Places. Visitors can run the model trains in the enormous railroad diorama upstairs, which is maintained by the Cape Fear Model Railroad Club (for membership information contact the museum). Children will also enjoy the railroad theaterette. Adult programming, children's workshops and group discounts are available. The museum also invites you to "conduct" your birthday parties on its caboose; the rental fee includes souvenirs and a tour of the museum, and train-theme refreshments can be arranged.

Museum hours are 10 AM to 5 PM Tuesday through Saturday and 1 to 5 PM Sunday.

Zebulon Latimer House
126 S. Third St. • (910) 762-0492

This magnificent Italianate building, built by a prosperous merchant from Connecticut, dates from 1852 and is remarkable for its original furnishings and art work. The house boasts fine architectural details such as window cornices and wreaths in the frieze openings, all made of cast iron, and a piazza with intricate, wrought-iron tracery.

Behind the building stands a rare (and possibly Wilmington's oldest) example of urban slave quarters, now a private residence. What sets the Latimer House apart from most other museums is the fact that it was continuously lived in for more than a century, until it became home to the Lower Cape Fear Historical Society in 1963. It has the look of a home where the family has just stepped out.

The Historical Society is one of the primary sources for local genealogical and historical research. For information on membership write to P.O. Box 813, Wilmington, NC 28402.

Guided house tours are offered Tuesday through Saturday 10 AM to 4 PM (adults $3, youths 11 and younger, $1). Walk & Talk Tours, which encompass about 12 blocks of the historic district and last 90 minutes, are given for $5 every Wednesday at 10 AM. The museum is open Tuesday 10 AM to 4 PM, Wednesday and Thursday 10 AM to 1 PM and by appointment by calling (910) 763-5869.

Around Wilmington

EUE/Screen Gems Studios Tour
1223 N. 23rd St., Wilmington
• (910) 343-3500

They don't call Wilmington "Wilmywood" for nothing, and Screen Gems Studios, the biggest film operation on the East coast, is the prime reason. At the head of the entire operation is Frank Capra, Jr., son of the great film director who brought us the Jimmy Stewart classics, *It's a Wonderful Life* and *Mr. Smith Goes to Washington*, as well as *It Happened One Night*, and *Lost Horizon*. You can tour the studios and visit working sets of current productions — actually see what the actors see from their side of the camera.

In Stage Four, you'll see the world's largest blue screen (which made Charles Durning appear to fall from his skyscraper office in *The Hudsucker Proxy*). Along the way, you may see vehicles and wagons used in feature films like *The Road to Wellville* or *The Wedding* or the gimble used for typhoon scenes in the movie Virus. You'll visit the backlot, which looks like a big-city street — here's the manhole cover seen at the beginning of the original Ninja Turtles movie.

Tour guides are film aficionados who will tell you more than you ever dreamed about the movie industry in Wilmywood. Take the tour again from time to time and the experience will likely be different — you may see stuntmen at their dangerous work, or dancers or rehearsals in progress, all depending on which productions are in town at the time. Tours last about one hour, and two are regularly scheduled each Saturday at noon and 2 PM. More tours may be added during the summer, given the demand. Admission costs $5, and reservations are strongly recommended; tours often fill weeks in advance.

Greenfield Lake and Gardens
U.S. 421 S.

In springtime the colors here are simply eye-popping. In summer the algae-covered waters and Spanish moss are reminders of the days when this was an unpopulated cypress swamp. In winter the bare tree trunks rise from the lake with stark verticality. Herons, egrets and ducks are regular visitors, as are hawks and cardinals. The 5-mile lakeview drive is a pleasure in any season, and there's a paved path suitable for walking or cycling surrounding the entire lake. Greenfield Lake is 2 miles south of downtown Wilmington along S. Third Street. (Also see our chapter on Sports, Fitness and Parks.)

Jungle Rapids Family Fun Park
5320 Oleander Dr., Wilmington
• **(910) 791-0666**

This self-contained amusement mecca includes the only true water park in eastern North Carolina plus more game attractions than a family could exhaust in a week. The quarter-mile-long Grand Prix GoKart track features bridge overpasses, banked turns, timing devices and one- and two-passenger cars. Children under 56 inches tall must ride with licensed adult drivers.

The water park includes five excellent slides — an open slide in which you ride down on a tube plus the four-tube slide called the Volcanic Express. Floating the Lazy River, which encircles the water park, is great for a relaxing bask. Lifeguards are always on duty, and there are plenty of lockers, lounges, tables and umbrellas.

Also worthwhile are a wonderful new wave pool, the Kiddie Splash Pool (with four kiddie slides), jungle-themed miniature golf, the adrenaline-pumping Alien Invader Laser Tag, the high-tech arcade featuring more than 100 games ranging from the classic to state-of-the-art and the air-conditioned Kids Jungle (Wilmington's largest indoor playground, for children 10 and younger).

Jungle Rapids caters kids' parties on site and off, offers meeting and function rooms (the largest accommodating 300 people) and even offers corporate outings and picnics for up to 3,000 people. The Big Splash Cafe and Pizzeria offers an ample menu during park hours. Bag lunches are also available for water-park guests.

The water park is open from 11 AM to 7 PM every day in the warm season. The "dry park" is open all year from 10 AM to 11 PM (until midnight on Friday and Saturday). (Also see our Kidstuff chapter).

New Hanover County Extension Service Arboretum
6206 Oleander Dr., Wilmington
• **(910) 452-6393**

This 6-acre teaching and learning facility is the only arboretum in southeastern North Carolina. An extension of the University of North Carolina, the arboretum was formally opened in 1989 and is still in the midst of development. These gardens rank among the finer theme gardens in the area. Boardwalks and paths wind through a profusion of plants, grasses, flowers, trees, shrubs, herbs and vegetables, and there is plenty of shaded seating. Several sections, such as the Herb Garden, with its variety of medicinal, culinary, fragrance and tea species, are sponsored by local garden clubs.

The arboretum assists commercial and private horticultural enterprises and helps residents create attractive home landscapes. This last mission is served by the Garden Hotline, (910) 452-6396, where volunteer master gardeners field questions about horticulture from 9 AM to 5 PM. The arboretum also sponsors and hosts seminars, classes (including hunting safety) and workshops. Some of the programs offer certificates upon completion.

Admission to the arboretum is free and hours are from 8 AM to dusk. Volunteer docents lead tours on request. Donations are

JUNGLE RAPIDS
WILMINGTON'S ONLY REAL WATERPARK!

Featuring Water Fun...
* North Carolina's Newest Waterslides
* Wave Pool
* Kiddie Slide
* Lazy River
* Kiddie Splash Pool

Birthday Parties
Family Reunions
Company Outings
Corporate Meetings

And More...
* Miniature Golf
* Alien Invaders Lazer Tag
* Grand Prix Go Kart Track
* Over 100 Arcade Games
* Kids Jungle Indoor Playgroun
* Big Splash Cafe and Pizzeria
* Meeting Rooms
* Full Service Catering

* Waterfun Open on a Seasonal Basis
For More Information or Group Rates call (910) 791-0666
5320 Oleander Drive Wilmington, North Carolina 28403
Open All Year, Everyday!

---

welcome and much needed. Enter the grounds from Oleander Drive (U.S. Highway 76) immediately east of Greenville Loop Road and west of the Bradley Creek bridge. And, yes, the arboretum is available for weddings.

Stadium Batting Cages
5570 Oleander Dr., Wilmington
• (910) 791-9660

Hallmarks of resort towns are the batting cages, and these are the only ones for miles around. The throwing machines are the armature type, not the kind with spinning wheels that throw wild every third pitch. There are baseball and softball cages pitching at a variety of speeds, and the fastballs are mighty fast. Helmets and bats are included. One $1 token gets you 12 pitches, and you can save on 72 for $5. It's a great way to practice your swing, vent some steam or spend an otherwise routine lunch hour. Hours are 2 to 10 PM weekdays, 10 AM to 10 PM Saturdays and 12 to 9 PM Sundays.

Outside Wilmington

Cape Fear River Circle Tour
Southport-Fort Fisher Ferry, U.S. Hwy. 421, south of Kure Beach
• (910) 457-6942

You can tour the history and culture of the Lower Cape Fear by incorporating the Southport-Fort Fisher ferry into a circular driving tour that could take several hours, given the most selective stopping, or could easily last several days if you choose to explore every stop in detail.

A brochure available from the ferry or the Cape Fear Coast Convention & Visitors Bureau, 24 N. Third St., Wilmington, (910) 341-4030, directs you around a loop that connects Wilmington, Pleasure Island, Southport and eastern Brunswick County and includes seven major attractions (all free unless otherwise noted): Battleship *North Carolina* (fee), Orton Plantation Gardens (fee), Brunswick Town/Fort Anderson, Southport Maritime Museum (fee), CP & L's Brunswick Nuclear Plant, North Carolina Aquarium (fee), and Fort Fisher Civil War Museum.

Total driving time is about two hours, including about 40 minutes on the ferry. The brochure provides information on the attractions and ferry schedule.

Poplar Grove Plantation
10200 U.S. Hwy. 17, Scotts Hill
• (910) 686-9518

This 1850 Greek Revival house and the 628-acre plantation were supported by as many as 64 slaves prior to the Civil War. Today, costumed guides lead visitors and recount the plantation's history. Skills important to daily 19th-century life, such as weaving, smithery and basketry, are frequently demonstrated. A restaurant and country store add to Poplar Grove's attraction, as do the many events held here throughout the year, including Halloween hayrides and the Medieval Festival in June.

Listed on the National Register of Historic Places, Poplar Grove Plantation is 8 miles outside Wilmington on U.S. 17 at the Pender County line. It is open to the public Monday through Saturday 9 AM to 5 PM and Sunday noon to 5 PM. Fees are $7 for adults, $6 for senior citizens 62 and older and military personnel with active IDs and $3 for students ages 6 to 15.

Wrightsville Beach

Blockade Runner Scenic Cruises
Waynick Blvd. • (910) 350-2628

In the warm season, a cruise aboard the 40-foot pontoon vessel along the calm Intracoastal Waterway affords a fine view of the landscape and wildlife of the tidal environment. The Blockade Runner Resort Hotel sponsors nature excursions and shuttles to Masonboro Island at 10 AM daily during the summer.

Excursions cost $25 per adult, $15 for children 12 and younger. Shuttles cost $10 per person. One-hour harbor cruises are available all day and cost $10 per person. Sunset cruises ($18 per adult, $10 per child) sail from 6:30 to 8:30 PM, and coolers are welcome. Walk-ins are accepted, but reservations are recommended in the high season and required for narrated nature excursions.

Wrightsville Beach Museum of History
303 W. Salisbury St. • (910) 256-2569

The newest attraction on Wrightsville Beach, this museum is housed in the Myers cottage, one of the oldest cottages on the beach (built in 1907). The museum presents beach history and lifeways through permanent exhibits featuring a scale model of the oldest built-up section of the beach, photos, furniture, artifacts, a slide show and recorded oral histories, plus rotating exhibits on loggerhead turtles, surfing, the Civil War, shipwrecks, hurricanes and beach nightlife at such bygone attractions as the Lumina Pavilion. Admission is by donation.

Upon crossing the drawbridge, bear left at the "Welcome to Wrightsville Beach" sign; the museum is on the right near the volleyball courts beyond the fire station.

Carolina Beach and Kure Beach

Carolina Beach Boardwalk

Spanning the oceanfront in the middle of town, the boardwalk is the heart and soul of Carolina Beach. It includes the actual beachside boardwalk plus paved walks bordering a multitude of arcades, nightclubs, miniature golf courses, pubs, billiard parlors and novelty shops. Colorful and crowded in summertime, the entire area has the aura of an amusement park. Several restaurants are a short walk from the beach, and parking is nearby. The strand along the boardwalk is the site of Carolina Beach's annual Beach Music Festival, which draws thousands of shagging music lovers each July (see our Annual Events chapter).

Jubilee Amusement Park
1000 N. Lake Park Blvd., Carolina Beach • (910) 458-9017

With 20 rides, three water slides, kiddie pool, three go-cart tracks, an arcade, gift shop, picnic area and live entertainment, Jubilee Park is a mecca for families. New additions include the Rain Room (walk through a cooling mist without getting drenched), the Human Slingshot (an open, "reverse bunjee" capsule that shoots you safely 150 feet straight up!). Most of the rides are kiddie-size, and there is no admission fee.

Prices for individual rides start at a little over a dollar for kiddie rides. Money-saving all-day passes cost $12.95 ($8.95 for kids younger than 5) and permit rides. Season passes are the best bargain ($44.95). Waterslides and go-carts are priced separately. Height requirements apply for go-carts other than the junior racetrack ($2.95 per session), and the NASCAR track ($4 per session) also requires a driver's license. An all-day waterslide pass costs $7.95, and the price comes down after 5 PM.

ATTRACTIONS • 175

Fort Fisher was the site of the largest land-sea battle fought during the Civil War.

Fort Fisher-Southport Ferry
U.S. Hwy. 421, south of Kure Beach
- **(910) 457-6942**

More than transportation, this half-hour crossing is a journey into the natural and social history of the Cape Fear River. You'll have excellent views of Federal Point, Zeke's Island and The Rocks from the upper deck. On the Southport side, you'll spot historic Price's Creek Lighthouse at the mouth of the inlet. The crew are knowledgeable, and the cabin is air-conditioned. When traveling between Southport and New Hanover County, timing your trip to the ferry schedule makes getting there half the fun. (See our Getting Around chapter for schedules.)

One-way fees are 50¢ for pedestrians, $1 for cyclists, $3 for vehicles less than 20 feet in length and $6 for vehicles or combinations up to 32 feet long. The ferry can be part of a wide-ranging, self-directed car-and-foot circle tour that includes seven free attractions and museums in Wilmington, Southport and Pleasure Island. See our listing for the Cape Fear River Circle Tour in the Outside Wilmington section above.

Fort Fisher State Historic Site
U.S. 421, south of Kure Beach
- **(910) 458-5538**

Fort Fisher was the last Confederate stronghold to fall to Union forces during the War Between the States. It was the linchpin of the Confederate Army's Cape Fear Defense System, which included forts Caswell, Anderson and Johnson and a series of batteries. Largely due to the tenacity of its defenders, the port of Wilmington was never entirely sealed by the Union blockade until January 1865. The Union bombardment of Fort Fisher was the heaviest naval demonstration in history up to that time.

Today all that remains are the earthworks, the largest in the South. The rest of the fort has been claimed by the ocean. However, a fine museum, uniformed demonstrations and reenactments make Fort Fisher well worth a visit (in fact, it's the third most-visited historic site in the state). Don't miss the underwater archaeology exhibit, Hidden Beneath the Waves, housed in a small outbuilding beside the parking lot. Thirty-minute guided tours allow you to walk the earthworks, and slide programs take place every half-hour.

The Cove, a tree-shaded picnic area across the road, overlooks the ocean and makes an excellent place to relax or walk. However, swimming here is discouraged due to dangerous currents and underwater hazards. Since Fort Fisher is an archaeological site, metal detectors are prohibited.

Museum hours are 9 AM to 5 PM Monday through Saturday and 1 to 5 PM Sunday. It is open all year, and admission is free (donations are requested). The site, about 19 miles south of Wilmington, was once commonly known as Federal Point. The ferry from Southport is an excellent and timesaving way to get there from Brunswick County. Also close by are the North Carolina Aquarium (see next entry) and the Fort Fisher State Recreation Area (see our Sports, Fitness and Parks chapter).

North Carolina Aquarium at Fort Fisher
Ft. Fisher Blvd., Kure Beach
- **(910) 458-8257**

Housing the largest shark tank in the state, the aquarium at Fort Fisher also boasts an intriguing ray and skate tank. But the touch tank seems to elicit the greatest reaction from visitors — especially those who squeamishly pick up a horseshoe crab or get squirted by a startled conch. The outdoor pond is filled with fish and turtles, and the barn swallows that nest beneath the building zoom in and out just above visitors' heads. Field trips, films and live animal exhibits are offered, and nature trails loop through the grounds.

INSIDERS' TIP

UNCW's Ev-Henwood Nature Preserve at 6150 Rock Creek Road, (910) 962-3197 or (910) 253-6066, in the Town Creek community along the Cape Fear River, offers walking trails, interpretive displays and a picnic area. Admission is free!

Go Wild All Night — Join a Turtle Watch!

Summertime nightlife at our beaches also means wildlife. North Carolina's beaches are the northernmost nesting area for loggerhead turtles, fascinating creatures threatened with extinction. All along our shores, people concerned for the survival of these ancient denizens turn out on summer nights to help protect their nests and hatchlings.

The loggerhead (*Caretta caretta*) is among the largest of the sea turtles. Adults average more than 3 feet in length and weigh about 300 pounds. Between early May and late October, the mother turtle creeps ashore at the very spot where she herself was hatched to lay her eggs along the dunes above the high-water line. She covers them over to incubate them in the warm sand. A single female may lay 120 spherical eggs at once and repeat the process up to six times a season. The hatchlings begin to appear in July, with the peak hatching period being September. Hatching usually occurs at night, an entire nest erupting all at once into scores of cute, three-inch-long hatchlings.

Getting across the beach strand and into the water is a perilous journey for the little critters. The baby turtles make a great meal for ravenous crabs, gulls and raccoons, which is why loggerhead moms lay eggs in such great numbers. The hatchlings can even get stranded in a human footprint. This is where humans can help.

Under the auspices of the North Carolina Wildlife Commission, turtle conservation programs along our coast provide much-needed protection to turtles and education to humans. Certain volunteers are trained to render emergency medical services. It is otherwise illegal even to touch such federally protected species unless they're injured or in serious distress. Volunteers are always needed to assist with locating and marking nests. When nests are due to hatch, volunteers smooth out turtle runways to help the newborns in their run to the sea. The primary roles of the turtle project are to protect all

— continued on next page

A loggerhead mom lays her eggs in a nest high above the waterline.

marine turtles, to educate the public, to report turtle activity and to stay out of the turtles' way. As turtle-watchers are fond of saying, the right of a turtle to be is more important than our right to see.

The Topsail Turtle Project (TTP), organized in 1986, sponsors weekly talks for the public at the Surf City Town Hall, (910) 328-4131, on Thursday at 4 PM during the summer. It also provides free volunteer training in late April and maintains a small turtle exhibit at Town Hall. TTP is now in the process of establishing the Karen Beasley Sea Turtle Rescue and Rehabilitation Center, the first of its kind in the state, at Topsail Beach. Topsail Island gets an average of 100 turtle nests each year.

It's easy to help, mainly by observing a few simple guidelines:
- Avoid disturbing a turtle crawling to or from the ocean.
- Avoid leaving outdoor lights on all night, particularly at the oceanfront. Lights can disorient turtles and cause them to lose their direction.
- Keep a respectful distance from nesting turtles and don't shine lights in their eyes or harass them in any way. (Besides, it's illegal.) Sit quietly and watch nature take its marvelous course.
- Report turtle sightings and turtle tracks (they may indicate the location of a nest). Adult turtle tracks look like single bulldozer tracks heading straight into the water.
- Never disturb a nest. This also means avoiding the dune line in nesting season when driving off-road vehicles on the beach. Known nests are clearly marked with brightly colored ribbon.
- Pick up trash. That's right! Keeping beaches clean will help reduce the need for sanitation machinery that can crush turtle eggs.

You can help. Volunteering requires commitment and hard work (and some loss of sleep). Or you can simply notify qualified turtle watchers at the numbers below when you see turtles or signs of nests.

Wrightsville Beach, (910) 256-4913
Carolina Beach, Kure Beach, (910) 458-0015
Southport, Yaupon Beach, Long Beach, (910) 278-5518
Caswell Beach, (910) 278-4507
Holden Beach, (910) 842-7242; pager (910) 754-0766
Ocean Isle Beach, (910) 579-9513; pager (910) 754-1272
Sunset Beach, (910) 579-2994 or (910) 579-5862
Topsail Island, (910) 328-1000

To report dead turtles and violations anywhere in North Carolina call (800) 662-7137. For more information call the North Carolina Sea Turtle Project at (919) 729-1359.

The self-guided Marsh Nature Trail leads visitors to the World War II-era pillbox in which Robert Harrell, the Fort Fisher Hermit, lived from about 1955 until his death in 1972. Shark feedings take place at 3:30 PM on Tuesday, Thursday and Sunday. There is an outdoor picnic deck and beach access nearby. The Aquarium, 20 miles south of Wilmington, is open 9 AM to 7 PM daily in summer. The aquarium is closed on New Year's Day, Thanksgiving and Christmas.. Admission fees are $3 for adults, $2 for senior citizens 62 and older and active military personnel and $1 for children ages 6 through 17.

Winner Cruise Boats
Carl Winner Ave., Carolina Beach
- **(910) 458-5356**

The Winner family is as integral to Carolina Beach as Fort Fisher (and goes back about as far), and its fishing and cruise boats are rightly famous. You may choose from among four cruise ships: the *Winner Queen*, the *Winner Speed Queen*, the *Winner Cruise Queen* (all 150-passenger vessels) and the 400-passenger *Royal Queen*.

Suitable for people of all ages and launching from the Carolina Beach municipal docks, the Winner cruises make regularly scheduled 90-minute excursions of the Intracoastal Waterway (at 8 and 9:30 PM) practically every night of the week during the summer and on weekends in the off-season. The cost is as little as $5 per person. During spring and summer you may purchase cruises with or without dinner. All vessels have three public decks with dance floors, bars and full restaurants. The vessels are also available for private charter.

Bald Head Island

Bald Head Island Historic Tour
Departure from Indigo Plantation, W. Ninth St., Southport • (910) 457-5003

This guided-tour package may be the most convenient way for a daytripper to get to know Bald Head past and present. The 90-minute tour begins with a 10 AM ferry departure and includes Old Baldy Lighthouse and Captain Charlie's Station. Put into service in 1817, Old Baldy is the state's oldest standing lighthouse, the second of three built on the island to guide ships across the Cape Fear Bar and into the river channel.

The fee ($32 per adult, $27 per child younger than 12) includes parking at the ferry terminal, roundtrip ferry and lunch at the River Pilot Cafe. Diners may choose a specially prepared entree and a beverage from the chef's menu (gratuities included). You may choose a return ferry between 1:30 and 4:30 PM. Reservations are required.

Southport-Oak Island

The Deck Family Entertainment Center
5524 E. Beach Dr. at S.E. 58th St., Long Beach • (910) 278-4111

Open whenever school is out (primarily weekends and holidays in the off-season), the Deck is a focal point for youngsters on Oak Island and features a swimming pool, arcade, dance floor with disco lighting and jukebox, snack bar and pool tables. The Deck rents beach items (including surfboards and body boards) and sells gifts. Along with Lighthouse Miniature Golf, water bumper rides and the Go-Dog go-cart track, it keeps this end of Oak Island pretty lively. For information on the Deck's swimming pool, see the Swimming section in our Watersports chapter.

Fort Caswell
Caswell Beach Rd., Caswell Beach
- **(910) 278-9501**

Considered one of the strongest forts of its time, Fort Caswell originally encompassed some 2,800 acres at the east end of Oak Island. Completed in 1838, the compound consisted of earthen ramparts enclosing a roughly pentagonal brick-and-masonry fort and the citadel. Caswell proved to be so effective a deterrent during the Civil War that it saw little action. Supply lines were cut after Fort Fisher fell to Union forces in January 1865, so before abandoning the fort, the Caswell garrison detonated the powder magazine, heavily damaging the citadel and surrounding earthworks.

What remains of the citadel is essentially unaltered and is maintained by the Baptist Assembly of North Carolina, which owns the property. A more expansive system of batteries and a sea wall were constructed during the war-wary years from 1885 to 1902. Fort Caswell is open for self-guided visits Monday through Friday 8 AM to 5 PM and Saturday 8 AM to 4 PM. Admission is $2.

Summer Fun Beach Days
Long Beach Cabana, foot of 40th St. E., Long Beach • (910) 253-2670

One afternoon each month from May through September, Brunswick County Parks and Recreation sponsors live musical performances, volleyball and games at the Cabana, a public beach-access facility overlooking the ocean. Admission is free, and things start kicking around 1 PM. Featured musical styles tend toward island sounds as well as Parrothead (Jimmy Buffett-style) and beach music. Times and dates vary, so check with Parks and Recreation for up-to-the-minute schedules.

Old Brunswick Town State Historic Site
Off N.C. Hwy. 133, Southport
• (910) 371-6613

At this site stood the first successful permanent European settlement between Charleston and New Bern. It was founded in 1726 by Roger and Maurice Moore (who recognized an unprecedented real estate opportunity in the wake of the Tuscarora War, 1711-1713), and the site served as port and political center. Russelborough, home of two royal governors, once stood nearby.

In 1748 the settlement was attacked by Spanish privateers, who were soundly defeated in a surprise counterattack by the Brunswick settlers. A painting of Christ (*Ecce Homo*), reputedly 400 years old, was among the Spanish ship's plunder and now hangs in St. James Episcopal Church in Wilmington. At Brunswick Town in 1765, one of the first instances of armed resistance to the British crown occurred in response to the Stamp Act.

In time, the upstart upriver port of Wilmington superseded Brunswick. In 1776 the British burned Brunswick, and in 1862 Fort Anderson was built there to help defend Port Wilmington. Until recently, occasional church services were still held in the ruins of St. Philip's Church. The other low-lying ruins and Fort Anderson's earthworks may not be visually impressive, but the stories told about them by volunteers dressed in period garb are interesting, as is the museum.

Admission to the historic site is free. Hours from April 1 through October 31 are 9 AM to 5 PM Monday through Saturday and 1 to 5 PM Sunday. From November 1 through March 31, visit between 10 AM and 4 PM Tuesday through Saturday and 1 and 4 PM Sunday. The site is closed Monday during winter. From Wilmington, take N.C. 133 about 18 miles to Plantation Road. Signs will direct you to the site (exit left) that lies close to Orton Plantation Gardens.

Orton Plantation Gardens
Off N.C. Hwy. 133, Southport
• (910) 371-6851

Orton Plantation represents one of the region's oldest historically significant residences in continuous use. The family names associated with it make up the very root and fiber of Cape Fear's history. Built in 1725 by the imperious "King" Roger Moore, founder of Brunswick Town, the main residence at Orton Plantation underwent several expansions to become the archetype of Old Southern elegance. It survived the ravages of the Civil War despite being used as a Union hospital after the fall of Fort Fisher. Thereafter it stood abandoned for 19 years until it was purchased and refurbished by Col. Kenneth McKenzie Murchison, CSA.

In 1904 the property passed to the Sprunt family, related to the Murchisons by marriage, and the plantation gardens began taking shape. In 1915 the family built Luola's Chapel, a Doric structure of modest grandeur available today for meetings and private weddings.

The gardens, both formal and natural, are among the most beautiful in the east, comprising ponds, fountains, statuary, footbridges and stands of cypress. The elaborately sculpted Scroll Garden overlooks former rice fields. Elsewhere are the tombs of Roger Moore and his family.

The best times to visit Orton Plantation are from late winter to late spring. Camellias, azaleas, pansies, flowering trees and other ornamentals bloom in early spring; later, oleander, hydrangea, crepe myrtle, magnolia and annuals burst with color. Bring insect repellent in the summer. If you're lucky, you may catch a glimpse of Buster, the 10-foot gator who has lived in the lagoon near the house for many years. He's been known to sun himself in front of the gardens.

Touring the gardens takes an easily paced hour or more. They are open every day from March through August 8 AM to 6 PM, September through November 10 AM to 5 PM. Admission is $8, $7 for seniors 62 and older and $3 for children ages 6 through 12. Orton Plantation is off N.C. 133, 18 miles south of Wilmington and 10 miles north of Southport. Nearby are the historic sites of Brunswick Town and Fort Anderson.

Fort Johnson
Davis and Bay Sts., Southport
• (910) 457-7927

The first working military installation in the state and reputedly the world's smallest, Fort

Johnson was commissioned in 1754 to command the mouth of the Cape Fear River. A bevy of tradespeople, fishermen and river pilots soon followed, and so the town of Smithville was born (renamed Southport in 1887). During the Civil War, Confederate forces added Fort Johnson to their Cape Fear Defense System, which included forts Caswell, Anderson and Fisher.

Fort Johnson's fortifications no longer stand, but the site is redolent with memories of those times and is one of the attractions listed on the Southport Trail (below). The remaining original structures house personnel assigned to the Sunny Point Military Ocean Terminal, an ordnance depot a few miles north.

The Grove
Franklin Square Park, E. West and Howe Sts., Southport

Shaded by centuries-old live oaks and aflame with color in spring, this is a park to savor — a place in which to drink in the spirit of old Smithville. The walls and entrances that embrace the Grove were constructed of ballast stones used in ships more than 100 years ago. Set back among the oaks, stately Franklin Square Gallery, (910) 457-5450, now displaying art in several media, was once a schoolhouse and then City Hall. The park is a place to indulge in local legend by taking a drink of well water from the old pump — a draught that is sure to bring you back again.

Keziah Memorial Park
W. Moore and S. Lord Sts., Southport

A shady little park with a gazebo, benches and a partial view of the waterfront, Keziah Park is notable for its uncannily bent live oak. Estimated to be 800 years old, the tree is called the "Indian Trail Tree" after the legend that it was curved while a sapling by ancient natives who used it to blaze the approach to their preferred fishing grounds beyond. It later rooted itself a second time, completing an arch.

Maritime Museum
166 N. Howe St., Southport
• (910) 456-0003

Read "Gentleman Pirate" Stede Bonnet's plea for clemency, delivered just before he was hanged; view treasures rescued from local shipwrecks; see a 2,000-year-old Indian canoe fragment; learn about hurricanes, sharks' teeth, shrimping nets and much more in one of the region's newest and most ambitious museums. Many of the exhibits are hands-on, and a Jeopardy-style trivia board is a favorite of history buffs of all ages. The museum is within walking distance of restaurants and shopping. Hours are 10 AM to 4 PM Tuesday through Saturday. Admission is $2 for adults 16 and older; $1 for seniors 62 and older and children.

Old Smithville Burial Ground
E. Moore and S. Rhett Sts., Southport

"'The Winds and the Sea sing their requiem and shall forever more. . . .'" Profoundly evocative of the harsh realities endured by Southport's long-gone seafarers, the Old Smithville Burial Ground (1804) is a must-see. Obelisks dedicated to lost river pilots, monuments to entire crews and families who lived and died by the sea and stoic elegies memorialize Southport's past as no other historic site can. Many of the names immortalized on these stones live on among descendants still living in the area.

Southport Trail
Southport • (910) 457-7927

This mile-long walking tour links 24 historic landmarks, among them the tiny Old Brunswick County Jail, Fort Johnson and the Stede Bonnet Memorial. Architectural beauty abounds along the route, revealing Queen Anne gables, Southport arch and bow and porches trimmed in gingerbread. The free brochure describing this informal, self-guided chain of discoveries can be obtained at the Southport 2000 Visitor Information Center, 107 E. Nash Street, Monday through Saturday from 10 AM to 5 PM in summer. The tour begins at this location. Off-season, call for information.

St. Philip's Episcopal Church
E. Moore and Dry Sts., Southport
• (910) 457-5643

Southport's oldest church in continuous use, St. Philip's is a beautiful clapboard church erected in 1843, partly through the efforts of Colonel Thomas Childs, then commander of Fort Johnson, one block east. It stands beside Southport City Hall. The first vestry (elected 1850) ushered the church into the diocese as "Old St. Philips" in memory of the original church of St. Philip in colonial Brunswick Town. Within the present church flies every flag that has flown over the parish's two incarnations since 1741, including the Spanish, English and Confederate.

The building exhibits Carpenter-style Greek Revival elements, particularly evident in the pediments and exterior wooden pilasters, as well as English Gothic details. Entrance is made through the small, square tower, with its louvered belfry, simple exterior arcading and colored-glass lancet windows. The church's side windows of diamond-paned clear glass flood the sanctuary with light, illuminating the handsome tongue-and-groove woodwork on the walls and ceiling. It's a beautiful, quiet place that remains open 24 hours a day for meditation, prayer or rest.

St. Philip's Parish
Old Brunswick Town State Historic Site, off N.C. 133, north of Southport
• **(910) 371-6613**

After St. James Episcopal Church left Brunswick Town in favor of the rival port of Wilmington, the Anglican parish of St. Philip formed in 1741 and in 1754 began building a stone church at Brunswick, the seat of royal government in the colony. After struggling with finances and a destructive hurricane, the church was finally completed in 1768, only to be burned by the British in 1776 (the colony's first armed resistance to the Stamp Act occurred nearby at the royal governor's residence).

Today, all that remains of St. Philip's church, the only colonial church in southeastern North Carolina, is a rectangular shell — 25-foot-high walls, three feet thick — plus several Colonial-era graves (some of which are resurfacing with time). The ruin's round-arched window ports are intact and suggest Georgian detailing, but little solid evidence exists about the building's original appearance beyond some glazing on the brick. Three entrances exist, in the west, north and south walls, and three, triptych-style windows open the east wall.

Until recently, several local congregations held periodic services within the ruins. The body of North Carolina's first royal governor (Arthur Dobbs) is reputed to have been interred at St. Philip's, as he requested, but it has never been identified. St. Philip's Episcopal Church in Southport (above) was named after the colonial parish to perpetuate its memory. (Also see the listing for Old Brunswick Town State Historic Site above.)

Trinity United Methodist Church
209 E. Nash St., Southport
• **(910) 457-6633**

Built c. 1890 for a total of $3,300, this church is the third to occupy its site. Today the building features two of the area's best stained-glass windows (at either side of the sanctuary); handsome, diagonally paneled walls; and "beaded" ceiling (i.e., finished with narrow, half-round moldings), finished by a 15-year-old carpenter. Emblazoned across the original front-transom window is the abbreviation "M.E.C.S." - Methodist Episcopal Church, South — a remnant of the days when the church was split from its northerly brethren due to the Civil War.

The clapboard exterior includes Shingle-style detailing, cedar-shingled roof and gabled bell tower. Trinity Church stands at the corner of N. Atlantic Avenue, up the street from the Southport 2000 Visitors Center and the Fire Department.

Waterfront Park
Bay St., foot of Howe St., Southport

This is possibly the most relaxing vantage point in Southport. From the swings overlooking the waterfront one can see Old Baldy Lighthouse and Oak Island Lighthouse (the brightest in the nation). Take a seat on Whittlers' Bench at the foot of Howe Street, a great place to whittle and swap fish tales. Sitting here, Old Smithville is not difficult to imagine. Gone are the pirate ships and menhaden boats, but the procession of ferries, freighters, barges and sailboats keeps Southport's maritime tradition alive.

Stroll or cycle the Historic Riverwalk trail, an easy 0.7-mile scenic route that meanders from the City Pier, past the fisheries and the small boat harbor, and culminates at a 750-foot boardwalk, with benches and handrails,

Photo: Joe Swift

The battleship *North Carolina* is a must-see when you visit Wilmington.

over the tidal marsh near Southport Marina. Leave your bike in the rack and walk on for an unbroken view of the Intracoastal Waterway and the ship channel. It's a restful place on a breezy day, where the only sounds you're likely to hear are the croaking of crows and the clank of halyards.

Winds of Carolina Sailing Charters
Southport Marina, foot of W. West St., Southport • (910) 278-7249

The Winds of Carolina offers three customized daily trips along the Oak Island shoreline aboard the 37-foot, twin-cabin sloop *Stephania*. The morning sail ($27 per person) leaves at 9:30 AM and offers narration of Oak Island history and points of interest. The afternoon sail ($27 per person) leaves at 1 PM and includes an optional swim off Caswell Beach. The sunset/dolphin-watch sail ($30 per person) leaves at 5:30 PM and includes a cheese tray and cold hors d'oeuvres.

All trips include complementary beverages and last approximately two-and-a-half hours and all are under the command of a USCG-licensed captain. Fresh towels are provided for sun worshiping on the forward decks. Guests are welcome to take the helm while under sail. Space is limited to six passengers, and reservations are requested. Half-day and full-day private custom charters are available. Inquire about overnight "Boat and Breakfast" accommodations.

South Brunswick Islands

Capt. Sam's Sightseeing Cruises
**1268 Riverview Dr., Calabash
• (910) 579-3141**

From Memorial Day through Labor Day weekend, choose between a three-hour inshore cruise and a calm, one-hour waterway cruise aboard the 55-foot aluminum party boat *Mary B. III*. On three-hour excursions, Capt.

Sam Bierworth takes you out to watch shrimp boats at work while sharks, dolphins, gulls and pelicans cavort about, especially when the shrimpers' nets are hauled.

Three-hour trips leave at 9:30 AM Tuesday and Thursday, and tickets cost $12 per adult, $10 per child 12 and younger. A one-hour cruise takes you along the Calabash River to the ocean and back, leaving at 6:30 AM from Memorial Day to June 15th and twice daily from June 16 to Labor Day, at 6:00 and 7:15 AM. One-hour cruises cost $8 per adult, $6 per child 12 and younger. All trips leave from Capt. John's Seafood House at the waterfront in Calabash (foot of River Road). Reservations are requested. Popcorn to feed the gulls is included!

Museum of Coastal Carolina
Second St., Ocean Isle Beach
* (910) 579-1016

Standing on the ocean floor would be a wonderful way to experience the marine environment up close. Visitors to this museum can do the next best thing — visit the Reef Room, believed to be the largest natural history diorama in the Southeast. Above you, sharks, dolphins and game fish "swim in place" while all types of crustaceans creep below. The remains of a shipwreck, dating from about 1800, rest on the "sea" bottom.

Elsewhere, Civil War artifacts, tidal exhibits, a display of shark jaws and many other exhibits bring the natural history of the southern coast vividly to life. Substantially expanded in 1997, the museum is now affiliated with the Discovery Place in Charlotte.

Admission is $3 for adults and $1 for kids 12 and younger. Summer hours (Memorial Day through Labor Day) are 9 AM to 5 PM Monday through Saturday (until 9 PM Thursday) and 1 to 5 PM Sunday. In autumn, winter and spring, the museum is open only on weekends from 9 AM to 5 PM Saturday and 1 to 5 PM Sunday. From the bridge onto the island, turn left on Second Street.

Hurricane Fleet and Capt. Jim's Marina
Little River Marina, Little River
* (803) 249-7775

Little River is a stone's throw from Calabash, so when you're down that way and want a cruise, the Hurricane Fleet has an array of cruise options aboard the *Hurricane*. Most popular is the Adventure Cruise ($15 for adults; $12 for children 11 and younger), which brings passengers practically stem-to-stern with working shrimpers, who often give away interesting sea shells and souvenirs. Ocean Cruises are inshore coasting jaunts (same price).

Open-boat breakfasts (buffet or à la carte) are served on the aptly named Breakfast Cruises ($16, including tax and tip). Dinner Cruises depart four times a week year round, and dancing is added on Thursdays in season ($29.75 plus tax and tip). On Wednesdays in season, families will enjoy the well-priced Country Barbecue Cruises, which feature dinners with all the trimmings ($20 per adult; $15 per child.)

Ocean Isle Beach Water Slide
3 Second St., Ocean Isle Beach
* (910) 579-9678

You can't miss the water slides as you cruise across the causeway onto Ocean Isle Beach. From the tops of the slides you get a stunning view of the ocean and beach. The slides are open only during the summer, and hourly or daily tickets are available for less than $10 all day. Refreshments and snacks are available at shops nearby.

Topsail Island

The Patio Playground
807 S. Anderson Blvd., Topsail Beach
* (910) 328-6491

"What is that thing?" is the common refrain of folks new to the Patio when they first lay eyes on the Gyrogym. A printed handout explains that the Gyrogym is a "no-impact workout and a thrill to ride." Looking like an oversized gyroscope, the multiple steel hoops lock the rider into a whirling, 360-degree environment said to yield sensations of weightlessness without the side effects of motion sickness. There are some restrictions as to who may ride — no pregnant women, for example — and the ride doesn't come cheap: $5 for up to 5 minutes.

The Patio, with its arcade, pool tables and miniature golf course, is a popular hangout for youth, and it rents various recreational items such as bicycles, surf boards and umbrellas. You'll find it in bustling downtown Topsail Beach, 6.4 miles south of the bridge into Surf City.

The Topsail Island Museum: Missiles and More
720 Channel Blvd., Topsail Beach
- **(910) 328-4722, (800) 626-2780**

After World War II, the U.S. Navy transformed the sleepy island of Topsail into a test site for its missile-development program, code-named Operation Bumblebee. America's first ramjet-driven guided missiles were the project's legacy as well as the many concrete towers remaining along the length of the island.

The Assembly Building, where the missiles were put together, is now a National Historic Treasure and a museum, housing exhibits about Operation Bumblebee, nearby Camp Davis, local history and prehistory and area nature. Showing continuously is *An Oral History of Topsail Island*, featuring several longtime residents sharing their memories of the island's development.

The museum is open 2 to 4 PM Wednesday, Saturday and Sunday, April through October; other times by appointment. Admission is free. Guided tours can be arranged through the Greater Topsail Chamber of Commerce in Surf City (phone numbers above). The Historical Society of Topsail Island, P.O. Box 2645, Surf City, NC 28445, can also provide tours by appointment.

Topsail Scenic Boat Tours at Topsail Island Trading Company
201 New River Dr., Surf City
- **(910) 328-1905**

Utmost relaxation is yours when touring the Intracoastal Waterway and adjoining inshore waters in the 33-foot pontoon boat *Kristy's Kruiser II*. It's an excellent way to view local wildlife while enjoying conversation and cool breezes beneath a shady canopy. The tours leave the soundside dock behind the trading post every summer day at 1, 3, 5 and 7 PM. Tours last about 90 minutes and cost $13 per person; kids younger than 6 ride for half-price and kids under 2 ride free. Ice is furnished, and you may bring your favorite beverages or coolers.

The vessel is handicapped-accessible and is equipped with a private toilet. Reservations are recommended. Private charters for up to 20 people are available. For recorded information, call (910) 328-FUNN or (910) 328-TOUR.

Treasure Island Family Fun Park
N.C. Hwy. 210, Sneads Ferry
- **(910) 327-2700**

Grand Prix go-cart racing, water slides, bumper boats, kiddie rides and an 18-hole miniature golf course are the main attractions at this park, about 10 minutes north of Topsail Island. Ice cream, snacks and an arcade may make it difficult for parents to get away cheaply, so look for discount coupons (good before 6 PM) at visitors centers and wherever tourist information is distributed. All-day passes are available for as low as $12.95. Treasure Island Park is open every day until 10 PM in the warm season and is just a few minutes from the North Topsail bridge.

Other Islands

Masonboro Island

Evidence suggests that the first stretch of continental American coastline described by a European explorer may have been the beach now called Masonboro Island. The explorer was Giovanni Verrazzano; the year, 1524. During the Civil War, Masonboro's beaches were visited by the destruction of three blockade runners and one Union blockader.

Before 1952 Masonboro was not an island, but was attached to the mainland. In that year Carolina Beach Inlet was cut, giving

---

INSIDERS' TIP

Visit Bird Island, the state's southernmost barrier island, by wading across from Sunset Beach at low tide. Respect the fact it's private property.

Carolina Beach its boom in the tourist fishing trade and creating the last and largest undisturbed barrier island remaining on the southern North Carolina coast, 8-mile long Masonboro Island. Masonboro is now the fourth component of the North Carolina National Estuarine Research Reserve, the other three being Zeke's Island, which lies south of Federal Point in the Cape Fear River (see below), Currituck Banks and Rachel Carson Island, these last lying farther north.

Masonboro is unique for a number of reasons. Its proximity to a large population center and its undeveloped condition make it a "distant" getaway only 5 miles from Wilmington. It receives fresh water from upland runoff, not from a tidal river as most other estuarine systems do. The island is little more than a shifting ribbon of vegetated sand backed by 4,400 acres of salt marsh, tidal flats and creeks.

The oceanfront dune is capped in places by shrub thicket and a small maritime forest of live oak, loblolly pine and red cedar. But what impresses most is the profusion of wildlife, some abundant and some endangered, in an essentially natural state.

Endangered loggerhead turtles successfully nest here, as do terns, gulls, ghost crabs and brown pelicans. Their neighbors include gray foxes, marsh rabbits, opossums, raccoons and river otters. Several types of heron, snowy egrets, willets, black skimmers and clapper rails all forage in the creeks and mud flats at low tide. The estuarine waters teem with 44 species of fish and a multitude of shellfish, snails, sponges and worms. Its accessibility to UNCW's marine biology program, among the world's best, makes Masonboro an ideal classroom for the study of human impact on natural habitat.

The island is a peaceful place where generations of locals have fished, hunted, sunbathed, swum, surfed, camped and sat back to witness nature. Small wonder Masonboro Island has always been close to locals' hearts. Accordingly, the Coastal Management Division of the North Carolina Department of Environment, Health and Natural Resources administers the island with as little intrusion as possible. Camping, hunting and other traditional activities pursued here are allowed to continue, albeit under monitoring intended to determine whether the island can withstand such impact. So far, so good.

If you don't own a boat and can't rent one for getting to Masonboro, refer to the listing for Turtle Island Ventures in the Rowing and Canoeing section of our Watersports and Rentals chapter, or see the listing for the Blockade Runner Scenic Cruises, above.

The efforts to preserve Masonboro Island are spearheaded by the Society for Masonboro Island Inc., (910) 256-5777, a nonprofit membership corporation. Much of the island, especially at the north end, remains with private landowners who could at any time alter the natural habitat or prohibit use by the public. The society's goal is to see the island acquired for public purposes and maintained in its undeveloped state. This is accomplished by facilitating negotiations between the state and landowners for the purchase of island tracts, among other means.

The society sponsors public education through a newsletter, nature walks, volunteer island cleanups and a speakers bureau. Membership in the society is inexpensive, ranging from $5 for students and $10 for individuals to $100 for donors and $250 for lifetime members.

Information on Masonboro Island and barrier island habitats may also be obtained through UNCW's Center for Marine Science Research, 7205 Wrightsville Avenue, Wilmington, (910) 256-3721.

Zeke's Island

You can walk to this island reserve in the Cape Fear River, and you need not walk on water. Simply drive down by the boat ramp at Federal Point (beyond the ferry terminal) and

---

INSIDERS' TIP

Seek refuge on high ground during Riverfest and the Azalea Festival — Roy's Riverboat Landing Restaurant has outside balconies on the second floor.

at low tide walk the Rocks, a breakwater first erected in 1873 that extends beyond Zeke's Island for just more than 3 miles. You can go by boat if keeping your feet on the tricky rocks isn't your idea of fun.

This component of the North Carolina National Estuarine Research Reserve, totaling 1,160 acres, comprises Zeke's Island, North Island, No-Name Island and the Basin, the body of water enclosed by the breakwater. The varied habitats include salt marshes, beaches, tidal flats and estuarine waters. Bottle-nosed dolphins, red-tailed hawks, ospreys and colonies of fiddler crabs will keep you looking in every direction.

Fishing, sunbathing and boating are the primary pursuits here, and hunting within regulations is allowed. Bring everything you need, pack out everything you bring, and don't forget drinking water!

Air Tours

From the air, tours in this area may offer some surprises such as pods of dolphin offshore and the mysterious inland ellipses known as Carolina bays. All you need to do to go aloft is pick up the phone and reserve a flight with one of the fixed-based operators at the Wilmington International Airport. Very often they'll have a plane available that afternoon or the next day. Tours are available by the half-hour and by the hour and usually require a minimum of three passengers. Don't forget the camera.

Aeronautics
(910) 763-4691
Air Wilmington
(910) 763-0146

Aeronautics and its affiliate Air Wilmington will fly three passengers in a Piper Warrior for $85 per hour or in a Piper Arrow for $100 per hour (both Pipers are low-wing models). Also available is a two-passenger Beechcraft Skipper. One good flight follows the Intracoastal Waterway to Figure Eight Island and back, a half-hour flight, for $59. You may choose your own destinations as well, based on the same half-hour fare. Both operators are at the airport's General Aviation facility. From the airport's main entrance on 23rd Street, make the first left onto Gardner Avenue, then bear right to General Aviation.

ISO Aero Service Inc.
(910) 763-8898

ISO flies high-wing Cessna 172s, which yield greater downward visibility than low-wing planes. Tours begin at $12 per half-hour per person (three-person minimum). ISO is on the airport's East Ramp access on N. Kerr Avenue.

Kitty Hawk Air Services
East Ramp, Wilmington International Airport • (910) 791-3034

Ever land a plane on water? Kitty Hawk Air Services offers scenic seaplane flights and thrilling water landings beginning at around $20 per person for half-hour flights (minimum party of two). Kitty Hawk operates comfortable Lake amphibious aircraft with experienced pilots fully certified to land on any navigable waterway. It also specializes in a variety of business flights, including real estate appraisals, mapping, surveying, aerial photography, film location searches and more, seven days a week. Reservations are appreciated. You'll find the airport's East Ramp directly off N. Kerr Avenue (1.6 miles north of Market Street).

Ocean Aire Aviation
Brunswick County Airport, 380 Long Beach Rd., Southport • (910) 457-0710

Aviators Larry Ryan and John Martin own two certified aircraft — a high-wing and a low-wing — used for air tours. They can accommodate up to three passengers at a time for a base rate of $15 per person for 15 minutes. A variety of tours lasting up to an hour are available within the range from Wrightsville Beach to Little River (north of Myrtle Beach). Flights are available seven days a week during the summer and by appointment off-season. Brunswick County Airport is on the mainland side of the Oak Island high span.

Celebrate Wilmington! brings together a vast array of arts and entertainment from mid-October through late-November.

Annual Events

Timing a vacation with major festivals can transform it from mediocre to memorable — and we wouldn't want you smacking your forehead if you were to miss something special. If you're relocating, you'll find this chapter useful in familiarizing yourself with the region's more amusing "habits."

We've compiled the region's most popular annual events in one goof-proof, month-by-month list. Each listing provides the event's street location, an information phone number and admission fees. (Naturally, call ahead for events listed with unspecified fees.) All the events take place in Wilmington unless we've noted otherwise.

Should you require further information, call the appropriate chamber of commerce for the location (in the Area Overviews chapter). For events in the greater Wilmington area, you may also contact the Cape Fear Coast Convention & Visitors Bureau, (910) 341-4030 or (800) 222-4757. Annual fishing and golf tournaments, sailing regattas and athletic events are listed in their respective chapters.

January

Greater Wilmington Antique Show and Sale
Coast Line Convention Center, 501 Nutt St. • (910) 452-0680

Wilmington's largest show of its kind draws antique dealers from near and far to display and sell their wares. Admission is $4.

Martin Luther King Day March and Commemoration
Martin Luther King Center, 410 S. Eighth St. • (910) 341-7866

Martin Luther King Day has special resonance to Wilmingtonians because (among other reasons) Dr. King was scheduled to speak here the day he was assassinated. Wilmington honors his memory on the third Monday of January with a short commemorative march from Williston Middle School, 401 S. 10th Street, to the Martin Luther King Center, where celebrations include music, speeches, theatrical presentations and more. Participation is free.

Metaphysic Expo
Coast Line Convention Center, 501 Nutt St. • (910) 392-2909

Astrology, astral projection, crystal therapy, aural photography, parapsychology, psychic counseling, channeling, past-life exploration, herbology, health food — all this and more becomes mainstream, not marginal, at this annual exposition of the metaphysical and spiritual arts and practices. The expo runs for two weekend days in mid-January from 10 AM to 8:30 PM, and admission is $3.

St. John's Museum Art & Wine Auction
114 Orange St. • (910) 763-0281

This elegant fund-raising soiree is as prestigious as it is exciting. Art objects supplied by St. John's Museum of Art and individuals, plus rare and specialty wines donated by private collectors, go under the gavel while a silent auction proceeds throughout the evening. Wine-tasting, gourmet hors d'oeuvres, musical accompaniment, and sometimes a fine buffet, round out the event, usually held in late January. Proceeds benefit the museum.

Venues hosting the event change from year to year and have included the upscale Landfall Club and stately Graystone mansion. Seating is limited and early reservations are strongly recommended. Admission averages $50 per person. Dress to impress; even a tux would not be out of place.

February

Connoisseurs' Wine & Art Auction
Graystone Inn, 100 S. Third St.
• (910) 343-1640, (910) 763-0281

This elegant fund-raising soiree, hosted in one of Wilmington's stateliest mansions, is as prestigious as it is exciting. Rare specialty wines donated by private collectors and art objects supplied by St. John's Museum of Art and by individuals go under the gavel while a silent auction proceeds throughout the evening. Wine-tasting, gourmet hors d'oeuvres and musical accompaniment round out the event, which benefits public radio WHQR 91.3 FM and St. John's Museum. Seating is limited to 100. Admission is $40.

How Does Your Garden Grow? Show!
Coast Line Convention Center, 501 Nutt St. • (910) 452-6393, (910) 763-6739

Get an early jump on the long North Carolina growing season by viewing what's new in landscape design and know-how. Exhibits, lectures and demonstrations present innovative products, designs and techniques for improving the surroundings of your home or business. Door prizes are awarded, and the show offers plenty of gift items that gardeners and landscapers would enjoy. The two-day show takes place in early February and is sponsored by the New Hanover County Extension Service Arboretum, which is itself a wonderful place to visit any time of year (see our Attractions chapter). Admission to the show costs $3.50.

North Carolina Jazz Festival
Wilmington Hilton, 301 N. Water St.
• (910) 763-8585

The performers roster of the North Carolina Jazz Festival over the years reads like a Who's Who in Dixieland and mainstream jazz: Milt Hinton, Ken Peplowski, Art Hodes, Frank Tate, Bob Wilber, Kenny Davern and Bob Rosengarden. The Friday- and Saturday-night performances, for which tickets may sell out a year in advance, enjoy a cabaret setting at the Wilmington Hilton's ballroom. A preview performance takes place on Thursday night at Thalian Hall, 310 Chestnut Street, (910) 343-3664. Reserved seating is $25. Tickets for the Hilton performances cost $25 per evening.

March

A Day at the Docks
Jordan Blvd., Holden Beach
• (910) 754-6644

Ever hear of a Bopple Race? Care for a free boat ride with a charter fishing fleet? Combine these with live entertainment, crafts, free Coast Guard boat inspections, a sunset boat parade, a blessing of the boats, and you've got Holden Beach's way of welcoming the return of spring. Something of a floating festival, the event offers various entertainments at "ports of call" along the island; thus, the free boat rides. All the food on sale is prepared by local restaúrateurs as a showcase of local fare.

Sponsored by the Greater Holden Beach Merchants Association, the festivities take place on the last Saturday in March, and admission is free. (P.S.: A bopple is an apple boat that is assigned a number and three randomly selected "crew." The bopples are dropped from the bridge into the Intracoastal Waterway, and the one that passes the finishing line first earns its crew cash prizes. All other proceeds are channeled into community volunteer groups and community projects.

INSIDERS' TIP

Watch news listings in October for the Cape Fear Filmmakers' Accord's annual Haunted House. It's one of the region's best, put together by movie-industry pros, and it benefits a good cause. Information: (910) 763-8811.

And the event is fish-friendly, too; all the bopples the fish don't eat are retrieved.)

Long Beach Horse-A-Thon
Long Beach • (910) 278-1000

The only time horses are permitted on the beaches of Oak Island is for this early-March event sponsored by and benefiting the Long Beach Volunteer Fire Department. There is an admission fee.

Quilters By the Sea Quilt Show
Coast Line Convention Center, 501 Nutt St. • (910) 763-6739

The quilt show is Wilmington's major quilting extravaganza, sponsored by the area's guild of note, Quilters By the Sea. The show features an open competition with several categories, demonstrations, raffles, and sales. Finished quilts from around the state are displayed, and competitive "challenges" are posed in which quilters must create quilt elements that meet predetermined criteria. A $5 admission fee is charged.

Robert Ruark Chili Cookoff
Franklin Square Park, Southport • (910) 457-5494

The Robert Ruark Chili Cookoff in late-March is a competition featuring more varieties of the dish than the famous hunter and author ever dreamed of cooking in his Southport home. Arts, crafts and entertainment offer diversions for salivating spectators as they taste samples. Admission is free, but food costs extra. (The phone number above is for the Leggett's store.)

Southern Lights Festival
Various locations • (800) 222-4757 USA, (800) 457-8912 Canada

Southern Lights is a week-long series of events for which the greater Wilmington area plays host to our snowbound northern neighbors (particularly Canadians) in celebration of our shared heritage. The feast is an amalgam of performing arts, entertainment, recreation, golf packages and tours, and it embraces primarily the coast from Wilmington south to Kure Beach. Admission fees vary. Discounted air travel is provided through USAir, (800) 334-8644.

April

Azalea Sale
New Hanover County Extension Service Arboretum, 6206 Oleander Dr. • (910) 452-6393

For two weeks coinciding with the North Carolina Azalea Festival (see below), the arboretum hosts the Master Gardeners' Association's spectacular azalea sale, offering a profusion of colorful plants in a variety that's sure to astound. On the Friday of Azalea Festival weekend, the Arboretum also serves locally made southern barbecue at a nominal additional cost. All proceeds benefit the arboretum, a nonprofit organization. Admission costs $6 in advance, $7 at the door.

Cucalorus Film Festival
Downtown • (910) 251-8677, (910) 343-3664, (910) 762-4003

With four days of "native North Carolina" feature films, shorts, videos and live music that are so good you'll be amazed you haven't heard of them before, this festival is the brain child of Twinkle Doon, a collective of independent Wilmington filmmakers. Works by international filmmakers are sometimes featured also. This is the event that draws every local artist, actor, musician and poseur out of the woodwork — it's such a hit, it was extended by a day in 1998.

Shows take place at Thalian Hall, 310 Chestnut Street and a nightclub location to be

---

INSIDERS' TIP

When your Christmas tree has lost its needles, the New Hanover County Recycling Program can tell you where to take it — call (910) 341-4373. Trees left in the parking lot at the N.C. Aquarium at Fort Fisher, (910) 458-8257, are used to help protect beach dunes from erosion.

announced. Admission varies from about $6 for an entire night of shorts to $7 per feature film. Screening passes with and without brunch are also available. (By the way, a cucalorus is the filmmakers' device used on sets to create the effect of dappled light.)

Medieval Festival
Poplar Grove Historic Plantation, 10200 Hwy. 17 N. • (910) 686-9518

The Society for Creative Anachronism offers a merry old time of jousting and other tournament events, dancing, demonstrations, crafts (medieval and modern) and costumes plus plenty of fresh foods. Admission is free.

North Carolina Azalea Festival
Various locations • (910) 763-0905

Azalea Fest, the semiofficial opening of the season in Wilmington, features scores of musical and theatrical performances, garden tours and house tours throughout Wilmington and Wrightsville Beach. A grand parade downtown kicks off a weekend of free outdoor entertainment on several stages, a triathlon and a street fair filled with foods, crafts and throngs of people along the riverfront. You may tour public and private gardens throughout the area over a period of days. (Admission is $10, and children 11 and younger go along free with a paying adult.)

Musical performances typically feature several top-name performers each year. Recent headliners have included Aretha Franklin, Frank Sinatra, Liza Minelli, Alan Jackson, Lou Rawls, Gladys Knight, Kitty Wells and Reba McEntire. Tickets for festival performances are available by mail from The North Carolina Azalea Festival at Wilmington, P.O. Box 51, Wilmington, NC 28402. Concert ticket prices range from around $25 to $45.

Poplar Grove Herb Fair
Poplar Grove Historic Plantation, 10200 Hwy. 17 N. • (910) 686-9518

The Poplar Grove Herb Fair offers displays, workshops and class instruction in the many aspects of herb growing and use plus a plant and garden sale. Choose from single classes and whole-day classes, with or without lunch included (food is also available at vendors outside). Class registration costs about $35 per day. Admission to the fair is free.

Topsail Area Spring Fling
Surf City • (800) 626-2780

The annual Spring Fling celebrates the rites of spring on the last weekend in April with the Surf & Turf Triathlon, miniature golf and hole-in-one tourneys, arts and crafts, music and more. The Triathlon (bike/swim/5K run) requires a $20 preregistration fee; the other events are free.

May

Art in the Park
Franklin Square Park, Southport • (910) 457-5450

Local and regional artists working in many media present their work for sale beneath Southport's venerable live oaks on the second Saturday of May from 10 AM to 3 PM. The event is sponsored by the Associated Artists of Southport and is free.

Battleship North Carolina Memorial Day Observance
Battleship North Carolina, U.S. Hwy. 421 N. • (910) 251-5797

Memorial Day is observed aboard the monumental battleship *North Carolina* with free music, guest speakers and other special events. The memorial site is near the junction of highways 17, 74, 76 and 421 and is easily accessible from either bridge serving Wilmington. See our Attractions chapter for information about touring the "Immortal Showboat" during regular hours.

Memorial Day Observance
Fort Fisher State Historic Site, U.S. 421, Fort Fisher • (910) 458-5538

Fort Fisher State Historic Site is a fitting place for Memorial Day observances, being the location not only of the Confederacy's last fort to fall to the Union, but also a militarily important site from Colonial days right to the present. It is a site redolent with suffering and sacrifice. The Civil War Museum and the Underwater Archaeology exhibit are open to the public. The event is free but a donation is requested for the museum.

ANNUAL EVENTS • 193

Each March the Wilmington area plays host to our Canadian neighbors during the Southern Lights Festival.

Photo: Cape Fear Coast Convention and Visitors Bureau

Memorial Day Observance
Topsail Beach Assembly Building, 720 Channel Blvd., Topsail Beach
• (910) 328-0666

Topsail Island hosts Memorial Day celebrations featuring picnics, entertainment and a memorial service. It's free.

Pleasure Island Spring Festival
Cape Fear Blvd., Carolina Beach
• (910) 458-8434

This weekend festival is filled with live entertainment and arts and crafts. It is the spring "bookend" event to the Fall Festival in October. Admission is free.

June

Beach Music Festival
Beach Strand, Carolina Beach
• (910) 458-8434

Carolina Beach's Beach Music Festival is one of the largest music events of its kind, featuring live big-name bands and shagging right at the heart of Carolina Beach. Admission is $10.

Poplar Grove Summer Fair
Poplar Grove Historic Plantation, 10200 Hwy. 17 N. • (910) 686-9518

A vestige of the ancient Midsummer's Day festival, Poplar Grove's fair celebrates summer with offerings of food, refreshments, entertainment and pony rides.

July

Cape Fear Blues Festival
Various Wilmington locations
• (910) 350-8822

The Blues Society of the Lower Cape Fear sponsors this weekend-long festival celebrating one of the region's most popular musical styles. Performers include local unknowns, regional favorites and sometimes national name-brands, all plying their trade in a series of shows at venues around town (tickets average $5), as well as on the exceedingly popular Blues Cruise ($20 per person), an all-out waterborne party. Workshops in various blues instruments (guitar, slide guitar, harmonica, etc.) are also presented by accomplished performers, and the festival's talent contest is among the highlights of Wilmington's annual calendar. The festival usually takes place on the last weekend of July. Be sure to book your place on the cruise early.

Fourth of July Fireworks
On the waterfront • (910) 341-7855

Tens of thousands of people turn out for Wilmington's best fireworks of the year, viewing the rockets' red glare over the battleship *North Carolina* Memorial from every vantage point imaginable. Find a rooftop (legally), if you can. It's free.

Lumina Daze
Blockade Runner Beach Resort, 275 Waynick Blvd., Wrightsville Beach
• (910) 256-2569, (910) 256-2251

Recalling the days when the Lumina Pavilion was the focus of beachgoers' entertainment and imaginations, Lumina Daze offers movies right on the beach, 1930s-style swing music, a slide show of old Wrightsville Beach, a kayak "surf rodeo" and a full-moon ocean swim. The daze descends at 7:30 PM. Proceeds benefit the Wrightsville Beach Preservation Society, administrators of the Wrightsville Beach Museum of History. Admission is $8.

North Carolina Fourth of July Festival
Downtown Southport and Oak Island
• (910) 457-6964

Southport's Independence Day celebration is among the biggest and most spectacular in the state. It all begins the Friday of the holiday weekend on Long Beach with surfing, volleyball, sand castle building, watermelon eating, horseshoe tossing and tug o' war contests. Three more days of festivities follow, with live music, foot races, children's field events, a street dance, a firefighters competition, arts and crafts, antiques, a parade and more. The celebration culminates in one of the grandest fireworks displays on the coast, at the mouth of the Cape Fear River over the Southport waterfront.

Surf, Sun & Sand Celebration
Wrightsville Beach • (910) 256-7925

If you're up to playing a grueling tournament of beach volleyball in the sun, here's your chance to shine. If you'd rather watch, you'll have plenty of company while enjoying the live music and food. Tournaments require a registration fee per team, but spectating is free.

Wacky Golf Cart Parade
Bald Head Island • (910) 457-7500

At such a stylish location as Bald Head Island, it's refreshing to see golf carts decorated with such sober themes as "Tacky Tourist" in celebration of the Fourth of July. Other categories are "Patriotic," "Bald Head Island," and "Environmental." It's an accurately named event and great fun. More than 100 carts took part in 1997. The parade leaves Old Baldy lighthouse at 11 AM led by Uncle Sam — sometimes Auntie Sam — atop a fire truck. The parade ends at the Bald Head Island Club, where festivities continue until 4 PM, offering food, beverages, wacky activities and live music. Registration is required to parade your wacky cart (preregistration is encouraged), and "off-islanders" are welcome. The event is free. Be aware that ferry costs can be substantial for families (see our Getting Around chapter).

August

Sneads Ferry Shrimp Festival
Sneads Ferry Waterfront
• (910) 327-3343

This event, one of the bigger celebrations of one of earth's smaller critters, kicks off with a parade that launches a weekend of crafts, live music, dancing, boiled and fried shrimp, carnival rides and more. Sneads Ferry is about 15 minutes north of Topsail Island. Admission is $2 for adults and free for children 11 and younger.

September

Autumn with Topsail Beach Arts & Entertainment Festival
Downtown Topsail Beach
• (800) 626-2780

Topsail Beach may be at the south end of Topsail Island, but the entire region takes part in this celebration of hometown pride. The weekend features artwork and music; a pancake breakfast and fish dinner; the "Outdoor Taste of Topsail," a collection of fresh food concessions selling tasty fare from more than a dozen restaurants within a 30-mile radius; and live Saturday-night entertainment at the historic Assembly Building (fee charged). It all gets underway on the third weekend of September.

Bark in the Park
Wrightsville Beach Park, Wrightsville Beach • (910) 256-7925

The annual Bark in the Park is an opportunity to show off how well-behaved, well-groomed and smart your pooch is — and even how much it looks like you! Events include the Come 'n' Get It Frisbee disc competition, the dog/owner Look-Alike contest and demonstrations by local canine law enforcement divisions, grooming experts and obedience trainers. Prizes are awarded for some events. Admission is free.

David Walker Day Festival and Concert
Martin Luther King Jr. Center, 401 S. 8th St. • (910) 763-3935

This two-day fair memorializes the great African-American abolitionist, thinker and native of Wilmington by spotlighting regional entertainers and artists and promoting cultural awareness for all, with emphasis on African-American culture. The diversity of offerings is impressive and features live music, guest speakers, crafts and novelties, children's rides (fee required) and food concessions. It takes place during the last weekend of September at the Martin Luther King Jr. Center and adjoining Robert Strange Park. Events are free.

Greek Festival
St. Nicholas Greek Orthodox Church, 608 S. College Rd. • (910) 392-4484

The Greek Festival is a wonderful opportunity (and for some people the only opportunity) to sample homemade moussaka, baklava and other Greek delicacies. Live Greek music, cultural presentations, demonstrations, cooking classes, travel videos and souvenirs and even a Greek-style taverna round out this gala weekend-long celebration, which usually occurs the weekend following Labor Day. The event is free, but food costs extra.

Labor Day Arts & Crafts Beach Fest
Middleton Park, Long Beach
- **(910) 278-3708**

On day one of the Labor Day weekend, local and regional artists and craftsmakers display and sell their goods, all within sight of the ocean (or nearly so). The event lasts from 10 AM to 5 PM and is free. Food is available at concession stands.

National Beach Sweep
Area beaches • (910) 762-0965

This is a day for locals to clean up the area's beaches and put another tourist season behind them. Every year on the third Saturday in September, volunteers are asked to join in preserving the area's water and habitats for birds and fishes. For Topsail Island, call (800) 626-2780.

North Carolina Spot Festival
Topsail High School, U.S. Hwy. 17 N., Hampstead • (910) 270-4715

Here's a fabulous feast of fish (fried for this event), with arts and crafts, games, variety shows, all kinds of food, the North Carolina Spot Festival Pageant, and a bake sale as well as carnival rides (fee required). The event is sponsored by the Hampstead Volunteer Fire Department and is the area's only annual fund-raising event, benefiting senior citizen programs and fire-fighting and EMS providers.

Piney Woods Festival
Hugh MacRae Park, Oleander Dr. at Greenville Loop Rd. • (910) 762-4223

The Piney Woods Festival is a multi-ethnic celebration featuring international foods, music, dance, crafts and demonstrations. It's held every Labor Day weekend and is sponsored by the Arts Council of the Lower Cape Fear. It's free.

October

Bud Light Chili Cookoff
Hugh MacRae Park • (910) 763-6216

Now here's a competitive feast that truly does amount to a hill o' beans. You'll be able to sample the winning recipes beginning at 1 PM. Live musical entertainment begins at noon, and proceeds benefit the Domestic Violence Shelter and Services. Admission is $3.

Celebrate Wilmington!
Various locations • (910) 962-3547, (910) 762-4223

Celebrate Wilmington! brings together a vast array of arts and entertainment from mid-October through late-November. A colorful Beaux-Arts Parade kicks off five weeks of art exhibitions, concerts, stage plays, fetes, craft shows and sales and dance performances held throughout the city. Accommodations information is also available at the number above. Admission costs vary.

Fall Festival
Cape Fear Blvd., Carolina Beach
- **(910) 458-8434**

A great way to celebrate the turn of season, Fall Festival offers free live entertainment, pony rides and hay rides, plus plenty of food, crafts and activities.

Family Fest
Middleton Park, Long Beach
- **(910) 278-5518**

Family Fest takes place after the busy summer season, so kids can have all the food concessions and activities to themselves. Well, almost. They'll have to take turns with their parents dunking city officials in the dunking booth — all in good fun, of course. The events are free.

Festival By the Sea
Holden Beach • (910) 842-9790

Tens of thousands of people are discov-

INSIDERS' TIP

Riverfest features a Raft Regatta that's always good for a few laughs.

ering this two-day romp. On the last Saturday in October there's a parade on the causeway and a huge outdoor festival beneath the bridge, with live music, food and more than 160 craft booths. Contests on the beach (no fee) include kite flying, sand sculpture and horseshoe toss. The fleet of foot may participate in the 1K, 5K, or 10K races (for a nominal fee). Saturday night features an old-fashioned street dance with live music. Plan to arrive early and carpool. (Parking laws are relaxed for the duration.) Admission to the festival is free, and all proceeds benefit Holden Beach's volunteer groups and community projects.

Halloween Festival
Poplar Grove Historic Plantation, 10200 U.S. Hwy. 17 • (910) 686-9518

Kids love Poplar Grove's haunted barn and playground, spooky hay rides (by moonlight or sunlight), costume party, carnival rides, the palm reader, costume contest and games at the Halloween Festival. Admission is free, but some activities require a fee. Events take place the weekend prior to Halloween. A parking donation benefiting a local nonprofit organization may be requested.

Halloween History-Mystery Tour
Bellamy Mansion Museum, 503 Market St. • (910) 251-3700

This otherwise gorgeous mansion takes on an eerie aspect just for Halloween, and you can tour it from 4:30 to 8:30 PM the weekend prior to trick-or-treating. Proceeds benefit the museum. Tickets are $10 in advance, $12 at the door.

Harley-Davidson Charity Halloween Run
Start at 6615 Market St. • (910) 791-9997

Beginning at Carolina Coast Harley-Davidson, which sponsors the event, big-hearted bikers in full Halloween costume (hey, there's a stretch), ride their rigs to a chosen watering hole on Front Street, where tattoos are momentarily forgotten and the five best costumes are elected for cash prizes. The event benefits a local charity and begins at noon the weekend prior to Halloween. Admission is $10.

New Hanover County Fair
County Fair Grounds, Carolina Beach Rd. • (910) 763-4439

The New Hanover County Fair is about the area's biggest to-do when it comes to kids rides, a petting zoo, games, agricultural contests, exhibits, stage shows and food. The $8 ticket price includes admission and parking. The fair is open from 5 to 11 PM for two weeks in late October. The Fair Grounds are opposite the Echo Farms subdivision.

North Carolina Oyster Festival
West Brunswick High School, U.S. Hwy. 130, Shallotte • (910) 754-6644

If you can find a better oyster-shucking competition, go there, but the N.C. Oyster Shucking Championship at this Oyster Festival is hard to beat. It's so popular there's even an amateur division. Featuring mountains of the South Brunswick Islands' favorite food, in season at this time, the festival also offers continuous live music featuring a headline performance by The Embers, more than 100 arts and crafts vendors, and more. It's a three-day party on the third weekend of October. Admission is $1. The high school is just north of U.S. Highway 17 Bypass, off Whiteville Road (N.C. 130).

Riverfest
Various locations • (910) 452-6862, (910) 799-4867

Riverfest is Wilmington's citywide celebration of the river, something like autumn's answer to Azalea Festival. It features regattas, water races (including homemade rafts), an enormous street fair with food and crafts, stage shows, a beer garden, live arts performances and music, an ever-popular waiter's wine race (runners carry bottles and wineglasses on trays) and a cast of thousands. The events are free, and shuttle service is provided to downtown from Independence Mall.

November

Christmas By-The-Sea Parade
Yaupon Beach and Long Beach • (910) 457-6964

This colorful holiday parade, on the first

Friday of December, begins in Yaupon Beach and proceeds down Oak Island Drive. The event is accompanied by a merchant open house along the route.

Fall Native American Pow-Wow
Poplar Grove Historic Plantation, 10200 U.S. Hwy. 17 • (910) 686-9518

Celebrate the traditions and innovations on tradition of America's native peoples at this intertribal powwow in early November. Featured are colorful dance contests, native drumming and singing, storytelling, authentic tepee lodges, demonstrations, arts and crafts, and food and refreshments. Admission is $5 for adults, $2 for seniors 65 and older and $3 for children 11 and younger.

Festival of Trees
Wilmington Hilton, 301 N. Water St.
• (910) 763-4700

Festival of Trees, a benefit for Cape Fear Hospice, is a dazzling display of scores of dressed Christmas trees at the Wilmington Hilton. Accompanying this is Children's Festival Land, featuring Mr. and Mrs. Claus, holiday crafts and hands-on activities and entertainment. One week-long pass entitles you to enter both events repeatedly. Tickets are $8 for adults and $6 for children 12 and younger.

Holly Festival
Fire and Rescue Dept., U.S. Hwy. 17 N., Holly Ridge • (910) 329-7081

This affair, held outside the Fire Department in downtown Holly Ridge, fetes this small town with arts and crafts, entertainment, dances, clowns, food and a parade. The events are free, and concession proceeds benefit the Onslow County Parks and Recreation Department.

Marine Expo
Coast Line Convention Center, 501 Nutt St. • (910) 962-3351

This annual exposition, on the third weekend of November, touts all the latest and greatest in marine vessels, equipment and accessories, from floating docks to global positioning systems. If it has to do with boats and boating, you're bound to find it here. Admission is free.

Oak Island Tour of Homes
Long Beach • (910) 278-5518

Visit Oak Island's historic and lavish modern homes dressed in holiday regalia and partake of holiday spirit, Southern style. Homes are open for touring during the first weekend in December. Tickets are $5.

Robert Ruark Festival
Various locations, Southport
• (910) 457-5494

Of the two Ruark celebrations each year in Southport, this one, in early November, emphasizes the area's literary and artistic legacies. The centerpieces of the festival are the writing competitions (poetry and short fiction) and a juried art show, for which prizes are awarded. Literary symposiums and receptions (at which winners are recognized) round out the festival. Locations include area art galleries and Southport City Hall. The festival is free, but competitions require a fee to enter.

Wrightsville Beach Holiday Flotilla
Banks Channel • (910) 256-0722, (910) 256-0411

This floating parade of brightly lit and wildly decorated watercraft of all shapes and sizes is one of the true highlights of the holiday season. It's free and typically takes place on the last weekend of November. A holiday fair, an arts and crafts show, children's art show, rides, food and performing artists add to the festive atmosphere. Fireworks brighten the party, after which everyone hits the town. For information, write Flotilla, P.O. Box 713, Wrightsville Beach, N.C. 28480.

December

Island of Lights Festival
Various locations, Carolina Beach and Kure Beach • (910) 458-8434

The Island of Lights Festival at Pleasure Island features several events, most of them free, beginning with a holiday parade on the first Friday in December. On Saturday, a evening holiday flotilla in full seasonal regalia runs from Snow's Cut to Town Marina (Carolina Beach) and back. The Island of Lights Tour of Homes, held the following Saturday, features refreshments and Southern hospitality on a self-guided tour of some of Carolina Beach's most elegant homes. The Tour of Homes costs $15 per person.

Largest Living Christmas Tree
Hilton Park, Castle Hayne Rd.
- **(910) 341-4030**

The lighting of the world's "largest living Christmas tree," an enormous live oak, has been a Wilmington tradition since 1928. On a Friday evening in mid-December, the town turns out with the mayor, a brass band and a chorus, and the festivities begin at 6 PM. At 6:30, the tree is lit to the sounds of music and voices raised in song, and everyone joins in. The tree remains lit nightly from 5:30 to 10 PM until the end of December.

Old Wilmington by Candlelight
Various locations • (910) 762-0492

This is one of the most popular and atmospheric of the holiday home tours. Each year, nearly a score of Wilmington's most historic homes, churches and businesses are opened to guests for two days on the first weekend in December from 4 to 8 PM. Stroll into Christmases past and see how yesterday's lifestyles have been adapted to our time. You're invited to enjoy cider and cookies at the Latimer House as well. The tour is self-guided. Proceeds benefit Latimer House and the Lower Cape Fear Historical Society. Tickets cost $15.

Poplar Grove Christmas Celebration
Poplar Grove Historic Plantation, 10200 Hwy. 17 N. • (910) 686-9518

Few places evoke bygone days as well as Poplar Grove Plantation, especially at holiday time. The Christmas Celebration here features seasonal arts and crafts, a beautifully decorated historic open house ($4 fee required to tour) and appearances by Victorian-style Mr. and Mrs. Santa Claus. Admission is free.

Southport Christmas Home Tour and Flotilla
Various locations, Southport
- **(910) 457-7927**

Southport's Christmas Homes Tour and Flotilla in mid-December combines a candlelight walking tour of Southport's historic riverfront homes from 5 to 9 PM ($8 admission) and a lively regatta of seasonally decorated vessels that sail the lower Cape Fear River by Waterfront Park that same evening (inquire about registration to participate; viewing is free!). The events usually take place the second Saturday in December.

Toy Jam
Location varies • (910) 343-1640

Toy Jam is a night of live music of many styles and has become a very popular Christmas tradition. Admission requires a new, unwrapped toy, to be distributed to needy children by the Salvation Army. The event is sponsored by Public Radio WHQR and is held in a downtown Wilmington restaurant. Santa and Mrs. Claus typically make an early appearance. Volunteers to assist with the event are always needed.

Walk-In Messiah
Kenan Auditorium, University of North Carolina at Wilmington, 601 S. College Rd. • (910) 962-3500

The Wilmington Symphony Orchestra presents this concert sing-along featuring carols and Handel's classic cantata. If you'd like to join in with the chorus for *Messiah*, you may attend a matinee rehearsal. Scores are available for the singing public in advance. Be sure to buy tickets early; the event typically sells out by late October. Tickets are $20 and $16. If you miss out on tickets for the evening performance, inquire about matinee rehearsal ($4).

Wilmington Boys Choir
St. Paul's Episcopal Church, 16 N. 16th St. • (910) 799-5073

Since 1895, the Wilmington Boys Choir has distinguished itself with fine performances throughout the state, in Washington, D.C. and overseas. Its annual Christmas concert is always well-attended and features carols, hymns and popular holiday songs. Admission is by donation.

Winter Holiday Fest
Sneads Ferry Community Building, Sneads Ferry • (910) 327-3343

Sneads Ferry, the small seaside village known for its Shrimp Festival in August, offi-

A young Confederate waits to escort a Southern belle.

cially kicks off its holiday observances with a tree-lighting ceremony and a community music program at 7 PM on the second Friday of December. The next day features a pancake breakfast with Santa from 7 to 11 AM and a community lunch from noon to 4 PM (there is a charge for these activities).

Also on Saturday is a holiday craft show beginning at 10 AM and a children's music program beginning at 7 PM. The music and art continue on Sunday at noon. All programs are free. The Community Building is located on Park Lane, which is off Sneads Ferry Road (N.C. Highway 172) a few minutes north of Topsail Island.

. . . And for New Year's

Carolina Beach New Year's Eve Countdown Party
Carolina Beach Boardwalk
- **(910) 458-8434**

Ring in the new year with food, refreshments and a street dance accompanied by live music (beach music, naturally!), culminating in the descent of an enormous beach ball at midnight. Top it off with fireworks and you've got yourself a beach-style New Year to remember. The fun begins at 10 PM on December 31 at the public gazebo.

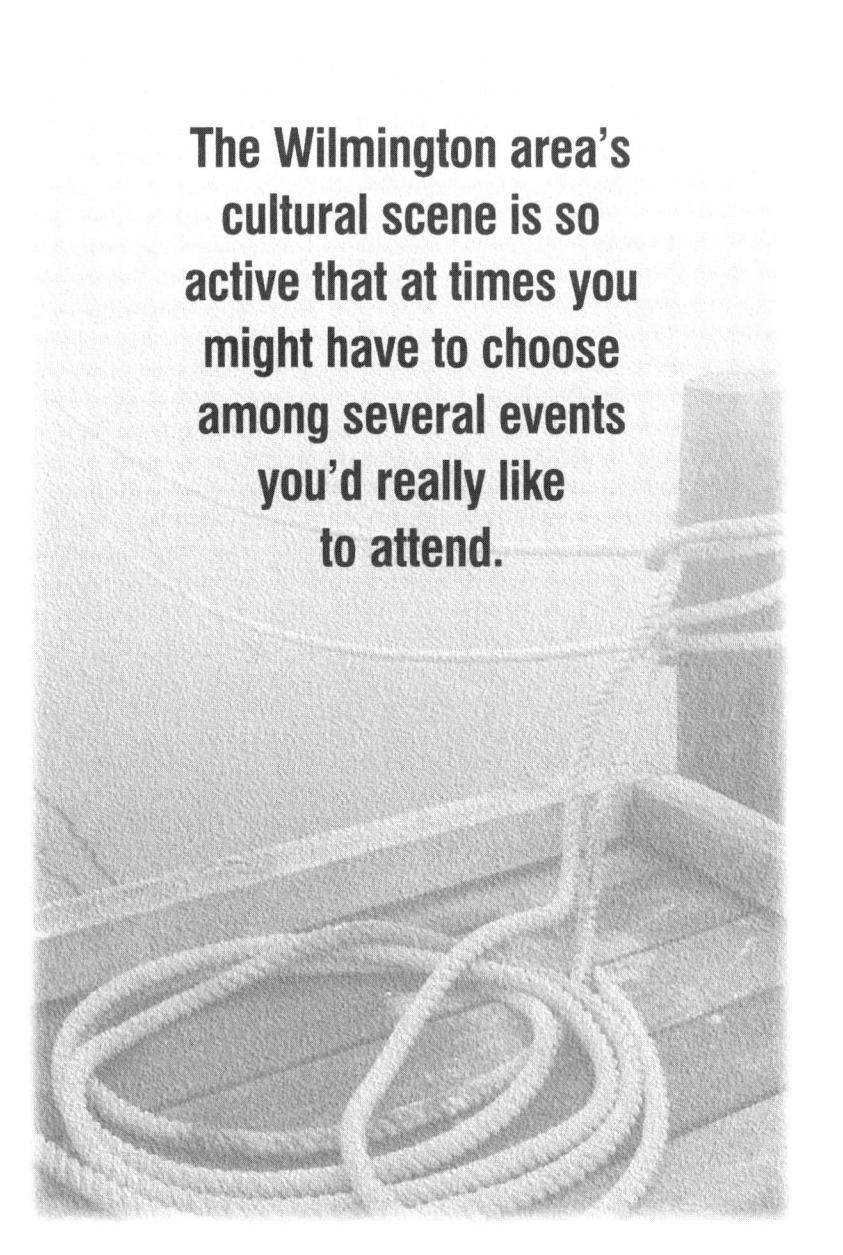

The Wilmington area's cultural scene is so active that at times you might have to choose among several events you'd really like to attend.

The Arts

Although Wilmington and the Cape Fear region are geographically far flung from the world's acknowledged cultural centers, the area boasts a lively professional arts scene that is the envy of many more-sophisticated cosmopolitan communities. Given the relatively small size of the city of Wilmington, its artistic offerings are disproportionately large — and have been since nearly the beginning.

Cape Fear people love to be entertained. Consequently, there are many established institutions devoted to the arts, including the Thalian Hall Center for the Performing Arts and St. John's Museum of Art. Touring exhibitions and artists, as well as an astonishing number of tremendously talented locals, keep everyone's social calender overbooked. The most commonly heard complaint about the arts scene is that there's just too much to do! It is no exaggeration to say there's something offered every night of the year and, often, one has to choose between events.

Downtown Wilmington is the hub of arts organizations and activities for the region, luring musicians, painters, actors, filmmakers, sculptors, paper-makers, and dancers to crowd the coffeehouses and cafes to discuss their crafts. Clubs and restaurants serve up a stimulating offering of live music and theater on a regular basis, including a long-running, live soap opera in a downtown basement bar. Cinematique, an ongoing film showcase for "classic, foreign and notable films" is jointly sponsored by public radio station WHQR and the Thalian Hall Center for the Performing Arts. Films are screened to capacity crowds and often a film has to be held over to accommodate interest.

Two dozen acting companies employ the talents of locals in writing, music and performance. Wilmington has its own symphony orchestra, a vibrant chamber music series, regular concert series and dozens of ensemble groups ranging from professionals to enthusiastic amateurs. There are several stages in town including Thalian Hall, Kenan Auditorium and Trask Coliseum at the University of North Carolina at Wilmington, the Scottish Rite Temple and even the lawn of the deRosset house, home to the Wilmington Historic Foundation.

Touring companies regularly visit Wilmington, particularly during the Azalea Festival in the spring and Riverfest in the fall. Over the centuries, Wilmington has hosted such notables as Lillian Russell, Maurice Barrymore, Oscar Wilde and John Philip Sousa. Come closer in time and consider these performers: Al Hirt, Peter Nero, the Paul Taylor Dance Company, Chet Atkins, Frank Sinatra, The Ciompi String Quarter, Judy Collins and Koko Taylor. Add in Itzak Perleman, Livia Sohn, the Alvin Ailey Repertory Company and James Galway. How about Roberta Flack, Reba McEntire, Kenny Rogers, the Beach Boys, The Embers and Ray Charles?

The visual arts occupy an important position in the region's cultural experiences. In addition to dozens of commercial art galleries, the region has St. John's Museum of Art, regarded as one of the finest small art museums in the southeast. The Arts Council of the Lower Cape Fear is a central facilitator and coordinator for the arts in the area. This organization works diligently to create opportunities for the arts to flourish, documenting the activities of various arts organizations, providing local artists with vital information and funding to further their professional development, and sponsoring innovative arts programs in area schools.

The Cape Fear region is a rich environment for the arts, offering a variety of opportunities for both creating and enjoying the cultural arts. Listed below is just a sampling of the arts scene in the region.

Unless otherwise indicated, all addresses are in Wilmington.

Museums, Performance Halls and Organizations

Acme Art
711 N. Fifth Ave. • (910) 763-8010

This is an artists' warehouse of working studios for rent at reasonable cost. Now and then, the warehouse opens to the public to show the works in progress. They hold an occasional Full Moon show where the community is invited to look at the work and enjoy performance arts and good company in a festive environment. Generally, it's a covered-dish affair, so bring your deviled eggs along and share in the fun.

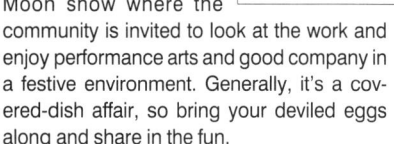

Arts Council of the Lower Cape Fear
807 N. Fourth St. • (910) 763-2787

The Arts Council of the Lower Cape Fear has a direct and an indirect impact on the growth of the arts. It stands as an advocate for regional creativity, searches for ways to locate funding through grants for exceptional artists and seeks to focus community attention on this resource. It administers the Emerging Artists Program annually, a project grant program that provides financial support to developing professionals.

The Arts Council also cosponsors Celebrate Wilmington, an effort to promote all arts in the area in October and November. The Piney Woods Cultural Heritage Festival, a two-day outdoor arts fair held in Hugh MacRae Park, is the major annual fund-raiser for this community organization. The Council publishes a monthly arts calendar for the entire area in the Sunday *Star-News* and mails a quarterly newsletter to members.

Associated Artists of Southport
(910) 579-4552

Housed in historic Franklin Square Gallery in Southport, this organization provides an increasingly rich environment for the growth and development of local visual artists. There are regularly scheduled workshops by recognized artists, as well as judged exhibitions and competitions. Monthly meetings are the third Monday of each month. Call for meeting information.

Brunswick County Arts Council
(910) 457-4330

Membership in the council is open to anyone interested in the arts. Range of interests include music, painting, pottery, photography, handwork, drama, dance, sculpture and woodworking.

The Community Arts Center
120 S. Second St. • (910) 341-7860

Managed by the Thalian Association, this Parks and Recreation center downtown is primarily a learning facility where anyone may go to take low-cost lessons in any of a full range of disciplines. Music, pottery, ceramics, dance, painting, drawing and more are offered at the center. For nominal fees, students of all ages can experience hands-on work under the direction of highly-skilled local artists and craftspeople. There is something for every age and level of ability.

Odell Williamson Auditorium
Brunswick Community College, 150 College Rd., Bolivia • (910) 343-0203 ext. 406

Built in 1993 on the campus of Brunswick Community College, this 1,500-seat proscenium auditorium offers entertainment opportunities in the heart of Brunswick County, only 22 minutes from the bridge at Wilmington. In its short history, the auditorium has presented the talents of the North Carolina Symphony, the U.S. Marine Band, the Kingston Trio, the North Carolina Shakespeare Festival, the Tommy Dorsey Orchestra, The Lettermen, Lee Greenwood, Pebo Bryson and, in 1997, a presentation of *The Odd Couple* starring Jamie Farr and William Christopher (Klinger and Father Mulcahey from the TV show *M*A*S*H*) and various national touring companies.

The auditorium has a subscription season each year as well as national dance competi-

MasonArt Showroom now open to the public!

MasonArt, eastern North Carolina's premier source for high-quality art and framing, now offers its beautiful frames and prints directly to the public at its new Dutch Square Industrial Park factory showroom! Come browse our selection — or visit us at the Whittler's Bench art and gift gallery in Wilmington's Cotton Exchange — today!

MasonArt
Wholesale pictures and framing
314 N.Greenmeadows Drive
Dutch Square Industrial Park
Wilmington, NC 28405
(910) 790-3990

The Whittler's Bench
ART, GIFTS AND ACCESSORIES
at The Cotton Exchange
(910) 762-6202

---

tions. In 1997 it initiated a Christian Contemporary Artists series. For tickets call (910) 754-3133.

St. John's Museum of Art
114 Orange St. • (910) 763-0281

This exceptional museum houses a stunning permanent collection of 18th-, 19th- and 20th-century North Carolina and American art, including the works of such artists as Mary Cassatt, Minnie Evans, Claude Howell, Elisabeth Augusta Chant, Jacob Marling, William Frerichs, Elliot Daingerfield, Hobson Pittman, Francis Speight and Will Henry Stevens. There is particular emphasis on three centuries of North Carolina art. Decorative arts from North Carolina include a major collection of Jugtown pottery.

The Sales Gallery represents more than 80 artists in the Southeast. The nonprofit museum offers presents temporary exhibitions and ongoing classes for children and adults in its Cowan House studio, as well as lectures, concerts, symposia and more on the visual arts and related cultural topics. A docent program provides guided tours and art appreciation talks to school and civic groups.

At this writing, St. John's is downtown but, thanks to a tremendous gift from a local family, plans are in the works for moving it into a grand new facility that will be constructed in another location in southern Wilmington within one to two years. (Read more about St. John's in our Attractions chapter.)

Thalian Hall Center for the Performing Arts
310 Chestnut St. • (910) 343-3660

Built in 1858, this majestic performance center has gone through several restorations and, at this time, offers three performance spaces. There is a 752-seat main theater, the 250-seat Council Chamber and a 136-seat studio theater. With a lively local performing arts community and the addition of touring companies, at least one of the spaces is in use each evening or afternoon. More than 35 area arts and civic organizations use the facility, and more than 250 performances in music, theater and dance are presented each year. (See our Attractions chapter.)

Wilmington Art Association
(910) 799-3702

This association is composed of local visual artists. The group holds juried exhibitions in the spring and fall; it also holds meetings on topics of interest and sponsors frequent workshops and critiques. A $20 annual fee entitles members to monthly meetings, participation in shows and a monthly newsletter. The Azalea Festival Show, held at St. Thomas Preservation Hall on Dock Street, is generally juried by a national arts figure.

"You Think You Have Sinus Problems!"

Curtis Krueger
PHOTOGRAPHIC ARTIST
Fine Art Photographs for Home or Office

2145 Wrightsville Avenue • Wilmington, NC 28403
(910) 762-2188
"Inside New Hanover Printing"

Galleries

American Pie
113 Dock St. • (910) 251-2131

Contemporary American crafts and folk art fill this lively gallery. There is a special section of one-of-a-kind small press, handmade books, unusual jewelry, handblown glass, paintings, papier-mâché sculpture and ceramics. Upstairs are the works of self-taught Southern artists and folk art.

Christie's Gallery
3308 Wrightsville Ave. • (910) 397-0094

Fine art, prints, posters, pottery, jewelry and restoration services are available at this relatively new and extremely interesting gallery, which carries the work of Ruth Franklin, Russell Yerkes, J. Baughman, Dan Goad, Gorge, Aldo Luongo and others. Originals by Picasso and Miro are occasionally available.

The Creative Resource
112 N. Cardinal Dr. • (910) 452-2073

This new gallery offers an eclectic collection of traditional and contemporary arts and also offers seminars on art collecting. Co-owner Cindy Golonka, degreed in art from the Art Institute of Pittsburgh and former teacher at the Art Institute of Dallas, also

WILMINGTON CONCERT ASSOCIATION

1998-1999

presents its 69th Season

Wednesday • November 11, 1998
San Francisco Western Opera Theater
presents *"La Traviata"*
Sung in Italian, English Supertitles

Tuesday • February 16, 1999
Moscow Philharmonic Orchestra

Monday • March 1, 1999
Arcadi Volodos, Pianist

Saturday • April 3, 1999
Harvard Glee Club

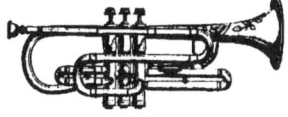

Bringing concert artists of international reputation to Southeastern North Carolina

Subscriptions may be ordered by telephone and charged to VISA or Mastercard by calling the Kenan Auditorium Box Office at 395-3500 or 1-800-732-3643.

teaches multimedia classes for children and drawing for adults. Featured artists in the gallery include Rudy Scheiner, Will Scheiner, Dave Sullins, Elizabeth Darrow, Jane Baldridge, Sharon Harris, Don Holmes, Thom Curtis, Joel Armstrong, Beth Aronson Meggs, Marianne Ewen, Candy Wilson, Michael Wolf, Cindy Galonka and Leah Fischer.

Deborah Jamieson and Associates Showroom/Gallery/Interior Design Services
Bradley Oaks Professional Park, 6317 Oleander Dr. • (910) 395-1818

Fine artwork by local, regional and national artists working in oil, watercolor and mixed media as well as sculptures, vases and other functional accessories are on display with periodic changes. The gallery features the works of local artists, including Elizabeth Darrow, Fritzi Huber, Sandra Brett, Jodie Rippy, Michael Costello and Hiroshi Sueyoshi.

Fidler's Gallery and Framing
The Cotton Exchange, 321 N. Front St.
• (910) 762-2001

Fidler's specializes in limited-edition reproductions by Bob Timberlake, Sallie Middleton, Bev Doolittle, Neil Watson, Robert Bateman, Charles Wysocki, James Gurney, John Stobart and others. This gallery also carries original works.

Franklin Square Gallery
Howe and West Sts., behind Franklin Square, Southport • (910) 457-5450

Operated by the nonprofit Associated Artists of Southport, this gallery is housed in an impressive historic building in the heart of Southport. The use of the building and a building next door that is utilized as a pottery studio was made possible by the farsighted City of Southport in a decision to rent it to artists for next to nothing. The expectation was that the artists would create and maintain an important cultural center and, indeed, they have. The building is filled exclusively with work by local artists ranging from paintings to pottery to dollhouse miniatures.

Golden Gallery
The Cotton Exchange, 321 N. Front St.
• (910) 762-4651

Mary Ellen Golden's original watercolors of the area scenery, son John W. Golden's exceptional photography and husband John C. Golden Jr.'s music cassettes are featured in this family gallery. Mary Ellen has been painting in watercolor since 1974 and has been in the Cotton Exchange since 1977. Her techniques and tips are featured in a video, *Watercolor Can Be Easy*, available for sale in the gallery.

Griffith Gallery
120-B, S. Front St. • (910) 815-0044

This gallery features the scenery of the North Carolina coast in a realistic style of paintings with heavy emphasis on maritime themes. Artist Ed Griffith paints scenes of downtown Wilmington, the beaches, North Carolina lighthouses and ships in acrylics with a sharp eye and a highly skilled hand. Both originals and limited-edition prints as well as select smaller prints are available.

Makado Gallery
The Cotton Exchange, 321 N. Front St.
• (910) 762-8922

The Makado Gallery specializes in contemporary fine arts, handblown glass, whimsical clocks, kaleidoscopes, fine woods, work by local wood-turners and handmade jewelry. It offers contemporary crafts by more than 300 American artists, including Tom Torrens, Josh Simpson, Corki Weeks, Tom Thresher and Henry Bergeson. Featured local artists include Floy Dawson, Mike Overton, Ed Jacobsen and Marshall Milton. Makado also features Fire Island Hotglass by Matthew Labarbera.

INSIDERS' TIP

The Community Arts Center in downtown Wilmington has outstanding pottery classes taught by Hiroshi Sueyoshi and Dina Wilde-Ramsing.

Chamber Music Society of Wilmington

1998-99 Season

Audubon Quartet

Ciompi Quartet

Dvorak Serenade

Carolina Piano Trio

Quartet for The End of Time

Sunday Evenings
September - March
Thalian Hall Ballroom

Ticket Info:
(910) 791-7331

New Elements Gallery
216 N. Front St. • (910) 343-8997
The Galleria, 6766 Wrightsville Ave.
• (910) 256-4707

New Elements offers changing exhibitions of fine art by regional artists and nationally recognized artists. Works in oil, watercolor, collage, mixed media and original arts are displayed. Decorative and functional pieces in glass, ceramics, jewelry, fiber and wood are also offered. Exhibiting artists include Virginia Wright-Frierson, Dorothy Gillespie, Claude Howell, Kyle Highsmith, Nancy Tuttle May, Hiroshi Sueyoshi, Michael Van Hout, Brian Andreas (creator of StoryPeople), Richard Garrison, Jodie Rippy, Dina Wilde-Ramsing, Gladys Faris, Betty Brown and Mary Shreves Crow. Jewelry by Patricia Locke is also featured.

New Elements opened a second location in 1997 at The Galleria. This store offers a different focus from the downtown gallery, featuring fine art, furniture and home furnishings, including lighting, that fall under the category of functional art.

North Fourth Collection
701 North 4th St. • (910) 251-0804

This exciting new entry in Wilmington's galleries market, affectionately known as NoFo, has staked out a spot on North Fourth Street, a redeveloping area that has received a lot of community revitalization attention in recent years and is home to the Arts Council of the Lower Cape Fear. NoFo carries modern and local art, as well as antiques. Artists represented include Elizabeth Darrow, Pam Toll, Sally Mason, Sharon Ihly, and Matthew Curtis.

Spectrum Gallery
Chandler's Wharf, 225 S. Water St.
• (910) 762-2327

Spectrum offers jewelry, contemporary art and glass with changing exhibits by local and national artists.

Wall's Fine Art and Framing
2173 Wrightsville Ave. • (910) 343-1703

In business since 1984, this recently expanded gallery carries works by national and international artists. The gallery component features oil paintings, watercolors, antique prints, woodcuts, stone lithographs and an impressive collection of glass from New Zealand. The framing component offers unusual, quality-finished framing that includes handcarved 23K gold frames. The gallery has plans for an ongoing lecture series aimed at helping people understand and appreciate fine art.

Music

Azalea Coast Chorus of Sweet Adelines
(910) 270-3313

Sweet Adelines, the female counterpart of the Society for the Preservation and Encouragement of Barbershop Quartet Singing in America (see Cape Fear Chordsmen, below), promotes and preserves the art of singing four-part harmony, barbershop style. The Azalea Coast Chorus chapter presents an annual show and membership is open to all women who enjoy this original American style of music.

Blues Society of the Lower Cape Fear
(910) 341-7350

Amateur and professional musicians devoted to the preservation and encouragement of the blues make up this lively group. There are free jam sessions locally, and the organization sponsors a major annual blues festival and a competition for amateurs (see our Annual Events chapter).

Cape Fear Chordsmen
1341 John's Creek Rd. • (910) 799-5850

This is Wilmington's chapter of the Society for the Preservation and Encouragement of Barber Shop Quartet Singing in America. Members practice male four-part harmony singing weekly at the Unitarian-Universalist Fellowship, 4313 Lake Avenue, Wilmington.

Chamber Music Society of Wilmington
Petrea Warneck, Exec. Dir., 233 Seagull Ln. • (910) 791-7331

A long-awaited addition to the Wilmington music scene, the Chamber Music Society of Wilmington is a nonprofit organization that brings world-class chamber music concerts to

Walls Gallery presents fine art from around the world, etchings from Germany and Italy, stone and hand-drawn lithographs from the former Soviet Union and US, and oils from NC to CA. With a substantial inventory, exhibitions are rotated on a more or less monthly basis. Walls offers periodic lectures by experts in their various fields directed toward those who love art and wish to learn a little more be it in restoration, gilding, printmaking, or art history. Walls offers framing to move a peice through the transition from the easel to its final beauty. Open Monday through Saturday 10am to 6pm, 2173 Wrightsville Avenue at Dawson St. 343-1703, fax 343-1802

Kosmachov - Stone Lithograph - 1957

Walls
FINE ART GALLERY & FRAMING

the Thalian Hall Ballroom. Past performances have included the Ciompi Quartet, East Winds, the Cassatt Quartet, the American Chamber Ensemble and the Scapati piano quartet as well as a series of children's concerts, including an Instrumental Petting Zoo (where children can touch the instruments).

Cape Fear Symphony Orchestra
8355 Vintage Club Cir. • (910) 686-1836

This orchestra, formed in June of 1996, is similar to the Wilmington Symphony Orchestra. In fact, about a third of the musicians play in both orchestras. The Cape Fear orchestra emphasizes familiar orchestral pieces that range from classical to popular and performs four concerts a year at Thalian Hall. Professional musicians from New Hanover, Brunswick and Pender counties are invited to audition.

Girls Choir of Wilmington
205 Dover Rd. • (910) 799-5073

It's about time Wilmington had a girls choir! This newly formed choral ensembles already has more than 100 girls enrolled. Girls ages 8 and older perform a variety of classical, folk, sacred, secular and popular music.

Harmony Belles
1341 John's Creek Rd. • (910) 799-5850

A local women's group formed in 1986, this group sings four-part harmony a cappella. Rehearsals are on Tuesday evenings at the New Hanover County Senior Center, 2222 S. College Road in Wilmington. The group performs frequently and stresses community service.

North Carolina Jazz Festival
The Wilmington Hotel, 301 N. Water St.
• (910) 763-8585

This weekend festival takes place in February and features mainstream jazz performances by national and international stars. The main event is held at the Wilmington Hilton, and a preview program is given at Thalian Hall the day before. (See our Annual Events chapter.) Good luck getting tickets to the main event if you don't have a standing order for them because this is a hugely popular festival with fiercely devoted fans.

North Carolina Symphony
805 N. Third St. • (910) 270-9812

This New Hanover County chapter of the state symphony sponsors five public concerts a year at UNCW's Kenan Auditorium. For tickets, call Kenan auditorium at (910) 962-3500 or (800)732-3643.

Suzuki Talent Education of Wilmington
4428 Mockingbird Ln. • (910) 395-0510

Independent piano and violin teachers in the Suzuki method of early childhood music education teach and assist in organizing recitals and workshops.

Wilmington Academy of Music
1635 Wellington Ave. • (910) 392-1590

The Academy is a private school, founded in 1987, that offers a full range of music instruction in voice, piano, guitar, harp, violin, viola, cello, percussion, horns, tuba, oboe, bagpipe and more for students of all ages. Theory, orchestration, arranging, Yamaha and Suzuki music education, jazz studies and other classes are available. Weekly private lessons and monthly group lessons, recitals and master classes are offered. The school has a community orchestra.

Wilmington Boys Choir
205 Dover Rd. • (910) 799-5073

This is a choral group for boys ages 8 to 15 with a repertoire of classical and traditional music. They perform in the area throughout the year and give special holiday concerts. Annual tours have taken the group to Washington, D.C., to perform at the Kennedy Center. Admission is by audition.

Wilmington Choral Society
(910) 458-5164

A large chorus for mostly classical vocal works, the society presents up to four major concerts each season. This group participates in the holiday Walk-In Messiah, a concert that encourages the audience to sing along. Members rehearse weekly and the organization is open to all interested singers.

Wilmington Concert Association
1203 Windsor Dr. • (910) 343-1344, (910) 962-3294

The Concert Association brings four or five classical music and dance concerts to Wilmington each year at UNCW's Kenan Auditorium. The association, established in 1929, regularly enjoys subscriptions of more than 800 people each season in a house that seats 960. Performers in recent years have included the San Francisco Western Opera Theatre, Alvin Ailey Repertory Ensemble, pianist Arcadi Volodos, the Ballet du Capitole de Toulouse and the Canadian Brass. The association's mission is to "bring internationally acclaimed musical artists to Wilmington."

Wilmington Concert Band
517 Bedford Forest Ave.
• (910) 799-5543

A volunteer community performing organization, this organization seeks musicians with a nearly-professional skill level. Auditions are not required but a minimum of two years instrumental experience is expected. The band performs at events and locations throughout New Hanover County from April through November.

Wilmington Symphony Orchestra
4701 Wrightsville Ave., Bldg. 3, Ste. 208
• (910) 791-9262

UNCW students and faculty members as well as musicians from the community comprise this all-volunteer symphony orchestra. They present five classical concerts per season. The 1996-1997 season marked the 25th anniversary of this orchestra.

Women of Wilmington Chorale (WOW)
205 Dover Rd. • (910) 799-5073

Classical and folk repertoire are the focus of this group, known by its initials, WOW. The group is most active in the summer, and no auditions are required.

Theater

Wilmington has a rich theatrical tradition that is continually expanding. Wilmington's Thalian Hall Center for the Performing Arts is home to the Thalian Association, the oldest continuous community theater in the country, dating from 1788. The theater hosts professional and amateur productions on an almost nightly basis.

Several local theatrical companies present original and popular productions at such area locations as Kenan Auditorium at the University of North Carolina at Wilmington, the Scottish Rite Temple on 17th Street, schools and churches. Additionally Wilmington is on the circuit for touring dance companies, symphonies and musicals.

Ad Hoc Theatre Company
1630 41st St. • (910) 791-2034

The Ad Hoc company offers experimental theater with plays by local writers.

Big Dawg Productions
1910 Wolcott Ave. • (910) 762-7182

Dedicated to producing experimental theater, this company stands outside of the mainstream in an effort to reach a more diverse audience than traditional theater. Auditions are announced in the *Star-News*.

Cape Fear Shakespeare
516 Dock St. • (910) 772-9188

Throughout the summer the Shakespeare festival offers free outdoor performances of the Bard's most familiar plays along with an Elizabethan "street fair." Audition are announced in the *Star-News* and performers of all ages are encouraged to try out.

Friends of David Walker
(910) 763-3935

Multicultural performances are sponsored by this nonprofit group, named for a 19th-century Wilmington abolitionist. An annual festival to celebrate David Walker's birthday is held the last Saturday in September at the Martin Luther King Center in Robert Strange Park. (See our Annual Events chapter.)

Minerva Productions
1118 Country Club Rd. • (910) 251-1310

Minerva Productions has a mission to give women of all ages and races an opportunity to showcase and expand their talent in all aspects of the theatre. It offers a mentoring environment for the production of original works by women and presents issues dealing with women and their relationship to the worlds in which they live.

Opera House Theatre
2011 Carolina Beach Rd.
• (910) 762-4234

A professional theater company presided over by artistic director Lou Criscuolo, this group stages seven major productions and two to three experimental works each season in Thalian Hall. Guest artists and directors are featured frequently. Auditions are open.

Playwrights Producing Company
(910) 763-7922

Playwrights is a nonprofit company that support emerging North Carolina playwrights. It looks for scripts-in-progress, which are read by actors and critiqued by the audience. Select productions or original plays are presented. Membership is open to all for a $10 fee.

Pride! Productions
(910) 343-8661

This production company finances a vari-

Thalian Hall is one of the focal points for theater in Wilmington.

ety of plays that offer multicultural impact and reflect alternative appeal. Interested directors with projects that need underwriting are invited to inquire.

Tapestry Theatre Company
228 N. Front St., No. 308
* **(910) 763-8830**

A nonprofit professional theater company, this group is dedicated to producing small, important works of contemporary and classical theater.

Thalian Association
120 S. Second St. • **(910) 251-1788**

The oldest theatrical group in the area, the Thalian Association stages five productions annually, including three musicals. The Second Stage Series, a group of small plays, is performed during the summer in Thalian Hall's Studio Theatre. An allied group, the Thalian Association Children's Theatre, stages performances by young casts and holds workshops for children.

Thalian Hall Concert Series
(910) 328-1654

This music series presents three to four classical music concerts a year and hosts touring opera and ballet productions in Thalian Hall. Coordinated master classes are held when possible.

University Theatre
University of North Carolina at Wilmington, 601 S. College Rd.
* **(910) 395-3446**

The University Theatre, produced by the school's Department of Fine Arts, is an educational theater devoted to the creative advancement of theater arts. Four major plays are produced during the academic year, with experimental work produced on demand. University Theatre provides an environment for students to participate in and learn about all aspects of theater.

Willis Richardson Players
508 Barclay Hills Dr. • **(910) 791-1584 ext. 209**

A community theater specializing in dramas by minority playwrights, the Willis Richardson Players perform works of particular interest to minority audiences.

Stageworks
4944 Marlin Ct. • **(910) 799-3069**

A youth repertory company, Stageworks offers young people ages 10 to 18 exposure to theater and training in the acting and technical aspects of play production.

Dance

Cape Fear Theatre Ballet
(910) 799-0900, (910) 395-3798

Founded in 1991, this company's mission is to bring dance theater to southeastern North Carolina. It offers public performances, educational workshops, master dance classes and community outreach special events. Approximately 35 dancers ages 10 to 17 are selected yearly through auditions.

Class Act Dance Company
(910) 452-4765

Class Act is a senior women's dance group that performs for local civic organizations, nursing homes, schools, churches and other community activities.

Writing

North Carolina Writers' Network
(919) 967-9540

This state organization, based in Carrboro, helps writers sharpen their skills in poetry, fiction, nonfiction, playwriting and technical writing. Writer workshops and conferences are often held in the Wilmington

---

INSIDERS' TIP

The Piney Woods Cultural Heritage Festival, held each Labor Day weekend in Hugh MacRae Park in Wilmington, is a great place to buy high-quality arts and crafts at good prices.

area. This organization is an important resource for local writers.

North Carolina Poetry Society
838 Everetts Creek Dr. • (910) 686-1751

The objectives of the society are to bring together in meetings of mutual interest and fellowship the poets of North Carolina; to encourage the study, writing and publication of poetry; and to develop a public taste for the reading and appreciation of poetry. Annual meetings are held in Southern Pines.

Playwrights Producing Company
(910) 763-7922

A nonprofit company supporting emerging North Carolina playwrights, this organization looks for scripts-in-progress, which are read by actors and critiqued by the audience. Selected productions or original plays are presented. Membership is open to all for a $10 membership fee.

Crafts

Azalea Coast Smockers Guild
228 Forest Rd. • (910) 395-5201

This group teaches smocking and heirloom sewing and publishes a newsletter for its members.

Quilters by the Sea
340 Bodega Bay Rd., Hampstead • (910) 452-2621

The Quilters encourage the highest standards of design and technique in all forms of quilting. Activities include quilt shows and exhibits as well as seminars and workshops on all levels. (See our Annual Events chapter.)

Port City Basketmakers
Poplar Grove Plantation, 10200 U.S Hwy. 17 N. • (910) 686-4868

The mission of this group is to stimulate interest in the art of basketry. It meets the fourth Sunday of every month at 2:30 at Poplar Grove Plantation. Special workshops are available for novice and advanced weavers.

Seashore Weavers and Spinners
418 Windemere Rd. • (910) 763-4804

Anyone interested in weaving, spinning, natural dyeing and other fiber-related crafts is invited to contact and join this organization.

Photography and Film

Cape Fear Camera Club
301 Honeycutt Dr. • (910) 392-5692

Founded in 1987, this club is a forum for photographic interests within the community. More than 50 members participate in education, travel, outings, workshops and friendly competition.

Cape Fear Filmmakers' Accord
21 Market St. • (910) 763-3456

A nonprofit organization of film industry professionals, this group promotes TV and film production in southeastern North Carolina. It publishes a directory of filming locations, serves as a liaison with business and government and provides help with initial location scouting.

OPEN EVERY DAY

Alligator Pie
A CHILDREN'S BOUTIQUE

CLOTHES—INFANT TO PRETEEN

TOYS

FURNISHINGS

MATERNITY

Beanie Babies

Lumina Station
1900 Eastwood Rd.
Wilmington, NC

YOU'LL LOVE US!

910-509-1600

Kidstuff

Among a parent's greatest area resources for entertaining kids (besides the beaches and waterways) are the various museums, which offer classes and workshops in arts and crafts, and the North Carolina Aquarium at Fort Fisher, which also offers classes and workshops as well as outdoor activities. Also, opportunities for adolescents to learn boating skills, participate in gymnasium and team sports and take part in many other activities, both physical and cerebral, exist with the various parks and recreation departments throughout the area. To contact these resources, see the listings in our chapters on Watersports and Sports, Fitness and Parks. (Information on child care can be found in our Schools and Child Care chapter.)

For this chapter, we've tried to ferret out some of the participatory activities that are easily overlooked as well as the bare necessities of kidstuff to balance the ubiquitous consumer-oriented offerings. Keep in mind that many of the activities listed here are not strictly for kids; conversely, many attractions and activities listed in other chapters are not exclusively for adults. Be sure to comb other chapters (especially Attractions) for great kidstuff ideas.

Each section in this chapter deals with a type of activity or interest: Amusements (including hobbies and toys), Animals, Arts, Birthday Parties, Eats, Exploring Nature, Farms, Holidays, Getting Physical, Getting Wet, Going Mental (for inquisitive minds) and Summer Camps.

Amusements

In this section we go slightly farther afield than you may expect in defining what constitutes "amusements." When the kids are in a funk that can only be shaken by gut-scrambling rides, go-carts, batting cages and the like, check our Attractions chapter to locate such opportunities. But for kids in need of a certain baseball card to complete the collection, a tube of cobalt blue to finish the painting or the newest interactive video game on CD, you're in the right place.

In the realm of sports cards and comics, the Wilmington Elks Lodge, 5102 Oleander Drive in Wilmington, (910) 799-2365, is noteworthy for its periodic card-and-comics shows, which attract collectors and vendors from miles around.

Coastal Sports Cards & Apparel
4830-B Main St., Shallotte
- **(910) 755-6100**

This well-stocked shop in the Vision Square shopping strip excels with its wide range of sports cards (including racing and hockey), magazines, autographed collectibles, official team shirts and hats and other curiosities.

Cool World Family Fun Center
5725 Oleander Dr., Wilmington
- **(910) 791-8700**

While tooling down Oleander Drive, your kids will undoubtedly notice this place. The arcade is as cool as any amusement park arcade, and equally pricey, but it's any kid's sensory overdose. They'll find all the popular (and often violent) video games and pinball machines, simulated racing games, gun games, Skee-Ball and air hockey. Outside is a "wacky" miniature golf course. The center is open every day 11 AM to 11 PM (midnight on Saturdays).

Fanboy Comics & Cards
419 S. College Rd., Wilmington
- **(910) 452-7828**

Offering a dazzling array of comic books for children and adults, Fanboy also carries collections, posters, role-playing games, collectors' cards (other than sports) and accessories. New releases are always stocked, and subscriptions can be arranged. Fanboy is in the University Landing strip mall (across the road from the Rock-ola Cafe) and is open seven days a week.

The Game Giant
1537 S. College Rd., Wilmington • (910) 792-0626

Specializing in new and used video games and game systems, The Game Giant accepts trade-ins for store credit, the amount of which varies according to the condition of, and demand for, the individual game. The store also rents games and carries every major brand. The Game Giant is beside Honey Baked Ham on the northbound side of S. College Road (south of Oleander Drive).

The Game Plan Video Game Exchange
4405 Wrightsville Ave., Wilmington • (910) 799-4386

Here, too, kids can exchange their old or unwanted video games and equipment for credits redeemable on a choice of secondhand but yet-unbeaten games in good playing condition. Credit for specific games fluctuates depending on supply and demand, and additional credits are earned for games in their original boxes or with instructions in good condition. The Game Plan trades all types of popular games and accessories, new and used, including Nintendo, Super Nintendo, Sega, Sega CD, Game Boy and others. New games and systems may be ordered. Games may be trial-run in the store.

Goldings Hobbies
4410 Market St., Wilmington • (910) 763-9395, (910) 343-9406

Goldings truthfully advertises itself as offering "one of Wilmington's largest and most complete lines of hobbies." The vast inventory goes well beyond plastic model kits, train supplies, radio-controlled models, dolls, art supplies and role-playing adventure games to include all manner of raw materials for the artist and craftsperson, from plaster molds to googly-eyes and aisles stuffed with every odd piece of whaddya-callits a creative mind could imagine. Don't miss it. Goldings is behind the Shell station at the intersection of Market Street and Kerr Avenue.

Hungate's Arts-Crafts & Hobbies
Independence Mall, 3500 Oleander Dr., Wilmington • (910) 799-2738

Hungate's stocks an impressive inventory of art supplies, including stretched canvas, model trains, rockets, toys, puzzles, novelties, miniature collectibles and a huge array of role-playing games and books. Located in the mall's JC Penney wing, this is a store for kids of all ages.

J & C Sportscards & Collectibles
3517 Wrightsville Ave., Wilmington • (910) 392-8550

J & C is among the premier card shops in the area, with its broad spectrum of collectibles, including sports plaques, commemorative bottles and cans, NASCAR die-casts and toys, college-team cards, cards derived from movies, TV shows and video games, puzzles and figurines. The store's appeal, therefore, draws as many adults as kids. For the completist, J & C stocks tens of thousands of common cards dating from 1981 as well as prized singles that are far older.

Learning Express
5704 Oleander Dr., Wilmington • (910) 397-0301

Learning Express, at the Courtyard on Oleander, is among those rare places that capture kids' imaginations with high-quality alternatives to the run-of-the-mill products for kids. Interactive and entertaining, the store succeeds in making learning fun for kids from infancy through early adolescence. The staff includes education and child-development professionals with broad knowledge of the products, which translates into excellent service.

Learning Express is organized in sections geared to particular interests, such as Whiz Kids (computer books and software), Science

Toys That Capture Imaginations

Awesome Art Supplies ◆ Dazzlin' Dress Up ◆ Great Games
Super Science ◆ Personalized Paraphernalia ◆ BRIO ◆ Thomas
Playmobil ◆ Outdoor Gear ◆ UPS Shipping & Lots More!

Learning Express

5704 Oleander Dr. (across from Pizza Inn)
(910) 397-0301

& Nature (including electronics and nature projects), Let's Pretend (fantasy dress-up), Great Beginnings (for infants and toddlers) and Transit (including wind-up race cars). This is the place to find that volcano your child needs for the diorama. Ask about professional discounts and gift services.

Memory Lane Comics
5751 Oleander Dr., Wilmington
- **(910) 392-6647**

Stocking one of the area's largest inventories of comic books (new and old), collections, non-sport and gaming cards and supplies, Memory Lane is an essential stopover for comics fans. Also stocked are animations, old toys and other oddities. You'll find the shop in the Philips' Azalea Plaza a short distance west of the Greenville Loop Road intersection. Memory Lane is open every day.

The Olde Wilmington Toy Company
309 N. Front St., Wilmington
- **(910) 251-1404**

This is a unique toy shop in the Danhardt Building at the Cotton Exchange. Proprietor Stephanie Carr, a former educator, specializes in hard-to-find games and toys, both classic and educational. Hers is a place where children are welcome to try out certain toys, provided they use the magic words, "please" and "may I?" You'll find few nationally advertised products and none that inspire aggression. From classic windups to doll houses to unusual kites, the Olde Wilmington Toy Company has something to inspire everyone.

Sears
Independence Mall, 3500 Oleander Dr., Wilmington • (910) 452-6200

Don't overlook Sears when shopping for toys, particularly video game systems.

Toys 'R' Us
4510 Oleander Dr., Wilmington
- **(910) 791-9067**

The inevitable hunt for a child's toy may well lead you to this gargantuan toy store near the intersection of S. College Road, not far from Independence Mall. Toys 'R' Us offers probably the largest selection of interactive video games in Wilmington.

U.S. Trolls
2305 Market St., Wilmington
- **(910) 251-2270**

Young children will enjoy stories performed with troll dolls handmade by Helena, Minna and Johannes Kuuskoski. Story time takes place every Saturday at 2 PM in a home just east of 23rd Street. Parents will appreciate the free admission. The trolls are cute, some are furry and all are for sale. There's parking in the rear of the building, with easy exit to 23rd Street.

Animals

Locals cherish the fact that our region is still not so urbanized as to have removed all wildlife from among us. In fact, it is not uncommon to witness hawks, ospreys and turkey vultures taking lunch breaks on roadsides within Wilmington city limits. Deer are frequently sighted in outlying areas at dusk. And watching dolphins cavort mere yards offshore can be endlessly entertaining. To be truly among animals, especially of the petting or feeding-by-hand variety, also check Ashton Farm, listed in the Summer Camps section below, and Greenfield Lake, listed under Exploring Nature in this chapter and in our Attractions chapter.

Hugh MacRae Park
Oleander Dr., east of S. College Rd., Wilmington

The resident wildlife at the duck pond here provides wonderful educational entertainment for children year round. Ducks march around the pond frequently, quacking as they go, especially when the park employees put out their weekly feed or when visitors offer bread. You'll often find ducks sleeping in the shade on warm afternoons. From the footbridge traversing the pond you get an excellent view of the many frogs, snapping turtles — from newborns to moss-backed elders — and fish that live beneath the water lilies. Some of the carp are of astounding size. Frogs are easiest to spot on the ground on damp mornings. Also look for spider webs, often quite large, among the bushes, but stay on the paths to avoid poison ivy. Plenty of shade trees and a gazebo invite picnicking. Be sure to bring your own beverages as there is no drinking water available at the pond. Park restrooms and playgrounds are a five-minute walk away.

North Carolina Aquarium at Fort Fisher
Ft. Fisher Blvd., Fort Fisher
- **(910) 458-8257**

The touching tank is not the aquarium's only eye-popping attraction for children of all ages. The outdoor carp and turtle pond is also a riot of activity, especially with the many barn swallows that nest beneath the building's overhang swooping just inches above spectators' heads all day. A walk along trails through the salt marshes is also likely to offer sudden, delightful sightings of small marsh animals and birds. The aquarium is 20 miles south of Wilmington and is open 9 AM to 5 PM Monday through Saturday and 1 to 5 PM Sunday. Admission fees are $3 for adults, $2 for senior citizens 62 and older and military personnel, and $1 for children 6 through 17 years old. For more information about the aquarium, see the Exploring Nature section below and our Attractions chapter.

Tote-Em-In Zoo
5811 Carolina Beach Rd., Wilmington
- **(910) 791-0472**

With its lion's mouth entrance, this place is hard to miss. Tote-Em-In has been a Wilmington fixture since 1951. Within its small parcel of land (too small by today's zoo standards) live more than 100 species of animals, including a camel, a zebra, baboons, many types of monkeys, antelope, peacocks, parrots and wallabies, not to mention various waterfowl. There are also two museums, one featuring mounted specimens and the other a collection of artifacts of various pedigrees. The zoo is open from March through late November, 9 AM to about 5 PM every day. Admission is $4 for visitors 12 and older and $2 for children younger than 12.

Arts

Once again, checking with the various parks and recreation departments in your area can be rewarding, since many of them offer art classes. Two facilities hosting such activities are the Community Arts Center (see later entry) and the Martin Luther King Jr. Center, 410 S. Eighth Street, (910) 341-7866. The Davis Center in Maides Park on Manly Avenue (north of Princess Place Drive), (910) 341-7867, and administered by Wilmington Parks and Recreation, offers free after-school activities that include arts and crafts, language arts and creative writing.

Wilmington also has an abundance of dance schools catering to young children. We've included a few that come well recommended and offer a variety of styles.

Baldwin-Copeland Studio of Dance
4711-1/2 Oleander Dr., Wilmington
• (910) 791-0602, (910) 791-5834

Since 1960 this studio has been teaching children as young as 2 (as well as adults) the fundamentals of dance. The emphasis here leans toward modern, jazz and folk styles.

The Ballet School of Wilmington
2250 Shipyard Blvd., Wilmington
• (910) 799-0900

Anne Goodrum, whose background includes dancing with the Atlanta Ballet and working as artistic director of the Wilmington Civic Ballet, directs Wilmington's only school dedicated exclusively to classical ballet. This school emphasizes the fundamental basics, and Ms. Goodrum is known for setting pieces on the dancers, allowing them to witness and share in the evolution of the dance.

Brunswick School of Dance
920 Ocean Hwy. W., Supply
• (910) 754-8281, (910) 754-6106

Housed in a remodeled country store since 1982, Brunswick School of Dance specializes in teaching children from age 3 the basics of movement and strives to build self-esteem and confidence. Class size averages nine students. Most classes take place in the afternoon Monday through Thursday, but there are morning classes for preschoolers. Round-trip van pickup service is available. Styles taught to older students include ballet, tap, jazz, pointe and acrobatics. Adult classes include aerobics, ballroom dancing and shagging. The school is convenient to most of the South Brunswick Islands.

Community Arts Center
120 S. Second St., Wilmington
• (910) 341-7860

This city-owned facility (a former USO building of World War II-vintage) is the focal year-round arts facilitator for children. Its annual Arts Camp offers school-age children six weeks of hands-on creative fun in practically every medium imaginable, including painting, pottery, music, dance, acting and photography. Offerings change, so call for current information and register early. Some adult classes are open to young adults ages 13 through 17 with permission of the instructor.

The Center is managed by the Thalian Association, (910) 251-1788, the nation's oldest continuous theatrical organization. The Thalian Association Children's Theater stages performances by young casts during the school year. Thalian Association Forte, a youth singing group, is open to vocalists ages 15 through 18. Auditions are held in January.

Danceworks Studio for the Performing Arts
4209 Oleander Dr., Wilmington
• (910) 392-0375

In addition to teaching all the styles of dance commonly taught in our region — jazz, tap, ballet and pointe — founders Brad and Jenny Moranz specialize in the practical approach to teaching musical theater. This includes film work, which is their professional background (they are active performers on stage and film). Thus, Danceworks accepts dance students no younger than 4 and students of musical theater age 9 and older, including adults. Their studio features one-way viewing windows so parents can observe the classes unseen.

Finklestein's Jewelry and Music Company
6 Front St., Wilmington • (910) 762-5662

Finklestein's music store (not to mention its adjoining pawn shop) has stood in the same location longer than most trees in the area. Offering a wide array of new and used instruments, Finklestein's also offers lessons, catering primarily to students of popular and rock music.

Kindermusik
(800) 628-5687

Kindermusik is a program of music learning and movement for children ages 18 months through 7 years, designed to facilitate children's creative expression, listening, communication and group skills. It incorporates singing, movement, musical play and a practical approach to writing and reading the language of music. This program is a four-semester, sequential curriculum structured in three age tiers. The program is published by Music Resources International, P.O. Box 13765, Greensboro, NC 27415. In the greater Wilmington area, there are three licensed

The Music Loft
413 S. College Rd., Wilmington
- **(910) 799-9310**

The Music Loft is among the better music shops in town. It carries electronic instruments and equipment, including recording equipment, and lessons are available. Master luthier Steve Gillhame provides expert repair of acoustic string instruments such as guitars, dulcimers and banjos.

Oak Island School of Dance & Art
210 Yaupon Dr., Yaupon Beach
- **(910) 278-6110**

The only dance school on Oak Island, this one teaches a spectrum of styles, including ballet, tap, jazz, creative movement and "danceplay."

St. John's Art Academy
St. John's Museum of Art, 114 Orange St., Wilmington • (910) 762-0281

Designed as a supplement to basic art instruction for children from elementary through high-school age, St. John's Art Academy offers several excellent opportunities, including the Exploring Visual Arts classes for 4th and 5th graders, Beginning Drawing and Design for 6th through 8th graders and Portfolio Preparation for 9th through 12th graders. Studio classes, multiple series and workshops for children ages 5 through high-school age are ongoing. Costs average $75 per semester plus materials.

Suzuki Method Music Education
Lorraine Westermark, Suzuki Talent Education of Wilmington, Wilmington
- **(910) 395-0510**

UNCW, Fine Arts Dept., 601 S. College Rd., Wilmington • (910) 395-3415
Wilmington Academy of Music, 1635 Wellington Ave., Wilmington
- **(910) 392-1590**

This tried-and-true method of early-childhood music education accepts students as young as 3 (for violin) and older students as well. The method relies heavily on parental involvement during young students' lessons and is well-represented in the area by independent teachers affiliated with several groups.

Wilmington Boys Choir
16 N. 16th St., Wilmington
- **(910) 799-5073**

Formed in 1985, the Wilmington Boys Choir regularly performs classical and traditional vocal music throughout the area and elsewhere in the state. A nonprofit organization, the choir stresses education and musical appreciation as well as performance technique and is directed by Ms. Sandy Errante. The Choir is actually two choruses in one: a soprano-alto group for boys ages 8 through 13 and a tenor-bass group for ages 14 through 17. Auditions are required, and candidates are expected to fulfill a 10-month commitment involving two rehearsals per week plus performances and a yearly $125 tuition. Rehearsals are held at St. Paul's Episcopal Church, at the address above, but the choir is nondenominational.

Wilmington Children's Museum
1020 Market St., Wilmington
- **(910) 254-3534**

The Children's Museum's various arts programs include Tot Art (for kids ages 3 through 5), Recycling to Art (ages 5 through 12) and Young Artists (age 7 through 12), all designed to introduce children to various arts media and methods and to enhance their capacity for learning and creativity. Ongoing performing arts series bring in storytellers, jugglers, puppeteers, musicians and dancers.

The Children's Museum encourages parental involvement in all the activities. Regular admission to the museum is $2.50 per child and $2 per adult with no time limit; there is an additional fee for some programs. (Other museum highlights are listed in various sections below.)

Wilmington Dance Academy
3333 Wrightsville Ave., Wilmington
- **(910) 791-7660**

This academy accepts children as young as 3, who participate in creative movement classes, something of a pre-dance class. With four teachers on staff, Wilmington Dance has been operating since 1986 and teaches a variety of styles, including ballet, tap, jazz and

Kids go loco over the Wilmington Railroad Museum's locomotive.

Birthday Parties

If you're looking for an extra-special place to give your child a memorable birthday party, look into these venues, all of which offer colorful party rooms and services, some including the use of the arcades, games and more. Also don't overlook your local bowling center — per-game prices for children younger than 12 are often discounted (see the Bowling section in our chapter on Sports, Fitness and Parks for listings).

Athletic Zone
4405 Northchase Pkwy., Wilmington • (910) 452-5020

You can combine a game of soccer, basketball, volleyball or roller hockey with your child's birthday party at this indoor sports facility. You supply the party goods and protective sport gear.

Cape Fear Museum
814 Market St., Wilmington • (910) 341-4350

The Cape Fear Museum designs educational theme parties for children. Craft activities and museum exhibitions may be incorporated into the celebration.

Coastal Tumblegym
915-C N. Lake Park Blvd., Carolina Beach • (910) 458-9490, (910) 458-8384

Coastal Tumblegym hosts 90-minute birthday parties, usually on Saturday or Sunday afternoons (weekdays by special arrangement), featuring a certified professional instructor to lead the children in various physical activities. These may include tackling an obstacle course, playing on a trampoline, running relay races, working out on gymnastic equipment or traversing a 40-foot-long "Moon Walk" floor. Costs begin at $75 for use of the entire facility for the first 10 guests (not counting the birthday child), with an additional $5 for each additional guest. Parents supply food and refreshments.

Jelly Beans Family Skating Center
5216 Oleander Dr., Wilmington • (910) 791-6000

Rain or shine, indoor roller skating can be a great way to celebrate birthdays, and Jelly Beans will provide everything you need for the party, including place settings, ice cream, refreshments — even the cake if you wish — plus a host to serve and clean up afterward. Ask about other provisions, too, such as pizza (additional costs may apply). Choose among several skating sessions lasting two, three or four hours, depending on day and time. Costs begin at $65 for the first eight guests (not counting the birthday child and his or her parents); add $7 for each additional guest.

Jungle Rapids Family Fun Park
5320 Oleander Dr., Wilmington
• (910) 791-0666

Jungle Rapids offers several birthday packages that vary according to age and price. Choose from packages that include go-carts, laser-tag (for older children), water slides, video games or minigolf. Two-hour packages can feature play time, a party in a private party room with a hostess, lunch, cake, a T-shirt for the birthday child, all paper products and balloons.

Putt-Putt Golf & Games
4117 Oleander Dr., Wilmington
• (910) 392-6660

Putt-Putt offers special deals for two-hour birthday parties that feature all the golf kids can play in that time. In addition, each partygoer receives 16 tokens for video games (20 tokens for the kid of honor). Ice cream, soft drinks, a group photo, use of the party room and a special pizza deal are also included.

Wilmington Children's Museum
1020 Market St., Wilmington
• (910) 254-3534

There are few birthday venues as educationally stimulating as the Children's Museum, where kids can play pirate on a genuine pretend-pirate ship, play dress-up with trunks full of costumes, or get into any number of creative, artistic and entertaining activities with dedicated adult supervision. The Children's Museum strives to make the pursuit of fun as educational as possible (and vice versa).

Eats

The vast majority of restaurants in our region caters to young people by offering well-priced children's menus. Several among them are notable.

Causeway Cafe
114 Causeway Dr., Wrightsville Beach
• (910) 256-3730

This is an extremely popular breakfast spot on Wrightsville Beach, just east of the drawbridge. The specialty pancakes and waffles are delectable and can be made in a variety of amusing shapes for children. Arrive early and be sure to ask about the fresh fruit toppings of the day. The recently expanded lunch and dinner menus are worthy of adults' attention.

Chuck E Cheese's Pizza
4389 Oleander Dr., Wilmington
• (910) 392-1234

The ubiquitous Chuck E Cheese's has plenty of diversions to make eating a kid's least concern.

Elizabeth's Pizza
4304 Market St., Wilmington
• (910) 251-1005

Kids like the pizza and other Italian dishes, but are fascinated by the several fish tanks that divide the room.

El Vaquero
4238 Market St., Wilmington
• (910) 815-0706

The quesadilla and the other items on the children's menu offer a nice change-up from other run-of-the-mill choices, and the virgin daiquiri makes for a colorful, cold dessert.

Katy's Great Eats
1054 S. College Rd., Wilmington
• (910) 395-5289

Katy's is well-liked by locals and provides families the opportunity to dine together with

---

INSIDERS' TIP

Some activities for kids on rainy days: bowling, movies, indoor hockey, indoor soccer, indoor skating, museum classes, the North Carolina Aquarium at Fort Fisher, library story times.

few diversions beyond some interesting memorabilia, TV and a Foosball table nearby. If your child is lucky, the one kid-size booth may be available when you visit.

Rock-ola Cafe
418 S. College Rd., Wilmington • (910) 791-4288

Rock-ola takes a tack similar to that of the famous Hard Rock Cafe, with classic rock 'n' roll and decorations, but less noise. Its menu includes several selections for children.

Sweets

No discussion of kidstuff would be complete without something for the sweet tooth. By sweets we mean not only candy but also baked goods and ice cream. As you travel the coast, you'll be tempted by all manner of strategically placed retailers who will dulcify your day; what follows here are some of the kings and queens of confectionery, the barons of bonbon. Read on at the risk of your waistline. Your kids will love you for it.

Apple Annie's Bake Shop
Outlet Mall, S. College Rd., Wilmington • (910) 799-9023
Landfall Shopping Center, Wrightsville Beach • (910) 256-6585

Two locations mean that satisfying a sugar craving will seldom take you too far out of your way. Baking everything fresh daily, Apple Annie's offers a sumptuous array of specialty cakes and cupcakes, cookies and plenty more. Don't pass up the hazelnut-cream-filled Paris brest! This is one of those shops in which the air itself is intoxicating. (Outlet Mall is opposite the south perimeter of the UNCW campus.)

Back Deck Grill
311 S. Topsail Dr., Surf City • (910) 328-0500

Thick shakes and large fresh-baked brownies that stand up well to ice cream are just some of the delights your kids will enjoy at the Back Deck. You can also get egg creams (a Yankee concoction containing no egg), 24 flavors of soft and hand-dipped ice cream as

---

Did You Say (gulp!) G-g-ghosts?

Mysterious footsteps . . . misty apparitions . . . playful pranks . . . empty rockers rocking . . . . Some say the true soul of an old town is its ghosts, and the southern coast region has more specters than golfers. (We're not complaining.) Sleep in a historic house long enough — a night or two might do it — and you're likely to make an acquaintance! Insiders take their ectoplasms seriously because, as the following oft-told tidbits suggest, wraiths have been a coastal way of life (and death) for a long, long time.

Capt. Harper's Ghostly Rescue
Back in 1897, Captain John M. Harper, a renowned Cape Fear River skipper, found he didn't need a dark and stormy night for a convincing ghost story — but it sure didn't hurt. He used to tell this story himself.

While making the passage from Wilmington to Smithville (now Southport) through a terrible winter storm, Harper was regaled by his sole passenger, a Scot, within the ferry's pilot house. The Scot told a tale about an ancestor of his, one of three Highlanders captured by the British during the American Revolution and imprisoned nearby at colonial Brunswick Town. The three captives were condemned to die, but one of them, the passenger's ancestor, made his escape. The other two were not so lucky.

Soon after the tale was told, Capt. Harper's steamer ran hard aground on a shoal opposite the site of old Brunswick Town. There was nothing to do but wait for the tide

— continued on next page

Many Insiders believe that a ghost called the Gossamer Lady is a frequent visitor at Thalian Hall.

to change and keep warm below decks. While they were there, a deck hand burst in, terrified. On deck moments before, he said, he had seen an unkempt man, dripping wet, his face contorted as if in pain. The apparition held the rail with one hand and pointed into the darkness with the other, and when the deck hand went to touch his arm, the man vanished.

Harper doubted the crewman's sobriety. But when the tide had shifted and the ship was again under way, Harper, too, witnessed the impossible. After distinctly hearing a human cry, he and his entire crew spied an old rowing barge with two emaciated men on deck, their injured legs and arms manacled and chained. Harper ordered a rope cast to them, but the barge disappeared into the darkness.

Harper continued on his course and very soon came upon a capsized ship to which two men clung for their lives in the icy, black waters. They were found in the direction in which the first apparition on deck had pointed. With the Scotsman's tale fresh in their minds, Harper's crew rescued the two survivors, the last of a riverboat's crew of seven. Evidently some ghosts, despite their own former suffering, believe in doing good deeds.

The Maco Light

Until the Atlantic Coast Railroad tore up the tracks running west through Maco, many locals living today had witnessed the strange swaying light at the old Maco crossing. President Grover Cleveland spoke about it publicly during his 1888 reelection campaign. *Life* magazine even reported it to the nation in 1957. The story is that of Joe Baldwin, a flagman who, one pitch-dark night in 1867, was riding a caboose that lost its coupling pin. Separated from the train, the caboose had slowed nearly to a halt when Joe spied the light of a speeding passenger train coming right at him. He stood at the back of the caboose waving a lantern in warning, but the oncoming train couldn't stop.

In the collision Joe was killed instantly, decapitated. His head was never found, but ever since then, a single swaying light could be seen over the tracks at that very spot.

— continued on next page

It was seen so frequently that trainmen routinely mounted two lights on their trains, one red and one green, so as not to be confused with the Maco Light, which hasn't been seen since the tracks were lifted. It seems Old Joe Baldwin's warnings are no longer needed.

The House on Gallows Hill

It is said that back when Wilmington barely stretched beyond what is now Third Street, the high ground just off the main road, past the old St. James burial ground, was a hanging ground. Criminals, we're told, who went to their Maker on the hill were buried nearby. But when the town outgrew its former bounds, the old gallows were dismantled and houses constructed, among them the Price-Gause House, built in 1843. Fortunately for its residents, this home's invisible guest is a playful one, occasionally mischievous but never baleful.

The ghost, who is lately called George, seems to favor phantom pipe tobacco and spectral sweet potatoes — judging by the smells that occasionally greet the living occupants, employees of an architectural firm. Other incidents? A rocker that rocks itself no matter where it's placed, clearly audible footsteps when no one's there, mysteriously clouding mirrors and, perhaps best of all, quilts yanked from beds while people lie sleeping. It's a wonder no one hears hearty laughter too.

There are many other ghostly yarns to spin about North Carolina's southern coast — the Edwardian thespians of Thalian Hall; the visitations of Samuel Jocelyn to prove he was buried alive; the phantom Confederate General William Whiting, still leading the defense of Fort Fisher. You can read the stories in books available at regional public libraries and stores: *Tar Heel Ghosts* by John Harden (Chapel Hill: University of North Carolina Press, 1954); *Haunted Wilmington . . . and the Cape Fear Coast* by Brooks Newton Preik (Wilmington, N.C.: Banks Channel Books, 1995); and *Ghosts of the Carolinas* by Nancy Roberts (Columbia: University of South Carolina Press, 1962).

---

well as full lunches and dinners with a can't-miss kids' menu ranging from PB&J sandwiches to fish 'n' chips and steaks.

The Back Deck Grill has an excellent soundside view and is open seven days a week in summer. (There's even live music in the evenings on Friday and Saturday. Don't tell the kids!) The Grill is a quarter-mile south of the Surf City traffic light.

Back Porch Ice Cream Shoppe
1572 Thomasboro Rd., Calabash
• **(910) 579-1533**

Back Porch, across from Callahan's Gift Shop, serves 21 hand-dipped ice cream and yogurt flavors, homemade waffle cones and plenty of other delights. Try the Hawaiian Ice.

Baskin-Robbins 31 Flavors Ice Cream and Yogurt Store
3809 Oleander Dr., Wilmington
• **(910) 791-7192**

Baskin-Robbins offers the typical wide variety of flavors, plus frozen yogurt, fat-free desserts and low-fat yogurt cakes.

The Candy Barrel
309 N. Front St., Wilmington
• **(910) 762-3727**

Situated in the Cotton Exchange down-

INSIDERS' TIP

Azalea Festival in April always brings a world-renowned circus to Wilmington — in a real big top!

Bring the entire family to the aquarium at Fort Fisher, where the sea really comes ashore.

Photo: Cape Fear Convention and Visitors Bureau

town, The Candy Barrel specializes in taffy, fudge and candy by the pound, including scrumptious homemade chocolate clusters of many kinds. The treats don't come cheap here, but the quality and selection are such that a little goes a long way.

Candy Express
Independence Mall, 3500 Oleander Dr., Wilmington • (910) 791-5089

A dieter's nightmare and a kid's dream come true, Candy Express is a good place to shop for that gumball machine you've always wanted as well as dessert sauces, gift tins and coffee mugs.

Dairy Queen
201 N. Fort Fisher Blvd., Kure Beach
• (910) 458-9788

This "full treat" establishment, one block from the ocean, features a spacious, shady porch with plenty of bench seating, handicapped access and ample parking. Did we mention great ice cream?

Fudge Company
201 New River Dr., Surf City
• (910) 328-1905

The Fudge Company at Topsail Trading Company makes a variety of fresh, cream-

---

INSIDERS' TIP

"Motherwell" is New Hanover Regional Medical Center's maternity fitness program for expectant mothers. It includes exercises and valuable discussions, and participation is on a monthly basis ($45 for one month, $25 each additional month). Call (910) 343-7000, ext. 7106 for information.

Kohl's Frozen Custard
92 S. Lumina Ave., Wrightsville Beach
- **(910) 256-3955**

Not ice cream, but the more full-bodied custard is Kohl's claim to local fame. Whipping up homemade-style custard in two flavors daily, plus a special flavor of the day, Kohl's creates some mouth-watering concoctions with its custard and serves light lunch fare as well. You'll find Kohl's a few steps from the foot of the fixed bridge, or a few more steps from the beach.

Ms. Muffet's Yogurt Shop
7110 Wrightsville Ave., Wrightsville Beach • (910) 256-6031

One of the few yogurt shops around with a drive-up window, Ms. Muffet's offers a great selection of rich frozen yogurts, a smorgasbord of toppings and fat-free and cholesterol-free indulgences. Ms. Muffet's, in the Cross Point Plaza shopping center, is convenient to Wrightsville Beach and has indoor seating and plenty of parking.

The Scoop Ice Cream & Sandwich Shoppe
309 N. Front St., Wilmington
- **(910) 763-3566**

For frozen confections as well as snacks and sandwiches a short walk from Wilmington's riverfront, there's The Scoop in the Cotton Exchange. Seating just outside the tiny shop offers an extremely pleasant shaded place in which to enjoy dessert in practically any season. It's a fine stopover for the weary shopper.

Seven Seas Ice Cream
126 N. Fort Fisher Blvd., Kure Beach
- **(910) 458-8122**

Seven Seas offers locally made hand-scooped ice cream and ice-cream desserts. Treats can be enjoyed at tables out front. Seven Seas is part of the Seven Seas Inn, and it's open seven days a week in summer.

Swensen's
620 S. College Rd., Wilmington
- **(910) 395-6740**

San Francisco's contribution to calorie-collecting, Swensen's ranks high (some say highest) among local ice cream parlors. The Outrageous Sundaes are often too much for all but the most voracious. The kids' treat called Mr. San Francisco is an ice cream creation shaped like a clown, with bubble-gum eyes and nose and a chocolate-dipped cone hat. Swensen's is a full-service restaurant and serves a children's menu. A miniature train circles the ceiling of the dining room.

Toms Drug Company
1 N. Front St., Wilmington
- **(910) 762-3391**

We often wonder how many children and their parents walk away from Riverfront Park craving sweets and leaving empty-handed because they didn't know that Toms stocks plenty of candies. Buying sweets in a drugstore makes sense, particularly if chocolate is your drug of choice. Toms offers a good selection.

Vic's Corn Popper
1616 Shipyard Blvd., Wilmington
- **(910) 452-2869**

Popcorn in a sweets listing? You bet, especially if it's Vic's freshly made caramel corn. Vic's is an award-winning popcorn franchise, and you'll find more different kinds of popcorn than you may have seen before.

Yogurt Plus
208 N. New River Dr., Surf City
- **(910) 328-1224**

The yogurt here tastes so good, the kids may not care that it's good for them. Fat-free, sugar-free and cholesterol-free desserts are the specialties, and it all tastes wonderfully sinful.

Exploring Nature

The most accessible, most affordable and most attractive source of fun for kids on the southern coast is the same one that draws adults in droves: the beaches and nearby waterways. So no matter what your kids' ages, get 'em down to the water, from Topsail to Calabash. Try a different beach now and then to pique their interest; there's

230 • KIDSTUFF

a great difference in character from beach to beach.

Combining activities with beach visits may also be worthwhile. Driving a four-wheel-drive vehicle on the beach at the Fort Fisher State Recreation Area is a bouncy jaunt most kids love. The area offers pristine surf, calm tidal waters on the inland side suitable for toddlers, great fishing and, just minutes away, a fine Civil War museum and historic site. (See the Off-Roading section in our Sports, Fitness and Parks chapter.)

Carolina Beach State Park
Dow Rd., Carolina Beach
- **(910) 458-8206**

In addition to all there is to do and see in this park (see our chapter on Sports, Fitness and Parks), the Sugar Loaf sand dune is one place that kids love. Running up and tumbling down is a simple pleasure, to be sure — perhaps the best kind. Elsewhere in the park, kids are challenged to locate the several carnivorous plants indigenous to the area: sun dews, pitcher plants and the famous Venus's flytrap. Be sure to instruct the children about the plants' rarity and delicacy, and leave them as you found them. You can visit the park from dawn to dusk.

Greenfield Lake and Gardens
U.S. 421 S., Wilmington • (910) 341-7855

Greenfield Lake and Gardens, a short drive down Third Street from downtown Wilmington, offers ideal outdoor entertainment for children. Toddlers will certainly enjoy feeding the many ducks and geese that gather at the lake shore. In fact, Greenfield Lake attracts many types of wildlife that will challenge a child's imagination and naming skills.

Most youngsters love taking excursions in the paddle boats or canoes that can be rented at the dock on the north side of the lake off Third Street. Rates are reasonable: Paddle boats cost $2 per half-hour; canoes cost $3 for the first hour and $1.50 each additional hour. Life jackets are included. Playgrounds and picnic areas abound near the dock. Older children can enjoy a day's fishing from any of the lake's several small piers and bridges or from your own johnboat, which can be launched from the ramp on W. Lake Shore Drive, just off Third Street. The park is open from dawn until dusk.

North Carolina Aquarium at Fort Fisher
Fort Fisher Blvd., Fort Fisher
- **(910) 458-8257**

Besides everything else the aquarium is famous for (see our Attractions chapter), it also specializes in excursions and learning programs designed with kids in mind. Typical programs here may address topics such as Animals Without Backbones, Shark Bites and Nature Crafts. The aquarium's Ocean Odyssey series allows children ages 7 through 10 to learn about ecology, marine animals and coastal wildlife (children should be prepared to get wet on certain excursions).

Children's Discovery sessions offer storytelling and "critter creating" for preschoolers. Outings are ongoing, vary widely and are led by qualified personnel. Recent programs have included hunting for shells, the Japanese art of fish-printing, surf fishing, cleaning and cooking coastal cuisine, salt-marsh hikes and canoeing the marshes, explorations of local plant life and sand casting.

Costs range from free to $7. Special events often mark holidays and seasons with appropriate crafts. Contact the aquarium for seasonal brochures. For weekly listings, also check the community calendar in the "Neighbors" section of the Wednesday *Wilmington Star-News*. Regular aquarium hours are 9 AM to 7 PM daily in the summer. Winter hours)Labor Day to Memorial Day) are 9 AM to 5 PM daily. Admission is $3 for adults, $2 for seniors 62 and older and active military personnel, and $1 for children ages 6 through 17.

Wilmington Children's Museum
1020 Market St., Wilmington
- **(910) 254-3534**

Nature Time is a series of one-hour sessions designed for children ages 3 through 5 to learn about and to explore nature. Meetings are held at the museum as well as off site. Representative topics include "Finding the Science of Spring" and "Endangered Species of Wilmington." Participation costs $2.50 per session.

Farms

Holden Brothers Farm Market
5600 U.S. Hwy. 17 W., Shallotte
• (910) 579-4500

Bring the kids to pick strawberries, sweet corn, cantaloupes, watermelons, pumpkins and other vegetables in season. The fields and market are open from April 1 through Christmas and are located 3 miles south of Shallotte.

Lewis Farms
6517 Gordon Rd.

Not long after the strawberries at Lewis' Strawberry Nursery appear, Lewis' Gordon Road location repeats the feat in blueberries and strawberries, with the added attractions of ice cream, potted plants and flowers for sale. Lewis Farms is open to the public only in the spring from 8 AM to 6 PM. Gordon Road intersects Market Street (U.S. 17) just south of the Military Cutoff Road intersection and N. College Road near the junction with I-40.

Lewis Strawberry Nursery
Castle Hayne Rd.

Picking berries can be almost as much fun as eating them. In late spring, peaking in May, the strawberries at Lewis' Nursery ripen into succulent concentrations of juicy, deep-red sweetness that almost defy belief. Whether you and the kids pick them yourselves or buy them by the quart, this is a treat you'll want to repeat. The nursery is less than 3 miles north of the 23rd Street intersection on Castle Hayne Road (Highway 117), and it's open for picking (depending on the supply of berries) every day.

Getting Physical

Check our chapter on Sports, Fitness and Parks for information on field and team sports for children of school age. Included below are physical activities that either apply specifically to young children or would otherwise fall through the cracks of the sports categories.

The Boxing & Fitness Center
602 N. Fourth St., Wilmington
• (910) 341-7872

Administered by the Wilmington Parks and Recreation Department, the Boxing Center welcomes grade school-age children to participate in fitness training and professionally supervised boxing. Six-week sessions in fitness for overweight youths ages 10 through 15 take place throughout the year after school hours, Monday through Friday. Fitness equipment here includes treadmills, Lifecycles, free weights, a universal gym, jump ropes, heavy bags, boxing gloves and scheduled exercise classes — all this for the bargain-basement annual membership price of $10 for city residents, $13 for others.

Fit For Fun
UNCW campus, Wilmington
• (910) 341-7855

This is a program sponsored by the Wilmington Parks and Recreation Department that affords children ages 18 months through 5 years the opportunity to exercise two days a week, with parental accompaniment. Two sessions, divided by age, take place each Monday and Wednesday morning. Soft-soled shoes (sneakers) are required, and class size is limited to 30 children and 30 parents. Cost is low — $1 for Wilmington residents, $1.50 for nonresidents — and preregistration is required.

Jelly Beans Family Skating Center
5216 Oleander Dr., Wilmington
• (910) 791-6000

Roller skating can be family fun at its best and perhaps simplest, and Jelly Beans ap-

---

INSIDERS' TIP

Fans of model trains can get on the right track with the Cape Fear Model Railroad Club, (910) 763-2634, which meets at the Wilmington Railroad Museum, 501 Nutt Street, and welcomes novices as well as experts.

peals especially to kids of middle-school age and younger and their parents. Grown-ups may appreciate the top-40 music on Wednesday and Thursday nights. The rink is a clean, well-kept place with a well-stocked pro shop providing rentals (standard skates $1.50, in-line skates $2.50), sales and repairs, a snack lounge and the Stuff Shop, which sells toys costing from 25¢ to $3.

Skating sessions cost $3 per person at all times except Friday and Saturday nights, when the admission is $5.50. Jelly Beans is open every day from 2 to 5 PM, plus 7 to 10 PM Wednesday and Thursday and 7 to 11 PM Friday and Saturday. The rink hosts its own roller-hockey league for kids age 12 and younger. Pick-up games are available during the summer. Jelly Beans also hosts skating birthday parties and a summer day camp (see our Kidstuff chapter). Jelly Beans is near the intersection of Oleander Drive and Forest Park Road, 5 miles from downtown.

The Kids' Gym
5710 Oleander Dr., Ste. 211, Wilmington
- **(910) 799-2553**

The Kids' Gym offers a variety of noncompetitive, educational gymnastics classes for ages 4 months through the teens. Classes also feature numbers, colors and music through the use of obstacles and games — what the staff of certified teachers and gymnasts calls "a physical Sesame Street" — all in a clean, positive atmosphere. A full-day preschool program is also available. Kids' Night Out gives kids and parents an evening to themselves each weekend.

The Kids' Gym also facilitates birthday parties hosted by Teddy Tumblebear; half- and full-day summer camps for children ages 3 through 12 (open to nonmembers on a weekly basis and useful to visitors); karate; morning preschool (9 AM to noon); postnatal exercise classes for moms; an after-school program; and a gymnastics demonstration team that emphasizes performance rather than competition. Nursery service is also available. Memberships cost $25 per month for one child, $30 a month for two or more children. The Kids' Gym is a member business of U.S. Gymnastics.

The Martin Luther King Jr. Center
410 S. Eighth St., Wilmington
- **(910) 341-7866**

On the third Thursday of each month, the Wilmington Parks and Recreation Department sponsors a sports night, essentially an evening of basketball, from 6 to 8 PM. Other activities include karate, field trips and table tennis (perhaps not everyone's idea of "getting physical").

Scooter's Family Skating Center
341 Shipyard Blvd., Wilmington
- **(910) 791-8550**

Scooter's is the current name for this classic rink, founded in 1959 and now totally remodeled. On a typical Friday evening, the empty parking lot gives no indication that there may be scores of skaters inside, "talking in circles," "figuring things out," rolling to rock music. Among Scooter's offerings are all-night skating sessions lasting from 7 PM to 7 AM.

Skating at Scooter's is affordable: sessions cost from $3.50 to $4, and skate rentals are only a buck. There's a pro shop on the premises and a full snack bar. Scooter's also offers private skating parties and group sessions, fund-raiser sessions and plenty of video games. The rink is open Wednesday through Sunday from 1 to 5 PM, Tuesday and Wednes-

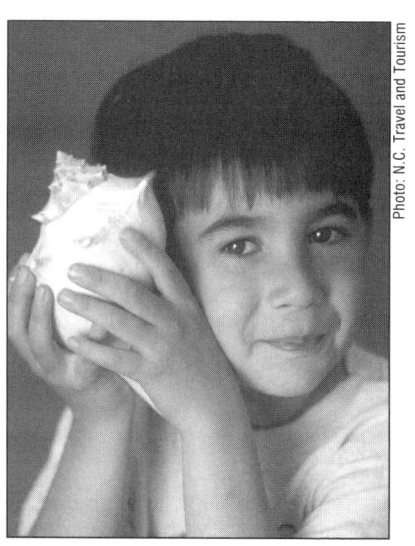

If you listen closely, you can hear the ocean.

day from 7 to 9 PM and Friday and Saturday from 7 to 11 PM.

Topsail Skating Rink
714 S. Anderson Blvd., Topsail Beach
• (910) 328-2381

An institution since the 1950s, this quaint, unpretentious, upstairs roller rink is in a lime-green house above the town's tiny post office. It is open 7 to 10 PM seven nights a week between Easter weekend and Labor Day. Sessions are inexpensive, $3.50 to $4.50, as are the skate rentals. The building is near Flake Avenue, an easy walk from the Patio Playground.

Getting Wet

As if the ocean weren't enough, Cape Fear offers plenty of other opportunities for kids to douse themselves, and some of them are downright thrilling. We're referring to water slides. One of the best is at the Jungle Rapids Family Fun Park, 5320 Oleander Drive, (910) 791-0888, in Wilmington. Jubilee Park, 1000 N. Lake Park Boulevard in Carolina Beach, (910) 458-6067, features a popular slide and the "Rain Room," a place to get nicely misted on a hot day. (Both locations are described in our Attractions chapter.)

In South Brunswick, the Magic Mountain Water Slide in Holden Beach, (910) 842-2727, has five killer flumes, and Ocean Isle Beach hosts its own water slide on Causeway Drive.

Most of these attractions are open seven days a week between Memorial and Labor days. Prices hover around $3 and $4 per half-hour, with discounts for longer sessions, ranging from about $8 to $12 for the whole day. Prices usually drop after 5 PM.

Beyond these, kids can find places to get wet in our Watersports chapter or our Sports, Fitness and Parks chapter.

Going Mental

Babbage's Software
Independence Mall, 3500 Oleander Dr., Wilmington • (910) 791-8168

Babbage's carries a fine selection of video games, CD-ROMs and computer accessories — many of them educational — in addition to its wide range of other computer software for IBM-compatibles.

Books-A-Million
3737 Oleander Dr., Wilmington
• (910) 452-1519

This book superstore adjacent to Office Depot hosts story hours for young children every Saturday at 3 PM. When the children's section is otherwise quiet, kids enjoy playing on the "train-car" benches. The locomotive houses a TV that shows ongoing children's videos to keep kids entertained while mom and dad browse nearby.

Brunswick County Library
Southport Library, 109 W. Moore St., Southport • (910) 457-6237
Leland Library, 487 Village Rd., Leland
• (910) 371-9442
G.V. Barbee Branch, 818 Yaupon Dr., Yaupon Beach • (910) 278-4283
Rourk Branch, 5068 Main St., Shallotte
• (910) 754-6578

Story times for children ages 2 through 5 are offered at these Brunswick County public libraries at 10 AM on Monday at Southport, Tuesday at Leland, Wednesday at Yaupon Beach and Thursday at Shallotte. The Brunswick County Library also hosts a summer reading program for school-age children. The six-week program involves weekly meetings and activities at the branch libraries and awards incentive prizes.

Be sure also to inquire about the library's weekly Preschool Music Hour, offering children the opportunity to sing, move creatively, play instruments and, in doing so — believe it or not — very possibly improve their spatial abilities and math skills. (Music really does make you smarter!) Participation in all library programs is free.

Cape Fear Astronomical Society
(910) 762-1033

Kids old enough to understand that those bright objects in the night sky are incredibly distant will appreciate the occasional sky observations, using members' telescopes, sponsored by the Astronomical Society to raise interest in membership. Viewing sessions are announced in the calendar of the *Wilmington Star-News*.

The public is also invited to the society's monthly meetings, which feature interesting films and presentations. Meetings take place on the first Sunday of each month (or the second, if delayed by a holiday) and are also announced in the newspaper. The society is open to everyone of any age, regardless of any astronomical knowledge, and young teenagers are among its current members.

In addition to the popular public viewing sessions, the society also undertakes periodic school talks and trips to planetariums. Membership has one prerequisite, if you could call it that: a sincere interest in astronomy and in learning more about it. Memberships cost $20 per year ($25 for families) and include the society's monthly newsletter, *Cape Fear Skies*. Members also participate in picnics and an exhibition booth at Riverfest. The society's mailing address is 305 N. 21st Street, Wilmington, NC 28405.

Carolina Kite Club
Wrightsville Beach

Is kite-flying an amusement, a physical activity, an art or a nature exploration? We decided it was all of these and therefore deserving of our Going Mental section.

There are no better places to fly kites than at the beach, with its steady winds. The Carolina Kite Club is an informal clutch of devotees who gather at the south end of Wrightsville Beach on Sunday mornings in the warmer seasons. Meetings are often announced in the calendar sections of the *Star-News*. For additional information on local kite flying, see the section by that name in our Sports, Fitness and Parks chapter.

L Bookworm
3004 Holden Beach Rd. S.W., Holden Beach • (910) 842-7380

Barbara and Jim Lowell's bookstore, housed in a converted former church building, is a community gathering place that offers story times for children ages 4 through 8 on Wednesdays at 11 AM in the summer. The store also features a good children's section that includes used books at low prices.

New Hanover County Public Library
Main Branch, 201 Chestnut St., Wilmington • (910) 341-4392
Carolina Beach Branch, 300 Cape Fear Blvd., Wilmington • (910) 458-5016
Myrtle Grove Branch, 5155 S. College Rd., Wilmington • (910) 452-6414
Plaza East Library, Plaza East Shopping Center, Wrightsville Beach
• (910) 256-2173

The Children's Rooms at these libraries are excellent resources for stimulating entertainment that isn't limited to story times. Activities are designed for children in three age groups. Toddler Time offers stories, songs and interactive finger plays just for babies ages 18 months through 3 years and their parents. Preschooler Storytime may include films and is geared for ages 3 through 5. Book Break is intended for children 6 through 10 and presents longer stories, read-alouds, activities and films. All events are offered weekly on different days at different branches of the library, giving you a choice of schedules. The main branch is the only one offering activities all year long. All programs are free and open to the public.

Other library programs are cut from a wide and colorful cloth. Recurring programs include a Babysitter's Workshop, designed to teach young people ages 12 through 15 about babysitting, safety, child development, simple snacks and activities. Family programs may present history as related in song, African dance or readings by children's authors. Call the library's Youth Services office at the number above to inquire about schedules and registration, which may be limited for some workshops.

School Room
Shallotte Plaza, #7 Main St., Shallotte
• (910) 754-2345

Sure, the professional teacher will find plenty of educational supplies and materials here, but School Room is also a real bonanza for the inquisitive child. It stocks a stimulating variety of games ranging from traditional board games to state-of-the-art computer games, science projects, puzzles, educational posters and foreign-language workbooks. There's also a children's section complete with small desk and blackboard (which we're told the kids love to erase).

This small shop is jammed with interesting stuff catering to children from pre-K through junior high. It's next door to Dairy Queen (a potential bargaining chip for parents).

Seahawk Chess Club
UNCW, University Union 105, 601 S. College Rd., Wilmington
• (910) 395-3841

This club, based on the UNCW campus and facilitated by advanced competitors, is a great place for players to sharpen their skills and learn new tactics. Novices and nonstudents are welcome.

Sneads Ferry Public Library
242 Sneads Ferry Rd., Sneads Ferry
• (910) 327-6471

This branch of the Onslow County Public Library, convenient to northern Topsail Island, invites children ages 3 and older to participate in stories, cartoons, crafts and short movies every Wednesday at 10:30 AM throughout the year, except for six weeks in the summer when the summer reading program kicks in. Reading for the summer program adheres to predetermined themes appropriate for a range of reading levels. All programs are free.

Wilmington Children's Museum
1020 Market St., Wilmington
• (910) 254-3534

The Children's Museum is a colorful, exciting space where kids up to age 12 can engage in activities that will enhance lifelong learning and creativity. Programs focus on the arts, science and technology, health and safety, mathematics, multicultural studies and the environment. In its muralled storefront setting, the museum features a two-deck pirate ship complete with flags, canon and costumes; computer terminals with educational software; a grocery store where kids learn to count by handling play-money and merchandise; and a costume theater where they can don a different personality with every stitch of clothing.

The medical room teaches kids about their bodies and internal organs through the use of ingenious visual aids, blood-pressure cuffs and stethoscopes. Kids learn about the weather through exhibits designed by kids. And the water-play room features two kid-size tanks filled with things that float, fill, spill and sink, plus life-size cardboard models of various marine life on the walls overhead. You'll find few chairs in the Children's Museum because it encourages adults to engage their kids in the process of learning through play.

Program highlights include the Science Saturdays series, in which kids learn about kitchen chemistry, the weather, the mechanics of simple machines and toys and much more. Puppet shows and programs about international foods and etiquette introduce kids to humanity's global diversity. Check the museum's calendar for special events.

Daily admission to the museum costs $2.50 per child, $2 per adult. An annual 12-visit membership costs $35 and includes discounts on birthday parties, special events and a bimonthly newsletter. Patrons ($100 per year) are entitled to additional benefits. The Children's Museum is entirely volunteer-driven and welcomes new participants. The museum is open Tuesday, Thursday and Saturday from 10 AM to 2 PM and Sunday 1 to 4 PM.

Wilmington Table Tennis Association
Tileston School, Fifth and Ann Sts., Wilmington • (910) 395-5644

Table tennis players of all ages and skill levels are welcome to join the association on Monday and Wednesday nights from 7 to 9 PM. There is no fee to join, and if you don't have your own paddle, the association can usually provide one.

Wrightsville Beach Summer Reading Program
1 Bob Sawyer Dr., Wrightsville Beach
• (910) 256-7925

Wrightsville Beach Parks and Recreation sponsors summer reading programs for high school students, where they read and explore several works of their choice from a select list. Meetings occur two mornings per week from late June through July. Fees range from about $175 for Wrightsville Beach residents to $260 for nonresidents.

Holidays

Several holiday events geared for kids are listed in our Annual Events chapter. Listed here is a cross-section of lesser-known offerings grouped by holiday. Be sure to stop by the Cape Fear Coast Convention & Visitors Bureau at 24 N. Third Street in Wilmington, (910) 341-4030 or (800) 222-4757, (800) 457-8912 in Canada, to request the latest publications for holiday events, particularly the Christmas season brochure, which includes information on festivities in Carolina and Kure beaches.

New Hanover County Public Library
201 Chestnut St., Wilmington
• **(910) 341-4392**

The public library hosts programs for several holidays. Offerings include ghostly tales at Halloween, teachings about Thanksgivings past and present, and a look at the many ways Christmas is celebrated around the world. Children also help make decorations and trim the library tree. Story sessions are geared for particular age groups ranging from ages 6 through 10 and last from 30 minutes to just under an hour. Call the library for schedules and events at locations other than the main branch. Admission is free.

Easter

Easter Egg Hunt
Poplar Grove Historic Plantation, 10200 U.S. Hwy. 17 N., Scotts Hill
• **(910) 686-9518**

Young children always get a big thrill out of the annual Easter Egg Hunt. The setting is attractive, and historic Poplar Grove offers other diversions for the entire family.

Halloween

Cape Fear Filmmakers Accord Haunted House
21 Market St., Wilmington
• **(910) 763-3456**

The Accord sponsors perhaps the most flamboyant Halloween haunted house in the region as a fund raiser and publicity vehicle, putting its talents for movie magic to work to create a truly impressive and often convincing abode of ghouls and ghosts. Locations change from year to year. Admission is $4.

Kwanzaa

This eight-day African-American cultural celebration is observed yearly in the Wilmington area during the week between Christmas and New Year's Day. The word refers to the harvest's "first fruit." For information on events, call the Cape Fear Coast Convention & Visitors Bureau, (910) 341-4030. Public radio WHQR 91.3 FM, (910) 343-1640, broadcasts its own Kwanzaa production, *Season's Griot*, created and performed by local storyteller and musician Madafo Lloyd Wilson each year. Tune in or call for details.

Christmas

Christmas Lights at Calder Court

Calder Court, a cul-de-sac in the Kings Grant subdivision off N.C. Highway 132 (College Road), is a must-see for kids and adults during the weeks prior to Christmas. Each year, residents of Calder Court (and, increasingly, the entire subdivision) adorn their homes with an incredible array of lights and decorations, attracting caravans of people who turn off their headlights to view the spectacle in all its glory. To get there from S. College Road, turn right onto Kings Drive, which is about 1.25 miles north of the Market Street overpass. Then make two left turns. Just follow the line of cars ahead; you can't miss it.

Christmas for Kids and Others Concert
Thalian Hall Center for the Performing Arts, 310 Chestnut St., Wilmington
• **(910) 343-3664, (800) 523-2820**

The Wilmington Choral Society presents this seasonal concert program in early December. Tickets cost $8 for adults and $6 for children 12 and younger, students and senior citizens 62 and older.

The Enchanted Toy Shop
Thalian Hall Center for the Performing Arts, 310 Chestnut St., Wilmington
- **(910) 343-3664**

The Enchanted Toy Shop is a ballet staged annually by the Cape Fear Theatre Ballet in mid-December. Performed by local dancers, some of them quite young, it makes a festive bookend to Thalian's other great holiday production, *The Nutcracker*. Call for tickets early on — October's not too soon — for ticket information and schedules. Ticket prices range from about $12 to $18.

Santa Claus at Independence Mall
3500 Oleander Dr., Wilmington
- **(910) 392-1776**

Santa Claus arrives at the mall every year in mid-November and remains ensconced in winter glory in the mall's central plaza until his midnight ride on Christmas Eve. Also featured is a month-long program of live, seasonal music.

Summer Camps

Day camps and sports camps (rather than overnight camps) are the norm in the southern coastal region. For sports camps, children must own basic personal equipment, including protective gear. Team items such as bats and balls are provided. Be sure to review our chapter on Sports, Fitness and Parks as well. Day campers generally need only swim suits, towels and sneakers to get the most out of their camp experiences.

An extremely useful publication, *Summer Alternatives*, lists dozens of summer activities for school-age children in our area. It is published in late April by the New Hanover County School Board and may be obtained free at any middle and elementary school office and at the Board of Education offices, 1802 S. 15th Street in Wilmington.

Ashton Farm Summer Day Camp
5645 U.S. 117 S., Burgaw
- **(910) 259-2431**

Ashton Farm is 72 acres of historic plantation about 18 miles north of Wilmington. Owners Sally and Jim Martin provide children ages 5 through 13 with down-to-earth fun. Kids participate in farm life, sports with minimized competition and nature. Among the activities are swimming, canoeing, riding, softball, hiking, crafts, animal care, rodeos, archery and ice cream-making.

One-week sessions ($75 per week) from June to August are available (daily with permission). Discounts apply for additional weeks and/or additional children registered. A special "Mini Camp" ($40) is available for three days in June for preschoolers. The camp provides round-trip transportation to Wilmington, camper health insurance and drinks; children should pack their own lunches. Single-day camps have been added to coincide with school holidays and weekends.

Brigade Boys and Girls Club
2759 Vance St., Wilmington
- **(910) 791-4282**

Between the last day of school and the first day back in the fall, children may share in games, computer activities, arts and crafts and library activities at the club, Monday through Friday 10 AM to 6 PM. An early program is also available from 6:30 to 10 AM. Cost is about $150 for the summer plus a $25 annual membership.

Brunswick County Parks and Recreation Department
Planning Bldg., Government complex, Bolivia • (910) 253-4357, (800) 222-4790

Summer sports camps in baseball, soccer and wrestling are offered at various parks in Brunswick County from June through August. Register early.

Cape Fear Museum
814 Market St., Wilmington
- **(910) 341-4350**

A variety of activities involving dinosaurs, local history and nature are available to children ages 5 through 12 in half-day and full-day camps at the museum, five days a week from June 10 through August 16. Fees range from $50 to $85 (discounted for museum members).

Girls Inc. Day Camp
1502 Castle St., Wilmington
- **(910) 763-6674**

Girls Inc. offers half-day and full-day camps in Wilmington and Burgaw. Activities include sports, crafts, swimming, computer classes, sewing, field trips, career exploration, science projects and cooking; guest speakers are brought in from time to time. The Wilmington camp accepts only girls from kindergarten to age 18. The Burgaw camp accepts boys and girls from kindergarten through age 15. Fees are approximately $40 per week for full-day camp, $25 for half-days plus a $10 registration fee.

Hammerheads' Soccer Clinic and Camps
1630 Military Cutoff Rd., Ste. 200 G-H, Wilmington • (910) 341-5102

In cooperation with the Cape Fear Youth Soccer Association, Wilmington's professional soccer team, the Hammerheads, offers camps and clinics led by Hammerhead players and staff, with coaches from around the country. Sessions are open to boys and girls of all ages, and some begin in January. Offerings include coach's clinics, training sessions, individual technical training, specialized sessions for strikers and goalkeepers, small-sided and 11-vs.-11 play and scholarship opportunities. Full-week camps (9 AM until 1 PM) cost $75 per player, T-shirt included. Call for schedule information and register early.

Jelly Beans Family Skating Center
5216 Oleander Dr., Wilmington • (910) 791-6000

Jelly Beans' summer day camp, for kids ages 4 through 15, is especially convenient (and affordable) because your child can just drop in for a single day at a time, and daily fees can be as low as $12. While roller skating is a natural part of regular activities, Jelly Beans concentrates heavily on outdoor and educational field trips. A typical camp day runs from 7 AM to 6 PM.

The Kids' Gym
5710 Oleander Dr., Ste. 211, Wilmington • (910) 799-2553

The Kids' Gym offers summer camp for children ages 3 through 12. Programs include gymnastics, exercise, arts and crafts and field trips, and run in two-week sessions or longer. Check in early spring for schedules and program information.

National Youth Sport Program at UNCW
601 S. College Rd., Wilmington • (910) 395-3262

Eligibility for this free camp, for children ages 10 through 16, is determined by application (available from school counselors and physical education instructors). Offerings include golf, soccer, swimming, tennis, drug and alcohol awareness, nutrition and career choices. Medical exams are given prior to attendance, and transportation and lunch are provided. The camp runs five days a week from mid-June through mid-July.

UNCW Athletic Department
601 S. College Rd., Wilmington • (910) 395-3232

UNCW sponsors one-week summer sports camps in baseball, basketball, tennis, swimming, volleyball and soccer. Attendees may be as young as 3 years old or as old as seniors in high school. These sessions give younger players a good foundation for the games and emphasize fundamentals. Camps are also available for men's and women's basketball. Camps can be arranged for full or half days and for team or individual instruction. Deposits are required, and prices range from about $75 for a half-day junior session to $250 for full-week adult camps. Call for information early in the season, as these camps tend to be quite popular.

UNCW Children's Academy Camps
601 S. College Rd., Wilmington • (910) 395-3195

For children in kindergarten through grade 6, UNCW offers a variety of music camps and arts-and-crafts camps, the latter including basic drawing and investigating cultural art through stories and crafts. Also available are environmental camps that explore the rain forest and endangered, extinct and existing animals for ages 9 through 12. A camp about fairy tales and folk tales is offered for ages 9 through 12 in which participants write and publish their own stories. Fees range from $65 to $85. Most camps last one week, some longer, and meetings range from 90 minutes to four or more hours in the morning.

UNCW Summer Science by the Sea Day Camp
601 S. College Rd., Wilmington
* **(910) 395-3193**

Children ages 7 through 12 who are interested in the marine environment and the outdoors may enjoy this university-sponsored day camp. Choose from among nine weekly sessions beginning in early June. Weekly fees begin at $65 for early registration (a bit higher later).

In-depth studies of marine life, college-level field and laboratory science, tropical ecosystems, dolphin behavior and even Australia's Great Barrier Reef are also open to more motivated students, ages 11 through 15, through UNCW's various camp offerings. Fees range from $450 to $3,625. Airfare, lodging, meals and amenities may be included, depending on the program. Call for details.

Wilmington Children's Museum
1020 Market St., Wilmington
* **(910) 254-3534**

The Children's Museum's Summer Soul Patch Program is a series of week-long performing arts camps in June and July for children ages 6 through 16. The program is directed by a professional actor and meets from 8:30 AM to noon and includes tours of the Thalian Hall Center for the Performing Arts and Screen Gems Studios, plus daily snacks. The fee is $35 per week per child.

Wilmington Family YMCA
2710 Market St., Wilmington
* **(910) 251-9622**

The Y hosts several day camps, including sports camps for soccer (April through July), basketball (two week-long sessions, June and July) and T-ball (April). Day camp sessions as short as four days are available and begin in early June.

Camp Tuscarora is a summer day camp for children ages 5 through 11 and offers daily trips to nearby Poplar Grove Plantation. Archery, swimming, music and overnight trips are among the many offerings. Camp Koda meets at the North Chase subdivision (north of Wilmington) and offers similar activities, except no field trips.

Kiddy Korner Kinder Kamp is a half-day preschool day camp offering age-appropriate activities to a maximum of 25 participants. An additional registration fee of $20 for members ($25 nonmembers) is required for this camp. Weekly and three-day sessions are offered.

Inquire about camper scholarships and their counselor-in-training programs (ages to 15). Camp costs begin at $65 per week for members ($75 nonmembers), plus a onetime registration fee of $25. Discounts apply when registering more than one child per family. Call to request a special-programs brochure for the most up-to-date information.

City of Wilmington Summer Traditions Camp
302 Willard St., Wilmington
* **(910) 341-7855**

Arts and crafts, swimming, sports, drama, field trips and other activities for children ages 5 and older are available through the Wilmington Parks and Recreation Department at Johnson Elementary School (1100 McRae Street) from mid-June through early August for less than $70 per week for full days, $40 per week for half days. Children with mental and physical handicaps are welcome.

Wrightsville Beach Parks and Recreation Department
1 Bob Sawyer Dr., Wrightsville Beach
* **(910) 256-7925**

Summer Day Camp orchestrates a variety of activities for children ages 6 through 11, including organized games, arts and crafts, field trips and beach fun. Two-week sessions run June through August and require fees beginning at less than $100 for residents.

YWCA of Wilmington
2815 S. College Rd., Wilmington
* **(910) 799-6820**

YWCA summer day camps for tots and juniors from kindergarten through age 12 operate weekdays from June through August. Activities include swimming, skating and field trips. Fees begin at $15 per day ($57 per week) plus a parent or guardian membership of $20 and a nonrefundable annual registration fee. Membership is $15 for children 12 and older.

The Murray House

Bed & Breakfast Inn • Plantation Tours

A plantation home built in 1850 has been fully restored to its original splendor

Tour Hrs.: Tues. - Sat.10am-4pm Sun.1pm-4pm
201 NC Hwy. 24 & 50 • Kenansville, NC
(910) 296-1000 • (800) 276-5322

Country Squire
Vintage Inn/Guest House

"A Superb Restaurant & Inn"

Rustic & Relaxed Setting
Weekend Package

748 NC HWY 24-50
Warsaw, NC 28398

Dinner Served Nightly 5:30
Lunch Sun. thru Fri.
Groups Welcome
All ABC Permits

(910) 296-1831

Southern Plantations in Historic Duplin County

Experience southern history and culture first hand. Visit the mid-1800s plantation homes of the wealthy planters and hear their Civil War stories. Many properties listed on the National Register of Historic Places.
Call 1-800-276-5322

MURRAY HOUSE PLANTATION
Murray House Plantation. Located on Hwy.24-50 between Kenansville and Warsaw. 910-296-1000. Admission.

BUCKNER HILL PLANTATION
Buckner Hill Plantation. 522 Taylor Town Road, Faison, NC. 910-293-6902. Admission.

LIBERTY HALL RESTORATION
Liberty Hall. 309 S. Main Street, Kenansville. 910-296-2175. Listed on the National Register of Historic Places. Admission.

BED & BREAKFAST
The Murray House Bed and Breakfast Inn. Located on Hwy. 24-50 between Kenansville and Warsaw. 910-296-1000 or 800-276-5322.

The Vintage Inn is located adjacent to the famous *Country Squire Restaurant* in the heart of Duplin County
Located on Hwy. 24-50 between Kenansville and Warsaw. 910-296-1831.

DINING
The Country Squire Restaurant.
Hwy. 24-50, between Warsaw and Kenansville. 910-296-1727.

The Mustard Seed. 127 W. Main Street in Wallace. 910-285-8375.

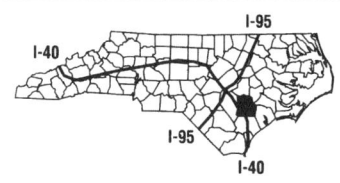

Other Attractions

Acorn of Golden Grove. 910-296-1717
The Cowan Museum. 910- 296-2149
Dickson Farm House. 910-289-4171
Duplin Outdoor Drama.
1-800-793-3726 or 910-296-2345

Duplin Winery. - 1-800-774-9634
Has been producing award winning wines and champagne from a 200 year-old recipe for many years. The winery has earned an enviable reputation for its outstanding wines made from Muscadine grapes. Tours & tastings Mon. - Sat. 9am-5pm. Dinner shows also available. Located on Hwy. 117 in Rose Hill.
1-800-774-9634.

Farm House Antiques. 910-293-3294
Southerland House. 910-296-1104
Visitor Center and Civil War Museum.
1-800-276-5322.
Westwater Country Hams. 910-293-7294.

Daytrips

It's hard to imagine that anyone would want to go beyond North Carolina's southern coast when there's so much to do and see right here. Yet an urge comes now and then to explore and, luckily, other interesting places are close enough for a daytrip. The following are teasingly brief overviews of two coastal destinations: Myrtle Beach, South Carolina, and North Carolina's Central Coast. Use them as pointers for planning your daytrip. For complete information on these areas, pick up copies of *The Insiders' Guide® to Myrtle Beach and the Grand Strand* and *The Insiders' Guide® to North Carolina's Central Coast and New Bern*, or call (800) 955-1860 to order either book.

Myrtle Beach

For decades, the Grand Strand, stretching nearly unbroken for 60 sun-drenched miles from the Little River south to historic Georgetown, has been the standard by which all other beach resorts are measured. As a tourist destination, it rivals Orlando and Las Vegas. Myrtle Beach's permanent, year-round population of only 28,000 hosted an estimated 13 million visitors in 1996. On a single summer's day that year, a cool 572,000 visitors were counted. Such magnetism is undoubtedly due to the town's abundance of lodging, dining and shopping opportunities, its world-class golf courses, a profusion of amusements, and its ideal weather and magnificent beaches.

It's understandable that Wilmingtonians look upon Myrtle Beach with equal amounts of interest and relief that their hometown is so different. Incidentally, Myrtle Beach hosts more visitors from North Carolina than from any other state — including South Carolina.

Myrtle Beach is approximately 72 miles from downtown Wilmington, a drive of little more than 90 minutes. U.S. Highway 17 is the artery that gets you there.

For the daytripper, Myrtle Beach is the Strand's entertainment nerve center. For a mile on either side of the Pavilion Amusement Park (see Attractions, below), the focus of downtown Myrtle Beach is Ocean Boulevard, a hotbed of activity. Before entering Myrtle Beach proper, the length of U.S. 17 (here called Kings Highway) is known as Restaurant Row, where dining establishments stand shoulder to shoulder.

There are more than 1,500 restaurants along the Grand Strand. Along with all the usual regional specialties, you'll find other samples of Southern fare such as chicken bog (chicken, seasoned rice and sausage), she-crab soup, alligator stew and crawfish. All-you-can-eat buffets are ubiquitous, so bring your appetite.

The Myrtle Beach Area Chamber of Commerce operates four information centers where you can pick up or order scads of information about the area: Myrtle Beach Office, 1200 N. Oak Street, Myrtle Beach, (803) 626-7444; North Myrtle Beach Office, 213 U.S. Highway 17 N., North Myrtle Beach, (803) 249-3519; South Strand Office, 3401 S. Highway 17 Business, Murrells Inlet, (803) 651-1010; and Official Grand Strand Welcome Center, 2090 U.S. Highway 501 E. at Horry-Georgetown Technical College, Conway, (803) 626-6619. To just request brochures from the Chamber, call (800) 356-3016.

A useful publication for planning a visit around one of Myrtle Beach's many annual events is *Grand Strand Festivals, Events, and Tournaments: The Myrtle Beach Area*, published by the Myrtle Beach Area Chamber of Commerce, (803) 626-7444. The booklet includes information on fishing and golf tournaments as well as sport, art, and cultural festivals.

The South Carolina Welcome Center on U.S. 17 near Little River is a convenient place for daytrippers from the Cape Fear area to gather brochures about the Grand Strand or about South Carolina in general. Many of the publications contain discount coupons that are good at dozens of Grand Strand locations.

Shopping

Shopping is probably tied for first place with sunshine when it comes to the Grand Strand's most popular attractions. The area is replete with shops and boutiques of every description and specialty, but it's the discount shops and factory outlet stores that are most renowned.

More than at any other single location, shoppers wear their plastic thin at the mammoth **Outlet Park at Waccamaw**, a three-mall complex equal in size to five football fields. The park houses 125 factory stores, movie theaters and an enormous food court. It's the home of Waccamaw Pottery (a home decor superstore) and Waccamaw Linen. Outlet Park is on Highway 501 immediately west of the Intracoastal Waterway. There's even an on-site hotel for those who live — and vacation — to shop.

Another popular shopping mecca, consisting of 120 shops, factory-direct stores and restaurants (along with rides for the children) is the attractive **Barefoot Landing** on U.S. 17 in North Myrtle Beach. The complex also houses the **Alabama Theatre**, (803) 272-1111, home of the musical group of the same name, the *Barefoot Princess* **Riverboat**, (803) 272-7743, and **Alligator Adventure**, (803) 361-0789, a zoo of regional and exotic reptiles, amphibians and birds. All of it surrounds a lake and borders the Intracoastal Waterway.

Forty-seven discount outlets await you at the **Myrtle Beach Factory Stores** on Highway 501 N., (803) 236-5100, about 3 miles west of the Intracoastal Waterway. Among the newer outlet complexes, this one includes "Off Fifth" Saks Fifth Avenue and Lenox China.

Attractions

Along the oceanfront, the boardwalk offers an array of shops, food stands and nightlife. Myrtle Beach is also home to some of the more outrageous miniature golf courses you'll see anywhere — more than 40 in all. Simply cruising Ocean Boulevard is so popular among the swimsuit-clad that at peak hours traffic seldom approaches the 25-mph speed limit. Visitors are drawn by the thousands to the batting cages, go-cart tracks, arcades, water parks, amusement rides, wacky museums, and souvenir shops.

More than a mere attraction, the **Myrtle Beach Pavilion Amusement Park** on the oceanfront at Ninth Avenue N., (803) 448-6456, is the symbolic heart of Myrtle Beach. Just a few blocks south, the **Family Kingdom Amusement Park**, 300 Fourth Avenue S., (803) 626-3447, is another classic.

Myrtle Waves Water Park, 3000 10th Avenue N. Extension, (803) 448-1026, open from mid-April to mid-September, is among the larger and more popular water parks. The **Myrtle Beach Grand Prix**, 3201 S. Kings Highway, (803) 238-4783, features go-carts, speed boats and the exhilarating Hydro Racer. A single fee to Myrtle Waves also grants admission to **Wild Water and Wheels**, 910 U.S. 17 S., (803) 238-9453, in Surfside Beach, about 6 miles south of Myrtle Beach. Don't overlook the boating, kayaking and sightseeing opportunities available on the nearby waterways. There are also some worthwhile historic attractions.

Brookgreen Gardens, 1931 Brookgreen Gardens Drive, Murrells Inlet, (803) 237-4218, demands a visit. Brookgreen, which is listed on the National Register of Historic Places, is a 9,000-acre arboretum, wildlife preserve, aviary and museum rolled into one, so pack a picnic lunch. Brookgreen boasts the first and largest permanent outdoor installation of American figurative sculpture. It features over 500 works by hundreds of top-name sculptors and continues to expand in scope. Guided tours, lectures and occasional workshops and concerts are offered. Brookgreen Gardens is 18 miles south of Myrtle Beach, off U.S. 17. The gardens are open daily, except Christmas, from 9:30 AM to 4:45 PM, and there is an admission charge.

Myrtle Beach Speedway, 4300 U.S. 501, (803) 236-0500, is, for auto-racing fans, the real thing: a nationally ranked track that hosts weekly races from March through September, including the NASCAR Winston Racing series, the NASCAR Dash, the Busch Grand National in mid-June and the 400-lap All Pro in late November.

The **Hurricane Fleet**, (803) 249-3571, offers a variety of cruise opportunities originating at the Little River Marina, (803) 249-7775, in Little River, South Carolina (a short drive from Calabash). Its "Adventure Cruises" take passengers to inshore waters where they can get a close-up glimpse of fishing vessels and shrimpers at work. Breakfast cruises offer an open-boat buffet or à la carte morning meals for $16, which includes tax and tip. Dance cruises sail Tuesday, Thursday, Friday and Saturday evenings and cost $29.75 per person. Country Barbecue cruises take place weekly in season and include dinner with all the trimmings for $20 per adult and $15 per child. Inquire about other cruises.

Head boats are also available at **Captain Dick's Marina**, 4123 U.S. 17 Business in Murrells Inlet, (803) 651-3676. Captain Dick's also offers sightseeing cruises, ocean speedboat rides, watercraft rentals and parasailing.

Entertainment

Nightlife and Myrtle Beach are practically synonymous. Live music, dancing, dinner attractions and stage shows form the core of one of the most active seaside scenes anywhere, and there are plenty of open-air bars along the boardwalk in which to relax over a drink with the sound of the surf as the backdrop.

All the fun is not reserved for adults. Nonalcoholic nightspots such as **The Attic**, (803) 448-6456, a club at the Pavilion, cater to kids younger than 21 who enjoy dancing, music and socializing.

The preeminent dinner attractions and live theaters in the area are quite touristy, and ticket prices pack a wallop, but the shows are consistently well-done and family-friendly. Reservations are recommended for all of them. The first of its kind in the area, the **Carolina Opry** at the north junction of U.S. 17 Bypass and U.S. 17 Business, (803) 238-8888, is one of the state's top tourist attractions. Shows offer a mix of comedy and music — standard country hits, bluegrass, gospel and medleys drawn from popular oldies — plus special Christmas shows.

A new attraction is the **Eddie Miles Theater**, 701 Main Street in North Myrtle Beach, (803) 280-6999, featuring impressions of Elvis and a different musical program each night.

Legends in Concert, 301 U.S. 17 Business S. in Surfside Beach, (803) 238-7827, is a Vegas-style musical extravaganza featuring impersonations of famous performers of yesterday and today. For reservations call (800) 960-7469.

In the 1970s, a then-unknown group named Alabama played for tips at the Bowery in downtown Myrtle Beach, earning a loyal following. Having since achieved superstardom, Alabama has made its home base the 2,200-seat **Alabama Theatre**, 4750 U.S. 17 S., (803) 272-1111 or (800) 342-2262, at Barefoot Landing in North Myrtle Beach. The "American Pride Show," performed there six nights a week, features music (country and rock), comedy and dancing.

One of the area's two dinner attractions, the **Dixie Stampede**, 8901-B U.S. 17 Business, (803) 497-9700, owned by Dolly Parton, is a theatrical icon of Southern culture, complete with music, horsemanship and a colorful depiction of the conflict between the North and South. The 90-minute show is complemented by dinner. Shows are staged from February through December at 5 PM (7 PM during the summer).

Fantasy Harbour-Waccamaw, on U.S. 501, is one of Myrtle Beach's largest entertainment complexes and includes the **Gatlin**

INSIDERS' TIP

Residents of Harker's Island on the Central Coast are descendents of a whaling community that existed on Shackleford Banks before a hurricane swept over their community in the late 19th century.

While in Beaufort, take a look across Taylor's Creek on the downtown waterfront for a glimpse of the wild horses.

Brothers Theatre, (803) 236-8800, showcasing the Grammy Award-winning country music trio; the **Ronnie Milsap Theatre**, (803) 236-1303; **Snoopy's Magic On Ice**, (803) 236-4400, a glitzy, professional ice-skating and illusions show; and the **Cercle Theatre**, (803) 236-1740, with world-famous impressionist Rich Little presiding. One booking service can handle ticket orders for these attractions: call (803) 236-8500 or (800) 681-5209. Also at Fantasy Harbour is **Medieval Times Dinner & Tournament**, (803) 236-8080 or (800) 436-4386, a medieval version of the dinner attraction.

One of the grandest entertainment complexes anywhere is **Broadway at the Beach** on U.S. 17 Bypass at 21st Avenue N. This 350-acre attraction includes no fewer than nine nightclubs, the 2,700-seat **Carolina Palace Theater**, **Ripley's Sea Aquarium**, the **IMAX Discovery Theater**, twelve restaurants (including a Planet Hollywood and a pyramidal Hard Rock Cafe), a 23-acre lake featuring water taxi tours and pedal boats, the Carolinas' largest movie complex (the sixteen-screen Carmike Cineplex), a Hampton Inn and oodles of shopping. For information call (800) FUN-IN-MB. Call (803) 444-3200 for a free visitors guide.

The shag was named South Carolina's Official State Dance in 1984. It is so closely identified with beach music (a derivative of old rhythm and blues) that locals contend the dance came first. The dance did engender the **Society of Stranders** (S.O.S.), (803) 782-7582, an organization of the Association of Carolina Shag Clubs. The society's annual Spring Safari in April and the Autumn Migration in October attract thousands of shaggers doing their thing on Main Street in North Myrtle Beach, the reputed birthplace of the shag. In January, shaggers compete in the National Shag Dance Championships, part of the S.O.S. Mid-Winter Classic.

Studebaker's, 21st Avenue N., (803) 448-9747, is a popular place to shag and attracts a relatively mature crowd. It features a large dance floor, and DJs spin 30 years of "non-stop bop." Studebaker's is open every day until the wee hours.

Golf

With nearly one hundred courses, some designed by the top names in the game, the area's self-proclaimed title as the Golf Capital of the World is well justified. And although the courses' popularity sometimes translates into crowds and waiting time, their prices are too competitive to be ignored. There are also plenty of driving ranges, par 3 courses and pro shops scattered up and down the Strand. Greens fees are lowest from November through February, and golf packages are accordingly most affordable during that time.

The Chamber of Commerce, (803) 626-7444, can provide details on golf packages, or you can call (800) 845-4653 for Myrtle Beach Golf Holiday's free 152-page *Golf Vacation Planner*. You may also want to pick up a copy of *The Insiders' Guide® to Golf in the Carolinas* to find detailed information about some of the area's best courses.

Among the annual golf highlights is the four-day, 72-hole **DuPont World Amateur Handicap Championship**. Played on 50 area courses, it is the largest tournament of its kind. Call (800) 833-8798 for information.

Other local annual tournaments include the **Mark A. Sloan Memorial Cancer Benefit Golf Tournament**, (803) 449-0015, played in August. The **Energizer Senior Tour Championship**, (803) 444-4782, is played in November. The **Charles Tilghman Junior Tournament**, (803) 249-1524, is played in early December.

North Carolina's Central Coast

Within a two-hour drive north by northeast up the Ocean Highway (U.S. Highway 17) from Wilmington are a multitude of daytrip possibilities. The area known as the Crystal Coast (Bogue Banks, Morehead City and quaint Beaufort) and historic New Bern, as well as the waters that surround and connect them, promise delightful opportunities.

The Crystal Coast shares much in common with the Cape Fear Coast. Both boast beautiful rivers, miles of oceanside communities, great restaurants and, of course, deep historical roots. However, they are different enough to make visiting each of them a unique experience.

Boaters visiting this area will be charmed by its amenities. Most marinas are just a short stroll from shopping, dining, historic sites and services. A fast powerboat can reach the area from Wilmington in several hours. Although some people make this a daytrip on the water, you'll have more time to enjoy the local attractions if you drive.

By car simply head up U.S. 17. Veer off onto N.C. Highway 172 and cut through the Marine base (Camp Lejeune) near Jacksonville. People who have never been on a military base will find this an unusual environment, with tank-crossing signs and trucks filled with Marines training in artillery practice. The sentries at the gate used to issue passes but they seem to have decided to do away with paperwork and just give a continual salute.

After crossing the base, go east on N.C. Highway 24 toward Beaufort. It is a trip of less than 100 miles from Wilmington, and there are many views of North Carolina's waters and coastal communities along the way.

Swansboro

Swansboro, an historic coastal town that dates back to the early 18th century, is a pleasant stopover after about an hour of car travel from Wilmington. Situated on the White Oak River and the Intracoastal Waterway, this lovely little town is surrounded on three sides by water.

Swansboro has a particularly attractive downtown historic area lined with antiques shops, art galleries and restaurants. Look for signs leading to the district just off N.C. 24. The area is concentrated within three blocks on the shores of the White Oak River. Parking is free, the merchants are friendly, and there are lots of interesting things to buy.

The historic district is a great stopover for lunch or dinner. **Captain Charlie's Seafood Paradise**, 106 Front Street, 326-4303, is a memorable place to enjoy some of North Carolina's best fried seafood. It serves dinner only. For breakfast or lunch, check out **Yana's Ye Olde Drug Store**, 119 Front Street, 326-5501, where you can enjoy omelets, pancakes and old-fashioned milkshakes.

Bogue Banks

Back on N.C. 24, travel another 20 minutes until N.C. Highway 58 appears on the right. This is the southern entrance to Bogue Banks island. You can choose to continue straight ahead or cross the bridge to take a parallel route on the barrier island. The bridge is worth the detour because its high arc gives the motorist a dramatic view of the Intracoastal Waterway.

The beach communities along approximately 20 miles of the island are widely varied in tone. **Emerald Isle, Indian Beach and Salter Path** offer an astonishing diversity of neighborhoods, ranging from expensive beach homes and condominiums to fishing trailers. There are also a few attractions for the kiddies, including miniature golf, waterslides and bumperboats.

Pine Knoll Shores is an exclusive residential area of windswept live oaks and kudzu with attractive single-family homes and condominiums as well as hotels and the occasional restaurant. This beach also offers the **North Carolina Aquarium at Pine Knoll Shores**, (919) 247-4003, a lively facility that includes a "Living Shipwreck," a touch tank, salt-marsh explorations and workshops on surf fishing. At the northern end of the island is **Atlantic Beach**, a smorgasbord of beach amenities that includes an amusement park with a Ferris wheel, a Civil War fort, a fishing pier, shopping opportunities, boat rentals, fast food places, full-service restaurants and motels.

Morehead City

Cross over the bridge at the northern end of Bogue Banks and enter Morehead City, home to the North Carolina State Port Authority — something Wilmington and the Crystal Coast have in common — and a multitude of restaurants specializing in fresh seafood. The undisputed traditional leader of dining in Morehead City is the **Sanitary Fish Market**, 501 Evans Street, (919) 247-3111. The restaurant seats 600 diners and serves fresh broiled or fried seafoods, homemade chowders and Tar Heel hush puppies that truly melt in your mouth.

The Charter Restaurant, (919) 726-9036, also on the waterfront, serves delicious crab cakes, stuffed shrimp and flounder, prime rib and a salad bar seven days a week. **The Plant Restaurant**, 105 South Seventh Street, (919) 726-5502, occupies the former headquarters of the Morehead Gulf Oil Company. Dine outside on nice days and enjoy the view from a second-story deck.

Beaufort

Just a few miles from Morehead City is the magical town of Beaufort. Beaufort is so gorgeous it seems more like a postcard than a real place. This little laid-back coastal community nestles up to international waters and is a gateway from the Atlantic Ocean to America's waterways. Taylor's Creek, the body of water in front of the town's quaint commercial district, is filled with sailcraft and powerboats from all over the world. Just up Taylor's Creek, you can catch sight of a menhaden fishing fleet. Beyond that is Core Sound and a view of Harker's Island, home to some of this country's earliest shipbuilders.

Beaufort boasts a very unusual view: wild horses on Carrot Island across from the waterfront. The horses are stocky, furry steeds that pretty much care for themselves on their little windswept island. In a world where horses are rarely seen running free, this is a stirring sight. If you want a closer vantage point, the **Shackleford Banks and Carrot Island Ferry Service**, 728-6888, will be happy to take you over for a fee. There are also boat tours that depart from the Beaufort Docks.

The island chain across from the Beaufort Waterfront is part of the **Rachel Carson Estaurine Research Reserve**. Free guided tours are offered each month from April to August. Inquire at the North Carolina Maritime Museum (see below) about tour times. One catch: You have to provide your own water transportation to get to the island. If you use the ferry service, expect to pay up to $12 for a round-trip journey, but remember the island tour is free.

The sheer beauty of the scenery at the Beaufort waterfront is enough to lull a visitor into sitting in a pleasant trance for a long time, but there is also the allure of nearby shops and attractions. Within an easy walk are stores, many appealing restaurants, the **North Caro-**

lina Maritime Museum, 315 Front Street, (919) 728-7317, the **Beaufort Restoration Grounds** on Ann Street two blocks from the waterfront, and a delightful neighborhood of historic homes. The museum now boasts the **Harvey W. Smith Watercraft Center** just across the street, a facility where students and craftsmen build wooden boats in traditional North Carolina design and welcome visitors to take a peek at boats-in-progress.

Shoppers will enjoy a variety of stores along the waterfront. **The Rocking Chair Bookstore**, 400 Front Street, (919) 728-2671, has a fine selection of books for children and adults. **Scuttlebutt Nautical Books and Bounty**, 433 Front Street, (919) 728-7765, sells a large selection of books about the sea and boating. NOAA charts, cruising guides and chartbooks make this a must-stop for passing boaters. **La Vaughn's Pottery, Coffee, Wines**, 517 Front Street, (919) 728-5353, is a show-stopper for shoppers interested in ceramics. **The General Store**, 515 Front Street, (919) 728-7707, has hand-dipped ice cream for your summer daytripping pleasure.

Diners will be overwhelmed with restaurant possibilities. The **Beaufort Grocery Co.**, 117 Queen Street, (919) 728-3899, a lunch and dinner restaurant, offers fine dining and a full delicatessen. Breads and desserts are baked daily. The **Front Street Grill** on the Beaufort waterfront at 419A Front Street, (919) 728-3118, has a reputation as an interesting restaurant that uses unusual spices in fresh presentations of seafood, chicken, pasta and homemade soups.

Spouter Inn, 218 Front Street, (919) 728-5190, is a charming spot that recently underwent a change of ownership, but diners can still enjoy a memorable clam chowder, creative seafood specialties and a great view thanks to its waterfront location. **Clawson's Emporium Restaurant**, 429 Front Street, 728-2133, long a dining fixture on the Beaufort waterfront, expanded dramatically in 1996 and serves wonderful all-American fare. It's coffee bar, known as **Fishtowne Java**, serves high-octane caffeine, baked goods and ice cream.

If you just can't bear to end the day by leaving, downtown Beaufort has many overnight accommodations. **The Cedars**, 305 Front Street, (919) 728-7036, the **Pecan Tree Inn**, 116 Queen Street, (919) 728-6733 and **The Inlet Inn**, 601 Front Street, (919) 728-3600 are just a few of the great spots to spend the night.

New Bern

The small city of New Bern lies along North Carolina's largest river, the Neuse. The Neuse River is the state's premier sailing area because of the width and depth of the water. It's tough to go aground in a sailboat unless you try hard.

Car travelers will appreciate the lovely view of the river and will certainly enjoy the many opportunities to shop, dine and stay overnight in historic New Bern, which was settled by the Swiss in 1710. Reach it by car from Beaufort by taking U.S. 70 North and slipping off immediately onto U.S. 17 into New Bern. You may be interested to know that New Bern is the place where Pepsi Cola was invented. This rather sleepy little town was the site of the first public schools in North Carolina, the first meeting of the North Carolina Legislature and the state's first bank.

The biggest tourist attraction in New Bern is **Tryon Palace**, 600 Pollock Street, (919) 514-4900 or (800) 767-1560. Built in 1770 for Colonial governor William Tryon, the palace burned in 1798 but was reconstructed in the 1950s according to the original architectural plans. The palace is furnished with rare English and American antiques dating from the late 18th century. These pieces were selected based on an inventory of Gov. Tryon's possessions made two years after he left New Bern to become governor of the colony of New York.

Tryon Palace and its many historic sites

INSIDERS' TIP

The City of Myrtle Beach provides 10 beach wheelchairs and maintains dune crossovers to the beach at 15 locations between 28th Ave. S. and 81st Ave. N. Inquire at lifeguard stations or the Police Department.

Waters off North Carolina's coast beckon visitors from all over the world.

are open year round, with the exception of major holidays, and include tours, historical dramas and crafts demonstrations. For information, call or write Tryon Palace Historic Sites and Gardens, P.O. Box 1007, New Bern 28563.

The **New Bern Academy Museum** at the corner of Haddock and New streets, (919) 514-4874, is a great place to introduce your kids to the origins of public education in North Carolina. The **New Bern Historical Society**, 511 Broad Street, (919) 638-8558, offers tours of the 1790 Attmore-Oliver House, which features a fascinating collection of 18th- and 19th-century furnishings. You can also visit the **New Bern Civil War Museum**, 301 Metcalf Street, (919) 633-2418 and the **New Bern Fireman's Museum**, 410 Hancock Street, (919) 636-4087. For expert touring advice, drop by the Craven County Visitors Information Center at 316 Tryon Palace Drive, or call (919) 637-9400 or (800) 437-5767. Ask for the "New Bern Heritage Tour" map.

Once you've museumed to your satisfaction, it's time to eat. For a small town, New Bern has an abundance of outstanding restaurants across the full price spectrum. The **Harvey Mansion Restaurant and Lounge**, 211 Tryon Palace Drive, (919) 638-3205, is open for dinner only, but what a dinner it is! Seafood and veal dishes, served in an upscale atmosphere, are exquisitely prepared. It isn't inexpensive, but people who regard a dining experience as the basis for travel will be delighted with their choice.

Fred and Claire's Restaurant, 247 Cra-

INSIDERS' TIP

Visit Myrtle Beach on a budget: Ten private campgounds and two state parks provide ample and affordable options.

ven Street, (919) 638-5426, is a great lunch spot with sandwiches and lunch specials. **Sonny's Raw Bar and Grill**, 235 Craven Street, (919) 637-9000, is an excellent restaurant with a large lunch and dinner menu. It has a soup and salad bar and serves up some of the best fried softshell crabs around. The pork ribs are a sight to behold.

If shopping is your reason to travel, New Bern has antique stores and gift shops galore. **Elegant Days**, 236 Middle Street and 517 Tryon Palace Drive, (919) 636-3689, is a "treasure trove of old things." **Jane Suggs Antiques**, 228 Middle Street, (919) 637-6985, carries period furniture and reproductions, silver, porcelain and glassware. **Lancing House**, 225 Tryon Palace Drive, (919)637-6595, features fine gifts and home accessories, including Waterford lamps, bath and tabletop accessories, and home fragrances. Not to ignore the kids, there's **Snapdragon Toys**, 214 Middle Street, (919) 514-6770, a shop of toys than range from educational to just plain fun.

New Bern is such a pleasant and interesting spot, it invites the daytripper back for long weekends of exploration. There are ample hotels and inns in the historic downtown area on the water, including the **Sheraton**, **Ramada** and **Comfort Suite**s. These hotels are particularly convenient to all the attractions and restaurants mentioned in this brief overview.

The Southern coast is blessed with clean, relatively clear, refreshing waters and a long outdoor season.

Watersports

It is said that once you get salt water in your veins, you'll never leave here — and no wonder. North Carolina's beaches are arguably the finest on the Eastern seaboard, given the combination of mild weather, warm water temperatures, good water quality, clean, uncrowded beaches and availability of services. Our coastal waters are warmed by the Gulf Stream, which not only makes for long seasons for watersports, but also brings a surprising array of tropical sea life. Watersports enthusiasts can splurge. The opportunities are limited only by your desire and stamina.

But you need to be aware of local ordinances. For example, swimming and surfing are forbidden within 100 feet of most fishing piers, and walking on protected dunes carries a minimum $50 fine. Some beaches do not allow dogs during the summer season, while others are more accommodating if the animals are leashed.

The sections that follow tell you more about local variations. The Boating section of this chapter includes details on safety, rentals and boaters' maps and charts. Be sure to check the Fishing chapter for information on the locations of boat ramps. The point is, every section relating to water activities will complement your primary interest.

Personal Watercraft

If you have your own water buggy, there are beach access points on Wrightsville Beach suitable for beach trailers. One of the easiest is at the foot of Causeway Drive (straight ahead from the fixed bridge), but parking here is rarely available in the high season. Another is the paved access to the left of the Oceanic Restaurant on S. Lumina Avenue, provided there are no volleyball tournaments that day.

On Topsail Island access points are fewer, largely due to dune erosion. Your best bet would be the crossover near the center of Surf City. Smooth riding is also available in the Northeast Cape Fear River, accessible from the several public boat ramps listed in our Boating section, but these waters are frequently busy with other boaters, fishermen, and swimmers in summer. Exercise courtesy and extreme caution.

All the rental craft available in our area launch into the Intracoastal Waterway. Be sure to respect the limitations set by the individual rental services. They must operate within the parameters of their permits.

Wrightsville Beach, in cooperation with the local flotilla of the U.S. Coast Guard Auxiliary, occasionally offers a personal watercraft safety course. Costs range from about $12 to $15. Call the Wrightsville Beach Parks and Recreation Department, (910) 256-7925, for information.

Regulations

If you own your own jet watercraft, be aware that North Carolina requires that it be registered (see the Boat Registration section below).

The use of personal watercraft in certain New Hanover County waters is restricted to safeguard people, property, and the environment. Note the following rules.

• Operators must be at least 16 years of age. Persons 13 through 15 may operate water scooters provided they are accompanied by someone over 18 or they have passed a boating safety course approved by the state, the Coast Guard Auxiliary or the National Association of State Boating Law Administrators.

• Watercraft must have a self-circling capability or an engine-cutoff device attached to the operator.

• When operating in the Intracoastal Waterway from Carolina Beach Inlet north to Mason Inlet or within the sounds and channels behind Masonboro Island and Wrightsville

Beach, watercraft speed is strictly limited to 5 mph within 50 feet of the marsh or shore, a surf fisherman, a person in the water, an anchored vessel, a posted waterbird sanctuary or piers or docks.

• Operators may not chase or harass wildlife unless lawfully hunting or fishing.

These restrictions have led many jetcraft operators to move into the waterways north of Wrightsville Beach, where there are currently no rules. But common sense is called for: Refrain from operating at speeds over 5 mph when in shallow water, especially at low tide; otherwise you will probably contribute to the destruction of oyster beds, plant life and other marsh wildlife. Be especially wary of watercraft larger than your own and of water skiers, since jet craft are more maneuverable, and respect waterfront property.

Rentals

Performance Watercraft
Wilmington • (910) 799-WAVE

Performance delivers jet craft (sit-down models) to Wilmington-area waterways from April through October, weather permitting; at least a day's notice is your best bet. It also organizes jet-craft tours of the Cape Fear River and the Northeast Cape Fear, and an experienced guide will accompany you if you desire. Crafts are Yamaha Wave models. Rates begin at $55 per hour and are discounted after the first hour. Safety equipment, tax and fuel are included. A credit card and a driver's license are required to place a deposit. Patrons must be 25 years old to rent and 16 years old to operate the craft. Travelers' checks and credit cards (MasterCard or Visa) are welcome, and group rates are available.

Dockside Watersports
100 Spencer Farlow Dr., Carolina Beach
• (910) 458-0220

Dockside rents Polaris and Yamaha craft beginning at less than $50 per hour and offers special three-hour packages. Board right at the dock at Snow's Cut Marina. Reserve in advance to ride any day of the week, April through October, from 9 or 10 AM until dusk. (Off-season, ask about availability.) A credit card is required. (Dockside also rents boats, canoes and windsurfers; check the appropriate sections in this chapter.) Spencer Farlow Drive is beneath the Snow's Cut bridge; when driving south, make a 180-degree turn at the first exit.

Watersports, Inc.
1045 B-Var Rd. S.W., Holden Beach
• (910) 842-5588

Launch into the Intracoastal Waterway from 10 AM until dusk in season on watercraft suitable for up to three passengers. Life vests and instruction are included. Watersports, Inc. is located at Betty's Waterfront Restaurant, off Old Ferry Road, on the mainland side.

Ocean Isle Marina
43 Causeway Dr., Ocean Isle Beach
• (910) 579-0848

You can rent Waverunners from the marina office/tackle shop starting at around $40 for the first hour. Most major credit cards are accepted but not required.

Sunset Watersports
301 Sunset Blvd., Sunset Beach
• (910) 579-7365

Sunset has a limited supply of Waverunners, so make your reservation early.

INSIDERS' TIP

Coastal Camera & Photo, 4609 Wrightsville Avenue in Wilmington, (910) 392-0730, stocks underwater photography supplies for divers.

Crosstown traffic got you down?

Topsail Water Sports
1184 N. Anderson Blvd., Topsail Beach • (910) 328-1141

This service has been popular since the mid-1980s. It rents late-model Waverunners and Jet Skis starting at around $30 per half-hour and $50 per hour. Reservations are suggested, and most major credit cards are accepted. It's located opposite the Topsail Motel and is open seven days a week from April to October.

S & S Water Sports Inc.
Davis St. and Channel Blvd., Topsail Beach • (910) 328-7751

S & S Water Sports is at the Breezeway Motel and rents Waverunners for $30 per half-hour and $50 per hour. It is open seven days a week during the warm season starting at about 9:30 AM. Grab one of S & S's rack cards at visitors centers and restaurants and receive a $5 discount on the hourly rate.

Boating

At times, boating in the lower Cape Fear involves competition with oceangoing vessels, thin water or the treacherous shoals that won the Carolina coast the moniker "Graveyard of the Atlantic." In contrast, the upper Cape Fear River, its northeast branch and the winding creeks of the coastal plain offer a genuine taste of the old Southeast to those with small boats or canoes. Tannins leached from the cypresses keep these waters the color of coffee.

Many creeks are overhung by trees, moss and, in summer, the occasional snake. Early spring and late autumn are particularly good times to go, since they are bug-free. See our Fishing chapter for boat ramp locations.

The U.S. Coast Guard Auxiliary conducts free Courtesy Motorboat Examinations (CME). The exams are not required for boat registration. For information, call (910) 395-1865 or the Marine Safety Office at (910) 343-4882. You will be referred to the examining flotilla officer nearest you.

Various flotillas of the local Coast Guard Auxiliary offer Safe Boating courses five times a year (autumn, winter, spring and twice in summer). Locations include the Wrightsville Beach Recreation Center (at Wrightsville Beach Park) and Cape Fear Community College in downtown Wilmington.

These courses are strongly recommended for everyone who operates a motor boat. Two-hour classes meet twice weekly for seven or eight weeks. The fee averages $25 and includes all materials. Also inquire about Basic Coastal Navigation, a course of two three-hour sessions offered three times yearly. For information call (910) 458-4518 for Carolina Beach,

(910) 686-9777 or (910) 392-5614 for Wilmington, (910) 256-7925 for Wrightsville Beach and (910) 270-3029 for Hampstead.

Local chapters of the nonprofit U.S. Power Squadrons (USPS), America's largest private boating association, also offer the USPS Boating Course on a regular basis in Wilmington, Wrightsville Beach, Hampstead, Southport and Shallotte. The fee ($20) includes materials, and you need not be a USPS member to participate. For information on the USPS classes closest to you, call (800) 336-BOAT.

For ship-to-shore calling along the Cape Fear Coast, contact the Wilmington Marine Operator on channel 26. For shore-to-ship calls dial (910) 726-1070. To report emergencies to the Coast Guard, all initial radio calls should be made on channel 16/158.8 MHz. The Wrightsville Beach Coast Guard station's telephone number is (910) 256-3469.

An excellent resource for boaters of all kinds is the *North Carolina Coastal Boating Guide*, compiled by the N.C. Department of Transportation. Obtain a free copy by calling (919) 733-2520; ask for the Map Department.

Among the several marine communications servicers in Wilmington, Ship and Shore Communications Inc., 6337 Oleander Drive, (910) 350-0014 or (910) 350-0015, is one to note. Dealing in complete two-way electronics, Ship and Shore sells and services navigation and positioning devices (including GPS), depth finders and fish finders. It carries a complete line of CB and VHF radios, radar, LORAN and auto pilot. The store, across from Bradley Creek Marina, is open every day except Sunday in the high season.

Boat Registration

North Carolina requires that motorized craft of any size (including water-jet craft) and sailboats 14 feet and longer be registered. The cost is $8 per year, $20 for three years. Renewal forms are mailed about two months prior to expiration. Titles are optional ($20). Further information on boating regulations may be obtained from the N.C. Wildlife Resources Commission Boat Registration Section, 512 N. Salisbury Street, Raleigh, N.C. 27604-1188, (800) 628-3773. The following businesses and offices can provide the necessary forms and information:

Canady's Sport Center, 3220 Wrightsville Avenue, Wilmington, (910) 791-6280

Johnson Marine Services, 2029 Turner Nursery Road, Wilmington, (910) 686-7565

N.C. Department of Motor Vehicles License Plates Office, 14689 U.S. Highway 17 S., Hampstead, (910) 270-9010

Stewart Hardware, 1635 Howe Street, Southport, (910) 457-5544

Shallotte Marine Supplies, Main Street, Shallotte, (910) 754-6962

Motorboat Rentals

If you would like to rent a power boat, note that advance reservations are essential in summer. Most proprietors require a deposit, a valid driver's license or major credit card, plus a signed waiver of liability.

Dockside Watersports
100 Spencer Farlow Dr., Carolina Beach • (910) 458-0220

Dockside Watersports rents 14-foot john boats and 19-foot center-console outboards. Rentals are available any day of the week, April to October 1, from 9 or 10 AM until dusk, and off-season by appointment. Four-hour rentals begin at around $70 for the smaller craft and around $170 for the larger. Dockside is at the Snow's Cut Marina. Reserve in advance. Major credit cards are accepted.

Entropy Rentals & Charters
Wrightsville Beach • (910) 395-2401

On the Intracoastal Waterway at Wrightsville Beach and at Johnson Marine in Hampstead, Entropy rents its own line of Sea Mark power boats, manufactured in Rocky Point, N.C. Fully equipped center-console vessels are available by the day or week. For a nominal fee, Entropy also rents water skis and equipment. The twelve-hour day rate is about $240. Most major credit cards are accepted. Call ahead for reservations and location information.

Ocean Isle Marina
43 Causeway Dr., Ocean Isle Beach • (910) 579-0848

This shop rents fishing boats, pontoon boats and ski boats as well as sailboats starting at around $125 per half-day.

WATERSPORTS • 255

Topsail Water Sports
1184 N. Anderson Blvd., Topsail Beach
• (910) 328-1141

When in Topsail Beach you may rent 14-foot power boats for $50 per hour, 22-foot cabin cruisers starting for $135 per hour and pontoon boats for $125 per hour. Day rates offer savings. All craft come with regulation safety equipment, and the folks at Topsail Water Sports will provide basic instruction if needed. You'll find them across the road from the Topsail Motel every day from April to October. Reservations are recommended.

Canoeing

Touring the lower Cape Fear River in a canoe isn't recommended for beginners because the river is a commercial shipping channel. But for the experienced canoeist, the lower Cape Fear holds some nice surprises. Paddlers who frequent these waters have been known to gather wild rice bequeathed by the vanished rice plantations of the past. The Black River, a protected tributary of the Cape Fear River noted for its old-growth stands of bald cypress, is an excellent, scenic canoeing choice, as are several of both rivers' tributaries. And a canoe makes excellent transportation for exploring the tidal marshes and barrier islands all along our coast.

In 1997, the town of Long Beach, on Oak Island, dedicated some 24 miles of canoe "trails" as the Long Beach Canoe Trail System. Actually, four trails make up the system: Lockwood Folly (4.2 miles), Montgomery Slough (7 miles), Howells Point (6.5 miles) and Davis Creek (6 miles). Conditions range from calm, protected waters to rough, exposed waters near inlets, and all are remarkably scenic, quiet (considering that Long Beach is the county's largest town) and full of wildlife. For information visit or call the Long Beach Parks & Recreation Department, 4601 E. Oak Island Drive, (910) 278-5518.

Cape Fear Outfitters
Plaza East Shopping Center, Wrightsville Beach • (910) 256-1258

Cape Fear Outfitters rents canoes starting at $25 per hour. It is convenient to the protected waters on the soundside of Wrightsville Beach. Safety equipment is included.

Dockside Watersports
100 Spencer Farlow Dr., Carolina Beach
• (910) 458-0220

Dockside rents canoes and all safety equipment beginning at $10 for the first hour and about $5 per hour thereafter. Major credit cards accepted. It's at the Snow's Cut Marina.

Island Passage
Bald Head Island Marina
• (910) 457-4944

An interesting area to explore by canoe is Bald Head Creek and salt marsh, the state's largest single expanse of salt marsh, on Bald Head Island. The creek is a tidal waterway, so excursions should be planned accordingly. "Full Creek Safaris" can be arranged at the marina through Island Passage, who will also ferry your golf cart to your take-out point. The unguided safari lasts two hours and costs $30 per canoe, each of which is suitable for up to three adults.

Holland's Shelter Creek Fish Camp
N.C. 53, Burgaw • (910) 259-5743

For paddling on the winding, blackwater Holly Shelter Creek, Holland's rents canoes for a flat $15 fee per day. You launch right behind the restaurant. The building at Holland's is a colorful restaurant and sporting supply store adjoining a camp ground. You'll find it a few miles east of I-40.

Rowing and Kayaking

The popularity of kayaking continues to grow and offers unparalleled opportunities for enjoying the local coastal wetlands and scenic rivers. Some enterprises, such as Wilmington's Turtle Island Ventures (below), emphasize ecological responsibility and education, and bring paddlers into intimate contact with wildlife and a silence that, for some, may be unfamiliar.

Cape Fear River Rowing Club
Wilmington • (910) 762-2878

Team rowing, a favorite pastime on the Cape Fear River for ages, was revived locally in 1989 with the formation of the Cape Fear River Rowing Club. Members cruise past shipwrecks, historic downtown Wilmington and old

Area sailing organizations hold local regattas throughout the year.

rice fields upriver — all the while enjoying plenty of exercise and friendly company. By becoming a CFRRC member you are entitled to use the club's boats, share in activities such as group rows and annual "tip drill" exercises and compete in regattas.

For insurance purposes, members are required to join the U.S. Rowing Association, which costs $40 annually for individuals, $75 for families and $25 for students. This is the only nonrefundable fee involved. After an initial dry lesson, you must sign a waiver of liability and pay the dues ($150 annually for singles, $225 for families, $100 for students). If you change your mind, your dues will be refunded. A series of free lessons will get the uninitiated started. The club's quarterly newsletter contains the latest news on club events, regattas and related items.

Turtle Island Ventures
(910) 392-4243, (800) 64-KAYAK

Ecologically focused tours of salt marshes, barrier islands and the Cape Fear River are TIV's specialty, the dual goal being the enjoyment of the sport and the broadening of stewardship of our natural resources. Guides are registered and have backgrounds in environmental education and the sciences. Novice kayakers are as welcome as experts, and the craft are lightweight and stable.

Tours lasting two-and-a-half hours cost $30; half-day excursions including lunch, $50. Longer trips afford opportunities for swimming, snorkeling, photography and more. Special tours, such as overnights with gourmet vegetarian meals, can be designed for you, and persons with disabilities or special needs can be accommodated. Depart from sites throughout the greater Wilmington area, including Hampstead, Topsail Island, Carolina Beach and Oak Island, seven days a week year round. Visa and MasterCard are accepted. Remember to bring your own water shoes or sandals, sun protection and water bottle.

Cape Fear Outfitters
Plaza East Shopping Center, Wrightsville Beach • (910) 256-1258

This business sells and rents a variety of sit-on-top and cockpit kayaks (and canoes), including Mad River, Dagger, Ocean Kayak and North Carolina's own Wilderness Systems touring boats, made in High Point. Kayak rentals cost $35 per day, $20 per half-day. Visa or MasterCard is accepted, all accessories and basic instruction are included, and kayaks put into Banks Channel. Reservations are preferred, and rentals are available every day in the summer. Plaza East Shopping Center is between Eastwood Road and Wrightsville Avenue near Wrightsville Beach.

Ship's Store Windsurfing & Sailing Center
275 Waynick Blvd., Wrightsville Beach
- **(910) 256-9463**

Ship's Store rents sea kayaks (SeaYaks, tandems and sit-on-tops) starting at $15 per hour from its dock on Banks Channel, opposite the Blockade Runner Hotel. The company offers tours (two or three hours and half-day) on Tuesdays, Thursdays and Sundays and by appointment. Lessons are offered on Mondays, Wednesdays and Saturdays in the summer at 9 AM, 1 PM, 5 PM and by appointment. The Center is open seven days a week. Reservations are recommended.

Beach Fun Rentals
Holden Beach Rd. S.W., Holden Beach
- **(910) 842-9600**

Beach Fun Rentals recently added kayaks to its wide inventory of beach-related paraphernalia. Rates are competitive, and the shop is open every day in the summer.

Ocean Isle Beach Rentals at The Winds Clarion Inn
310 E. First St., Ocean Isle Beach
- **(910) 579-7575, (910) 754-4538**

Ocean Kayak rentals here are competitively priced. A credit card is required for deposit. Ocean Isle Beach Rentals is open 9 AM to 5 PM seven days a week May through September and by appointment in spring and autumn.

Julie's Rentals
2 Main St., Sunset Beach
- **(910) 579-1211**

Julie's is a complete beach-rental shop that rents kayaks (singles and doubles) as well as many other recreational items. Rates begin around $30 for four hours for singles, $45 for doubles.

Herring's Tackle & Beach Shop
701 New River Dr., Surf City
- **(910) 328-3291**

On Topsail Island, Herring's rents and sells canoes and tandem kayaks (as well as many other beach items). Rentals cost $35 for a full day (sunup to sundown) and $25 for a half-day (sunup to 1 PM or 1 PM to sundown).

Topsail Water Sports
1184 N. Anderson Blvd., Topsail Beach
- **(910) 328-1141**

Topsail Water Sports rents kayaks for $20 per half-hour, $30 per hour. It's located opposite the Topsail Motel and operates every day from April to October.

Sailing

An event eagerly awaited by salts and lubbers alike is the Holiday Flotilla at Wrightsville Beach, held just after Thanksgiving, in which boaters (power and sail) adorn their craft in the most flamboyant seasonal decoration possible for an evening cruise through Motts and Banks channels. Prizes are awarded for the best-decorated craft at the Post Flotilla Awards Dance, and fireworks are an added attraction. Check local listings for information, or call the Cape Fear Coast Convention and Visitors Bureau, (910) 341-4030.

It's useful to note that anchorage in Banks Channel, Wrightsville Beach, is free. Thirty days seems to be the average limit before the authorities pay a visit or post a nastygram, but boaters have been known to stay longer. Find complete information on anchorage and marina services in our chapter on Marinas and the Intracoastal Waterway.

Wrightsville Beach Ocean Racing Association
P.O. Box 113, Wrightsville Beach, NC 28480

For serious competition sailors and those who just love to cruise, WBORA (wuh-BORE-ah) is the local organization of note. Founded in 1967, it is an active, nonprofit organization that promotes and sponsors sailboat cruising and racing in the Cape Fear region

---

INSIDERS' TIP

Early spring and late fall are the best times of year for canoeing the region's inland waterways.

Seashells washed up by the waves offer learning opportunities for kids of all ages.

and elsewhere along the North Carolina coast. Its members are a decidedly fun-loving bunch. WBORA provides race and cruise schedule management and development, hosts sailing seminars, participates in community programs, assists in youth sailing and organizes social activities around sailing events.

Sailing events span the season from spring to fall, with social events sprinkled throughout the year. Among the highlights are the Coca-Cola Regatta, the Governor's Cup, The Bald Head Island Cruise and Race (which is followed by the year's landmark party), a year-end awards banquet, and the Mid-Summer Cruise from Masonboro Island to the Cape Lookout Light. Boats of various types may compete, and a performance handicap racing factor is figured into the standings. There is one specialty-class race in which only J-24s compete.

WBORA is a member of the U.S. Sailing Association, the South Atlantic Yacht Racing Union and a charter member of the North Carolina Yacht Racing Association. Membership is open to all, and dues depend on the extent of your participation. An annual handbook and frequent newsletter are published for members. WBORA does not maintain permanent offices. Information may be obtained from the association's officers. For 1997 they were Commodore Bob Cowen, (910) 791-5616, Vice Commodore Rona Garm, (910) 452-1817, and Race Committee Chair Sam Barfield, (910) 251-2133.

Hobie Fleet 101
Wrightsville Beach • (910) 256-6468, (910) 256-6624

Hobie Fleet 101 is a local sailing club open to anyone interested in sailing Hobie Cats. It is part of Division 9 (which includes both Carolinas plus Virginia and Georgia) of the North American Hobie Cat Association. Ownership of a Hobie is not required, since qualified members can obtain use of the fleet boat for the summer for a mere $40. Family membership costs $25 annually, and meetings are held monthly. Among the events are the Mid-Summer Offshore Regatta in July, open to Hobies of all classes, and the Frostbite Series, which runs from October through Christmas.

Sailing Instruction and Rentals

Water Ways Sailing School
7110 Wrightsville Ave., Wrightsville Beach • (910) 256-4282, (800) 562-SAIL

Jerry Outlaw's Water Ways Sailing School is the only sailing school in the Carolinas certified by the American Sailing Association. The ASA awarded Water Ways its highest honor two years in a row by naming the school the 1995 and 1996 School of the Year. Capt. Outlaw has also received the ASA's Outstanding Instructor award three years consecutively, 1993 through 1995.

Water Ways offers a battery of sailing courses taught entirely by USCG-licensed captains. Courses include Basic Sailing (2 days), Basic Coastal Cruising, Intermediate Coastal Cruising (Bareboat Charter), Coastal Navigation and Advanced Coastal Cruising. The Water Ways fleet boasts a variety of craft, ranging from a Catalina 22 to a Hunter 335. The boats are available for rent. Captained and bareboat charters are also available for local excursions.

Carolina Yacht Club
401 S. Lumina Ave., Wrightsville Beach • (910) 256-3396

This is the oldest private sailing club on Cape Fear. The club sponsors regional competitions, regattas and other events, a few of which are open to the public, and it offers training to members. Membership is not expensive, but the number of members nearly always exceeds the established cap of 1,000. About the only way to become a full member is to have a blood relative who is a member propose that your membership be conferred. Otherwise you may get on the waiting list by participating in the club's regattas as the guest of a member. Recently added to the club's calendar of annual regattas that are open to the public is the fund-raising Leukemia Cup in mid-April.

Ship's Store Windsurfing & Sailing Center
275 Waynick Blvd., Wrightsville Beach • (910) 256-9463

Among the most complete enterprises of its kind, the Sailing Center rents Hobie Cats, 14-foot DaySailors, Sunfish and more. Prices range from $20 per hour to $100 for four hours. The center also offers lessons and group discounts. The minimum age to rent is 18; the minimum age to ride is 6. Boats launch from the center's dock opposite the Blockade Runner Resort Hotel.

Dockside Watersports
100 Spencer Farlow Dr., Carolina Beach • (910) 458-0220

Dockside rents small sailboats (14-foot Hobie Cats and Sunfish) for about $70 per half day, $125 per full day. Ask about off-season specials, and reserve in advance. Major credit cards are accepted. Dockside Watersports is at the Snow's Cut Marina.

Cape Fear Boat Rentals
Long Beach • (910) 278-1880

Oak Island residents and visitors may rent a variety of small sailboats, including Sunfish and Butterfly craft (great for kids) and have them delivered, too, seven days a week from May through August. Life preservers are included. Rentals are by the day ($50) or week ($325) only. Credit cards are not accepted.

Ocean Isle Beach Rentals at The Winds Clarion Inn
310 E. First St., Ocean Isle Beach • (910) 579-7575, (910) 754-4538

This shop rents a 14-foot Aquacat for $30 per hour or $110 per day with a credit card deposit. Lessons are included. (It also rents beach items such as umbrellas and chairs.) Ocean Isle Beach Rentals is open seven days a week, May through September, from 9 AM to 5 PM, and by appointment in spring and autumn.

INSIDERS' TIP

Glass containers are not welcome on any beach strand. At Wrightsville Beach, having one can cost you an $85 fine!

Topsail Water Sports
1184 N. Anderson Blvd., Topsail Beach
• **(910) 328-1141**

John and Gay Maxwell's shop is a local favorite. You can rent Hobie Cats (14-foot and 16-foot) and other small craft at fees ranging from $30 per hour to $90 per day. Half-day and full-day sailboat charters with a certified captain and lessons are also available. Reservations are necessary, and most major credit cards are accepted. The shop is open seven days a week April through October.

Supplies, Accessories and Repair

There are many more businesses in the area that provide good service for marine supplies and repair than are listed here, but those below come recommended.

Boater's World Discount Marine Center
University Commons Shopping Center, S. College Rd., Wilmington
• **(910) 452-3000**

When it comes to marine supplies, accessories, gear and clothing, there's very little that Boater's World doesn't carry. And as if an inventory that's well-displayed, comprehensive and well-priced weren't enough, the staff is expert and polite. It's open seven days a week.

Overton's Discount Boating Supplies
5912 Oleander Dr., Wilmington
• **(910) 313-0022**

Overton's is among the more trusted suppliers of boating equipment and accessories, including electronics, hardware and cleaning supplies. It even carries water skis and swim wear and has recently moved to more spacious digs. It's closed on Sunday.

Pennington's Marine
97 Heathcliff Rd., Wilmington
• **(910) 392-7488**

Pennington's has a reputation for honesty and competence when it comes to marine (including outboards) repair. Pickup service is available.

Scuba Diving and Snorkeling

Diving the southern coastal waters offers rewarding experiences to collectors, nature-watchers and wreck divers, despite there being no true coral reefs in these latitudes. A surprising variety of tropical fish species inhabit these waters, including blue angel fish, damsel fish and moray eels as well as several varieties of sea fans, some as large as three feet in height. Spiny oysters, deer cowries, helmet shells, trumpet tritons and queen conchs can be found here.

Among the easiest places to find tropical aquatic life is 23 Mile Rock, part of a 12-mile-long ledge running roughly perpendicular to the coast. Another 15 miles out, the Lobster Ledge, a low-lying formation 120 feet deep, is a collectors' target. There are several smaller ledges close to shore in shallower water better suited for less-experienced divers and more bottom time. Visibility at offshore sites averages 60 feet and often approaches 100 feet, but inshore visibility is seldom better than 20 feet. The coastal waters can be dived all year long, since their temperatures range from the upper 50s in winter and low 80s in summer. However, many local charters typically end their diving season in early fall. Some charters organize destination trips after that.

Good snorkeling in the region is a matter of knowing when and where to go. Near-shore bottoms are mostly packed sand devoid of the rugged features that make for good viewing and collecting, but a good guide can lead you to rewarding areas. When the wind is right and the tide is rising, places such as the Wrightsville Beach jetty offer good viewing and visibility. The many creeks and estuaries support an abundance of life, and the shorter visibility, averaging 15 to 20 feet, is no obstacle in water so shallow.

The waters around piers in Banks Channel at Wrightsville Beach are fair but often murky, and currents are strong. Only experienced snorkelers should attempt these waters or those in local inlets, which are treacherous, and then only at stopped tides. It is neither safe nor legal to swim beneath oceanside fishing piers. When in doubt, contact a local dive shop for information.

WATERSPORTS • 261

This region of the "Graveyard of the Atlantic" offers unparalleled opportunities for wreck divers. From Tubbs Inlet (near Sunset Beach) to New River Inlet (North Topsail Beach), 20 of the dozens of known shipwrecks resting here are accessible and safe. Most are Confederate blockade runners, one is a tanker torpedoed by the Nazi sub U-158, and several were sunk as part of North Carolina's artificial reef program (see the Fishing chapter for more on artificial reefs). These and higher-risk wrecks can be located with the assistance of dive shops.

Wreck diving is an advanced skill. Research prior to a dive is essential in terms of the target, techniques and potential dangers, which in this region include live ammunition and explosives that may be found on World War II wrecks. Contact the proper authorities if you observe anything suspicious, and leave it alone! Under state law, all wrecks and underwater artifacts that remain unclaimed for more than 10 years are declared state property. Anyone interested in searching for artifacts should file for a permit with the North Carolina Department of Cultural Resources, 109 E. Jones Street, Raleigh, NC 27611.

Six-person dive charters range in price from about $225 to $600, depending on the distance of your destination. Charter boats can be arranged for dive trips through all the dive shops listed here, but there are others. Also check the marinas for fishing charters that accommodate dive trips.

Hanover Fishing Charters, (910) 256-3636, and Sea Lady Charters, (910) 452-9955 or (800) 242-2493, both out of Wrightsville Beach, and the Flo-Jo out of Carolina Beach, (910) 458-5454 or (800) 356-5669, are good resources for charters run by experienced crew. Many charter boats are primarily fishing boats, so if you need custom diving craft, be sure to inquire.

Most dive shops can lead you to a certification class if they don't offer one themselves. Also, proof of diver's certification is required by shops or dive masters when renting equipment, booking charters or purchasing air fills.

Aquatic Safaris & Divers Emporium
5751-4 Oleander Dr., Wilmington
• (910) 392-4386

This PADI training facility is one of Wilmington's largest full-service charter services and dive shops, offering daily dive charters and air fills, including Nitrox. It carries a full range of equipment for sale and rent. Snorkeling equipment is for sale only. The shop is certified by major manufacturers to perform repairs on all life-support equipment and most other equipment as well. It's open seven days a week during the summer and six days a week in the off-season.

Entropy Rentals & Charters
Wrightsville Beach • (910) 395-2401

PADI-certified Capt. Pete Klingenberger guides wreck- and reef-diving trips for up to six persons at a time. His Sea Mark vessels, equipped with full electronics, dock on the Intracoastal Waterway at Wrightsville Beach and at Johnson Marine in Hampstead.

Offshore Adventures
301 Wood Dale Dr., Wilmington
• (910) 799-2895

Offshore Adventures offers dive charters with professional crew aboard its custom 31-foot Bertram and scuba instruction during the warm season. It also provides equipment rentals. In winter, destination dives are organized for those willing to travel.

Bottom Time
6014 Wrightsville Ave., Wilmington
• (910) 397-0181, (800) NITROX1

This is a PADI five-star facility and among the largest sport diving and snorkeling facilities in the region. Services include rentals, repair, sales, air (standard and Nitrox), guided snorkeling tours and instruction in diving and snorkeling. Local charters and customized dive travels to warmer climes during the winter are available. The staff is fully certified, and the business is a National Association of Underwater Instructors (NAUI) facility. In summer, Bottom Time is open Monday through Saturday. Its Cape Fear season closes by early November.

Scuba South Diving Company
222 S. River Dr., Southport
• (910) 457-5201

Among the most respected diving experts in the Southport area is Wayne Strickland, who specializes in dive charters to some of the less-frequented targets off the Cape plus such well-known sites as the *City of Houston*, a passenger freighter that sank in 1878 and which Strickland salvaged for the Southport Maritime Museum. (Artifacts are on display.) Strickland will arrange dives to any site along the southern coast. Trips are aboard his custom 52-foot *Scuba South II*. Scuba South sells and rents a full store of equipment, including wet and dry suits, and provides air fills.

Southport Scuba and Water Sport
610 W. West St., Southport
• (910) 457-1944

Southport Scuba specializes in sales and rentals of equipment, instruction, charters and commercial diving. It also provides local information to divers. It shares retail space with Ocean Outfitters, a purveyor of nautical apparel and accessories, in a shop at the foot of W. West Street near the Southport Marina.

Holden Beach Surf & Scuba
3172-4 Holden Beach Rd. S.W., Holden Beach • (910) 842-6899

Bob Huey's dive and surf shop, on N.C. 130 in the Palmetto Plaza shopping strip on the mainland side of the waterway, carries practically everything needed for diving, including air fills and computers. Bob is a USCG-certified boat captain and diver, and his wife is a PADI-certified dive master. They conduct lessons at a nearby pool during the summer. Their shop is open seven days a week March through December and on weekends in January and February.

East Coast Discount Dive Center
Causeway Dr., Surf City • (910) 328-1887

Doug Medlin's East Coast Discount Dive Center is part of his East Coast Discount Bait & Tackle Shop. The Center provides complete dive services, including sales, rentals, certification classes and air. The shop is staffed by certified divers and is open seven days a week during the high season. Charter excursions include dives on various World War II wrecks, 23 Mile Rock, 18 Mile Rock and many other sites on request. Trips to common dive sites are well-priced.

Ocean Ray
1315 S. College Rd., Wilmington
• (910) 392-9989, (800) 645-5554

Ocean Ray is a manufacturer of quality custom-fit wet and dry suits. Wet suits are made in 3 mm and 6 mm thicknesses. Dry suits are 6-mm-thick G231 nitrogen-blown Rubatex. All suits carry a three-year warranty. Ocean Ray ships throughout North America and Europe and does alterations and repairs on all name-brand suits. Direct sales to the public are available at the retail outlet at the address above.

Water-Skiing

The protected waters of the lower Cape Fear River, from Carolina Beach south, are the most popular for water-skiing the greater Wilmington area. These waters are convenient to public boat ramps in Carolina Beach, including those at the marina at Carolina Beach State Park and at Federal Point. Throughout most of the region, the wider channels of the Intracoastal Waterway and adjoining sounds offer skiing opportunities, boat traffic allowing. The wide mouths of the Shallotte River and Lockwood Folly near Varnumtown are just adequate.

The relatively hushed surf along the Brunswick Islands is well-suited to skiing, yielding about 22 miles of shoreline from Ocean Isle Beach to Sunset Beach. Big Lake, in the community of Boiling Springs Lakes 8 miles northwest of Southport on N.C. 87, is a long, narrow body of water that's excellent for water-skiing. There is a free public boat ramp off Alton Lennon Drive.

Check with the rental services listed in the Motorboat Rentals section above if you need to rent a towing craft. Many, if not most, services and some boating supply shops also rent skis and equipment.

Surfing

California surfers who come to the southern coast of North Carolina agree: The surf may be less spectacular than on the West Coast, but the water is warmer and the season is longer. Conditions were considered good enough for the U.S. Amateur Surfing Championships's Mid-Atlantic Regionals to be held at Wrightsville Beach in 1996. And surfers from here are making their mark worldwide.

Wrightsville Beach's own Ben Bourgeois became the 1996 Junior Men's Amateur World Champion, having won the Quicksilver Grommet World Championship in Bali the year before. Former Men's World Champion Bill Curry is a local resident and one of six local members of the Eastern Surf Association's All-Star team (which includes his son, Chris).

With surfing joining the pantheon of Olympic events (beginning in the year 2000), local surfing has naturally gained further status. Surf shops throughout the region can provide information on regional surfing competitions.

The beaches running north-south — Topsail Island down to Fort Fisher — experience consistently better surf, especially when a nor'easter blows, than the Brunswick beaches, with their east-west orientation. (The Brunswick beaches are fine for bodyboarding.) A favored surfing spot is Masonboro Island's north end near the jetty; however, it's not an easy place to reach, since Masonboro Inlet is an active boat channel with dangerous currents. Crossing over from the soundside (the Intracoastal Waterway) and hiking to the beach is a good idea.

Wrightsville Beach has the most stringent rules governing surfing. Between 11 AM and 4 PM during the summer (Memorial to Labor Day), surfing is restricted to surf zones (also called sounds), which are two-block segments of the beach that move south, two streets at a time, each day. Any lifeguard can tell you where the zone currently stands. Zones do not apply during the off-season. Leash laws, however, are in effect year round. Surfing within 150 feet of fishing piers is prohibited. On northern Topsail Island, surfing is prohibited near Onslow County's Public Beach Access pavilions.

Surfers on the Brunswick Islands say the surfing near the piers is best, but on Ocean Isle Beach (where there are no restricted zones), an ordinance require surfers to remain a full 1,000 feet away from the pier (though it's not consistently enforced). Staying clear just makes good sense, given the amount of lost fishing tackle and barnacle-encrusted pilings that lie in wait for reckless surfers. The occasional feat of shooting the

Banks Channel behind Wrightsville Beach offers smooth sailing for windsurfers.

pier is like a train wreck — terrifying yet fascinating to watch.

Wrightsville Beach Parks and Recreation Department
1 Bob Sawyer Dr., Wrightsville Beach • (910) 256-7925

June through August, weekly beginner surfing lessons for advanced ocean swimmers 10 and older are available. The course covers surfing etiquette, paddling, wave-catching, maneuvers and basic surfing principles.

The Eastern Surfing Association
(910) 256-8604, (910) 395-5865

The ESA, the largest surfing association in the world, is well-represented in the Wilmington area, having more members than anywhere else on the Eastern seaboard. The ESA promotes amateur competitive surfing and fair play worldwide and environmental interests locally (the latter often in cooperation with the Surfrider

Foundation — see below). The local chapter sponsors five to six contests yearly, provides a framework for ranking amateur surfers and is your best source of information about non-ESA surfing events.

The East Coast's first all-women's surfing competition, the Wahines Championship, an ESA event, debuted at Wrightsville Beach in August 1997. Annual ESA membership costs $20, which includes a newsletter and subscription to *Surfing* magazine. Write: ESA/SNC, P.O. Box 542, Wrightsville Beach, NC 28480.

The Surfrider Foundation
Cape Fear Chapter • (910) 350-8282, (910) 256-0233 (infoline)

Headquartered in California, the Surfrider Foundation is a nonprofit international environmental organization that works to preserve the world's beaches through direct action (primarily cleanups), conservation and education. The Cape Fear Chapter sponsors beach sweeps, the Adopt-A-Beach-Access program and Storm Drain Stenciling in association with the Wrightsville Beach Parks and Recreation Department. Open meetings are held regularly.

Surf Reports

Daily surf reports for Wrightsville Beach are broadcast by radio station Surf 107-FM at 7:25 AM and 3:30 PM. Aussie Island Surf Shop, (910) 256-5454, maintains a 24-hour surf report phone line, (910) 256-5757, for conditions at Wrightsville Beach. Reports by phone are also provided by Surf City Surf Shop, (910) 256-4353; Sweetwater Surf Shop, (910) 256-8184; and Star-Line, (910) 762-1996 ext. 2213, all for conditions at Wrightsville Beach. For Topsail Island, call Spinnaker Surf & Sport, (910) 328-2311. Also check the local surf shops listed below.

Surfboard Rentals

There is no shortage of places to rent a stick if you don't have one of your own. Check with the surf shops below or these specialty watersports shops.

S & S Water Sports, Davis Street and Channel Boulevard, Topsail Beach, (910) 328-7751

Beach Fun Rentals, 3324 Holden Beach Road S.W., Holden Beach, (910) 842-9600

Ocean Isle Beach Rentals at The Winds Clarion Inn, 310 E. First Street, Ocean Isle Beach, (910) 579-7575 or (910) 754-4538

Topsail Water Sports, 1184 N. Anderson Boulevard, Topsail Beach, (910) 328-1141

Surf Shops

The many surf shops in the area offer a complete selection of surf gear, apparel and accessories, including wet suits and videos. You can buy a new or used stick, rent one by the day and get yours repaired. Shops can lead you to local people who customize boards too. Most surf shops also are the best place to find everything you'll need for skateboarding and in-line skating, including parts and accessories, as well as surfwear and skatewear, designer eyewear, shoes and sandals, jewelry and Boogie boards. Most area shops are open seven days a week in season.

Aussie Island Surf Shop, 1319 Military Cut-off Road, Wilmington, (910) 256-5454

Bert's Surf Shop, 5740 Oleander Drive, Wilmington, (910) 392-4501; U.S. Highway 421, Carolina Beach, (910) 458-9047; Norton Street and Yaupon Beach Drive, Yaupon Beach, (910) 278-6679; N. New River Drive, Surf City, (910) 328-1010

Hot Wax Surf Shop, 4510 Hoggard Drive, Wilmington, (910) 791-9283

Surf City Surf Shop, 530 Causeway Drive, Wrightsville Beach, (910) 256-2265

Sweetwater Surf Shop, 10 N. Lumina Avenue, Wrightsville Beach, (910) 256-3821

The Cove Surf Shop, 107 Cape Fear Boulevard, Carolina Beach, (910) 458-4671

Local Call Surf Shop, 609 Yaupon Beach Drive, Yaupon Beach, (910) 278-3306

Holden Beach Surf & Scuba, 3172-4 Holden Beach Road S.W., Holden Beach, (910) 842-6899

Salty's Surf Shop, First Street, Ocean Isle Beach, (910) 579-6223

Spinnaker Surf & Sport, 111 N. Shore Drive, Surf City, (910) 328-2311

Swimming

The Southern coast is blessed with clean, relatively clear, refreshing waters and a long outdoor season. Water temperatures become comfortable usually no later than the middle of spring, generally hovering in the 75 to 80 degree range by summer. Only at the end of the season do temperatures approach those of the waters farther south. Most beaches consist of fine, clean sand. Together with the shores of the Outer Banks and farther north, the southern coast gives evidence that North Carolina does indeed have the finest beaches in the east.

Except during storm surges, the surf is generally moderate. Most beach communities employ lifeguards during the summer, but the beaches are unstaffed otherwise. Swimming in a few areas is hazardous, such as at the extreme east end of Ocean Isle Beach and along the Fort Fisher Historic Site because of either strong currents or underwater debris. All hazardous areas are well-marked. (See our chapter on Sun, Sand and Sea for more on beach-going.)

Check the facilities listed below if pool swimming is more to your liking.

City of Wilmington Public Swimming Pools
(910) 341-7855

The City of Wilmington maintains three public pools, open only during the summer: Shipp Pool at Southside Park (beside Legion Stadium), Carolina Beach Road, (910) 341-7863; Jackson Pool at Northside Park, 750 Bess Street, (910) 341-7866; and Murphy Pool at Robert Strange Park, 410 S. 8th Street, (910) 341-7866. Admission fees are nominal.

YMCA
2710 Market St., Wilmington
• (910) 251-9622

The YMCA boasts two pools to accommodate its many members, and it has extensive hours. Classes in water aerobics is among its many offerings.

YWCA
2815 S. College Rd., Wilmington
• (910) 799-6820

The YWCA has excellent facilities, water aerobics and swimming instruction by highly qualified staff. Instruction in lifesaving is one of its specialties.

The Deck Family Entertainment Center
5524 E. Beach Dr., Long Beach
• (910) 278-4111

The Deck operates a pool that is open to the public. All-day passes are $3.50 for kids up to age 18 and $4.50 for adults and are good 10 AM to 5 PM — come and go as you please. Weekly passes ($15 any age) are good seven days from the day of purchase and include admission to night swims, 7 to 11:30 PM (see also our Attractions chapter). The Deck is open every day from Memorial to Labor Day.

Wrightsville Beach Parks and Recreation Department
1 Bob Sawyer Dr., Wrightsville Beach
• (910) 256-7925

Wrightsville Beach Parks and Recreation offers beginner and advanced-beginner swimming lessons for youth ages 4 through 11. Lessons are conducted June through August in two-week sessions at the pool at Channel Walk Condominiums on Driftwood Court. The cost is $28 for Wrightsville Beach residents, $42 for nonresidents.

Camp Lejeune
MWR Recreation Division's Athletics Branch, Jacksonville • (910) 451-5430

The MWR Recreation Division of the local Marine Corps base sponsors stiff swimming competitions as part of its annual Grand Prix Series of sporting events. These include the Masters Swim I held in January, the Masters Swim II in June and the Davy Jones Open Ocean Swim in July. These events (and others listed in our Sports, Fitness and Parks chapter) take place within the confines of Camp Lejeune in Jacksonville, about 20 minutes from North Topsail Beach.

INSIDERS' TIP

Learn to sail. Cape Fear Community College, (910) 251-6942, 411 N. Front Street in Wilmington, offers two sessions each spring for under $90. Register early!

All events are open to military personnel and the general public of all ages, and they typically draw a nationwide field of competitors. Entry forms and information can be obtained by contacting the division's Fitness Director at the number above — fax: (910) 451-2093 — between 8 AM and 4 PM, Monday through Friday.

Windsurfing

One of the best and most popular windsurfing areas is the Basin, the partially protected body of water off Federal Point at the southern end of Pleasure Island. Accessible from a public boat ramp down the road from the ferry terminal, the Basin is enclosed by the Rocks, a 3.3-mile breakwater that extends to Zeke's Island and beyond. Mott's Channel and Banks Channel on the soundside of Wrightsville Beach are popular spots, but you'll have to contend with the boat traffic. Advanced windsurfers prefer the oceanside of the jetty at the south end of Wrightsville Beach, where action is fairly guaranteed.

Around Topsail Island, the choices are the Intracoastal Waterway and the ocean. The inlets north and south of the island are not well-suited to uninterrupted runs. Along Oak Island and the South Brunswick Islands, the ocean is your best bet, although limited stretches of the ICW are OK for beginners (near the Ocean Isle Beach bridge when it's not busy, for example). Shallotte Inlet and River are narrow but worth a shot. Up-to-date information on windsurfing competitions, usually held in the fall, may be available at the shops listed here.

Ship's Store Windsurfing & Sailing Center
275 Waynick Blvd., Wrightsville Beach
• **(910) 256-9463**

Ship's Store rents sailboards at reasonable rates by the hour ($15 for the first hour) and in blocks of hours. Surfers put in at Banks Channel opposite the Blockade Runner Hotel. Instructors are available Thursdays and Fridays during the summer to teach four-hour windsurfing classes ($60). The store, located in the Atlantic View Retail Center on Wrightsville Avenue, is open for sales all year.

Ocean Isle Beach Rentals at The Winds Clarion Inn
310 E. First St., Ocean Isle Beach
• **(910) 579-7575, (910) 754-4538**

Windsurfers are available for rent at $20 per day. A credit card deposit is required.

Dockside Watersports
100 Spencer Farlow Dr., Carolina Beach
• **(910) 458-0220**

Dockside Watersports rents sailboards beginning at $15 for the first hour from Snow's Cut Marina. The craft are already in the water, ready to go. Reserve in advance when possible. Major credit cards are accepted.

Topsail Water Sports
1184 N. Anderson Blvd., Topsail Beach
• **(910) 328-1141**

You can rent windboards for $15 per half-hour or $40 per hour, and this shop also offers lessons. Reservations are recommended.

Beach Access

Public beach access is a state-regulated system of pedestrian right-of-ways, dune crossovers, parking lots and, at some locations, restroom and shower facilities. A few have food concessions. Except in the public lots on Wrightsville Beach, where parking meters must be fed during the summer only, parking everywhere is free. At Wrightsville Beach, signs indicating beach access paths are readily visible, marked with a large orange sun over blue water.

Note that most beach communities strictly prohibit glass containers and vehicles on the strand. Kure Beach also prohibits dogs and alcohol. Keep in mind that, in most communities, crossing dunes at places other than approved crossovers can earn you a minimum $50 fine.

On Wrightsville Beach, public access with restrooms, metered parking and a shower are across S. Lumina Avenue from the Oceanic Restaurant and Crystal Pier near Nathan Avenue. Restrooms and a shower are at the foot of Salisbury Street near Johnny Mercer's Pier. To the north, parking is also available adjacent to the soon-to-be-rebuilt Holiday Inn (a Hurricane Fran victim) and on either side of the Duneridge Resort, about 1 mile north of

Salisbury Street. One of the Duneridge lots has restrooms. At the north end of Wrightsville Beach, there is parking on both sides of Shell Island Resort. On summer weekends, unless you're parking a bicycle, arrive before 10 AM or after 2 PM to find a space.

At Carolina and Kure Beaches, public beach access points and parking generally are situated at the foot of every second street. Public restrooms and showers are also available along the boardwalk, the most popular being at the foot of Cape Fear Boulevard.

On Oak Island, beach accesses are managed separately by each of the three towns occupying the island. On Caswell Beach Road along eastern Oak Island, about a half-mile east of the Fort Caswell Lighthouse at Caswell Beach, the only public beach access consists of a large gravel parking lot with no facilities. The area is open 5 AM to 11 PM, and prohibitions include camping, the use of alcohol, firearms and fires and cars on the strand.

In Yaupon Beach there are nine beach access points with parking. The less-crowded ones are naturally the ones farther from the pier, especially to the west.

There are 52 public beach accesses along the 8 miles of Long Beach oceanfront. The Cabana at the foot of 40th Street E. is one of the liveliest access points, being the site of Brunswick County Parks & Recreation's Summer Fun Beach Days (see our Attractions chapter). There's plenty of parking, a concession stand and showers. Most other access points have no services except the one at the foot of S. Middletown Avenue, where retail and food stores are an easy walk from the beach. Most of the public accesses in Long Beach have limited parking, especially close to S. Middletown Avenue.

The majority of beach accesses on 11-mile-long Holden Beach are private, but public access points abound at the East end (Avenues A through E), near Jordan Boulevard, and at Ferry Road. Several others are west of the bridge. Parking along Ocean Boulevard is prohibited. A Regional Beach Access facility with showers, restrooms and parking, open 6 AM to 11 PM, is located nearly under the bridge off Jordan Boulevard, where limited parking and covered tables are available.

On Ocean Isle Beach, access is concentrated around the center of town, near the foot of the causeway.

Beach access on Sunset Beach is indicated by small white posts about 100 yards apart. There are no sidewalks and little parking. The paved parking lot adjacent to Sunset Fishing Pier is convenient to the beach and pier facilities.

In Surf City, Topsail Island, access with parking and restrooms is at the foot of New Bern Avenue. Handicap access extends only to the dune-top deck. New restrooms are also at the foot of Roland Avenue. Along Topsail Beach, access with limited parking is available at the foot of nearly every cross street. South of Florida Avenue, a series of stairways provides crossovers, with street parking along Ocean Boulevard.

Onslow County Parks and Recreation operates four beach access pavilions along the strand of North Topsail Beach. All were damaged by the hurricanes of '96. While only Access #2 has been rebuilt and reopened, free parking at all sites is still available. All sites are open April 1 to September 30 from 9 AM to 8 PM daily; off-season they close at 5 PM. (Note: The numbers assigned to Onslow County's beach accesses reflect the order in which the sites were constructed, not their location along the beach. Yes, we think it's odd, too.)

Onslow County's southernmost public beach access, #2, stands about 2 miles north of Tilghman's Square, a short drive north of Surf City. The facility has ample parking, a handicap ramp that extends to the building only, showers, restrooms and phones. Snack vendors are usually nearby. Little more than 4 miles north (just south of Villa Capriani Resort) is Access #4, once the county's largest beach facility on Topsail. Farther north, Access #1, at 1795 New River Inlet Drive, has very limited parking.

At the New River Inlet, where River Road ends, lies Access #3. Parking here is on mostly packed sand, but four-wheel-drive vehicles are recommended. Swimming or wading is prohibited here due to treacherous currents. The nearest telephone is about one mile south, next to Topsail Reef condominiums.

Look for all-white skeletal sand dollars, and return the brown, furry ones to the water — they may be still alive.

Sun, Sand and Sea

Ask native residents or newcomers why they're willing to overlook the difficulties of a tight job market along the Cape Fear coast and you'll get the same answer: It's just so great to live by the ocean. Nothing soothes the spirit like lazing around on a sunny beach under a Carolina-blue sky, taking an occasional dip in the beautiful, clean waters off North Carolina's southern coast or cruising down the Intracoastal Waterway (ICW) on a powerboat, sailboat or kayak.

In the philosophy of locals, this great natural resource provides incomparable riches in terms of the quality of daily living. Our unofficial community slogan is, "You couldn't pay me to move."

Small wonder hundreds of thousands of vacationers choose this region for their play time year after year. Vacationing by, on, or in the water is the most popular way for Americans to relax, which probably explains why many visitors end up being residents on the coast by retirement age, if not before. It's the lure of island-style living; it's the simplicity of bare feet and casual clothing; it's the worry-free attitude of paradise. But everyone, including Insiders, needs to be reminded that even in such a paradise, there are some good tips to follow for a safe, enjoyable vacation.

The Sun

Everybody knows the sun's rays can cause skin damage, but you'd never guess it by looking at area beaches, where — despite years of warnings from medical professionals — the sand is packed with bodies in search of a golden tan or a darker skin tone. If you're determined to tan, some common sense guidelines are in order. Wear sunscreen. Take an umbrella and set up a shade camp — particularly important for small children. Make sure everybody has a hat and good quality sunglasses as standard beach gear.

You can burn even on a cloudy day because up to 90 percent of the sun's rays penetrate clouds and can still damage your skin. Surfaces such as sand, concrete and water can reflect up to 85 percent of the sun's rays. Applying sunscreen with an appropriate SPF should be a daily habit. No matter how immune you think you are to sunburn, you should slather yourself in the best protection you can find, especially when on the open beach. After swimming, put more on.

More than half of the skin damage done by the sun happens in the first 18 years of life. Children need a sunscreen with an SPF of at least 15. Using waterproof sunblock will save you from having to constantly reapply it on your kids as they dart back and forth between the sand and the water.

Wide-brimmed straw hats are very popular in the area, so you can enjoy their protection and look cool at the same time. In the heat of summer, wear light-colored clothing for maximum comfort. Look for linen and cotton clothing because these fabrics breathe better than synthetics. Stay out of the sun in the hottest part of the day in the summer, generally between 11 AM and 3 PM. You can have a long morning on the beach and hours in the afternoon without exposing yourself to the depleting effects of excessive summer heat.

Alcohol, which isn't allowed on area beaches anyway, is debilitating in the heat and can set you on the path to dehydration. Take a cooler of soft drinks or lemonade, and you'll enjoy yourself much more on the beach or on the water. Also, the Coast Guard doesn't take kindly to drunk boaters, so if you must drink, be moderate. If the long arm of the law doesn't worry you, think of this: beer will just make you thirstier under the hot sun. Distilled spirits, such as gin and rum, will incapacitate you in short order.

The Sand

Beaches in the Wilmington area vary in width and shell diversity, but they all have one thing in common: even after two hurricanes in 1996, they have beautiful expanses of sand. Repairs were done so swiftly that it's hard to see evidence of hurricane damage on most of the beaches directly adjacent to Wilmington.

Sand is a great natural pumice, so regular strolls during your vacation can gently sand the soles of your city-worn feet to smoothness. Access to area beaches is free because North Carolinians are rigid in their belief that the shores belong to the people. Note orange and blue signs at frequent intervals along beach roads — they point out easements between homes where you can freely cross someone's property to get to the beach. Stick to these paths.

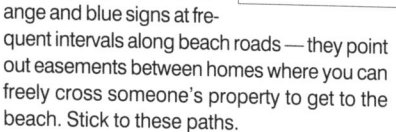

You are free to walk the length of all area beaches, including those on private islands such as Bald Head and Figure Eight (although you'll need a private boat or, in the case of Bald Head Island, a passenger ferry to get there). Everyone's property line stops at the high-water mark.

Beach hospitality includes public restrooms, showers and rinse-off spots located conveniently along most beaches. Restaurants that offer everything from hot dogs to prime rib to vegetarian dining are an easy walk from the sand. Parking is generally free on the street and in public lots in the off-season after Labor Day, when the meters are retired until Memorial Day. At the peak of summer, be sure to bring a pocket of quarters for parking on Wrightsville Beach, where 25¢ will buy you 15 minutes. The meters can be filled for several hours, so you don't have to race back and forth to stay legal.

You can see all kinds of amazing things on the beach. Keen observers on Topsail Island will spot shark teeth, ebony in color and varied in shape, by their characteristic glint in the sand or at the water's edge. Brunswick beaches yield other interesting treasures — whole sand dollars are frequent finds. Look for the all-white skeletal sand dollars, and return the brown, furry ones to the water — they may be still alive (they will also smell terrible if you put them in your car to take them home). Arrowheads from ancient Native American tribes can be found on these beaches if you are very observant and lucky.

The sand dunes bear important mention: Please stay off them. The dunes are a vital part of the beach environment and provide homes for a variety of beach animals. Particularly as the area made its recovery from the summer storms of 1996, the value of the dunes in retarding erosion and protecting homes was vividly recognized. Also, on the purely practical side, there is a stiff fine if you climb in the dunes or disturb any of the vegetation. A wild romp through the dunes could put as much as a $500 dent in your vacation allowance. So, be forewarned and stay off them.

Some other laws worth noting: don't take glass containers on the beach; don't let your dog run loose until you check local ordinances (and in all cases pick up its "business" so other people don't step in it); don't let your parking meter expire; don't take alcohol to the beach; and don't litter. Take a portable ashtray with you if you plan to smoke because, as inconsequential as a butt or two may seem, millions of them cause a litter/environmental problem. Filters are not biodegradable and can harm sea life. Also, they're just not pretty and you're not spending all this vacation money to look at trash, right?

An interesting phenomenon occurs on the beaches drop in the fall. At times, on a night walk, you can kick up a phosphorescent light show in the sand with your bare feet. It sort of

---

INSIDERS' TIP

When combing the beaches for shark teeth, scrutinize the coarse sand most carefully. The teeth show up best when they are wet.

There are beautiful shells for the careful seeker on Cape Fear-area beaches.

makes you feel like you're walking through stars. Night on the sand is a special time. Many a person has been inspired to take a moonlight stroll and a dip in the ocean. However, a word of warning about taking a swim in the buff. As daring and romantic as this sounds, it's not allowed and, worse, it's easy to lose your bearings regarding the whereabouts of your clothing after the current moves you quickly up or down the beach.

The Sea

The sea is the key to all of North Carolina's coastal beauty, and two of the state's three most reliable inlets are situated in the heart of the southern coastline. Mason Inlet at Wrightsville Beach and the mouth of the Cape Fear River both offer quick, sure routes from the mainland to the Atlantic Ocean. And whether you plan to swim, boat, surf, fish, or sit and stare at it, the sea offers endless possibilities for exploration, education and contemplation.

A visit to the North Carolina Aquarium at Fort Fisher makes a great outing for the whole family. Exhibits of sharks and other area fish, sea turtles, eels, sea urchins, alligators and more makes this a great introduction to the sea creatures of the region. The aquarium also has regular hands-on workshops where participants can learn crabbing, surf fishing, and how to identify marsh creatures. Call the aquarium at (910) 458-8257 for a schedule of events and read more about it in our Attractions chapter.

Wilmington is a major shipping port where international freighters and other exotic ships can be seen navigating Frying Pan Shoals and the Cape Fear River. The North Carolina State Ports Authority is located just minutes south of downtown Wilmington. A pair of binoculars is a handy aid for spotting ships still at sea. As ships enter Wilmington, be sure to wave to the sailors on deck because in-bound ships have probably been at sea for months and the guys seem anxious for a friendly greeting.

If swimming is your water sport or relaxation of choice, you've come to the right place. The ocean offers limitless possibilities for everyone from the wader to the long-distance swimmer. For our safety in the spring and summer, lifeguards are posted at many of the beaches in the area. If you see someone running into the water with an orange or red float in hand, it's probably a lifeguard. You can be called closer to shore if the lifeguard thinks you're getting too far out for your own safety, but don't take it badly. These trained professionals are just looking out for your best interests.

Riptides and undertows are unseen dangers lurking beneath the waves — dangers that Insiders respect. If you are swimming and are suddenly pulled in a frightening way by the currents, the most important thing to remember is to stay calm. Panic leads to exertion, which leads to fatigue. If you find yourself in a riptide, relax and let it carry you on its natural course toward the sea. Within a few minutes, it will dissipate. Then you can swim parallel to the shoreline to get out of the riptide area and back to shore. Do not try to swim straight back into shore against the riptide . . . you'll only tire yourself out.

A few don'ts: don't swim in inlets because you may not be spied by a speeding boat; don't swim alone; and don't swim in the Cape Fear River at and below Wilmington unless you can tolerate the company of alligators and big ships. Although the river is not particularly wide, it is deep — 38 feet on average — and has fast currents that have to be experienced to be believed.

Wrightsville Beach is a popular place for surfing, but there are some regulations, and you should ask the lifeguard about designated surfing zones, which shift each day. (See our Watersports chapter for more information on surf zones.) You must wear a leash and will be immediately chastised if you are not attached to your board. Lifeguards are fastidious about enforcing this rule.

The tides are such an important factor in coastal communities that their comings and goings are part of the daily weather forecast. Be aware of them if you splash out to sandbars or islands at low tide. Changing tides could make the trip back to shore a daunting swim.

Regarding weather, take storms seriously. Get out of the water and off the beach when these often-spectacular weather events take place. Lightning on the beach means business, and you should seek immediate shelter inside a building or in your car. Also, a hurricane watch is a good reason to leave an area and the worst reason to arrive to watch nature in upheaval. Area beaches are often evacuated when hurricanes threaten.

There are many opportunities for boating along the southern coast. If you trailer your own boat, there are ample public boat ramps throughout the entire area. If you choose to leave your boat at the water, more than 70 marinas offer a variety of services, including dry-dockage, wetslips and storage (see our Marinas and the Intracoastal Waterway chapter). Boating possibilities include the Cape Fear River and its adjacent branches, the Atlantic Ocean, the ICW, and area lakes. Fuel and other amenities are available on the southern coastline, generally on the ICW. If you don't have a boat of your own, you can take advantage of one of the charter services for sailing craft and, of course, tour and deepsea fishing boats that cater to all cruising needs (see our Watersports and Fishing chapters for listings).

Boaters should understand the rules of the road when operating their own boat or chartering someone else's. Many waterways, especially the ICW at Wrightsville Beach and Carolina Beach, can become heavily congested. Educate yourself on basic navigation. A Power Squadron course, probably available

INSIDERS' TIP

The best way to cook firm-fleshed fish such as snapper or grouper is on the grill, wrapped in bacon and basted with melted butter, lemon juice and pressed garlic.

in your city or town, is an invaluable experience before boating.

Perhaps the most important thing about boating is preparation. File a float plan; it can be as official or informal as your circumstances require. The point is that you should tell someone where you're going and when you expect to return. Motors don't always work, and tides never stop. Don't make your loved ones on shore worry about your whereabouts if you're late returning. You are required to have one life jacket for each person on your boat, and the Coast Guard is within its rights to stop you and see that you have proper equipment. Adults may use their own judgment about wearing a life jacket; children should automatically be strapped into one. It isn't comfortable, but these things save people's lives.

Carry sufficient nonalcoholic liquids, not only for the humans aboard but for your dog if you choose to take Rover along. Discourage your pet from drinking sea water, and have fresh water available. Carry an emergency kit that contains flares, a fire extinguisher, first aid supplies, and various repair items. Understand how to use your ship-to-shore radio and practice in advance of an emergency. Channel 64 is the hailing channel but, in nonemergency situations, advise the person you're contacting to another frequency to keep 64 clear. If you're going to be out after dark, turn on your running lights. The ICW is also a highway for commerce, and you want to be sure that barges know you're out there.

Boats under sail always have the right of way over powercraft. If power is your chosen method of boating, be aware of the instability your wake can create for sailboats. If you find yourself in the shipping lanes, give big ships a wide berth. Yielding the right-of-way is often necessary because big ships require at least a mile to stop.

If you're a Ski-Doo or personal watercraft fan who has regularly ripped down the waters at high speed, take note that some things have changed. There are no-wake zones near homes at Wrightsville Beach, and other beach communities are studying the issue at this writing. Just be alert to the zones, marked by signs, and keep your speed down. Also, stay out of delicate sidewaters where your craft may damage the nurseries of shellfish and fish.

Emergencies happen on the water. The Coast Guard is particular about what constitutes an emergency, and it will not immediately come to your rescue in all situations. Generally, only life- or environment-threatening situations will get its attention. Running aground in the waterway is rarely considered an emergency because if you get stuck, it is commonly understood that you can walk to shore. Commercial towing companies, such as SeaTow, (910) 452-3798, will arrive if you get stuck on a sandbar and call for help on your radio; and, believe this Insider who has been stuck hard aground a few times, their service is worthwhile. A sailboat with a fixed keel is virtually guaranteed to go aground at some point, and it isn't always possible to get loose without a sturdy towboat. Yearly membership with SeaTow — sort of the AAA of the water — is a good investment.

The area's waters are full of shoals, so keep an eye on your depth-sounder. If you don't have one and charts suggest shallow waters, steer clear of questionable areas. The ICW is susceptible to shoaling near inlets, and you can't rely on charts for accuracy because changes occur frequently. The markers entering the Cape Fear River from the ocean were renumbered in 1997, so be alert to the fact that these changes haven't been made on current NOAA charts.

The southern coast of North Carolina boasts the best that sun, sand and sea have to offer. Come prepared to enjoy a safe and fun visit.

The fastest-growing niche in fishing these days seems to be saltwater fly-fishing.

Fishing

For anglers, the southern coast is very nearly paradise. Blue-green inshore waters tempered and cleansed by the Gulf Stream, the deep-blue offshore waters of the Gulf Stream itself, saltwater estuaries where many saltwater species breed, and dozens of winding freshwater creeks teeming with life await. Whether you're interested in lazing alongside a shady creek in slow pursuit of catfish, surf-casting for blues, or pitting yourself against mighty deep-sea game fish, it's all here. Even at Wilmington's Greenfield Lake, where one lucky guy hauled in a 40-pound carp in 1995, opportunities abound. Strict catch limits and catch-and-tag programs have helped several saltwater fish populations thrive and keep the fishing prospects looking good.

Since the early 1970s, the Division of Marine Fisheries has been involved in creating artificial reefs that provide habitat for a plethora of sea life. These reefs consist of old ships, railroad cars, bridge rubble, concrete and FADs (fish-attracting devices, whatever they may be). Using the motto "We sink 'em — you fish 'em," reef-builders have created 20 such structures along the coast to date. Judging by the number of sheepshead, mackerel and billfish landed on an average day, the program seems to be paying off. (Surely the men who landed the 937-pound tiger shark in the Poor Boy Shark Tournament in August 1993 think so.) A chart will lead you to these sites as well as to the scores of fish-filled wrecks littering this area.

After being decimated by hurricanes Bertha and Fran in 1996, the fish in the Cape Fear and Northeast Cape Fear rivers seem to have returned to pre-storm levels. Good catches of striper and shad were being reported in spring of 1998. Ocean anglers who prefer pier fishing should still consider surf casting again this year rather than face overcrowding at the piers that survived the storms or have since been rebuilt.

Of the seven oceanside piers on Topsail Island, only three have been rebuilt. Most other piers are likely gone forever; cherish your photographs. Brunswick County piers, from Southport to Sunset, were essentially untouched by the storms.

Note that fishing from most bridges in the area is restricted (prohibited at Wrightsville Beach) because bridges often transverse boat channels. Be certain to check the signs on particular bridges before casting.

Small-boat owners have many fishing opportunities — around the pilings of Pfizer Pharmaceutical Company's pier in the Cape Fear River north of Price's Creek, for example. The mouths of most creeks and some inlets are good spots, especially during incoming tides when you and your bait can drift in with the bait fish. Use caution at ocean inlets during outgoing tides.

If you're traveling without tackle, rental gear is fairly abundant. Among the places to check are these shops in addition to the fishing piers listed below: Herring's Tackle in Surf City (Topsail Island), (910) 328-3291; and Beach Fun Rentals on Holden Beach Road S.W. (on the mainland side of the bridge), (910) 842-9600. Tackle shops abound along the coast. Be sure to inquire whether particular shops rent equipment.

For a wide range of information on boating access, inland fishing, species information (especially trout), lake and stream stock and maps, call the North Carolina Wildlife Resources Commission at (919) 733-3634 or write to 512 N. Salisbury Street, Raleigh, N.C. 27604-1188.

What follows is information on fishing licenses, up-to-date fishing reports, fishing piers, surf fishing, fly-fishing, boat ramps, a cross-section of head boats and charters, and annual fishing tournaments. Of course, we've included recommendations for some special places to cast your lure or net.

Fishing Licenses

Although licenses are not currently required for hook-and-line saltwater fishing, authorities are currently considering them. A decision could be made within the shelf life of this edition of *The Insiders' Guide®*, so check with the businesses below that handle licenses for updates. (Individual recreational saltwater licenses are expected to cost about $15 annually, if authorized.)

In any case, you must observe size and bag limits. Familiarize yourself with regulations, which are posted at most piers and marinas. Freshwater licenses are issued by the North Carolina Wildlife Resources Commission, (919) 662-4370. Licenses range greatly in price and privileges and may be combined with a hunting license. Licenses may be obtained at the following retailers.

Wilmington
- Kmart, 815 S. College Road, (910) 799-5360
- Tackle Express Tackle Mart, 4100 Oleander Drive, (910) 392-3472
- Wal-Mart, 352 S. College Road, (910) 392-4034

Pender County
- Hampstead Village Pharmacy, in the Hampstead Village Shopping Center, U.S. Highway 17 (about 2 miles north of town center), (910) 270-3411
- Holland's Shelter Creek Fish Camp, N.C. Highway 53, (910) 259-5743

South Brunswick
- Holden Beach True Value Hardware, 3008 Holden Beach Road, (910) 842-5440
- Island Tackle and Gifts, N.C. Highway 179 between Ocean Isle Beach and Sunset Beach, (910) 579-6116
- Pawn-USA, 5001-4 Main Street in Shallotte, (910) 754-7918
- Stewart Hardware, N.C. 211 near the Sandfiddler Restaurant in Southport, (910) 457-5544
- Wal-Mart, 4540 Main Street in Shallotte, (910) 754-2880

Fishing Reports

The most up-to-date sources of fishing information are charter captains, fishing piers and tackle shops. Beach 106.3 FM (WCCA) airs fishing reports twice a day on weekdays at 7 AM and 5 PM. Star-Line, a telephone service of the *Wilmington Star-News*, provides daily fishing and weather reports for the price of a local call, (910) 762-1996 extension 2212. Digh's Country Sports Gallery, 1988 Eastwood Road in Wrightsville Beach, (910) 256-2060, also reports fishing conditions.

Fishing Piers

Each pier in the area has its own personality. Some — of those that have survived — have been made crooked by years of battering by the ocean and gales. Some are festooned with odd novelties and memorabilia. Most proudly display photographs of trophies reeled up from the sea. Sad to say, every pier on Topsail Island, which once boasted seven ocean piers, was lost to Hurricane Fran in 1996. Only two ocean piers have been rebuilt, bringing the total number of rebuilt piers to three, counting the Sound Pier on the sound side of Topsail Beach. On Pleasure Island, only Kure Beach Pier has been rebuilt. On busy days, expect to be rubbing elbows with other pier-fishers between Kure and Topsail.

Almost all piers charge a fee for fishing permits, good for a 24-hour period beginning at 6 AM. Bottom fishing generally costs $3 to $5 per day and king fishing about twice as much. Most piers offer season fishing permits, tackle shops, snack bars, wet cleaning tables and restrooms.

Wilmington

River Road Park
6300 River Rd. • (910) 341-7198

River Road Park, south of the State Port about 8 miles from downtown Wilmington and

COASTAL CAROLINA'S FINEST
fly shop & light tackle outfitters.

LOCATED ON THE WAY TO
Wrightsville Beach.

GUIDE SERVICES AVAILABLE:

Inshore
Offshore
fly
Spin
or plug

INTRACOASTAL ANGLER
WILMINGTON NC

Lumina Station
1900 Eastwood Rd. #7
910•256•4545
888•325•4285
www.saltwaterfly.com

opposite Sugar Pine Drive, features a 240-foot, handicapped-accessible fishing pier on the Cape Fear River. The park is handicapped-accessible and is open from 8 AM to dusk.

Wrightsville Beach

Johnnie Mercer's Pier
Foot of E. Salisbury St. • (910) 256-2743

Almost half of this popular pier was lost to Hurricane Fran. Reconstruction of the pier in concrete, complete with a new, handicapped-accessible pier house, should be in full swing by the time you read this. Completion is expected by Spring 1999. That means there'll be no pier to fish from until then, but the existing pier house, with its bait-and-tackle shop and arcade, will remain open until the new one is completed.

Kure Beach

Kure Beach Pier
Ave. K, Kure Beach • (910) 458-5524

Kure Beach Pier is fully operational, perhaps better than before, and permits are good from midnight to midnight. The new facilities include a grill, complete tackle shop, souvenir store and an arcade with four pool tables. It's handicapped accessible. No alcoholic beverages (including beer) are permitted.

Southport-Oak Island

City Pier
Waterfront Park, Bay St., Southport

This small, handicapped-accessible pier near the mouth of the Cape Fear River is a municipal facility, and usage is free.

Long Beach Pier
2729 W. Beach Dr., Long Beach
• (910) 278-5962

Located near the far west end of Oak Island, Long Beach Pier is the longest pier in the state, measuring 1,012 feet. Some folks use shopping carts to move their gear the distance. Three things are not welcome here: shark fishing, net casting and profanity. The owners perform rod-and-reel repairs on the premises, and there is good handicapped access.

Ocean Crest Pier
1411 E. Beach Dr., Long Beach
• (910) 278-6674, (910) 278-3333

This 1,000-foot pier near 14th Place E. has a tackle shop and allows handicapped anglers to fish for free. The owners do not allow shark fishing but do provide a shelter of sorts at the T-shaped far end that is reserved for king fishers. Season permits cost $75 for bottom fishing and $125 for kings. The Windjammer restaurant adjoins the pier.

278 • **FISHING**

Photo: Bill DiNome

The character of each pier is a reflection of the storms it survives.

Yaupon Pier
Foot of Womblie Ave., Yaupon Beach
- **(910) 278-9400**

Yaupon is not only the highest pier in the state, it also boasts the state record for the largest fish caught from a pier to date — read it and weep — a 1,150-lb tiger shark caught on rod and reel. The pier is handicapped-accessible. The adjoining Pirate's Cove Restaurant is known for its ocean view and homemade clam chowder, and the pier lounge is a small, friendly place featuring live entertainment, karoake, and plenty of fish tales. (Who needs to stand in the rain?)

South Brunswick Islands

Holden Beach Pier
441 Ocean Blvd. W., Holden Beach
- **(910) 842-6483**

Holden Beach Pier prohibits the use of nets and the consumption of alcoholic beverages. It sells three-day and seven-day fishing permits and live bait. A grill and snack counter adjoins a game room, which is fairly busy in summer. This is one of only three area piers (including Ocean Isle and Sunset Beach, below) that charge spectators a fee (25¢) for walking the pier. Handicapped access is good.

Ocean Isle Pier
Foot of Causeway Dr., Ocean Isle Beach
- **(910) 579-6873**

The steep ramp to the pier gets slippery when wet and is not handicapped-friendly. The large game room and small grill are popular in summer.

Sunset Beach Pier
Foot of Sunset Blvd., Sunset Beach
- **(910) 579-6630**

There is no running water at the cleaning table, but amenities include a snack bar, game room and bait for sale. It's handicapped accessible, but the cramped rest rooms could prove a little difficult.

Topsail Island

Jolly Roger Pier
Foot of Flake Ave., Surf City
- **(910) 328-4616**

The Jolly Roger stands 6 miles south of Surf City, and its patio is what remains of a launch pad built for Project Bumblebee, the Navy's historic, top-secret missile development program of the late 1940s. Rebuilt following Hurricane Fran, the pier now has a new handicapped-accessible side ramp.

Topsail Sound Pier
1520 Carolina Blvd., Topsail Beach
- **(910) 328-3641**

This is the only soundside pier on Topsail Island, part of the Topsail Sound Pier Market & Marina at the foot of Florida Avenue. The original pier was destroyed by Hurricane Fran in 1996 and now, at a length of 200 feet, the pier is longer and better than ever for fishing (net-fishing, too) in the relatively placid sound. At the market and marina you'll also find bait and tackle for sale, a boat ramp, charter boat service, and a fully stocked grocery store, owned and operated by the affable former town mayor, Kip Oppegaard.

Surf City Pier
N. Shore Dr., Surf City • (910) 328-3521

One block south of Roland Avenue in the heart of Surf City, this handicapped-accessible pier is a busy, family-oriented establishment that prohibits alcohol and drunks. Indoors, a large game room will keep the kids twitching their joy sticks. Special bottom-fishing rates apply to children: $2 daily, $15 per season (April 1 to November 30). Because of the pier's popularity, the management enforces a two-rod limit per person (for king rigs, one per person) from dawn to dark. After dark, only bottom rigs are permitted. Spectators are charged 50¢ per day ($20 per season; season fishing permit-holders are exempt).

INSIDERS' TIP

Do not land swordfish no matter how big a prize, and don't eat it at restaurants. The current over-harvesting of swordfish has been likened to that of the American bison.

Surf Fishing

We've all heard this type of exchange between anglers: "Where'd you catch it?" asks the hopeful one. "In the mouth," replies the successful one. Well, we can't reveal every secret fishing hole in the region either (we're still learning them ourselves), but we can recommend a few to get you started.

On Wrightsville Beach, when swimmers and surfers rule the rest of the strand, an exceptional surf-fishing spot is behind the jetty at Masonboro Inlet, on the south end of the island. Do not fish from the jetty itself; it's dangerous and illegal.

The Fort Fisher State Recreation Area is an undeveloped 4-mile stretch of beach and tidal marsh approximately 6 miles south of Carolina Beach that is accessible by four-wheel-drive vehicle. At the entrance to the area, off U.S. Highway 421 before the Aquarium (bear left at the fork), there is a public beach access with restrooms, a shower and snack bar, and a new ranger contact station. Otherwise, there are no services, so bring everything you'll need and pack out everything you bring (also see "Off-Roading" in our Sports and Fitness chapter).

Another good spot, Carolina Beach Inlet at the north end of Pleasure Island, is also accessible by four-wheel-drive. A less-known and more restricted fishing spot on Pleasure Island lies off Dow Road. For 3 miles south of Spartanburg Avenue, foot paths enter the woods from the roadside (you may notice vehicles parked there). Foot traffic only is permitted since this is an environmentally sensitive area, which is owned by the federal government (the "No Trespassing" warnings are not enforced). The trails lead to the Cape Fear River, but the northernmost trails open upon a secluded inlet where bait fish are often stirred into a frenzy by the unseen feeders or netted by anglers. It's also a good place to picnic and relax if the mosquitoes aren't too voracious.

Fishing The Rocks is a unique outing. The Rocks is a 3.3-mile breakwater extending from Federal Point, south of the Fort Fisher Ferry terminal. The enclosed water around Zeke's Island is called the Basin, and fishing on both sides of the barrier can be excellent. Walking The Rocks can be hazardous; they're often slippery and awash at high tide. Enter upon them only at low tide.

The Point, at the west end of Oak Island bordering Lockwood Folly Inlet, is a productive spot for surf fishing. It's a fairly long walk to the water, but you can drive there if you've got an off-road vehicle and a permit ($50 from the town of Long Beach). Beach driving there is permitted only off-season, from September 15 to April 15.

Access to the Intracoastal Waterway and New River Inlet, at the north end of Topsail Island, can be gained from the boat ramp parking lot directly beneath the N.C. Highway 210 high span. It's usually a very quiet place. You'll find it at the last turnout from the northbound side of N.C. 210 before the bridge. Unmarked footpaths also wind through the brush to the water.

When fishing the beaches, observe local dune ordinances and keep off the dunes except at established crossovers. Most beach communities levy fines for trespassing on the dunes. In North Topsail Beach, for example, you may be tagged with a hefty $500 fine for ignoring the warning signs, which apply equally to private property.

Fly-Fishing

The fastest-growing niche in fishing these days seems to be saltwater fly-fishing, which combines all the artistry of freshwater fly-fishing plus the adrenaline rush of ocean game fishing. Neophytes and aficionados of the sport should take note of the following resources in the Wilmington area and in many tackle shops throughout the region.

Digh's Country Sports Gallery
1988 Eastwood Rd., Wrightsville Beach • (910) 256-2060

Wilmington's exclusive Orvis dealer, Digh's (rhymes with "dyes") offers the services of full-time, expert fly-fishing guides for any type of local fly-fishing action. Gulf Stream trips are aboard a Bertram sportfisherman, and inshore trips are aboard Boston Whalers and custom flat boats. Digh's is also the local sponsor of the Orvis saltwater fly-fishing school. Arranging worldwide hunting, fishing (salt and freshwater) and travel packages is among Digh's specialties. The handsomely designed store stocks casual and sport clothing and original sporting art in various media. You'll find Orvis rods and reels, fly-tying materials, books and luggage. You can even call for the day's fishing report. In the summer Digh's is open 10 AM to 7 PM Monday through Friday, 9 AM to 5 PM Saturday and 11 AM to 4 PM Sunday.

Intracoastal Angler
1900 Eastwood Rd., Ste. 7, Wrightsville Beach • (910) 256-4545

Intracoastal Angler has attracted the attention of national fishing publications and for good reason. Boasting perhaps the most elaborate fly-tying department in the state, this full-service fly shop and outfitter provides expert guide service, boat charters, clinics, lessons and a full line of apparel, equipment and tackle for both salt and fresh water, including light tackle for spinning and bait fishing. It stocks top-name rods and reels as well as books and videos in a visually appealing shop at Lumina Station on the mainland side of the bridge. The staff is friendly and professional. The shop is open Monday through Saturday from 10 AM to 8 PM and noon to 5 PM Sunday during the warm season.

From mid-April through the warm season, owner Tyler Stone captains his own 20-foot center-console vessel, *Misguided*, for inshore and offshore charters geared for everything from Atlantic bonita and Spanish mackerel to barracuda, amberjack and tarpon.

Boat Ramps

The North Carolina Wildlife Resources Commission maintains free ramps for pleasure boaters and anglers. Parking is generally scarce in the summer months at the busier locations such as Wrightsville Beach. The ramps are identified by black-and-white, diamond-shaped "Wildlife" signs. For information on public boat access, call (919) 733-3633. Included here are some private ramps as well.

Wilmington

Dram Tree Park on the corner of Castle and Surry streets off Front Street in downtown Wilmington is almost beneath the Cape Fear Memorial Bridge and gives access to the Cape Fear River.

Castle Hayne

Access to the Northeast Cape Fear River is by a ramp next to the N.C. Highway 117 bridge.

Pender County

The Northeast Cape Fear River and its tributary creeks are accessible by three public ramps:

A ramp that allows access to the west bank of the river from I-40 can be reached by taking N.C. 53 east about 1.7 miles, then County Road 1512 to its end.

A public ramp on the east bank is off County Road 1520 about 7.7 miles north of N.C. 210. The intersection of N.C. 210 and Secondary Road 1520 lies about 3 miles east of I-40 (Exit 408).

Holland's Shelter Creek Campground and Restaurant, (910) 259-5743, is 7.5 miles east of I-40 down N.C. 53. Canoes are for rent ($15 flat fee), and the restaurant offers a memorable glimpse of local style. The private ramp gives access to Holly Shelter Creek (see our chapters on Camping and Restaurants).

The Beaches

At Wrightsville Beach next to the U.S. Highway 74/76 drawbridge is a public ramp accessible from either side of the main road. This access to the Intracoastal Waterway is very busy in summer months, especially on weekends.

On Pleasure Island, there are four ramps east of U.S. 421 at Snow's Cut. Coming south, make a hairpin right turn at the south end of Snow's Cut bridge onto Bridge Barrier Road. Turn right at Spencer Farlow Road and follow it less than a half-mile to the Wildlife sign. The lot is down a short road on your left. If you're coming north from Carolina Beach, exit U.S. 421 at Lewis Road just before the bridge and take an immediate left onto Access Road. Spencer Farlow Road is less than a half-mile ahead. Another ramp is at the end of U.S. 421, south of the Fort Fisher ferry terminal and gives access to the Basin off Federal Point.

Also on Pleasure Island, Carolina Beach State Park, off Dow Road, (910) 458-8206, has four ramps ($3 per day), a marina and ample parking.

The ramp directly beneath the N.C. 210

North Carolina Fishing: What's Hot and When!

January: Trout, sea bass, some grouper, some snapper, bluefish, oysters, clams

February: Trout, sea bass, some grouper, some snapper, bluefish, oysters, clams

March: Grouper, sea trout, sea bass, bluefish, croaker, oysters, some snapper, some clams

April: Bluefish, channel bass, grouper, snapper, croaker, sea trout, sea mullet, some king mackerel, some oysters, some clams

May: King mackerel, bluefish, grouper, some flounder, cobia, tuna, some sharks, crabs, soft crabs, some sea mullet

June: Blue marlin, white marlin, dolphin, wahoo, cobia, king mackerel, bluefish, tuna, summer flounder, snapper, grouper, some Spanish mackerel, crabs, soft crabs, sharks

July: Dolphin, wahoo, tuna, blue marlin, white marlin, snapper, grouper, summer flounder, bluefish, Spanish mackerel, crab, some soft crabs, some sea mullet, sharks

August: Dolphin, wahoo, tuna, grouper, snapper, Spanish mackerel, bluefish, some speckled trout, some spots, some sea mullet, sharks, crabs

September: Grouper, snapper, Spanish mackerel, king mackerel, spots, sharks, bluefish, some speckled trout, sea mullet, some channel bass

October: King mackerel, bluefish, snapper grouper, channel bass, spots, speckled trout, some flounder, sharks, some oysters

November: King mackerel, bluefish, speckled trout, flounder, snapper, grouper, clams, some sharks, some sea mullet

December: Bluefish, flounder, speckled trout, oysters, clams, sea trout, some snapper, some sea bass, some grouper

Courtesy of N.C. Department of Environment, Health & Natural Resources, Division of Marine Fisheries

---

high span in North Topsail Beach is generally uncrowded. It is accessible from the last turnout from the northbound side of N.C. 210 before the bridge. Access is to New River Inlet.

Across the Intracoastal Waterway from North Topsail Beach is a ramp at the foot of County Road 1529. From U.S. 17, drive east from Folkstone on Old Folkstone Road (County Road 1518), which intersects 1529 about 2 miles on.

For freshwater fishing in north Brunswick, a public ramp gives access to historic Towne Creek and its tributaries at the eastern end of County Road 1521, about 1.5 miles east of Winnabow, off U.S. 17.

Brunswick Islands

At the foot of County Route 1101, accessible from N.C. Highway 133 on the mainland side of Oak Island, the public ramp gives direct access to the Intracoastal Waterway.

At Sunset Harbor, east of Lockwood Folly River, a public boat ramp gives access to Lockwood Folly River and Inlet and the Intracoastal Waterway. From N.C. 211, take County Route 1112 about 6 miles south and turn right at Lockwood Folly Road. Follow to its end.

At Holden Beach, public boat ramps are under the N.C. Highway 130 bridge on the island side.

Low tide on the barrier islands of North Carolina's Southern coast reveals oyster beds.

Freshwater anglers may launch into the east bank of the Waccamaw River at the N.C. Highway 904 bridge at Pineway, about 5 miles north of the South Carolina border.

Head Boats and Charters

From Topsail's Treasure Coast to Calabash, there are fishing vessels aplenty. Choose among head boats (a.k.a. party boats) accommodating dozens of people and "six-pack" charters accommodating up to six passengers.

Head boats average $50 to $75 per person for full-day excursions, and walk-ons are always welcome. They are equipped with full galleys and air-conditioned lounges. Handicapped accessibility to most large head boats tends to be good, but varies from ship to ship and with weather conditions.

Charters offer a variety of trips, typically half-day and full-day, inshore and offshore, and sometimes overnight; most are available for tournaments and diving trips (reserve early). If you can't find enough friends to chip in to cover the cost, ask about split charters; many captains book them. Most charter captains prefer reservations but will accept walk-ons when possible. Charters range anywhere from $300 for half-day excursions to $1,200 for an entire day of Gulf Stream fishing. From our shores, the Gulf Stream can be 40 to 70 miles offshore, depending on currents and the marina from which you embark.

Certain provisions are common to all charters: first mate, onboard coolers and ice, all the bait and tackle you'll need for kings, tuna, dolphin, wahoo, billfish and more. With advance notice, many will arrange food packages, and some may even arrange hotel packages. Optional electric reels may be available, usually costing about $10.

Although most six-pack charters are unable to bring wheelchairs aboard, crews are often very accommodating of handicapped passengers, sometimes leaving the wheelchair ashore and providing secure seating on deck, right where the action is. Call the vessel of your choice in advance for details.

Remember that no one can guarantee sea conditions. If your captain decides to turn back before you've landed a smoker, rest assured he knows what he's doing. Captains reserve the right to cancel trips if conditions are unsafe for the vessel or passengers.

Carolina Beach is the Gulf Stream fishing hub between Bald Head and Topsail islands. A large number of vessels run out of the Carolina Beach Municipal Docks at Carl Winner Street and Canal Drive. Parking ($3 per day in summer) is available on the marina's west side. Sea captains being the rugged individualists they are, there is no central booking office for these vessels. But since you should know something about what you're chartering in advance, your best bet is to simply walk the docks and eye each one. Signs and brochures there will give you all the booking information you'll need in lieu of the Old Man himself.

Charters in southern Brunswick County are concentrated at the Southport Marina, Blue Point Marina at the western tip of Oak Island, at Holden Beach and Ocean Isle Beach. Head Boats dock only in Calabash and at nearby Little River, South Carolina. There are no charters running directly out of Wilmington. Look instead for charters and head boats running from Wrightsville Beach and Carolina Beach.

So many fishing vessels are available all along our coast, we've listed below only those locations (marinas mostly) booking several charters from one office (check our Marinas chapter for more options). The types of vessels available at each location — six-packs or head boats — are indicated.

Carolina Sport Fishing Charters (six-packs), Wrightsville Beach, (910) 799-8144

Hanover Fishing Charters (six-packs), Wrightsville Beach, (910) 256-3636

Gung-Ho and Flapjack (six-packs), Carolina Beach, 458-4362, (800) 288-3474

Outer Limits Fishing Adventures (six packs), Carolina Beach, (910) 395-4943.

Pirate Fishing & Cruise Charters (head boats), Carolina Beach, (910) 458-5626

Winner Gulf Stream Fishing & Cruise Boats (head boats), Carolina Beach, (910) 458-FISH

Southport Marina (six-packs), Southport, (910) 457-9900, (910) 457-5261

Blue Water Point Marina (both), Long Beach, (910) 278-1230

Holden Beach Marina (both), Holden Beach, (910) 842-5447

Capt'n Pete's Seafood Market (both), Holden Beach, (910) 842-6675

Ocean Isle Marina (six-packs), Ocean Isle Beach, (910) 579-0848

Capt. Jim's Marina (head boats), Calabash, (910) 579-3660

Hurricane Fleet (head boats), Little River Marina, Little River, South Carolina, (803) 249-4575, (803) 249-7775

Swan Point Marina, Sneads Ferry (north of Topsail Island) (six-packs), (910) 327-1081

Topsail Sound Pier Market & Marina (six-packs), Topsail Beach, (910) 328-3641

Southern Coast Saltwater Fishing Tournaments

Tournament fishing has been luring ever-larger schools of anglers, and no wonder: the prize bait can be as much as $200,000 in a single tournament. Proceeds often benefit worthwhile charities. Many contests recognize tag-and-release as part of the Governor's Cup Billfishing Conservation series. The major events are listed below. Check current listings at tackle shops, marinas and visitors centers.

Flapjack & Gung Ho Fishing Charters

Catch
Tuna • Dolphin • Wahoo • Sharks • King Mackerel • Spanish Mackerel • Sailfish • Marlin • Barracuda • Amberjack

Rod, Reel, Tackle, Bait, Ice for your fish
Mate Provided, Up to 6 persons - 4 to 24 Hour Trips

Make Reservations on one of the best charter boats located in the Heart of Carolina Beach at the Municipal Marina.

**Captain Chuck Harrill • P.O. Box 2140, Carolina Beach, NC 28428
(910) 458-4362 • 1-800-288-FISH
Visit Our Web Site at: http://gungho.wilmington.net**

May
Bald Head Island Fishing Rodeo, Bald Head Island Marina, (800) 234-1666

June
King Classic, Blue Water Point Marina, Long Beach, (910) 278-1230

July
East Coast Got-Em-On King Mackerel Classic, Carolina Beach Yacht Basin, Carolina Beach, (910) 458-9576

Hampstead King Mackerel Tournament, Harbor Village Marina, Hampstead, (910) 270-4017

August
Long Bay Lady Anglers King Mackerel Tournament, Sure Catch Tackle Shop, Southport, (910) 457-4545

Poor Boy Shark Tournament, Hugh's Marina, Shallotte Point, (910) 754-6233

Sneads Ferry King Mackerel Tournament, New River Marina, Sneads Ferry, (910) 327-2106 or (910) 327-9691

Topsail Offshore Fishing Club King Mackerel Tournament, Topsail Marina, Topsail Beach, (910) 328-5681

September
South Brunswick Isles King Mackerel Tournament, call for location, (910) 754-6644

U.S. Open King Mackerel Tournament, Southport Marina, Southport, (910) 457-6964

Wrightsville Beach King Mackerel Tournament, Bridge Tender Marina, Wrightsville Beach, (910) 392-3666

October
Pleasure Island Surf Fishing Tournament, Carolina Beach, (910) 458-8434

Wrightsville Beach Storage, Inc.
"A private facility for boat & R.V. owners"

"Slip Memberships available to purchase or Lease
24 hour electronic gate
24 hour video cameras monitoring activity
7 day a week on site manager
Showers/TV room/bathrooms
10 minutes from Wrightsville Beach
2 minutes from I-40 *(Gordon Rd. exit)*
Washdown area

Custom Transporting Coast to Coast

Inhouse services offered
Detailing
Winterized/De-Winterizing
Local Hauls
Hurricane Haul-outs
Bottom painting/pressure washing
Gelcoat repair
Custom Transporting Coast to Coast

Please Call for further information or questions that you may have about our facility.

Murrayville Station
(910) 791-6414
2010 Capital Dr.
(Gordon Rd. exit off I-40)

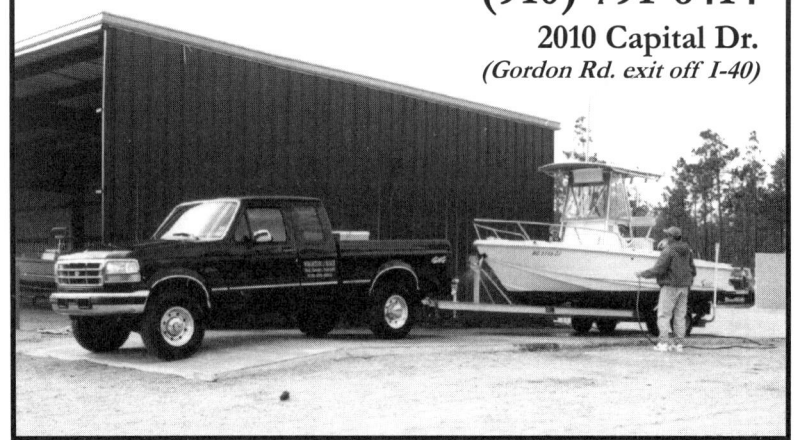

Marinas and the Intracoastal Waterway

The Intracoastal Waterway

For residents and visitors alike, part of the pleasure of life along North Carolina's southern coast is boating, and there is no more immediately accessible or friendlier setting for boaters than our portion of the Middle Atlantic Intracoastal Waterway (ICW). Built during the Roosevelt years, the ICW was created as a commercial waterway to move goods up and down the coast. Secondarily, but more importantly now, the water trail known affectionately as "the ditch" is a protected, scenic route for pleasure craft.

The ICW runs from Norfolk, Virginia, to Miami, Florida, and is maintained by the U.S. Army Corps of Engineers. It links sounds and rivers into the most extensive system of inland waters in the country and provides charted cruising waters for every kind of boater. The Cape Fear region portion of the ICW — quite different from the broad sounds to the north that flank the Outer Banks — generally lies close between the mainland and the barrier islands. It's shores are largely undeveloped throughout the southern North Carolina coast, so boaters can get great views of coastal wildlife.

The area's mild temperatures make pleasure boating on the ICW comfortable from March until the latter part of December, so there is a very long season in which to enjoy this special part of the coast.

Marinas

After a long cruise or even a short daytrip into the Atlantic, marinas are probably one of the most beautiful sights a boater can see. Fuel, beverages, restaurants, overnight berths, ship's stores, repair facilities and nearby services make the boating experience much more pleasant.

Although there are more than 90 marinas along North Carolina's southern coast, what follows is a condensed listing, from north to south on the ICW with a side trip up the Cape Fear River to downtown Wilmington. Although some addresses may be confusing (for example, a Wilmington address for a Wrightsville Beach marina), they are grouped according to boating area.

In the case of Wrightsville Beach, nearby marinas to the south of the mainland side of the ICW have Wilmington land addresses but are service-linked to Wrightsville Beach. Carolina Inlet Marina above Snow's Cut, also addressed as a Wilmington location by the post office, is regarded as part of the Carolina Beach boating scene, so it's included in the Carolina Beach section.

For maps and detailed and candid infor-

INSIDERS' TIP

Most of the navigational markers on the Cape Fear River have been renumbered, and the changes won't show up until new NOAA charts are printed in another year or so.

mation on all these marinas, pick up a copy of native North Carolinian Claiborne Young's *Cruising Guide to Coastal North Carolina*.

As of this writing, Topsail Island no longer has a marina. Hurricane Fran wreaked havoc on Topsail's marina business in 1996 and, although one may return in the future, it's obvious to locals that it won't be for a while — if ever.

Pender County

Harbour Village Marina
101 Harbour Village Dr., Hampstead
• **(910) 270-4017**

Just off U.S. Highway 17 north of Wilmington at Belvedere Plantation, turn into Harbour Village and follow the road and signs to the marina. From the water, this marina is located to the north of flashing daybeacon #96. The marina has all of the amenities a boater could want, including a boater's lounge, transportation to restaurants, showers and a laundry. Boating guests can also enjoy swimming, tennis and golf for a fee.

New Hanover County

Canady's Marina, 7624 Mason's Landing Road, Wilmington, (910) 686-9116

Johnson Marine Services, 2029 Turner Nursery Road, Wilmington, (910) 686-7565

Scott's Hill Marina, 2570 Scott's Hill Loop Road, Wilmington, (910) 686-0896

Oak Winds Marina, 2127 Middle Sound Loop Road, Wilmington, (910) 686-0445

Carolina Yacht Yard, 2107 Middle Sound Road, Wilmington, (910) 686-0004

Mason's Marina, 7421 Mt. Pleasant Drive, Wilmington, (910) 686-7661

Pages Creek is home to a cluster of marinas and marine services. You can reach all of them by taking Middle Sound Loop Road off U.S. 17 at the light at Ogden. On the water, the creek is north of flashing daybeacon #122 and 0.7 nautical miles south of the Figure Eight Island bridge, which has a private marina just for the use of the island's residents.

None of the marinas in Pages Creek should be regarded as regular transient stops, but they are usually very accommodating. You won't generally find overnight dockage except at Scotts Hill Marina. You will find extensive repair services as well as fuel at Carolina Yacht Yard, Johnson Marina and Scotts Hill Marina. Waterway Marine Service, (910) 686-0284, specializes in below-the-waterline repairs. The others mostly provide slips or dry-dockage to regulars. Johnson Marina also has a ramp.

Wrightsville Beach

You'd never know hurricanes paid a visit to this beach in 1996. Not only is everything repaired, but it's actually even nicer than it has ever been. This is one of the best places along the coastline not only for services but also for a tremendous amount of fun. The area is rich in marinas that welcome, in most cases, transient boaters.

To get to these marinas, take Eastwood Road from U.S. 17 or, if coming from downtown Wilmington, take Oleander Drive or Market Street, both of which intersect with Eastwood. Several marinas are located just before the first bridge leading to Wrightsville Beach on Airlie Road to the right. Others are across the bridge on Harbour Island, also to the right.

For those with trailered craft, there's a free Wildlife Access Ramp just to the north of the first bridge over to Harbour Island. A note of caution: this ramp is not in good shape at this writing and the storms had nothing to do with the situation. Hopefully, government promises for funding to get it in good repair will be honored soon.

Wrightsville Marina Yacht Club
1 Marina St., Wrightsville Beach
• **(910) 256-6666**

Located on the eastern shore of the ICW just south of the bridge, this marina is a luxurious place to dock for the night. It offers

A cruise on the *Henrietta II* will help you discover Wilmington from the river.

power, water, telephone, cable TV connections, fuel and mechanical repairs. There is even a swimming pool available for transients. Pusser's Restaurant overlooks the docks, welcoming famished boaters to enjoy prime rib and seafood.

Atlantic Marine
130 Short St., Wrightsville Beach
• **(910) 256-9911**

Just past Wrightsville Marina, Motts Channel opens in the direction of the Atlantic Ocean. This marina offers repair services and is oriented to serving locals with its dry-docked small-craft facilities. Gasoline is the only service for transients.

Seapath Yacht Club
330 Causeway Dr., Wrightsville Beach
• **(910) 256-6681**

Next up on Motts Channel and just down the road from Wrightsville Marina, this well-appointed marina has some transient dockage with power, water, fuel, waste pump-out and cable TV connections. A store provides many essential supplies, and George, the manager, is a heck of a nice guy. Seapath is very close to Banks Channel and is the nearest approach to the Atlantic Ocean, although Bradley Creek Marina farther south is just about as close to Masonboro Inlet. You can't miss Seapath because it adjoins a high-rise condo that clearly marks the spot for miles.

Bridge Tender Marina and Restaurant
Airlie Rd., Wrightsville Beach
• **(910) 256-6550**

On the western shore, directly across from Wrightsville Marina on Airlie Road, is a marina with a bonus — a great local seafood and steak restaurant. The marina offers all amenities, including gas and diesel fuel. One word of caution: The current is very swift here, so mind your slippage on entering and be ready with a boathook to fend off some very expensive craft docked nearby.

Dockside Marina
1306 Airlie Rd., Wrightsville Beach
• **(910) 256-3579**

Overnight space and amenities for boaters are also available at this small marina, which also boasts the Dockside Restaurant, a great place to get a shrimpburger in a basket. It has a small ship's store, fuel and power/

water connections. Again, mind the fast current as you're docking.

Bradley Creek Boatominium
6338 Oleander Dr., Wilmington
• (910) 350-0029

As you travel south on the ICW or take Airlie Road from Wrightsville Beach and a left onto Oleander Drive, you'll come upon the Boatominium just south of the bridge on Bradley Creek. Located on the western shore of the ICW, this is a large, dry-dock and wetslip facility that serves the local community and, sadly for the transient, is not a place to stop for the night. Fuel is available.

Boathouse Marina
6334 Oleander Dr., Wilmington
• (910) 350-0023

Boathouse Marina is a dry-dock facility with haul-outs and repair service just past the Bradley Creek facility. It offers gasoline and has a ship's store. The marina's main business is dry-dock storage.

Masonboro Boatyard and Marina
609 Trails End Rd., Wilmington
• (910) 791-1893

Masonboro took a severe hit with Fran but, in the resilient way of coastal people after a storm, the owners of this marina got it back together in grand style. In early 1997, the channel was dredged and new concrete floating docks were installed. Masonboro is a delightful place to spend the night. Some boaters dock and end up staying for years. The scenery is absolutely lovely from the front row of floating docks.

This facility specializes in repairs and has haul-out services as well as below-the-water repairs and other maintenance services. It has one of the largest inventories of diesel engine parts in the region. If you want to do your own out-of-the-water repairs, you can do them here. There's a ship's store with a friendly staff at this special marina, and you are guaranteed to find some interesting conversation among the residents. Masonboro Boatyard Marina has been operated by the same people since 1968.

On land, travel down Oleander Drive toward Wilmington until you come to Piner Road at Hugh McRae park on the left. Take the left and when you come to a fork in the road take the right fork onto Masonboro Loop Road. After a couple of miles, take note of a small bridge and a road to the left with a sign that points out Masonboro Marina and the Trails End Steak House.

Carolina Beach

Below Masonboro Sound, there is a stretch with no marinas. The shoreline becomes residential in character, and there is not another port until you get close to Carolina Beach.

Carolina Inlet Marina
801 Paoli Ct., Wilmington
• (910) 392-0580

Located just north of Snow's Cut, this marina has fuel, a ship's store, parts and a full assortment of repair services. There is limited transient dockage; call the Inlet Watch Yacht Club at 392-7106 for transient reservations. To get there by land, go down Oleander Drive and take a left on S. College Road. Drive through Monkey Junction where U.S. Highway 421 converges, and pick up this highway heading south. Carolina Inlet Marina is on the left just before crossing the bridge over Snow's Cut into Carolina Beach.

Harbour Point and Pleasure Island Marina & Resort
Spencer Farlow Dr., Carolina Beach
• (910) 458-7368, (800) 989-2589

Approved by CAMA permit in early 1997, this is the newest marina along the southern North Carolina coast. It will offer 92 slips for sale or long-term lease, as well as space for transient dockage. The floating piers will be fitted with power and freshwater lines. At this point, look to the nearby Carolina Beach Park marina for fuel. The marina will offer a ship's store, casual restaurant, showers and an outdoor eating area. Yacht club memberships are open to residents and nonresidents. It is located south of Snow's Cut Landing Marina to starboard.

Snow's Cut Landing Marina
100 Spencer Farlow Dr., Carolina Beach
• (910) 458-7400

This friendly marina is on the channel's

western shore, just south of Snow's Cut as it makes its way into Carolina Beach's harbor. Although transients are welcome, some big changes are taking place in this area. Townhomes are being built, and it is becoming more of a residential marina community. Fuel and boatyard services are no longer offered.

Carolina Beach Municipal Marina
207 Canal Dr., Carolina Beach
• (910) 458-2985

Fuel is available, but mooring is tight at this city marina, located at the southern end of the channel in Carolina Beach, off the ICW. The marina seems mostly dedicated to fishing charter and party boats, and the southern side of it is packed with ticket booths. You can sometimes find an overnight berth, but not always. It's a good spot for a brief visit, particularly if you want to disembark in the heart of Carolina Beach and avail yourself of the fare at several restaurants and fast-food places.

Coquina Harbour at Carolina Beach
Carolina Beach • (910) 458-5053

Coquina Harbour marina lies across from Snow's Cut Landing Marina. It has a harbour enclosed by a breakwater and floating piers. Transients may or may not be able to find a berth for the night, but the facility offers water/power connections, showers, a laundromat and a swimming pool.

Carolina Beach State Park Marina
Carolina Beach State Park, Carolina Beach • (910) 458-7770

Leaving Carolina Beach and heading toward the Cape Fear River, Snow's Cut is the passage. On land, just go over the Snow's Cut Bridge on U.S. 421 S. and take the first right into the campgrounds. This marina offers a ramp, fuel and ample overnight dockage. If you're weary of being on a boat, you can pitch a tent and roast marshmallows over a campfire in the park.

Wilmington

It can be a very bumpy 15-mile ride from Snow's Cut across the Cape Fear River into Southport and the more protected ICW. This is a major shipping lane to the State Port at Wilmington as well as the route for the Southport-Fort Fisher Ferry. Before crossing over, take a northerly route up the Cape Fear River, where you will find increasingly improved opportunities to dock and visit Wilmington's historic center.

Something of great importance to boaters entering the Cape Fear River from Snow's Cut or the ocean is that all of the navigational markers have been redone. It's a confusing situation at best because NOAA charts won't show these corrections for at least another year. When in doubt, just fall back on the boater's rule: Keep red markers to your right going toward Wilmington and keep them to your left when returning to the sea.

Wrightsville Beach Storage, Inc.
2010 Capital Dr., Murrayville Industrial Park, Wilmington • (910) 791-6414

Wrightsville Beach Storage is a drydock marina with a full range of services, including 15-foot-high storage in sizes 12 x 36 and 14 x 46 with water and power for $150 to $200 per month respectively. It stores boats and RVs and also offers pre-fueling, refueling, bottom-painting, pressure-washing, detailing and other services on site. With 24-hour access and six-days-a-week management, it also features security systems with staff and cameras. It has an exceptionally nice clubhouse with TV, showers and bathrooms, and membership is included with storage. The company also offers land and water transport services.

Wilmington Marine Center
3410 River Rd., Wilmington
• (910) 395-5055

This excellent marina comes into view to starboard several miles up the Cape Fear River from Snow's Cut. It can also be reached by leaving U.S. 421 just north of the Snow's Cut Bridge or veering off onto River Road at the N.C. State Ports on Burnett Boulevard. This facility, the sole marina on the Cape Fear (until Bennett Brothers Yachts builds its new marina north of downtown Wilmington on the river in 1998), specializes in service and storage of larger yachts and offers repairs and lift-out services as well as fuel. Dockage, power, water, showers and fuel are available to transients and regulars.

A salty sea cat watches over provisions.

Downtown Wilmington Waterfront

Although downtown isn't a marina and there is no fuel available, it bears mentioning as a very interesting stopover. Also, look for a new marina going in north of the Wilmington waterfront in 1998 owned by Bennett Brothers boatbuilders.

The Hilton
301 N. Water St., Wilmington
• (910) 763-5900

The Hilton offers water and power to overnight boating guests on docks in front of the hotel. At 50¢ a foot, it's a wonderful bargain to be in immediate proximity to historic downtown Wilmington. If you're docked here, please look through the Restaurants, Shopping, and various entertainment chapters in this guide. Happy news for previous visitors who had to climb the ladder at low tide: This section of the Riverwalk now has floating docks.

City of Wilmington Municipal Docks
302 Willard St., Wilmington
• (910) 341-7855

The municipal docks to the south of The Hilton are available for brief visits but are not set up for extended stays. The general rule seems to be a limit of 48 hours of free dockage all along the downtown waterfront. Longer stays may be arranged through the City of Wilmington by special permit but, frankly, nobody official seems to pay much attention unless a yacht is docked for months and the tax people happen to notice. The situation on the downtown Wilmington waterfront for transients is very much improved this year with new floating docks, and plans are in the works to continue to make downtown a boating destination.

Bald Head Island

Bald Head Island Marina
Bald Head Island • (910) 457-7380

Bald Head Island Marina offers slips, fuel, restaurants and lift-out service as well as a gracious welcome to this lovely island. The marina is not reachable by road and the only way you're going to get there is by boat. Odds are you're not going to take the ferry if the marina is your destination for boating. You'll just boat right in and be delighted you did. This marina primarily serves a private, residential community where many of the homes are also vacation rentals, but it has the welcome mat out for visitors. Stop by for a rest in a beautiful setting, provisions, fuel and the opportunity for a walking adventure on this historic island. Be sure to visit the Bald Head Island lighthouse for a brisk climb and a panoramic view of the area.

Southport-Oak Island

Mother Nature was kind to Brunswick — both 1996 hurricanes went to the north into Wilmington. Local marinas took absolutely no hit at all.

Southport Marina Inc.
W. West Place, Southport
• (910) 457-5261

This immaculate marina is on the Southport waterfront just south of downtown. By land, take U.S. 17 from Wilmington and a left onto N.C. Highway 132 to Southport. At the intersection of N.C. Highway 211, take a left and go as far as you can without going into the water. Then take a right and drive a few blocks until the marina comes into view on the left. This marina's extensive docks welcome the cruising boater with fuel, power, transient slips, restaurants, repair service, a clubhouse and supplies. It is one of only about a dozen North Carolina marinas with pump-outs. Interestingly, this marina is owned by the federal government and leased to operators.

Blue Water Point Marina Resort
W. Beach Dr. to 57th Pl., Long Beach
• (910) 278-1230

Blue Water offers slip rentals, boat rentals, gas and diesel fuel, bait, tackle and ice. It also has deep sea fishing charters and party boats. As if that weren't enough, there are also airboat rides. The marina is located at ICW marker #33. The new owners seem particularly accommodating to boating visitors.

South Brunswick Islands

Hughes Marina
1800 Village Point Rd., Shallotte
• (910) 754-6233

Hughes Marina is available for overnight accommodations, with transient slips, fuel and shore power. However, the current is particularly swift here, so boaters need to pay careful attention while docking. If you'd like a night ashore, the marina has a motel and restaurant on the property.

Holden Beach Marina
3238 Pompano St., Holden Beach
• (910) 842-5447

This marina at the tip of Oak Island is regarded as one of the friendliest on the North Carolina coast. Located on the waterway's northern banks in Supply, it has a full range off services, including fuel and transient slips.

Ocean Isle Marina
43 Causeway Dr., Ocean Isle Beach
• (910) 579-0848

Ocean Isle Marina has gas and diesel fuel, bait and tackle, boat equipment and ice. Launch your own boat from it or charter a half-day or all-day fishing boat. You can also rent pontoon boats, wave runners, and rods and reels.

Pelican Pointe Marina
2000 Sommersett Rd., Ocean Isle Beach
• (910) 579-6440

This full-service marina at marker #98 on the ICW offers gas and diesel fuel, extensive dry indoor boat storage for boats up to 32 feet, and a staff of certified mechanics; there's a nine-ton boat forklift standing by. Pelican Pointe has a ship's store complete with boat parts and supplies, beer, ice and fishing tackle. It also offers boat rentals.

Marsh Harbour Marina
10155 Beach Dr. S.W., Calabash
• (910) 579-3500

Prepare to be impressed. This large marina has 221 slips, gas and diesel fuel, complete repair service, supplies and even a pump-out station. There are shoreside showers and a small ship's store just behind the fuel dock. The marina has shore power and water. It welcomes transients to berth in a spot a mere-minutes stroll from one of three dozen Calabash restaurants — and there's even a laundry facility along the way. The marina is particularly well-sheltered for overnight dockage.

The River Keeper

Bouton Baldridge works in a small, even cramped, office in downtown Wilmington and ponders the future of the Cape Fear River, flowing less than 50 yards from his desk. Two volunteers pore over documents nearby. There are no windows and very little in the way of office furniture, so the visitor is immediately struck by the fact that this must be a struggling venture.

The walls are covered with maps of the river as it makes its way from Greensboro to the ocean, a journey of hundreds of miles. A few newspaper articles tacked to the walls proudly demonstrate the media attention paid to the work of this organization. Inexpensively produced newsletters and brochures are stacked on old tables.

This is the office of Cape Fear River Watch, the workplace of one paid staff member — courtesy of a recent grant by the Z. Smith Reynolds Foundation — and 600 volunteers who all share one thing in common: a determination to protect the Cape Fear River. Although the office is modest, the organization's goals are ambitious.

Cape Fear River Watch came into being in 1995 when Baldridge was struck with a notion that Wilmington's river needed protection as much as the highly publicized Neuse River to the north. Baldridge, a onetime graduate student in environmental sciences, read an article about the environmental problems in the Neuse River — unexplained fish kills, high algae levels, agricultural pollution, industrial pollution — and was heartened to note a river keeper had been hired by a grass roots organization in Raleigh (also funded with seed money from Z. Smith Reynolds) to search for the source of these and other problems.

"I read this article by *Star-News* reporter Kirsten Mitchell," says Baldridge, "and I found myself thinking the Cape Fear, although very different from the Neuse, also needed a river keeper. So several of us started talking, and we got to work on it. After two years, we were able to get a grant that would allow me to do this work full time as the Cape Fear river keeper.

"The Neuse is important, but so is the Cape Fear. More people in Raleigh were familiar with the Neuse because it flows from Raleigh [the seat of the government] to New Bern. We weren't getting as much attention as the Neuse, and I felt it was important to make the needs of our river known."

The importance of the Cape Fear to Wilmington, as well as to North Carolina, is profound. "Fayetteville upstream relies on this river for 60 percent of its municipal water. Wilmington draws on it 100 percent.

— continued on next page

Bouty Baldridge keeps a close eye on waters from this canoe.

Many smaller communities on the way look to this river for their needs," says Baldridge. "This is a great natural resource that is in danger from overdevelopment, hog farm overspill, industrial pollutants, chemical spills and overuse, and the problem is nobody really knows what kind of shape it's in now compared to the past."

The grant money for Baldridge's river keeper job came with a requirement he embraced: regular testing of the waters along 80 miles of the Cape Fear over time to determine a baseline. No one knows what shape the river is in because there is nothing upon which to base comparisons. "We really don't know what our readings should be for it to be for a healthy river," says Baldridge, "So our work involves trying to determine where we are now. We don't have the obvious problems of the Neuse but now is when we should start making sure we never do."

The Cape Fear River is very different from the Neuse River because the Wilmington river is connected directly to the ocean and the Neuse isn't. The Neuse is relatively slow-moving, even stagnant in areas, so fish kills tend to stay in place and algae isn't flushed out with a rapidly moving tide. The Cape Fear's fast currents tend to disperse pollution rapidly. Additionally, the extensive wetlands that lie alongside the Cape Fear have excellent filtration powers.

"Unfortunately, rapid residential development, hog farms and confusion over jurisdiction are causing real problems," says Baldridge. "We have a concern with the fact that hog farms, a major contributor to increased nitrates in the water supply, are allowed to operate under relaxed legislative conditions. Then there's the concern that water quality isn't overseen by one agency. There are different rules, for example, for the Forestry Department and the Department of Water Quality Control. The people in charge of water quality don't have jurisdiction over what's happening on the land. The people in charge of the land issues don't have control over what's happening in the water."

There are more questions than answers about the river's health, and Baldridge notes that without serious commitment from government it's going to be a long process to gather information, analyze it and take steps to protect the Cape Fear as well as the other rivers and streams of the state.

For now, Cape Fear River Watch operates with a fleet of five boats — one canoe and four small powercraft — as well as 100 individual small craft on call from volunteers to keep an eye on the Cape Fear. The group relies on people who use the water recreationally to report unusual sightings such as fish kills, water discoloration, oil spills, fishing violations and dredging or filling in wetlands. Some volunteers monitor creeks and streams.

Raising public awareness is high on the list of goals for Cape Fear River Watch because, unfortunately, it's like that line in Joni Mitchell's song "Big Yellow Taxi" — "You don't know what you've got 'til it's gone." That's one reason the group has labeled storm drains downtown with stenciled lettering that announces the fact the drains empty into the river. If people can be made to understand that the pollutants they flush back into the water supply can cause environmental problems, that awareness will go a long way toward stopping abuses of the river.

"People take the Cape Fear River for granted," says Baldridge. "We're so used to having it that we can't imagine not having it. People need to remember that Wilmington wouldn't even be here if it were not for that river."

To join the effort to protect the river, observers of spills and kills are encouraged to call the river keeper at (910) 762-5606. People who want to join the effort may become members of the Cape Fear River Watch by calling the same number or writing to the organization at 119 S. Water Street, Wilmington, NC 28401.

YMCA

THE WILMINGTON FAMILY YMCA HAS EVERYTHING YOU NEED TO GET STARTED:

Gym, 2 Indoor Pools, Jacuzzi, 4 Racquetball Courts, 1/4 Mile Outdoor Track, Locker Rooms, Aerobic, and Water Aerobic Classes, Whirlpool, Steam Room, Sauna, Towels, Cybex, Nordic Track, Lifecycles, Step Climbers, Rowing Machines and Much, Much, More!

Ask about our special rates for Senior Citizens

* The Wilmington Family YMCA is New Hanover County's largest child care provider, providing several summer day camps, and school-age child care at 10 local elementary schools.

> The Wilmington Family YMCA is a non-profit association committed to a mission of putting Judeo-Christian principles into practice though programs that build healthy body, mind and spirit for all.

We Strengthen More Than Muscles

2710 Market Street • 251-9622

Sports, Fitness and Parks

Except for snow skiing, rappelling and rock climbing, just about every kind of sport you could ask for is offered in the southern coastal region. (There is a club, the Cape Fear Ski & Outing Club, (910) 799-8035, that organizes snow ski trips.)

In this chapter, we've included information on where to find or join just about every sport and recreation except golf and watersports, which have their own separate chapters in this book. Following the sports listings, we've included a section on fitness centers and descriptions of area parks and their facilities. Useful businesses and services are described along the way.

The daily "Lifestyles" pages of the *Wilmington Star-News* also provide a handy guide to recreation throughout the region, so check them periodically. Also check the Summer Camps section in our Kidstuff chapter for information on summer sports camps for youth.

Parents should note that registration fees for youth league sports are often discounted when registering more than one child in the same league. Be sure to inquire.

Recreation Departments

Local and county parks and recreation departments organize a staggering selection of activities, including team sports for all ages. Check with them when looking into the sport of your choice. They specialize in seniors activities that may include archery, croquet, tae kwon do and water aerobics. Addresses and phone numbers of the local offices are listed here.

Wilmington Parks & Recreation, 302 Willard Street, Wilmington, (910) 341-7855

Wilmington Athletics, Empie Park, 3405 Park Avenue, Wilmington, (910) 343-3680

Wrightsville Beach Parks & Recreation, 1 Bob Sawyer Drive, Wrightsville Beach, (910) 256-7925

Carolina Beach, 1121 N. Lake Park Boulevard, Carolina Beach, (910) 458-7416

Long Beach, 4601 E. Oak Island Drive, Long Beach, (910) 278-5518

Southport, Stevens Park, 107 E. Nash Street, Southport, (910) 457-7945

New Hanover County, 414 Chestnut Street, Room 103, Wilmington, (910) 341-7198

Brunswick County, Planning Building, Government Complex, Bolivia, (910) 253-2670

Onslow County, 1250 Onslow Pines Road, Jacksonville, (910) 347-5332

Sports and Recreation

Baseball and Little League

The region has several baseball youth leagues, but there are no public leagues for

---

INSIDERS' TIP

Of the two bridges leading into Wilmington, cyclists prefer the U.S. Highway 421 N. bridge, which is wider and safer than the Cape Fear Memorial Bridge.

adults. The youth leagues offer divisions from T-ball for toddlers to baseball for teens through age 18, and some offer softball too. Registration generally takes place from early February through mid-March and carries a modest fee (about $25 to $45). Registrants need to present their birth certificates. The playing season begins in April. Contact one of the following organizations for specifics.

Wilmington
Optimist Club of Cape Fear , (910) 762-7054

New Hanover Youth Baseball, (910) 791-5578

Wilmington Family YMCA, (910) 251-9622

Winter Park Optimist Club, (910) 791-7907

Brunswick County
Brunswick County Parks and Recreation, (910) 253-2670, (800) 222-4790

Onslow County
Onslow County Parks and Recreation, (910) 347-5332

The Wilmington Sharks, one of 16 teams in the new Coastal Plain League, debuted in 1997. This summer league features undergraduate college players competing in six North Carolina cities. The level of play is said to be between that of A and AA minor league teams, and the entertainment is ideal for the entire family. A number of Sharks players are also known as players for UNCW, NC State, and Old Dominion University. The league's 50-game regular season is capped by a best-of-three championship playoff in mid-August.

The Sharks play their 25 home games, beginning around Memorial Day, at Legion Stadium on Carolina Beach Road, 2.3 miles south of Market Street. Single-ticket prices range from $3 to $5. Season tickets go on sale in early March and cost $75 for box seats, $65 for reserved. For more information, write to P.O. Box 15233, Wilmington, NC 28412, or call (910) 343-5621.

Basketball

Athletic Zone
4405 Northchase Pkwy. N.E., Wilmington
- **(910) 452-5020**

The Zone is an indoor facility that organizes and hosts basketball games and leagues. Playing schedules may vary according to participation.

Winter Park Optimist Club
Masonboro Loop Rd., Wilmington
- **(910) 791-7907**

Winter Park Optimist offers a seasonal basketball league for boys and girls ages 13 through 15.

Wilmington Family YMCA
2710 Market Street, Wilmington
- **(910) 251-9622**

The Family Y hosts leagues for boys and girls ages 6 through 12 during the winter and offers inexpensive court passes to teenagers who wish to join informal games. It also offers men's leagues throughout the year.

Wilmington Parks & Recreation
302 Willard St., Wilmington
- **(910) 343-3680**

The Wilmington Parks & Recreation Department organizes weekly and Saturday games for adults and seniors from December through March.

Wrightsville Beach Parks and Recreation
1 Bob Sawyer Dr., Wrightsville Beach
- **(910) 256-7925**

The Wrightsville Beach Department offers four-on-four league games for adults on weeknights from June through August.

INSIDERS' TIP

The Breakfast Club, (910) 815-5006, is an outdoor walking club for people 55 and older in Wilmington. It meets every Tuesday and Thursday at 8:30 AM in the New Hanover Regional Medical Center lobby.

Brunswick County Parks and Recreation
Planning Bldg., Government Plaza, Bolivia • (910) 253-4357, (800) 222-4790

The Brunswick County Department conducts one-week youth basketball camps in summer for ages 6 through 15. Referee clinics are offered to persons of any age. There is also an adult men's basketball league with separate spring and fall divisions. Registration is open to teams only. A youth basketball league for children ages 5 through 13 runs from December through March.

Onslow County Parks and Recreation
1250 Onslow Pines Rd., Jacksonville • (910) 347-5332

Onslow County offers youth basketball for children ages 7 through 18.

Bicycling

Touring most of North Carolina's southern coastal plain by bicycle can be as ideal as touring gets. Roads tend to be lightly trafficked, and most motorists have a fairly good awareness of cyclists.

It's a different story within Wilmington city limits, where large protests were mounted in 1997 to raise awareness of the lack of safe roadways, the most glaring example being Market Street. But that shouldn't scare you off from visiting Wilmington by bicycle or from touring the rest of our coastal region. State-funded touring routes are well planned and marked by rectangular road signs bearing a green ellipse, a bicycle icon and the route number.

One such route is the River-to-Sea Bike Route (Route 1), stretching from Riverfront Park at the foot of Market Street in Wilmington to Wrightsville Beach, a ride of just less than 9 miles. Exercise caution on the Bradley Creek bridge: The shoulder is ridged by uneven road seams.

The state-funded Bicycling Highways are worth trying. The Ports of Call route (Route 3) is a 319-mile seaside excursion from the South Carolina border to the Virginia line. Approximately 110 miles of it lie within the southern coastal region, giving access to miles of beaches and historic downtown Wilmington.

The Cape Fear Run (Route 5) links Raleigh to the mouth of the Cape Fear River at Southport. This 166-mile route crosses the Cape Fear River twice and intersects the Ports of Call route. Free maps and information can be obtained from the North Carolina Department of Transportation Bicycle Program, (919) 733-2804. Although the maps are updated regularly, be ready to improvise when it comes to information on private campgrounds and detours.

A curiosity about Wilmington: According to city code, it is unlawful to ride an unregistered bicycle on public streets and alleys within the city (yes, we were dazzled by this, too). And although that's a law we've never, ever, heard of being enforced — or obeyed — it's worth noting if only because registration with the city police may actually help you recover your ride in the event of theft. Police reports suggest that some 700 bikes are ripped off each year — nearly $200,000 worth. (They used to hang horse-thieves, didn't they?) Most bikes recovered by the police are never claimed and are auctioned off at year's end. You can register your wheels at police headquarters downtown, 115 Redcross Street, (910) 343-3600, or at any of four neighborhood stations; it's free to Wilmington residents, one buck for New Hanover County residents.

A great way to tour our region for a good cause is to take part in the Coastal Carolina Bike Trek, sponsored by the American Lung Association of North Carolina. This is a fundraising event in which participants ride 70 or 100 miles of the area's most beautiful roadways over a two-day period in April (when the weather is typically gorgeous). The route begins and ends in Kure Beach, looping through Southport and Wilmington. Riders can choose their own pace. Meals, technical support and the ferry to Southport are provided.

Participants may take time to visit historic sites along the way, relax on the beach or by the pool and spend Saturday evening dancing on an Intracoastal Waterway cruise. What you are asked to do in return is raise funds to fight lung disease. Prizes are awarded. Organizers require all riders to wear helmets. For complete information and registration forms, contact Trek Headquarters Wilmington, P.O. Box 3577, Wilmington 28406, (910) 395-5864 or (800) 821-6205.

The Cape Fear Cyclists Club, (910) 799-6444, is a good social and information network, and it's an active sponsor of a number of tours, training rides and races as well as a racing team. It provides opportunities to join the U.S. Cycling Federation and obtain discounts on equipment at local shops.

The club also sponsors the annual By-The-River Biathlon series of three races taking place January through March. Each race consists of a 3.1-mile run and a 15-mile bike ride. The entry fee of $20 includes a sweatshirt and T-shirt. It's a good idea to register early; races are limited to 150 entrants each. More information may be obtained by calling Two Wheeler Dealer at (910) 799-6444 or writing to Cape Fear Cyclists, Box 3466, Wilmington 28406.

The Wilmington Bike Map is a must for local cycling. Free copies can be obtained by contacting the City Transportation Planning Department, P.O. Box 1810, Wilmington 28402, (919) 341-7888.

Several excellent bicycle specialty shops in our area sell new and used bicycles and provide repair services. Many businesses also offer rentals; competitive rates are typically around $15 per day. Try the following stores.

Aussie Island Surf Shop
1319 Military Cutoff Rd., Wilmington
• (910) 256-5454

Aussie Island, in the Landfall shopping center at the intersection of Eastwood Road, rents Earth Cruisers by the hour, day or week. Rentals begin at $5 per day and $50 per week.

Bicycle Works
4547 Fountain Dr., Wilmington
• (910) 313-1415

Bicycle Works is near the UNCW campus and is open seven days a week. In addition to renting mountain bikes and beach cruisers, the shop sells new and used bicycles and provides repair services.

Bill Curry's Cycling and Fitness
2509 S. College Rd., Wilmington
• (910) 392-4433

Bill Curry's is among the finer bike shops in the region and carries a varied inventory of bicycles and accessories. The shop also offers professional repair service, but no bike rentals. It also specializes in Schwinn cardiovascular-fitness equipment sales and service.

Chain Reaction Bicycling Center
7220 Wrightsville Ave., Wilmington
• (910) 256-3304

Chain Reaction, in the Atlantic View shopping center immediately west of the drawbridge to Wrightsville Beach, carries mid-line and low-end mountain bikes and beach cruisers. It also sells new high-performance cycles, components, accessories and used bikes, and does repairs.

Pedal Pump & Run
5629 Oleander Dr., Wilmington
• (910) 392-8020

In addition to carrying all kinds of fitness equipment, this shop sells new top-name bikes and performs repairs on bikes of any make. It's open every day and is located in the Bradley Square strip mall.

Two Wheeler Dealer
4406 Wrightsville Ave., Wilmington
• (910) 799-6444

One of the largest bicycle shops around, Two Wheeler stocks a vast array of bicycles, including some vintage models and second-hand bikes, plus touring equipment, tricycles, bike trailers, infant seats — practically anything that rolls on spoked wheels — and accessories. Professional repair work and fitting are done on the premises. Two Wheeler is also a place to find racing information and equipment and to connect with the Cape Fear Cyclists Club.

Win City of Wilmington
127 S. College Rd., Wilmington
• (910) 452-3190

The studio-cycling craze that first hit the west coast in 1987 has finally hit Wilmington. Win City, in Marketplace Mall, offers studio-cycling classes using Cycle Reebok-brand cycles — stationary apparatus that closely simulate the feel and challenge of actual road bikes but with three big differences: there's no coasting (cycles feature locked-gear, direct drives), no foul weather and no traffic. To musical accompaniment, certified trainers lead classes through guided visualizations of outdoor rides, while each cyclist adjusts the resistance of his or her own bike (it feels like shifting gears) to simulate various outdoor conditions such as riding uphill, through mud or across flat ground.

If you're looking for a high-aerobic, indoor workout or cross-training option that is impact-free, this could be the ticket. As racers know, studio cycling is serious training; its results compare favorably with actual road work. Each fully adjustable cycle provides a close biomechanical fit to your body, and its 37.5-lb. flywheel yields the sensation of momentum.

Other Win City amenities include lockers, showers, nursery service, a small pro shop, and light free weights and treadmill for warm-ups. Win City does not sell memberships; you pay as you go or you can buy class packages to suit your needs. Schedules and payment options are flexible — the introductory "4 pack," four classes for $20, has no time limit and is transferable (bring your partner twice!). Ask about student rates, the rider referral program, the frequent rider program and other specials.

Rainbow Bike Rentals
215 Atlanta Ave. #3C, Carolina Beach
* **(910) 458-9115**

Rainbow delivers rental bikes — all one-speed Earth-Cruisers — anywhere from Kure Beach to Figure Eight Island. Bicycles with baskets and child carriers are available. A deposit is required.

Ocean Rentals
4014 E. Beach Dr., Long Beach
* **(910) 278-4460**

Ocean Rentals is more than just a place to rent beach-cruising bikes on Oak Island. You may rent four bikes for less than $100 for an entire week. (The shop also rents practically anything you could possibly need for the beach.) Delivery and pickup are free with a $10 minimum order.

Boomer's Bikes & More
111 Jordan Blvd., Holden Beach
* **(910) 842-7840, (910) 579-1211**

Boomer's rents bicycles and tandems and other models by the hour, day and week (as well as many other beach items). It's at Tarheel Video next to the Post Office. Boomers also sells bikes and does repairs.

Julie's Rentals
2 Main St., Sunset Beach
* **(910) 579-1211**

Affiliated with Boomer's (above), Julie's is a bicycle-cum-beach-rental shop that offers beach cruisers, tandems, adult trikes (which are excellent for some handicapped persons) and Suncycle recumbent bikes. Julie's is open year-round, although you may need to call ahead in the off-season.

The Patio Playground
807 S. Anderson Blvd., (N.C. 50), Topsail Beach • (910) 328-6491

You can rent bicycles for a measly $2 per hour up to $45 per week, tax included. There is no deposit, but identification is required.

Bowling

Most bowling centers in our area not only host leagues but also host private parties. Some have even added live music and dancing to their lounge entertainment, and all are family-oriented. Competitive prices average about $2.65 per game for adults on weekends. Prices on weekdays and for children 11 and younger may be lower. Try Cardinal Lanes, with two locations: 3907 Shipyard Boulevard, Wilmington, (910) 799-3023, and 7026 Market Street, Scotts Hill, (910) 686-4223; or Brunswick County Bowling Center, 630 Village Road, Shallotte, (910) 754-2695.

Boxing

Wilmington Parks & Recreation Fitness Center
602 N. Fourth Street, Wilmington
* **(910) 341-7872**

For more than 20 years, the Boxing & Fitness Center has been teaching children and adults the techniques and sportsmanship of boxing and physical fitness. Equipped with a regulation-size ring, free weights and a basic fitness center, it offers memberships that are among the best bargains in town.

Flying

The local dearth of sizable hills, and therefore reliable updrafts, limits local aviation to powered flight. Among the surprises of a bird's-eye view of the area is sighting the so-called "Carolina bays," enormous elliptical depressions in the earth first "discovered" from the air (see Lake Waccamaw State Park in our Camping chapter). There are several places where you can rent a plane, take flying classes, or book a sightseeing flight.

Flyers can rent conventional aircraft at Wilmington International and Brunswick County airports. Most companies offer 24-hour charter service and flight training.

Aeronautics/Air Wilmington
Wilmington International Airport, 1740 Airport Blvd., Wilmington
- (910) 763-4691 Aeronautics
- (910) 763-4691 Air Wilmington

Aeronautics and its affiliate, Air Wilmington, offer flight instruction, aircraft rentals and sightseeing tours.

ISO Aero Service Inc. of Wilmington
1410 N. Kerr Ave., Wilmington
- (910) 763-8898, (910) 762-1024

Offering rentals, instruction and sightseeing, ISO is also located at Wilmington International Airport.

Blue Yonder Flying Machines
Brunswick County Airport, 380 Long Beach Rd. (N.C. Hwy. 133), Southport
- (910) 278-8277

Some say that unless you feel the wind in your face, you're not really flying. Among that faction you might find Adam Parsons, who promotes the flying of Quicksilver ultralights. They look like a cross between a hang glider and a Wright brothers' original. Quicksilver aircraft meet all aviation requirements, even though the pilot (and passenger, in some models) is suspended in an open cockpit. Adam offers introductory flights and training with a certified instructor and sells a variety of Quicksilver aircraft.

Ocean Aire Aviation
Brunswick County Airport, 380 Long Beach Rd. (N.C. Hwy. 133), Southport
- (910) 457-0710

Larry Ryan and John Martin offer flight instruction and other flight services and can also arrange aircraft rentals.

Football

League football beyond the scholastic realm is the focus of two organizing bodies, the Pop Warner league and Brunswick County Parks and Recreation. Look into registration during June; most teams commence practice in August.

Pop Warner Football
Wilmington • (910) 799-7950

Pop Warner organizes tackle football teams for boys and girls age 7 through 14 in Pee Wee, Midget and Mighty Mights divisions.

Brunswick County Parks and Recreation
Planning Bldg., Government complex, Bolivia • (910) 253-4357, (800) 222-4790

Brunswick County's league is open to kids ages 10 through 13. If you're interested in becoming a referee, inquire about Brunswick County's referee clinics.

Horseback Riding

Although English (hunt seat) style is favored in this region, Western is available. Most stables and riding academies offer

INSIDERS' TIP

The Cape Fear Fencing Association, (910) 762-2962 or (910) 686-2956, is a Wilmington club open to anyone with an interest in the sport. Open fencing, group and individual instruction in fundamentals and tactics, and equipment are available for a modest fee.

boarding, instruction, rentals and trail rides. Some stables do their own shoeing. Tack shops are scarce. Most stables and academies will assist you in locating the equipment you need.

Canterbury Stable
6021 Wrightsville Ave., Wilmington
• (910) 791-6502

Canterbury specializes in private and group riding instruction, boarding, training and showing but no rentals.

Castle Stables
5513 Sidbury Rd., Castle Hayne
• (910) 675-1113

English-style instruction is offered on a plush 120-acre spread a few minutes north of Wilmington. A lighted training ring and a jumping ring are available.

Fox Fire Farm
7724 Sidbury Rd., Castle Hayne
• (910) 686-4495

The folks at Fox Fire train riders and their horses in English riding and help find horses for purchase and lease.

Hanover Stables
5901 Bizzel Ave., Castle Hayne
• (910) 675-8923

Offering 19 acres of pasture and lighted ring trails, Hanover Stables teaches English and Western styles of riding. Also available are sales, boarding and professional training.

Lo-Di Farms
610 Old Folkstone Rd., Sneads Ferry
• (910) 327-2040

Convenient to Topsail Island, Lo-Di boards, leases and rents horses and ponies. Horses for special occasions can be reserved, and the owners will haul if needed.

Cottonpatch Farms
Cottonpatch Rd., Shallotte
• (910) 754-9288

Judy Hilburn's farm is a high-quality training facility that sells horses and teaches owners to ride and show. Judy occasionally breeds horses. Youth riders are welcome.

Sea Horse Riding Stables
Boonesneck Rd., Holden Beach
• (910) 842-8002

Sea Horse provides English and Western lessons, shoeing and training. Its 18 acres, 3 miles off Holden Beach Road, are laced with shady trails, and the kids will love the pony rides.

Peachtree Stables
810 Hickman Rd., Calabash
• (910) 287-4790

With 120 acres nearly adjacent to the South Carolina state line, Peachtree Stables is convenient to the entire southeastern corner of Brunswick County and northeastern South Carolina. The trails traverse 70 acres, much of it shady. Peachtree offers hourly trail rides, full boarding facilities, a tack shop, two outdoor riding rings and an indoor riding arena. Group and private instruction is given in English and Western styles. Horses are available for lease and for sale, and moonlight rides along the beach can be arranged.

Tuscarora Tack Shop
5751 Oleander Dr., Wilmington
• (910) 791-0900

Tuscarora specializes in English riding apparel and equipment, including saddlery, boots and grooming supplies. The shop, next to Kelly's Coffee Pub in Philips Azalea Plaza, is closed on Thursdays and Sundays.

The Castle Hayne Saddle Shop
11975 U.S. Hwy 17, Castle Hayne
• (910) 675-1805

This friendly full-service shop is a few minutes north of Wilmington. It carries everything necessary for riding (English and Western) and instructional videos. Feed is available and expert leather repair can be arranged.

Hunting

There are several game lands in the region where hunters may pursue big and small game, including dove, deer, rabbit, wild turkey and black bear. Game lands are typically leased from individual landowners and companies by North Carolina Wildlife Resources Commission, Division of Wildlife Management,

512 N. Salisbury Street, Raleigh 27604, (919) 733-7291. Some lands are owned outright by the commission. Most game lands are accessible from public roads, while some have only water access.

The 48,795-acre Holly Shelter Game Land in Pender County is the largest local game land. It is a varied wetland of pocosins (peat-bottomed lowlands) and pine savannas threaded by winding creeks and existing in some noncontiguous parcels. It's located north of Wilmington, roughly between U.S. Highway 17 west to the northeast Cape Fear River and between N.C. Highways 210 and 53.

The Green Swamp Game Land, a 14,851-acre expanse lying in nearly one contiguous block bordered by Highway 211 in Brunswick County, is among the most isolated areas re-

Cape Fear's Celebrity Roster

Wilmington and the Cape Fear area have played well-known roles throughout the nation's history, but few people are aware of the famous and talented folks who once called this area home:

David Brinkley, TV journalist
John Cheek, operatic baritone
Charlie Daniels, country-rock musician
Sammy Davis, Sr., stage performer
Edward B. Dudley, first popularly elected governor of North Carolina
Mary Baker Eddy, founder of Christian Science Church
Nelson Eddy, singer
Minnie Evans, visionary painter
Roman Gabriel, NFL Player of the Year, 1969, L.A. Rams
Althea Gibson, tennis champion (U.S. Open 1957-58, Wimbledon 1957-58, French Open 1956)
Thomas Godfrey, first American playwright
Cornelious Harnett, patriot of the American Revolution
William Hooper, signer of the Declaration of Independence
Caterina Jarboro, operatic soprano
Michael Jordan, basketball star, Chicago Bulls
Sonny Jurgenson, NFL Hall of Famer
Charles Kuralt, TV commentator and author
Meadowlark Lemon, basketball star, Harlem Globetrotters
Sugar Ray Leonard, Olympic gold medalist boxer
Robert Ruark, author and safari hunter
Anna McNeill Whistler, "Whistler's Mother"
Woodrow Wilson, 28th president of the United States

A teenaged Michael Jordan, then playing football for Laney High School, Wilmington.

maining in southeastern North Carolina, an easy place in which to get turned around for a couple of days. Foot travel only is permitted here. The Nature Conservancy owns the land, and much of it, as the name suggests, is low-lying wetland and pocosin.

Lying in New Hanover County, the Sutton Lake Game Land is a 3,322-acre land leased from CP&L. It is bordered by N.C. Highway 421 and the Cape Fear River.

The newest local game land came into state ownership in early 1998. Roan Island is a 2,757-acre island situated at the confluence of the Cape Fear and Black rivers in Pender County. The North Carolina chapter of the Nature Conservancy purchased the land with a $1 million donation from the National Heritage Trust Fund, then turned it over to the state.

The island lies in the flood plain and has the oldest stand of bald cypresses in the eastern United States. The Black River is also a National Scenic River, still in relatively pristine condition. The island is partly covered by water and supports wild turkey and black bear as well as various smaller game, including some rare and endangered species such as the shortnose sturgeon. Access to Roan Island is only by boat.

Hunting, mainly for fowl, is allowed on Zeke's Island Coastal Preserve, which lies across the Basin from Fort Fisher. Access to it is only by boat or by foot across the Rocks, a tricky 3-mile breakwater that is awash at high tide.

Hunting licenses are issued by the North Carolina Wildlife Resources Commission, License Section. They can be purchased specifically for small game ($15), big game ($25) and combined with fishing licenses ($20; small game only). The sportsman's license ($40) permits the holder to pursue all types of hunting, including bow hunting and game land use, and saves money in the long run. Call the License Section of the North Carolina Wildlife Resources Commission at (919) 662-4370 for more information. Licenses may be purchased at the following locations:

Kmart, 815 S. College Road, Wilmington, (910) 799-5360

Pawn USA, three Wilmington locations: 3922 Market Street, (910) 763-7682; 2392 Carolina Beach Road, (910) 251-1200; 4127 Oleander Drive, (910) 392-1177

Tackle Express Tacklemart, 4100 Oleander Drive, Wilmington, (910) 392-3472

Wal-Mart, Wal-Mart Shopping Center, 352 S. College Road, Wilmington, (910) 392-4034

Mobile Home Store & Hardware, 5601 Castle Hayne Road, Castle Hayne, (910) 675-9205

Hampstead Village Pharmacy, N.C. 17, Hampstead, (910) 270-3411, (910) 270-3414

Holland's Shelter Creek Fish Camp, N.C. Highway 53 east of Burgaw, (910) 259-5743

Roses, 1505 N. Howe Street, Southport, (910) 457-9573

Stewart Hardware, 1635 Howe Street, Southport, (910) 457-5544

Holden Beach True Value, 3008 Holden Beach Road, Holden Beach, (910) 842-5440

Island Tackle & Gifts, 6855-3 Beach Drive SW, Ocean Isle Beach, (910) 579-6116

Pawn USA, 5001-4 Main Street, Shallotte, (910) 754-7918

Wal-Mart, 4540 Main Street, Shallotte, (910) 754-2880

Canady's Sport Center
3220 Wrightsville Avenue, Wilmington
• **(910) 791-6280**

Canady's is among the best one-stop retail shops for hunters, whether rifle or bow; staffers are practiced and knowledgeable in each. Clothing, field gear and a good selection of binoculars are stocked. Canady's is open Monday through Saturday.

In-line and Roller Skating

The popularity of in-line skating continues to grow along with the population, despite the fact that skating conditions within towns such as Wilmington, Southport and Shallotte are relatively poor. In 1996 the city of Wilmington completely banned in-line skating (and skateboarding) in the downtown historic district. Recreational and commuter skaters on city streets and sidewalks can be fined, so consider practicing elsewhere and drive to work like everybody else.

So where do you go to skate? The 'burbs, of course! where the pavement is new and traffic is light. But the 'burbs aren't all there is. The

UNCW campus offers long stretches of wide, paved walks, including smooth, curvy stretches surrounding the newly built lake at the university commons. The nearly 5-mile-long bike path around Greenfield Lake in Wilmington is as picturesque as any place in the state, particularly in early spring; just be watchful of nasty bumps and breaks in the asphalt due to tree roots.

The pavement in the few Wilmington parks that have any was mostly damaged by the hurricanes of '96, so parks are out — except for basketball courts (they're small, but not bad for beginners). A word of warning: Skating on city tennis courts can earn you a fine and community service. Avoid it.

One of the best places to skate is the Loop at Wrightsville Beach. Consisting of paved walks totaling approximately 2.5 miles, the Loop runs along Wrightsville Beach Park, Causeway Drive, Lumina Avenue and Salisbury Street. There are plenty of places to stop for a cool refreshment or a dip in the ocean along the way.

The No. 1 place to skate on Oak Island consists of nearly 7 miles of municipal sidewalks along Oak Island Drive in Long Beach. Ramps (rather than curbs) meet every intersection. Recently paved Yacht Drive, which stretches the length of Long Beach on the north side of the island, is also an excellent choice. On the south side, Dolphin Drive, just one block from the ocean, is an OK choice, but you'll have to deal with some motor traffic. Avoid Beach Drive altogether, with its heavy traffic and gravel. Bald Head Island is a true skate haven, where the only other traffic on the smoothly paved byways is golf carts and bicycles.

It seems as if anyone who's not interested in skating for its own sake (or for commuting) is playing roller hockey. Enter the Cape Fear Roller Hockey League, (910) 791-1572, the area's first organized in-line skating venture. A participating member of the new North Carolina Inline Hockey League, the Cape Fear league is open to youth and adults in two divisions: ages 7 through 14 and 15 and older.

The 11-game season is played at locations throughout five states from Virginia to Georgia. Participation costs $95 for youth, $80 for adults, and does not include equipment. Registration and information may be obtained at Play It Again Sports, 3530 S. College Road, (910) 791-1572, and at the Athletic Zone (below).

Athletic Zone
4405 Northchase Pkwy N.E., Wilmington
• (910) 452-5020

New to the area in 1996, Athletic Zone has two indoor rinks offering open skating nights, in-line roller hockey and in-line skating lessons (as well as several other indoor sports). The hockey rink is regulation size, and players of all ages are welcome. The Zone is the nerve center of the Cape Fear Roller Hockey League (see above). Registering entire teams offers vast per-person savings. The Zone has some skates available for rent and a small pro shop operated by Play It Again Sports, but players must expect to supply all their own equipment. Pick-up games cost $5 per hour.

Instructor Certification Program of the International In-Line Skating Association
201 N. Front St., #306, Wilmington
• (910) 762-7004

Now headquartered in Wilmington, the ICP promotes the health and longevity of the sport by offering skating lessons for groups and individuals, producing certified instructors and advocating safe skating, public skate paths and nonaggressive skating practices. The ICP is the service-oriented educational wing of the International In-Line Skating Association, the trade organization representing the interests of in-line skate manufacturers. Fees for lessons vary widely according to locale and number of pupils.

INSIDERS' TIP

Walking, cycling, skating and riding in electric carts are the only ways to get around on Bald Head Island, where gasoline engines aren't allowed.

Jelly Beans Family Skating Center
5216 Oleander Dr., Wilmington
• **(910) 791-6000**

Jelly Beans hosts its own roller hockey league for kids age 12 and younger, offering instruction, practice and game time. The fee for each 10-week session is $45 per player, which includes helmet, shin guards, gloves and stick. Also note that non-league, pick-up games may be played during the summer.

Julie's Rentals
2 Main St., Sunset Beach
• **(910) 579-1211**

Julie's is a complete beach-rental shop that rents in-line skates as well as many other recreational items all year long.

Kite Flying

Steady beach winds are ideal for kite flying. Of course, it pays to use common sense; beware of power lines, piers, boat masts and homes. Stunt kites, which can fly close to the ground, may annoy some beachgoers. Fort Fisher, the north ends of Topsail Island and Carolina Beach, and the south end of Wrightsville Beach are fitting places to tie your hopes and dreams to a colorful swatch and send them aloft.

The Carolina Kite Club (no phone) is an informal club that meets Sunday mornings from 9 AM to noon at the south end of Wrightsville Beach. In summer get there early: The small, metered parking area fills quickly. Gatherings are usually listed in the *Wilmington Star-News'* Sunday calendar.

Blowing In the Wind
115 N. Front St., Wilmington
• **(910) 763-1730**

If you're a kite lover, this is your kind of store. Its wide selection, from wind sleds to box kites to parafoils and beyond — kites of every shape and size, for every skill level and age — will make your eyes pop. Also available are flags, windsocks and wind chimes.

Lacrosse

Call it bagataway, lax, or just plain cool, this rugged and almost legendary game, like soccer, has been making great strides recently in the greater Wilmington area, spearheaded by a strong program at Cape Fear Academy and recently aided by the fledgling Hoggard Lacrosse Club. Ten regional middle schools and four high schools now field lacrosse teams. UNCW fields two teams, a men's team and the only all-female team currently in our area. The listings below describe playing opportunities beyond school teams.

Athletic Zone
4405 Northchase Pkwy. N.E., Wilmington
• **(910) 452-5020**

Indoor lacrosse is hosted at this facility on the north side of town. The playing "field" doubles as a regulation-size roller-hockey rink. Players must supply their own equipment. The Zone also organizes league play.

Cape Fear Academy Lacrosse Camp
3900 S. College Rd., Wilmington
• **(910) 791-0287**

This summer day camp for boys ages 11 through 18 in two age divisions runs for about one month beginning in mid-June. Four-hour sessions begin at 4:30 PM and are directed by the Academy's head lacrosse coach with assistance from members of the UNCW Lacrosse Club, the Cape Fear Lacrosse Club and coaches from the New Hanover County Schools. Instruction emphasizes fundamentals, rules and team play, and the camp culminates in a round-robin tournament. The cost is exceedingly reasonable (about $80 per camper), and equipment is available (campers should supply their own cleats).

Hoggard Lacrosse Club
(910) 395-1183 (ask for Terry Finnegan)

Not yet a varsity club (it hopes to be), this rapidly growing coed club is at present open to all players of middle school and high school age. The club is a true grassroots project with an enormous amount of dedication at every level (two players earned lacrosse scholarships in 1996). The club competes locally and sometimes outside the area. There are two squads, including an all-female team.

The club keeps a fairly stiff practice schedule during the season, and home games are

Sailors enjoy a reach in the Atlantic on a perfect fall afternoon.

played at Hoggard High School in Wilmington, usually on Saturday afternoons. Players supply their own equipment, and no fee is required (donations are welcome). The club is always in need of additional hands-on support, especially in terms of fund-raising, transportation and referees.

Marksmanship and Riflery

Shooting enthusiasts may like to note the periodic gun shows held at the National Guard Armory at 2221 Carolina Beach Road in Wilmington, (910) 762-0214. Vendors carry everything from antique and replica black-powder firearms to state-of-the-art rifles and pistols, plus ammunition.

Water & Woods Hunting & Fishing
4405 Wrightsville Ave., Wilmington
• **(910) 791-4855**

This small shop offers new and used guns and hunting and reloading supplies, as well as fishing tackle.

Digh's Country Sports Gallery
1988 Eastwood Rd., Wrightsville Beach
• **(910) 256-2060**

In the autumn, owner Bobby Digh, a professional gun fitter and certified shooting instructor, provides laser-assisted custom tailoring of high-quality Orvis shotguns, which are then manufactured to your body's specifications. Digh's is in the Plaza East Shopping Center, west of the drawbridge.

Rocky Point Shooters World
14565 Ashton Rd., Rocky Point
• **(910) 259-7333**

This small (50-foot) indoor pistol range offers automatically retrievable targets in a comfortable, safe, air-conditioned setting. Rifles no larger than .22 caliber are allowed. Safety training and marksmanship can be arranged by the staff. Rocky Point is about 25 minutes north of Wilmington.

Off-Roading

Although most beaches prohibit vehicles, there are a couple of relatively unspoiled areas where off-road enthusiasts (especially those who fish) can indulge themselves. But driving off-road is a two-edged sword: The vehicles that make these beautiful areas accessible also erode them. Observe regulations closely and use common sense when off-roading. This is your living room.

The best off-roading around is at the Fort Fisher State Recreation Area, an undeveloped 4-mile reach of strand and tidal marsh 5 miles south of Carolina Beach, off U.S. 421. The earth within the marsh area is firm at low tide, and fiddler crabs, egrets, ibis and herons are common. The deeper tidal pools are suitable for bathing, especially for toddlers. Passage onto the beach is through marked crossovers only. The sand here is loose and deep. At high tide, the strand becomes very narrow and may even prevent you from turning around. Also, the marsh floods at high tide. Plan accordingly.

The north end of Carolina Beach at the end of Canal Drive is also open to off-roading. This area becomes quite busy in the warmer months.

Fishermen and beachgoers can drive the beach at the west end of Long Beach (Oak Island) at Lockwood Folly Inlet. This gives access to the Point, a popular surf-fishing area. The "catch" is this: A permit is required from the town of Long Beach, 4601 E. Oak Island Drive, (910) 278-5011, and it costs a whopping $50. Beach driving is permitted only between September 15 and April 15.

Racquetball

In addition to the listing here, check the Fitness Centers section, below, to locate those that have racquetball courts.

Wilmington Family YMCA
2710 Market Street, Wilmington
• **(910) 251-9622**

Each year the Family Y sponsors racquetball and handball tournaments The Y has four courts that are available to members by reservation.

Rugby

Cape Fear Rugby Club
Laney Football Stadium, N.C. Hwy. 132, Wilmington • (910) 395-2331

This club has more than 100 members and is the three-time defending Division II state champion. Members play and practice Tuesday evenings at Laney Football Stadium on Highway 132 North in Wilmington. The club produces the Cape Fear Sevens Rugby Tournament each July. Considered one of the finest showcases of Sevens rugby in the East, the event attracts 70-odd teams from Europe, Canada, Japan and South Africa — well over 700 players. Games are held at UNCW on College Road and are free. Ranked second in the state in 1993, the club is always interested in recruiting new members. Other numbers to call are (910) 762-8324 and (910) 763-0902.

Running and Walking

Sure, you can run or walk just about anywhere in creation. But you may want to check out some of the following prime locations or participate in one of the area's several annual racing events. Also check our Track and Field section below for similar listings.

Greenfield Park
U.S. Hwy. 421 (Carolina Beach Rd.), Wilmington

Among the most beautiful places in Wilmington to jog or walk is the 4.5-mile loop around Greenfield Lake, south of downtown. The scenic paved path bears mile markers and follows the undulating lake shore across two wooden foot bridges (slippery when wet).

"The Loop" at Wrightsville Beach

This scenic sidewalk circuit is an approximately 2.5-mile circuit popular among locals. It encompasses a portion of the perimeter of Wrightsville Beach Park along Causeway Drive, plus Lumina Avenue and Salisbury Street. The park itself also features an outdoor fitness trail in the field off Causeway Drive. Bring the pooch — there's a free Dog Bar (serving only water) beside Bryant Real Estate, corner of N. Lumina and Salisbury.

Wilmington Roadrunners Club
c/o YMCA, 2710 Market St., Wilmington
• (910) 251-9622

The Roadrunners, based at the Y, sponsors races, picnics, fun runs and evening runs; provides information on technique and safety; and welcomes entire families. Also sponsored by the club is the Cape Fear Flyers youth track organization. Membership in the Roadrunners Club includes newsletter and magazine subscriptions, discounts on gear, the opportunity to take a discounted corporate membership in the YMCA, plus other perks. Yearly individual membership costs $20, families $25.

Island Walking Club
Carolina Beach Parks and Recreation
• (910) 458-7416

The Island Walking Club organizes daily invigorating beach strolls. Meet at 7 AM weekdays at the Carolina Beach Community Building at Third and Raleigh streets.

Walking Classes with Freddie J. King
Assembly Building, 720 Channel Blvd., Topsail Beach • (910) 328-1532

Walking classes incorporating stretching techniques are led by personal trainer and fitness counselor (Ms.) Freddie J. King every Tuesday morning at 9 AM. Everyone is welcome, and a small donation is requested.

Annual Tournaments

The Wilmington Tri-Span Run
The Wilmington Roadrunners Club, c/o YMCA, 2710 Market St., Wilmington
• (910) 251-9622

Sponsored by the Wilmington Roadrunners Club, the Wilmington Family Y and several area businesses, the Tri-Span is an 8K run that takes place in July. The course crosses all three bridges along the Wilmington waterfront and is sure to test your mettle. The event also includes a 1-mile fun run/walk. Early registration costs $12, and there are 13 age divisions for the 8K run.

The Reindeer Romp
The American Lung Association
• (800) 821-6205

The American Lung Association sponsors this double event, a 1-mile and 5K walk or run, held each December along Greenfield Lake. Prizes are awarded for performance as well as for costumes. Registration fees begin at $8 for children and $12 for adults.

Leprechaun Run
Medical Society Alliance
• (910) 452-7486, (910) 251-1198

Sponsored by the New Hanover-Pender Medical Society Alliance, the Leprechaun Run consists of two events held at Wrightsville Beach each March. The 1-mile walk is an out-and-back course entirely on the beach strand. Half of the 5K run is on paved road and half is on the beach. Cash prizes go to the top men and women overall winners in the 5K run, and other prizes go to top three men and women in 12 narrow age groups ranging from 12 to older than 60. Special awards are given to kids age 12 and younger for the best St. Patrick's Day costume, and there is a post-race awards party. Early entry fees range from $8 for individual children to $35 for families. Proceeds benefit local health care projects.

MS Walk
National Multiple Sclerosis Society, Greater Carolinas Chapter
• (800) 477-2955

The MS Walk in early April is a fund-raising event in which participants of all ages raise and collect pledges and walk the loop around Greenfield Lake. Incentives and prizes are awarded.

Halloween Moonlight 5K Run
UNCW Athletics Department
• (910) 962-3889

The Halloween Moonlight 5K Run takes place on the UNCW campus beginning at 8 PM on Halloween night. Late registration is accepted beginning at 6:30 PM, and food and beverages are served following the race. Registration costs $10 in advance, $12 after October 21.

North Carolina Oyster Festival Road Race
South Brunswick Islands Chamber of Commerce • (800) 426-6644

The Oyster Fest Road Race in October is Sunset Beach's contribution to footrace frenzy. Open to runners of all ages, the event comprises three races — a 10K, 5K and a 1-mile Fun Run (this last has no age divisions). The race takes place at serene Sunset Beach. Preregistration deadline is mid-October.

Bald Head Island Maritime Classic Road Race
Bald Head Island Management • (910) 457-7500

The Maritime Classic takes place in November and features a 10K and 5K foot race along some of the most scenic byways in the region, ranging through dense maritime forest, open meadow, and through a manicured golf and beach community. Preregistration is $20 and includes the ferry ride.

Camp Lejeune Oktoberfest Family 5K Fun Run
Mike Marion • (910) 451-1799

Camp Lejeune's Oktoberfest Family 5K Fun Run is one of three runs designed to promote family wellness. It is open to anyone who can walk, run, jog, stroll or be carried the distance. The course is suitable for strollers and carriages and is entirely within the confines of Camp Lejeune, near Jacksonville (about an hour north of downtown Wilmington). The event is sometimes scheduled in late-September. Also see the Track and Field section for information on the highly-competitive Lejeune Grand Prix Series.

Skateboarding

The City of Wilmington dealt a controversial blow to skateboarders and in-line skaters in 1996 by banning those activities downtown where, it so happens, there are paved hills best suited to these sports. There is still a strong skateboarding presence on the UNCW campus, where responsible boarders who respect property may ride freely.

The Skate Barn
Pansy Ln., Hampstead • (910) 270-3497

This is the area's indoor skateboarding facility of note. Formerly known as the Middle School Indoor Skate Park, the Skate Barn features a 6-foot ramp, a 3-foot-deep bowl and a full street course, as well as a full accessories shop, snack machines, video games and a foosball table. "Cheapie" nights are Monday and Thursday, when skaters with helmets ride for $3; without helmets for $5. Other days it's $5 with helmet, $8 without. Release forms must be signed to use the facility (parents or guardians must sign for children younger than 18). To get there, take U.S. 17 to Hampstead, turn west onto Peanut Road, then right onto unpaved Pansy Lane.

Soccer

Soccer fever continues to sweep this area. Youth and adult leagues continue to grow in popularity, and the fields are constantly busy on weekends. Wilmington is home to the U.S. Independent Soccer League professional team, the Wilmington Hammerheads, who use Laney High School as their home field until the team's own complex is completed. The Hammerheads also conduct affordable, specialized clinics, camps and individual instruction for players and coaches for as little as $5 per day for clinics and $10 per hour for individual lessons. Clinics run year-round and include spring break and summer sessions.

The team also provides some coaching for the Cape Fear Youth Soccer Association's "classic" games. For information about programs and matches, call the Hammerheads office at (910) 256-0975 or write to Wilmington Hammerheads, 1630 Military Cutoff Road, Wilmington, NC 28403.

Perhaps the best news for parents and players is that the investment necessary to play soccer is fairly low, generally limited to a one-time registration fee averaging $25 and shin guards that can cost less than $20.

Beyond the Goal Soccer Camp
c/o Dawn Crow, 5016 Hunt Club Rd., #14, Wilmington, NC 28403 • (910) 793-5799

This is the only soccer camp around exclusively for females, and participation is limited to 70 players and eight goalkeepers. Several instructors are semipro and are assisted by distinguished college players from around the state. Each participant must supply a ball, shoes, shin guards, water, lunch, and a good attitude. The camp's two-day sessions meet in February at Ogden Soccer Park, a few minutes north of Wilmington, from 9 AM to 4:30 PM. Camp costs range from $110 to $125 per player, and discounts apply to groups of six who register early. Applications are due by the end of January.

Cape Fear Youth Soccer Association
(910) 675-2713

Boasting 134 teams and roughly 1,800 players in the recreational division alone, the CFYSA, a member of the U.S. Soccer Federation, is the area's predominant soccer organization. Programs include a coed adult league. The league seems to expand every season, so don't be surprised when it drops the word "youth" from its name. League play proceeds in two yearly cycles, fall and spring, with the year-end Hanover Cup tournament beginning in late April.

The CFYSA offers every child and adult the opportunity to play at his or her own skill level. Teams are provided in two recreational leagues (one for youth through age 19 and one for adults), a classic league and a challenge league. Recreational League teams are open to all players without tryouts.

The Youth Recreational League is a participation league in which coaches are required to play every player who constructively participates in at least one practice a week. (No scores or records are kept for the noncompetitive U6 teams.)

Classic and challenge league teams are formed through trials and may travel around and outside the state, as tournaments determine. Licensed coaches lead all teams, and all matches are refereed.

Most CFYSA games are held at the Hugh MacRae athletic fields (behind Hoggard High School off Shipyard Boulevard) and at Emma Trask Middle School fields (2900 N. College Road) on Saturdays and some Sunday afternoons. Register in July and in January. In addition, the association sponsors an indoor league that plays at Athletic Zone, 4405 Northchase Pkwy NE, (910) 452-5020, on the north side of Wilmington. Athletic Zone is fitted with plexiglass walls and set-in goals.

The CFYSA also offers coaching clinics, uniforms, access to supplementary insurance, newsletters, summer camps and more.

Soccer Stop
5424 Oleander Dr., #103, Wilmington
- **(910) 792-1500**

The only dedicated shop of its kind in the area, the Soccer Stop is co-owned and operated by a former professional player with the Wilmington Hammerheads, someone who knows soccer inside-out. Apparel, accessories, equipment, even some field equipment . . . it's all here. Discounts apply for registered league players, including those with Cape Fear Youth Soccer. The store is in the Willow Woods Arbor strip mall a few doors from Overton's.

Wilmington Parks & Recreation Athletic Office
302 Willard St., Wilmington
- **(910) 343-3680**

An adult soccer league plays from May through July. The league's growing popularity often makes it difficult for new teams to enter, especially late in the preseason. Games are held at Legion Stadium on Carolina Beach Road, 2.5 miles south of downtown Wilmington.

Wilmington Family YMCA
2710 Market St., Wilmington
- **(910) 251-9622**

The Y sponsors league games for boys and girls ages 3 through 11 during the spring and fall.

Wilmington Hammerheads/Athletic Zone Indoor Soccer Tournament
1630 Military Cutoff Rd., Wilmington
- **(910) 256-0975, (910) 256-0975, (910) 256-0927 fax**

Marking its second year in 1998, this annual tournament spans three weekends in January and is open only to players still in high school and younger. Games take place at Athletic Zone (see above) and last only 20 minutes each with no break at halftime except to switch ends. Each team fields five field players and one keeper. Mandatory shin guards must be provided by the players, who must also sign waivers of liability. Registration costs $155 per team.

Brunswick County Parks and Recreation
Planning Bldg., Government Complex, Bolivia • (910) 253-4357, (800) 222-4790

From September through November, Brunswick County Parks and Recreation organizes youth soccer for players ages 5 through 14 (the older players must still be in middle school). Soccer camps are popular from June through August. Early registration is recommended.

Onslow County Parks and Recreation
1250 Onslow Pines Rd., Jacksonville • (910) 347-5332

Onslow Parks and Recreation hosts a coed league for adults 30 and older. Teams with up to 20 players can register for $170. Play starts in February and continues through mid-May. Games are played at Hubert Bypass Park in the town of Hubert, convenient to the northern reaches of this guide's coverage.

Softball

Refer also to the section on baseball in this chapter for information on the Optimist clubs and the Wrightsville Beach and Onslow County Parks and Recreation Departments, which also sponsor softball leagues.

Wilmington Parks & Recreation
302 Willard St., Wilmington • (910) 341-7855

Wilmington Parks & Recreation hosts adult men's, women's and coed leagues and a league for seniors during the spring and fall. The adult leagues run in two seasons. Team registration for the fall season is in August. Registration for the spring season is in March. Fees range from $200 to $400 per team.

Optimist Club of Cape Fear
3420 N. Kerr Ave., Wilmington • (910) 762-7065

This group sponsors the Cape Fear Belles softball league for girls in two age groups: 13 through 15 and 12 and younger.

Wilmington Senior Softball Association
7231 Lounsberry Ct., Wilmington • (910) 791-0852

Well-established for years in the north, senior softball for players 55 and older made its quiet debut in the Wilmington area in 1995. Now the local association boasts two teams. Some players are in their 70s. The association organizes games every Tuesday and Thursday at Empie Park, beginning with warm-ups at 9 AM, before the day grows hot. Doubleheaders are played on Thursdays. Spring training commences the first Tuesday in March, and the season of seven-inning games spans the month of May. Certain safety rules apply, such as no tag plays at home. A nominal registration fee may apply, and "unofficial" games with teams from neighboring counties are sometimes organized.

Wrightsville Beach Summer Softball League
1 Bob Sawyer Dr., Wrightsville Beach • (910) 256-7925

Wrightsville Beach Parks and Recreation organizes league play for teams of all skill levels. Registration opens in March, and games start May 1. The regular season is followed by an interdivision, double-elimination tournament. The cost is $245 per team, plus a nominal additional fee for each player not a resident of Wrightsville Beach, up to $120 per team.

INSIDERS' TIP

Brunswick County beaches are some of the nicest family-oriented beaches anywhere.

Carolina Beach Parks and Recreation
1121 N. Lake Park Blvd., Carolina Beach
- **(910) 458-7416**

Carolina Beach hosts a two-day, open softball tournament in August. If you can scrape up a team, your own softballs and the $100 entry fee, you're in.

Brunswick County Parks and Recreation
Planning Bldg., Government Complex, Bolivia • (910) 253-2670

The county sponsors two separate leagues. The summer league for men only begins play around the first of July and ends by the first of September. The coed league in the fall starts its season September 1 and plays to the end of October. Registration for both leagues costs $350 per team of 20 and begins six weeks prior to seasonal play.

Tennis

Practically every larger public park in the region has at least two courts (see the Parks section at the end of this chapter).

Greater Wilmington Tennis Association
3209 Amber Dr., Wilmington
- **(910) 452-2941**

The GWTA organizes tournaments for serious players. The tournaments are open to all in singles, doubles and mixed-doubles divisions. Registration fees vary, beginning around $10. You can also call Wilmington Parks & Recreation for information, (910) 343-3680.

USTA Team Tennis Association
3209 Amber Dr., Wilmington
- **(910) 452-2941**

With more than 100 teams and nearly 1200 players in Wilmington alone, this organization plays a major role for tennis in the region. The association organizes adult- and senior-league team tennis tournaments, played from March through May. Match-winners may go on to compete at the district, sectional and national levels. All players must be computer-rated to play, and rating clinics take place from October through early January. Players must be USTA members ($25 per individual, $40 per family). The association's local dues are $35 per person, which includes (among several benefits) a T-shirt and an end-of-season dinner dance.

Wilmington Parks & Recreation
302 Willard Dr., Wilmington
- **(910) 341-7855**

The Department offers tennis for youth and seniors from March through November. Mr. PeeWee tennis for ages 4 through 7 takes place September through November and March through May.

Wrightsville Beach Parks and Recreation
1 Bob Sawyer Dr., Wrightsville Beach
- **(910) 256-7925**

Wrightsville Beach sponsors all levels of group instruction for adults and children age 5 and older from March through October, and a Women's Tennis Day every Thursday 9 AM to noon year round, weather permitting. Fees range from about $22 to $35 for Wrightsville Beach residents and about $33 to $52 for non-residents.

Brierwood Golf Club
10 Brierwood Rd. near Shallotte city limits • (910) 754-4660

This private club offers its four outdoor tennis courts for public play for a nominal fee (about $3).

Ocean Isle Beach Golf Course
Ocean Isle Beach Dr. (on the mainland)
- **(910) 579-2610**

Two outdoor tennis courts are available to the public for a very small fee.

INSIDERS' TIP

Use the outdoor shower if your beach house has one. It will really help keep sand from being tracked inside and make cleanup easier.

Brunswick County Parks and Recreation
Planning Bldg., Government complex, Bolivia • (910) 254-4357

All six Brunswick County District Parks maintain tennis courts for public use. See the section on Parks below.

Sickle Cell Open Tennis Tournament
WSTA Tennis Tournament, 226 Normandy Dr., Wilmington • (910) 392-0568, (910) 341-7841 days, (910) 251-5676 days

The Wilmington Seagulls Tennis Association sponsors this annual tournament, which takes place at a Wilmington park in mid-September and is governed by USTA rules. Singles and doubles matches are the best of three sets. Evening play could be under lights. Entry fee is $12, and awards are presented.

Tennis With Love Ltd.
4303 Oleander Drive, Wilmington • (910) 791-3128

If your racket needs repair or you need a new pair of shorts, stop by Tennis With Love in the easy-to-miss Landmark Plaza near Oh!Brian's restaurant. This shop specializes in restringing tennis and racquetball frames and carries clothing, shoes and accessories. It's a shop that lives up to its name.

Track and Field

Track and field is mostly school-related in this region, but there are a few other ways to participate. Also check the section on Running and Walking above.

Brunswick County Parks and Recreation
Planning Bldg., Government complex, Bolivia • (910) 254-4357

Brunswick County has a program for youth in the Leland area (northern Brunswick County). The program operates in summer and emphasizes fun and technique more than winning.

Wilmington Triathlon
Wilmington Family YMCA, 2710 Market St., Wilmington • (910) 251-9622

Superheroes can tackle the annual Wilmington Triathlon, sponsored by the Wilmington Family Y, in mid-September. The combination 2K saltwater swim, 45K bike race and 10K run may be entered by individuals and three-member teams, ages 14 and older. Call the Y or call (910) 762-3357.

Lejeune Grand Prix Series
Mike Marion • (910) 451-1799

Camp Lejeune, the Marine Corps base near Jacksonville, hosts this annual series of events from January through October. The 11 series challenges are grueling and draw a highly competitive field of athletes from across the nation. Among the events are the Tour d'Pain (February), the European Cross Country (March), the Armed Forces Day 5K (May), the Mud, Sweat & Gears Duathlon (June), the Wet & Wild Biathlon (August), and the Lejeune Triathlon (September). Events take place within the confines of Camp Lejeune and are open to civilians of all ages.

Azalea Festival Triathlon
Set-Up, Inc., 641 Sloop Point Ln., Kure Beach • (910) 458-0299

This triathlon, sanctioned by the U.S. Triathlon Association, coincides with Wilmington's most famous annual festival, usually occurring on the second weekend in April. The event consists of a 300-yard pool swim, a 20K bike race, and a 5K run. Except for some of the bike leg, the entire triathlon takes place on the UNCW campus in Wilmington. Contestants are divided into the nationally standard age and gender brackets. Registration is $35.

Carolina Beach Triathlon
Set-Up, Inc., 641 Sloop Point Ln., Kure Beach • (910) 458-0299

Now that triathlon is an official Olympic sport, this particular event, an Olympic-distance triathlon held in mid-May, could be a good place to judge how you measure up for the big time. Spanning most of Pleasure Island, the Carolina Beach Triathlon is a 1.5K swim, 40K bike, and 10K run sanctioned by the U.S. Triathlon Association. Contestants are

Kure Beach Double Sprint Triathlon
Set-Up, Inc., 641 Sloop Point La., Kure Beach • (910) 458-0299

Here's an event tailored for overachievers. After you get through the 400-meter swim, the 1.5K run and the 10K run, guess what: You get to do the entire thing all over again, in reverse — bike, run and swim. The overall distance is less than half that of an Olympic triathlon, but considering that this U.S. Triathlon Association-sanctioned race is in late-July, the challenge is formidable. Contestants are divided into the nationally standard age and gender brackets. Registration is $35.

Surf & Turf Triathlon
Topsail Area Chamber of Commerce and Tourism • 205 S. Topsail Dr., Surf City • (910) 328-4722, (800) 626-2780

The Surf & Turf's special challenge consists mainly in two of its components: the half-mile swim is in open ocean, and half of the 5K run is on the beach strand — that is, in loose sand. The bike leg is 12 miles. This competition coincides with the Greater Topsail Area Spring Fling, a festival held at Topsail Island on the last weekend of April. Registration costs $20.

Ultimate

Like any beach community worth its salt, we take Frisbee seriously. Two teams in the 1993 World Championships came from Wilmington: the UNCW's men's team (1993 national champs) and the Port City Slickers, (910) 791-8623, an unaffiliated men's team, half of which is made up of UNCW grads. The UNCW's women's team was 1991-92 national collegiate champ and it remains a top-ranked force. All three of these powerhouses participate in a sport that is undergoing a surge in popularity, even to the point that talk is focusing on whether to introduce referees.

Volleyball

If you're not accustomed to playing in sand, you're in for a workout. Some say it will either whip you into shape or kill you. But not all volleyball in the area is outdoors. If you survive the summer playing in sand, your improved agility and jumping may manifest themselves dramatically on a hard court in winter. As you might expect, competition is fairly stiff, and local players generally take their games seriously.

Athletic Zone
4405 Northchase Pkwy. N.E., Wilmington • (910) 452-5020

This indoor facility on the north side of town offers a good place to play during the winter. Team registration is the most economical way to play, but pickup games may be available at nominal cost.

Wilmington Family YMCA
2710 Market St., Wilmington • (910) 251-922

In conjunction with the Federal Outdoor Volleyball Association, the Y sponsors one tournament each month from March to October at Wrightsville Beach. There are three doubles divisions — novice, intermediate and advanced — and sign-up is at 8:30 AM on weekends. Games begin at 9 AM.

Capt'n Bill's Backyard Grill
4240 Market St., Wilmington • (910) 762-0111

These are the only sand courts within city limits. They are behind the North 17 shopping center. Join a pickup game for a buck per player, or register your team in one of Capt'n Bill's leagues. Hot food and cold drinks are served by the courtside grill.

Wilmington Parks & Recreation
302 Willard St., Wilmington • (910) 343-3680

Wilmington Parks & Recreation has fall and spring coed volleyball for adults. Teams must register early to participate in this crowded league, usually by the end of July for the fall season and by early January for the spring.

Wrightsville Beach Parks and Recreation
1 Bob Sawyer Dr., Wrightsville Beach • (910) 256-7925

Wrightsville Beach Parks and Recreation sponsors doubles tournaments with round-

SPORTS, FITNESS AND PARKS • 317

robin play in men's, women's and mixed categories. Games are held March through October on the beach strand.

If you'd like to put up your own net on Wrightsville Beach, you'll have to get permission from the folks at Parks and Recreation. It's easy.

Brunswick County Parks and Recreation
Planning Bldg., Government complex, Bolivia • (800) 222-4790

Adult team volleyball in Brunswick County is sponsored by the Parks and Recreation Department. Players must be 18 or older and out of high school. The season runs from late October through March. Inquire early about registration.

Onslow County Parks and Recreation
1250 Onslow Pines Rd., Jacksonville • (910) 347-5332

Folks 16 and older from Onslow and northern Pender counties may enter teams in Onslow County Parks and Recreation's volleyball league. Contact the department in July for registration information. The indoor matches commence during the third week of September.

Sharky's Pizza & Deli
Ocean Isle Beach Cswy., Ocean Isle Beach • (910) 579-9177

Sharky's has a sand court, and you can even arrive by boat (docking facilities are available). Food and refreshments are within easy "serving" distance.

Wrestling

Brunswick County Parks and Recreation
Planning Bldg., Government complex, Bolivia • (910) 253-4357, (800) 222-4790,

Brunswick Parks and Recreation is about the only agency that sponsors wrestling teams outside the schools. The league boasts two national champs among its alumni. The county has a scholastic league (ages 5 through 14) and a freestyle league (any age). Inquire early about the availability of summer wrestling camp.

Martial Arts

Whether it's the sword technique of iaido, the open-hand style of karate or the throws and take-downs of jujitsu that interest you; whether it's self-defense, physical fitness, mental focus or competition you desire; all that and more is available in our region. Martial arts schools generally offer classes on a term basis, usually monthly or yearly.

Bushin-Kai Karate
2875 Carolina Beach Rd., Wilmington • (910) 395-2170

Del C. Russ, an instructor since 1966, teaches traditional martial arts, including Japanese sword art (iaido), aiki-kai aikido, toyama and ko-dachi. Inquire about family rates.

Champion Karate Centers
127 S. College Rd., Wilmington • (910) 792-1131

Owner/instructor John Maynard welcomes physically-challenged students, including the sightless. Maynard was personally trained by Chuck Norris, and his studio is part of Norris's United Fighting Arts Organization. Champion offers instruction in self-defense for men, women and children, contact and non-contact kick boxing, a weight room and guidance for those interested in competition. Maynard also operates at Wyatt Fitness in Hampstead (see the Fitness Centers section). Champion Karate's College Road facility is inside the Market Place Mall beside Gold's Gym.

Choe's Hapkido
7419-C Market St., Wilmington • (910) 686-2678

Grandmaster Jong Hyun Choe is a ninth-degree black belt in hapkido, an eighth-degree black belt in tae kwon do, and an Olympic tae kwon do referee who teaches only those who, through an interview and trial course, demonstrate positive attitude, dedication and respect and are interested in holistic self-improvement. Remarkably, Master Choe can directly trace his family's martial arts tradition back 2,000 years. He specializes in teaching the use of empty hands and weapons as well as women's self-defense. Students of all ages are welcome. Choe's studio is in the Market Street Center on the northeast side of town.

Jung's Tae Kwon Do Academy
4623 Market St., Wilmington
- **(910) 392-6980**

Jung's teaches traditional karate, kung fu and hapkido as well as tae kwon do. Instructor Yong Jung is a ninth dan-degree black belt with more than 40 years of teaching experience. He is assisted by a fifth dan black belt instructor. The Academy also sells supplies and equipment.

South East Karate
145 S. College Rd., Ste. 109, Wilmington
- **(910) 313-2788**

Jim Irwin, a sixth-degree black belt, has been teaching martial arts in Wilmington since 1985. His certified instructors lead day and evening classes for children and adults, including special classes for girls, in a roomy, air-conditioned space. Specialties include kempo and kobudo. The school's approach emphasizes traditional family values, safety and fun. South East Karate offers child development programs for children with ADD, and the school is endorsed by local police departments. Private instruction is available, schedules permitting.

Stover's Martial Arts
2505 S. College Rd., Wilmington
- **(910) 791-3656**

Stover's is Wilmington's oldest school of martial arts. Mr. Stover, a seventh-degree black belt, stresses fundamentals in a variety of styles, including karate, kempo, jujitsu, kung fu and traditional weapons. Classes meet evenings, Monday through Thursday.

Wilmington Family YMCA
2710 Market St., Wilmington
- **(910) 251-9622**

The Family Y offers karate, t'ai chi and judo classes, with U.S. Judo Association membership included. Costs range from $25 to $40 per month, excluding memberships and gear.

YWCA of Wilmington
2815 S. College Rd., Wilmington
- **(910) 799-6820**

Evening karate classes for adults are offered twice weekly for a $30 per month ($20 for members). A small registration fee is extra. T'ai chi ch'uan is offered periodically.

Kure Beach Aikido
Kure Beach Community Center, 3rd St., Kure Beach • **(910) 799-6955**

This dojo is an affiliate of the Aikido Association of America and trains Kure Beach police officers in the "responsible" art of using the minimum effective force necessary to neutralize an attacker. Chief instructor Richard Price, himself a Kure Beach policeman, is a third-degree black belt. Monthly rates are reasonable and prorated for students ($20), adults ($35), couples ($40), and families ($50).

Forever Fit Fitness Center
214 Sneads Ferry Rd., Sneads Ferry
- **(910) 327-2293**

Forever Fit offers tae kwon do within convenient reach of northern Topsail Island. Visitors can take advantage of daily and weekly rates, and individual memberships begin as low as $40 per month.

Yoga

In addition to the listings below, fitness centers occasionally offer classes. For individual instructors, information and contacts, check the bulletin boards at the Tidal Creek Food Co-op, 4406 Wrightsville Avenue, (910) 799-2667, and Doxey's Market & Cafe, Landfall Shopping Center (Eastwood and Military Cutoff roads), (910) 256-9952, both in Wilmington.

Wilmington Family YMCA
2710 Market St., Wilmington
- **(910) 251-9622**

The Y offers regular yoga classes for members and is a good resource for locating private instructors.

Haren (Ed Pickett)
(910) 395-4431

A proponent of Kripalu, or "posture-flow," yoga, Haren instructs informal weekly classes in Wilmington. Kripalu yoga emphasizes spontaneous movement rather than static form and is thought to be a rediscovery of yoga's most ancient traditions. Classes are open to anyone for a voluntary donation.

Wrightsville Beach Parks and Recreation
1 Bob Sawyer Dr. • (910) 256-7925

Wrightsville Beach Parks and Recreation offers year-round morning and evening classes emphasizing flexibility, alignment, conditioning and stress-reduction techniques. Classes meet twice weekly for six weeks. Drop-ins are welcome. The six-week fee is $26 for residents, $39 for nonresidents.

Fitness Centers

The many fine fitness centers along the coast generally offer state-of-the-art apparatus and certified instructors. Aerobics classes have become standard, as has the use of bikes, treadmills, free weights and stair-climbers. Membership costs usually include a one-time registration fee plus a monthly fee for a required term, but many local centers cater to the short-term visitor by offering daily, weekly and monthly rates.

Cory Everson's Aerobics & Fitness for Women
4620 Oleander Dr., Wilmington
• (910) 791-0030

Among the newest facilities in the area, Cory Everson's focuses on women's health exclusively. Aerobics classes with certified instructors and child care are included in memberships, as is a half-hour fitness evaluation with a personal trainer to help you get started. Longer-term personal training is available at additional cost, and the center maintains several certified professional on staff.

The center is clean, nicely laid out, and features state-of-the-art equipment, including Cybex and Nautilus equipment designed especially for women. Headphones connected through each cardiovascular machine allow members to hear any one of six TV sets without disturbing their neighbors. Tanning and free weights are also available.

There are special rates for guests, corporate groups, seniors 65 and older, students and families. It's located near the southeast corner of Oleander Drive and S. College Road.

Gold's Gym
4310 Shipyard Blvd., Wilmington
• (910) 350-8289
127 S. College Rd., Wilmington
• (910) 392-3999

Meticulously equipped and maintained, and deservedly popular, Gold's is a full-service fitness center known for its attentive staff and its array of equipment. It was voted Wilmington's most popular fitness center two years in a row (1995 and 1996) in a local poll.

Offerings at both locations include personally designed exercise programs and one-to-one training; cardiovascular equipment, including StairMaster and the Reebok SkyWalker; a variety of aerobics classes; resistance and free-weight training; tanning (at extra cost); dry sauna; child care (free to full members and staffed by CPR-certified personnel); and a pro shop. Circuit equipment is sequentially arranged for a complete body workout.

An Aerobics Hotline, (910) 350-6778, makes daily class schedules readily available. Gold's also offers the "FAST Track" food and exercise management system. Members of Gold's Gym are entitled to use any other Gold's Gym anywhere (500 nationally). Memberships are available by the day, week, month and year. The Shipyard Boulevard location is at Long Leaf Mall; the College Road facility in the Marketplace Mall, immediately east of the Market Street overpass.

The Physiological Edge
3115-E Wrightsville Ave., Wilmington
• (910) 343-1661

Exclusively offering one-on-one personal training in a private, even elegant, atmosphere, the Physiological Edge boasts a highly qualified staff under the direction of founder and trainer Trey Wyatt. Service and results are the two operative words here. Half-hour and full-hour sessions are by appointment only, and the staff will meet your schedule. One workout is free; all are custom-tailored to your needs. Trey Wyatt is also the founder of Wyatt Fitness in Hampstead (see below).

Pro-Fit
23 N. Front St., Wilmington
• (910) 763-7224

Wilmington's downtown professional

crowd enjoys Pro-Fit (Professional Fitness) as much for its chic location, celebrity clientele (many film and TV actors) and ground-floor view of Front Street as for its excellent facilities and services, which include free weights, cardiac equipment and personal trainers.

PT Connection
5710 Oleander Dr., Wilmington
• (910) 792-1200, (800) 750-7384

For the utmost in personal attention, PT Connection specializes exclusively in high-end personal training tailored to the individual. State-of-the-art equipment and staff expertise come together in a positive, upbeat atmosphere where the work is hard, the quality high, and the clientele predominantly affluent. Fees are set on a per-session basis. Massage therapy is also available. You'll find it in the Oleander Business Center, suite 210, next to the Kids' Gym.

Pulse Athletic Club
2026 S. 16th St., Wilmington
• (910) 763-9655

Formerly known as the Wilmington Athletic Club, Pulse is still everything it has always been since people called it "the Wac" — an attractive, family-oriented fitness and recreational center hosting sports, including basketball, racquetball and coed volleyball. It offers a steam room, sauna, an outdoor pool, a nursery with CPR-trained staff and swimming lessons. Fitness consultations and nutritional lectures are frequently offered. Short-term contracts and personalized training for members and nonmembers are available.

Walden's Gym
North 17 Shopping Center, Market St., Wilmington • (910) 763-7444
6400 Carolina Beach Rd., Wilmington
• (910) 395-7002

Can't sleep at night? Can't seem to fit your hours to any fitness center's? One of Walden's two locations could be for you. Walden's is the area's only health club with doors open around the clock, seven days a week. Somewhat less glitzy than some other clubs (and proportionally priced), Walden's offers all the free weights and cardiovascular training equipment you'd expect, plus personal training, circuit training and tanning. You'll find the North 17 Shopping Center just west of Kerr Avenue. The Carolina Beach Road location is in the Masonboro Commons shopping center.

Wilmington Family YMCA
2710 Market St., Wilmington
• (910) 251-9622

Offering a wide variety of fitness and educational activities, the Family Y features ample facilities, such as a large gym, two indoor pools, a Jacuzzi, four racquetball courts, Nautilus equipment and even sunbathing decks. Athletic fields with a track and playground are also available. Aerobics (including water classes), t'ai chi ch'uan, arthritis aquatics classes and massage therapy are just a few of the Y's vast offerings. League sports for adults and youth are organized seasonally, and youth are eligible for limited, reduced-rate gym passes in the summer.

Wilmington Parks & Recreation Fitness Center
602 N. 4th St. • (910) 341-7855

Wilmington Parks & Recreation offers special exercise classes for youth who are overweight, physically impaired and inner-city bound. Senior adults will find fitness classes tailored to their needs, plus low-impact aerobics, water aerobics and floor Slimnastics for adults 55 and older.

YWCA of Wilmington
2815 S. College Rd., Wilmington
• (910) 799-6820

The YW's elaborate swimming programs include full-scale ocean lifesaving, and the facility trains and certifies more lifeguards that any other in eastern North Carolina. Indoor activities include low-impact, step and water aerobics; toning classes; dance in many styles for kids 2 and older; karate for kids and adults; kids' gymnastics; water basketball for teens; and t'ai chi ch'uan. Child care is also available.

Exercise Today
6832 Market St., Ogden • (910) 397-0003

A fitness center for women only, Exercise Today features a full array of cardio equipment designed specifically for women's bodies and physiologies, plus a bright, clean, state-of-the-art facility. Emphasis is given to holistic wellness, nutritional guidance and safety. Fitness counselors and certified personal trainers work one-on-one with patrons for at least eight sessions following the initial fitness/stress evaluation and fat analysis. Classes include aerobics, jazzercise and yoga. Chiropractors periodically present health seminars on the premises.

Also available are seniors classes, pre/postnatal exercise classes, sauna, whirlpool and steam room. Child care is provided by CPR-certified nursery staff for kids at least six months old. Exercise Today offers long-term memberships as well as monthly specials. Be sure to inquire about the daily guest fee for friends of members. Look for Exercise Today directly behind McDonald's.

Wyatt Fitness
14653 U.S. Hwy. 17, Hampstead
• (910) 270-9300

Worldwide, only 24 Resistance Training Specialists (RST), experts in the education of resistance-training instructors, have been certified; Trey Wyatt, CPT, founder and chief trainer at Wyatt Fitness, is one of them. His staff of NASM-certified personal trainers have also undergone Wyatt's own, more rigorous Physiological Edge certification training. Wyatt Fitness probably has the most extensive array of cardio equipment in the region, an entertainment system that could shame some night clubs and even a full-service cappuccino bar serving fresh juices, smoothies, power shakes, supplements, and fruits.

Great stuff, all of it, but the interior design of this place deserves the word "stunning." Wyatt designed his center with a boldly modern aesthetic that makes good use of burnished stainless steel (the work of a renowned local artist), richly hued finishes, curving sightlines and tiered workout areas.

Members are entitled to two free personal training sessions in order to design individually tailored exercise programs. Offerings include treadmill classes, non-contact cardio kick boxing and the 12-week Apex fitness and nutritional program. Martial arts instruction is available on site from Champion Karate Centers. Annual memberships are offered with a five-day "try before you buy" option, and day rates, short-term memberships and out-of-town memberships are also available. Wyatt Fitness is on the south-bound side of U.S. 17, near the heart of Hampstead.

Coastal Tumblegym
915-C N. Lake Park Blvd, Carolina Beach
• (910) 458-949, (910) 458-8384

The certified instructors at Coastal Tumblegym specialize in gymnastics, tumbling and trampoline instruction for children ranging from preschoolers to high schoolers. The facility's location is a particular boon to those living or vacationing on Pleasure Island. Friday nights bring open-gym sessions (a.k.a. Parents' Night Out) from 7 to 10 PM, which are open to nonmembers as well. Coastal Tumblegym also offers a variety of party services, including birthday parties, team parties and parties for church and youth groups. (Also see our Kidstuff chapter.)

The Crest Fitness Center
38 N. Lumina Ave., Wrightsville Beach
• (910) 256-5758

This long-lived establishment, under new management since 1997, is the only fitness center on Wrightsville Beach. Despite that, the Crest's prices are more than reasonable, and day passes are available for those fitness-conscious travelers just passing through. A complete Nautilus program is available, as well as aerobics classes, free weights, personal training, tanning beds and a nursery. Because of its location, The Crest boasts that it's the fitness center with the "largest outdoor swimming area" (you guessed it, saltwater fans).

A variety of memberships are offered, including corporate, student, weekly, monthly, daily — even passes for motel lodgers.

Body Dimensions
5241 Main St., Shallotte • (910) 754-3808

Emphasizing the natural approach to lifelong fitness, the folks at Body Dimensions offer a full line of free weights, aerobics classes, treadmills, stair climbers and Badger/Magnum strength systems. Visitors to the area benefit from daily, weekly, monthly and other short-term rates. The center is open every day except Sunday and is located in the South Park Plaza, the first shopping plaza when traveling north into Shallotte along U.S. 17 Business (Main Street).

The Fitness Zone
5140 Sellers Rd., Shallotte
• (910) 754-2772

This small facility, not far from the South Brunswick Islands, has separate rooms for free weights and exercise machinery such as treadmills, Lifecycles, and Climbmax steppers. There is also a massage therapist on the premises. Daily and weekly memberships are available — great for visitors. Tanning beds, tae kwon do and sauna are offered, as are CPR classes and health supplies. Sellers Road, on the south side of Shallotte, is the first right-hand fork from U.S. 17 Business when traveling north into Shallotte (just beyond South Park Plaza).

Brunswick County Parks and Recreation
Planning Bldg., Government complex, Bolivia • (910) 253-2670, (800) 222-4790

For $15 per month or $4 per drop-in, you may participate in step aerobics classes (provide your own step) twice each week at two Brunswick County locations: the Town Creek and Leland community buildings. Low-impact aerobics is also offered twice weekly at the Lockwood Folly Community Building. Registration is available on location, and the one-hour classes usually get underway at around 6:30 PM.

Aerobics with Freddie J. King
Surf City Baptist Church, 304 Wilmington Ave., Surf City • (910) 328-1532

Personal trainer and certified fitness counselor Freddie King leads weekly (nondenominational) aerobics classes on Friday mornings. Participants are welcome to register at the door, and you don't have to sign up for a specific number of classes. A small donation is requested.

Forever Fit Fitness Center
214 Sneads Ferry Rd., Sneads Ferry
• (910) 327-2293

Stressing a balanced regimen for fitness, Forever Fit offers strength training, a full line of cardio equipment, step and aerobic classes, circuit training, tae kwon do, dance (line, ballet, tap, jazz), tanning, a personal trainer on staff and AFAA-certified instructors. Water aerobics are offered in June, July and August. Visitors can pay daily and weekly rates; individual memberships begin as low as $40 per month. Forever Fit is convenient to the northern Topsail Island area.

Parks

We've grouped state, county and city parks by location since all three types can be found within Wilmington or Carolina Beach city limits. Refer to the Index if you're unsure of a park's location.

Wilmington

The 32 public parks maintained by the City of Wilmington differ widely. From the historic Riverwalk of downtown's Riverfront Park and the athletic fields of Empie Park to the sculpted benches of Carolina Courtyard and sunken cypress stands of Greenfield Lake, there is always a park nearby with the kind of recreation or quiet you desire. Of city parks, we list a cross-section of the larger ones.

Inquiries about particular facilities at Wilmington parks should be directed to the Wilmington Parks & Recreation Department's athletic office, (910) 343-3680. To reserve picnic shelters at any of the New Hanover County parks, call (910) 341-7181.

Empie Park
Park Ave. at Independence Blvd.

Empie has lighted baseball fields, picnic shelters, a playground, bike racks and a concession stand. Due to popular demand, tennis courts here must be reserved in advance ($3 for city residents; $4 nonresidents) by calling the Wilmington Athletics office at (910) 343-3860.

Greenfield Park
U.S. Hwy. 421 (Carolina Beach Rd.)

Greenfield Lake and its surrounding gardens are the centerpiece of Wilmington's park system and a scenic wonder that changes character from season to season. Among the city's oldest parks, it was at one time a working plantation and, later, a carnival grounds.

The Southern North Carolina coast is a haven for golfers, with dozens of professional courses.

The lake attracts a wide variety of birds and is rumored to contain alligators. When the azaleas bloom in early spring, the area explodes in a dazzling profusion of color. Stands of flowering magnolia, dogwood, long leaf pine and live oak — many hung with Spanish moss — line the shady 5-mile Lake Shore Drive.

On the north side of the 158-acre park are lighted tennis courts, playgrounds, picnic areas, a concession stand and docks where canoes and paddleboats are available for rent. A free public boat ramp is on W. Lake Shore Drive immediately east of U.S. 421. The benches at mid-span on Lions Bridge are a wonderful spot to relax on a breezy day. Open-air performances are presented in summer at the amphitheater off W. Lake Shore Drive, adjacent to the Municipal Rose Garden.

An excellent place to observe wildlife is from the Rupert Bryan Memorial Nature Trail, an easy one-third-mile looped boardwalk through dense cypress swamp. The trail head is through the parking lot off E. Lake Shore Drive between Yaupon and Cypress drives.

Legion Stadium
Carolina Beach Rd. (U.S. Hwy. 421)

Beside Greenfield Lake, approximately 1.75 miles south of the Cape Fear Memorial Bridge, Legion Stadium is home to several local high school sports teams. The site also has lighted athletic fields, tennis courts and a swimming pool as well as plenty of parking. The pool fee is $1 for adults and 50¢ for children.

Hugh MacRae Park
Oleander Dr., east of S. College Rd.

This county park of tall pines is, appropriately, the site of the extremely popular Piney Woods Festival in early September (see our Annual Events chapter). Playgrounds, lighted tennis courts, athletic fields, sheltered picnic areas, a scenic pond (an altered Carolina bay) and a concession stand explain this park's popularity.

Northside Park
Between Sixth and MacRae Sts., north of Taylor St.

The pool is the main attraction at this city park, and sheltered picnic areas are available. The pool fee is $1 for adults and 50¢ for children.

Ogden Park
7069 Market St., Ogden

This 125-acre county park, located between Wilmington and Wrightsville Beach and still under development, is destined to be the flagship park of the county's north side, as Hugh MacRae Park is to the south side. So far, the four baseball fields and the concession building are complete. Ogden Park is being developed in stages and will include several combination football-soccer fields (which may be completed by the time you read this), hiking trails, tennis courts, playgrounds, and more. The entrance is on the west (southbound) side of Market Street, about 0.2 miles north of the intersection of Military Cutoff Road, a few minutes north of Wilmington city limits. Look for the entrance beside Mt. Ararat AME Church at Planter's Walk.

Riverfront Park
Water St.

For many locals, this park epitomizes Wilmington life. Once congested with the wharves of the state's busiest port, the Riverwalk is now a place for quiet strolls, sightseeing, shopping, live outdoor music and dining. The sternwheeler *Henrietta II* and the tour boat *Capt. Maffitt* dock here. You'll also find a visitors' information booth. Historic sailing ships visiting town often dock here and usually offer tours.

Robert Strange Park
Eighth and Nun Sts.

The heart of this park is its swimming pool ($1 adults, 50¢ children). Other facilities include a recreation center, restrooms, playground, picnic shelters, softball fields and lighted tennis and basketball courts.

Snow's Cut Park
River Rd., near Snow's Cut Bridge

Divided into two sections along River Road, one directly beneath the bridge and the other some 100 yards west, this county park offers shady picnic grounds, sheltered tables, a gazebo and pedestrian access to Snow's Cut. It is very near Carolina Beach Family Campground. For shelter reservations call (910) 341-7198.

Wrightsville Beach Park
Causeway Dr., Wrightsville Beach

This sprawling recreation and athletic facility is impossible to miss when traveling Causeway Drive. Thirteen acres in breadth, it includes tennis courts, basketball courts, a softball field, a football/soccer field, sand volleyball courts, playground equipment and a fitness trail. The 2.5-mile sidewalk Loop bordering much of the park and traversing both of the island's bridges is popular among walkers and joggers.

Carolina Beach and Kure Beach

Carolina Beach State Park
Dow Rd., Carolina Beach
• (910) 458-8206

This is one of the most biologically diverse parks in North Carolina and a contender for the most beautiful park in the area. Maritime forest, sandhill terrain, waterfront and sand ridges support carnivorous plants and centuries-old live oaks. Five miles of easy trails wind throughout the park. The marina offers boat ramps ($3) and 42 boat slips off the Cape Fear River. Excellent overnight camping facilities are available. The park is on Pleasure Island, 1 mile north of Carolina Beach and less than a half-mile from U.S. 421, off Dow Road. Day use is free.

Carolina Lake Park
Atlanta Ave. and U.S. Hwy. 421, Carolina Beach

Primarily a picnic site, this 11-acre park has four gazebos, sheltered picnic tables and a playground.

The Cove at Fort Fisher State Historic Site
U.S. Hwy. 421 S., Kure Beach
• (910) 458-5538

The Cove is a beautiful getaway, about 6 miles south of Carolina Beach. Bordering the beach and a rocky sea wall, a grove of windswept live oaks provides shade for the picnic tables and grills. Come to fish and sunbathe — but don't swim: dangerous currents and underwater hazards make it risky. Parking is available south of the museum, near the Ft. Fisher Memorial and at the museum itself, across the road. The nearest restrooms are at the Fort Fisher Recreation Area Public Access, 1 mile south. Otherwise, there are no facilities.

Mike Chappell Park
Dow Rd., Carolina Beach

Two lighted ball fields and a football/soccer field make up the largest area of this 10-acre park, which also offers picnic tables, two tennis courts, two lighted sand volleyball courts and a playground. The park is bounded by Sumter Avenue and Clarendon Boulevard.

Joe Eakes Park
K Ave. at Seventh St., Kure Beach

This small park, not a long walk from the beach, offers a playground, two tennis courts and volleyball and basketball courts.

Brunswick County

The following six District parks are maintained by the Brunswick County Parks and Recreation Department. All have excellent facilities, including tennis courts, ball fields, football/soccer fields, basketball courts, playgrounds and picnic shelters. Most of them also feature shuffleboard courts and horseshoe pits, plus community buildings for use by groups for such occasions as reunions, exercise classes and other events.

For specific information about any of the district parks, or to reserve picnic shelters and community buildings, call (910) 253-2670. Tennis players at Ocean Isle Beach also may note the town's public courts on Third Street across from the Museum of Coastal Carolina.

Leland District Park
Village Rd., Leland

This is a 13-acre community park, situated behind the Leland Post Office. Facilities include a community building, playground and sand volleyball courts.

Lockwood District Park
N.C. Hwy. 211, a mile north of U.S. Hwy. 17

The park is a mile north of the town of Supply. Its community building, however, is at Holden Beach. The park offers shuffleboard and horseshoes.

Northwest District Park
U.S. Hwy. 74/76, 2 miles west of the Leland overpass.

This park lies 15 minutes west of Wilmington, on the south side of the highway.

Smithville District Park
N.C. Hwy. 133 near Southport

Smithville District Park includes beach-style volleyball courts.

Shallotte District Park
Old Hwy. 17, 1 mile south of Shallotte

To find this park from U.S. 17, follow signs for U.S. 17 Business.

Town Creek District Park
U.S. Hwy. 17, near Winnabow

You can't miss this park on the east side of the road, about 15 or 20 minutes south of Wilmington.

E. F. Middleton Park
E. Oak Island Dr. at S.E. 47th St., Long Beach

The primary city park in Long Beach, Middleton Park offers a large playground with sand pits, swings and climbing bars, plus two tennis courts, basketball courts, a baseball field and picnic tables with some shade. The park is across the street from Town Hall and the emergency medical station.

Ev-Henwood Nature Preserve
6150 Rock Creek Rd., Town Creek
• (910) 253-6066, (910) 962-3197

This nature preserve, owned and administered UNCW, comprises 174 acres of lush woodland with marked trails and educational displays. Among the many natural points of interest is an old tar kiln of the type once ubiquitous throughout the region. At present, only about 74 acres are open to the public. Suitable for families, the preserve is open during daylight hours seven days a week. Picnic tables and a restroom are available, and there's an on-site caretaker. Don't forget the camera and lunch! Admission is free.

*They say it's not nice to fool Mother Nature...
So we chose not to.*

*Come visit Carolina National Golf Club
and experience Golfing and Nature,
at their finest.*

Carolina National
GOLF CLUB

SIGNATURE COURSE

1-888-200-6455   (910) 755-5200

Golf

More new golf courses sprout up along our southern coast than anywhere else in North Carolina. Brunswick County already boasts nearly 30 facilities, many located in residential golf communities. Courses throughout the southern coastal region receive more accolades, nominations and citations from the national golf press than you can shake a 9-iron at. The area features several world-class course designs bearing the signatures of Tom Fazio, P.B. Dye, Dan Maples, Hale Irwin, George Cobb and Willard Byrd.

Players familiar with the Myrtle Beach area know that our courses offer less crowded and less hurried playing at prices that encourage multiple rounds per day, all year long. PGA and fund-raising tournaments are increasingly finding host clubs locally. And if there's one other essential factor affecting golf in this region, it's the wind — sometimes steady and but often capricious — which makes play along this coast an especially challenging treat.

Most local courses are semiprivate, which means they're open to the public and club memberships are available. Membership, of course, offers various benefits and privileges, such as lower fees or preferred tee times. Greens fees vary according to season and location. At semiprivate courses they range widely, from about $20 to $100 and more, but average between $30 and $40. Fees are highest during the peak months (late March to early May and mid-September to early November) and at the more exclusive clubs. Many courses offer practice ranges.

Overall, the region's courses offer an excellent balance between price and playing conditions. Summer rates and discounts for seniors, corporations and groups are commonplace. Many pro shops at the courses rent clubs.

Below we describe some of the better courses, judged by overall beauty, location and variety of challenges. We've also included a few independent driving ranges throughout the area, retail shops that offer equipment and repairs and come highly recommended by Insiders, information on golf package and services, and local annual tournaments. Complete listings of courses can be found at local chambers of commerce.

Courses

Wilmington

The Cape Golf & Racquet Club
535 The Cape Blvd. • (910) 799-3110

A mile north of Carolina Beach, this semi-private, meticulously landscaped, par 72 championship course sits amid 24 lakes, ponds and marshland. The Bermuda grass fairways comprise 6800 yards, with a 73.5 rating from the blue tees and a slope of 135. Signature double greens grace the 15th and 17th holes.

The grounds include a driving range and putting and chipping greens, as well as a fully stocked pro shop, locker rooms with showers, a cocktail lounge, the full-service Mulligans Pub, banquet facilities and a snack bar. Club members also have access to the Cape's swimming pool and tennis courts. Greens fees range from inexpensive to moderate.

Echo Farms Golf & Country Club
4114 Echo Farms Blvd. • (910) 791-9318

Stands of moss-draped hardwood and some of the finest bentgrass greens in Wilmington distinguish this semiprivate course, designed by Gene Hamm. A former dairy farm (the original farmhouse near the 17th hole is still occupied), it's now a par 72 challenge rated between 69.6 and 72.7, with slopes from 121 to 131. Lakes come into play on nine holes.

A driving range, practice greens, full restaurant, bar and snack lounge are open to all.

The pro shop does regripping. Echo Farms has developed a fine teaching facility, offering clinics and private lessons. The course is 5 miles south of downtown Wilmington on Carolina Beach Road (N.C. Highway 421).

Inland Greens
5945 Inland Greens Dr. • (910) 452-9900

Sharpen your short game ($7 per) on this public par 3 course. Holes average just over 100 yards, and the greens are in good condition. It's strictly a walking course, but pull-carts are available for rent. Almost midway between Wrightsville Beach and downtown Wilmington, the course is hidden off Cardinal Drive between Eastwood Road and Market Street.

Landfall
1550 Landfall Dr. • (910) 256-8411

Golfing on Landfall's two superlative courses, designed by Jack Nicklaus and Pete Dye and situated along the Intracoastal Waterway, is restricted to members (and members' guests) of the exclusive Landfall Club. Membership is available to Landfall property owners and non-owners, and the rewards for golfing members include challenges unparalleled in the majority of area courses.

The par 72 Nicklaus course is perhaps the more forgiving of the two. With a rating of 72.6 and slopes ranging from 120 to 137, it looks easier on paper than it really is, thanks largely to the many carries over marshes and water. The 6th hole, for instance, is a tough par 3 playing 190 yards from the back, with little more than marsh all the way to the green. Hole 17's island green is backed with a bunker with a 5-foot forward lip — aim well!

Another island green is the signature hole on the Dye course. Completely waterbound, the kidney-shaped 11th (135 yards, par 3) slopes away from the sand trap that collars half its perimeter. The Dye course is a par 72 rated at 73.9 from the back (slope: 116-135). Plenty of uneven lies, marshes and pot bunkers demand that players push the envelope of their game to the utmost. Fairways and roughs stay green all year.

Members also have access to Landfall's elaborate sports center, which has 14 tennis courts, a croquet course, an NCAA short-course pool and many indoor facilities.

Porters Neck Plantation and Country Club
1202 Porters Neck Rd. • (910) 686-1177

Porters Neck is an aficionado's course, aesthetically picture-perfect and strategically challenging. Designed by Tom Fazio, this is a championship course (par 72, slope 130) that emphasizes careful club selection and pin placement. Impeccably maintained fairways undulate in sometimes deceptive fashion. Enormous waste bunkers and lakes abound, some of which span from tee to green (holes 11, 13, 14). Distinctive waste mounds planted with native grasses add to the course's character. Each hole presents conditions to make the most accurate golfer uncomfortable, yet leave no player unfulfilled.

About 6 miles from Wilmington, this course winds through a private residential development on the Intracoastal Waterway. Greens fees are at the high end of the local scale. Public play is invited but limited. The pro shop offers a few services such as regripping. The entrance gate is a little over a mile in from the property limit on Porters Neck Road.

Wilmington Golf Course
311 Wallace Ave. • (910) 791-0558

Relatively flat and among the more populated courses, the "Muni" features a practice fairway left of the 9th hole. Enter this par 71 facility from either Oleander Drive or Pine Grove Drive, a seven-minute drive from downtown. Compared to other local courses, the Muni has a relative dearth of water hazards, but the stream crossing the fairways of holes 2 (495 yards, par 5) and 12 (519 yards, par 5) is in just the wrong place for many golfers. The clubhouse and pro shop are open every day from 7 AM until sundown.

The clubhouse has showers and lockers in the men's room only. Greens fees are about the cheapest you'll find, especially for city resi-

The Cape Golf & Racquet Club has a proud history...which includes hosting two past U.S. Golf Tours. Our Gene Hamm designed course offers visitors a challenging and unique golf experience. Numerous vistas provide spectacular views of our par 72 course which include 24 lakes, ponds, coastal terrain and natural surroundings.

The Cape
GOLF & RACQUET CLUB

535 The Cape Blvd.
Highway 421 South
Wilmington NC. 28412
Pro Shop 910-799-3110
Group Outings 800-291-9847

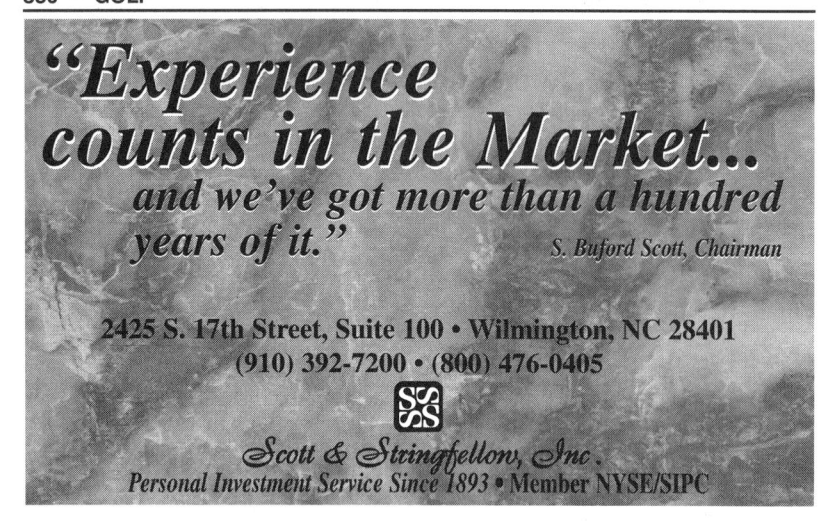

> "Experience counts in the Market...
> and we've got more than a hundred years of it."
>
> S. Buford Scott, Chairman
>
> 2425 S. 17th Street, Suite 100 • Wilmington, NC 28401
> (910) 392-7200 • (800) 476-0405
>
> *Scott & Stringfellow, Inc.*
> Personal Investment Service Since 1893 • Member NYSE/SIPC

dents, and nine-hole rounds are available. Groups are limited to fours, and no onesomes or twosomes are permitted before 1:30 PM.

Outside Wilmington

River Landing Country Club
116 Paddle Wheel Dr., Wallace
• **(910) 285-6693, (800) 959-3096**

Rated one of the best public courses in the state by *North Carolina* magazine in 1998, River Landing combines artful landscape design and horticultural diversity with a variety of challenges from its four sets of tees. Slope-rated at 135 from the popular blue tees, the Clyde Johnston-designed course totals 7000 yards from the back, with mixed elevations and carries over a variety of water hazards, including creeks, ponds and a river.

The 6th hole hugs the banks of the northeast Cape Fear River (and requires a carry over it, too), while the 9th features par-resistant ravines. The signature 18th is a 402-yard, par 4 (from the blue) with a multi-tiered green; it's a dogleg left sloping downhill that dares you to avoid the ball-hungry bunker on the right. The elegant brick bridge there is one of many aesthetic delights. Also featured are a driving range, putting greens, and snack bar.

River Landing is a tranquil, semiprivate course (play is open to club members and the public) in a golf community about 35 minutes north of Wilmington. The management welcomes corporate outings, group functions and fund-raisers. To get there from Wilmington, drive north on I-40 to exit 385, NC 41 East. Paddle Wheel Drive is a quarter-mile ahead on the right.

Carolina Beach

Beau Rivage Plantation Golf & Country Club
6230 Carolina Beach Rd.
• **(910) 392-9022, (800) 628-7080**

Elevations up to 72 feet and scads of bunkers (including two waste bunkers) place this course among the more dramatically landscaped in New Hanover County. It is a semi-private par 72 course (slope: 114-136) in which water hazards come into play on eight holes. Hole 4 (206 yards, par 3) is notable for its island tee box for women and a carry that is entirely over water. Its well-watered bentgrass green is protected on three sides.

A bar and grill and restaurant provide attractive settings for post-round analysis. Beau Rivage is a residential development, but club memberships are available to nonresidents. A 32-suite hotel adjoins the clubhouse.

A NEW LANDMARK IN NORTH CAROLINA GOLF

RIVER LANDING
A Clyde Johnston Course

CALL FOR TEE TIMES
OR GROUP OUTINGS
1-800-959-3096
910-285-6693

LOCATED IN WALLACE. I-40 EXIT 385. HWY 41 E. 1/4 MILE ON RIGHT.
Visit our Web Site: www.riverlanding.com

Bald Head Island

Bald Head Island Club
Bald Head Island • (910) 457-7310, (800) 234-1666

Extremely demanding, due as much to the ocean wind as to the late George Cobb's brilliant design, this par 72 course is among the scenic gems on the East Coast. Exposed greens on its ocean side contrast sharply with interior holes lined with palms and maritime forest, separated from fairways with virtually no playable rough. Four sets of tees yield course lengths up to 7040 yards. The finishing holes run alongside the ocean. The club currently hosts its own pro-am tournament, to which spectators are welcome.

Bald Head Island is accessible only by ferry or private yacht, and tee times are required. A driving range and snack bar are available. Golf Getaway packages can be arranged year-round by calling (800) 432-RENT. A Day Golf Package includes parking, ferry, transfers, cart and greens fee for 18 holes.

Southport-Oak Island

Carolina National Golf Links at Winding River Plantation
1643 Goley Hewett Rd., Bolivia
• **(910) 755-5200**

Within sight of the Lockwood Folly River, this brand-new course, Fred Couples' first North Carolina design, is full of dramatic elevations and bunkering nestled amid forest, scrub and wetland. Five holes feature waste bunkers. The signature hole, number 14 (205-yard, par 3) features an island green set in the middle of the marsh — not the kind of place you'd want to retrieve a ball from. The toughest hole is probably the 16th, with its right-hand approach to the green heavily fortified by timber and sand.

This is a course of great beauty — one among a handful of courses certified by the Audubon Society for the designers' efforts to leave wetland habitat undisturbed — and a course of admirable challenge as well.

The elegant, gabled clubhouse, planned

INSIDERS' TIP

If you're still on the course when lightning threatens, remove your spiked golf shoes and get rid of your umbrella, even if it has a fiberglass shaft.

GOOD CHEER FOR OVER A QUARTER CENTURY

Experience Echo Farms... recent course redesign in the Scottish tradition by European golf architect Ian Scott Taylor offers a new challenge to golfers of all skill levels. Plus you will enjoy the best in casual Club fare and good cheer among friends in the Restaurant and Roost. New ownership offers a commitment to excellence and friendly customer service. We are open to the public and invite you to stop by.

GOLF • RESTAURANT • BANQUETS

Tee Times: **910-791-9318**

MEMBERSHIP INFORMATION: 910-799-0324

Call for Tee Times
910-799-0324

ECHO FARMS
Golf & Country Club

ALL FACILITIES OPEN TO PUBLIC

4114 ECHO FARMS BOULEVARD • WILMINGTON, NORTH CAROLINA
OWNED AND OPERATED BY MATRIX HOSPITALITY
HOME OF THE NGA HOOTERS PRO TOUR

---

for fall 1998 completion, will house the pro shop and offer a wide view of the surroundings from its high veranda, a great place to relax after a round with a drink or meal from the grill. You'll find the course off Zion Hill Road, about 2.5 miles east of St. James Plantation along N.C. 211 (Southport-Supply Road).

The Gauntlet Golf Club
N.C. Hwy. 211, Southport
• **(910) 253-3008, (800) 247-4806**

With a championship slope of 142, it's no wonder designer P.B. Dye called this "My most challenging course yet." Its carries over many water hazards have been described as heroic, while its multilevel fairways, bulkheads

The first Golf Community in the South Brunswick Islands!

- 18 hole par 72 course
- Fully stocked Pro Shop
- Blue Heron Bar & Grill
- Semi-private
- Pro Shop - (910) 754-4660
- Tee times required
- Real Estate Info - (910) 754-7077

BRIERWOOD GOLF CLUB

Route 179 at Shallotte City Limits

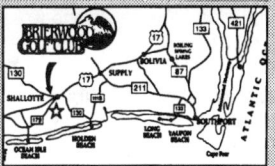

---

and variety of grasses are stamped with the Dye hallmark. The final three holes, which include the No. 1 handicap (the 9th), play into and over a series of marshes and lakes for a spectacular finish. Five sets of tees present a variety of plays. Most tee boxes are elevated. The Gauntlet and its new companion course, the Members Club (see below), are 4 miles outside Southport and offer fine views of the Intracoastal Waterway. Caddies, a complete practice facility and lessons are available. A restaurant and lounge are close by.

The Members Club at St. James Plantation
N.C. Hwy. 211, Southport
• (910) 253-9500, (800) 474-9277

New in 1996, this Hale Irwin-designed par 72 course utilizes the natural lay of the land to good effect, forgoing flashy, amusement-park landscaping. The course has been called user-friendly (73.5 slope from the back), although its proximity to the Intracoastal Waterway means winds that can prove deeply trying. Watch out for the 15th hole, a par 5 with lateral water hazards squeezing the fairway into a bottleneck about 200 yards down, and more water in front of the green — potentially an express ticket to bogeyland.

The entire facility has all the amenities of the most exclusive clubs, such as practice greens and sand traps, a driving range, and on-site professionals. The Members Club invites nonmembers to be "members for a day."

Oak Island Golf & Country Club
928 Caswell Beach Rd., Caswell Beach
• (910) 278-5275, (800) 278-5275

One of Brunswick County's vintage courses, this George Cobb creation is home to the Southport-Oak Island Masters Putting Tournament. It is a forgiving course, 6608-yard par 72, that can be enjoyed by players of varying skills. Its wide bermuda grass fairways are relatively short, lined with live oaks and tall pines, and not overly fortified with water hazards. But that ocean wind!

The clubhouse is less than 200 yards from the Atlantic, and sea breezes can frustrate the best players. Hole 9 may send you to Duffers Restaurant and Lounge early. Even so, the bermuda grass greens, driving range, putting green and swimming pool make this course quite popular.

South Brunswick Islands

Lockwood Golf Links
19 Clubhouse Dr., Holden Beach
• (910) 842-5666, (800) 537-9043

This is a classic Willard Byrd-designed par 72 course. Beautifully set at the confluence of Lockwood Folly River and the Intracoastal Waterway, it has no parallel fairways. Undulating, sloping greens are protected by ample clear ponds, particularly at the 11th hole (best approached from below). The unique "beaches" of oyster shells lining some water hazards make for handsome landscaping but difficult sighting of white balls and potentially frustrating wedge work.

Amenities include a restaurant and lounge, driving range, putting green and pro shop. Lockwood plays host to the Carolina's PGA Seniors Pro-Am Golf Tournament each November and the Cheerwine College Tournament in June.

Brierwood Golf Club
27 Brierwood Rd., Shallotte
- **(910) 754-4660, (910) 754-7076**

Brierwood was the first golf community built along the South Brunswick Islands. Located about 7 miles north of Ocean Isle Beach, it is a player-friendly, par 72, championship course (slope 129) distinguished by plenty of freshwater obstacles and surrounded by residential properties. Fourteen holes present water hazards, including part of a 3-acre lake that traverses the 10th fairway.

The clubhouse includes a pro shop and the Blue Heron Bar & Grill, with its superb outdoor balcony seating above a lake. Calls for tee times are received 24 hours a day. The entrance to this semiprivate course is just off N.C. Highway 179 at the Shallotte town limit.

Brick Landing Plantation
N.C. Hwy. 179, Ocean Isle Beach
- **(910) 754-5545, (800) 438-3006**

With 41 sand traps and 12 water holes, this handsome waterfront course was rated by *Florida Golf Week* magazine as among the top 50 distinctive golf courses in the Southeast. The Brick's fairways wind among freshwater lakes and through salt marshes, offering striking visual contrasts and championship challenges. The 17th hole finishes dramatically along the Intracoastal Waterway. Total course length is 6943 yards, a par 72 rated at 72.1. Amenities include a snack bar, lunch and cocktail lounge and practice facilities. Instruction is available, as well as tennis and family vacation packages and memberships.

Oyster Bay Golf Links
N.C. Hwy. 179, Sunset Beach
- **(910) 579-3528, (800) 697-8372**

The signature hole (17th, par 3) is one of two island greens that are sure to push you to excel. This is an exceedingly challenging and imaginative public course (par 70, slope 134, rating 71.6), featuring stark elevations, deadly lakes and even a few trees smack in the middle of some fairways. Oyster Bay is one of the area's two Legends courses. It was voted Resort Course of the Year (1983) and among the top 50 public courses in the country (1990) by *Golf Digest*. The notorious 3rd hole (460 yards, par 4) presents the course's toughest two greens — one is designated daily.

As with other Legends courses, Oyster Bay features computerized golf carts that tell you precise distances to greens from where the cart stands. Each cart is also equipped with club and ball cleaner, a cooler and ice; beverage carts roam the course. The management enforces a dress code, and fees tend toward the medium-to-high.

Sea Trail Golf Resort & Conference Center
211 Clubhouse Rd., Sunset Beach
- **(910) 287-1100, (800) 624-6601**

With its three par 72 courses and overnight accommodations, Sea Trail is an all-out golf resort known locally for its attractive balance of price, friendliness and outstanding playing conditions. Located about a mile from the beach, Sea Trail has its share of wind and water and three sets of tees on each course: the Dan Maples (slope: 129), Rees Jones (132) and Willard Byrd (128). Maples' 17th hole (190 yards, par 3) is the signature hole, with its scenic appeal, a large oak tree blocking the right-hand approach and deep bunkers.

A restaurant (at the Maples clubhouse), two lounges and many meeting facilities add to Sea Trail's appeal. Two clubs, one for members and one for resort guests, offer tennis and swimming.

Calabash Golf Links
820 Thomasboro Rd., Calabash
- **(910) 575-5000, (800) 841-5971**

New in 1996, this par 72 course features

Best Kept Secret In Wilmington

INLAND GREENS

5945 Inland Greens Dr.

18 Hole Regulation Par 3 Golf Course
For All Ages and Skill Levels
Group & Business Outings Available

JAMESBURG
FARMS
MANAGEMENT
GROUP

Call 452-9900
visit our Web site at:
www.jamesburg-farms.com

---

large greens, soft doglegs and some lateral water hazards, but no over-water carries. Fairways are lined mostly with saplings. Greens fees are on the low end of average. Designed by Willard Byrd, the course offers four tee positions, few substantial elevations and an overall slope of 128.

Carolina Shores Golf & Country Club
99 Carolina Shores Dr., Calabash
• **(910) 579-2181, (800) 762-8813**

This par 72 Tom Jackson creation, built in 1974, will reward even moderately careful golfers with better-than-usual games without killing themselves, so it tends to be popular. With a slope of 128 from the back, it's an attractive, traditional, well-bunkered course set within a residential community. There are four par 5 holes (1, 7, 13, 18), and the 570-yard 18th, crowded with traps, is appropriately named The Last Mile. You'll find the clubhouse off Country Club Road.

Marsh Harbor Golf Links
N.C. Hwy. 179, Calabash
• **(910) 579-3161, (800) 552-2660**

It wouldn't be enough to describe Marsh Harbor as the course with the toughest hole on the southern coast (according to a formal survey). Although the par 5 17th certainly is redoubtable, this championship par 71 Dan Maples creation is better known as one of the most lavishly beautiful courses on the Brunswick coast. It's among *Golf Digest*'s top 50 public courses in America. The design em-

---

INSIDERS' TIP

Watch the clock when traveling to and from Wrightsville Beach. The drawbridge rises on the hour and can substantially delay summertime traffic.

phasizes shot-making and trickiness, yielding a blue tee rating of 73.3 (slope 134).

Holes tend to be short and tight off the tees. Greens are well-bunkered, perhaps to compensate for the relative lack of water hazards. Five fairways are marsh-bound. There are some excellent par 3s, and players with single-digit handicaps will be formidably challenged. The much-touted 17th hole (570 yards from the back) demands two virtuoso carries over marshes before reaching the well-protected green. Greens fees lie at the medium-to-high end of the local average.

A Legends course, Marsh Harbor's upscale character is also evident in the well-stocked pro shop, roving beverage carts and computerized golf carts complete with club-and-ball cleaners, coolers and ice. Management enforces a dress code.

The Pearl Golf Links
N.C. Hwy. 179, Calabash
• (910) 579-8132

These two par 72 courses, east and west, will have you wanting to play 36 straight, so start early. Architect Dan Maples endowed these links with theatrical bentgrass island greens, washboard fairways and solid challenges that yield ratings of 73.1 (east) and 73.2 (west). Course lengths are on the long side (6895 east, 7011 west), so break out the lumber and let 'er rip. A pro shop, snack bar, cocktail lounge and driving range are open year-round.

Topsail Island

Belvedere Plantation Golf & Country Club
2368 Country Club Dr., Hampstead
• (910) 270-2703

Developed in 1975 and designed by Russell Burney, Belvedere is a narrow par 71 with plenty of water and small greens. Hole 3 (180 yards, par 3) stands out for its carry over water to an elevated green. This is a busy course, with affordable greens fees and discounts for residents of local counties. The clubhouse has a limited pro shop.

Although part of a golf community, Belvedere offers club memberships to nonresidents as well. Golf schools lasting three to four days are available, with overnight accommodations. Belvedere is less than a mile from Topsail Greens Country Club (see below), about 18 miles north of Wilmington off U.S. Highway 17 N.

Olde Point Golf and Country Club
U.S. Hwy. 17 N., Hampstead
• (910) 270-2403

The 11th hole here has been called Jezebel for its wicked ways. Considered one of the two toughest holes on all the southern coast by many area pros and amateurs (the other being the 17th at Marsh Harbor in Calabash), this long, narrow 589-yard par 5 is a gradual dogleg right that slopes laterally downward to the right into the woods and consistently defies players' depth perception. The course is buffeted by winds almost year-round, especially at the second hole (372 yards, par 3), where the wind is usually in your face and the bunkered green is surrounded on three sides by water. Olde Point is among the finer challenges in the area.

Topsail Greens Golf and Country Club
19774 U.S. Hwy. 17 N., Hampstead
• (910) 270-2883

Although its overall length is not particularly daunting, this semiprivate par 71 course presents respectable challenges and several birdie opportunities to blue tee players. Five holes require sizable carries over water and two others have water beside the fairways. Greens are mostly elevated. The 8th is the signature hole, a 159-yard par 3 played to an island green protected on both forward flanks by sand traps. The course is laid out on a roughly east-west axis, and hole 14 is about 200 yards from the Intracoastal Waterway.

The club is located about 18 miles outside

INSIDERS' TIP

Save your score cards! And be sure to ask about duffers' discounts when dining out along our "golf coast."

North Carolina's Southern coast offers a wide variety of golfing opportunities.

Wilmington. Greens fees are on the low end of average, making the course popular yet not overrun. The annual benefit Kool Aid Golf Tournament is played here in mid-December.

North Shore Country Club
N.C. Hwy. 210, Sneads Ferry
• **(910) 327-2410, (800) 828-5035**

Notorious for its long carries over water, North Shore is among the best-conditioned courses in the Topsail Island area. With a championship slope of 137, it is also among the most challenging. Not very long ago it was rated among the top 20 new courses of the decade by *Golf Reporter* magazine. It is also quite affordable. The fairways are fraught with extensive mounding, tall pines and menacing waters. Occasionally, strong sea breezes will greet you as you step up to the elevated tee boxes. The 9th hole (412 yards, par 4) is memorable for its required 250-yard tee shot — anything less is in the drink.

North Shore is on the mainland side of the North Topsail Beach bridge. Late-day discounts are available. The club hosts two annual tournaments: the Stump Sound Rotary Golf Tournament in May and the Kiwanis Loggerhead Golf Tournament in October. Preregistration opens about one month prior to each. Call for further information.

Driving Ranges

Wilmington

Coastal Golf Center and Carolina Custom Discount Golf
6987 Market St. • **(910) 791-9010**

More than a driving range, Coastal is a superior one-stop facility for practicing, instruction, equipment and repairs. Stations on the lighted 257-yard driving range feature well-kept grass mats and tees. Three PGA instructors are on staff, and the pro shop offers all repair services, including shafting, refinishing and customizing.

Located 4 miles outside Wilmington on U.S. 17 (Market Street) near the intersection with Military Cutoff Road, Coastal is one of five affiliated stores based in Raleigh. It's open Monday through Saturday during the summer; hours are somewhat curtailed throughout the rest of the year.

Oleander Golf and Family Center
5026 Oleander Dr. • (910) 791-7155

This lighted facility offers an undulating grassy field with raised greens, complete with flags, to imitate course conditions. Stations are grass only (no fixed tees) and include club stands. Club repair and PGA lessons can be arranged on site. Oleander is open year-round, seven days a week in the summer.

Valley Golf Center & Driving Range
4416 S. College Rd. • (910) 395-2750

Convenient to Carolina Beach and Wilmington, this large range has 40 lighted tee stations plus mats and a grass hitting area as well as sand trap areas. A covered hitting area allows practice during inclement weather. The fully stocked pro shop offers repairs, accessories and instruction with PGA staff professionals. The center, which is just north of Monkey Junction, is open every day year-round.

Southport-Oak Island and South Brunswick Islands

Oak Island Sports Center
4836 Long Beach Rd. (Hwy 133), Southport • (910) 457-5105

With 40 mats and 40 grass tees, this is among the largest driving ranges in the area. Amenities include a pro shop, lessons and clinics, and a miniature golf course. The range stays open until 7 PM from March 1 through October.

Holden Beach Driving Range
N.C. Hwy. 130, Holden Beach
• (910) 842-3717

This lighted practice facility offers lessons by Class-A PGA professionals, a small pro shop and, as any good resort-area attraction should, batting cages next door. A unique feature is that when unattended by staff, the range operates on the honor system. Instructions for payment are posted beside the ball baskets.

Pro Tee Practice Range
N.C. Hwy. 179, Ocean Isle Beach
• (910) 754-4700

Two 18-station tee areas flank a mat area with rubber tees, all fully lighted. The pro shop stocks basic accessories, refreshments and snacks, and the management performs minor equipment repairs. Pro Tee is a half-mile west of the Brick Landing Plantation Golf Course and is open daily during the summer.

Equipment and Repairs

Nevada Bob's
5629 Oleander Dr., Wilmington
• (910) 799-4212

Nevada Bob's is a chain store that boasts a broad selection of new equipment and accessories and a knowledgeable staff. It has the air of a connoisseur's shop, right down to the indoor netted tee station on which to test clubs. There is also an artificial indoor putting green. Nevada Bob's is in the Bradley Square shopping center on the westbound side of Oleander. The store is open seven days a week.

Pro Golf Discount
914 S. Kerr Ave., Wilmington
• (910) 392-9405

Affiliated with the nationwide Pro Golf chain, this shop stocks a complete line of major brand equipment and accessories, including "experienced" golf balls and rental clubs. It maintain a full club repair department, and regripping and customizing of metal clubs are done on the premises (woods are sent out). The store is attractively designed and includes a carpeted putting area. You will find Pro Golf a few doors south of the Wilshire Boulevard intersection, and it's open Monday through Saturday.

Tee Smith Custom Golf Clubs
1047 S. Kerr Ave., Wilmington
• (910) 395-4008

Tee Smith has been customizing and repairing clubs commercially since 1975 and carries the approval of pro shops throughout the area. Simple repairs often have a one-day turnaround. The shop carries a full line of top-name brands and is open all year Monday through Saturday.

Golf Tech
6408 Beach Dr. (N.C. Hwy. 179), Ocean Isle Beach • (910) 579-3446

Keith Steagall's method of custom club design, which promises "lower scores through advanced club technology," is coming into increasing demand in several states. Keith builds and fits clubs and performs all kinds of repairs. His full-line pro shop carries major brands, including Harvey Penick and Golfsmith. Golf Tech also stocks used balls and rental clubs. The shop is open from 8 AM to 6 PM Monday through Saturday most of the year.

Packages and Services

Most travel agencies and local hotels arrange golf packages. Some people prefer central reservations services for the convenience and discounted rates.

3D Golf Vacations, (800) 377-2985, offers two all-inclusive packages, premier and regular, as part of either a "fly-drive" or "drive-in" program. Packages include play at the more exclusive courses in southeastern North Carolina and representatives who escort you to your destination upon arrival in the area. The mailing address is P.O. Box 4874, Calabash, NC 28467.

Hobbs Realty, (800) 655-3367, books golf packages and tee times at prime courses throughout our coverage area at competitive rates.

The American Lung Association Golf Privilege Card offers discounts for one year on more than 135 rounds of golf at 123 courses throughout North Carolina. There's unlimited play on four courses within the range of this guide, plus hundreds more rounds in Virginia and South Carolina — nearly 300 courses in all, including nine in nearby Myrtle Beach. The card costs $40; buy three and get one free. Some restrictions apply. Contact the American Lung Association of North Carolina, Southeast Area, P.O. Box 40236, Fayetteville, NC 28309, or call (910) 486-5864 or (800) 821-6205.

Brunswick County Parks and Recreation, (910) 253-4357 or (800) 222-4790, sponsors a youth golf program affiliated with the national Hook A Kid On Golf program. Registration is limited, so inquire in April about the upcoming season, which runs from June through August.

Coastal Golfaway, (910) 791-8494 or (800) 791-8497, books customized packages in all price ranges, from Wilmington to Hilton Head, South Carolina.

Tee-Times Inc., (910) 256-8043 or (800) 447-0450, is a Wilmington-based service that can arrange everything for your golf vacation: tee times, accommodations, airline tickets and rental cars.

Twin Travel & Cruises, (910) 799-5225 or (800) 365-8003, offers complete golf packages for more than 80 courses from the greater Wilmington area south to Pawley's Island, South Carolina. It can handle everything from air fare and accommodations to tee times, restaurants, group outings, golf clinics, meetings and conventions.

The Wilmington Golf Association, (910) 256-2251 or (800) 545-5494, disseminates information on, and accepts reservations for, packages provided by the area's leading courses and hotels.

For more information on golfing in North and South Carolina, pick up a copy of *The Insiders' Guide® to Golf in the Carolinas*.

Annual Tournaments

The annual American Cancer Society Tournament, played in August, pits four men or women per team in a scramble. Winners are eligible to compete in the state championship

---

INSIDERS' TIP

Check various visitors' guides, available at local chambers of commerce, for discount golf coupon offers.

340 • GOLF

If you're golfing on a crowded course, you're not on North Carolina's Southern coast.

tournament in early autumn. The tournament is played each year at one of three courses in the Topsail-Hampstead area (north of Wilmington): Topsail Greens, Belvedere or Olde Point. Call one of those courses (listed above) for information.

The Kool Aid Golf Tournament in mid-December is a team event that brings together golfers, veterans and lovers of "golden oldies" rock 'n' roll. It is played at Topsail Greens Golf Club in Hampstead. Prizes for the three top-placing teams may include free golf packages and concert tickets. The tournament is handicapped to level the field. Teams of four may register for $180 and individuals for $45. Registration includes lunch and beverages. For information, call (910) 488-1133 or contact the Topsail Area Chamber of Commerce, 205 S. Topsail Drive, Surf City, NC 28445, (910) 328-4722 or (800) 626-2780.

North Shore Country Club, N.C. Highway 210, Sneads Ferry, (910) 327-2410 or (800) 828-5035, hosts two annual tournaments: the Stump Sound Rotary Golf Tournament in May and the Kiwanis Loggerhead Golf Tournament in early October. Preregistration opens about one month prior.

Welcome to Brunswick County, *Our* Home

Whether you are buying your first home, building a vacation home or purchasing investment property, our loan professionals will make sure you get the best loan to meet your needs.

We also offer a full array of checking and savings accounts and competitive rates on our certificates of deposit.

So, don't make a move without checking with us.
Call 1-800-457-7438 and let us help you become a permanent member of our community.

The Community Bank in Brunswick County Since 1911.

SECURITY SAVINGS BANK

Southport • Shallotte • Oak Island • Leland • Calabash

Member FDIC

Real Estate

Real estate is one of the biggest businesses in the southern coastal region and for good reason: This is a great place to live. The climate, the amenities of North Carolina's largest coastal city within an hour's drive of all beaches, a thriving university, unlimited shopping and dining, first-rate medical services, attractions, historical sites, varied recreational opportunities, and beautiful coastal scenery conspire to lure newcomers and maintain a lifelong hold on residents.

With the population booming in the 1990s, it is no surprise that the cost of real estate has escalated considerably. Since the entire region from Topsail Island to Sunset Beach hugs the shore, land is limited to an approximately 180-degree angle. Naturally, the closer a property is to the water, the higher the price. Local real estate company representatives report that as of 1997 it was very hard to find a desirable half-acre piece of land in any location for less than $60,000. Prime lots can go for as little as $150,000 and as high as $2 million in some sites on or near the water.

Prospective home or land buyers who thought the problems caused by two hurricanes in 1996 would drive down prices will discover this is not the case at all. In fact, the opposite is true. The damage has been repaired and, frankly, the upgrades have only made the beach communities more appealing.

Housing is still remarkably affordable throughout the Cape Fear region compared to some more affluent parts of the country. There is also tremendous diversity in terms of neighborhoods, housing styles, scenery and price. There are smaller, new homes for as low as $80,000; there are truly vintage homes in need of repair for even less. At the top end, one may spend well into the millions for a fine new home in an upscale neighborhood, but $175,000 to $200,000 will buy a nice home in a number of fine neighborhoods.

It would be impossible in this guide to write about every neighborhood because, even as we go to press, new neighborhoods are sprouting in the area. What follows is information about established neighborhoods, average prices and other general facts. For specific information, contact an area Realtor (a partial list of agencies is included in this chapter) or visit the sales office of a community that appeals to you.

Neighborhoods

Downtown Wilmington

It has been said by many a native that downtown Wilmington is a separate place from the rest of the city and New Hanover County. The tone is absolutely different from any other neighborhood in the region. If you appreciate being at the crossroads of the community, downtown is the place for you. If you are looking for history and charm as well as an energetic and culturally/socially inspirational atmosphere, downtown is definitely the place to be. It's lively, warm and relentlessly interesting.

Many of the homes date from the mid- to late-1800s and the first quarter of the 20th century. There are stunning examples of Victorian, Italianate, Renaissance, Neoclassical and Revivalist architecture. Homes in the area — small cottages and large mansions alike — feature high ceilings, hardwood floors, fascinating detail, front porches and all of the interesting characteristics one would expect of vintage homes.

The population is as eclectic as the architecture. Downtown is a very interesting melting pot of natives and newcomers. What the entire neighborhood seems to have in common is a mutual appreciation for the particular amenities of downtown: easy accessibility to

Two To Six Acre Private Estates

WhiteBridge offers the best of everything in its recreation facilities, surroundings and its distinguished quality homes. And just as important, it has an atmosphere that appeals to those rare people who expect a level of personal privacy within a protected community and have the ability to obtain it.

Discover uncommon choices in residential living at WhiteBridge. Expertly developed estate sites, from two to six acres, provide a lush backdrop for distinguished homes. At WhitBridge, lifestyle choices are diverse. Homesites overlook elegant ponds, pristine meadows or are tucked into hardwood forests.

- Only 75 lots on 300 acres of land, with finished homes also available.
- A neighborhood protected by architectural controls and restrictions without confining your lifestyle. Privacy with social amenities including swimming pool with outdoor pavilion, tennis courts, miles of natural trails and a 20-acre bird sanctuary
- Custom homes by WhiteBridge Construction available.
- Homes on estate-sized lots from the 300's.

WHITEBRIDGE

The Alternative To Heavily Restricted Half-Acre Living
Located on Hwy. 17, just 11 minutes North of Wilmington
For more information, stop by or write: P.O. Box 963, Hampstead, NC 28443
(919) 270-2000 • (800) 480-2007
WILCOX & WILCOX BUILDERS/DEVELOPERS
BROKERS PROTECTED

Tee Time ~ Anytime

Cypress Island
GOLF AND RAQUET CLUB

Developed and Marketed by:
**Cypress Green, Inc.
(910) 790-8010**

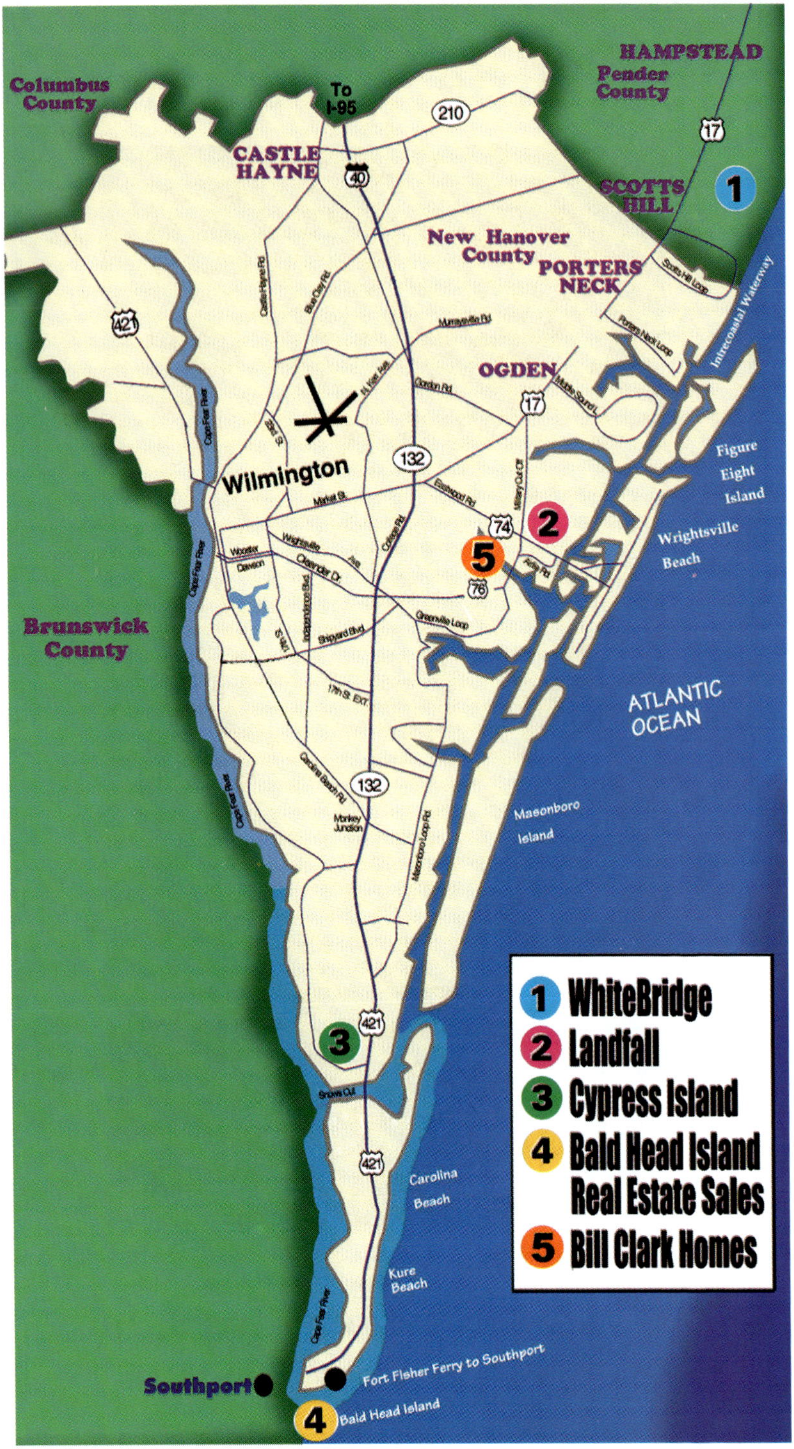

Columbus County
To I-95
210
CASTLE HAYNE
40
HAMPSTEAD
Pender County
17
SCOTTS HILL
1
New Hanover County
PORTERS NECK
421
OGDEN
17
Wilmington
132
74
2
5
76
Figure Eight Island
Wrightsville Beach
Intracoastal Waterway
Brunswick County
ATLANTIC OCEAN
132
Masonboro Island
421
3
421
Carolina Beach
Kure Beach
Southport
Fort Fisher Ferry to Southport
4
Bald Head Island
1 WhiteBridge
2 Landfall
3 Cypress Island
4 Bald Head Island Real Estate Sales
5 Bill Clark Homes

REAL ESTATE

Moving to Wilmington?
Have a trained & experienced *Buyer's Agent* work for you!

HARBOUR TOWN ASSOCIATES Real Estate

Harbour Town Associates
7040 Wrightsville Ave. Suite 101
Wilmington, NC 28403

Bob Jamieson, ABR, GRI
Accredited Buyer Representative
(910) 313-1307
email:egscrow@aol.com

---

cultural arts opportunities, fine dining, friendly shopping, city and county government centers, a beautiful riverfront for strolling, and a strong sense of community identity.

Relatively few homes come on the market in the more established center of the neighborhood, and the ones that do aren't available for long unless they are very large and, therefore, quite expensive. Larger homes in the district are fetching upwards of $400,000. Small cottages can command $175,000.

Within the Historic District proper, most homes have been restored, but there are still handyman bargains to be had in the areas outside of the district in the Historic Overlay. It takes a person with vision and to redo some of the deteriorated architectural gems in these neighborhoods. The level of downtown neighborhood restoration is most stable at the river and diminishes as you head east toward the ocean at about 8th Street.

The residential neighborhoods to the north of Market Street are generating high interest at this time and are seeing quality restoration

---

Home Sweet Home.
We can build your home from our plans or your plans
- Residential Builder
- General Contractor

For more information and free estimates please call 910-452-1058
E-Mail: vasqz@coastalnet.com

JJR Builders and Renovators, N.C., L.L.C.

N.C. License #36747 with offices in Long Island, NY and Wilmington, NC

The Business Location That Does The Most For Your Business.

Landfall Executive Suites, next-door to the prestigious Landfall community and just minutes from 1-40, offers a truly innovative office alternative to traditional business environments.

Whether you are an entrepreneur beginning a new business, or a national company requiring a regional presence, Landfall Executive Suites can accommodate the most discriminating tenant.

Landfall Executive Suites provides professionalism and flexibility without the expensive overhead of furnishing, staffing and maintaining your own office. It's the business location that does the most for your business.

Call (910) 256-1900 to arrange a tour and to receive our full-color brochure.

Landfall Executive Suites
1213 Culbreth Drive, Wilmington, N.C. 28405
(800) 647-9119 • (910) 256-1900

MEMBER EXECUTIVE SUITE ASSOCIATION

---

efforts. The North 4th Street Business District Project, a renewal effort supported in part by the City of Wilmington, business owners and residents along this corridor, promises to open new options to people who want to live downtown. To the south, the natural boundary of the neighborhood is the Cape Fear Memorial Bridge. Quality restorative development has taken place on South 2nd, Queen and Castle streets.

The general downtown real estate market consists of single-family homes. There are also a few condominium or duplex developments and some opportunities to have a rental apartment within one's own home. Also, if the notion of living over a storefront or in a urban, loft-type space has appeal, ask your Realtor to show you buildings in the downtown commercial district.

Some solidly rediscovered older neighborhoods beyond downtown are the Mansion District and nearby Carolina Heights and Carolina Place. Both flank Market Street beyond 15th Street. These neighborhoods date from the 1920s, and architectural styles vary. In the Mansion District you can certainly purchase a mansion-style home, but there are also appealing cottages. In Carolina Heights and Carolina Place you'll find bungalows priced in the low $70,000s. Yes, homes at this price need some fix-up, but this neighborhood has become the new magnet for urban pioneers in search of an investment payoff.

Carolina Heights and Carolina Place begin roughly at 17th Street and continues to 23rd Street. It is widely regarded as the new frontier for not only residential investors but also homeowners, largely thanks to its rela-

INSIDERS' TIP

Go see the home you're considering buying right after a big rain to make sure flooding isn't a problem.

tively new status as an Historic Registry District. It also is comfortably close to venerable Forest Hills.

Wilmington and New Hanover County

Suburbs

Forest Hills is, without dispute, a fine address. This large and very stable neighborhood was once a suburb of downtown. Today it is a conveniently located neighborhood of older homes that date from as early as the 1920s. Well-maintained lawns, large setbacks, quietness, alleys for backyard access and trash pickup, and gorgeous live oaks are the hallmarks of this neighborhood. There are ambling canopied lanes and lots of southern shade.

You'll find relatively few resales in this neighborhood. There is diversity in square footage and architectural style, so there is diversity in price. You may find a home for as low as $150,000 or you could spend more than a half-million. An attractive feature of this neighborhood is its proximity to shopping and services. It is minutes from the largest mall in the region.

Pine Valley, near S. College Road around Longleaf Mall, is about three decades old as a development. It has attracted many Wilmingtonians to its quiet, pine tree-dotted blocks. A nearby golf course and clubhouse are easily accessible to people who want to live in a stable neighborhood that isn't necessarily exclusive in terms of price. Homes, largely brick ranches, range from $120,000 to more than $300,000.

Intracoastal Waterway Communities

Mainland

On the mainland side of the ICW from Wrightsville Beach is the planned community of Landfall, 1801 Eastwood Road, (910) 256-6111. This gated community offers a pristine environment of immaculate lawns, beautiful homes, three clubhouses, private golf courses designed by Jack Nicklaus and Pete Dye, a

NEW HOME · MARKETPLACE

The Area's Only Full Service Realtors

Specializing in New, Newer and Newly Renovated Homes.

Exclusive Agents for the Area's Finest Builders & Developers

NEW HOME · MARKETPLACE

email: newhome@wilmington.net

3501 Market St.
Wilmington, NC 28403

251-2288
800-200-2466
Fax:(910)-251-2299

WELCOME SERVICE OF WILMINGTON

FREE!!!
Welcome & Referral Service for Newcomers

We'll bring you:
Gift Package, Map, & Information
from some of the best business and
professional people in Wilmington!

Special family & retiree packets available.

Nancy Wilcox, owner
910-793-0950

Island Appliance

- We sell to Builders
- Factory Authorized Service

KitchenAid • Whirlpool • JENN-AIR • Amana

Main Showroom
5946 Carolina Beach Rd.
Wilmington, NC • 790-8580

tennis facility overseen in person by Landfall resident (and tennis legend) Cliff Drysdale, an eight-lane Olympic-size swimming pool and more. Single-family homes range from $325,000 to $3 million; homesites range from $70,000 to $1.5 million. Landfall currently has 900 homes. The Landfall Club, a large banquet/dining/special occasions complex of 31,000 square feet, opened in 1997.

Greenville Loop and Masonboro Sound are to the south of Wrightsville Beach on the mainland. This land along the sound is home to many attractive neighborhoods, several of which have direct access to the water and, in some cases, their own boatslips for use by community residents. At this writing, these county neighborhoods have the economic advantage of being outside of the city of Wilmington, which means there are no city property taxes, but annexation plans are afoot for many outlying neighborhoods in the immediate future.

A word about services in the county (water, sewer and waste disposal come as a package

STONEBRIDGE REALTY

- **Real Estate Sales**
- **Houses & Condos**
- **Vacation Rentals**
- **Investment Property**

AREA SPECIALISTS ~ TWO LOCATIONS

Wilmington	Carolina	Toll Free
910/397-9373	Beach	888/428-4428

WILMINGTON ❖ WRIGHTSVILLE & CAROLINA BEACH

Where are you?

Are you getting ready to move? Would you like a hand? Would a free change-of-address service that notifies everyone help? How about $100 of free and discounted financial services along with it? We are here. To make things a bit easier. Just make one simple call to Wachovia Address Express at 1-800-430-4418 to get started. Even if you're not a Wachovia customer. Moving is tough enough. At least you don't have to do it alone. We are here.

WACHOVIA

www.wachovia.com

Wachovia Bank is a member FDIC.

Let's get started.℠

---

for city residents): Depending on where you live outside the city, sewer service is provided either by the county sewer service or individual septic tanks. Some communities have private water companies; there are also private wells in some neighborhoods. Waste-disposal companies are hired by county residents either individually or collectively as a neighborhood.

North of Wilmington

Porters Neck Plantation, 1202 Porters Neck Road, (910) 686-7400 or (800) 423-5695, is north of Wilmington and Wrightsville Beach just off U.S. Highway 17. The Tom Fazio-designed golf course is a key feature of this very attractive neighborhood of homes that appeals to active people. There is a sports complex, complete with heated lap pool, clay tennis courts and a fitness center. The new clubhouse was completed in 1996.

Traditional single-family homes are available in sizes ranging from 1,600 to 2,000 square feet and prices beginning at $190,000. A 2,000-square-foot home on the golf course begins at $250,000. Homes away from the course with 3,000 square feet start at $240,000. Homesites begin at $50,000.

Figure Eight Island is a private neighborhood of very expensive homes and homesites. Lots range from $125,000 to $400,000; home prices average $700,000. There is a yacht club and private harbor for residents of this lovely island, where there is no commercial development. Shopping is available in nearby Ogden and Hampstead. Call your favorite Realtor for information.

INSIDERS' TIP

The value of property across the area's beach communities actually increased after the hurricanes of 1996 because so many damaged homes were upgraded during repairs.

REAL ESTATE • 353

Enjoy the serenity of a stroll along the beaches of the South Brunswick islands.

Photo: N.C. Travel and Tourism Division

354 • REAL ESTATE

Locals take the future of the endangered loggerhead turtle very seriously.

WhiteBridge at Hampstead, 101 Whitebridge Road, Hampstead, (910) 270-2000, is a development of larger homes on larger lots. With an average home size of 3,600 square feet and lots ranging from two to six acres, WhiteBridge is located on 300 acres of land near the ICW. The neighborhood offers a swimming pool with outdoor pavilion, lighted tennis courts, miles of bridle and nature trails and a 20-acre bird sanctuary. This is the site of two annual matches held by the Wilmington Polo Club. Lot prices range from $85,000 to $130,000.

River Landing, 116 Paddlewheel Drive, Wallace, (910)285-4171 or (888) 285-4171, is located just over the Duplin-Pender counties line off Interstate 40 about 35 minutes from Wilmington. It is a semi-private, residential golf community consisting of primary residences and second homes with a wide variety of recreational facilities. Club memberships include an 18-hole championship golf course designed by Clyde Johnston, a swim and tennis center, private guest cottages, fishing and boating and walking/jogging/nature trails. Homesites throughout the 1,500-acre community with its seven neighborhoods range from $33,900 to $200,000.

South of Wilmington

Travel south of Wilmington on U.S. Highway 421 toward Carolina Beach and notice all of the different neighborhoods along the

INSIDERS' TIP

If fixing up an historic home interests you, contact the Historic Wilmington Foundation at (910) 762-2511 for information about low-interest loans that may be available in certain neighborhoods.

MINI-STORAGE

CLIMATE CONTROLLED UNITS AVAILABLE

Closed Circuit & TV Security Controlled Access

- Commercial
- Personal
- Wide Driveways
- On-Site Live-In Manager
- Well Lighted
- Low Monthly Rates
- Open 7 Days
- Boxes & Packing Supplies

ONLY MINUTES FROM ANYWHERE IN WILMINGTON

392-8100
901 Shipyard Blvd.

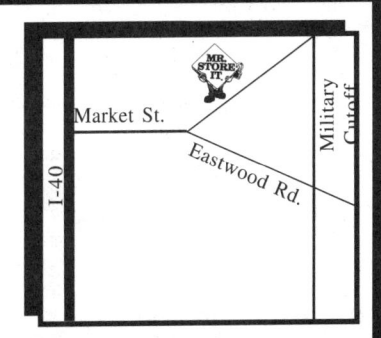

791-2323
6974 Market St.

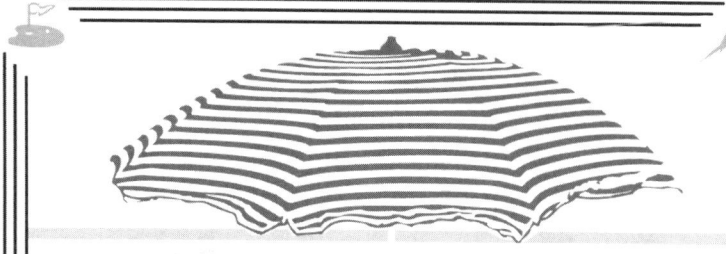

It's A Shore Thing.

With the largest selection of rental homes & condos, we can help you plan a perfect vacation. We offer daily, weekly, and year round rentals. Our 46 years' experience in sales & rentals assures you the expertise & resources to make your stay at the beach a shore thing.

Bryant Real Estate

800.322.3764 • 910.256.3764
P.O. Box 899, Wrightsville Beach, NC 28480 • rental@bryantre.com

---

way. Notice, too, that two themes dominate this area: golf and water. The increasingly narrow strip of land where the Cape Fear River rushes to meet the Atlantic Ocean is heavily residential, with recreation a constant consideration.

There are retirement and general lifestyle communities situated around golf courses, including the sprawling developments of single-family homes at Echo Farms and, a few miles down U.S. 421, The Cape. Paralleling U.S. 421 closer to the river is River Road, a previously remote area that has been discovered and is now home to several major residential developments.

Just north of the Snow's Cut Bridge on River Road is the new development of Cypress Island. It consists of 1,400- to 1,700-square-foot single-family homes and 1,200- to 1,800-square-foot townhomes. Homes and lots are offered as a package deal starting at $138,900 for single-family homes and $114,900 for townhomes. The community has a 14-acre nature preserve with a nature trail that meanders beside Telfare Creek, three stocked fishing lakes, a clubhouse, pool and tennis courts. It has a 9-hole, par 3 golf course.

Wrightsville Beach

Wrightsville Beach is highly residentially developed. For the most part, houses are close together, and a person who craves the mythical remote island life is not going to find it here. Happily, development has been largely controlled, thanks to vigilance on the part of local residents, and the relative density of development is quite palatable. In 1998, the community put new building ordinances into effect that limit the size of new houses based on square footage relative to lot size.

This is a pretty beach town. It's clean, there is little in the way of garishness, and the local constable does a fine job keeping order in the face of masses of visitors. A person who appreciates small-town living in a beach atmosphere with the convenience of a nearby city will adore this place. There are 5 miles of clean

Coastal Condo-Let

FREE BROCHURE

Vacation Rentals and Sales
Federal Point Shopping Center
1020 N. Lake Park Blvd. #12
Carolina Beach, NC 28428

http://www.condolet.com
email: condolet@wilmington.net

1-800-994-5222 • 910-458-5658

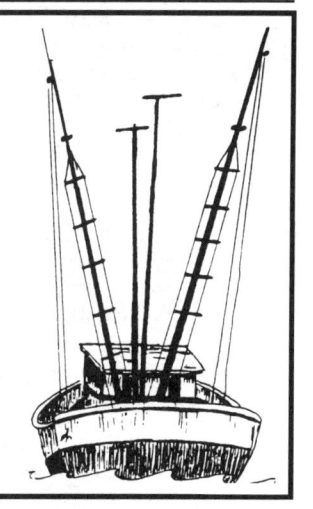

beach on which to jog or simply stroll. On just about any day of the year, you'll see surfers waiting for the big one.

There is very little for sale on this popular beach these days as far as single-family homes are concerned. Many of the existing homes stay in families generation after generation. Quite a few of them are used only as summer homes because they're not heated. When homes do go on the market, the price tag is large. Expect to pay an average of at least $500,000 for any single-family home, and don't be surprised by much higher prices.

Since the available land is all but exhausted in terms of development on the island — and since locals are not appreciative of high-rises — most of the opportunities for purchase are either replacement of older houses with new ones or, more likely, in condominiums. You could easily spend $200,000 to $350,000 for a two-bedroom condominium on Wrightsville Beach.

Something to note is that the northern end of the beach, an area called Shell Island, is in danger from erosion unless continual expenditures are made to keep the ocean at bay. Since there has been considerable development at this end of the beach, presumably the erosion problems will continue to be addressed by dredging of the channel and renourishment of the sand, but it's hard to predict at this writing.

Carolina Beach, Kure Beach and Fort Fisher

Cross over the bridge on U.S. 421 at Snow's Cut, a U.S. Army Corps of Engineers project that connects the ICW with the Cape Fear River and waters to the south, and you fall right into Carolina Beach.

This island represents some interesting prospects for home ownership in the Cape Fear region. Prices are considerably lower than in the rest of New Hanover County because the island is perceived to be somewhat outside the immediate Wilmington area. The truth is it only takes 20 minutes of easy highway driving to get from Carolina Beach to downtown and suburban Wilmington.

Carolina Beach is a very pleasant beach town with clean, wide beaches, an abundance of fishing opportunities, several nice restaurants and a growing sense of community pride that makes living here a charming prospect. Carolina Beach is one of the new-growth areas for New Hanover County's coastal dwellers and offers excellent value to the first- or second-home owner. The assortment of ownership opportunities range from condominiums to cottages. There are several high-rises, many multistory buildings on the northern end, an abundance of small homes and, particularly toward the south end at Fort Fisher, quite a few larger homes.

Homes can be purchased for as low as $80,000 and as high as a half-million dollars along Carolina Beach, Wilmington Beach, Kure Beach and Fort Fisher.

The farther south you go on this island, the more fascinating the scenery becomes. Down at Fort Fisher, beautiful live oak foliage seems to have been sculpted over the centuries by the sea breezes. At the most southerly tip of this strip of land, the watery panorama of the Cape Fear River converges with the Atlantic Ocean near Bald Head Island.

Bald Head Island

It takes 20 minutes to cross from the ferry landing at Indigo Plantation to Bald Head Island, a beautiful bit of land where there are no high-rises, no shopping malls and no crowds. There are also no cars. Everyone travels by electric golf cart or bicycle. You'll find a clubhouse with a pool, a George Cobb-designed golf course, tennis courts, a marina, limited shopping and opportunities for fine and casual dining. There is a resort atmosphere and, to be sure, the year-round residential population count is quite low, about 150. It is largely a vacation spot where most of the homes are available for weekly rental.

Homesites range from $50,000 to several hundreds of thousands of dollars. New cottages start as low as $260,000 but can rapidly rise toward the $500,000 range to more than a million. Single-family homes, townhouses and villas dot the island and are connected by a meandering golf cart path. There are now 600 homes on the island.

Southport-Oak Island

The charming fishing village of Southport attracts not only retirees but also families and folks who have decided to get out of the rat race. Southport's geographical location on the Cape Fear River near the Atlantic Ocean provides some lovely coastal scenery. Bald Head Island lies between Southport and the ocean. Oak Island serves as a barrier to the ocean on the south side.

Southport's quaint historic neighborhood of homes dates from the late 1800s and offers mostly restored, single-family residences. The handyperson can find a smaller dwelling for around $50,000 but, as a local Realtor says, you can also expect to put another $50,000 into it before you move in.

Houses on the waterfront are larger, and a 2,500-square-foot home may run from $250,000 to $300,000. Newer homes may cost more. Along River Drive, one can spend up to $500,000. Naturally, the farther back from the water, the lower the price. A nice finished house in Southport will average around $150,000 for 1,500 square feet.

Subdivision areas are growing rapidly in and near Southport. These include Indigo Plantation, Arbor Creek, St. James Plantation, Winding River and Marsh Creek. These neighborhoods offer a broad range of surprisingly affordable new homes in attractive settings with some very pleasant amenities. New homes are nestled in lovely settings that can cost as little as $120,000 for a home/site package or more than $500,000 for a 2,500-square-foot home in a prime location.

Across the ICW from Southport is Oak Island. This island has three beach communities: Caswell Beach, Yaupon Beach and Long Beach. All these communities have resort rentals, but they are overwhelmingly occupied by permanent residents. There is very little in the way of commercial development, and activity on the island is generally limited to families getting together at the church or the firehouse for social occasions.

Prices for single-family homes range from $70,000 to $600,000. At the center of the island, you can expect to pay from $80,000 to $140,000 for a small home. Long Beach, the biggest geographical area on Oak Island, has oceanside properties for less than $160,000.

South Brunswick Islands

Holden Beach

The next island down the coast is Holden Beach. A remarkable bridge connects the mainland with Holden and some say it's a surprise attraction in itself. You get a breathtaking view of the whole island, the marshes, the ICW and the Atlantic Ocean from the top of this fixed bridge as it rises 65 feet above the mainland (at high water) and careens dizzily to the island. Holden Beach is another family beach. In fact, every beach we'll tell you about in the rest of the chapter, which will geographically take us to the South Carolina line, fits into the family-beach category.

Prices for real estate are climbing rapidly. An oceanfront cottage of 1,800 square feet may cost $190,000 and more. An oceanfront lot with wide beach strand ranges from $140,000 to $300,000. Second-row lots, depending on view and water access by way of a canal, begin at $40,000 and may be as high as $70,000. Duplexes, condominiums and other multifamily dwellings on the oceanfront begin at $150,000.

Ocean Isle

Ocean Isle is an 8-mile-long island approximately a quarter-mile wide that lies at the center of South Brunswick's three barrier islands. The sandy beaches face directly south, providing sunshine all day. Beach residents are accustomed to seeing the sun rise and set over the ocean, but it's a little disorienting for newcomers at first. The island has a stable year-round population of about 650 residents, ensuring a sense of community.

The island, identifiable from a distance by virtue of a solitary high-rise, is an appealing residential environment of largely single-family homes. They range in price from several hundred thousands on the oceanfront to $100,000 in the middle of the island. Naturally, properties on the ICW side facing the mainland also fetch higher prices.

Sunset Beach

This beach may have thousands of visitors in the summer, but it is home to only about 720 year-round residents. It is overwhelmingly occupied by single-family dwellings, but there is a trend toward large duplexes on the oceanfront. This is because the island homes are on septic systems, and the oceanfront lots are the only ones that can accommodate two systems on one lot. Lots may range from $50,000 to $300,000 depending on location. Four finger canals, regularly dredged, escalate the cost of interior lots. Duplexes of 2,000 square feet can cost $300,000. Single homes may range as high as $400,000. In general, homes average between $135,000 and $160,000.

Calabash

Carolina Shores is a golf-oriented neighborhood that attracts a high proportion of retired folks to its appealing setting. Homes, mostly one-story plans, average between $100,000 and $165,000. Calabash and Carolina Shores has been having some disputes that essentially amount to the development trying to secede from the town.

The town of Calabash is a fishing village with its share of famous restaurants that specialize in Calabash-style seafood. Calabash homes range from $80,000 to $180,000 and attract a wide range of families and individuals who appreciate the easy pace of the area.

Topsail Island

Topsail Island is rumored to have some of the best opportunities for beach real estate. Located 45 minutes north up U.S. 17 from Wilmington, this community has surprising diversity in housing. Unlike the pricier beaches to the immediate south, Topsail Island offers homes for $100,000 or less in some cases. New 2,000-square-foot homes can cost as much as $250,000 to $350,000 on the ocean, although there are not yet many homes this large on the island. The norm is more 1,500 to 1,800 square feet, and prices average $175,000 to $200,000. Lots across the waterway on the mainland can still be purchased for as low as $10,000 for a half-acre site.

Topsail is still mostly a second-home market. There are only about 2,000 year-round residents on this quiet island. Recent development has put all of the necessities of life close to residents with ample grocery stores, convenience marts and other services either available on the island or the mainland.

Real Estate Agencies

Any one of an abundance of area real estate agencies will be happy to assist you in your search for a new home. The agencies included here represent a fraction of the reputable companies working along the Cape Fear Coast. Although we've grouped

Orton Plantation is a fine example of Greek Revival architecture.

the agencies geographically, many of them sell properties in other communities and some have offices in several locations throughout the area. Regardless of the location of the office, choose a Realtor who is knowledgable about the areas you're interested in and with whom you feel comfortable working.

Wilmington

Adam and Hilliard Realty
3912 Shipyard Blvd. • (910) 799-7500, (800) 628-7089

This company, established in 1979, specializes in sales in Wilmington and New Hanover County. It represents the Birch Creek development on Wrightsville Avenue and Howell Builders in Snug Harbour, Wessex in Covil Estates, Crosswinds and Windward Oaks. Adam and Hilliard Realty is a member of Genesis Relocation Services. The Wilmington Regional Association of Realtors has named this company its Most Cooperative Firm eight times since 1980.

Bachman Realty
2413 Middle Sound Loop Rd.
- **(910) 686-4099, (800) 470-4099**

The broker-in-charge of Bachman is a long-term resident of Figure Eight Island and is intimately familiar with properties on this attractive island. The company also offers properties along the waterfront throughout New Hanover and Pender counties as well in Historic Downtown Wilmington. It is a member of RELO relocation service.

Century 21
Coastal Communities

More POWER to you

800 Shipyard Boulevard Suite 17　5653 Carolina Beach Rd.
Wilmington, NC 28412　　　Wilmington, NC 28412
Business (910) 395-4770 • Brunswick County 579-4770
Fax (910) 395-1715
Toll Free (888) 395-4770
www.century21.com　　email: CoastalXXI@aol.com

Century 21-Brock Mills
802 S. College Rd. • (910) 395-8266,
(800) 521-4746
Bypass 117, Burgaw • (910) 259-7717

Gardner and Associates Realty merged with Brock Mills in early 1996 to create this larger company. It offers properties throughout New Hanover and Brunswick counties. Established in 1977 as Brock Mills, it sells more than 500 properties a year and is an International Centurion company. It specializes in relocation and received the Quality Service Award by Century 21 International, special recognition given to the top 5 percent of all Century 21 firms in the country.

Century 21 Coastal Communities
800 Shipyard Blvd., Ste. 17
• (910) 395-4770, (888) 395-4770
5653 Carolina Beach Rd. (same telephone numbers)

This residential and commercial real estate company merged with Gulf Stream Realty Group in 1998. It covers an unusually large territory, ranging from Topsail Island in the north to Sunset and the other Brunswick County islands in the south. It specializes in residential recreational properties and has an extensive listing of finer homes as well as mid-range ones. Relocation service is provided through Century 21 Relocation and Referral.

Century 21, Sweyer & Associates
1630 Military Cut-off Rd., Ste. 110
• (910) 256-0021, (800) 848-0021
14865 Hwy. 17 N., Hampstead
• (910) 270-3606

This company has been in business since 1987, meeting residential housing needs in New Hanover, Pender and Brunswick counties. Designated as the top Century 21 producer in both Carolinas in 1997, it is projected to sell up to 1,000 homes in 1998. In addition to general representation, it also represents new homes in Courtney Pines, Demarest Landing and Cornerstone. The company has a full-time, in-house relocation service, a property management division and a prelicensing school for aspiring Realtors. A mortgage bank is conveniently located beside the office.

INSIDERS' TIP

If your new home isn't on city or community water systems, you may want to investigate installing a water treatment system.

Clark-Teachey Realtors
1430 Commonwealth Dr., Landfall Center
• (910) 256-1155, (800) 497-7325

Established in 1991 as a residential company, this partnership of native Wilmingtonians traces its roots to 1970. It represents Sun Coast Villas, Emerald Cove, Bishop's Park, Berkleigh, Lakemoor, Regency Manor, Willougby Park, The Cottages, The Commons, Sentry Oaks, Tidalholm Village, Tidalholm and Old Cape Cod. It has an in-house relocation service.

Coldwell Banker Baker Properties
6209 Oleander Dr., Ste. 1
• (910) 395-5566, (800) 776-6110
25 Market St. • (910) 251-2234,
(800) 232-7719

This company focuses on residential sales throughout the region and is heavily involved in sales of new construction. Greenway Village, Alamosa Place, Regency Manor, Courtney Pines, Williamsburg Place, Shinn Creek Estates, Legacy at Brittany Lakes, Purviance Landing, Belmar Forest, Middle Point and Newbury Woods are some of the developments it represents. This company is a member of five separate relocation services.

Coldwell Banker Sea Coast Realty
5710 Oleander Dr. Suite 200
• (910) 799-3435, (800) 522-9624

Sea Coast handles properties in Wilmington and New Hanover County in diverse locations, including Abbey Glen at Futch Creek, Arrondale, Brooks Landing, Mason Bend, the Summit at Telfair Forest, Halcyon Forest, Stonegate at Pine Valley, Heathfield Hall and Evergreen Park. Sea Coast Realty was awarded the Premier Office Designation by Coldwell Banker in 1998.

Coldwell Banker Hanover Realty, Inc.
3901 Oleander Dr., Stes. E and F
• (910) 395-2244, (800) 441-4595

Hanover Realty handles properties in Wilmington and New Hanover, Brunswick and Pender counties. It represents the new neighborhoods of Lucia Point, Windward Oaks, Harvest Grove, Brewster Place, Creeks Edge at Jackey's Creek, and Stonington Court.

Dal-Har Real Estate and Construction, Inc.
401 Endicott Ct. • (910) 686-5123

Dallas Harris has been building in the Wilmington area since 1978 and was an innovator in the patio-home market. The company builds and sells single-family and patio homes near Wrightsville Beach. Current exclusive properties represented include Glen Ridge at West Bay Estates at Ogden and Seaspray Landing patio homes. Homes range between $99,500 and $125,500, and are from 1,034 to 1,390 square feet.

Dunlea Realty
2005 Eastwood Rd., Ste. 100
• (910) 256-3063, (800) 438-6532

In business since 1956, this is one of the area's oldest real estate companies. Dunlea Realty handles both commercial and residential properties in New Hanover, Brunswick and Pender counties. Its focus is on properties that range from $150,000 and up. It is a member of the HMS Relocation Service.

Figure Eight Realty
15 Bridge Rd. • (910) 686-4400,
(800) 279-6085

While other companies may sell Figure Eight houses, this is the only real estate company located on this exclusively residential island. It focuses on island housing, a neighborhood composed of luxury, single-family homes. Figure Eight Realty is a small company housed in the private marina's yacht club. This company also offers vacation rentals on the island.

G. Flowers Realty
602 Castle St. • (910) 762-7146,
(800) 421-6063

Properties represented by this small company range all over New Hanover County but are concentrated heavily in downtown/urban residential and commercial areas in developing neighborhoods. G. Flowers Realty also offers investment counseling services.

Harbour Town Associates Real Estate
7040 Wrightsville Ave., Ste. 101
• (910) 256-0032, (800) 521-8132

In business since 1995, this relatively young

Life quickly becomes elemental at the seashore.

company has high visibility. A full-service brokerage, Harbour Town Associates covers the territory both geographically and in terms of price. It is the exclusive listing agent for Westgate at Georgetown, Maritime Square in downtown Wilmington, Trolley Park, Saponas Point and Orchard Park and has many new projects underway. It is a member of RELO/The International Relocation Network, the oldest and largest network of independent real estate brokers.

Howard, Perry and Walston Realty, Inc.
803-G S. College Rd. • (910) 799-1194, (800) 768-1194, (910) 791-8874 new home sales

This company is part of a network of more than 600 real estate associates from the coast to the Raleigh area. The Wilmington office is the fourth-largest real estate company within the Better Homes and Gardens national network and 37th-largest brokerage in America. Exclusively representing more than nine communities in Wilmington, it also lists and sells properties in New Hanover, Pender and Brunswick counties.

Intracoastal Realty Corporation
1900 Eastwood Rd., Ste. 38, Lumina Station • (910) 256-4503, (800) 533-1840
534 Causeway Dr., Wrightsville Beach • (910) 256-4503

This market leader has been in business in the area since 1974. An exclusive affiliate of Sotheby's International Realty, it is a resort and residential property specialist. This company has listings throughout the region. It is a member of the RELO relocation service. Neighbor-

INSIDERS' TIP

When searching for a home builder, ask other new home owners about their experiences.

hoods exclusively represented include Marsh Oaks, Kensington Place, and Masonboro Forest, a new 260-lot subdivision near Masonboro Sound. It also represents Carleton Place, Craven Point, Westwood at Echo, Highgrove, Bay Shore Estates, Scotts Hill Bluff and Turnstone.

Jeanette Golder Realty
7208 Wrightsville Ave. • (910) 256-6659, (800) 642-6443

This small company specializes in residential sales and development in New Hanover, Brunswick and Pender counties, selling homes that range from $35,000 to nearly $2 million. In addition to general properties, it also represents the Deerfield community at Hampstead, Mill Creek and Old Baymeade.

Laney Real Estate
4918 Randall Pkwy. • (910) 799-9660, (800) 628-3021
The Galleria, 6800 Wrightsville Ave.
• (910) 256-0056, (800) 733-1428
140 Harper Ave., Carolina Beach
• (910) 458-3739, (800) 235-9068
201 Yaupon Dr., Oak Island
• (910) 278-9800, (888) 708-9800
Topsail Island • (910) 452-7219, (910) 270-2202

Laney was founded in 1978 and handles residential, commercial and property management divisions that range New Hanover, Brunswick and Pender counties from its five offices. Laney Real Estate is a member of RELO, an international relocation network.

Landfall Associates
1985 Eastwood Rd., Ste. 100
• (910) 256-6111, (800) 227-8208

Landfall Associates deals exclusively with the fine properties in Landfall, a private neighborhood of single homes, villas, patio homes, condominiums and homesites. The community boasts numerous amenities, including Jack Nicklaus and Pete Dye golf courses and the Cliff Drysdale tennis/sports center. The new 31,000-square-foot Landfall Club opened in early 1997.

New Home Marketplace
3501 Market St. • (910) 251-2288, (800) 200-2466

New Home Marketplace is the only full-service real estate company in the area that specializes in selling new, newer and newly renovated homes. The company offers full general brokerage services for the entire Wilmington area, including Pender and Brunswick counties. Developments represented include Bexley, The Enclave, Churchill Estates, Cassimir Commons, Tifton Park at Merestone and Pointe Summerset at Wrightsville.

Port City Properties
1209 Market St. • (910) 251-0615

Established in 1995, Port City Properties represents residential and commercial properties in New Hanover, Brunswick and Pender counties. Many of this company's agents have direct experience in historic property renovation of their own homes. The company covers the full geographical and price spectrum and specializes in downtown properties as well as beach properties. Port City Properties renovated its own turn-of-the-century building in the downtown area, the former Yopp Funeral Home, beside New Hanover High School.

Prudential Carolinas Realty
4130 Oleander Dr., Ste. 100
• (910) 395-2000, (800) 336-5654
530 Causeway Dr., Wrightsville Beach
• (910) 256-9299, (800) 562-9299

This large company covers the Greater Wilmington area. It specializes in corporate relocation services provided by certified relocation experts. It handles new residential developments such as Georgetowne.

Nancy Rassier Real Estate
217 S. Second St. • (910) 762-4272

This small company specializes in historic

INSIDERS' TIP

Most gated golf course communities welcome club members who don't live within the community and all of them invite guests to play for a fee.

residential as well as waterfront residential properties. The broker spent 18 years in Bucks County, Pennsylvania prior to moving to downtown Wilmington in 1993. She received the Pennsylvania Association of Realtors Lifetime Excellence Award. Nancy Rassier Real Estate focuses on New Hanover County and coastal Pender County properties that range from $150,000 to $1 million.

Select-Internet Realty
14710 Hwy. 17 N., Hampstead
• (910) 270-2017, (800) 535-6538
712 Country Club Rd., Hampstead
• (910) 270-3312

This company is primarily involved in relocation sales and services in the Pender County area, although it also has a number of properties located in Wilmington and New Hanover County.

Stonebridge Realty
432 Landmark Dr., Ste. 4
• (910) 397-9373, (888) 428-4482

Stonebridge Realty handles brokerage in Wilmington, New Hanover and Brunswick counties, specializing in beach property that ranges from residential to commercial. It is the exclusive builder and marketing agency for Harbour Point Villas and Yacht Club beside Snow's Cut north of Carolina Beach, which offers 66 end-unit townhomes ranging from 2,200 to 2,400 square feet and beginning at $269,500. Boat slips at the community's Pleasure Island Marina and Yacht Club are available for sale. Margaret Young, Stonebridge's broker-in-charge, has been in real estate in the Lake Norman area for 12 years and has been a coastal property owner for more than two decades.

Wrightsville Beach

Bryant Real Estate
1001 N. Lumina Ave. • (910) 256-3764, (800) 322-3764
501 N. College Rd., Wilmington
• (910) 799-2700

Bryant Real Estate is a small company that has specialized in Wrightsville Beach properties since its founding in 1952. It is a full-service real estate company, offering waterfront properties, acreage, homes, condominiums and lots throughout New Hanover and Pender counties.

Intracoastal Realty Corporation
534 Causeway Dr. • (910) 256-4503, (800) 322-3764

This market leader has been in business in the area since 1974. An exclusive affiliate of Sotheby's International Realty, it is a resort and residential property specialist. This company has listings throughout the region. It is a member of the RELO relocation service. Neighborhoods exclusively represented include Marsh Oaks, Kensington Place, and Masonboro Forest, a new 260-lot subdivision near Masonboro Sound. It also represents Carleton Place, Craven Point, Westwood at Echo, Highgrove, Bay Shore Estates, Scotts Hill Bluff and Turnstone.

ERA Brittain and Associates Realtors
1322 Airlie Rd., Crocker's Landing
• (910) 256-2224, (800)362-9031

This company is located across the ICW from Harbour Island. Established in 1988, it became an ERA franchise in 1996, becoming part of an international real estate company of more than 3,000 offices. ERA Brittain and Associates Realtors sells single-family homes, condominiums, resort property and land in New Hanover County.

Carolina Beach, Kure Beach and Fort Fisher

Bullard Realty
1404 S. Lake Park Blvd., Carolina Beach
• (910) 458-4028, (800) 327-5863

Bullard Realty has been in the business of listing and selling homes, condominiums, beach properties and commercial properties since 1985. Broker Beth Bullard has 18 years of experience in real estate. Her company also handles rentals on Carolina and Kure beaches.

Coldwell Banker United Realty Group
1001 N. Lake Park Blvd., Carolina Beach
• (910) 458-4401

This company, on the island since 1984,

Walk the nature trail behind the North Carolina Aquarium at Fort Fisher.

specializes in sales not only on the island from Carolina Beach to Fort Fisher but also on the beach and mainland communities in New Hanover, Brunswick and Pender counties. Formerly United Resorts, it joined Coldwell Banker in late 1996 and now offers the services of the extensive Coldwell Banker Referral Network.

Davies Realty
809 N. Lake Park Blvd., Carolina Beach
• **(910) 458-0444, (800) 685-4614**

This family-owned firm has been focusing its residential and commercial real estate sales on Pleasure Island from Carolina Beach in the north to Fort Fisher in the south since 1996. It is also branching out into the greater Wilmington area, but it concentrates on Carolina Beach, Kure Beach and Fort Fisher. In-house relocation services.

Gardner Realty
C-4 Pleasure Island Plz., Carolina Beach
• **(910) 458-8503, (800) 697-7924**

Gardner Realty sells homes, duplexes and condominiums throughout the Wilmington area, including properties on Carolina Beach, Wilmington Beach, Kure Beach and Fort Fisher. It also offers property management services.

Lighthouse Realty
201 Fort Fisher Blvd., North Kure Beach
• **(910) 458-3300**

This small real estate company sells both residential and commercial properties on all of Pleasure Island and throughout New Hanover County. It is centrally located in Kure Beach, the community that lies between Carolina Beach to the north and Fort Fisher to the south.

Tucker Bros. Realty
201 Harper Ave., Carolina Beach
• **(910) 458-8211**

Tucker Bros. Realty has been in real estate on the island since 1973, selling homes from Federal Point just south of Monkey Junction to Fort Fisher at the southern tip of Pleasure Island. The owners are Carolina Beach natives with family roots on the island.

Bald Head Island

Bald Head Island
5079 Southport-Supply Rd., Southport
• **(910) 457-5000, (800) 888-3707**

This company sells single-family homes, cottages, condominiums and homesites on Bald Head Island, as well as Indigo Plantation in Southport. Available areas include property along the Cape Fear River, the Atlantic Ocean, the ICW, the creek side of Bald Head Island, a maritime forest at Bald Head, as well as a professional golf course. Indigo Plantation homes, similarly priced, are situated on the mainland in a neighborhood of wooded lanes, tidals creeks and marshlands.

Southport-Oak Island

Coldwell Banker Southport-Oak Island Realty
607 N. Howe St., Southport
- (910) 457-6713, (800) 346-7671
300 Country Club Dr., Yaupon Beach
- (910) 278-3311, (800) 841-4950

This company covers Southport, Oak Island and Boiling Spring Lakes and Brunswick County selling single-family homes, condominiums, duplexes and land. This is the largest franchise firm in Brunswick County. A member of the International Resort Property Network, it specializes in finding temporary accommodations for corporations in need of this service for their employees.

Century 21 Dorothy Essey and Associates Inc.
6102 E. Oak Island Dr., Long Beach
- (910) 278-3361, (800) 849-2322
105 E. Moore St., Southport
- (910) 457-4577, (800) 469-4577

This real estate company covers Southport and Oak Island as well as Boiling Spring Lakes. It offers general brokerage and services for single-family homes, condominiums, duplexes, lots and commercial properties. The company has a new-home specialist on staff. It is currently marketing Harbor Oaks in Southport near the Fort Fisher ferry landing and the Arboretum in Caswell Beach.

Margaret Rudd & Associates Inc., Realtors
210 Country Club Dr., Yaupon Beach
- (910) 278-5213, (800) 733-5213
1023 N. Howe St., Southport
- (910) 457-5258, (800) 733-5258

This large and firmly established real estate company covers Southport, Long Beach and Brunswick County. It offers diverse properties that range from Southport's historic district to properties on the beachfront, ICW, marshfront and wooded areas of Oak Island. The company is currently marketing a new development called Barnes Bluff on the ICW.

Walter Hill & Associates
6101 E. Oak Island Dr., Long Beach
- (910) 278-5405

Formerly known as Scruggs & Morrison Realty, this company changed its name in 1997. It continues to serve Southport, Oak Island's three beach communities and Brunswick County through the sale of residential and commercial properties near the water and on the mainland. The company also specializes in property management.

South Brunswick Islands

Alan Holden Vacations/RE/MAX at the Beach/Sea Castles Construction
128 Ocean Blvd. W., Holden Beach
- (910) 842-6061, (800) 720-2200
6900 Ocean Highway 17 South, Sunset Beach • (910) 575-7355

This is the largest and oldest real estate company handling sales and rentals on Holden Beach. The Holden family bought the island from King George of England in 1756. Mr. Holden, broker-in-charge, was the first baby born to a Holden Beach resident, in 1949. This company built a large percentage of homes on the island. The new office on Sunset Beach just handles sales and construction. Sea Castles Construction has an unlimited residential and commercial license.

Coastal Development and Realty
131 Ocean Blvd. W., Holden Beach
- (910) 842-4939, (800) 262-7820

Coastal Development and Realty has been on the island since about 1985. It built its large oceanfront office in 1992. In addition to general real estate services, the owner is a builder/developer/designer who has brought new architecture to Holden Beach with his Summerville Collection. These homes have a Charleston flair.

Hobbs Realty
114 Ocean Blvd. W., Holden Beach
• (910) 842-2002, (800) 655-3367

On the island for more than 20 years, Hobbs Realty offers properties on and off Holden Beach. The company specializes in resort properties, including single-family homes, duplexes, condominiums and lots and also offers commercial sales. The company has an in-house relocation service. The office is located at the end of the bridge on Holden Beach on the left.

Cooke Realtors
#1 Causeway Dr., Ocean Isle Beach
• (910) 579-3535, (800) 622-3224

This company, on the island since 1976, specializes in sales and construction on Ocean Isle Beach. It does a brisk business in new and resale condominiums, as well as cottages and larger single-family homes.

Sand Dollar Realty
102 Causeway Dr., Ocean Isle Beach
• (910) 579-7038, (800) 457-7263

In business since 1985, this real estate company sells properties on Ocean Isle Beach and along the coast of Brunswick County. It is an agent for Seaside North and Branchwood Village, two manufactured home subdivisions, and Riverhills, a single-family, site-built development on the backwaters of the Shallotte River. Homes and sites at Riverhills are priced beginning around $95,000 for a 1,440 square-foot home.

Sloane Realty
16 Causeway Dr., Ocean Isle Beach
• (910) 579-1144, (800) 237-4609

The first permanent family to live on Ocean Isle Beach owns this company. It represents waterway communities, as well as homes and lots on the beach. Club Villas at Baytree and the Colony II at Oyster Bay Plantation are its exclusive residential golf course developments.

Century 21 Sunset Realty
502 N. Sunset Blvd., Sunset Beach
• (910) 579-1000, (800) 451-2102
(Island Office) 401 S. Sunset Blvd.
• (910) 579-5200

Founded in 1982, this large company handles residential and commercial properties on Sunset Beach, throughout the South Brunswick Islands as well as North Myrtle Beach. It is licensed in both North Carolina and South Carolina. It is the exclusive marketing developer for Sunset Beach. Two properties it represents are Waterway Oaks, an upscale waterway community, and Sea Trail Plantation at Oyster Bay. Relocation services are available through Century 21 Relocation.

Simmons Realty
1021 Beach Dr., S.W., Sunset Beach
• (910) 579-0192

This small real estate company has been working in sales on Sunset Beach since 1990, but broker Beth Simmons is a lifelong native of the area. The company offers general real estate services on the island and the adjacent mainland. It handles single-family homes, cottages and condominium units.

Sunset Properties
419 S. Sunset Blvd., Sunset Beach
• (910) 579-9900, (800) 446-0218

On the island since 1988, this company regularly handles properties only on Sunset Beach. Single-family homes dominate this quiet residential island that attracts second-home investors, retirees and people who simply appreciate living away from it all.

ERA Callihan, Peal, Skelley and Assoc. Realty and Pinehurst Builders
10239 Beach Dr., S.W., Calabash
• (910) 579-4097, (800) 833-6330

This company handles commercial and residential properties through nine offices. Its range is from Wilmington to Pawley's Island south of Myrtle Beach. Pinehurst Builders built approximately 80 percent of the homes in Carolina Shores, an exclusive retirement community in Calabash. It is a member of the ERA Relocation Service.

Topsail Island

Beach Properties of Topsail Island Inc.
(910) 328-0719, (800) 753-2975

This is a relatively new business in name,

but the broker, a permanent resident on the island, has been handling Topsail Island, Sneads Ferry and Holly Ridge properties since 1988. Owner Patsy Jordan was awarded the 1997 Realtor of the Year Award.

Jean Brown Real Estate
522-A and B New River Dr., Surf City
- **(910) 328-1640, (800) 745-4480**

This small and personable company sells properties on Topsail Island, including Topsail Beach, North Topsail and Surf City as well as mainland properties in Onslow and Pender counties. It also offers property management services on Topsail Island through its rental department.

Coldwell Banker Coastline Realty
965 Old Folkstone Rd., Topsail Way Shopping Center, Sneads Ferry
- **(910) 327-7711, (800) 497-5463**

This company, established in 1994 and owned and operated by Duplin County native Bud Rivenbark, handles mostly oceanfront condominiums and soundside properties on Topsail Island and in the Sneads Ferry area. It offers single-family homes, townhomes and lots. It is a member of the Coldwell Banker Relocation Network. The company also handles commercial sales.

Cathy Medlin Real Estate
405 Roland Ave., Surf City
- **(910) 328-2323, (800) 622-6886**

Cathy Medlin has been selling properties on Topsail Island and the mainland in Onslow and Pender counties since 1979. She was one of the founders of the Topsail Island Board of Realtors in 1992. This small company sells beach, waterway and mainland homes and lots.

Topsail Realty
712 S. Anderson Blvd., Topsail Beach
- **(910) 328-5241, (800) 526-6432**

Topsail Realty specializes in south Topsail Island's finer sales and rental properties. It is located in Topsail Beach at the south end of Topsail Island on N.C. Highway 50, 6.3 miles south of the stoplight in Surf City.

Turner Realty
Surf City (IGA) Shopping Center, Surf City • (910) 328-1313, (800) 326-2926

Turner Realty has focussed on residential and commercial sales on all of Topsail Island since 1988. It lists and sells single-family homes, cottages and condominiums on the island, which spans two counties: Pender and Onslow. It is one of the few real estate companies that doesn't offer vacation rentals. The Broker-in-Charge, Rick Turner, makes his home on the oceanfront in Surf City. The office is located at the corner of South Topsail and Roland avenues, at the island's only traffic light

Ward Realty
116 S. Topsail Dr., Surf City
- **(910) 328-3221, (800) 782-6216**
101 N. Front St., Wilmington
- **(910) 763-8222**

This company was the original developer of Topsail Island in 1947. Channel Bend and Pirate's Cove are two of the 19 subdivisions this company has developed. Alva Hill Ward, Jr., was the first President of the Topsail Island Board of Realtors as well as mayor of Surf City in 1954. His brother David now runs the agency and continues the family tradition of longtime real estate service to Topsail Island.

IS IT TIME TO MAKE OUR HOME YOUR HOME?

THE CATHERINE KENNEDY HOME

Of course you'd rather spend your golden years in the comfort of your own home. Unfortunately, sometimes living alone isn't the safest or most beneficial situation. At the same time, a full service nursing facility often isn't necessary either. If you're 62 or older, still independent and quite capable of taking care of yourself, you should consider our Home as an option.

At the Catherine Kennedy Home, you'll enjoy an active, healthy and fulfilling lifestyle, without all the aggravations associated with living alone. We do the cooking, the dishes, the housekeeping, the yardwork and best of all, you'll be surrounded by other active peers. Our full-time Activities Director will definitely keep you busy, and our 24-hour staff will provide the security of knowing that someone is always there when you need them.

We are NOT a nursing home. We are an Independent Living Retirement Community. We don't even look like the hospital-like environments you're probably imagining right now. Instead, the whole look and feel of our community is warm and homey, just like what you're used to. You'll have your own private bedroom and bathroom while sharing the multitude of common areas throughout the Home.

The Catherine Kennedy Home is the oldest retirement community in the country and has been caring for your friends and family for over 153 years. As one of the few non-profit communities in the Wilmington area, our rates are very affordable, and our reputation is unsurpassed.

Call us to schedule a no-obligation personal tour of our Home or even join us for lunch sometime. Take a look for yourself why so many seniors have chosen to call Our Home, Their Home. We'd love to have you as a member of our family.

- Respite Care
- Full-time Activities Director
- All Meals and Snacks Provided
- Free Personal Laundry Facilities
- Transportation for Physician Appointment
- Convenient Downtown Location
- Non-denominational Chapel

- 24-Hour Staff
- Private Rooms and Suites
- Utilities Provided
- Housekeeping Provided
- Beauty and Barber Shop
- Fitness Center and Library
- Beautifully Landscaped Grounds

Our Non-Profit Organization has been serving Wilmington since 1845

The CATHERINE KENNEDY Home
207 South Third St. • Wilmington, NC 28401
(910)762-5322 • Fax (910)762-8489
WebSite Address: http://www.ckh.org

Managed by Life Care Services Corporation, the industry leader.

EQUAL HOUSING OPPORTUNITY

Retirement

North Carolina's southern coast is tremendously attractive to retirees from around the country and even the world because of its beautiful scenery, services, recreational opportunities, cultural resources, relatively low taxes, low crime rate and, perhaps most importantly, mild weather.

Throughout most of this century, especially during the latter half, many a winter-weary Northerner has gone to latitudinal extremes in search of respite from snow and ice. Snow and ice are rare in New Hanover, Pender and Brunswick counties, making a snow shovel about as useful as a wool coat in the Caribbean.

Although many retirees settle in Florida, land of sunshine, some are viewing the year-round warmth as too much of a good thing. As a result, North Carolina is experiencing a rebound effect as retirees leave Florida and head here for more seasonal variety within reasonable temperature ranges. A year-round average temperature of 68.7 makes our climate extremely pleasant.

Wilmington's temperature range is moderate due in large part to its maritime location. Afternoon sea breezes make the summer heat more comfortable. Although there can be some beastly hot days with high humidity, there is nothing to match Florida's excessively relentless summer heat. Afternoon temperatures in this area may reach 90 or more a third of the days in midsummer, but several years may pass without reaching the 100-degree mark. The average temperature in July is 79.8.

Most winters here are short and mild. Polar air masses heading for the Atlantic Ocean must pass over the Appalachian Mountains first, which takes the bite out of the bitter cold before the air masses reach North Carolina's coastal area. According to records kept since 1870, there is only one entire day each winter when the temperature fails to rise above freezing. The mean temperature in January is 47 degrees.

Rainfall in the area is usually ample and well-distributed throughout the year, concentrated mostly in summer thunderstorms between June and August. Retirees who enjoy gardening will appreciate the fact that the growing season may be as long as 302 days for some flowers and vegetables.

In addition to agreeable weather patterns, the southern coast has much to offer its retired population. There is ample shopping, first-rate medical care, affordable housing opportunities, a full range of cultural activities, the benefits of a progressive university and a robust industry developing around services to older citizens.

The median age of the overall population was 36 in 1995 and it is projected to move to 40 within two decades, a statistic that suggests what most people here know instinctively. At this writing, New Hanover County/Wilmington is experiencing an increase of 10 percent per year in the population of citizens who are 60 and older. More than 16 percent of the residents of New Hanover County were in this age bracket in 1995 according to projections by the U.S. Department of Commerce and the North Carolina Office of State Planning.

Frankly, these figures are probably conservative. Until a full census is done in 2000, the possibly much larger percentage of citizens who make up the growing senior population will not be known. But ponder this: According to state projections, there will be more than 26,000 people age 60 and older in New Hanover County alone in 1997-98. Almost 2,000 will be 85 and older. New Hanover, Pender, Brunswick and nearby Columbus counties combined will have nearly 60,000 people older than 60 by 1998.

Seniors are increasingly being attracted to North Carolina on the whole. North Carolina ranks fifth in the nation for migratory retirees, according to the North Carolina Division

Deciding Where To Live

People from all walks of life and all socioeconomic circumstances will discover attractive options for living in the Wilmington area. If you are fortunate enough to have good health and a comfortable financial situation, you have many neighborhoods from which to choose. You may not wish or need to move into a retirement community at this point in your life. In fact, there seems to be a trend that suggests older people want to live in communities with a full range of ages and household configurations.

These living options range from exclusive gated neighborhoods with security guards and golf courses to lower-cost patio-home communities with built-in maintenance services. There's also the artsy, urban neighborhood in Wilmington's downtown historic district for senior adults who favor afternoon strolls to one of several coffee shops or evening walks to restaurants or theaters.

There are vast choices in terms of the view thanks to the coastal scenery and, although beach real estate is quite expensive near Wilmington, there are some extremely reasonable condominium developments along the Brunswick beaches and Topsail Island. Both Pender and Brunswick counties, as well as New Hanover, have excellent golf course communities where homes range from large mansions to condominiums to doublewides.

If you're considering retiring to this region, you might do well to go ahead and purchase land for later building, particularly in the less-expensive counties adjacent to New Hanover and Wilmington.

Whether you're buying or renting, visit with a local Realtor for information (see our Real Estate chapter.) Also, the Cape Fear Council of Governments publishes a free booklet, *Community Resource Guide for Senior Services* (see the Government Agencies section at the end of this chapter).

of Aging. Given the special attributes of coastal North Carolina, it would not be surprising to see this area rank higher than the overall state.

Retirement Communities

Senior adult retirement communities — neighborhoods with congregate housing intended specifically for older occupants — offer a variety of social and recreational amenities. These communities feature single homes or apartments centered around several services, which may include meals in a central location, a pool, transportation and activities. They may or may not offer healthcare services.

Several of these communities are described below. You can also contact the chamber of commerce in the area you choose for relocation (see our Area Overview chapter) or one of the government agencies listed at the end of this chapter

Brightmore of Wilmington
2324 41st St., Wilmington
- **(910) 350-1980, (800) 556-6899**

Brightmore welcomes active retirees who wish to combine "independence with a small-town atmosphere." A basic package includes a complete apartment with utilities (except for phone service), 24-hour security services and medical-emergency call, housekeeping and flat linens, regularly scheduled transportation, daily choice of meals, an ice-cream parlor and recreational programs. Studio, one-bedroom, one-bedroom deluxe, two-bedroom and two-bedroom deluxe apartments are available.

Monthly rates begin at $1,295 for a studio apartment with a onetime membership fee of $10,000 under Plan A. Plan B offers monthly rates beginning at $1,550 for a studio apartment and no membership fee. Prospective residents can make reservations through a $1,000 deposit. Due to Brightmore's affiliation with nearby Liberty Commons Assisted Living and Liberty Commons Nursing Center, home-care services may be contracted within one's own apartment.

Capeside Village
1111 The Cape Blvd., Wilmington
- **(910) 458-7603**

This community at The Cape Resort and

Join An Association So Exclusive It Takes 50 Years To Get In!

More than 300,000 individuals age 50 and over benefit from this national membership program which promotes healthy living through education, social events and other special membership privileges.

You Gotta Have FRIENDS...

Call **(910) 452-8373** for more information.

National Association of Senior Friends

Cape Fear Memorial Hospital • (910) 452-8100
5301 Wrightsville Ave • Wilmington, NC 28403

Golf Club has manufactured homes in a landscaped, golf course setting. Three-bedroom, two-bath homes begin at around $90,000, and one resident must be at least 55 years of age (children younger than 18 may visit but are not allowed to be permanent residents). Residents enjoy full lawn maintenance, in-ground utilities and irrigation systems. Close to shopping, entertainment and the beach, this community south of Wilmington is pleasantly secluded. The ability to drive is important in this location.

Catherine Kennedy Home
207 S. Third St., Wilmington
• (910) 762-5322

The Catherine Kennedy Home in downtown Wilmington is a nondenominational, nonprofit private home operated by a self-perpetuating board of directors. Organized in 1845 by Catherine deRosset Kennedy, and known then as The Ladies Benevolent Society, it is the oldest home for the aged in the United States. In 1995, impressive renovations were made to the residential wings. Residents enjoy three meals a day, stimulating activities and comfortable private rooms or suites with private baths.

An attractive feature of this home is its location on a beautiful campus in historic downtown Wilmington. It is a pleasant stroll to shopping, dining and entertainment. Additionally, all of the city bus lines converge just a few blocks away.

This is not a nursing home, and residents must be 62 years of age or older, ambulatory and in good health upon admission. Residents may retain their own personal assistants. There is a nonrefundable fee of $2,500 upon moving into the home. A schedule of fees (based on type of accommodation) is available by calling or writing. Rates begin at $1,015 per month.

Coastal Plantation
U.S. Hwy. 17 N., Hampstead
• (910) 270-3520

Just north of Wilmington, Coastal Plantation is a beautifully landscaped community of individual manufactured homes. Residents purchase the house and lease the land. These quality homes range in price from the high $80,000s for a two-bedroom, two-bath plan and high $90,000s for a three-bedroom home. The price includes quite a few amenities. Each home has a utility shed, peripheral plantings, a cement driveway, carport, all appliances, energy-efficient heating and cooling systems, a screened porch and more.

This is a community for healthy individuals who are at least 55 years of age and appreciate independence within the context of a planned community. A clubhouse, swimming pool, regular potluck suppers and activity groups provide social opportunities.

There's so much to do on North Carolina's Southern coast, there's not much time for rocking.

Lake Shore Commons
1402 Hospital Plaza Dr., Wilmington
• **(910) 251-0067**

This neighborhood is in a park setting on picturesque Greenfield Lake near downtown Wilmington. The lake is a tremendously interesting ecosystem of cypress trees, Spanish moss and assorted amphibians, birds and reptiles. Sidewalks surrounding the lake allow for interesting walks or jogs. Three meals a day in an elegant dining area, housekeeping, all utilities and no-charge personal laundry are some of the features of this community.

A monthly fee includes apartment rental, use of a private dining room on occasion and regular use of the main dining room, library, chapel, television lounge, transportation and scheduled activities. There is an on-site beauty/barber shop. No healthcare service is provided, but the complex has a personal-care wing staffed by Certified Nurse's Aides and supervised by a Registered Nurse. There is no buy-in fee and the only upfront cost is a fully refundable security deposit equal to one month's rent.

Apartments include studio, one-bedroom and two-bedrooms, ranging from $1,075 to $2,075. Lake Shore Commons plans to build a second facility on the 17th Street Extension in 1998-99.

Liberty Commons
2320 41st St., Wilmington
• (910) 392-6899

Assisted living in a home-style environment is the focus here. Each of the spacious and airy rooms is individually climate-controlled and each has a private bathroom with shower, a large closet and residential-quality furniture. Residents who wish to create their own decor are welcome to do so. Every room is equipped with a bedside and bathroom emergency call-response system. Cable television and private telephones are optional. Liberty Commons has 85 beds in its assisted-living residence and 50 in its special-care center.

Monthly rates for assisted living are $2,275 for private and $1,545 for semiprivate rooms. Personal-care rates are $2,745 and $2,020, and special-care rates are $3,585 and $2,810. These rates include meals, housekeeping and linens, personal laundry, the administration of physician-directed medication and free transportation to the doctor.

Residents may choose among optional services such as barber and beauty shops, physical and speech therapy, dining out, theater and shopping trips and more. Licensed practical nurses and assistants are on call 24 hours a day. Various activities programs are available to meet individual needs.

Plantation Village
1200 Porter's Neck Rd., Wilmington
• (910) 686-7181, (800) 334-0240 in state, (800) 334-0035 out of state

Plantation Village is a life-care retirement community on 50 acres within Porter's Neck Plantation. The campus has a library, bank facilities, auditorium, swimming pool, woodworking shop, crafts room and many more amenities.

The complex has 170 private apartments and villas in place, with more construction on additional duplexes with garages ongoing. Although the entry fee ranges from $96,000 to $237,000, there is a 90-percent return-of-capital plan. Monthly service starts at $1,200 and tops off at $2,200 for an individual. Add an additional $680 for a second person. This full-service package includes everything except assisted-living services.

Plantation Village is a unique retirement community in that it receives people in good health age 62 and older and is able to offer professional, long-term nursing care services from nearby Cornelia Nixon Davis Center as a part of the monthly service fee. Before nursing care is needed, residents have access to a wellness center on the campus, a 24-hour nurse on call and the visit of a doctor each week. For the monthly service fee, residents may also receive 240 hours of assisted-living services.

Garden spaces are provided for those inclined to poke about in the dirt. Gardeners will appreciate the fact that this was once a working plantation where peanuts, rice and cotton were grown in abundance.

Senior Centers

The following senior centers maintain lively schedules of entertainment and other services. Many offer exercise programs (including aerobics and jazzaerobics), bingo, shuffleboard, line and ballroom dancing, covered-dish suppers, fitness checks and a multitude of other

INSIDERS' TIP

Bridge tournaments are held regularly at the New Hanover County Senior Center, 2222 S. College Road in Wilmington. The per-session fee ($7 per player, $68 per team) includes lunch. Call (910) 256-6207 or (910) 762-1435 for more information.

activities. Call the one closest to you for information about its programs and calendar of events.

Burgaw Senior Center, 312 W. Williams Street, Burgaw, (910) 259-9119

Katie B. Hines Senior Center, 308 Cape Fear Boulevard, Carolina Beach, (910) 458-6609

New Hanover County Senior Center, 2222 S. College Road, Wilmington, (910) 452-6400

Shallotte Senior Citizens Center, 11300 Seven Creeks Highway, Shallotte, (910) 754-8776

Topsail Senior Center, 20959 U.S. Highway 17, Hampstead, (910) 270-0708

Employment Services

Senior AIDES Program
709 Market St., Wilmington
• (910) 251-5040

The Senior AIDES program offers job counseling and training for senior citizens and places people 55 and older into employment situations in the expectation that the jobs will become permanent.

Volunteer Opportunities Just for Seniors

Although our area offers a wide range of volunteer opportunities (see our Volunteers chapter), there are some jobs that can only be handled by people with a lifetime of experience. Following are several organizations that would appreciate your help.

Retired Senior Volunteer Program (RSVP)
2222 S. College Rd., Wilmington
• (910) 452-6400

RSVP puts the talents of retired members of the community to work. Its motto is "Sharing the Experience of a Lifetime." This is the largest RSVP in North Carolina, with more than 1,000 active volunteers working in local non-profit agencies.

Seniors Health Insurance Information Program (SHIPP)
2222 S. College Rd., Wilmington
• (910) 452-6400

Volunteers with this organization are trained by the North Carolina Department of Insurance to help people with Medicare problems, questions about Supplemental Insurance or long-term care issues.

Service Corps of Retired Executives (SCORE)
Alton Lennon Federal Bldg., 2 Princess St., Wilmington • (910) 815-4576

Retired executives share their knowledge with new business owners in a mentoring relationship.

Just for Fun

Gold's Gym
127 S. College Rd., Wilmington
• (910) 392-3999

Gold's Gym offers special programs for seniors, including aerobics classes, senior strengthening classes, the largest selection of workout and cardiovascular equipment in New Hanover County and special rates for people age 50 and over.

Region O Senior Games
2222 S. College Rd., Wilmington
• (910) 452-6400

Seniors compete in sports events including archery, golf, running, swimming and more. The local group competes in national events and is known to bring home quite a few awards. The New Hanover County Senior Center sponsors these yearly games.

INSIDERS' TIP

Cape Fear Memorial Hospital has a national membership program called Senior Friends for people age 50 and over who are interested in healthy living through education, social events and other special membership privileges, (910) 452-8373.

Twin Travel & Cruises
5751 Oleander Dr., Ste. 10, Wilmington
• (910) 799-5225

Twin's "LJ Tours" are geared (but not limited) to people age 55 and older. This full-service travel agency creates attractive package tours to Myrtle Beach shows, the Spoleto Festival in Charleston and the Biltmore House in Asheville.

University of North Carolina at Wilmington
601 S. College Rd., Wilmington
• (910) 962-3000

The university offers a lecture series, concerts, plays, continuing education and other programs geared to the retired population. Call for a calender of events.

Government Agencies

County departments of aging offer a variety of services, including congregate meals, home-delivered meals, transportation, minor home repairs, Senior Tar Heel Cards for area discounts, senior center operations, in-home aide, health promotion/disease prevention, and fan/heat relief. Contact one of the following agencies for more information.

Brunswick County Department of Older Adults, Brunswick County Government Complex, Bolivia, (910) 253-2080

Cape Fear Council of Governments, Department of Aging, 1480 Harbour Drive, Wilmington, (910) 395-4553. This organization's Area Agency on Aging administrator is a rich resource. The agency oversees senior services in New Hanover, Pender, Brunswick and Columbus counties.

New Hanover County Department of Aging, 2222 S. College Rd., Wilmington, (910) 452-6400

WHEN VISITING WILMINGTON, QUICK, CONVENIENT MEDICAL CARE IS AS CLOSE AS OUR NEAREST OFFICE.

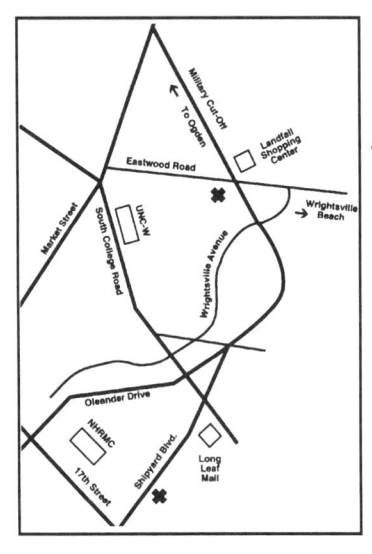

Medac provides a variety of Affordable, Professional, Urgent Care Medical Services for injury or illness, including:

- Minor Accidents and Injuries
- Lacerations, Sprains, Fractures
- Burns, Bites and Stings
- EKG, X-ray and Lab Services
- Sports and School Physicals
- Employment Health
- Drug & TB Screening
- Flu & Pneumonia Shots
- Referrals to Specialists
- Private Physician Assistance
- Medical Records Transfer
- Workman's Comp Cases
- Occupational Health Services

medac

CONVENIENT + COURTEOUS + CARING

Now With Two Easy-to-Find Locations

3710 SHIPYARD BLVD • 910-791-0075
1442 MILITARY CUTOFF RD • 910-256-6088

WILMINGTON NC 28403

·OPEN 7-DAYS-A-WEEK • 8AM-8PM • WALK-INS WELCOME

Most Insurance Plans and Credit Cards are Welcome. For a complete List of our Medical Services, including Corporate Health Services, please contact Meredith Billman, Administrator, at 910-452-1400.

Owned and Operated by Eastern Carolina Emergency Physicians, PA.

Healthcare

The Cape Fear area offers excellent healthcare facilities and services. In the first half of this century, residents generally went inland to more sophisticated medical facilities in search of state-of-the-art technology to treat serious illness. That trend has changed and even reversed itself as inlanders now come here for exceptional healthcare services.

More than 360 practicing physicians in Wilmington and New Hanover County have access to some of the most technologically progressive facilities and equipment in the state by way of two large hospitals that serve the area.

Several small hospitals dot the southern coast. Care beyond the scope of their services is referred to Wilmington's larger hospitals, but these smaller facilities also offer a broad and excellent range of healthcare services. Vacationers along the Brunswick beaches and Topsail Island sometimes find these smaller hospitals more convenient if they need medical attention.

Hospitals

Wilmington

Cape Fear Memorial Hospital
5301 Wrightsville Ave. • (910) 452-8384

Cape Fear Memorial is an acute-care hospital with 142 beds. It provides medical, surgical and ambulatory care, and 24-hour emergency services. Outpatient surgery, radiology, ultrasound, magnetic resonance imaging, laboratory facilities and a sleep disorder center are some of the hospital's expanded service areas. It also offers pain management services, neurological services and orthopedic surgery.

Women's Services, a hallmark of patient care at Cape Fear, presents classes and seminars where women can learn about their own health issues as well as those that might affect their families. The Birthing Center, the hospital's family-oriented labor, delivery and postpartum services unit, offers a homelike setting with the advantage of immediate access to state-of-the-art medical care and equipment.

Neuroscience is one of this hospital's many medical specialties. This field includes endovascular coil occlusion, the process in which a catheter is used to close off an aneurysm and prevent it from rupturing. Cape Fear is only the third hospital in North Carolina to have performed this procedure. The hospital offers a full range of neurodiagnostics, including an updated CT scanner with spiral capability. This equipment allows a technologist to scan an internal organ in a matter of seconds.

The hospital offers a program called Senior Friends for people age 50 and older that stresses wellness. For a yearly membership fee of $15 for an individual or $25 for a couple living at the same address, seniors can attend monthly meetings, enjoy discounts on particular services, get discounts on meals in the cafeteria and have a private room at a semi-private rate. Members are also entitled to national pharmacy discounts, discounted health screenings, travel opportunities and special promotions through area merchants.

Regularly held health-related classes focus on nutrition, cardiopulmonary resuscitation certification, exercise, smoking cessation and stress management. Safe Sitter, a national program for young adults, provides a comprehensive course on safe, responsible child care and teaches its students rescue breathing and choking techniques, and helps them understand the fundamentals of babysitting.

Cape Fear Memorial Hospital is accredited by the Joint Commission on Accreditation of Healthcare Organizations, the world's largest provider of healthcare services.

New Hanover Regional Medical Center
2131 S. 17th St. • (910) 343-7000

New Hanover Regional Medical Center is a 628-bed hospital with five intensive care units, including one for neonatal. It also includes several specialized care facilities and programs on site and at various locations throughout the city. The center is operated by trustees appointed by the New Hanover County Board of Commissioners and offers high-quality care with an increasing emphasis on more critical illnesses and conditions. The hospital is staffed by 2,850 employees, making it one of the largest employers in New Hanover County.

New Hanover Regional's Coastal Heart Center, which has become a magnet for patients with heart disease from New Hanover and surrounding counties, provides some of the best physicians, surgeons and support staff in the state of North Carolina. Services of particular importance to a community with a booming retirement population include cardiac catheterization, angioplasty, open-heart surgery, cardiac rehabilitation and a new cardiovascular laboratory, diagnostic testing and outpatient services.

Cancer services include chemotherapy, radiation, surgical and medical treatments as well as participation in clinical trials. CanSurvive, a support group for those who are coping with cancer, was created to allow these individuals and their families to share their experiences. Construction began on new 30,000 square foot Coastal Cancer Center in late 1996, and this facility, adjacent to the main hospital building, will open in 1998. It will consolidate all cancer services in one location, including radiation therapy.

Designated by the state as one of eight regional trauma centers, this hospital provides a mobile intensive care unit, VitaLink, that can transport the most seriously ill and injured patients from the region's community hospitals at any hour of the day or night. Equipped with life-sustaining systems and trained staff, the vehicle is also in constant communication with the hospital until the patient arrives. A paramedic and registered nurse are always on board.

New Hanover Regional BirthPlace specializes in obstetrical services, offering more than two dozen rooms that combine homelike decor with sophisticated facilities to allow a family-centered birthing experience. In Women's Health Specialties, a team of perinatologists care for women with high-risk pregnancies. The area's only Board-certified reproductive endocrinologist works with women who are having difficulty conceiving, and a gynecologic oncologist specializes in cancer care for women.

The Center for Successful Aging is an outpatient department staffed by a geriatrician, nurses, social workers, therapists and a pharmacist. The hospital also has an inpatient Geriatric Unit.

The Medical Mall at the intersection of 17th Street and Glen Meade Drive makes outpatient services such as MRI, X-rays, mammography and lab tests convenient.

The Coastal Rehabilitation Hospital, (910) 343-7845, is situated on New Hanover Regional Medical Center's sprawling 70-acre campus. Patients include those with traumatic brain injury, spinal cord injury, orthopedic conditions and stroke.

Another component of New Hanover Regional Medical Center is the Coastal Diabetes Center, 1201 S. 16th Street, (910) 763-6111, an American Diabetes Association-approved facility specifically devoted to diabetes education and management.

A freestanding psychiatric hospital on the hospital campus, The Oaks, (910) 343-7787, attracts patients from the entire region. The Oaks' staff of 125 provides specialized care for 62 adult and adolescent inpatients in a serene, landscaped setting. The Oaks' partial hospitalization program provides day therapy and the outpatient program provides counseling services. Psychiatric evaluations are available 24 hours a day.

New Hanover Home Health, (910) 815-5310, provides professional services to individuals and their families as an alternative to inpatient care. Services include skilled nurs-

A comprehensive, community oriented hospital, Cape Fear Memorial Hospital has expanded its services and enhanced its facilities to combine the latest in medical technology with an abiding belief in personalized compassionate care.

Serving the area since 1957, Cape Fear Memorial Hospital now offers the community a Wound Care Center, a Senior Health Center, Neurodiagnostic Imaging, plus Outpatient Health Services and a Family Birthing Center.

Cape Fear Memorial Hospital • (910) 452-8100
5301 Wrightsville Ave • Wilmington, NC 28403

---

ing, home infusion, medical social service, pediatric care, physical and occupational therapy, nutritional counseling and speech/audiology therapies.

New Hanover Regional Medical Center has the only Pediatric Unit in a six-county region and a new unit specifically designed for children started construction in 1997.

VitaLine is a 24-hour health-information line where callers can get confidential and prompt answers to health-related questions. Experienced registered nurses and other professionally trained staff can help determine your need to see a physician, provide physician referral information and suggest community health resources. The Automated Health Information component allows callers to listen to tapes on health topics. At the touch of a button, the caller can interrupt the taped information and speak directly to a nurse. This free service is available by calling (910) 815-5188 or (888) 815-5188.

The hospital also sponsors The Healing Arts Network, (910) 815-5870, a collaboration of complementary therapies directed toward helping patients heal and better handle transitions and losses related to illness. HAN offers a variety of individualized interventions such as relaxation, communication of feelings and development of coping skills. Therapies include art, music, movement, expressive arts, horticulture, storytelling, creative writing, massage, energy and yoga. These services are available to all patients of New Hanover Regional Medical Center and affiliated facilities by a physician referral.

New Hanover Regional Medical Center is accredited by the Joint Commission on Accreditation of Healthcare Organizations.

Outside Wilmington

Brunswick Community Hospital
U.S. Hwy. 17, Supply • (910) 755-8121

Brunswick Community Hospital, which is owned by the county and leased by Columbia/HCA, is located in central Brunswick County at Supply, near Long Beach and Ocean

Isle. It is licensed for 60 beds. The hospital has a 24-hour physician-staffed emergency department, full medical and surgical services and an inpatient adolescent psychiatric care program. A chest pain emergency center is also in the hospital.

Included among its comprehensive medical services are general medicine and a broad range of specialties, including obstetrics/gynecology, opthalmology, nuclear medicine, pain management, urology and pediatrics. New programs include Senior Friends, Safe Sitter and Alzheimer's Disease and Neurological Support Groups.

Brunswick Community offers a Physician Referral Service, (910) 755-1400, and also operates the Brunswick Shores Children's Center within the facility. The hospital is accredited by the Joint Commission on Accreditation of Healthcare Organizations.

J. Arthur Dosher Memorial Hospital
924 N. Howe St., Southport
- (910) 457-5271 (emergency ext.: 351)

J. Arthur Dosher Memorial Hospital is a 40-bed, acute care hospital that offers extensive outpatient services. Established in 1930, this small public hospital serves the Smithville Township area, attracting patients from Oak Island, Southport, Boiling Springs Lake, Bolivia and Leland. A public, tax-based facility, Dosher Memorial is focused on its community, offering outreach programs in the schools and working with local citizen organizations to promote healthy lifestyles.

The hospital has a 24-hour, physician-staffed emergency room. There are 12 medical specialties, including diagnostic imaging, cardiopulmonary services, speech and physical therapy and comprehensive surgical services. Support groups sponsored by Dosher Memorial include diabetes, head injury, hospice, stroke and weight control.

The hospital provides a valuable free publication, *Safe Vacation Guide*, distributed to hotels, motels and condominiums in the area. It advises visitors about potential health hazards related to sunburn, dangerous aquatic life and rusty fish hooks. It also gives safety tips about avoiding alligators and checking the Intracoastal Waterway at low tide for obstructions before you go tearing along in a boat. It offers a healthcare reference manual that explains all services of the hospital, as well as a physician guide according to specialty.

Pender Memorial Hospital
507 Fremont St., Burgaw
- (910) 259-5451

Pender Memorial Hospital is a general acute medical and skilled nursing facility with a bed capacity of 66. It offers inpatient and outpatient services, including ambulatory/same day surgery, laparoscopy, laboratory tests, radiology, respiratory therapy and physical therapy.

Immediate Care

For nonsurgical medical services, the Cape Fear area has an ample number of immediate care centers. Vacationers or residents with relatively minor injuries, illnesses or conditions may prefer the convenience of visiting these centers over making an appointment to see a personal doctor. Illnesses and injuries beyond the care centers' capabilities are referred to area hospitals.

These are convenient places to get flu and tetanus shots or to have a limited variety of tests or physicals for school, sports or insurance purposes. Most have their own labs and X-ray services, and all are staffed by qualified, licensed physicians and nurses. Be advised that most of the centers operate on a first-come basis, so don't expect to be able to make an appointment. However, serious illnesses, injuries or conditions will receive first priority.

These medical service facilities offer emergency care but are not open 24 hours a day. In many cases, they are not open seven days a week. If you need attention and choose one of these centers, you're advised to phone ahead.

INSIDERS' TIP

An enormous range of support groups are listed in the daily calendar in the "Lifestyles" section of the *Wilmington Star-News*.

HEALTHCARE • 383

Visitors to Topsail Island are within a one-hour drive to hospitals and clinics in Wilmington. For serious injuries and illnesses, the coastal region has ample EMT services that can be reached by calling 911.

Wilmington

Doctor's Immediate Care, 4606 Oleander Drive (central Wilmington), (910) 452-0800

Doctor's Urgent Care Centre, 4815 Oleander Drive (central Wilmington), (910) 452-1111

MEDAC Convenient Medical Care, 3710 Shipyard Boulevard (south side of Wilmington), (910) 791-0075

MEDAC II Convenient Medical Care, 1442 Military Cutoff Road (Landfall area of Wilmington), (910) 256-6088

Northside Medical Center, 502 N. Fourth Street (downtown Wilmington), (910) 251-7715

Photo: Scott Taylor

Old Baldy on Bald Head Island is restored and open for touring.

Outside Wilmington

Express Care, U.S. 17, Shallotte, (910) 579-0800

Federal Point Medical Center, 1300 Dow Road, Carolina Beach, (910) 458-8201

Hampstead Medical Center, 14980 US Highway 17, Hampstead, (910) 270-2722

Urgent Care Center, North Brunswick, 117H Village Road, Leland, (910) 371-0404

Penslow Medical Center, 206 N. Dyson Street, intersection of U.S. 17 and N.C. 50, Holly Ridge, (910) 329-7591

Home Healthcare

There is an increasing demand for in-home care in the region. The following list is a representative sampling of private businesses and nonprofit agencies that offer in-home nursing care services such as nurses' aides, LPNs, RNs, companions and other assistance depending upon individual need.

Assisted Care, 4010 Oleander Drive, Suite 2, Wilmington, (910) 395-9998 or (800) 293-9380

Comprehensive Home Health Care, 3311 Burnt Mill Road, Wilmington, (910) 251-8111 or (800)-800-0622; 602 US Highway 117 N., Suite F, Burgaw, (910) 259-1150

Eldercare Convalescent Service, 5003 Randall Parkway, Wilmington, (910) 395-5003

Lower Cape Fear Hospice, 725 Wellington Avenue, Wilmington, (910) 762-0200

New Hanover Home Health, New Hanover Regional Medical Center, Long Leaf Mall, Wilmington, (910) 815-5310

Well Care and Nursing Services Inc., 2424 S. 17th Street, Wilmington, (910) 452-1555

Drug and Alcohol Abuse

There are numerous organizations and agencies in the area to help people struggling with substance abuse. Under new laws, mental health counselors are required to be licensed and certified by the State of North Carolina, and to hold at least a masters degree from an accredited institution. So make it a point to inquire into these important credentials. All the following organizations are located in Wilmington.

A Center for Counseling, 306 Windemere Road, (910) 392-5915

Alcoholics Anonymous, 3130 Wrightsville Avenue, (910) 762-1230

Alpha Counseling and Development Center, 3415 Wrightsville Avenue, (910) 791-5171

Southeastern Center for Mental Health, Developmental Disabilities and Substance Abuse, 2023 S. 17th Street, (910) 251-6440

Wilmington Treatment Center, 2520 Troy Drive, (910) 762-2727

Chiropractors

Chiropractors are available in astonishingly high numbers in the Cape Fear region. A national movement toward alternative health care and nontraditional medical treatment of pain, as well as an approach to wellness, have focused attention on chiropractic care. Some well-established chiropractic offices are listed here.

Alternative Health Care Center, 4706 Oleander Drive, Wilmington, (910) 392-3770

Friedman Chiropractic, 1033-A S. Kerr Avenue, Wilmington, (910) 350-2664

Reese Family Chiropractic, 2003 Carolina Beach Road, Wilmington, (910) 763-3611

Dr. Glenn Weckel, Chiropractic Physician, 3015 Market Street, Wilmington, (910) 762-9000

Massage Therapy

The Cape Fear region has an abundance of practitioners of massage therapy for wellness, chronic pain, strain and injuries. Every therapist or practice offers particular methods that range through Swedish, deep tissue, myofascial release, neuromuscular, craniosacral therapy, trigger point, foot reflexology, polarity, shiatsu, acupressure, prenatal and sports. The service averages

INSIDERS' TIP

The New Hanover-Pender County Medical Society, 2259 S. 17th Street in Wilmington, (910) 251-8455, offers a physician referral service.

around $40 per hour, but you can certainly find a therapist who charges less or more. Some massage therapists work in their homes, others in offices and a few will be happy to come to your own home. The following therapists are listed because their work has been personally experienced or conveyed by knowledgeable friends. However, the phone book reveals a long list of alternatives for consideration.

Deborah Flora, CMT, Wilmington, (910) 762-9073

Wilmington Center for Therapeutic Massage, The Cotton Exchange, 321 N. Front Street, Wilmington, (910) 762-9484

Elizabeth Bryson, LMT, The Cotton Exchange, 321 N. Front Street, Wilmington, (910) 343-0807

Theresa Jones, CMP, Wilmington, (910) 763-1882

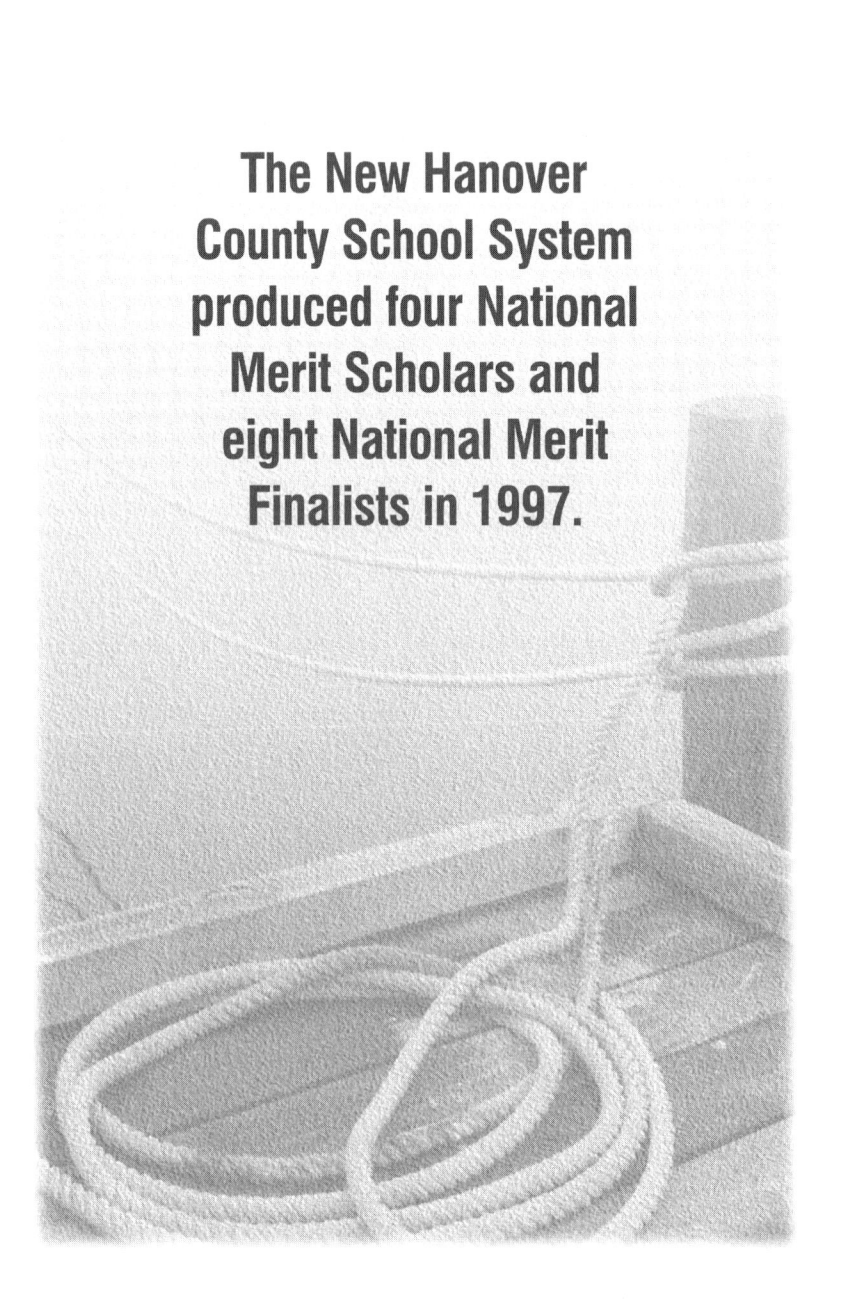

The New Hanover County School System produced four National Merit Scholars and eight National Merit Finalists in 1997.

Schools and Child Care

The southern North Carolina coast is served by three separate public school systems. New Hanover County has the largest system, as it encompasses the largest city on the state's entire coastline. Brunswick County Schools and Pender County Schools serve largely the rural populations to the southwest and north of New Hanover.

Additionally, the region offers a growing list of private schools, both secular and religion-based, that meet a broad range of educational requirements

School-age children in New Hanover County should immediately be enrolled in a public or private school. To enroll a child in the public schools, the parent or guardian must bring a birth certificate along with the child's Social Security card and immunization records to the school system office.

Children entering kindergarten must be 5 years old on or before October 16 of that year. Parents of students who were enrolled in a different school should bring the student's last report card to the new school.

Schools

Public Schools

New Hanover County School System
1802 S. 15th St., Wilmington
• **(910) 763-5431**

The New Hanover County School System, the 10th-largest public school system in the state, serves the city of Wilmington and the county, including the beach communities of Figure Eight Island, Wrightsville Beach, Carolina Beach, Kure Beach and Fort Fisher. In 1997-1998, the system served 21,324 students from kindergarten through grade 12 in 33 schools. The mission of New Hanover County Schools is "to provide a high quality education that prepares all students to be productive and contributing citizens of a global society."

The system faces the familiar challenges encountered by most American school systems. There is a constant need for more funding and better facilities, and there's a continuing pursuit of educational excellence to serve the needs of children in diverse socioeconomic circumstances. In November of 1997, the citizens of the county voted in favor of a $125 million dollar school bond referendum. New Hanover earned an exceptional rating on accreditation standards applied by the Southern Association of Colleges and Schools.

North Carolina basic skills test scores for 1997 placed New Hanover County Schools slightly ahead of the state average for grade 4 writing (53% scoring 2.5 or better compared to 48.6% for the state) and above the state average for Grade 7 writing (65.3% scoring 2.5 or better compared to 54.9% for the state.) On the Iowa Achievement Test, students scored above the national average in grade 3.

Combined SAT scores averaged 1004, compared to 978 for the state and 1016 nationally. Although New Hanover's average is lower than the national average, it is important to consider that more students take the test in the South than in other regions of the country. Sixty-four percent of New Hanover County seniors take the SAT compared to a national average of 41 percent.

In 1997-1998, 83.2 percent of the system's graduates planned to continue their education beyond high school. More than $5.7 million in scholarships and financial aid was awarded to 1997 graduates. The system produced four National Merit Scholars and eight National Merit Finalists in 1997. Twenty-two students were selected for enrollment in the North Carolina Governor's School, and five were selected to attend the North Carolina School of Science and Math. North Carolinas Scholars recipients, students recognized by the state for superior academic achievement, numbered 386.

The system has had the benefit of tremendous support from the business community and community volunteers. Volunteers in 1997 numbered more than 4,200 and contributed a whopping 183,000 documented hours of service to the system. These individuals contributed in many different ways, including tutoring, working to lower the dropout rate and offering opportunities for students to gain exposure to the corporate realm beyond the classroom.

Much of the assistance from businesses comes through the Greater Wilmington Chamber of Commerce Education Foundation, a community education support organization that provides funding for mini-grants to supplement system-funded education each year. It sponsors "Best Foot Forward," a variety show put on by the schools at Thalian Hall each March. Proceeds from this lively event fund the mini-grant program. As of 1997, this event had generated $120,000 for grants, funding 126 projects. Other programs under the auspices of this foundation include Project Business, Cape Fear Careers, Community Resource File, ROCAME (Region O Council for the Advancement of Minorities in Engineering) and a Scholars Reception.

The 1997-98 budget for New Hanover County Schools was $127.7 million, with 65 percent coming from the state, 31 percent from local monies and 4 percent from the federal government. Per-pupil expenditure was $4,687. Of the total budget, more than 70 percent was used directly for instructional costs.

The system is organized as kindergarten through grade 5, grades 6 through 8 and grades 9 through 12, using the middle school concept instead of junior high schools. The school year runs from the end of August until the first part of June, although year-round schooling is now available at five elementary schools and one middle school. The year-round program is voluntary for students and teachers. After considerable investigation, the Board of Education found the advantages of year-round schooling include increased learning, a reduction in stress levels for both students and teachers, more time, greater opportunity for effective enrichment and remediation, and higher motivation.

While still in high school, students in New Hanover County schools may engage in advanced studies at the University of North Carolina at Wilmington or enroll in courses at Cape Fear Community College for part of the instructional day. In 1993, the Gregory School of Science, Mathematics and Technology opened its doors to allow elementary school students to experience a high-tech program of study that integrates science and mathematics throughout the curriculum. This was the first magnet school in the system, and it has been enthusiastically received within the community. Other magnet schools are Codington Elementary and Eaton Elementary.

Lakeside Alternative School takes students with special needs, primarily those identified as at-risk. This school operates an extended-day program for students who also work.

There are four senior high schools in New Hanover County, and the middle schools that feed into these operate according to district lines, which are available for inspection at the school system office. In no case should a new resident assume his/her child will attend a neighborhood school. The county student population is 31.3% minority enrollment, and lines are periodically shifted to ensure balanced racial populations at all schools.

More than 288 courses are available to

CAPE FEAR ACADEMY

THE ART OF DISCIPLINE

Member of NAIS, NCAIS, SAIS
Accredited by Southern Association of Colleges and Schools

Contact Director of Admissions
(910) 791-0287
Fax: (910) 791-0290

Whether it's hitting the right note or the right key on a computer, mastering a skill requires discipline. At Cape Fear Academy, supportive teachers and a nurturing environment can help your child develop a sense of personal responsibility.

We help turn hard work into accomplishment, because we believe that self-discipline leads to self-confidence – and to a successful future.

Cape Fear Academy practices a nondiscriminatory admissions policy.

---

senior high school students, including social studies, mathematics, computer science, English, foreign languages and the full range of sciences. Students can participate in Army, Navy and Air Force JROTC Honor units as well as a broad range of extracurricular activities and programs. There are many programs in vocational education, including marine sciences and oceanography. A cultural arts curriculum includes band, orchestra, chorus, drama, art and dance.

Middle schools offer a similar, though more limited, curriculum to that of the senior high schools. Elementary schools emphasize hands-on experience in all disciplines. Elementary school students participate in a curriculum based on the use of manipulatives to build a foundation that will support the learning of concepts in the middle grades and high school. A comprehensive program has been designed for exceptional children at all grade levels.

Basketball and football figure largely in interscholastic athletic programs. What else would you expect from the sports-minded city that produced such athletes as Michael Jordan, Meadowlark Lemon and Roman Gabriel on its public school courts and fields? Volleyball, baseball, soccer, wrestling, golf, tennis and track are also offered.

Brunswick County School System
35 Referendum Dr., N.E., Bolivia
• (910) 253-2900

The Brunswick County School System has a student population of approximately 10,000 and operates three high schools, three middle schools and six elementary schools. It offers an alternative high school, the Brunswick Learning Center, that provides education for students who have left the regular program or have not had success in other programs. There is also one combined elementary-middle school housing grades 1 through 8. A new elementary school is under construction on Highway 211, slated to open in 1998-1999, and a 10-year building needs project was initiated in 1998 to accommodate anticipated rapid growth of the population.

Some things never change: hunting for seashells, Wrightsville Beach, c. 1916.

In addition to the basic K-12 instructional program, Brunswick County Schools offer a comprehensive program of instructional services for the exceptional child, vocational education, remediation and courses for the North Carolina Scholar.

The system's budget for 1997-98 was approximately $54,757 million and per-pupil expenditure was $5,848. The average SAT score for Brunswick County in 1997 was 929. SAT scores have increased by 25 points since 1995. In end-of-course tests for all grade levels, students improved in 11 of 12 subject areas with one area, math, remaining about the same. Shallotte Middle School 7th and 8th grade students, participating in the North Carolina Math Quiz Bowl for the first time in 1998, brought home the second-place prize.

The Center for Advanced Studies, a joint partnership with Brunswick Community College, encourages and offers more advanced courses in all arenas of the curriculum, including vocational coursework and AP programs. Juniors and seniors who have excelled in high school can get license credit toward trades occupations. In addition to assisting students

CREATIVE WORLD PRE-SCHOOL

Ages 6 Wks-12 Years
Providing An Educational Setting
Devoted To Fostering Growth
Of The "WHOLE" Child

EXTRA-CURRICULAR
ON-SITE WATERSLIDE & GYMNASIUM
BALLET • SKATING • SWIM LESSONS
BOWLING • MOVIES • PICNICS • FIELD TRIPS • GYMNASTICS

SUMMER CAMP PROGRAM
AFTER SCHOOL PICK-UP AT MOST ELEMENTARY SCHOOLS
HOURS: 6:30am-6pm
*"WE INVITE YOU TO TOUR OUR FACILITIES
AND MEET OUR EXPERIENCED AND CARING STAFF"*

791-2080
4202 Wilshire Blvd
(Off College Rd)

799-5195
2411 Flint Dr.
(Near New Hanover Memorial Hospital)

ELEMENTARY SCHOOL
- Extensive Education
- 1st-4th Grades
- Learning Labs
- Computer Science
- Foreign Language Studies

2409 Flint Drive
(Near New Hanover Memorial Hospital)

799-9765

---

pursue vocational careers, the program also is intended to expose students to college life and make them aware of higher education options. In 1998, fifty-three students were enrolled in the program.

The system's technology plan is directed at not only student but also parental computer literacy. Leland Middle School, Old Fayetteville Road, Leland, (910) 371-3030, offers night courses in computer education free of charge to parents as well as students.

Pender County School System
925 Penderlea Hwy., Burgaw
• **(910) 259-2187**

The Pender County School System has 11 schools with an enrollment of approximately 6,100 students. It comprises six elementary schools, three middle schools, two high schools and one alternative school that serves students in grades 7 through 10. The system also offers one year-round school, Penderlea. It participates in the A+ Arts Program, a widely acclaimed program devised to integrate the arts into the academic experience.

The curriculum includes 20 major areas covered by more than 150 course selections. Students are afforded the opportunity to specialize in college preparatory, Tech Prep or any blend of courses to address individual needs. Both high schools operate on the block schedule, a system that compresses a full course into one semester by extending each class from 50 minutes to 90.

The Board of Education is beginning a campaign to construct and renovate school facilities and has recently identified more than $58 million in facility needs for the next decade. The total budget for the system in 1997-98 was in excess of $30.6 million. The citizens of Pender County passed a $25 million school bond referendum in 1996, and an additional sum of $13 million from the state puts the facility upgrades well ahead of schedule. Per-pupil expenditure is approximately $5,000. The 1997 SAT scores averaged 904 with 48.9 percent of seniors taking the test.

Pender county was selected by the North Carolina School of Science and Mathematics to host a Cyber Campus. One of seven in the state, it is housed at Pender High School.

Private Schools

The Cape Fear region's private schools offer curricula and activities for children from preschool to high school. While tuition and expenses are the responsibility of the parent or guardian, most of these schools offer financial aid or easy-pay plans. In many cases, having more than one child in a particular school allows a discount on tuition for other children within the same family. All private schools aren't shown here, but the following list suggests some alternatives to public education.

Cape Fear Academy
3900 S. College Rd., Wilmington
• (910) 791-0287

Cape Fear Academy is the dominant secular private school in the region. Established in 1967, this coeducational day school is open to students interested in a traditional, college preparatory education. There are approximately 470 students in pre-kindergarten through grade 12. Pre-kindergarten and kindergarten students participate in half-day programs, with after-school care available. The Lower School comprises pre-kindergarten through grade 5. Instruction by a professional faculty includes art, music, science, foreign language (Spanish), drama, computer science and physical education.

The Middle and Upper schools concentrate on college preparation in the classroom coupled with individual development through extracurricular activities. Students in grades 6 through 8 must satisfactorily complete courses in English, science, social studies, math, physical education, art, music, computer science and foreign language. At grade 9, students begin to fulfill graduation requirements. Challenging, Outward Bound-type ventures are part of the Middle and Upper schools curricula. Ropes courses, rock-climbing and rappelling are among the activities that culminate with each student attending the North Carolina Outward Bound School for a week at the beginning of the senior year.

Community service is a key component of the Middle and Upper schools programs as well. The Upper School student government organization has an entire branch devoted to community service. Group and individual activities are planned as students work to serve a minimum number of hours required for graduation. The school also has seven acres of wetlands that have been developed into an outdoor science education area. Nature trails have been established, and teachers have participated in extensive training through the North Carolina Wildlife Commission.

As far as success rates for Cape Fear Academy go, 100 percent of graduates attend four-year college programs, and approximately 85 percent of those students are accepted into their first-choice college or university. The 1997-98 average composite SAT score (all students were tested) was 1,226, more than 200 points higher than North Carolina's average of 978.

Helen Alice Higgins Montessori School
4915 Oriole Dr., Wilmington
• (910) 392-7007

This private school offers instruction based on the Montessori principles of education, encouraging children to exercise independence, initiative and responsibility. Children work at their own pace and are able to choose appropriate work in an environment specially designed for them. The role of the teacher in this setting is to guide children, motivating them gently when necessary and giving only the help they need to progress. As long as the children are engaged in a learning activity, they are allowed to work without interruption.

The school offers a Toddler Program, Primary Program for ages 3 to 6 years, Junior

HELEN ALICE HIGGINS MONTESSORI SCHOOL

Eighteen Years of Proven Success

If Your Child's education is a priority, do not choose a school before walking through our doors.

4915 Oriole Drive • Wilmington, NC 28403 • 392-7007

Elementary Program (Cosmic Education) for grades 1 to 3 and a Senior Elementary Program (Birth of Culture) for grades 4 to 6. The school comprises a toddler room for 2-year-olds, three primary classrooms for 3- to 6-year-olds, junior and senior elementary classrooms for 1st through 6th grade, an art room, libraries, an atrium, a piano lab, a computer lab and a science lab.

Wilmington Christian Academy
1401 N. College Rd., Wilmington
• (910) 791-4248

This is the largest private school in southeastern North Carolina. Founded in 1969 as a ministry of Grace Baptist Church, more than 660 students are enrolled in this academy, which serves kindergarten through 12th-grade students. The school is on a 40-acre campus at the eastern terminus of Interstate 40.

Wilmington Christian Academy's focus is on providing conservative Christian education. The school is committed to "offering our students an academically challenging course of study in an environment that is conducive to spiritual growth. Our goal is to produce students who will glorify God with their lives while successfully competing in today's world."

Academics, athletics and the fine arts are combined to give students a well-rounded educational experience. The academy's sequenced curriculum begins with phonics in kindergarten and progresses through physics and calculus in high school.

The elementary curriculum strongly emphasizes the basic skills of reading and math, augmented by studies in English, spelling, science, history and health. Phonics-based reading instruction begins early and continues through the entire curriculum. Hands-on learning projects and practice drills are combined to enhance math instruction. Students are also taught art, music, physical education and foreign language. Piano lessons are available during school hours. Each elementary classroom is equipped with a computer with a Pentium processor and CD-ROM capabilities for classroom instruction and tutoring.

The junior-senior high days consist of seven class periods covering five core academic subjects, one Bible class and one elective. Students in grades 9 through 12 follow one of three academic tracks: general, college preparatory or honors. The math curriculum progresses through calculus, while the science program culminates with physics. Mandatory computer training gives all graduates a working knowledge of word processing, spreadsheets and graphics. Most students graduate with 26 high school credits. Graduates gain acceptance into major Christian colleges and state universities across the country.

St. Mary School
217 S. Fourth St., Wilmington
* **(910) 762-6517**

St. Mary serves approximately 300 students in grades 1 through 8. The school's mission is to "ensure learning for all our students within the framework of Catholic Christian values, to help our students grow in a manner consistent with their needs, interests and abilities, and to prepare them to live in a changing world as self-directing, caring, responsible citizens."

Grades 1 through 5 are structured, self-contained classes. The curriculum includes science, social studies, computers, Spanish, music, art, physical education, religion, reading, phonics in grades 1 and 2, creative writing and math. Grades 6 through 8 have departmental teachers who rotate to different classrooms. Classes include religion, science, social studies, math, language arts, literature, writing, computers, Spanish, music, art and physical education.

St. Mary School graduates are prepared to enroll in the honors courses offered by area high schools. The school's emphasis is on preparing students to be independent learners who maintain high academic achievements and standards throughout their high school and college years.

St. Thomas Pre-School Child Development Center
109 S. Second St., Wilmington
* **(910) 762-7764**

This center specializes in kindergarten, serving 3-, 4- and 5-year-old children who will go on to attend St. Mary School. It is historically notable as the first North Carolina Catholic school for girls, founded in 1868 — although the location was changed to the present one in 1973.

Special Education

Child Development Center, School for the Developmentally Disabled
6743 Amsterdam Way, Wilmington
* **(910) 392-6417**

The Child Development Center serves children ages 2 through 7 who have developmental disabilities. The center can serve 52 children in a full-time educational setting. There are no fees for students from ages 3 to 7, as this center operates under the auspices of the public school system. The center is open weekdays 8 AM to 5 PM, and the educational day is 8 AM to 2 PM. Call for information on financial needs.

United Cerebral Palsy Developmental Center
500 Military Cutoff Rd., Wilmington
* **(910) 392-0080**

Children from New Hanover and surrounding counties who have physical impairments can be referred by a parent, physician or community agency to this special education center. Known as "The Exceptional Preschool," the center serves children from birth to 5 years old who have cerebral palsy or other physical developmental delays.

The center also accepts children without disabilities because the administration believes it is beneficial to bring students with and without physical disabilities together in a quality preschool program. Educators and therapists facilitate learning through play and promote development in areas such as gross and fine motor skills, speech and language, and social-emotional, cognitive and independence skills.

Home Schooling

The State of North Carolina allows schooling outside both public and private schools for children whose parents prefer to administer their education. Supervised under the auspices of the Division of Nonpublic Education, home schooling requires participation in standardized testing and immunization programs and that the educational program be administered for nine months a year by a person with a high school diploma or equivalency certificate.

Wilmington Homeschool Organization provides information for parents interested in educating their children at home. A few queries around the community can produce a contact person reasonably quickly, but a call to the Division of Nonpublic Education in Raleigh, (919) 834-6243, is probably a surer way to find this information. The group is relatively informal at the moment since only about 100

An Educational Oasis...

WILMINGTON CHRISTIAN ACADEMY...
your refreshing school alternative

- Christian Philosophy
- Challenging Academics
- Qualified, Caring Faculty
- Biblical Teaching
- Conservative Values
- Excellent Facilities
- Affordable Tuition
- Championship Athletics
- Fine Arts Instruction
- Serving Wilmington since 1969
- Grades K4-12

1401 North College Road • Wilmington, NC 28405 • (910) 791-4248

---

students were being home-schooled in New Hanover County last year.

Child Care

Child care is an increasing concern and, consequently, a business opportunity in the area. The phone book is flooded with possibilities, including church-affiliated day-care centers, preschool development centers and after-school care, making the choices somewhat bewildering for parents.

The Child Advocacy Commission, 1401 S. 39th Street, Wilmington, (910) 791-1057, maintains a detailed data bank of child-care resources in the area. This organization does not make recommendations, but it offers information and referrals that allow parents to make informed decisions. There is no charge for this service.

The commission also works to develop cooperative efforts with governmental and other community service agencies to promote an awareness of children's issues. It sponsors community service activities, educational information and gives assistance to community agencies, civic groups and individuals. The commission offers on-site child-care training for providers and businesses.

The Child Advocacy Commission provides helpful guidelines for deciding which center or service is right for you and your children. It offers detailed lists of things to look for when you go to investigate the suitability of a center such as staff qualifications, programs offered, amount of space, health and safety concerns, meals and fees. Parents can take great comfort in knowing this kind of organization exists because, if its information packets are an indication, this organization takes a keen interest in the well-being of children. Ask for a general information packet that contains the important tips referred to above.

There are approximately 50 day-care centers and services in the area as well as 92 day-care homes, although these numbers regularly fluctuate. The North Carolina Department of Human Resources regulates these businesses and establishes guidelines for enrollment capacity, as does the City of Wilmington. A small day-care home can serve a maximum of five preschool children or up to eight children if at least three are school age, but there are various stipulations that may affect each situation. Check with the Child Advocacy Commission for information.

The following list of day-care centers is partial, and no recommendations are made. However, these centers have demonstrated consistent efforts in terms of longevity and quality of service.

South Brunswick High School's Aquaculture Program

The first words the instructor gives seem to be odd ones for a high school program: "Suit up and put your boots on."

When instructor Barry Bey gives that directive to the nine students in his Aquaculture 3 class at South Brunswick High School, he gets an immediate response. These students, juniors and seniors, bolt from their desks and scramble down the stairs to get to the day's assignment.

Close-up

Brunswick County Schools is a rural system with approximately 10,000 students. The Aquaculture program launched by Mr. Bey in 1987 has brought the system into North Carolina's educational spotlight. It is one of only 13 successful programs of its kind in the nation. The work of the instructor and students has been honored for seven consecutive years with a "Best in Show" award in education at the New Hanover County Fair.

In Mr. Bey's classroom, students tend several large fish tanks filled with trout, brim, goldfish or whatever species of fish is required for a particular project. The walls are lined with aquariums that contain larger fish. Outside on the school grounds, a ditch is filled with netted areas containing various fish at several stages of development. Beyond the school campus, the class tends clam rafts in the intake canals at the nearby Brunswick Nuclear Plant.

"It's all experimental," says junior Royce Potter, a descendent of several generations of Brunswick County shrimpers. "In the case of the clams, we take small clams from South Carolina and see how we can make them thrive in the waters of the canal. We've had a 90-percent success rate so far and our knowledge, based on trial and error, is helping establish some guidelines."

— continued on next page

Students at South Brunswick High School take their study of aquaculture into the field.

Student Mike Mitchem was part of a project to stock tilapia at a golf course to eat algae and keep the pond healthier. Jason Reis and Jon Griffee came up with a plan to empty multiple aquariums faster than the standard and shared this knowledge with the school's oceanography class. Edmund Randolph suited up on a very cold January day and wandered into the ditch to carefully release young trout. The whole class participated in a project to transport and introduce catfish to a pond in Arbor Creek, a nearby residential development. The development paid for the fish, and the students had another opportunity to experience practical application of their classroom experience in the real world.

All of Mr. Bey's students seem completely engaged with the class and that, in itself, is a major accomplishment. "This is an important area of research and my students appreciate that fact," he says. "They know this work will land them jobs one day, but they also understand they're on the cutting edge of something very valuable. Aquaculture is something we need to address on this planet and it's only going to grow in importance. It's a food source, a pet store source, a sports source. We need to learn to protect it in ways we never considered before because it's going to matter to all of us."

Mr. Bey's enthusiasm for his subject matter and his concern for helping his students find a meaningful, practical link between education and employment power the program, which suffers from a lack of adequate funding. In search of grant money on a regular basis, Mr. Bey has faith it will eventually come.

"My students are helping to lay the groundwork for a technology that will have enormous impact in the future in terms of how we feed populations. This is the equivalent of agriculture, and it will have the same profound impact on the world. I think aquaculture isn't well understood at this point, so that makes grants a little harder to come by."

The North Carolina Department of Agriculture reports that aquaculture is the fastest growing component of American agriculture. It provided nearly 12 percent of edible fish and shellfish production in 1990. By 1994, catfish production alone was valued at $439 million. North Carolina supplies about 10 percent of the fish market, with 17 producers. As the oceans are overfished and pollutants have more impact on coastal waters, the significance of this young industry will become more apparent. Eventually, thanks to the persistence and vision of teachers like Mr. Bey, the economic value of aquaculture will catch the eye of state legislators, and funding will become more readily available.

In the meantime, South Brunswick High School's aquaculture students are preparing themselves for successful jobs. After learning the skills of tending to the young fish and clams, they can look forward to continuing education or immediate employment in fields that range from fisheries management to wildlife conservation and more. As they learn fish identification, water quality assessment, pond management and construction, disease identification treatment and more, they expand their career horizons.

Higher education in Aquaculture Technology is conveniently available to Mr. Bey's graduates at nearby Brunswick Community College, where students can earn a two-year degree as an Associate in Applied Science. As part of the Tech Prep Track, high school students can go on to Brunswick Community College and then transfer for a bachelor's degree at North Carolina State University in Raleigh or UNCW in Aquaculture, Mariculture or Fisheries Biology.

Classy Bears Learning Center
6620 Windmill Way, Wilmington
• (910) 791-7872

Located near Blair School on Market Street north of Wilmington, this center accepts children between ages 6 weeks and 11 years. It concentrates on child development and independent learning. Computer classes and gymnastics are offered. The Stretch and Grow program for 3- to 5-year-olds emphasizes physical fitness and health. Capacity is 179.

Creative World
4202 Wilshire Blvd., Wilmington
• (910) 791-2080
2411 Flint Dr. (near New Hanover Regional Medical Center), Wilmington
• (910) 799-5195
Elementary School, 2409 Flint Dr., Wilmington • (910) 799-9765

This child care center and preschool has two convenient locations directed at fostering growth of the whole child. It cares for children ages 6 weeks to 12 years. Extracurricular activities include an on-site waterslide and gymnasium, dance, foreign language, arts and crafts, bowling, skating, picnics, field trips and gymnastics. It offers a summer camp program as well. The elementary school, grades 1 through 4, provides extensive education and includes learning labs, computer science and foreign language studies.

Early Childhood Learning Center
4102 Peachtree Ave., Wilmington
• (910) 392-4637

Located in the Winter Park area since 1983, this center accepts children from 2 to 5 years of age into its child development, independent learning and academic programs. Call to ask about extended-care hours and summer camp programs. Capacity is 88. This center is the only area school accredited by the National Academy of Early Childhood Programs.

Granny's Day Care Center
7010 Market St., Wilmington
• (910) 686-4405

Serving New Hanover County to the north and east of Wilmington, this center accepts children from 6 months to 5 years of age in a child development program. Field trips and dance are part of the fun. The center offers two nutritional snacks each day; children bring their own lunch. Capacity is 80.

Headstart Program of New Hanover County
New Hanover County Community Action, 507 N. Sixth St., Wilmington
• (910) 762-1177

Headstart is a nonprofit child development and academic program that serves children who are 4 years old by October 16. Located in downtown Wilmington, it also has an extensive free food program for children from low-income families. Call to inquire about fees for additional programs. Capacity is 245.

Park Avenue School
1306 Floral Pkwy., Wilmington
• (910) 791-6217

Near Independence Mall off Oleander Drive, this school has preschool programs for children from 6 weeks to 4 years of age. It also houses a private elementary school for students from kindergarten through grade 5. The child-care component emphasizes child development, independent learning and academic development. Two snacks and lunch are provided, and there is an indoor swimming pool. Capacity is 200.

Shaw Speakes Child Development Center
718 S. Third St., Wilmington
• (910) 343-1441

Shaw Speakes is in downtown Wilmington right beside the Cape Fear Memorial Bridge. It accepts children from 2 weeks to 12 years of age. The nonprofit center's program is based on child development and independent learning. Capacity is 99.

Total Child Care Center
4304 Henson Dr., Wilmington
• (910) 799-3556

This center is in the Northchase neighborhood near Laney Senior High and Trask Middle schools at Wilmington's northeast corner by incoming I-40. It accepts children from 6 weeks to 12 years of age. Computer classes, dance and gymnastics are offered. Child development and independent learning are the focus of the program. Two snacks and lunch are provided. Capacity is 127.

YWCA After School Program
2815 S. College Rd., Wilmington
- **(910) 799-6820**

The YWCA, a United Way agency, offers extensive after-school, school out and summer camp programs that serve children in kindergarten through 8th grade. The After School Program operates from 2:30 to 6 PM Monday through Friday and costs $37 a week, including transportation. The School Out Program, offered on teacher workdays and holidays, is a full-day schedule beginning as early at 6:30 AM and lasting until 6 PM.

Participation in these programs requires parent or guardian membership in the YWCA at a cost of $20 per year. Call about registration fees, financial assistance and program availability in other locations in the region. Gymnastics, dance and karate programs are available to participants in the After School Program for an additional fee.

Home Child Care

There is a robust cottage industry in child care in the area, evidenced by browsing through offers for child-care services in local newspapers and tabloids. According to the Child Advocacy Commission, the care providers list changes on an almost weekly basis, and a parent must be especially cautious in selecting home child care.

In-home care has some obvious advantages. If you have an infant, it's very nice to have a person come into your home. Live-in help or an in-home caregiver are the alternatives in this case. Word of mouth is an important way to learn about good nannies. Ask people with in-home child care about their experiences.

Since Wilmington is a vacation area, there are companies that specialize in both resort child-sitting services and regular sitting services for locals. The Sitter Network Inc., (910) 392-5899, has sitters trained in child CPR, and it offers quality child care for vacationers and locals who need a break for short or extended times. It also offers nanny placement services and temporary sitting. Established in 1991, this agency has just become the area's AuPair in America representative, offering long-term child care through a respected international program. The central, national AuPair office in Salt Lake City may be reached at (801) 255-7722.

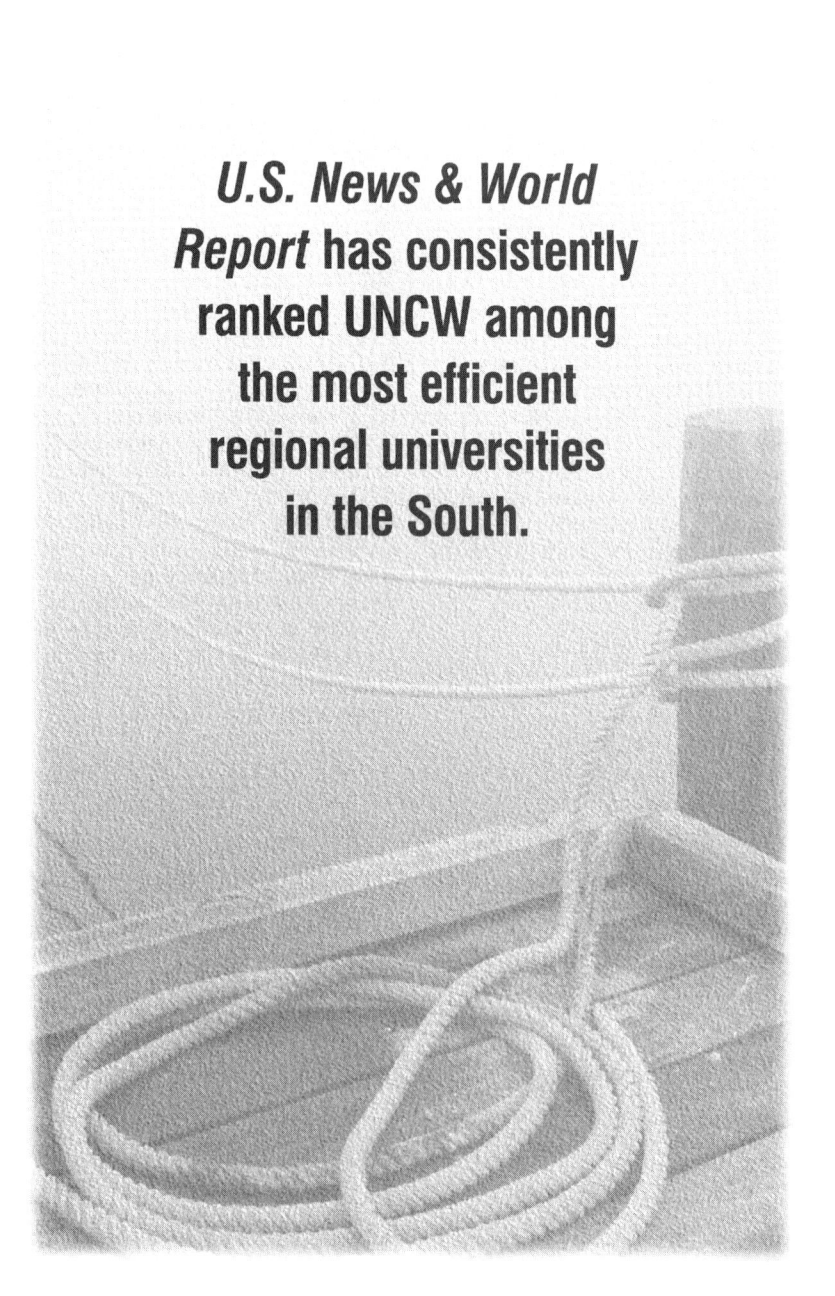

U.S. News & World Report has consistently ranked UNCW among the most efficient regional universities in the South.

Higher Education and Research

Before Wilmington became the tourist mecca it is today, the Port City had always been a major commercial hub. Early centers for higher learning were accordingly of the vocational ilk, and it wasn't until the mid-1900s that institutions of broader education were established.

The southern coast's growing economy and desirable location are again attracting industry, creating the need for higher levels and greater specialization of learning as never before. Wilmington is now a true college town, being home not only to a campus of the University of North Carolina system, but also to an excellent community college, a business college, and two satellite campuses. The Topsail Island, Jacksonville, and South Brunswick areas are all served by community colleges.

Not surprisingly, the major emphases of the research performed in the area are in the fields of oceanography, wetland and estuarine studies, marine biomedical and environmental physiology, and marine biotechnology and aquaculture.

Universities and Colleges

University of North Carolina at Wilmington
601 S. College Rd., Wilmington
• (910) 962-3000

Celebrating its 50th anniversary last year, UNCW is successfully living up to its responsibilities as the only public university in southeastern North Carolina. *U.S. News & World Report* has consistently ranked UNCW among the most efficient regional universities in the south.

The university originated as Wilmington College in 1947 and became a senior four-year college in 1969, expanding from three buildings in 1961 to the more than 70 that today occupy a 661-acre tract of land bordering S. College Road. UNCW is now a fully-accredited, comprehensive level I university in the state's 16-campus University of North Carolina system. Seventy percent of the nearly 500 instructional and research faculty members hold doctoral degrees. Class size averages less than 30 students, with a faculty-to-student ratio of 1-to-17. There are approximately 9,100 students currently enrolled.

UNCW comprises four schools: the College of Arts and Sciences, the Watson School of Education, the School of Nursing and the Cameron School of Business Administration, which is accredited by the American Assembly of Collegiate Schools of Business, a distinction earned by only 20 percent of the nation's business programs.

Four-year undergraduate programs lead to the Bachelor of Arts and Bachelor of Science degrees. The many master's degree programs now include the Master of Fine Arts in Creative Writing, the university's first true terminal-degree program. A cooperative program with North Carolina State University leads to a Ph.D. in marine science. There is also a variety of preprofessional programs and special programs in several areas, including marine science research and continuing education.

Through the Contract Extension Program, students may study freshman- and sophomore-level courses at three regional community colleges and be eligible to apply for admission to UNCW as baccalaureate degree candidates.

UNCW is one of two sites nationwide to offer regular faculty training in hypermedia classroom instruction, and was the first university connected to the state's information highway, a boon to distance learning programs.

The university's marine sciences program, utilizing sites at estuaries and the ocean, was ranked fifth best in the world by *The Gourman Report*, and is undergoing a landmark expansion with a new $18-million facility. The program's primary site has been its four-acre Center for Marine Science Research (see our write-up in the Research Facilities section below). The Center is dedicated to fostering a multidisciplinary approach to marine research. Basic and applied research programs available at the undergraduate and graduate levels make use of the Center's 15 laboratories, video equipment/editing facilities, machine tool shop, aquatic specimens holding room and USDA-licensed animal facility. Additional lab space is available for research requiring constant flow-through seawater.

UNCW's William Randall Library, (910) 962-3760, contains more than 415,000 volumes, subscribes to more than 5,000 serial titles and employs state-of-the-art electronic informational resources. Its 73-seat auditorium is equipped for various types of audiovisual use. The library is a partial repository for U.S. government publications and has a current inventory of 490,000 items in hardcopy and microtext. Randall Library is a full repository for North Carolina documents, which are available to all users, including nonstudents. Nonstudent memberships are available for $15 annually.

Other instructional and research resources at UNCW include the 10-acre Bluethenthal Wildflower Preserve, the Upperman African-American Cultural Center, elaborate campus-wide computing services with Internet access, an internship program with EUE/Screen Gems film studios, the Ev-Henwood Nature Preserve at Town Creek, and the Division for Public Service and Extended Education. The latter division offers continuing adult education comprising noncredit programs and courses in art, languages, investment and estate planning, scuba diving, photography, professional development, adult scholar enrichment, music and more. Programs may be custom-designed to fit particular needs.

Student life on campus is enhanced by a full battery of services and entertainment, food-service facilities, three student periodicals, and a music-format radio station. Kenan Auditorium hosts theatrical, symphonic and instructional events year round. The university holds NCAA Division I membership and competes in the Colonial Athletic Association. The university fields 19 varsity teams, men's and women's, including golf, basketball, tennis, soccer, swimming and diving. Both UNCW Ultimate Frisbee teams (men and women) are top-ranked nationally.

Sports facilities include a 1,200-seat baseball stadium; tennis, volleyball, and outdoor basketball courts; a track-and-field complex; an Olympic-size swimming pool with a diving well; and the 6,000-seat Trask Coliseum.

UNCW's school year is divided into four sessions consisting of the standard fall and spring semesters plus two summer sessions. For information on undergraduate admissions call (910) 962-3243; for graduate studies call (910) 962-3135. For information on Public Service Programs and Extended Education call (910) 962-3193.

INSIDERS' TIP

When you're in need of a tutor for your child, call the University of North Carolina at Wilmington, (910) 962-3000, and ask for the appropriate academic department office. They may be able to refer you to a graduate student who tutors.

Just a few reasons to consider CFCC ...

Associate in Arts (College Transfer) - Accounting - Air Conditioning, Heating & Refrigeration Technology - Architectural Technology -Associate Degree Nursing - Automotive Body Repair - Automotive Systems Technology - Basic Law Enforcement Training - Boat Building - Business Administration - Carpentry - Chemical Technology -Computer Engineering Technology - Cosmetology - Criminal Justice Technology - Culinary Technology Diesel Mechanics Technology - Dental Assisting - Drafting & Design Technology - Early Childhood Associate - Electrical/Electronics Technology - Electronics Engineering Technology - Environmental Science Technology - Instrumentation - Hotel & Restaurant Management - Industrial Maintenance Tech. - Information Systems - Interior Design - Machining Technology - Manicuring - Manufacturing Engineering Tech. - Marine Technology - Masonry - Mechanical Engineering Tech. - Medical Transcription - Office Systems Technology - Paralegal Technology - Pharmacy Technology - Phlebotomy - Practical Nursing - Radiography - Real Estate - Real Estate Appraisal - Speech-Language Pathology Asst. - Truck Driver Training - Welding Technology

Apply now for the summer and fall! Call 251-5118!

Cape Fear Community College

411 N. Front St., Wilmington NC 28401

http://cfcc.wilmington.net

AA/EOC

Cape Fear Community College
411 N. Front St., Wilmington
• **(910) 251-5100**

Dedicated to providing workforce training through more than 40 trade, technical and college transfer programs, full-time and part-time, Cape Fear Community College exerts a major educational presence in the area. It is among the state's most technologically advanced and fastest growing community colleges, serving over 21,000 students yearly.

There are now three campuses: the main campus on the river in historic downtown Wilmington, which is currently undergoing expansion, and two Pender County satellite campuses, one in Burgaw, about 21 miles north of Wilmington, (910) 259-4966; the other in Hampstead, on U.S. 17, (910) 270-3069. Classes are also held at area industry facilities.

Two-year programs, some leading to associate degrees, include business, chemical technology, microcomputing, criminal justice, college transfer, electrical and nautical engineering, hotel and restaurant management, nursing (RN) and paralegal technology. Among the one-year programs are administrative office technology, a renowned boat-building curriculum, dental assistance, industrial electricity and industrial mechanics, practical nursing, marine and diesel mechanics and welding. A broad range of extension certificate courses are offered during the day and night throughout the area to meet the continuing education needs of adults.

CFCC maintains small and large oceangoing vessels for its quality marine technology curriculum, which is enhanced by a deepwater pier on the Cape Fear River at the Wilmington campus. One of these vessels was integral to the recovery of artifacts from the wreck of the pirate Blackbeard's flagship, the *Queen Anne's Revenge*.

The college offers free courses in high-school equivalency (GED), English as a Second Language (ESL) and adult literacy. Many other special programs and seminars are free or very reasonably priced. Day and evening classes in semester-long cycles are available at all campuses, and financial aid is available for eligible applicants. Cape Fear Community College is one of 59 colleges in the North Carolina Community College System and is accredited by the Southern Association of Colleges and Schools.

Miller-Motte Business College
606 S. College Rd., Wilmington
• (910) 392-4660, (800) 868-6622

Miller-Motte is a well-respected 79-year-old collegiate alternative for students desiring employment-targeted training. The school is an accredited institution that maintains a strongly monitored job-placement service to assist its graduates in becoming employed — Miller-Motte's primary mission. With the help of a board of advisors made up of faculty, employed former students and regional employers, Miller-Motte's curricula are constantly updated to keep pace with changes in the regional job market. The school is well known and trusted among employers in southeastern North Carolina.

Miller-Motte offers 15- and 18-month diploma programs in business management, accounting, administrative assistance, medical assistance and microcomputer specialties. Nine-month and 12-month certificate programs are available in word processing, general office accounting, general office technology and medical unit clerk studies. Financial assistance, student services and internships in some programs are available.

Mt. Olive College, Wilmington Campus
1422 Commonwealth Dr., Wilmington
• (910) 256-0255, (800) 300-7478

Founded in 1951 by the Freewill Baptist Church, Mt. Olive College is a private, four-year, liberal arts institution that operates two fully accredited distance learning centers designed to help nontraditional students complete their associate's or baccalaureate degrees. Schedules are designed with students who must work full time in mind. The distance learning centers maintain their own registration offices. Enrollment at the Wilmington campus has tripled since it opened in 1995.

The Wilmington campus offers two degree-completion programs, in criminal justice and in management and organizational development. Both programs confer Bachelor of Science degrees.

Mt. Olive's has a tradition of student-focused, supportive programming and teaching styles. Courses are discussion-oriented, emphasizing critical thinking and research papers more than tests. Classes meet at night and on weekends and are limited to 20 students, who proceed through the curriculum together as a cohesive group, or "cohort." New cohorts are formed seven or eight times a year in a cycle of rolling admissions, and admissions requests are typically answered quickly, within a couple of weeks or so. Tuition includes all books and fees.

Most students attending Mt. Olive's Wilmington campus are in-state transfer students, and many are working to complete undergraduate requirements in preparation for career changes or further study.

Mt. Olive's Wilmington campus is at the intersection of Military Cutoff and Eastwood roads, between McDonald's and the First Union building.

Shaw University The Wilmington CAPE
224 N. Front St., Wilmington
• (910) 763-9091

The Wilmington Center for Alternative Programs of Education (CAPE) is one of nine accredited satellite programs of Shaw University in Raleigh designed to offer a viable opportunity to the working adult who, because of personal or job obligations, has been unable to attend other institutions of higher education. The Wilmington CAPE has been operating since 1986, offering night classes that lead to bachelor's degrees in psychology, sociology,

BRUNSWICK COMMUNITY COLLEGE

Visit Brunswick Community College's campus on Highway 17 at College Road, just 25 miles south of Wilmington, three miles north of Supply.

Brunswick Community College offers more than 20 curriculum programs, computer software and Internet classes

- Smaller class sizes with personal assistance from instructors
- A 1500-seat community auditorium with musical and dramatic performances
- Specialized training for new and expanding industry on-site or at Leland Center
- Small Business Center services

(800) 754-1050 or 343-0203

Visit our website at www.brunswick.cc.nc.us/Brunswick

---

criminal justice, religion and philosophy, public administration, business management and liberal studies.

Transfer credits from two- and four-year institutions are accepted, and life experience can earn students up to 27 credit-hours. Classes tend to be small, and total enrollment is less than 200. Founded in 1865, Shaw University is affiliated with the Baptist church.

Brunswick Community College
U.S. Hwy. 17 N., Supply
- **(910) 343-0203, (910) 754-6900, (800) 754-1050**

With three locations — the main campus north of Supply, a site in Southport and the Industrial Education Center in Leland — BCC serves more than 1,300 curriculum students and more than 3,000 others in continuing education courses.

Established in 1979, the college offers one- and two-year certificate, diploma and associate degree programs. These include aquaculture, various business studies, cosmetology, turf management, practical nursing, medical records and the Early Development Associate program (child development).

The College Transfer program leads to an associate of arts or associate of science degree and, to expedite transferals from Brunswick's two-year curricula to four-year programs at any of the 16 member universities in the UNC system, course content, classroom instruction, textbooks, testing, grading procedures and academic support services meet university transfer standards.

Through its New and Expanding Industry Program and its Small Business Center, BCC works closely with area businesses and industry to tailor curricula to their needs. The college assists industry in seeking, evaluating, training and retraining employees according to changing standards. BCC will custom-design courses to fit various needs and typically conducts industrial courses at the job site to upgrade employees to associate degree levels.

BCC is widely known as a educational value for the tuition dollar. The Supply campus is at the intersection of U.S. Hwy. 17 and College Road, about 25 miles south of Wilmington.

Research Facilities

UNCW Center for Marine Science Research
7205 Wrightsville Ave., Wrightsville Beach • (910) 256-3721

The University of North Carolina at Wilmington is the primary local marine research organ with its Center for Marine Science Research. Research facilities and equipment at

The Fort Fisher Hermit

During the turmoil of the 1960s, people often came to the old man who lived alone on the salt marsh south of Fort Fisher to ask his opinions about those troubled times, which the man said were "a wave of mental illness sweeping the country."

The man was Robert Edward Harrell who, for 17 years until his death in June 1972, lived in a World War II-era concrete bunker not far from where the North Carolina Aquarium at Fort Fisher now stands. It's an inhospitable place, scorched and mosquito-ridden in summer, frozen and wind-scoured in winter. It's also beautiful, serene and teeming with wildlife. In the late 1950s it was desolate. The windowless bunker was stuffed with the hermit's ragtag accumulations of driftwood, Styrofoam surfboards, newspapers and tin cans. Steepled planks of wood sheltered the entrance. The 1929 Chevy in which he slept during his early years there was Fort Fisher's first dune buggy. The hermit's abode was everything to him, except when Hurricane Helene in 1958 drove him to hitchhike to Wilmington. "I like to be alone," he said, "but not that alone."

The hermit could talk a blue streak. Visitors were treated to endless conversation and were asked to sign his guest register. The hermit's frying pan, always seeded with small change, stood in plain sight, and if people added to it or paid him for his

— continued on next page

Robert Harrell fished with a seine net.

photograph, he always gave something back, even his "millionaire's ration" made from any number of foods abundant on the tidal flats: crabs, oysters, fish, shrimp, turtles, raccoons, opossums. Sometimes he gave youngsters Civil War artifacts he had found.

Robert Harrell was born on Ground Hog Day in 1893 near Gaffney, South Carolina. He eked out a living as a sidewalk tinker in Shelby, North Carolina, and as a Linotype operator. He married and had four sons and a daughter who died young. When one of his sons committed suicide in the 1930s, the family moved north, but Harrell stayed behind.

His first sojourn at Fort Fisher ended sometime prior to 1955 when his brother retrieved him from a Wilmington jail. The trouble had begun when Harrell went scurrying about, looking for something live to feed his pet jay bird. A local woman happened to inquire about his frantic behavior, and he asked, "Have you got anything that will wiggle?"

The earliest confirmed date of Harrell's permanent residence on the salt marsh is 1955, but he was fond of claiming that he "rode out Hazel"—Hurricane Hazel, that is—one year earlier. He subscribed to an unaccredited discipline called biopsychology and claimed to have come to Fort Fisher to write a book, A Tyrant in Every Home. He claimed to have finished a 500-page manuscript, but it has never been found. Some people speculate that Harrell came to get away from his troubles; he had been institutionalized in the past.

At an age when most people think about collecting Social Security, Harrell began a new life with little more than the clothes on his back. He quickly became something of an attraction in Kure and Carolina beaches. He took to his celebrity well and recorded his visitors' signatures in old registers. One register survives, a 1949 calendar book containing about 2,500 signatures dated between November 1971 and June 1972, now part of the Cape Fear Museum's hermit collection.

Robert Harrell appealed to the hermit in everyone, that part of us that wants to be left alone, to live in harmony with nature, to escape our entanglements. But even he couldn't escape it all. Mystery surrounds his death—foul play is suspected—and the investigation remains open to this day. Some of the hermit's artifacts are on display at the North Carolina Marine Resources Center at Fort Fisher. His final resting place, always strewn with flowers and seashells, is in the Federal Point Methodist Cemetery in Carolina Beach. His headstone bears the epitaph, "He Made People Think."

Robert Harrell lived for more than 17 years in the salt marshes of Fort Fisher.

INSIDERS' TIP

Adults can continue their education for credit or simply for fun through UNCW's Division of Public Service and Extended Education, (910) 962-3193.

the Center not mentioned in the description of the university (above) include a low-temperature aquarium room, an atomic absorption spectrophotometer and an extensive microscopy capability. The Center also maintains nine research vessels ranging in size from 13 to 29 feet and highly specialized, state-of-the-art equipment that includes a robotic data-gathering vehicle.

A new state-of-the-art research facility (now under construction) will be the largest of its kind between Massachusetts and Key West and heralds a new era for cooperative programs among the state's major research universities.

The Center serves as host for the NOAA-sponsored National Undersea Research Center (NURC) for the southeastern United States. NURC annually supports fisheries management, ocean-floor processes and other research projects from the Gulf of Maine to the Gulf of Mexico. This support is based upon competitive proposals. The Center also assists with local research for the North Carolina Division of Marine Fisheries, the agency that acts as steward for the protection of all coastal wetlands, waterways and the ocean within a 3-mile limit.

North Carolina National Estuarine Research Reserve
UNCW Center for Marine Science Research, 7205 Wrightsville Ave., Wrightsville Beach • (910) 256-3721

The National Estuarine Research Reserve system was created by Congress to preserve undisturbed estuarine systems for research into and education about the human impact on coastal habitats. The reserves are outdoor classrooms and laboratories for researchers, students, naturalists and hobbyists.

The headquarters of the North Carolina National Estuarine Research Reserve (NCNERR) is housed at the UNCW Center for Marine Science Center in cooperation with the N.C. Division of Coastal Management. The NCNERR program manages four estuarine reserve sites as natural laboratories and coordinates research and education activities. Masonboro Island and Zeke's Island are two of the four components of NCNERR, the others being Rachel Carson Island near Beaufort and Currituck Banks in northeastern North Carolina.

Masonboro Island is the last and largest undisturbed barrier island remaining on the southern North Carolina coast and one of the most productive estuarine systems along the coast. The Zeke's Island component of the Reserve, immediately south of Federal Point in the Cape Fear River, actually consists of three islands — Zeke's, North Island, No-Name Island — and the Basin, the body of water enclosed by the breakwater known locally as the Rocks. Because the Basin has been relatively isolated from the river so long, it exhibits a salinity level nearly that of the ocean, presenting something of a huge ocean aquarium.

NCNERR has limited its presence on Masonboro and Zeke's islands by allowing traditional activities to continue, including hunting within regulations, pending future conclusions that may result from monitoring. (For further information about these islands, see our chapters on Attractions; Camping; and Sports, Fitness and Parks.)

Another preserve that has received its share of scientific scrutiny is Permuda Island (the name is an obvious corruption). This string bean of a spit bears substantial archaeological significance in that large tracts consist essentially of huge shell middens created by prehistoric inhabitants over a vast span of time. Such sites are rare in the ever-shifting, acidic soils of barrier islands. Despite decades of farming, the archaeological resources survived fairly intact. The island passed into state ownership several years ago.

Of further interest is the theory that Permuda Island represents an original barrier island later eclipsed by the growth of what today is called Topsail Island. A similar theory has been posited for North Island, mentioned above, and other privately-owned islands along the Pender County coast such as Hutaff and Lee islands. (The only other islands behind the barriers are dredge spoil mounds.) Permuda Island is not open to the public. It remains in a natural state and is managed by the North Carolina Department of Environment, Heath and Natural Resources, NCNERR and the Department of Marine Fisheries.

To inquire about NCNERR's Cape Fear components and other coastal resource issues, call the Coastal Reserve Coordinator at the number above.

North Carolina State Horticultural Crops Research Station
Castle Hayne Rd., Castle Hayne
• (910) 675-2314

Another field of research important to the region is horticulture. Between them, the North Carolina Department of Agriculture and North Carolina State University run 15 horticultural research stations around the state. The state-run station in Castle Hayne is the primary local research site. Its varied, ongoing programs concentrate on crops of local economic importance, such as blueberries, strawberries, grapes, sweet corn, sweet potatoes and cabbage. Variety trials, breeding and herbicide tests are among the studies performed.

The station works in limited association with the New Hanover County Extension Service arboretum, especially regarding soil studies, but primarily serves local horticulturists by making useful publications available to them.

LaQue Center for Corrosion Technology Inc.
702 Causeway Drive, Wrightsville Beach
• (910) 256-2271

When driving along U.S. Highway 421 through Kure Beach, you may wonder what that large array of strange-looking racks on the ocean side of the road is all about. Another cluster stands across the road. Curiously, these are historical landmarks (in place since 1935) designated by the American Society of Materials Testing and used for atmospheric testing. They are the property of the LaQue Center for Corrosion Technology. LaQue (pronounced "luh-KWEE") conducts tests on any material subject to corrosion, particularly alloys and coatings, under various corrosive conditions, whether atmospheric, marine or artificial.

Testing makes up about 98 percent of the lab work, but LaQue also performs related research into corrosion technology. Through an internship program affiliated with UNCW and Cape Fear Community College, the center employs students as operating assistants for round-the-clock test monitoring.

The LaQue Center sponsors seminars such as the ever-popular "Fundamentals of Corrosion and Its Control," which is offered four times a year at a local hotel. Open-house tours of the Wrightsville Beach facility are conducted periodically and may be arranged for groups on request.

WOMEN MEAN BUSINESS

BPW / NC

Making a Difference Through...

- Leadership
- Networking
- Professional Development
- Advocacy

BPW Objectives:

To elevate the standards for women in business and the professions; To promote the interests of business and professional women; To bring about a spirit of cooperation among business and professional women of the United States; To extend opportunities for business and professional women through education.

Please join us if you are a visiting BPW member from out of town or interested in attending a meeting of the North Carolina Federation of Business & Professional Women (BPW / NC). Our local organization meets the second Thursday of every month at Charlotte's Downtown Eatery, 130 N. Front St. (910-343-9883).

For more information please contact us through Laura Schauer, president (Coastal Realty, 910-763-5411) or BPW / ILM P.O. Box 2324 Wilmington, NC 28402.

WOMEN MEAN BUSINESS

Volunteer Opportunities

When there is a need, Cape Fear people are there. While that's surely true of every community in the world to a degree, there is something particularly intense about the high level of commitment local people bring to volunteer projects. Part of this dedication to helping others may stem from the fact that even our largest city, Wilmington, is still a small town socially. This intimate environment makes it impossible to look the other way when someone is in need of help.

Newcomers will quickly discover that involvement with good causes and organizations not only helps the community but also helps strangers become members of the family. People are known by their works, and those who involve themselves in doing good works will be welcomed into many social and business circles. Newcomers looking for employment would do well to involve themselves in philanthropic efforts because the volunteer arena offers a good and fast lesson on the intricacies of community relations.

The demand for volunteer time and talent is extremely high year round. Regardless of your particular interests, you are likely to find plenty of places where you can contribute. It is, in fact, very easy to become overrun with requests for your help once you present yourself as a concerned individual. Although tens of thousands of people volunteer annually — and this is a conservative estimate — Wilmington still lacks a central coordinating agency to match volunteers with tasks and organizations.

The Cape Fear United Way Information and Referral Service, (910) 251-5020, can provide information about human service organizations throughout the region. The Community Services pages of the phone books contain a listing of all the human service agencies. Both of these information sources are limited, however, because many organizations that use volunteers aren't listed.

The arts, the senior population, health services, nutrition, historic preservation, the environment, minority interests, business development, human relations, housing, schools and education, special festivals and more make up the volunteer possibilities in the region. The following is a very condensed list of some of the organizations that would appreciate your involvement.

Human Services

American Red Cross, Cape Fear Chapter
1102 S. 16th St., Wilmington
• (910) 762-2683
Volunteer positions include blood services aides, registered nurses, disaster team mem-

---

INSIDERS' TIP

Watch the *Star-News* for information about Big Sweep, a yearly event in September that involves the whole community in picking up trash on area waterways. Call (910) 762-5606 for information.

bers, service to military case workers, health and safety class instructors and office aides. This very active organization has a high community profile and is extremely responsive to people in need. It responds to emergencies both inside and beyond the region with shelter, food and funds. The simple act of giving blood is an easy way to volunteer, and this is a critical need because only 2 percent of the population donates blood. Give a pint and save a life.

Brunswick Family Assistance Agency
(910) 754-4766

Formerly named the Brunswick County Volunteer Information Center, this organization needs volunteers to help families in need of food, shelter, furniture and other necessities. It distributes nearly 500 Christmas baskets across Brunswick County and has a food pantry that distributes more than 22,000 pounds of food each year.

Brunswick County Literacy Council Inc.
104 Ocean Hwy. E., Supply
• (910) 754-7323, (800) 694-7323

The Council helps adults in Brunswick County learn to read by pairing them with interested volunteers. Volunteers are carefully screened, trained and matched with adult students. Volunteers are also needed in a variety of functions, including publicity, office help and newsletter publication.

Cape Fear Area United Way
709 Market St., Wilmington
• (910) 251-5020

As with most United Way agencies, this is the funding body for a large number of community organizations. It has an Information and Referral Service to direct interested volunteers to various human service organizations. It needs community volunteers to conduct and allocate an annual fund-raising program.

Cape Fear Literacy Council
1012 S. 17th St., Wilmington
• (910) 251-0911

Like the Brunswick County Literacy Council, this organization pairs volunteer tutors with adults who are learning to read. It also provides a computer literacy lab, training for parents and caregivers and a readers support group. Additionally, it offers Babies and Books, a program provided through the prenatal clinic at New Hanover Regional Medical Center, to encourage expectant parents to begin reading to their children at birth. More than 300 tutors are needed on a yearly basis.

Cape Fear Memorial Hospital
5301 Wrightsville Ave., Wilmington
• (910) 452-8373

Senior Friends and Volunteer Services are housed together in one office, so expect the phone to be answered this way. (See our chapters on Healthcare and Retirement for information about Senior Friends, a wellness program for people older than 50.) Volunteers at Cape Fear are needed to work in the gift shop, the general information desk, the surgical information desk, the outpatient rehabilitation center, central supply, purchasing, the pharmacy, imaging services, the patient representative program, the emergency center, the Lifeline program and as needs arise. The hospital's auxiliary has approximately 150 members.

Coastal Horizons Center
721 Market St., Third Floor, Wilmington
• (910) 343-0145
Crisis Line/Open House • (800) 672-2903
Rape Crisis Center • (910) 392-7460

This private, nonprofit service agency serving the tri-county area is for individuals who need assistance recovering from chemical dependency/substance abuse, sexual assault and other crisis situations. There is also an emergency care shelter for youths 8 through 18. Other programs include HIV/AIDS Outreach, pregnancy testing, criminal justice alternatives and food vouchers.

Domestic Violence Shelter and Services Inc.
(910) 343-0703

Women and children who have suffered domestic violence are sheltered by this agency. Volunteers are needed to help with direct services, work in the office and in Vintage Values (the recycled clothing and goods shop), provide transportation, serve as court advocates and children's advocates, and act as on-call workers in emergency situations. More than 1,400 women and children are assisted yearly by the shelter.

Gay Rights of Wilmington (GROW)
341-11 S. College Rd. #182, Wilmington
• (910) 799-7111

GROW provides information on activities of particular interest to the gay and lesbian communities. It is also involved in HIV-related services such as resources, transportation, information and referral, and patient advocacy. The switchboard number provides extension numbers for a variety of organizations and services.

Good Shepherd House
511 Queen St., Wilmington
• (910) 251-9862, (910) 763-5902

This day shelter for homeless people needs volunteers to work at the front desk greeting guests, answering the phone and distributing toiletry items for the shower. Volunteers are also needed to sort clothing, distribute fresh clothing, do laundry and drive the van to take clients to work or on errands. People interested in working in the kitchen are needed to set up for lunch, serve meals and clean up.

Hope Harbor Home
(910) 754-5726, (910) 754-5856 24-Hour Crisis Line

Volunteers are needed at this domestic violence shelter in Brunswick County to serve as client advocates, work on the speakers bureau and help organize and implement fund-raising activities.

Hospice of the Lower Cape Fear
725 Wellington Ave., Wilmington
• (910) 762-0200

Hospice serves the needs of clients and their families when terminal illness occurs. Volunteers who will visit terminally ill clients, do office work and help with fund-raising events are needed. The Annual Festival of Trees is a major fund raiser for Hospice.

New Hanover Regional Medical Center
2131 S. 17th St., Wilmington
• (910) 343-7704

The Medical Center has 70 set areas of volunteer involvement, but opportunities are actually limitless. An average of 800 active volunteers work in the hospital each year in almost every sector of hospital activity. Direct patient service people, oncology volunteers, mailroom clerks, flower deliverers, transportation providers, lobby receptionists, gift shop clerks, clerical assistants and courtesy van drivers are all needed.

Volunteers may also be involved in helping care for newborns at the birthing center or, in the case of Kangaroo Kapers, helping children come to terms with a new baby in the house. People with ideas for new volunteer activities are encouraged to call.

Salvation Army
820 N. Second St., Wilmington
• (910) 762-7354

The Salvation Army provides shelter for the homeless and assistance for people in difficult circumstances. It needs volunteers in fund-raising activities and public relations efforts. Volunteers may serve on the Advisory Board and Ladies Auxiliary and in the shelter, which serves men, women and children. Volunteers may also work at the thrift store, on the Woodlot Project, Christmas fund raisers, the toy and food distribution center, the annual Coats for the Coatless drive and on disaster relief teams.

The shelter provides emergency housing to more than 20,000 individuals each year and has a Soup Line serving meals seven days a week between 5:30 and 6 PM for the public. This food program serves nutritious meals to more than 60,000 people each year in Bladen, Brunswick, Columbus, Pender and New Hanover counties.

St. James Shelter
25 S. Third St., Wilmington
• (910) 763-1628

This cold-weather homeless shelter in the

basement of St. James Episcopal Church is a relatively new addition to Wilmington's humanitarian services for people who need a place to sleep. Volunteers are needed to spend an occasional night welcoming guests and making sure the evening goes smoothly. The shelter is open from 8:30 PM to 7:00 AM for women, men and children from November through March. Guests are referred by the Good Shepherd House (see listing above).

Southeastern Sickle Cell Association
508 Castle St., Wilmington
• (910) 343-0422

Volunteers provide support services as well as fund-raising activities and community education for this organization, which concentrates its efforts on a disease that affects 1 in 400 African-Americans. Volunteers with public relations and promotions experience are needed to develop community awareness. Nurses are needed to do screenings.

Children

Public Schools

School systems offer a variety of volunteer opportunities that are essentially the same from system to system: helping in the classroom, tutoring, serving as a mentor for at-risk students, working in dropout prevention programs, helping minority students achieve success in engineering/science careers, getting involved with the PTA/PTO.

If you want to volunteer your time to the public schools, contact the Community Schools/Public Information Office in each system: New Hanover County School System, 1802 S. 15th Street, Wilmington, (910) 763-5431; Brunswick County School System, Central Office, Southport, (910) 457-5241; Pender County School System, 925 Penderlea Highway, Burgaw, (910) 259-2187.

Boy Scouts of America, Cape Fear Council
110 Long Street Dr., Wilmington
• (910) 395-1100

This organization requires a tremendous number of volunteers to assist the many Boy Scouts in the Cape Fear area. Board and committee members are needed as well as a host of leaders, coaches and advisors. Volunteers are needed for the Sports Club Program, which combines traditional Scout activities with a basketball league for inner-city boys from four housing developments.

Brigade Boys and Girls Club
2759 Vance St., Wilmington
• (910) 791-4282

Now a century old, this venerable organization needs volunteers to serve as photographers, class instructors, arts and crafts teachers, coaches, tutors and group club leaders for both boys and girls. The club provides behavioral guidance and promotes the social, recreational, cultural, vocational, physical and mental health of youth.

Community Boys and Girls Club
901 Nixon St., Wilmington
• (910) 762-1252

The Community Club primarily serves minority youth and it has produced some exceptional adults over the years. Basketball great Michael Jordan played here when he was a child. Meadowlark Lemon did too. The club relies on volunteer involvement for fund raising, implementing special programs and working as adult role models.

Child Advocacy Commission
1401 S. 39th St., Wilmington
• (910) 791-1057

This organization works as an advocate for children in three main areas: child care resource and referral, the juvenile restitution program and Project First Stop, an educational/counseling program for first offenders younger than 16 and their parents. Volunteer assistance in many areas is needed, including a relatively new family nurturing program that helps Wilmington Housing Authority residents develop better parenting skills if their children, ages 4 through 12, are identified as at risk for behavioral problems.

Girls Inc. of Wilmington
1502 Castle St., Wilmington
• (910) 763-6674

Girls Inc. is an after-school and summer

Waterbirds like this heron are a common sight in the area's marshes, lakes and waterways.

program primarily for minority girls ages 5 to 18. It offers programs in career and life planning, health and sexuality, leadership and community action, sports, cultural heritage and self reliance. Volunteers are needed as tutors, group leaders and fund-raisers, as well in many other capacities.

Girl Scout Council of Coastal Carolina
(910) 458-5164

The Girl Scouts need volunteers in many positions. Troop leaders, consultants, organizers, trainers, product sales coordinators (we're talking cookies here) and communicators are needed. This council serves girls in Brunswick, Columbus, New Hanover and Pender counties and offers leadership development for girls through fun and rewarding programs.

Family Services of the Lower Cape Fear
4014 Shipyard Blvd., Wilmington
• **(910) 392-7051**

This organization offers family counseling, consumer credit counseling, Travelers Aid and the Big Buddy program for the lower Cape Fear area. Volunteers are needed as office helpers, child sitters (while parents are in counseling sessions) and Big Buddies. The Big Buddy program provides reliable, trusted friends to boys and girls in need of positive role models and requires a minimum commitment of one year.

Wilmington Family YMCA
2710 Market St., Wilmington
• **(910) 251-9622**

If you're a real hands-on volunteer, this is certainly the place for you. Be a youth sports volunteer, nursery attendant, Special Olympics volunteer or a person who helps maintain the facility. The Y has a great aquatics program that offers activities for individuals with a variety of disabilities, and volunteers who like to get in the water will enjoy this opportunity to help.

YWCA
2815 S. College Rd., Wilmington
• **(910) 799-6820**

Youth programs, clerical and maintenance are just a few of the areas where the YWCA needs your volunteer assistance. If you would like to be a tutor at one of six locations throughout the Cape Fear area, this organization can use your help. The Y offers an extensive after-school program and a child-care center as well as programs addressing youth development, women's health issues, racial justice, employment training and counseling.

The Arts

Arts Council of the Lower Cape Fear
807 N. Fourth St., Wilmington
• (910) 762-4223

The Arts Council has a number of programs that need volunteers. The annual Piney Woods Celebration of the Arts, a two-day cultural arts event held at Hugh MacRae Park, needs a host of volunteers to help with parking, admission, preparation, publicity and more. The Arts Council has a volunteer Board of Directors with administrative committees in the areas of advocacy, finance, fund raising, membership and publications/information.

St. John's Museum of Art
114 Orange St., Wilmington
• (910) 763-0281

This extraordinarily fine museum of visual arts needs volunteers to work in many capacities. Things are always happening at this lively center, and volunteers are needed to serve as docents and in membership, publicity, fund raising, the gift shop and much more. The museum constantly has new projects underway, such as a cookbook, art trips to other cities, film series, art sales, exhibitions, educational programs and special events. If you love the visual arts, this is a wonderful place to offer your volunteer services. (Some of the organizations listed in our Arts chapter also use volunteers.)

Historic Preservation and Community Development

Downtown Area Revitalization Effort (DARE)
201 N. Front St., Wilmington
• (910) 763-7349

DARE concentrates on revitalization of the Central Business District in downtown Wilmington. Thirty-six volunteers representing a cross-section of the community serve on the Board of Directors. Thirteen are designated by other organizations, seven are elected based on their profession and 16 serve as at-large members. This body expedites quality development of the commercial district by offering a wide range of services and detailed information to potential downtown businesses.

Habitat for Humanity, Cape Fear
1515 S. Front St. • (910) 762-4744

Thanks to former president Jimmy Carter, this organization enjoys a high profile. Call this number to find out about construction projects in progress and volunteer your skills in a wide array of areas ranging from hands-on carpentry to office assistance to clerking in the used construction materials store at the same address as the main office.

Historic Wilmington Foundation
(910) 762-2511

Volunteers interested in preserving the architectural heritage of the region are invited to work in public relations, membership, education, preservation action, urban properties and gardens. There is a yearly gala, the primary fund raiser, that relies on lots of volunteers for logistics, publicity, entertainment, food and everything else required to throw a major, glittering party and auction.

Lower Cape Fear Historical Society
126 S. Third St., Wilmington
• (910) 762-0492

Volunteers are needed for publicity, fund raising, membership drives and planning at this venerable organization, which seeks to accurately preserve the history of the area. Volunteers also work as docents and archivists in the society's home, the Latimer House. The society sponsors the yearly Olde Wilmington by Candlelight Tour of Homes.

Wilmington Community Development Corp.
511 Cornelius Harnett Blvd., Wilmington
• (910) 762-7555

A relatively new endeavor, this organization nurtures business development through the Small Business Incubator and other programs aimed at economic development. It looks for volunteers interested in broadening the area tax base by helping launch new businesses by offering low-cost office space, financial advice, marketing advice and more.

Wilmington Harbor Enhancement Trust
(910) 251-9438

The Trust exists to support the orderly development of property and recreational activities in and along the Cape Fear River and the Northeast Cape Fear River adjacent to the Wilmington city limits. Efforts of WHET focus on "development which is functional and attractive to all types of boating and river activities while considering the environmental, historic and natural beauty of the river." If you have an interest in working to protect the river, this organization will welcome you.

U.S. Coast Guard Auxiliary
272 N. Front St., Wilmington
• (910) 343-4882

The Auxiliary relies on volunteers to inspect recreational vessel, conduct tours of visiting Coast Guard vessels and participate in activities related to boating safety.

Senior Citizens

Brunswick County Department of Older Adults
(910) 253-4746

The county offers congregate and home-delivered meals, transportation, minor home repairs and other services to Brunswick County's senior population.

Elderhaus Inc.
1950 Amphitheater Dr., Wilmington
• (910) 251-0660

Elderhaus provides structured and stimulating day care for the elderly, including programs for those with Alzheimer's and dementia. Volunteers are needed as program aides, activity assistants, meal servers and van assistants. Volunteer board members oversee fund raising, public relations, educational activities and more. Elderhaus is building a new center in 1998 to serve the area's increasing need for these services.

New Hanover County Department of Aging
2222 S. College Rd., Wilmington
• (910) 452-6400

This government organization can point you in many directions if you wish to become involved in volunteer efforts that both serve and involve senior citizens. The department was formed in 1983 to serve older adults by promoting visibility and representation, providing support services that encourage independent living and operating as the focal point of aging services in the community.

Retired Senior Volunteer Program
2011 Carolina Beach Rd., Wilmington
• (910) 341-4555

RSVP taps the talents of retired people by sharing their experience with the needs of the community. Volunteers have special assignments matching their interests, skills and abilities in schools, libraries, hospitals, nursing homes and other places. Volunteers in this program are 60 and older.

Senior AIDES Program
709 Market St., Wilmington
• (910) 251-5040

Volunteers serve this program in an advisory council capacity, donating their time to public speaking, representing the agency at community fairs, preparing publicity materials, giving management and technical assistance and assisting in personnel placement of Senior AIDES through resume preparation, job interview skills enhancement, job search assistance and more.

Senior Citizen Services of Pender Inc.
312 W. Williams St., Burgaw
• (910) 259-9119

This Pender County organization provides services for the elderly, including transportation, in-home care, congregate meals and home-delivered meals. Volunteers are needed to deliver meals five days a week to homebound senior citizens and provide transportation to and from the center, doctor appointments, and the grocery store.

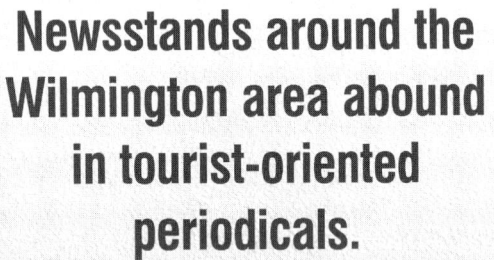

Newsstands around the Wilmington area abound in tourist-oriented periodicals.

Media

Wilmington's media scene largely remains the same year after year in terms of staying power. Owners may come and go, but the area's dominant newspapers, magazines, and radio and television stations are stable sources of information.

In the print medium, visitors will notice an abundance of tourist-oriented publications in street racks. We haven't listed them here, but they are generally handy guides to the area's attractions. Some of them have been around for years while others seem to drift in one day and out the next. There's a robust business in publications on real estate; in fact, these magazines or booklets are so pervasive you can't go anywhere without encountering them.

Choices for radio listening are eclectic, ranging across talk, country music, beach music, urban contemporary, Top 40 and the diverse offerings of the city's own National Public Radio affiliate. There's a general feeling that other successful formats could be added to those already on the air, but surely time will change this situation to satisfy everyone.

Television is a somewhat limited medium unless one has cable or satellite services, in which case the whole spectrum of channels becomes available. TV 26 changed affiliation from CBS to Fox several years ago and, at this writing, it's difficult to get a clear picture of CBS transmission without cable. Public Television, broadcast from Jacksonville by way of Chapel Hill, has a strong signal.

The media listed below have settled into their own niches on what seems to be a permanent basis. In a volatile industry, these information/entertainment outlets have proven themselves over time.

Newspapers

Brunswick Beacon
106 Cheers St., Shallotte
- **(910) 754-6890**

A weekly community newspaper published on Thursdays, the *Beacon* has won dozens of awards during the past decade for advertising and editorial content. It covers and is distributed to all of Brunswick County, with particular emphasis on the southwestern portion of the coast. The *Beacon* is among the last of the small independents still produced and printed entirely at one location. About 13,000 copies are circulated each week to subscribers, retail outlets and news racks.

The Challenger
514 Princess St., Wilmington
- **(910) 762-1337, (800) 462-0738**

The Challenger is a statewide, African-American-focused publication based in Wilmington and Fayetteville. Published weekly on Wednesdays, it is a subscription-based periodical with limited news rack distribution. Circulation is about 5,000, with some free distribution.

The Island Gazette
Pleasure Island Plaza B-4, Carolina Beach • (910) 458-8156

If you're looking for real estate on Pleasure Island, the *Gazette* is probably your best first source. It is a weekly, published on Wednesdays and available at news racks throughout Carolina Beach. Its focus is on southern New Hanover County, with an emphasis on Pleasure Island. Circulation is about 5,000. Mail subscriptions are available.

INSIDERS' TIP

Check out *Reel Carolina Magazine* to find out which movie stars are in town for filming.

The Pender Chronicle
110 Courthouse Ave., Burgaw
- **(910) 259-2504**

Owned by H.L. Oswald Corporation, an area publishing family, this community paper first went to press in 1897. Published every Wednesday, it's available by subscription and in news racks throughout the Pender County area and beyond. It has a circulation of about 6,000. Its focus is local community and church news.

Pender Post
210 E. Freemont St., Burgaw
- **(910) 259-9111**

This small but venerable independent community newspaper has a circulation of 5,000 and is available by subscription and in news racks throughout Pender and New Hanover counties. Published every Wednesday, it covers Pender County people and news.

State Port Pilot
105 S. Howe St., Southport
- **(910) 457-4568**

Covering the six towns in the Southport-Oak Island sphere, this weekly newspaper concentrates on community perspectives, carrying news on government, society and sports. With a circulation averaging more than 7,000, the *Pilot* includes a classifieds section and is available by subscription and at news racks throughout its coverage area every Wednesday.

Topsail Voice
14888 U.S. Hwy. 17 N., Hampstead
- **(910) 270-2944**

This weekly, established in 1991, is published on Wednesdays and is the largest newspaper in the greater Topsail Island area. The *Voice* covers local politics, commerce and sports (often emphasizing fishing) throughout the region from Sneads Ferry south to Ogden. It includes classifieds and op-ed pages. With a circulation of about 5,000, the *Voice* is a fast-growing periodical available by subscription and at news racks throughout its coverage area and at a few locations in Wilmington.

The Wilmington Journal
412 S. Seventh St., Wilmington
- **(910) 762-5502**

This weekly describes itself as the voice and mirror of the area's African-American community in New Hanover, Brunswick, Pender, Onslow, Columbus, Jones and Craven counties. It is available each Thursday at news racks throughout the city or by subscription. Circulation is about 8,600.

Wilmington Star-News
1003 S. 17th St., Wilmington
- **(910) 343-2000**

The *Star-News*, offering two editions, is the only major daily paper in the region and dominates the print market along the southern coast of North Carolina. Owned by *The New York Times*, the *Star-News* concentrates on the local scene (New Hanover, Bladen, Brunswick, Columbus, Duplin and Pender counties, and Jacksonville and Camp Lejeune), as well as on national and international news. Established in 1867, it is the oldest daily newspaper in North Carolina. Wire services include the Associated Press, The New York Times News Service, Knight-Ridder-Tribune News Service, Los Angeles Times-Washington Post News Service, Cox News Service and Bloomberg Business News.

The *Star-News* is distributed throughout the Cape Fear region, and home delivery is avail-

---

www.insiders.com
See this and many other **Insiders' Guide®** destinations online — in their entirety.
Visit us today!

INSIDERS' TIP

Think Wilmington is lacking in foreign and art films? Cinematique, a film series sponsored by WHQR-FM Public Radio, offers the best of both at Thalian Hall on a regular basis.

able. Subscribers can receive all editions or the Sunday edition only. Daily circulation is around 55,500 and Sunday circulation around 66,500. StarLine, an audiotext service that makes information available 24 hours a day, can be reached by calling (910) 762-1996.

Entertainment Magazines

Encore Magazine
255 N. Front St., Wilmington
• (910) 762-8899

Publisher Wade Wilson describes this as a "general what's happening" magazine for the Wilmington area. Arts, entertainment, local sports and essays/fiction make up this free weekly, which has published each Tuesday since 1984.

Certainly the most widely distributed free entertainment periodical in the region, *Encore*'s many highlights include festival and holiday roundups, recipes, attractions, personal ads and Chuck Shepherd's syndicated "News of the Weird" column. Perhaps its most outstanding feature is a detailed calendar of weekly events.

The magazine is available at news racks practically everywhere in Wilmington, at many retail outlets elsewhere and by subscription. Circulation averages 18,000 year-round.

Encore co-sponsors an annual fiction contest in cooperation with the Lower Cape Fear Historical Society. In addition to the magazine, *Encore* also publishes a "Guide to Boating and Fishing," available at marinas; "Directions," a guide for students at

> **INSIDERS' TIP**
>
> National news anchor David Brinkley was born in downtown Wilmington. The late Charles Kuralt was born in Wilmington, too.

UNCW; and "Alternatives," a free summer and fall guide for school-age kids looking for interesting things to do. The "Guide to Cape Fear Leisure," available for perusal in hotel rooms around the area, is an annual *Encore* publication.

Reel Carolina Magazine
(910) 392-5445

This monthly keeps readers up to date on what's happening in the film industry in North and South Carolina. Production notes, a trades section, technical information, business profiles and interviews fill the pages. After four years of publication, circulation is at about 15,000. It is available by subscription and in racks across the Carolinas.

Wilmington Magazine
201 N. Front St., Wilmington
- **(910) 815-0600**

Published every other month, this attractive and lively full-color magazine, established in 1994, covers Greater Wilmington's people and places from a historical, cultural, business and personality perspective. It is available by subscription, at news racks and in bookstores, and has a circulation of about 7,500. The managing editor is Wilmington's former longtime mayor, Don Betz.

Wright Times
(910) 256-0477

This little magazine, launched in 1995, covers news about Wrightsville Beach. It has an average circulation of 8,000 and is distributed for free at various sites around the beach and in Wilmington. Content makes this publication tremendously appealing to locals and visitors alike, and it's a welcome addition to the area print scene. Gutsy, self-admitted "jarhead" publisher Grant Hoover doesn't mind taking punches at things that annoy him, and his brassy attitude can be a breath of fresh air. *Wright Times* includes features, town hall reports, a business section, a calendar of events and a police blotter.

Television Stations

WECT-TV 6, NBC
322 Shipyard Blvd., Wilmington
- **(910) 791-8070**

NBC-affiliated TV 6 is one of the major television stations in southeastern North Carolina. It offers full news coverage and exceptional meteorological programming.

WSFX-26, Fox
1926 Oleander Dr., Wilmington
- **(910) 343-8826**

There are no news programs on this channel, so there are no "personalities" associated with it. This station's strength is its Fox affiliation.

WSSN-TV 10, The Sun Channel
1536 Castle Hayne Rd., Ste. D-1, Wilmington • (910) 815-1030

Debuting in 1994, this low-power station has just affiliated with UPN, offering UPN night and nostalgia programming — old movies and television shows — by day. The air signal is weak, but you can get a clear picture on Cable Channel 2, Time-Warner Cable.

WUNJ-TV 39, PBS
Research Triangle Park, NC
- **(919) 549-7000**

Quality national and local public television programming is the hallmark of WUNJ-TV. Its yearly pledge drive is enthusiastically supported by southeastern North Carolinians.

WWAY-TV 3, ABC
615 N. Front St., Wilmington
- **(910) 762-8581**

ABC-affiliated TV 3 is another major television station in the region. It also offers full news and meteorological coverage.

Cable

Cable television in Wilmington is provided by Time-Warner Cable of North Carolina, (910)

INSIDERS' TIP

Local weather news always includes the times of high and low tides, as well as sea height and offshore weather information.

Photo: Scott Taylor

Snowmen are not standard equipment on Cape Fear area boats.

763-4638. Falcon Cable provides service to Pleasure Island, (800) 682-7814.

Radio Stations

Adult Contemporary: WGNI 102.7 FM (and Top 40)
Big Band: WZXS 103.9 FM
Christian: WWIL 90.5 FM, 1490 AM
Country: WKIX 99.9 FM; WWQQ 101.3 FM
Oldies and Beach Music: WCCA 106.3 FM; WKOO 98.7 FM
National Public Radio: WHQR 93.1 FM (classical, jazz, blues, news, National Public Radio and Public Radio International)
News, Talk, Sports: WAAV 980 AM and 94.1 FM; WMFD 630 AM
Rock: WRQR 104.5 FM; WSFM 107 FM
Urban Contemporary: WMNX 97.3 FM

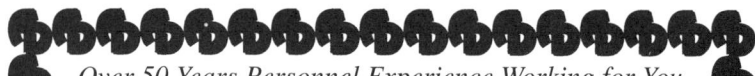

Over 50 Years Personnel Experience Working for You

Anderson & Daniel
PERSONNEL ASSOCIATES
A Division of Employment Solutions, Inc.

4900 Randall Parkway, Suite F • Wilmington, NC 28403
Telephone (910) 799-8500 • Fax (910) 791-0706
www.employment-solutions.com

Corporate • Division • Plant
National • Regional • Local

SERVICES OFFERED
- Temp-to-Perm Placement
- Payrolling
- Temporary
- Direct Hire
- Executive Search
- Outplacement Assistance

AREAS OF SPECIALIZATION
- Accounting & Finance
- Light Industrial
- Administrative
- Medical
- Banking
- Professional
- Clerical Support
- Sales & Marketing
- Data Processing
- Technical
- Engineering
- Warehousing & Shipping

"Recruiting your needs for tomorrow... today"

Commerce and Industry

During most of the 20th century, the Greater Wilmington area has experienced what some business leaders have described as an immunity to national and state economic trends. There have been good eras and bad eras, but the general Wilmington economy has neither performed as well in prosperous times nor as badly in recessionary times as regions with similar demographics. There seems to be a kind of unspectacular (but sometimes comforting) financial stability in the Cape Fear area.

This middle-of-the-road economic situation has made it hard for workers to get rich in traditional professional employment because there are no tremendous opportunities to work for large corporations. Manufacturing accounts for about 15 percent of the jobs and a quarter of the economy, suggesting how cherished this kind of employment is to Wilmingtonians.

Locals view the relatively few corporate professional employees with a degree of awe and speak with amazement of their high salaries and profuse benefits. By far, most people in the area work in smaller businesses for someone else or are engaged in some kind of enterprise of their own.

Geography seems to be the main factor that sets Wilmington apart from the overall North Carolina economy, and it is also driving some new trends that are positioning Wilmington to take advantage of a new and prosperous era at the end of the 20th century and beginning of the 21st. Its maritime environment creates opportunities for business based on what is naturally available — the sea, the river, the many beautiful views — instead of that which must be manufactured.

There have been, of course, significant times in history when Wilmington relied heavily on its natural resources for both manufacturing and agriculture. Early 18th century settlers used the area's lush pine forests to foster a lumber industry that continues today. The manufacture of lumber-related by-products, such as tar, turpentine and pitch, was the dominant business in the 19th century, but this type of manufacturing has since declined.

Rice and cotton were an early source of income for the area; the downtown wharves were once the site of the largest cotton exporting operation in the world. After the War Between the States, the economy shifted away from cotton and rice plantations because the labor supply was no longer available.

Railroads provided jobs for 4,000 families in the first part of the 20th century, as Wilmington became a major rail center. The Atlantic Coast Line, the evolution of the Wilmington and Weldon Railroad, was a technological marvel and the pride of the Wilmington economy at the time. Many an opulent downtown home was built on railroad dollars. Trains moved the area's products efficiently into the inland market, and there was popular speculation that the rails would move the economy into prosperity.

In 1955, the railroad announced the closing of its corporate office and sent a considerable segment of Wilmington's population south to Jacksonville, Florida in 1960. This was a severe economic loss that forced stunned Wilmingtonians to ponder their destiny. Not only were good-paying jobs lost with the railroad, but service businesses all over the area lost steady customers.

Although manufacturing is still an economic force in the region, statistics compiled by the University of North Carolina at Wilmington's Cameron School of Business indicate that the bulk of today's employment opportunities are in the services sector. This is a broad category that includes such diverse occupations as physicians, government workers, real estate brokers, educators and fast-food employ

The Port

The North Carolina State Port Authority established a deep-water terminal at Wilmington 51 years ago, initiating one of the region's early forays into the service realm. The facility now receives more than 550 ships annually from Mexico, Europe, South America, the Far East, the Mediterranean, the Red Sea and Arabian Gulf, Africa and the Caribbean, loaded with diverse cargoes.

Trade ports that do significant business through North Carolina ports include Japan, Korea, Hong Kong, Taiwan, Germany, France, Belgium, the Netherlands, the United Kingdom and South Africa. The main imports are metal products, general merchandise, tobacco and furniture. Leading exports are wood pulp, furniture products, general merchandise and food. The increasingly vital international trade industry at the ports at Wilmington and Morehead City and the two inland facilities at Greensboro and Charlotte provide a living for more than 26,000 North Carolinians.

Tourism

Tourism is one of the most important industries to arise in the latter half of the 20th century in the southern coastal area. Because the scenery is a constant and people are drawn to the sea, this industry provides a strong economic center. Even in the midst of economic downturns in more prosperous Raleigh, Greensboro and Winston-Salem, people in those cities still vacation at the beach. They may defer the mortgage payment, but they will not give up a week relaxing by the sea.

At this writing, more than 75,000 visitors a year drop by the Cape Fear Coast Convention and Visitors Bureau in downtown Wilmington, 24 N. Third Street, (910) 341-4030. On a typical summer weekend at Wrightsville Beach, more than 80,000 cars cross the bridge to the 5-mile-long island, and bridges to other area beaches frequently become clogged. And summer is no longer the sole tourism season. Visitors Bureau officials recognize that Wilmington has moved from a three-month to an eight-month tourism season that begins in March.

There are thousands of rooms, motels and inns in the Greater Wilmington area. Historic downtown Wilmington alone has more than two dozen bed and breakfast inns. One gets the sense someone sprinkled hotel/motel seeds all over the Cape Fear region because they seem to be springing up from the soil overnight, and statistics simply are not available for their numbers at this time. Still, it is often difficult to find lodgings on short notice during the summer and many facilities are experiencing nearly full occupancy on a year-round basis.

Other businesses that profit from the steady flow of tourists are also thriving. Visitors need a full range of services, and there are many entrepreneurs who are more than willing to provide them. Convention facilities and their attendant services represent a growing segment of the economy. Restaurants number in the hundreds and continue to proliferate at an astounding rate, with the best of them enjoying capacity dining on weekends. Special attractions and activities such as horse and carriage rides in the historic district, boat tours, sailing charters, a downtown Wilmington walking tour, and educational tours in the historic district continue to respond to high demand.

Trade

Wholesale and retail trade, linked strongly to tourism dollars, account for about 30 percent of the local economy, compared with 22.5 percent of the state's. Wilmington's retail businesses earned the city sixth place in retail sales

Tanker cars wait for transport to the North Carolina State Port Authority.

among all North Carolina cities in 1997. Sales figures are increasing at an annual rate of 10 percent, with a gross total of nearly $2.6 billion posted in 1996. Neighboring Brunswick and Pender counties posted $571.8 million and $175 million, respectively.

Recent years have seen the opening of such national and regional chains as Circuit City, The Gap, Barnes & Noble, and Target — stores Wilmingtonians never thought they would see. Belk-Beery, the city's premiere fashion department store, opened a second, though much smaller, store at Landfall Center in 1996. The city's retail corridor is pushing north, with extremely heavy development in the vicinity of Wrightsville Beach. On every corner, there seems to be a new shopping center going up, and retail stores that stock beachwear, vacation items and souvenirs are everywhere.

Office Space and Services

Because the region has a high percentage of single-staff entrepreneurs, there is a need for office space with secretarial services. Several office centers provide the individual or small company with turnkey services that include a central reception area, support staff services, use of office equipment and an opportunity to be in a professional setting. Utilities, excluding phone service, and janitorial services are included in the lease.

The region also has several employee services. For additional staffing needs, look in the Yellow Pages of the BellSouth phone book under Employment Agencies.

Landfall Business Center and Executive Suites
1213 Culbreath Dr., Wilmington
• **(910) 256-190**

Located adjacent to the residential neighborhood and shopping center of the same name, Landfall offers furnished office suites with long- or short-term leases near Wrightsville Beach. It is the largest center of its kind in Wilmington. Amenities include office supplies, a conference room and offices ranging from 130 to 300 square feet. Professional support services are available. It offers a corporate identity program to individuals or companies that are not housed on the site.

The Cotton Exchange
321 N. Front St., Wilmington
• (910) 343-9896

The Cotton Exchange has offices available for individuals or small companies in a center that overlooks the Cape Fear River in Historic Downtown Wilmington. It offers unfurnished offices with both long- and short-term leases as well as a corporate identity package that includes mailboxes, phone messages and receptionist answering services for businesses not physically located at the center. Professional support services are available.

Olsten Staffing Services
513 Market St. • (910) 343-8673

Olsten is part of an international company that specializes in a wide variety of temporary staffing assignments, including office services, legal support, accounting services, technical services, production/distribution/assembly and office automation.

SENC Technical Services
3142 Wrightsville Ave. • (910) 251-1925

SENC offers contract, permanent and contract-to-hire workers in technical fields such as engineering, designing/drafting, electronics, computer programming and more.

The Film Industry

In 1996, Wilmington captured $242 million of North Carolina's $410 million in revenues from filmmaking. According to the Wilmington Regional Film Commission, newly located on the Screen Gems lot, 1223 N. 23rd Street, (910) 343-3456, the film industry represents about 12 percent of the area's economic base. At this writing, only New York City and Los Angeles do more film business than Wilmington.

In 1996, movies filmed in the Wilmington area included *Virus*, *Bloodmoon*, *Day of the Jackal*, *This World* and *Then the Fireworks*. *Black Day* and *Oprah Winfrey Presents The Wedding* were filmed here in 1997. Since its purchase by Screen Gems, local studio Carolco is widening its focus to include the lucrative television commercial market. Under the guidance of Frank Capra, Jr., Screen Gems promises more activity in this sector. Commercials for BB&T, Nationwide Insurance and Dutch Boy Paints have been filmed locally.

Senior Services

A major industry is beginning to arise around the retirement population, thanks largely, of course, to our maritime location, which makes the climate unusually mild for our latitude. There are four discernible seasons, an important factor for northern retirees who have grown weary of Florida's almost single season. Warm summers and an occasional snow create a more interesting yearly cycle for retirees who yearn for a little diversity.

Nationally, North Carolina ranked fifth in 1996 as a retirement destination for people age 60. Figures suggest a 32-percent increase in this population between 1995 and 2000 according to the *1997 Fact Book* of the *Wilmington Star-News*. In response and expectation, planned retirement communities, senior services, recreational opportunities aimed at retirees, and other enterprises will represent a major component of the local economy.

As retirees flow into the area from more prosperous economies in the north and west, they bring their nest eggs with them and spend several decades buying local goods and services. An added benefit is their contribution of skills and knowledge to area volunteer organizations.

Healthcare

Healthcare is big business in the region. Three hundred physicians and five regional hospitals employ large numbers of medical personnel. One of the largest employers is the New Hanover Regional Medical Center, with more than 2,000 employees. In general, healthcare is one of the most lucrative employment sectors in the entire region.

Local healthcare services are extensive and many are comparable with the best state-of-the-art medical facilities and services in the nation. The Coastal Cancer Center at the New Hanover Regional Medical Center will provide complete cancer care at one site upon its completion in 1998.

The rapidly expanding seniors healthcare market is a national phenomenon, but it is particularly pronounced in coastal/resort communities. In addition to extensive medical services, New Hanover, Brunswick and Pender counties offer a large — and constantly growing — number of domiciliary care facilities.

Real Estate

After years of record growth, the area's new home building market is beginning to show signs of slowing down, but the real estate business in general is phenomenal. Driven partly by large numbers of retirees migrating to the area and non-retired newcomers who are drawn to the region for its weather and coastal orientation, the price of real estate has skyrocketed in the 1990s.

Manufacturing

The largest manufacturing companies in the area include Corning Glass Works (the Wilmington location is the largest manufacturer of optical fibers in the world); General Electric (aircraft engine parts, nuclear fuel and components); Carolina Power & Light; E.I. DuPont de Nemours (Dacron and polyester fibers); International Paper Board; and Trevira (dimethyl terephthalate, ethylene glycol and terate resins).

Smaller (in terms of employment) but still economically important companies include Pharmaceutical Product Development (clinical drug development services); Takeda Chemical Products USA (vitamins); Exide Electronics (uninterruptible power supply systems); Applied Analytical Industries (pharmaceutical products); Bedford Fair Industries (a women's apparel mail order company); Interroll Corporation (conveyor components and motorized pulleys); Sturdy Corporation (electronic and electromechanical control devices); and Occidental Chemical Corporation (sodium bichromate, chromic acid and sodium sulfate).

For a complete listing of manufacturers in Brunswick, New Hanover and Pender counties, drop by the Wilmington Chamber of Commerce, One Estell Lee Place, (910) 762-2611, and ask for a copy of the *Directory of Manufacturers*. The directory is produced by the Committee of 100, 1739 Hewlett Drive, (910) 763-8414, a component of Wilmington Industrial Development, Inc.

The University

The University of North Carolina at Wilmington accounts for 10 percent of the economic activity in New Hanover, Pender, Brunswick and Columbus counties — $360 million. Serving a student body of about 9,000, the university is among the fastest-growing and most technologically advanced in the 16-campus UNC system.

Organized into the College of Arts and Sciences (including a marine sciences program ranked fifth best in the world), the Cameron School of Business Administration, the Donald R. Watson School of Education, the School of Nursing and the Graduate School, the university offers bachelor's degrees in 38 areas of concentration, 10 pre-professional programs and 16 master's degree programs.

Greater Wilmington and the Cape Fear region offer great diversity in places and styles of worship.

Worship

Faith has always been a significant element of the Cape Fear region's identity. As is the case with most communities along the eastern seaboard, European settlers migrated to this area in the 18th century partly in search of religious freedom. The founding citizens of Wilmington brought their own beliefs with them, created spiritual homes for a broad array of nationalities, and eventually built stunning architectural monuments to their various faiths, some of which stand today as America's most significant religious buildings.

In the process, they also established a religious environment of absolute tolerance of each other's right to observe their beliefs. In the entire recorded history of Wilmington, there is not so much as one example of religious oppression. To the contrary, there are many examples of a congregation of one denomination coming to the aid of another, such as when the members of Temple Israel, the first Jewish Temple in North Carolina, freely shared their building with neighboring Methodists for two years after the Methodist church was destroyed by fire in 1886.

In the aftermath of the Civil War, many a white congregation offered financial and moral support to newly created black churches when black members decided the time had come to create their own houses of worship. Although churches are still largely segregated, there is a continuing respectful and supportive attitude among them.

Modern day Greater Wilmington and the Cape Fear region offer great diversity in places and styles of worship in more than 200 churches. One cannot view the Wilmington skyline without being instantly struck by the profusion of spires — even in the aftermath of the hurricanes of 1996, when the First Baptist Church on the corner of Market and 4th streets lost its 197-foot-high steeple (the city's tallest); restoration is underway.

The grander houses of worship in downtown Wilmington date from the 18th and 19th centuries and, in addition to providing opulent settings for large congregations, figure prominently on historic tours of the area. St. James Episcopal at the corner of Market and South 3rd, St. Mary Catholic on South 5th, Temple of Israel with its distinctive gold onion-shaped domes, St. Paul's Evangelical Lutheran on Market Street, First Presbyterian on South 3rd (whose minister from 1874 to 1885 was President Woodrow Wilson's father, the Rev. Joseph R. Wilson) and St. Stephen AME all represent fascinating history and architecture for the visitor. (See our Attractions chapter for more information on historic churches.)

In terms of identifiable religions throughout Wilmington and the entire Cape Fear region, a breakdown of churches in New Hanover County is a good indicator of who is worshipping where. The largest Christian denomination in sheer number of churches in Wilmington and New Hanover is Baptist, with Southern Baptists leading the way with at least 42. There are another 19 Baptist churches, including Free Will, Independent and Missionary. The next largest group is the Presbyterians, with 21 congregations. AME and United Methodist are next, with 16 houses of worship apiece.

Nondenominational Christian, Episcopal, Holiness, Pentecostal and AME Zion make up the next tier, with 11 to 12 churches each.

INSIDERS' TIP

Wilmington's Baha'i Center, at 15 N. Eighth Street, (910) 762-7074, holds frequent workshops to promote community understanding.

Experience the awe that the serene coast can inspire.

Other religions with a strong presence in the area include Jewish, Roman Catholic, Jehovah's Witnesses, Full Gospel, Greek Orthodox, Advent Christian, Christian Science, Islam, Lutheran, Quaker, Unitarian, Metropolitan Community, Seventh Day Adventist, Unity, Eckankar and others.

An unusual sight in Bolivia, in Brunswick County, is the Thai temple rising from the coastal forests. The North Carolina Association of Buddhists has been building this temple for nearly a decade and has relied on community donations to complete the work. It represents an important addition to the region's religious and philosophical centers.

Visitors to the area can expect to be heartily welcomed into its churches and temples. The Sunday edition of the *Wilmington Star-News* has a comprehensive listing that includes denomination, location and service hours. The yellow pages of the BellSouth telephone book and the business section of the community phone book provide listings of churches and temples by denomination. For detailed tour information on area churches, refer to our Attractions chapter.

If you want to attend church services while you're on vacation and you're wondering what to wear, here's some advice: Cape Fear coast people don't dress up too much for work, love to wear very casual clothes on the beach, but generally dress for worship. You'll probably be more comfortable at a local church or temple if you arrive in a suit and tie or dress for services, but, as one parishioner from St. James Episcopal remarked, "Oh, we don't mind how they dress as long as they come. In fact, when we see them in their vacation clothes, that lets us know they're from out of town and it gives us a chance to welcome them." Probably the only vacation dress not welcome in houses of worship is a swimsuit and flip-flops. Incidentally, beach attire is inappropriate for any place beyond the beach.

The history of churches in the Cape Fear area could fill several books. Many of the region's larger churches were occupied by British or Union troops, and historical commentary about those episodes conjure up dramatic pictures. Imagine, if you will, the courtyards of downtown Wilmington churches populated by weary soldiers for so long that their camp fires permanently blackened the steeples. If you want to know more, drop by the North Carolina Room at the New Hanover County Public Library in downtown Wilmington and ask for information.

Wilmington and the Cape Fear area have an abundance of spiritual resources in terms of bookstores. Mainstream Christian shoppers will enjoy The Bible Book and Gift Center, 5015 Wrightsville Avenue, Wilmington, (910) 791-3911, a store that serves all Christian denominations with bibles, tapes, and music. Cox Christian Bookstore, 75 South Kerr Avenue, (910) 762-2272, and 2222 South 16th Street, (910) 392-0410, is another good reference spot.

Alternative spirituality is evident in the Metaphysical Fair, held twice a year in January and August at the Coast Line Convention Center downtown. Channelers, fortune tellers, and meditation experts, among others, interact with the general public and display crystals, alternative books, and more at this weekend event. The Wilmington area is apparently a spiritual magnet, likened by some believers to Norfolk, Virginia, home of spiritual guide Edgar Cayce's institute.

Index of Advertisers

Ad Lib	146
Affordable Affluence	7
Alligator Pie	216
Anderson & Daniel Personnel	424
Annabelle's Restaurant & Pub	93
Atlantic Towers	46
Audio Visions	142
Audubon Village	138
Bald Head Island Real Estate, Inc.	inside cover map
Barney's Drinking & Dancing	120
Basket Case	21
Battleship North Carolina	163
Beds Express	6
Big Daddy's	107
Bill Clark Homes	color insert
Birkenstock Comfortable Soles	141
Blockade Runner	inside back cover
Bob Jamieson, ABR, GRI	347
BPW/NC	410
Bradley Square	133
Brierwood Golf Club	333
Brunswick Community College	405
Bryant Real Estate	356
Cape Fear Academy	389
Cape Fear Coast Convention & Visitors Bureau	color insert
Cape Fear Coffee & Tea	110
Cape Fear Community College	403
Cape Fear Memorial Hospital	373, 381
Cape Fear Musuem	167
Cape Golf & Racquet Club	329
Carolina National Golf Club	326
Carolina Temple Apartments	43
Carolina's Food & Drink	91
Catherine Kennedy Home	370
Catherine's Inn	56
Century 21 Coastal Communities	361
Chamber Music Society of Wilmington	209
Chandler's Wharf Inn	57
Clark-Teachey Realtors	color insert
Coastal Condo-Let	74, 357
Coast Line Inn	39
Country Squire	240
Courtyard by Marriott Wilmington	41
Creative World	391
Curtis Krueger Photographer	206
Cypress Green, Inc.	color insert
Daphna's House of Charms	5
Davies Realty	68
Down Island Traders	137, 143
Easy Living	140
Echo Farms	332
Elijah's Restaurant	color insert
ERA-Brittain & Associate Realtors	72
EUE/Screen Gems Studios	viii
Exercise Today	19
Fiddler's Gallery	145
First Citizens	color insert
Flapjack & Gung Ho Fishing Charters	285
Gold's Gym	3
Golden Gallery	145
Golden Sands Motel	45
Graystone Inn	59
Grouper Nancy's	18
Harbour Town Associates	347
Hobbs Realty	76
Howard, Perry & Walston	73
Howard RV Center	80
Incredible Pizza	94
Independence Mall	color insert
Inland Greens	335
Intracoastal Angler	277
Island Appliance	351
Island Passage	135
JJR Builders	347
James E. Moore, Insurance	color insert
Jungle Rapids	173
Katy's Great Eats	89
Landfall Associates	inside front cover

INDEX OF ADVERTISERS • 435

Landfall Business Center
   Executive Suites 348
Learning Express 219
Lumina Station 130
Makado Gallery 145
Manhattan Bagel 101
Marina's Edge 109
MasonArt 205
MEDAC 378
Montessori Schoo 393
Mr. Store It 355
Murray House 240
Murrow Furniture Galleries ...... color insert, 144
New Hanover Regional Medical
   Center .... color insert
New Home Marketplace 349
Oceanic Restaurant .... color insert
Olsten Staffing Services 11
Paradise Inn 47
Perry's Emporium .... color insert
Pilot House Restaurant .... color insert
Pleasure Island Merchants
   Association 12
Pinehurst Pottery 149
Pizza Bistro 99
Provence, Ltd. .... color insert
Red Dinette .... color insert
Reeds Jewelers .... color insert
River Landing 331
Romanelli's Restaurant .... color insert
Rosehill Inn 54
Rucker Johns Restaurant 16
Runway 148
Scott & Stringfellow, Inc. 330

Security Savings Bank 342
South Beach Grill 105
South Brunswick Islands Chamber of
   Commerce 33
Southport-Oak Island Chamber of
   Commerce 31
Stonebridge Realty 351
Stork's Nest 148
Subway 90
Surfside Motor Lodge 47
Sweet & Savory Bake Shop & Café 97
Szechuan 132/130 17
Taste of Country Buffet & Catering 95
Temptations 132
Tomatoz American Grill 88
Tom's Drug Company 148
Tryon Palace 165
United Beach Vacations 75
Verandas 60
Victoria's Interiors 21
WAAV 25, 70, 123, 169, 421
Wachovia Bank 352
Walls Fine Art Gallery 211
Welcome Service of Wilmington 350
WhiteBridge .... color insert, 344
Whittler's Bench 205
Wilmington Christian Academy 395
Wilmington Concert Association 207
Wilmington International Airport 4
Wilmington Star News 160
Winds Clarion Inn & Suites 51
Wrightsville Beach Storage, Inc. 286
Wrigley's Clocks 145
YMCA 296

Index

Symbols

219 South 5th 55
3D Golf Vacations 339

A

A & G Sportswear 141
A-Plus Taxi Service 5
AAA Motor Club 141
About Time Antiques 157
Acme Art 204
Ad Hoc Theatre Company 213
Adam and Hilliard Realty 360
Aerobics with Freddie J. King 322
Aeronautics 11, 187, 302
Affordable Affluence Inc. 5
After Dark Limousine Service 5
Air Tours 187
Air Wilmington 11, 187, 302
Airlie Moon 151
Alabama Theatre 242, 243
Alan Holden Realty 367
Alcoholics Anonymous 384
Alligator Adventure 242
Alligator Pie 150
Alpha Counseling and Development Center 384
Alternative Health Care Center 384
Alzheimer's Disease and Neurological
    Support Group 382
American Cancer Society Tournament 339
American Lung Association Golf Privilege Card 339
American Pie 132, 206
American Red Cross, Cape Fear Chapter 411
Angel's Antiques and Auctions 157
Annabelle's Restaurant 9
Annabelle's Restaurant & Pub 89
Annual Festival of Trees 413
Antique Emporium 157
Antique Mall, The 157
Antiques of Old Wilmington 157
Apple Annie's Bake Shop 225
Aquatic Safaris & Divers Emporium 261
Arbor Creek 358
Archibald's Delicatessen & Rotisserie 114
Ari Rang House 89
Art in the Park 192
Arts 203
Arts Council of the Lower Cape Fear 203, 204
Ashton Farm Summer Day Camp 237
Assisted Care 384
Associated Artists of Southport 204, 208
Association of Carolina Shag Clubs 244
At Easy Living 151
Athletic Zon 298

Athletic Zone 223, 306, 307, 316
Atlantic Beach 246
Atlantic Marine 289
Atlantic Towers 45, 74
Atlantic Vacations Resorts and Real Estate 77
Attic, The 243
Audio Visions 143
Audubon Village 140
Auld Stokley Antiques 157
Aussie Island Surf Shop 150, 264, 300
Autumn with Topsail Beach Arts &
    Entertainment Fes 195
Azalea Coast Chorus of Sweet Adelines 210
Azalea Coast Smockers Guild 215
Azalea Festival 22
Azalea Festival Show 205
Azalea Festival Triathlon 315
Azalea Plaza 140
Azalea Sale 191

B

B. Dalton Bookseller 141
Babbage's Software 233
Babies and Books 412
Bachman Realty 360
Back Alley Lounge, The 126
Back Deck Grill 225
Back Porch Ice Cream Shoppe 227
Bald Head Island 30, 358
Bald Head Island Club 331
Bald Head Island Club, The 109
Bald Head Island Conservancy 30
Bald Head Island Cruise and Race, The 258
Bald Head Island Ferry 7
Bald Head Island Fishing Rodeo 285
Bald Head Island Historic Tour 179
Bald Head Island Information Center 76
Bald Head Island Marina 292
Bald Head Island Maritime Classic Road Race 311
Bald Head Island Real Estate 366
Baldwin-Copeland Studio of Dance 221
Ballet School of Wilmington, The 221
Barbary Coast 122
Barefoot Landing 242
Barefoot Princess Riverboat 242
Bark in the Park 195
Barnes & Noble 129, 143
Baseball and Little League 297
Basket Case, The 136
Basketball 298
Baskin-Robbins 31 Flavors Ice Cream and
    Yogurt Store 227
Battleship North Carolina 162

INDEX • 437

Battleship North Carolina Memorial
    Day Observance 192
Beach Access 266
Beach Buggy Taxi 5
Beach Fun Rentals 257, 264
Beach Harbour Resort 46
Beach Music Festival 194
Beach Properties of Topsail Island Inc. 368
Beacon House Inn Bed and Breakfast, The 61
Beau Rivage Plantation Golf & Country Club 330
Beaufort 246
Beaufort Grocery Co. 247
Beaufort Restoration Grounds 247
Bed & Breakfast at Mallard Bay 67
Bed Express 158
Belk-Beery 141, 149
Bellamy Mansion Museum of Design Arts 164
Belvedere Plantation Golf & Country Club 336
Bert's Surf Shop 264
Bessie's 122
Best Holiday Limousine Service 5
Betty's Smokehouse Restaurant 117
Beverage Boutique, The 136
Beyond the Goal Soccer Camp 311
Bible Book and Gift Center, The 433
Bicycle Program, North Carolina Dept. of Transport 4
Bicycle Works 300
Bicycling 299
Big Daddy's Seafood Restaurant 105
Big Dawg Productions 213
Big Sweep 411
Bijoux 137
Bike Path 3
Bill Curry's Cycling and Fitness 300
Bird Island 35
Birkenstock Comfortable Soles 143
Birthing Center, The 379
Blockade Runner Resort Hotel 43
Blockade Runner Scenic Cruises 174
Blowing In the Wind 307
Blue Water Point Marina 284
Blue Water Point Marina Resort 293
Blue Water Point Marina Resort Motel 48
Blue Yonder Flying Machines 10, 302
Blues Society of the Lower Cape Fear 210
Bluethenthal Wildflower Preserve 402
Bluff Island 30
Boat House Gifts 153
Boat Registration 254
Boater's World Discount Marine Center 260
Boathouse Marina 290
Boating 253
Bocci 89
Body Dimensions 321
Bogey's At the Beach 127
Bogue Banks Island 246
Books-A-Million 140, 233
Boomer's Bikes & More 301
Bottom Time 261
Bowling 301
Boxing 301
Boxing & Fitness Center, The 231
Boy Scouts of America, Cape Fear Council 414
Bradley Creek Boatominium 290
Branchwood Village 368

Brass Pelican, The 127
Breakfast Café 106
Breakfast Creek Bed & Breakfast 62
Breaktime Sports Bar, Billiards & Grill 122
Breezeway Restaurant 117
Brick Landing Plantation 77, 334
Bridge Tender Marina and Restaurant 289
Bridge Tender Restaurant, The 101
Brierwood Golf Club 314, 334
Brigade Boys and Girls Club 237
Brigade Boy's Club 414
Brightmore of Wilmington 372
Bristol Books 150
Broadway At The Beach 244
Brookgreen Gardens 242
Brown Real Estate 78, 369
Brunswick 13
Brunswick Beacon 419
Brunswick Community College 405
Brunswick County Airport 10
Brunswick County Arts Council 204
Brunswick County Bowling Center 301
Brunswick County Department of
    Older Adults 377, 417
Brunswick County Library 233
Brunswick County Literacy Council Inc. 412
Brunswick County Parks and
    Recreation 299, 315, 322, 339
Brunswick County Parks and Recreation
    Department 237
Brunswick County School System 389
Brunswick Family Assistance Agency 412
Brunswick Hospital 381
Brunswick School of Dance 221
Brunswick Shores Children's Center 382
Brunswick Town 30
Brunswickland Realty 77
Bryant Real Estate 73
Bryson, Elizabeth, LMT 385
Bud Light Chili Cookoff 196
Buddy's Crab & Oyster Bar 126
Budget Rent A Car 6
Bullard Realty 74, 365
Burgwin-Wright House 164
Buses 4
Bushin-Kai Karate 317
Butterflies Castle Antiques 157
Butte's Antiques 157
By-The-River Biathlon 300

C

Cabana De Mar Motel 46
Cafe at Sweet & Savory Bake Shop, The 101
Caffe Phoenix 90, 122
Calabash 35, 359
Calabash Golf Links 334
Calabash Nautical Gifts 154
Calabash Seafood Hut 116
Calhoun's Celtic Import 136
Camellia Cottage 55
Camelot RV Park & Campground 82
Cameron School of Business Administration 401
Camp Lejeune 265
Camp Lejeune Oktoberfest Family 5K Fun Run 311

438 • INDEX

Canady's Marina 288
Canady's Sport Center 144
Canady's Sports Center 81, 254, 305
Candles Etc. 135
Candy Barrel 136
Candy Barrel, The 227
Candy Express 228
Canoeing 255
CanSurvive 380
Canterbury Stable 303
Cape Fear Academy 392
Cape Fear Academy Lacrosse Camp 307
Cape Fear Antiques Center 158
Cape Fear Area United Way 412
Cape Fear Astronomical Club 233
Cape Fear Blues Festival 194
Cape Fear Boat Rentals 259
Cape Fear Camera Club 215
Cape Fear Chordsmen 210
Cape Fear Christmas House, The 132
Cape Fear Coast Convention & Visitors Bureau 1
Cape Fear Coast Convention and Visitors Bureau 426
Cape Fear Coffee & Tea 110, 122
Cape Fear Community College 403
Cape Fear Council of Governments 377
Cape Fear Cyclists Club 300
Cape Fear Filmmakers Accord 26
Cape Fear Filmmakers' Accord 215
Cape Fear Filmmakers Accord Haunted House 236
Cape Fear Literacy Council 412
Cape Fear Memorial Hospital 379
Cape Fear Museum 165, 223, 237
Cape Fear Outfitters 81, 151, 255, 256
Cape Fear River 13
Cape Fear River Circle Tour 173
Cape Fear River Rowing Club 255
Cape Fear River Watch 294
Cape Fear Roller Hockey League 306
Cape Fear Rugby Club 309
Cape Fear Run 82, 299
Cape Fear Sevens Rugby Tournament 309
Cape Fear Shakespeare 213
Cape Fear Ski & Outing Club 297
Cape Fear Symphony Orchestra 211
Cape Fear Theatre Ballet 214
Cape Fear United Way Information and
  Referral Service 411
Cape Fear Youth Soccer Association 312
Cape Golf & Racquet Club, The 327
Cape Resort and Golf Club, The 372
Cape, The 356
Capeside Village 372
Capt. Jim's Marina 184, 284
Capt. Maffitt Sightseeing Cruise 165
Capt. Sam's Sightseeing Cruises 183
Capt. Willie's Restaurant 116
Captain Dick's Marina 243
Capt'n Bill's Backyard Grill 316
Capt'n Pete's Seafood Market 284
Car Rentals 6
Cardinal Lanes 301
Carolco Pictures 26
Carolina Beach 23, 357
Carolina Beach (910) 458-7416 314
Carolina Beach Boardwalk 174

Carolina Beach Chamber of Commerce 35
Carolina Beach Family Campground 82
Carolina Beach Municipal Marina 291
Carolina Beach New Year's Eve Countdown Party 201
Carolina Beach Realty 74
Carolina Beach State Park 83, 230, 324
Carolina Beach State Park Marina 291
Carolina Beach Triathlon 315
Carolina Heights 348
Carolina Inlet Marina 290
Carolina Kite Club 234, 307
Carolina Lake Park 324
Carolina National Golf Links 331
Carolina Opry 243
Carolina Palace Theater 244
Carolina Place 348
Carolina Shores 359
Carolina Shores Golf & Country Club 335
Carolina Sport Fishing Charters 284
Carolina Temple Apartments 43
Carolina Trailways 7
Carolina Yacht Club 259
Carolina Yacht Yard 288
Carolina's Food & Drink 103
Carolina's PGA Seniors Pro-Am Golf Tournament 334
Carson Cards and Gifts 154
Castle Hayne Saddle Shop, The 303
Castle Stables 303
Caswell Beach 32, 358
Catherine Kennedy Home 373
Catherine's Inn 56
Causeway Cafe 224
CD Alley 134
Celebrate Wilmington 204
Celebrate Wilmington! 196
Center for Counseling, A 384
Center for Marine Science Research 402, 405
Center for Successful Aging, The 380
Century 21 Coastal Communities 361
Century 21 Dorothy Essey and Associates Inc. 367
Century 21 Sunset Realty 368
Century 21, Sweyer & Associates 361
Century 21-Brock Mills 361
Cercle Theatre 244
Chadsworth Columns 134
Chadwick House 247
Chain Reaction Bicycling Center 300
Challenger, The 419
Chamber Music Society of Wilmington 210
Chamber of Commerce 1
Chambers of Commerce 35
Champion Karate Centers 317
Chandler's Wharf 134, 166
Chandler's Wharf Inn 56
Charles Tilghman Junior Tournament 245
Chart House, The 111
Charter Restaurant 246
Checkered Church 152
Cheerwine College Tournament 334
Chestnut Street United Presbyterian Church 166
Child Advocacy Commission 395, 414
Child Care 395
Child Development Center School for
  Developmentally Disabled 394
Children's Festival Land 198

Chiropractors 384
Choe's Hapkido 317
Chris's Restaurant 90
Christie's Gallery 206
Christmas By-The-Sea Parade 197
Christmas for Kids and Others Concert 236
Christmas Lights at Calder Court 236
Chuck E Cheese's Pizza 224
Cinematique of Wilmington 128
City Pier 277
Clark-Teachey Realtors 362
Classy Bears Learning Center 398
Clawson's 1905 Restaurant 247
Clockwise Clocks 149
Club Rio 123
Coast Line Convention Center 38
Coast Line Inn 37
Coastal Cancer Center 380
Coastal Cancer Center, The 428
Coastal Carolina Bike Trek 299
Coastal Condo-Let 75
Coastal Development and Realty 367
Coastal Diabetes Center, The 380
Coastal Golf Center and Carolina Custom
    Discount Golf 337
Coastal Golfaway 339
Coastal Horizons Center 412
Coastal Plantation, A Jensen's Residential
    Community 373
Coastal Rehabilitation Hospital, The 380
Coastal Sports Cards & Apparel 217
Coastal Tumblegym 223, 321
Cobb's Corner Lounge 126
Coca-Cola Regatta 258
Cockle Shell, The 154
Coldwell Banker Baker Properties 362
Coldwell Banker Coastline Realty 78, 369
Coldwell Banker Sea Coast Realty 362
Coldwell Banker Southport-Oak Island Realty 76
Coldwell Banker United Realty Group 365
Coldwell BankerSouthport-Oak Island Realty 367
Columbia Cape Fear Memorial Hospital 376
Comedy Club, The 123
Comfort Inn Wilmington 38
Commerce and Industry 425
Community Arts Center 204, 221
Community Boys and Girls Club 414
Comprehensive Home Health Care 384
Connoisseurs' Wine & Art Auctio 190
Cooke Realtors 368
Cooke's Inn Motel 50
Cool World Family Fun Center 217
Coquina Harbour at Carolina Beach 291
Cory Everson's Aerobics & Fitness for Women 319
Cottage, The 106
Cotton Exchange 428
Cotton Exchange, The 135
Cottonpatch Farms 303
Country Vogue 140
Courtyard Marriott 38
Cove at Fort Fisher State Historic Site, The 324
Cove Surf Shop, The 264
Cowboy's Texas Bar-B-Q 90
Cox Christian Bookstore 433
Crabby Oddwaters Restaurant and Bar 114

Crafts 215
Craven County Visitor's Information Center 248
Creative World 398
Creek, The 127
Crescent Moon Inn 66
Crest Fitness Center 321
Crystal Connection New Age Shop 137
Cucalorus Film Festival 191
Curran House 57
Currituck Banks 408
Cypress Island 356

D

Dairy Queen 228
Dallas Harris Real Estate Construction 362
Dance 214
Danceworks Studio for the Performing Arts 221
Daphna's House of Charms 144
DARE 16
David Walker Day Festival and Concert 195
Davies Realty 75, 366
Davis Center, The 220
Day at the Docks, A 190
Daytrips 241
Deborah Jamieson andAssociates Showroom/
    Gallery/Interior 208
Deck Family Entertainment Center, The 179, 265
Del's Restaurant 111
Deluxe Cafe 91
Dial-A-Sailor 22
Digh's Country Sports Gallery 280, 308
Directory of Manufacturers, The 429
Dixie Stampede 243
Dockside Marina 289
Dockside Restaurant 289
Dockside Watersports 252, 254, 255, 259, 266
Docksider Gifts & Shells 156
Docksider Inn-Oceanfront 47
Doctor's Immediate Care 383
Doctor's Urgent Care Centre 383
Domestic Violence Shelter and Services Inc. 413
Down Island Traders 136
Downtown Area Redevelopment Effort, The 65
Doxey's Market & Cafe 103
Doxey's Market and Cafe 149
Dragon Garden Chinese Cuisine 91
Driftwood Motel 49
Driftwood Shell Shop 154
Duffer's Pub & Deli 114
Dunlea Realty 362
DuPont World Amateur Handicap Championship 245

E

E. F. Middleton Park 325
Early Childhood Learning Center 398
Earth's Treasures 137
East Coast Discount Dive Center 262
East Coast Got-Em-On King Mackerel Classic 285
Easter Egg Hunt 236
Eastern Surfing Association 263
Easy Way Transport Service 5
Echo Farms 356
Echo Farms Golf & Country Club 327

440 • INDEX

Eckerd Drugs 141
Ecko Furniture 158
Eddie Miles Theater 243
Eddie Romanelli's 92
El Vaquero 224
Eldercare Convalescent Service 384
Elderhaus Inc. 417
Elegant Days 249
Elijah's 92, 134
Elizabeth's Pizza 92, 224
Ella's of Calabash 117
Embellishments 151
Emerging Artists Program 204
Empie Park 322
Enchanted Toy Shop, tThe 237
Encore Magazine 421
Energizer Senior Tour Championship 245
Enterprise Rentals 6
Entropy Rentals & Charters 254, 261
EUE/Screen Gems Studios 26
EUE/Screen Gems Studios Tour 171
Ev-Henwood Nature Preserve 402
Ev-Henwood Preserve 325
Exercise Today 320
Express Care 384
Expresso Cafe 110

F

Faded Rose, The 92
Falcon Cable 423
Fall Festival 196
Fall Native American Pow-Wow 198
Family Fest 196
Family Kingdom Amusement Park 242
Family Services of the Lower Cape Fear 415
Fanboy Comics & Cards 217
Fantasy Harbour-Waccamaw 243
Federal Point Medical Center 384
Ferries 6
Festival By the Sea 196
Festival of Trees 198
Fidler's Gallery and Framing 208
Figure Eight Island 28, 352
Figure Eight Island Vacation Rentals 74
Figure Eight Realty 74, 362
Film 215
Finkelstein's Jewelry and Music Company 136
Finklestein's Music 221
First Baptist Church 166
First Presbyterian Church 166
Fisherman's Wife, The 149
Fishing Licenses 276
Fishing Tournaments 284
Fit For Fun 231
Fitness Centers 319
Flo-Jo 261
Flora, Deborah, CMT 385
Flying 302
Football 302
Forest Hills 349
Forever Fit Fitness Center 318, 322
Formal Limousine Service 5
Fort Caswell 179
Fort Fisher 24
Fort Fisher State Historic Site 176
Fort Fisher State Recreation Area and Historic Sit 24
Fort Fisher-Southport Ferry 176
Fort Johnson 180
Fourth of July Fireworks 194
Fox Fire Farm 303
Fran Brittain Realty 73
Franklin Square Gallery 204, 208
Fred and Claire's Restaurant 248
Freddie's Restaurant 106
Friedman Chiropractic 384
Friends of David Walker 213
Front Street Brewery 92
Front Street Grill 247
Front Street Inn 38
Fudge Company 228
Furniture Patch of Calabash, The 158

G

G. Flowers Realty 362
Galleries 206
Game Giant, The 218
Game Plan Video Game Exchange, The 218
Gap 142
Garden Botanika 142
Gardner Realty 75, 366
Gatlin Brothers Theatre 243
Gauntlet Golf Club, The 332
Gay Rights of Wilmington (GROW) 413
General Assembly 110
Gift Basket, The 156
Gifted Gourmet, The 135
Girl Scout Council of Coastal Carolina 415
Girls Inc. of Wilmington 414
Girls Incorporated Day Camp 237
Glenn Weckel, Dr. 384
Gold Rose Apparel, The 152
Golden Gallery 208
Golden Sands Motel 46
Golder Realty 364
Goldings Hobbies 218
Gold's Gym 376
Gold's Gym Fitness & Aerobics 319
Golf 327
Golf, Myrtle Beach 245
Golf Tech 339
Golf Vacation Planner 245
Good Shepherd House 413
Goody Goody Omelet House 93
Goose Creek Bed & Breakfast 66
Governor's Cup, The 258
Granny's Day Care Center 398
Gray Gull Motel 49
Graystone Inn 58
Great Harvest Bread Company, The 144
Great Mistakes 152
Greater Wilmington Antique Show and Sale 189
Greater Wilmington Chamber of Commerce 35
Greater Wilmington Tennis Association 314
Greek Festival 195
Green Swamp Game Land 304
Greenfield Lake and Gardens 172, 230
Greenfield Park 309, 322
Greyhoun 7

INDEX • 441

Griffith Gallery 208
Grouper Nancy's Fine Dining & Spirits 93
Grove, The 181
Gung-Ho and Flapjack 284

H

Habitat for Humanity, Cape Fear 416
Halfmoon's Coffee Bar 110
Halloween Festival 197
Halloween History-Mystery Tour 197
Halloween Moonlight 5K Run 310
Hammerheads' Soccer Clinic and Camps 238
Hampstead Chamber of Commerce 35
Hampstead King Mackerel Tournament 285
Hampstead Medical Center 384
Hampstead Village Pharmacy 305
Handscapes Gallery 247
Hanover Center 141
Hanover Fishing Charters 261, 284
Hanover Stables 303
Harbour Point and Pleasure Island Marina & Resort 290
Harbour Town Associates Real Estate 362
Harbour Village Marina 288
Hard Rock Cafe 244
Haren (Ed Pickett) 318
Harley-Davidson Charity Halloween Run 197
Harmony Belles 211
Harris Teeter 141
Harvest Moon 93
Harvey Mansion Restaurant and Lounge 248
Headstart Program of New Hanover County 398
Healing Arts Network, The 381
Healthcare 379
Helen Alice Higgins Montessori School 392
Henrietta II 167
Herring's Tackle & Beach Shop 257
Hertz 6
Hilda Godwin's 137
Hilton, The 292
Hiro Japanese Steak and Seafood House 94
Historic District Commission 16
Historic Wilmington Foundation 416
Historic Wilmington Foundation, The 64
HIV/AIDS Outreach 412
Hobbs Real Estate 339
Hobbs Realty 77, 368
HobbyTown USA 150
Hobie Fleet 101 258
Hoge-Wood House Bed and Breakfast 58
Hoggard Lacrosse Club 307
Holden Beach 32, 358
Holden Beach Driving Range 338
Holden Beach Marin 284
Holden Beach Marina 293
Holden Beach Pier 279
Holden Beach Pier Family Campground 84
Holden Beach Surf & Scuba 262, 264
Holden Beach True Value 305
Holden Brothers Farm Market 231
Holden Realty 78
Holiday Inn 40
Holiday Inn Express Hotel & Suites 40
Holland's Shelter Creek Fish Camp 255, 305
Holland's Shelter Creek Restaurant 118

Holly Festival 198
Holly Shelter Game Land 304
Home Child Care 399
Home Healthcare 384
Home Schooling 394
Hope Harbor Home 413
Horse-Drawn Carriage Tour 167
Horseback Riding 302
Hospice of the Lower Cape Fear 413
Hot Wax Surf Shop 264
Hotel Tarrymore 25
How Does Your Garden Grow? Show! 190
Howard Johnson Plaza Hotel and Conference Center 40
Howard, Perry & Walston Better Homes and Gardens 73
Howard, Perry andWalston Realty Inc./ Better Homes and Gardens 363
Hugh MacRae Park 220, 323
Hughes Marina 293
Hungate's Arts-Crafts & Hobbies 218
Hunting 303
Hurricane Fleet 184, 243, 284

I

Ice House, The 123
IMAX Discovery Theater, 244
In-line and Roller Skating 305
Incredible Gourmet Pizza 94
Independence Mall 141
India Mahal 95
Indigo Plantation 358
Inland Greens 328
Inlet Watch Yacht Club 290
Inn at St. Thomas Court, The 41
Intracoastal Angler 281
Intracoastal Realty Corporation 74, 363, 365
Intracoastal Waterway, The 287
Island Appliance 152
Island Chandler Delicatessen 109
Island Gazette, The 419
Island of Lights Festival 198
Island Passage 137, 255
Island Realty Vacations 78
Island Resort 49
Island Super Store 156
Island Tackle & Gifts 305
Island Tackle & Hardware 152
Island Treasures 156
Island Walking Club 310
ISO Aero 187
ISO Aero Service Inc. 302
Iso Aero Service Inc. of Wilmington 11

J

J & C Sportscards & Collectibles 218
J. Arthur Dosher Memorial Hospital 382
J.S. Anderson 150
J/G's Country Bar-B-Que 114
Jackson's Big Oak Barbecue 95
Jacobi Warehouse 137
Jane Suggs Antiques 249
Java Lane 111
JCPenney 141

442 • INDEX

Jean Brown Real Estate 369
Jelly Beans Family Skating Center 223, 231, 238, 307
Joe Eakes Park 325
Joe's Barbecue Kitchen 115
Johnnie Mercer's Pier 277
Johnson Marina 288
Johnson Marine Services 254
Jolly Roger Motel, The 50
Jolly Roger Pier 279
Jones' Seafood House 112
Jones, Theresa, CMP 385
Jubilee Amusement Park 174
Jubilee Park 24, 233
Julia, The 150
Julie's Bike Rentals 301
Julie's Rentals 257, 307
Jungle Rapids Family Fun Park 172, 224, 233
Jung's Tae Kwon Do Academy 318

K

K-38 Baja Grill 95
Kangaroo Kapers 413
Katie B. Hines Senior Center 376
Katy's Great Eats 96, 124, 224
Kelly's Coffee Pub 111
Kenan Auditorium 402
Kennedy Company Realty and Management, The 79
Ken's Bagels & Deli 96
Keziah Memorial Park 181
Kids' Gym, The 238
Kid's Gym, The 232
Kindermusik 221
King Classic 285
King Neptune 103
King Neptune's Pirate Lounge 126
Kingoff's Jewelers 137, 140
King's Motel 46
Kitchen Shoppe, The 136
Kite Flying 307
Kitty Hawk Air Services 187
Kiwanis Loggerhead Golf Tournament 341
Kmart 305
Kohl's Frozen Custard 229
Kool Aid Golf Tournament 341
Kure Beach 24
Kure Beach Aikido 318
Kure Beach Double Sprint Triathlon 316
Kure Beach Pier 277
Kwanzaa 236

L

L Bookworm 234
La Costa Mexican Restaurant 96
Labor Day Arts & Crafts Beach Fest 196
Lacrosse 307
Lake Shore Commons 374
Lake Waccamaw State Park 86
Lancing House 249
Landfall 328, 349
Landfall Associates 364
Landfall Business Center and Executive Suites 427
Landfall Park Hampton Inn & Suites 44
Landfall Shopping Center 149

Laney Real Estate 364
LaQue Center for Corrosion Technology Inc. 409
Laredo's Neon Cactus 127
Laredo's Neon Cactus Restaurant & Cantina 112
Largest Living Christmas Tree 199
Larry's Calabash Seafood Barn 117
Latimer House 416
Learning Express 218
Learning Express, The 146
Legends in Concert 243
Legion Stadium 323
Lejeune Grand Prix Series 315
Leland District Park 325
Lenox China 242
Leon's Ogden Restaurant 96
Leprechaun Run 310
Lett's Taxi Service 5
Lewis Farms 231
Lewis Realty 79
Lewis Strawberry Nursery 231
Liberty Commons 375
Lighthouse Realty 76, 366
Linda's 153
Little Professor Book Center 154
Live Oaks Bed & Breakfast 58
Lo-Di Farms 303
Local Call Surf Shop 264
Lockwood District Park 325
Lockwood Golf Links 333
Logan's Cafe 103
Lois Jane's Riverview Inn 62
Long Bay Lady Anglers King Mackerel Tournament 285
Long Beach 32, 358
Long Beach Canoe Trail System 255
Long Beach Family Campground 84
Long Beach Horse-A-Thon 191
Long Beach Pier 277
Loop, The 309
Lower Cape Fear Historical Society 416
Lower Cape Fear Historical Society, The 65
Lower Cape Fear Hospice 384
Lowe's 142
Lucky Fisherman 112
Lula's 124
Lumina 25
Lumina Daz 9
Lumina Daze 194
Lumina Pavilion, The 8
Lumina Station 150
Lynne's Hallmark Shop & Treasure Room 154

M

Magic Mountain Water Slide 233
Makado Gallery 208
Manhattan Bagel 103
Mansion District 348
Marge's Restaurant & Waffle House 112
Marinas and the Intracoastal Waterway 287
Marina's Edge 107
Marine Expo 198
Maritime Museum 181
Mark A. Sloan Memorial Cancer Benefit
  Golf Tournament 245
Marksmanship and Riflery 308

INDEX • 443

Marsh Creek 358
Marsh Harbor Golf Links 335
Marsh Harbour Marina 293
Martha's Vineyard 142
Martin Luther King Day March and
    Commemoration 189
Martin Luther King Jr. Center 220
Martin Luther King Jr. Center, The 232
Masonart 137
Masonboro Boatyard and Marina 290
Masonboro Island 28, 82, 185, 408
Mason's Marina 288
Massage Therapy 384
McAllister & Solomon Books 143
McClure Realty Inc. 78
McMillan Real Estate 78
MEDAC Convenient Medical Care 383
MEDAC II Convenient Medical Care 383
Media 419
Medical Mall, The 380
Medieval Festival 192
Medieval Times Dinner & Tournament 244
Medlin Real Estate 79
Mega Mattress Super Store 158
Members Club at St. James Plantation, The 333
Memorial Day Observance 192, 194
Memory Lane Comics 219
Mermaid, The 127
Metaphysic Expo 189
Metaphysical Fair 433
Michael Moore Antiques 157
Michael's Seafood Restaurant & Market 107
Mickey Ratz 124
Middle Island 30
Mike Chappell Park 325
Miller-Motte Business College 404
Miss Patti's Porch 154
Mobile Home Store & Hardware 305
Mollye's Downtown Market 96
Morehead City 246
Motorboat Rentals 254
Movie Theaters 128
MS Walk 310
Ms. Muffet's Yogurt Shop 229
Mt. Olive College 404
Murrow Furniture Galleries 158
Museum of Coastal Carolina 184
Museums 204
Music 210
Music Loft, The 222
Myrtle Beach 241
Myrtle Beach Area Chamber of Commerce 35, 241
Myrtle Beach Factory Stores 242
Myrtle Beach Golf Holiday 245
Myrtle Beach Grand Prix 242
Myrtle Beach Pavilion Amusement Park 242
Myrtle Beach Speedway 243
Myrtle Waves Water Park 242

N

National Beach Sweep 196
National Car Rental 6
National Shag Dance Championships 244
National Youth Sport Program at UNCW 238

Neighborhoods 343
Nevada Bob's 338
New Bern 247
New Bern Academy Museum 248
New Bern Civil War Museum 248
New Bern Fireman's Museum 248
New Bern Historical Society 248
New Coastal Regional Coastal Heart Center 380
New Elements Gallery 210
New Hanover County 18
New Hanover County Department of Aging 377, 417
New Hanover County Extension Service Arboretum 172
New Hanover County Fair 197
New Hanover County International Airport 17
New Hanover County Public
    Library 129, 234, 236, 433
New Hanover County Schools 387
New Hanover Home Health 380, 384
New Hanover Regional BirthPlace 380
New Hanover Regional Medical
    Center 380, 413, 428–429
New Hanover Regional Women's Health Specialties 380
New Hanover Senior Center 376
New Hanover-Pender County Medical Society 384
New Home Marketplace 364
Newspapers 419
North Carolina Aquarium 25, 176, 271
North Carolina Aquarium at Fort Fisher 220, 230
North Carolina Aquarium at Pine Knoll Shores 246
North Carolina Association of Buddhists 433
North Carolina Azalea Festival 192
North Carolina Fourth of July Festival 194
North Carolina Fourth of July Festival, 30
North Carolina Jazz Festival 190, 211
North Carolina Maritime Museum 246
North Carolina National Estuarine Research
    Reserve 29, 82, 408
North Carolina Oyster Festival 197
North Carolina Oyster Festival Road Race 311
North Carolina Poetry Society 215
North Carolina Spot Festival 196
North Carolina State Horticultural Crops Research 409
North Carolina Symphony 212
North Carolina Writers' Network 214
North Carolina's Central Coast 245
North Fourth Collection 210
North Shore Country Club 337, 341
Northrop Mall 154
Northside Medical Center 383
Northside Park 323
Northwest District Park 325
Nuss Strasse Cafe 97

O

Oak Island 32, 358
Oak Island Golf & Country Club 333
Oak Island School of Dance & Art 222
Oak Island Senior Center Craft Shop 154
Oak Island Sports Center 338
Oak Island Tour of Homes 198
Oak Winds Marina 288
Oakdale Cemetery 168
Oaks, The 380
Occasions 135

444 • INDEX

Ocean 1 Realty 78
Ocean Aire Aviation 187, 302
Ocean Aire Aviation Inc. 11
Ocean Crest Motel 48
Ocean Crest Pier 277
Ocean Isle 359
Ocean Isle Airstrip 10
Ocean Isle Beach 32
Ocean Isle Beach Golf Course 314
Ocean Isle Beach Rentals 257, 259, 264, 266
Ocean Isle Beach Water Slide 184
Ocean Isle Inn 50
Ocean Isle Marina 252, 254, 284, 293
Ocean Isle Pier 279
Ocean Princess Inn 61
Ocean Ray 262
Ocean Rentals 301
Ocean Terrace Restaurant 104
Oceanic Restaurant, The 104
Oceanic, The 25
Oceanside Restaurant 118
Odell Williamson Auditorium 204
Off-Roading 309
Office Depot 140
Offshore Adventures 261
Ogden Park 323
Old Brunswick Town State Historic Site 180
Old Smithville Burial Ground 181
Old Wilmington by Candlelight 199
Old Wilmington City Market 137
Olde Point 336
Olde Wilmington by Candlelight Tour of Homes 416
Olde Wilmington Toy Company, The 219
Olsten Staffing Services 428
Onslow County Parks and Recreation 299
Opera House Theatre 213
Optimist Club of Cape Fear 313
Organizations 204
Original Calabash Restaurant, The 117
Orton Plantation 30
Orton Plantation Gardens 180
Outer Banks Hammocks 150
Outer Limits Fishing Adventures 284
Outlet Park at Waccamaw 242
Overton's Discount Boating Supplies 260
Oyster Bay 334

P

P.T.'s Grille 98
Paleo Sun Cafe 97, 124
Paradise Cafe 108
Paradise Inn 47
Park Avenue School 398
Parks 322
Patio Playground, The 184, 301
Paula's Health Hut 146
Pawn USA 305
Peachtree Stables 303
Pearl Golf LinksN.C. Hwy. 179, Calabash, The 336
Pedal Pump & Run 300
Pelican Pointe Marina 293
Pelican Square Books & Ball Cards 156
Pender Chronicle, The 420
Pender County School System 391
Pender Memorial Hospital 382
Pender Post 420
Pennington's Marine 260
Penslow Medical Center 384
Perfect Golf Practice Facility 338
Performance Halls 204
Performance Watercraft 252
Perry's Emporium 141
Phar-mor 142
Philomena Moultries Boutique 154
Photography 215
Physiological Edge, The 319
Pier 1 Imports 141
Pilot House, The 97, 134
Pine Knoll Shores 246
Pine Valley 349
Piney Woods Celebration of the Arts 416
Piney Woods Cultural Heritage Festival 204
Piney Woods Festival 196
Pink Palace of Topsail, The 67
Pirate Fishing & Cruise Charters 284
Pizza Bistro 98
PK's 153
Plantation Village 375
Playwrights Producing Company 213, 215
Plaza East Shopping Center 151
Plaza Motel 50
Pleasure Island Spring Festival 194
Pleasure Island Surf Fishing Tournament 285
Poetry Readings 129
Poor Boy Shark Tournament 285
Pop Warner Football 302
Poplar Grove Christmas Celebration 199
Poplar Grove Herb Fair 192
Poplar Grove Plantation 173
Poplar Grove Summer Fair 194
Port Charlie's 112
Port City Basketmakers 215
Port City Java 111, 124
Port City Properties 364
Port City Taxi Inc. 5
Porters Neck Plantation 352
Porter's Neck Plantation 375
Porters Neck Plantation and Country Club 328
Ports of Call 299
Ports of Call Route 82
Prestige Limousine Service 5
Pride! Productions 213
Pro Golf Discount 338
Pro Tee Practice Range 338
Pro-Fit 319
Project Bumblebee 29
Project First Stop 414
Proper Garden, A 134
Provenance Antiques & Interiors 157
Prudential Carolinas Realty 364
PT Connection 320
Public Swimming Pools 265
Pulse Athletic Club 320
Pusser's Landing 104
Pusser's Restaurant 289
Putt-Putt Golf & Games 224

INDEX • 445

Q

Quarter, The 150
Quilters by the Sea 215
Quilters By the Sea Quilt Show 191

R

R. Bryan & Company 135
R. Bryan Collections 150
Rachel Carson Estaurine Research Reserve 246
Rachel Carson Island 408
Rack 'M Pub and Billiards 124
Racquetball 309
Radio Stations 423
Rainbow Bike Rentals 301
Ramada Inn Conference Center 41
Rape Crisis Center 412
Rare Cargo 138
Rassier Real Estate 364
Real Estate 343
Real Estate Companies 359
Rebecca's Lingerie Ltd. 140
Recreation 297
Recreation Departments 297
Red Carpet, Dorothy Essey & Associates Inc., Realt 76
Red Dinette, The 158
Redix 152
Reel Carolina Magazine 422
Reese Family Chiropractic 384
Region O Senior Games 376
Reindeer Romp, The 310
Research Facilities 405
Retired Senior Volunteer Program 376, 417
Ripley's Sea Aquarium 244
River Inn, The 59
River Landing 354
River Landing Country Club 330
River Pilot Cafe 109
River Road Park 276
River-to-Sea Bike Route 299
Riverfest 22, 197
Riverfront Park 324
Riverhills 368
Riverside Motel 48
Riverwalk 22
Riverwalk, The 168
Roan Island 305
Robert Ruark Chili Cookoff 191
Robert Ruark Festival 198
Robert Strange Park 324
Roberto's Pizzeria & Restaurant 115
Rock-ola Cafe 225
Rockits Rhythm & Sports Grille 124
Rocky Point Shooters World 308
Rogers Bay Family Campway 85
Romax Shoes 135
Romax Shoppe 135
Ronnie Milsap Theatre 244
Ropa, Etc. 138
Rosehill Inn Bed and Breakfast 59
Roses 305
Rose's 141
Rowing and Kayaking 255
Rucker John's Restaurant and More 98

Rudd & Associates Inc., Realtors 76
Rudd &Associates Inc., Realtors 367
Rugby 309
Running and Walking 309

S

S & S Water Sports 264
S & S Water Sports Inc. 253
Safe Sitter 379, 382
Safe Vacation Guide 382
Sailing 257
Saks Fifth Avenue 242
Salon Deja Vu 134
Salty's Surf Shop 264
Salvation Army 413
Sam's Club 142
Sand Dollar Realty 368
Sandfiddler Seafood Restaurant 113
Sanitary Fish Market 246
Saratoga Restaurant 119
Sassy Glass 153
Scentsational 138
School Room 234
Scoop Ice Cream & Sandwich Shoppe, The 229
Scooter's Family Skating Center 232
Scott's Hill Marina 288
Scruggs & Morrison Realty 77, 367
Scuba Diving and Snorkeiing 260
Scuba South Diving Company 261
Scuttlebutt 247
Sea Captain Motor Lodge 48
Sea Captain Restaurant 113
Sea Horse Riding Stables 303
Sea Lady Charters 261
Sea Mist Camping Resort 84
Sea Trail Golf Resort & Conference Center 334
Sea Turtle Program 30
Sea Vista Motel 52
Seahawk Chess Club 235
Seapath Yacht Club 289
Sears 141, 219
Seashore Weavers and Spinners 215
Seaside North 368
Seasoned Gourmet, The 150
SeaTow 273
Select-Internet Realty 365
SENC Technical Services 428
Senior AIDES Program 376, 417
Senior Citizen Services of Pender Inc. 417
Senior Friends 379, 382
Seniors Health Insurance Information Program 376
Service Corps ofRetired Executives 376
Seven Seas Ice Cream 229
Seven Seas Inn 48
Shackleford Banks and Carrot Island Ferry Service 246
Shallotte 35
Shallotte District Park 325
Shallotte Marine Supplies 254
Shannon's Services Inc. 77
Sharky's Pizza & Deli 115, 317
Shaw Speakes Child Development Center 398
Shaw University 404
Shell Island 27, 357
Ship and Shore Communications Inc. 254

446 • INDEX

Ship's Store Windsurfing & Sailing Center 257, 259, 266
Shuckers 127
Sickle Cell Open Tennis Tournament 315
Simmons Realty 368
Sitter Network Inc., The 399
Skate Barn, The 311
Skateboarding 311
Sleep Inn 42
Sloane Realty 78, 368
Small Business Incubator 416
Smithville District Park 325
Snapdragon Toys 249
Sneads Ferry King Mackerel Tournament 285
Sneads Ferry Public Library 235
Sneads Ferry Shrimp Festival 195
Snoopy's Magic On Ice 244
Snow's Cut Landing Marina 290
Snow's Cut Park 324
Soccer 311
Soccer Stop 312
Society of Stranders 244
Something Special Florist and Gifts 150
Sonny's Raw Bar and Grill 249
Sound Pier Market & Marina 284
Soundside 119
South Beach Grill 105
South Brunswick Islands Chamber of Commerce 35
South Brunswick Isles King Mackerel Tournament 285
South Carolina Welcome Center 241
South East Karate 318
Southeastern Center for Mental Health, Development 384
Southeastern Sickle Cell Association 414
Southern Lights Festival 191
Southport 29
Southport Christmas Home Tour and Flotilla 199
Southport Marina 284
Southport Marina Inc. 293
Southport Scuba and Water Sport 262
Southport Trail 181
Southport-Fort Fisher Ferry 6
Southport-Oak Island Masters Putting Tournament 333
Southport/Oak Island Chamber of Commerce 35
Southwinds Motel 49
Space Savers 142
Special Education 394
Spectrum Gallery 210
Spinnaker Surf & Sport 156, 264
Sports Club Program, The 414
Spouter Inn 247
St. James Episcopal Church and Burial Ground 168
St. James Plantation 358
St. James Shelter 413
St. John's Art Academy 222
St. John's Museum Art & Wine Auction 189
St. John's Museum of Art 169, 203, 205, 416
St. Marks Episcopal Church 169
St. Mary School 394
St. Mary's Roman Catholic Church 169
St. Paul's Evangelical Lutheran Church 170
St. Philip's Episcopal Church 181
St. Philip's Parish 182
St. Regis Resort 52
St. Thomas Pre-School Child Development Center 394

Stadium Batting Cages 173
Star-Line 264
Starlight, The 125
State Port Pilot 420
Steamers II Restaurant and Lounge 127
Stewart Hardware 254, 305
Stonebridge Realty 365
Stork's Nest, The 139
Stover's Martial Arts 318
Studebaker's 244
Stump Sound Rotary Golf Tournament 341
Sugar Shack 116
Summer Camps 237
Summer Fun Beach Days 179
Summer Sands Motel 45
Summer Traditions Camp 239
Sunset Beach 32, 359
Sunset Beach Pier 279
Sunset Celebration at the Hilton 125
Sunset Properties 78, 368
Sunset Vacations 78
Sunset Watersports 252
Surf & Turf Triathlon 316
Surf City 29
Surf City Pier 279
Surf City Surf Shop 264
Surf Fishing 280
Surf Reports 264
Surf Shops 264
Surf Suites 45
Surf, Sun & Sand Celebration 195
Surfboard Rentals 264
Surfing 262
Surfrider Foundation, The 264
Surfside Motel 52
Surfside Motor Lodge 47
Sutton Lake Game Land 305
Sutton-Council Furniture 158
Suzuki Method Music Education 222
Suzuki TalentEducation of Wilmington 212
Swan Point Marina 284
Swansboro 245
Swayne's Crafts & Things 154
Sweetwater Cafe 108
Sweetwater Surf Shop 152, 264
Swensen's 229
Swimming 264
Szechuan 132 99

T

T.S. Brown Jewelers 136
Tackle Express Tacklemart 305
Tapestry Theatre Company 214
Taste of Country II 99
Taverniers Jewelers 150
Taxicabs and Limousines 5
Taylor House Inn Bed and Breakfast 60
Teagues 139
Tee Smith Custom Golf Clubs 338
Tee-Times Inc. 339
Television Stations 422
Temple of Israel 170
Temptations 141
Tennis 314

INDEX • 447

Tennis With Love Ltd. 315
Texas Steakhouse & Saloon 99
Thai Peppers 113
Thalian Association 214
Thalian Association, The 221
Thalian Hall Center for the Performing Arts 170, 205
The Intracoastal Waterway 287
Theater 212
Theodosia's Bed and Breakfast 62
Time-Warner Cable 422
Tomatoz American Grille 100
Toms Drug Company 229
Toms Drug Store 139
Topsail Area Chamber of Commerce and Tourism 35
Topsail Area Spring Fling 192
Topsail Greens Golf and Country Club 336
Topsail Island 29, 270, 359
Topsail Island Museum 185
Topsail Island Trading Company, The 156
Topsail Island Vacation Rentals 78
Topsail Motel, The 52
Topsail Offshore Fishing Club King Mackerel Tourna 285
Topsail Realty 79, 369
Topsail Scenic Boat Tours 185
Topsail Skating Rink 233
Topsail Sound Pier 279
Topsail Turtle Project 29, 178
Topsail Voice 420
Topsail Water Sports 253, 255, 257, 260, 264, 266
Total Child Care Center 398
Tote-Em-In Zoo 220
Town Creek District Park 325
Townhouse Art & Frame Center 146
Toy Jam 199
Toys 'R Us 219
Track and Field 315
Trails End Steak House 100
Transportation Planning Department, City of Wilmington 4
Treasure Island Family Fun Park 185
Trends Home Furnishings 151
Triangle Rental 6
Trinity United Methodist Church 182
Tryon Palace 247
Tucker Bros. Realty 366
Turner Realty 369
Turtle Island Ventures 256
Tuscarora Tack Shop 303
Twin Lakes Restaurant 116
Twin Travel & Cruises 339
Twin Travel and Cruises 377
Two Sisters Bookery 136
Two Wheeler Dealer 300

U

U.S. Coast Guard Auxiliary 417
U.S. Open King Mackerel Tournament 20, 285
U.S. Trolls 219
UNCW Summer Science by the Sea Day Camp 239
UNCW's University Children's Academy Camps 238
United Beach Vacations 76
United Cerebral Palsy Developmental Center 394
Universities and Colleges 401
University of North Carolina at Wilmington 238, 429

University of North Carolina at Wilmington, The 401
University Theatre 214
Upperman African-American Cultural Center 402
Urgent Care Center 384
USTA Team Tennis Association 314

V

Valley Golf Center & Driving Range 338
Van Service 5
Verandas, The 60
Verrazano, Giovanni da 13
Vic's Corn Popper 229
Villa Capriani Resort 52
Vinnie's Steak House & Tavern 105
Vintage Values 413
Visitors Information Center 1
VitaLine 381
VitaLink 380
Volunteer Opportunities 376

W

WAAV 423
Waccamaw Pottery 242
Wacky Golf Cart Parade 195
Wal-Mart 142, 305
Walden's Gym 320
Walk-In Messiah 199
Walking Classes with Freddie J. King 310
Wall's Fine Art and Framing 210
Ward Realty 79, 369
Water & Woods Hunting & Fishing 308
Water Street Restaurant & Sidewalk Cafe 126
Water Street Waterfront Restaurant & Sidewalk Cafe 100
Water Ways Sailing School 259
Water-Skiing 262
Waterfront Park 182
Watersports, Inc. 252
Waterway Marine Service 288
Wave Hog Saloon 126
WCCA 423
Weckel, Dr. Glenn, 384
WECT 422
Weekly and Long-term Cottage Rentals 69
Well Care and Nursing Services Inc. 384
West Marine 151
WGNI 423
WhiteBridge 354
Whiting & Company 152
WHQR 423
Wild Water and Wheels 242
William Randall Library, The 402
Williams, Ronald 138
Willis Richardson Players 214
Wilmington 13, 14
Wilmington Academy of Music 212
Wilmington Adventure Walking Tour 170
Wilmington and Weldon Railroad 14
Wilmington Art Association 205
Wilmington Bike Map 4
Wilmington Boys Choir 199, 212, 222
Wilmington CAPE, The 404
Wilmington Center for Therapeutic Massage 385

Wilmington Chamber of Commerce 429
Wilmington Children's Museum
    222, 224, 230, 235, 239
Wilmington Choral Society 212
Wilmington Christian Academy 393
Wilmington Community Development Corp. 416
Wilmington Concert Association 212
Wilmington Concert Band 212
Wilmington Dance Academy 222
Wilmington Elks Lodge 217
Wilmington Espresso Co., The 111
Wilmington Family YMCA 239, 298, 320, 415
Wilmington Film Office 428
Wilmington Golf Association, The 339
Wilmington Golf Course 328
Wilmington Hammerheads/Athletic
    Zone Indoor Soccer 312
Wilmington Harbor Enhancement Trust 417
Wilmington Hilton 42
Wilmington Historic Foundation 16
Wilmington Homeschool Organization 394
Wilmington International Airport 9
Wilmington Journal, The 420
Wilmington Magazine 422
Wilmington Marine Center 291
Wilmington Municipal Docks 292
Wilmington Parks & Recreation Fitness Center 301
Wilmington Parks and Recreation 298, 320
Wilmington Polo Club 354
Wilmington Public Transit Guide 4
Wilmington Railroad Museum 171
Wilmington Roadrunners Club 310
Wilmington Senior Softball Association 313
Wilmington Sharks 298
Wilmington Star-News 420
Wilmington Symphony Orchestra 212
Wilmington Table Tennis Association 235
Wilmington Transit Authority 4
Wilmington Treatment Center 384
Wilmington Tri-Span Run, The 310
Wilmington Triathlon 315
Win City of Wilmington 300
Windjammer Restaurant & Lounge 113
Windrose Furniture Company 159
Winds Oceanfront Clarion Inn, The 50
Winds of Carolina Sailing Charters 183
Windsurfing 266
Wine House, The 60
Wings 153
Winner Cruise Boats 178
Winner Gulf Stream Fishing & Cruise Boats 284
Winter Holiday Fest 199
Winter Park Optimist 298

WKIX 423
WKOO 423
WMFD 423
WMNX 423
Women of Wilmington Chorale 212
Women's Services 379
Wonder Shop, The 140
Worship 431
Worth House, The 60
Wright Times 422
Wrightsville Beach 356
Wrightsville Beach Holiday Flotilla 198
Wrightsville Beach King Mackerel Tournament 285
Wrightsville Beach Museum of History 174
Wrightsville Beach Ocean Racing Association 257
Wrightsville Beach Park 324
Wrightsville Beach Parks and Recreation 298
Wrightsville Beach Parks and Recreation
    Department 239
Wrightsville Beach Preservation Society 9
Wrightsville Beach Storage, Inc. 291
Wrightsville Beach Summer Reading Program 235
Wrightsville Beach Summer Softball League 313
Wrightsville Beach Vacation Rentals 73
Wrightsville Marina 288
Write Place, The 136
Writing 214
WRQR 423
WSFM 423
WSFX 422
WUNJ 422
WWAY 422
WWIL 423
WWQQ 423
Wyatt Fitness 321
WZXS 423

Y

Yacht Basin Provision Company 113
Yaupon Beach 32, 358
Yaupon Pier 279
Yellow Cab 5
YMCA 265
Yogurt Plus 229
YWCA 265, 415
YWCA After School Program 399
YWCA of Wilmington 239, 320

Z

Zebulon Latimer House 171
Zeke's Island 408
Zeke's Island Coastal Preserve 305

Going Somewhere?

Insiders' Publishing presents 48 current and upcoming titles to popular destinations all over the country (including the titles below) — and we're planning on adding many more. To order a title, go to your local bookstore or call (800) 955-1860 and we'll direct you to one.

Adirondacks	Minneapolis/St. Paul, MN
Atlanta, GA	Mississippi
Bermuda	Myrtle Beach, SC
Boca Raton and the Palm Beaches, FL	Nashville, TN
Boulder, CO, and Rocky Mountain National Park	New Hampshire
Bradenton/Sarasota, FL	North Carolina's Central Coast and New Bern
Branson, MO, and the Ozark Mountains	North Carolina's Mountains
California's Wine Country	Outer Banks of North Carolina
Cape Cod, Nantucket and Martha's Vineyard, MA	The Pocono Mountains
Charleston, SC	Relocation
Cincinnati, OH	Richmond, VA
Civil War Sites in the Eastern Theater	Salt Lake City
Colorado's Mountains	Santa Fe
Denver, CO	Savannah
Florida Keys and Key West	Southwestern Utah
Florida's Great Northwest	Tampa/St. Petersburg, FL
Golf in the Carolinas	Tucson
Indianapolis, IN	Virginia's Blue Ridge
The Lake Superior Region	Virginia's Chesapeake Bay
Las Vegas	Washington, D.C.
Lexington, KY	Wichita, KS
Louisville, KY	Williamsburg, VA
Madison, WI	Wilmington, NC
Maine's Mid-Coast	Yellowstone

THE INSIDERS'® GUIDE

Insiders' Publishing • P.O. Box 2057 • Manteo, NC 27954
Phone (252) 473-6100 • Fax (252) 473-5869 • *www.insiders.com*